THE

HODDER

STAMP

DICTIONARY

To our son Robert and his wife Jean

The
Hodder
Stamp
Dictionary

Douglas Patrick

Fellow, Royal Philatelic Society, London

and

Mary Patrick

HODDER AND STOUGHTON

LONDON SYDNEY AUCKLAND

U.K. edition 1973

ISBN 0 340 17183 9

Printed in Canada for Hodder and Stoughton Limited,
St. Paul's House, Warwick Lane, London.

E C 4P   4 AH

PREFACE

TWENTY-FIVE YEARS AGO, when we began our work on stamp words, we had no idea that it would lead to a book. The work started when we set up a small reference file of questions that novice stamp collectors were asking at meetings of the stamp club in Mimico, near Toronto. With every question we filed a well-researched answer. The file began to grow more rapidly after we launched the weekly *CBC Stamp Club* on the Canadian Broadcasting Coporation's radio network, early in 1950. Still more impetus came from the inauguration in 1952 of our regular stamp column in the Toronto *Globe and Mail*. Radio listeners and newspaper readers were invited to ask questions. Every letter was answered and the answers added to the file of stamp-word definitions. Between 1947 and 1972 over 150,000 inquiries from collectors were handled. Letters came not only from every corner of Canada but from collectors in sixty other countries. Experts in many countries were consulted by mail. Visitors from abroad who came to Toronto to appear on the *CBC Stamp Club* gave freely of their help with difficult definitions.

Harold Gosney and Donald Sinclair, two advanced philatelists, and Mrs. Harold Jackson, a former school teacher, read and checked every English-language entry. Mrs. Jackson also did the currency research work. Staff members of the Berlitz Schools of Languages in Toronto translated the Spanish, Portuguese, and Italian philatelic words. Svend A. Karlfeldt provided the Swedish words, and Louis Lamouroux of Paris and Toronto translated the French terms. Paula Lischka edited and reduced the German text that the late Franz Gerhard had compiled in 1955. Dr. Frank O. Theubert checked and read all the German, French, and Dutch words. Melva Kenny did the geographical research, and with Dorothy Miller typed all the entries on individual cards.

The authors are deeply indebted to the following publishers and editors who helped with the compilation of this book in a great many ways, but especially by granting permission for the use of data from their materials:

Bernard D. Harmer, director of H. R. Harmer, Inc., New York, philatelic auctioneers.

Henry E. Harris, retail stamp dealer in Boston, publisher of stamp albums, catalogues, and other books.

James B. Hatcher, editor of Scott's postage stamp catalogues.

Robson Lowe, London, stamp auctioneer and publisher of philatelic books.

Jacques Minkus, present of Minkus Publications, publishers of stamp albums, catalogues, and philatelic books.

Stanley Phillips, former director of Stanley Gibbons, Ltd., London, editor of Gibbons' catalogues and author of several philatelic books.

DOMTAR *Fine Papers Ltd.,* Toronto, publisher of the *Howard Smith Dictionary of Terms Used in the Paper, Printing, and Allied Industries.*

The following have provided books and given permission to use information from them:

Cyril H. C. Harmer, director of H. R. Harmer, Ltd., London.

Duane Hillmer, president of Scott Publishing Co., Omaha, Nebraska, publishers of stamp catalogues, albums, and philatelic books.

A. L. Michael, chairman and managing director of Stanley Gibbons, Ltd., London.

The section on non-Latin European alphabets at the back of the book was prepared with the help of newspapermen of the foreign-language press in Toronto: Gregory Okulewich (Russian), Steve Miosich (Jugoslav), Elia Mitoff (Bulgarian), and Jim Zafeiropoulos (Greek). Michael Madesker, linguist and philatelist, checked all four languages for spellings and meanings.

At General Publishing Co. Limited under the direction of J. E. Stoddart, president, Tom Fairley, managing editor, Pam Joho, editor, and James Thompson, production manager, took the greatest care over many months to ensure maximum accuracy in this work.

Douglas and Mary Patrick
Toronto, Ontario
August 15, 1972

ABBREVIATIONS

Fr.	French
Ger.	German
her.	heraldry
insc.	inscription
It.	Italian
Lat.	Latin
N.	north
nick.	nickname
ovpt.	overprint
Port.	Portuguese
S.	south
Sp.	Spanish
sur.	surcharge
Swed.	Swedish
U.N.	United Nations
U.S.	United States
U.S.S.R.	Union of Soviet Socialist Republics
wmk.	watermark

A

A (insc.) for the Spanish word "anotación", indicating registered mail, as on the Colombia 1865 and 1870 registered-letter stamps.

A (ovpt.) for A.V.I.A.N.C.A., a Colombian airline, on airmail stamps of Colombia in 1950 and 1951-3.

A.A.A. Australian Airmail Association.

A.A.L. (airline) Adria Aero Lloyd, Italy.

A.A.M.S. American Air Mail Society. A number of airmail philatelists in this group compiled the popular *American Air Mail Catalogue.*

Aangebragt per Land-Mail (insc.) on 1945-6 postage-due stamps of the Dutch Indies used to pay the postal charges on mail to the former Dutch colony when the charges had not been prepaid.

aantal (Dutch) number.

A.B.A. (airline) A.B. Aerotransport. Former point of origin, Sweden. Amalgamated with DDL (Danish) and DNA (Norwegian) to form SAS, the Scandinavian Airlines System.

Abaco and Cays north group of the Bahama Islands, including Great Abaco and Little Abaco.

Abadan seaport in Persia (Iran), site of U.S. air field and base during Second World War.

abaissé (Fr.) dropped.

Abart (Ger.) variety.

Abbild (Ger.) copy.

Abbildung (Ger.) illustration.

Abbott, Sir John J. Caldwell Canadian prime minister 1891-2, portrayed on Canadian postage stamp of Nov. 3, 1952.

A.B.C. Powers a designation of three South American republics, Argentina, Brazil, Chili.

Abdruck (Ger.) impression.

A below Crown watermark frequently used by Australia 1913, by Papua 1907 and subsequent years; sometimes a double-line A, but may be single-line A.

Aberdeen, Miss. issued postmasters' provisional envelopes for this town in Mississippi in 1861, as part of the Confederate States of America.

abfaerben (Ger.) rub off.

abgefaerbt (Ger.) faded.

abgenutzt (Ger.) worn out.

Abingdon, Va. issued postmasters' provisional envelopes for this town in Virginia in 1861, as part of the Confederate States of America.

Abklatsch (Ger.) offset.

Abkuerzung (Ger.) abbreviation.

abnormals virtually any postage stamp or postal stationery item that differs from the regular or normal stamp or item of its kind; in Great Britain, some of the Queen Victoria stamps that were put into use despite differences in paper, watermarks, or other varying characteristics.

abonnieren (Ger.) to subscribe.

aborigines name given a topical collection of stamps showing aborigines, the earliest inhabitants of any land. Australia, Canada, the United States, and Mexico have portrayed aborigines on stamps.

abreviação (Port.) abbreviation.

abréviation (Fr.) abbreviation.

abschaetzen (Ger.) to value.

absenden (Ger.) to send.

Absender (Ger.) sender.

Abstempelung (Ger.) obliteration, cancellation, postmark.

abt. about.

Abteilung (Ger.) department, section.

Abteilungsstempel (Ger.) department cancel.

Abu Dhabi independent Arab sheikdom. Issued stamps 1964.

Abutshi a town in Nigeria on the Niger River. The name appears in a postmark with the words "The Royal Niger Co. C & L" (Chartered and Limited), used in 1899; these coloured cancels are not revenues used to cancel the British stamps.

abwaerts (Ger.) downward.

Abyssinia See ETHIOPIA.

Abyssinie (Fr.) Abyssinia.

Abzug (Ger.) copy.

Acadia a former French colony in North America including Nova Scotia and most of New Brunswick. Longfellow's *Evangeline* tells of the forced emigration of Aca-

1

dians. In 1930 on a 50-cent stamp, Canada depicted the church of Grand Pré, from where the Acadians emigrated.

Acapulco Mexican Pacific seaport famous as a resort and exporting centre.

accents marks put over, under, or through certain letters to indicate differences in pronunciation.

accepted design the design of a postage stamp accepted and approved by an authority, who may be the postmaster, one of his assistants, or a committee.

accessories the items stamp collectors use: hinges, albums, stamp tongs, catalogues, watermark detectors, perforation gauges, printed labels, or any similar materials other than postage stamps.

accidental grills or **incidental grills** grills formed by a method of perforating the stamps of Turkey in 1870-1 issues. These Turkish stamps were rouletted by a sewing machine, and were not made with holes punched in the margins like most postage stamps. The claws of the sewing machine that originally helped to move the cloth through the machine performed the same duty when the postage stamps were being prepared. The grills, three to five millimetres wide, appeared lengthwise and sidewise from the pin-perforating operation, and formed small frames around the edges of the stamps, leaving clear areas in the centre of some of them. Refer to *The Stamps of Turkey* by Adolph Passer (he uses the English spelling "grilles").

Accra capital of Ghana, seaport exporting rubber, cocoa beans, diamonds, and timber.

accum. accumulation.

A Century of Progress Flight (insc.) on 1933 U.S. airmail stamp issued in connection with the Graf Zeppelin flight to Miami, Florida, Akron, Ohio, and Chicago, Illinois, then to Europe.

Acheson's graphite a substance used on the back of British postage stamps to activate the automatic mail-handling machinery introduced as an experiment in 1957 in Southampton, England.

achievement (her.) the full coat of arms with external ornaments.

acht (Ger.) eight.

achteckig (Ger.) octagonal.

achtzehn (Ger.) eighteen.

achtzig (Ger.) eighty.

acid (1) the acid solution used for etching of plates in photo-engraving; (2) the cooking liquor in the sulphite process; (3) the acid of the fountain solution used on offset printing presses.

acid dye organic colouring substance in which the dye-base takes the place of the acid radical of a salt; acid dyes are used mostly for surface tinting or colouring; they are fast to light.

Açores (Port.) Azores, on overprints and inscriptions.

à côté de (Fr.) alongside, beside one another.

A countries in auction catalogues, refers to stamps of countries of the world with names beginning with A (Afghanistan, Aden, Albania, etc.).

Acropolis the high part of ancient Greek cities, frequently the citadel. The Acropolis of Athens appears on many Greek postage stamps.

A.D. anno Domini, Latin for "in the year of the Lord".

Adams & Co. Express in California, issued U.S. local stamps and envelopes in 1854.

Adams' City Express Post in New York, issued U.S. local stamps in 1850-1.

Adams, John (1735-1826) second president of the United States.

Adams, John Quincy (1767-1848) sixth president of the United States; son of John Adams, second president.

addendum (pl. addenda) additional matter placed at the back of the book to supplement the main body of the text or to supply omissions, shorter than a supplement.

Addis Ababa capital of Abyssinia (Ethiopia), 10,000 feet elevation, estimated 400,-000 population.

Adelie Land See TERRE ADÉLIE.

Adelaide capital of South Australia. First settlement made in 1836. Port Adelaide, about seven miles distant, is a principal port of call for European vessels.

Aden, Colony of on the southern coast of Arabia, included the Isthmus of Khormaksar and six islands. Capital: Aden. Area 75 square miles excluding islands. First stamps of Aden Colony were issued April 1937 and used throughout the Protectorate. In 1939, a restricted postal union was formed with Aden Colony, Qu'aiti, and Kathiri states as initial members. Later issues were inscribed "Aden" (1939) and then "Aden Kathiri State of Seiyun" (1942); other issues were inscribed "Aden Qu'aiti State of Shihr and Mukalla" and "Aden Qu'aiti State in Hadhramaut".

Aden Protectorate territory that encircled Aden Colony. In two parts: Western Protectorate and Eastern Protectorate. Area 112,000 square miles. For members of the Aden Postal Union stamps were interchangeable: Aden Colony, Aden Protector-

Advertising labels

ate, and the Qu'aiti State of Shihr and Mukalla and the Kathiri State of Seiyun (or Sai'un). The state stamps were inscribed with their names plus "Aden" in larger letters across the top of each stamp. Details can be found in *British Colonial Stamps in Current Use, 1955.*

adhesive referring to postage stamps, those made for sticking on mail as compared to stamps printed on cards or envelopes or to handstruck stamps in use before the advent of penny postage in 1840, when adhesive postage stamps were introduced for the prepayment of mail in Great Britain.

adhesive paper paper gummed with glue or dextrin for stamps, labels, or tapes.

Adler (Ger.) eagle.

Admirals (nick.) postage stamps of Canada 1912, New Zealand 1926, and Rhodesia 1913 portraying King George V in an admiral's uniform.

Admiralty Official (ovpt.) on 1903 stamps of Great Britain. The Admiralty, a department in British government subject to control of Parliament, directs naval affairs.

adressieren (Ger.) to address.

adulteration de la couleur (Fr.) colour changeling.

advance copies copies of stamps, books, or any printed works issued before the regular editions or issues, often intended for review.

ADVERTISED or **ADV** handstamps on mail used in Canada and the United States in the early days of postal services. When, in the opinion of the postmasters, mail remained too long at the post offices, they advertised for the owners and stamped the mail by various handstruck marks.

advertisements many countries employ advertising in booklets of stamps or in sheets where the stamps are se-tenant (side by side) with advertising labels.

advertising cancellations Like slogan cancellations, these announce something of interest to the public. But advertising cancellations are always sponsored by the public with authorized permission to use the text in the obliteration. Advertising cancellations are a part of duplex cancellations with the text in the obliteration. "Buy and use/crippled children/Easter Seals" is an example of three-line advertising cancellation. The sponsor determines the differ-

Advertising cancellation

ence between a slogan and an advertising cancellation.

advertising on the back of stamps on British and New Zealand stamps in certain issues.

A.E.F. Afrique Equatoriale Française (Fr.), French Equatorial Africa. First stamps issued in 1936.

A.E.F. American Expeditionary Forces, the entire body of U.S. troops in the European

Advertising on back of stamps

theatre during the First World War. Often refers to postmarks on mail from soldiers at that time.

A.E.F. Booklet Stamps postage stamps in booklets prepared for use of the U.S. forces during the First World War.

Aegean Islands islands in the Aegean Sea off coast of Greece, including the Cyclades, Sporades, and Dodecanese. See Italy and Greece listings in catalogues for postage stamp issues.

Aegean Sea the gulf between Asia Minor and Greece, approximately 400 miles long and 200 miles wide.

aehnlich (Ger.) similar.

Aenderung (Ger.) change, modification.

Aent also inscribed Aenta, Aenton. See EPIRUS.

aérea, aéreo a (Sp.) aerial or aeronautical.

aéreo (Sp.) by air; inscribed, overprinted or surcharged on stamps of Spanish-language countries for airmail use.

Aéreo Exterior 1931 (ovpt.) on regular issue of Guatemala 1929 for use as airmail postage for the Central American Airpost System inauguration on May 9, 1931. Subsequent overprinted stamps were for use on mail to foreign (exterior) countries.

AEREO SEDTA 0,65 (Sp.) Sociedad Ecuatoriana de Transportes Aéreos, and new value (sur.) on Ecuador postal tax stamps in November 1938 for Ecuador airmail.

Aerlinte Eireann (airline) Irish Air Lines. Point of origin, Dublin, Ireland.

aerograma (Port.) airmail letter, aerogramme.

aerogramme or aerogram, the Universal Postal Union name for airletters made from special light-weight paper, usually in blue colour with or without the government-authorized printed postage stamps on the forms. Aerogrammes have become so popular that special news bulletins are produced with news about them. The *Air Mail Entire Truth,* a newsletter published by LAVA in New York, is a popular example. The late F. W. Kessler, a former airmail stamp dealer and auctioneer, published a loose-leaf catalogue on aerogrammes in New York City.

Aerolineas Argentinas (airline) point of origin, Argentina.

aeronauta (Sp.) aeronaut.

Aeronaves de Mexico (airline) point of origin, Mexico City, Mexico.

aérophilatélie (Fr.) aerophilately.

aerophilately stamp collecting devoted to the study of airmail stamps, covers, and everything related to mail delivery by bal-

loons, planes, or any other type of aircraft.

aérostat (Fr.) airship.

Aerovias Nacionales de Colombia, S.A. (airline) Bogotá, Colombia.

AEROÿ (insc.) with dates 1923-43; Finland airmail stamps of 1944 to mark twenty years of Finnish airmail service.

AERPHOST (insc.) on Irish airmail stickers (etiquettes) by airmail.

AER-POST (insc.) on airmail stamps of Ireland.

Aesculapius god of healing in Greek mythology. An entwined serpent on a staff symbolizes this god. The design appears on many postage stamps.

Afars and Issas, French Territory of the a French overseas territory in East Africa, formerly named Somali Coast. Issued stamps under its new name for the first time in 1967. Stamps inscribed "TERRITOIRE FRANÇAIS DES AFARS ET DES ISSAS".

A.F.D.C.S. American First Day Cover Society.

afdruk (Dutch) imprint, print, impression.

affixing machines devices made to hold roll postage stamps (coils) for easy application to mail, usually in offices. Widely replaced by meter postage stamp machines.

affranchissement (Fr.) franking, postage.

affranchissement avec differentes valeurs (Fr.) combination franking.

Affranchissement – exceptionnel – (faute de timbres) handstamped impressions on bisects of Madagascar in 1904. Believed to be speculations.

affranchissement mixte (Fr.) mixed franking.

AFFt plus decorative cross and new values (sur.) on 1923 semi-postal stamps of Tunisia. A speculative issue.

Afghan, Afghanes (insc.) Afghanistan.

Afghanistan constitutional monarchy in Asia, bounded by India on the east, Baluchistan on the west, and Russia on the north. Capital: Kabul, or Cabul. First issued postage stamps in 1870. Ancient name of the capital was Ortospana.

Afghanistan (insc. in Persian or Arabic characters) The early circular issues have a quaint face representing an animal's head in the centre. Later issues depict a mosque gate with crossed cannons in front. Modern pictorials advertised the country since 1932.

AFRICA CORREIOS (insc.) appears on pictorial stamps in 1898 for use in any Portuguese possessions in Africa. In 1919 revenue stamps were overprinted "TAXA DE GUERRA" for use as charity tax stamps, and another issue of 1945 was for postage-due use in any of the Portuguese possessions in Africa.

Africa Occidental Española (Sp. insc.) appears on stamps of Spanish West Africa.

Africa Orientale Italiana (insc.) appears on stamps of Italian East Africa, issued stamps in 1938.

Afrikaans one of two languages inscribed on South African and Southwest African postage stamps.

Afrique centrale anglaise (Fr.) British Central Africa.

Afrique du Sud anglaise (Fr.) British South Africa.

Afrique Equatoriale Française overprint with bars on stamps of Gabon 1932 issue, French Equatorial Africa. Overprint occurs without bars but with overprint "TCHAD" (Chad, a republic in Central Africa).

Afrique Equatoriale Gabon (insc.) Gabon.

Afrique Française Combattante plus a large red cross and new values (sur.) on semipostal stamps, June 28, 1943, of French Equatorial Africa.

Afrique Occidentale Française (insc.) French West Africa.

Afrique Orientale allemande (Fr.) German East Africa.

Afrique Orientale anglaise (Fr.) British East Africa.

Afrique Orientale italienne (Fr.) Italian East Africa.

Afrique portugaise (Fr.) Portuguese Africa.

Afrique Sud-Ouest allemande (Fr.) German South-West Africa.

agency organization that sells or promotes the sale of the products of a manufacturer, or postage stamps from a country.

A.G.O. (airline) Estonia. Ceased operations in 1942. Merged with Aeroflot.

agora, agorot Israeli coins that replaced the pruta and prutot. (Courtesy of Harry Zifkin)

Agra city in India on the Jumna River, famous for the Taj Mahal located near by. India stamp of 1949 shows this famous mausoleum.

Agriculture (insc.) with Dept. of, and U.S. – United States official stamps, 1873, for the Department of Agriculture.

A. Grill name of one type of grill used in U.S. postage stamps. Grills were embossed impressions that absorbed cancellation ink to prevent stamps from being used a second time. Grills were named from A to J, plus Z.

Agüera, La south Rio de Oro region and Spanish administrative post in northwest

Africa. From 1920 to 1922 stamp issues of Rio de Oro were overprinted.

Aguinaldo, Emilio possibly born 1870, Filipino leader who commanded rebellion forces against Spain (1896-8) and led insur-

Aguinaldo: postage stamp

rection against U.S. authorities. Issued postage stamps that are listed in some catalogues.

A.I.F. and Nurse Australian Imperial Forces name of Australian issue of July 1940; features a sailor, soldier, and airforce man, and a nurse portrayed above them.

aigle (Fr.) eagle.

A.I.L. (airline) Avio Linie Italiane, Italy.

AIR (insc.) on airmail stamps of Canada, 1928-46.

Air Algérie (airline) Compagnie Générale de Transports Aériens Air Algérie, Algeria.

Air Canada (airline) formerly Trans-Canada Air Lines, Canada.

Air Ceylon Ltd. (airline) point of origin, Ceylon.

Air France (airline) point of origin, France.

airgraph service a method of photographing letters and transmitting the mail on film during the Second World War. Introduced by Great Britain in 1941. These are similar to aerogrammes, but are not aerogrammes in the Universal Postal Union official term for airmail letter sheets.

Air-India International (airline) point of origin, India.

air label a small phosphor-tagged airmail label used at Dayton, Ohio, and other post offices in the early days of the tagging experiments. (Courtesy of Alfred G. Boerger)

air leaflets publicity warnings, propaganda printed on sheets of paper or cards dumped from balloons or airplanes.

Air Liban (airline) port of origin, Lebanon.

airmail air post stamps, postage specially prepared for prepayment of airmail service.

airmail bond a light-weight bond paper used for correspondence to be transported by airmail; basis weight varies from 5 to 9 pounds per 5,000 sheets measuring 17 inches by 22 inches.

airmail covers envelopes with adhesive or imprinted postage stamps, mint or used, intended for, or used for, airmail service.

airmail inverts inverted overprints, surcharges, and centres that are airmail errors. The most famous is the U.S. 24-cent stamp of 1918.

airmail labels small stickers applied to mail to indicate delivery by air; also called "etiquettes".

airmail postal stationery a sheet of paper with or without a stamp printed on it for airmail use. The letter sheet is folded and sealed with pregummed flaps.

airmail rotary set (Panama) refers to the 1955 series issued to mark the fiftieth anniversary of the founding of the Rotary (Club) International.

airmails (nick.) refers to airmail postage stamps, covers, or related items flown by any type of aircraft, usually specified, for example, as pioneer, balloon, or Zeppelin.

airport dedication covers envelopes mailed on the days of airport dedications. These became popular through the late 1920s and through the next decade while airports were still novelties.

AIR POST (insc.) on airmail stamps of Newfoundland.

Air Vietnam (airline) point of origin, Vietnam.

Airwork (airline) point of origin, England.

Aitutaki one of the larger Cook Islands (about 7 square miles) northeast of New Zealand in the South Pacific, a dependency of British Dominion of New Zealand since 1901. Issued stamps in 1903, with surcharged stamps on New Zealand 1902 and subsequent issues to 1917-20. Issued inscribed stamps, 1920-32, then used Cook Islands stamps.

Ajánlás, or **Ajl. 1.** (ovpt.) meaning "registered letter", overprinted in 1946 on former regular-issue stamps of Hungary.

Akassa part of postmark used by the Royal Niger Company, Chartered and Limited, sometimes used to cancel British postage stamps 1888-97. Akassa is a seaport in Nigeria on the western side of the Nun mouth of the Niger River.

Akyab town of Burma where aviators stopped in experimental flights from Great Britain to Australia and other routes.

ALALC (insc.) appears with a design of flags in a circular chain covering most of the airmail stamp of Uruguay issued Nov. 23, 1970, for the Asociación Latinoameri-

cana de Libre Comercio (Latin American Association for Free Trade).

Alaouites (ovpt.) on stamps of France and Syria. Stamps issued under French mandate, 1925.

Alaouites, Territory of the division of Syria under French mandate in western Asia of about 2,500 square miles. Capital: Latakia.

Alaska-Yukon vending machine perforated stamps commemorative stamps with private perforations. See Scott's U.S. Specialized catalogue for details.

Albania republic east of Yugoslavia and Greece on Adriatic Sea of about 10,629 square miles. Capital: Tirana. Issued stamps in 1913.

Albania (sur.) in 1902-7 on stamps of Italy used by Italian offices in Albania, a part of the Turkish Empire at that time.

Albanie (Fr.) Albania.

Albany, Ga. issued postmasters' provisional envelopes for this town in Georgia in 1861, as part of the Confederate States of America.

albino a type of error; a colourless, embossed area on postage stamps or postal stationery where colour should appear. Many adhesive postage stamps, such as those of the Gambia and some European countries, were intentionally printed without colour.

albumen (1) substance obtained from white of eggs and used for coating glass or metal plates, sensitized for photographic reproduction; (2) also used in book-binding as size in gold stamping and application of gold leaf to edges.

albums (1) books of various types for stamp collections. Justin H. Lallier produced the first postage stamp album in 1862 in France. (2) type of binding in which the loose leaves are separated by stubs at binding edge to take up bulk of stamps or covers mounted on the leaves.

Album Weeds title of three editions of the same book, enlarged each time. Last edition published in 1906 by Stanley Gibbons of London. The works, by Rev. R. B. Earé, still remain the outstanding references on forged stamps of the world.

ALCANCE y U.H. (insc.) on late fee stamps of Uruguay.

ALDABRA (insc.) on stamps of British Indian Ocean Territory. Aldabra is a group of small islands forming an atoll in the Indian Ocean. Leased to the Royal Society until 1985.

alemán (Sp.) German.

alemão (Port.) German.

Aleppo a town of northern Syria about mid-way between the Mediterranean Sea and the Euphrates. Used as an important stopping place on pioneer flights between England and India.

Alerta (Sp. script ovpt.) meaning "on the alert". On regular-issue stamps of Peru for use in 1884 in the Department of Ancachs (now spelled "Ancash") following the war between Chili and Peru, 1879-82.

Alexandretta formerly administrative district of Turkey, became Republic of Hatay in 1938, and incorporated in Turkish Republic in 1939; about 5,000 square miles. Chief towns: Alexandretta and Antioch. Issued stamps in 1938.

Alexandria, Va. issued postmasters' provisional stamps for this city in Virginia in 1846.

Alexandrie (insc.) Alexandria. Appears on stamps used by French offices in Alexandria, Egypt.

Alexandroupolis seaport city in western Thrace on the Aegean Sea. Annexed by Bulgaria 1915-18 and returned by treaty after the First World War to Greece. Greece issued occupation stamps in 1913. Also known as Dede Agach (spelled "Dedeaghatch" – Scott's, "Dedeagatz" – Gibbons).

ALFABETIZACION (ovpt.) and other spellings on regular-issue and airmail stamps of Ecuador in 1950 as propaganda for adult education.

Alfonso XII (1856-85) proclaimed king of Spain by the Spanish army in 1874, following a civil war. He suppressed the Carlist opposition in 1876. Spanish stamps of 1875-82 portrayed Alfonso XII and continued in use until his death. See CARLIST ISSUES.

Alfonso XIII king of Spain 1886-1931, portrayed on Spanish and colonial stamps as a child, a youth, and a man. His mother, Maria Christina, was his regent from 1886 to 1902.

Algeria country in northwest Africa, constituting a government-general of the French Union until independence in 1962; about 113,883 square miles. Capital: Algiers. Issued stamps in 1924.

Algérie (Fr. insc.) Algeria.

Alitalia (airline) Linee Aeree Italiane. Point of origin, Italy.

Allan Line mail route named after Hugh Allan, of Montreal, Quebec, who got the contract to transport mail in 1855 between Canada and England, by the Montreal Steamship Company.

Allemagne (Fr.) Germany.

Allemagne/Duitschland (ovpt. in French and Flemish) on stamps of Belgium during the Belgian occupation of Germany in 1919-21.

Allemand (Fr.) German.

Allen, Ralph a postal reformer in England and postmaster of Bath in 1720. Became the farmer (operator) of the bye and cross posts in England. Farmers of the post were men who paid an annual rental fee for the privilege of carrying the mail in England. Bye posts were these which passed from one town to another on a direct post road but not to London. Cross posts, as the name implies, were mail deliveries between two direct post roads.

Allen's City Dispatch in Chicago, Illinois, issued U.S. local stamps in 1882.

Allenstein former government district in southeast Prussia joining Germany by plebiscite in 1920; about 4,458 square miles. Capital: Allenstein. Issued stamps in 1920.

allgemein (Ger.) general(ly).

Allgemeine Bemerkungen (Ger.) general remarks.

ALLIED MILITARY POSTAGE (insc.) Appears above the inscription "Italy" and the values, on stamps issued in 1943 by the Allied Military Government of Great Britain and the United States for civilian use in Italy under Allied occupation.

Allied Occupation Issues Second World War refers to numerous stamps issued by Great Britain, France, United States, Russia, and Australia for regions these countries occupied mainly in Europe, but in 1946-7 Australian stamps of 1937-46 were overprinted "B.C.O.F./Japan/1946" in three lines for occupation use (initials stand for "British Commonwealth Occupation Force").

allseitig (Ger.) on all sides.

Alsace and Lorraine frontier region between Germany, France, Belgium, and Switzerland. Under Germany 1871-1918. Restored to France by treaty in 1919; occupied by Germany 1940-4, then restored to France. Stamps were issued under German occupation in 1870. German stamps surcharged for use in 1916. Again in 1940 German stamps were overprinted "Elsas" for Alsace, and others "Lothringen" for use in Lorraine. In 1944-5 the Allied Military Government of the United States and Great Britain issued two series of stamps inscribed "France" over the Arc de Triomphe for use by the people of Alsace and Lorraine.

alt (Ger.) old.

A.L.T. (airline) Aer Lingus Teorante. Irish International Airlines. Point of origin, Dublin, Ireland.

Altbrief (Ger.) pre-philatelic letter, stampless cover.

alteração de côr (Port.) change of colour, or colour changeling.

alteración de color (Sp.) change of colour.

altezza (It.) height.

alto (It.) top.

ALT-ORSOVA river quarantine station for ships ascending the Danube at the frontier of the Banat and Walachia, now Jugoslavia. (Courtesy of Herbert Dube)

altura (Port.) height.

Alwar Indian feudatory state of about 3,158 square miles in Jaipur Residency southwest of Delhi. Capital: Alwar. Issued stamps 1877-1901, then used India stamps.

A.M. (Latin) ante meridiem (before noon), set after the figures for the hour.

AMBULANCE LAQUINTINIE (sur.) and new values, on two stamps of Cameroun 1939 issue. Semi-postal stamps were issued in 1941 with a surtax to raise money to buy ambulances for the Free French army.

ambulante (Fr.) travelling; found in French and Belgian postmarks to indicate a mobile post office, truck, or railroad.

American Airlines, Inc. (airline) point of origin, United States.

American Bank Note Company New York City firm of security printers who have produced postage stamps and securities for more than a century.

American Express Co. in New York City, issued U.S. local stamps in 1857.

American Journal of Philately publications by John W. Scott. These magazines were the forerunners of *Scott's Standard Postage Stamp Catalogues*. They were published in two series. The second series, published monthly from 1888 to 1895, contained valuable data not available elsewhere.

American Letter Mail Co. issued U.S. local stamps in 1844.

American Philatelic Association. (APA) former name of American Philatelic Society. The name was changed to avoid confusion with an anti-Catholic group that used the same initials for its name and was said to be an Anti-Popery Association.

American Philatelic Congress founded by Eugene Klein and James Waldo Faucet in 1935. This organization holds annual meetings and publishes excellent philatelic studies. Serious collectors are invited to associate with the A.P.C.

A.M.G. Allied Military Government. The United States and Great Britain after the Second World War issued postage stamps for civilian use in Austria, France (Lorraine), Germany, Italy, Trieste.

A.M.G. F.T.T. (ovpts.) Allied Military Government, Free Territory of Trieste. On stamps of Italy issued under the military

authority of Great Britain, the United States, and Jugoslavia for use in Trieste in 1947-54.

A.M.G.-V.G. overprinted on stamps of Italy, allied occupation of Venezia Guilia.

Amharic the official and court language of Ethiopia, a Semitic language related to ancient Ethiopic.

A. M. Hinkley's Express Co. in New York City, New York, issued U.S. local stamps in 1855.

aminci, amincissement (Fr.) thin, thinned. The French word "clair" has a similar meaning.

ampersand correct name for the usual contraction "&" for "and".

A M post (insc.) appears on stamps issued by the Allied Military Government of the United States and Great Britain, for use by civilians in Allied occupation areas of Germany during 1958.

A.M.S. airmail service, a term that postal employees use to distinguish the type of postal service.

amtlich (Ger.) official.

amtliche Lochungen (Ger.) official perforations.

amtlicher Verkehr (Ger.) official stamps of Württemberg. The translation is "official business".

an, année (Fr.) year.

analogue (Fr.) similar.

anastatic process a printing method of producing facsimiles by a transfer process from zinc plates. Gibbons editors of the Great Britain Specialized stamp catalogue reported: "The British Post Office experimented with new colours for the one-penny stamps (1852) owing to alarm that persons named Glynn and Appel professed ability to make imitations of the one-penny by the anastatic process." British experimental printings were done in dull greyish black and dull pale purple on wove paper dipped in prussiate of potash.

Anatolia the part of Turkey in Asia equivalent to the peninsula of Asia Minor. Postage stamps issued 1920-3.

anbieten (Ger.) to offer.

Ancachs city in Peru. Issued stamps in 1884.

Anchor watermark frequently used in postage stamps of Cape of Good Hope, Great Britain, and certain British colonial stamps. In 1907, some 1-penny carmine stamps of Transvaal were issued with a Cape-of-Good-Hope type of anchor watermark while other stamps in the series of 1905-10 had multiple Crown and C.A. watermarks. Some of the Cape triangular stamps have double anchor watermarks sideways instead of one in vertical position.

ANCIENS COMBATTANTS RF (sur.) with new values and surtax charges; on Tunisia semi-postal stamps for benefit of war veterans.

ancre (Fr.) anchor (as a type of watermark).

A.N.D.E. (airline) Aviación Nacional Del Ecuador.

andersfarbig (Ger.) of different colour.

Anderson Court House, S.C. issued postmasters' provisional envelopes for Anderson, South Carolina, in 1861, as part of the Confederate States of America.

Andorra a state on the southern slope of the east Pyrenees, of about 191 square miles, between France and Spain, under the joint control of Spain and France. Capital: Andorra. Money of both countries is used. Stamps were issued under both administrations: under Spain in 1928 and France in 1931.

Andorre (Fr.) Andorra.

Andorre (ovpt.) Andorra, on stamps of France in 1931.

Anfang (Ger.) beginning.

angeklebt (Ger.) pasted on, affixed, stuck on.

ANGL. B.M. in octagonal or circular postmarks from the Channel ports of Granville, St. Malo, and Le Havre in France. Ships of the L. and S.W. Ry. Co. (London and South Western Railway Co.) sailing from St. Helier on Jersey, Channel Islands to St. Malo, and to Granville on alternate weekdays took the regular mails between the islands and to France. The ships carried "Boîtes mobiles" (Fr., mobile boxes or moveable post boxes) that were taken ashore in France; and the letters, with English stamps, were cancelled but not handled by the British Post Office. ANGL. is an abbreviation for the French word "Angleterre",

England. Known postmarks are dated 1859-79.

ANGL EST (Fr.) postmark used approximately 1815-49 on mail from Paris to London, England. (Courtesy of Herbert Dube)

Angola a Portuguese colony in southwest Africa of about 481,226 square miles. Capital: Luanda. Issued stamps in 1870.

Angra a district of Portugal; about 275 square miles. Capital: Angra do Heroismo. Issued stamps from 1892 to 1905; used Azores stamps 1906-31, and then Portugal stamps. Angra do Heroismo is the full name of the town and commune in the Azores islands. The "Do Heroismo" was added to the town name for its patriotic opposition (1830-2) to the pretender Dom Miguel.

Anguilla an island of the Leeward Islands, British West Indies. Formerly used the stamps of St. Christopher, Nevis, and Anguilla (concurrently with the general issues of the Leeward Islands until July 1, 1956). St. Christopher, Nevis, and Anguilla were granted Associated Statehood on Feb. 27, 1967, but following a referendum Anguilla declared her independence and the St. Christopher authorities withdrew. Stamps were issued by the governing Council and have been accepted for international mail. (Courtesy of Stanley Gibbons)

Anhang (Ger.) addendum.

Anilin (Ger.) aniline.

aniline ink made by dissolving organic dyes in a quick-drying vehicle; used in printing certain postage stamps (Papua, 3d of 1916), on glassine, cellulose, and other substances.

Anjouan one of the Comoro Islands southeast of Great Comoro, of about 89 square miles. Capital: Mossamondu. Issued stamps in 1892.

Anlage (Ger.) enclosure, investment.

anna a small copper coin of India, Aden, British East Africa, Burma, Indian Native States, Mesopotamia, and Zanzibar. Sixteen annas equal one rupee, about 2½ pence, or 4 pice or 12 pies. The two-anna piece was of silver.

Annam and Tonkin French protectorate of about 97,503 square miles on the east coast of Indo-China. The capital of Annam was Hué and the capital of Tonkin was Hanoi. First stamps were issued in 1888, then Indo-China stamps were used.

Annapolis, Md. issued postmasters' provisional envelopes for this town in Maryland in 1846.

anniversaire (Fr.) anniversary.

anniversary cancels postmarks that contain some data pertaining to anniversaries. The twentieth anniversary 1857 cancel of Streetsville, Upper Canada (now Ontario), to honour Queen Victoria's reign is a rare example of an impressive anniversary cancel. An example is in the Royal Ontario Museum stamp collection. The year 1857 was carved in a crude circle with a small crown and a few lines.

annotation notes or comments written in the margins of a printed work.

annulé (from Fr. verb "annuler") cancelled, made void.

annulé par barres (Fr.) barred.

annullamento (It.) cancellation, obliteration.

annullamento a mano (It.) handstamp.

annullato (It.) cancelled.

annullato a penna (It.) pen-cancelled.

annullo (It.) postmark.

annullo a sbarra (It.) bar cancel.

ano (Port.) year.

anode in electrotyping, the copper, zinc, or nickel plate that serves as the positive pole in the electrolytic bath. The metal from the positive pole is transferred to the cathode, or negative pole, constituted by the wax or lead mould.

ANOTACION (insc.) appears on registration stamps of Colombia, 1870.

Anotado vertical Spanish overprint reading top to bottom on Mexican stamps with distinct names, 1872: Vera Cruz, Puebla, Monterey, and many others. The *Holkar Mexico Catalogue* note reads: "As the stock of the stamps of the new issue was found too small to supply all the post offices the Government caused some of the stamps of 1868 [which had already been withdrawn from circulation] to be surcharged ANOTADO, which means: noted, registered; and replaced in circulation."

ANSETT-ANA (airline) operated by Ansett Airways (AA) and Australian National Airways, Victoria, Australia.

Antananarivo (insc.) Madagascar British Consular Mail postage stamps of 1884-6. Listed in the British sections of stamp catalogues. British consulates in the community named Antananarivo handled the mail, and in 1884 W. C. Pickersgill, British Vice Consul, organized the Consular Mail and then issued adhesive stamps.

anteado (Sp.) buff-coloured.

Anti-Graham Wafers small circular paper wafers used to seal the flaps of envelopes. British laws since the time of Queen Anne, who reigned 1702-14, prohibited the postal employees from detaining or opening letters without a warrant. In 1844 some Britons thought their privacy was being invaded by Sir James Graham, the Home Secretary, when he caused some letters of the Italian patriot Giuseppi Mazzini to be opened. Mazzini had been banned from Italy, moved to France, and then to England, where he continued his work to unify Italy. Sir James intercepted some mail that Mazzini had written and mailed in England, and sent it to Austria. When the British people learned of the censorship of Mazzini's mail, Parliament investigated Sir James' activities, but found no reason for the people to fear for their privacy. In typical British humour, people bought the little seals they used to stick down the flaps. These wafers were embossed "By the Kind Permission of Sir James Graham". Now known as Anti-Graham Wafers.

Antigua British colony of about 171 square miles in the West Indies southeast of Puerto Rico. Capital: St. Johns. Issued stamps 1862.

Antilles danoises (Fr.) Danish West Indies.

antimony metal used in the manufacture of type-metal alloy to harden it; also used in manufacture of stereotype metal.

Antioquia a department of Republic of Colombia in South America, issued stamps 1868 to 1904. See COLOMBIA, UNITED STATES OF.

Antwortschein (Ger.) reply coupon.

anulado con barras (Sp.) barred.

använd (Swed.) used.

Anvil Seal Issue (nick.) for 1914 stamps of Sonora State in Mexico. Design shows an anvil.

ANZAC (insc.) Australian and New Zealand Army Corps. On stamps of Australia, March 18, 1935, and New Zealand, April 14, 1965, commemorating the anniversary of the landing of the Australian and New Zealand Army Corps at Gallipoli in Turkey on April 25, 1915.

A.O. (ovpt.) Afrique Orientale, on semipostal stamps of the Congo for the Belgian occupation of German East Africa in 1918.

AOF (ovpt.) appears on French semi-postal stamps 1945, and French West Africa 1945 semi-postal stamps for charities.

A.O.I. (ovpt.) Africa (or Afrika) Orientale Italiana – both spellings are inscribed on various stamps of the former Italian colony. Appears on Italian postage-due stamps for Italian East Africa.

AOPU (insc.) appears on stamps of China for the Republic of Formosa, April 1, 1963. Issued to mark the first anniversary of the formation of the Asian-Oceanic Postal Union. Stamp design features two swallows, a pagoda, and the AOPU emblem.

A PAYER (Fr.) part of insc. on stamps of Belgium, means "to pay".

A PAYER TE BETALEN postage due; bilingual inscriptions on postage-due stamps of Belgium, the Congo, Ruanda-Urundi.

A.P.C. American Philatelic Congress.

apêndice (Port.) tablet – part of stamp design.

à percevoir (Fr.) postage due. On stamps of France, Canada, Belgium, and French colonies.

à percevoir (insc.) appears with values, but

without a country name on stamps of Guadeloupe, 1876-9.

A PERCEVOIR and **POSTAGE DUE** bilingual inscription on Canadian postage-due stamps since 1933.

A.P.O. Army Post Office. The letters sometimes appear in markings on mail from army men and women.

Aportación Voluntaria (Sp. insc.) voluntary contribution.

appraisals the work of placing selling values on postage stamps, collections, or entire philatelic holdings. Postage stamp dealers with years of experience appraise philatelic materials for a percentage of the value based on an offer to purchase. Thus the man or estate is assured of a true market value. Large or extremely valuable items are often appraised, then sold by auction. Owners should not rely on the retail prices quoted in stamp catalogues.

approval books or sheets inexpensive sheets or booklets often printed with rectangular spaces for postage stamps. Dealers mount stamps, then send them to collectors for their inspection and purchase.

approvals postage stamps sent to collectors for their inspection. Collectors buying stamps from dealers make a habit of handling the approval stamps with the greatest care, and always return them promptly, with money to pay for the stamps they keep. Every year hundreds of thousands of

dollars pass through the mails in payment for postage stamps and collectors' supplies. Such large purchases by mail are a tribute to the integrity of stamp collectors.

après le depart (Fr.) handstamp impression meaning "after departure" or "too late". Known on some French letters mailed after the last collection from post boxes for the day. An extra charge would assure that such mail would be processed and dispatched that day, not on the next day. A French law of May 9, 1863, authorized the surtax.

A.P.S. American Philatelic Society, an international organization of the highest standards. Publishes the monthly magazine *The American Philatelist* (address: State College, Pennsylvania).

Apurimac (ovpt.) appears on stamps of Peru, one of many provisional issues during the Chilean-Peruvian War, 1879-82.

aquatint (1) an etching process by hand work that prints; imitates the broad flat tints of India ink or sepia drawings; (2) the print produced by the aquatint process. Gravure printing is based on the aquatint process.

A.R. Aviso de Recepción, acknowledgment-of-receipt stamps. Colombia, Chile, Salvador, and Montenegro stamps bear the letters "A R", indicating their specific use for which a special fee is paid in advance. The U.P.U. recognizes the service.

arabesque a design of interlacing lines and figures of plants, flowers, foliage. Examples of stamps with such designs include Denmark 1870 and Danish West Indies 1873-96.

Arabia peninsula of Southwest Asia of about 1,000,000 square miles. See SAUDI ARABIA.

Arabic inscriptions appearing without pictures or English words on stamps of Hejaz.

Arad city in west Romania on the Mures River that runs through Hungary and Romania. In 1919 stamps issued under French occupation of Hungary were called the Arad issue. Hungary stamps were overprinted "Occupation Française".

arancio (It.) orange.

ARBC American Revolution Bicentennial Commission, established by the U.S. Congress to plan, encourage, develop, and co-ordinate the 200th anniversary of the United States. The ARBC issued a combination philatelic-numismatic memento with help from the U.S. Mint and the U.S. Postal Service, and offered a first-day cover with four postage stamps dated July

4, 1972, postmarked with the usual first-day-of-issue cancellation. The price was $5 for insured mailing.

Arbe (ovpt.) appears on stamps of Fiume, 1920, for use on the island that had been in Jugoslavian territory. Stamps for the other two islands, Carnaro and Veglia, were also overprinted or surcharged in 1920. The islands as part of the city of Fiume were annexed to Italy in January 1924, when stamps of Italy were used.

ARC types of exchange markings used by Canada and the United States, some with paid or collect rates indicated.

arc lamp an electric lamp in which the light is produced by heating the ends of carbon rods to incandescence by an electric arc; sometimes formerly used as source of light in photographic work in studios.

arc roulette, perce en arc (Fr.) sometimes called serrated roulette; type of separation in small curves. Arc-rouletted stamps in singles appear with edges concave on one side and convex on the opposite sides.

Arce, Dr. José President of the Argentine delegation to the United Nations, proposed a U.N. postal service. Dr. Arce was former President of the U.N. General Assembly. Postage stamps for the United Nations went on sale for the first time on United Nations Day, Oct. 24, 1951.

Archer, Henry In October 1847 Henry Archer told British Postmaster General, the Marquis of Clanricarde, of his invention of a machine to perforate stamps.

Archer wrote in part: "I have contrived an inexpensive plan whereby the postage stamps may be instantly detached from the sheet." After years of experimenting and perfecting his invention, Archer received £4,000 from the Treasury Department for his perforating machine and patent rights. On January 28, 1854, the British postage stamps with perforation gauge 16 went into use officially.

Archer roulette series of slits in wavy lines between rows of postage stamps. It was the first method to facilitate separating postage stamps. In 1847, before most countries had introduced adhesive postage, an Irishman named Henry Archer invented a rouletting machine.

Arc roulette

Archipel des Comores Grand Comoro Island, located in the Mozambique Channel between Madagascar and Mozambique, Africa. French colony. First issued stamps in 1897. Three others in the Archipelago – Mayotte, Moheli, and Anjouan – each issued stamps prior to 1914.

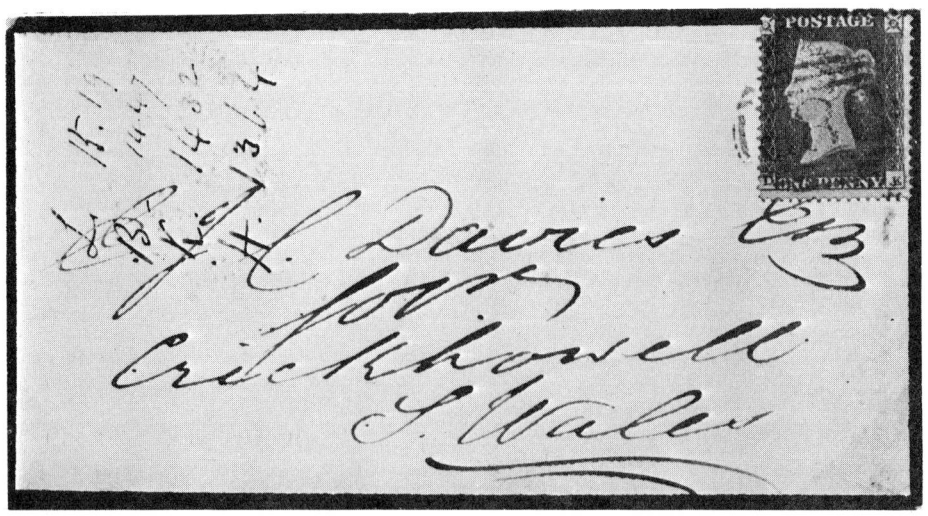

Archer: experimental perforation gauge 16 (1852)

A.R.C.O. (airline) Aerovias Ramales Colombianas; point of origin, Colombia. Now A.V.I.A.N.C.A.

ardoise (Fr.) slate, dark bluish, or greenish-grey colour of the rock, sometimes used as a postage stamp colour.

a receber (Port. insc.) appears on postage-due stamps of Portugal and Portuguese colonies.

Arequipa (ovpt.) appears on stamps of Peru. One of many provisional issues during Chilean-Peruvian War, 1879-82.

Arequipa provisional issues of Peru used during the Chilean-Peruvian War of 1879-82. Stamps were used from 1881 to 1885. The city is located in southwest Peru near the foot of Misti volcano.

argent (Fr.) silver.

Argentina republic of about 1,072,700 square miles in South America. Capital: Buenos Aires. Issued stamps 1858.

Argentine Airlines (airline) Aerolineas Argentinas, Buenos Aires.

Argentine Republic official stamps for governmental use, various regular-issue stamps overprinted with initials for the department names.

ark (Swed.) sheet.

armed (her.) with teeth and claws, or beak, of a distinctive tincture.

Armenia an ancient country of about 11,945 square miles in western Asia now divided among Russia, Turkey, and Iran; issued stamps from 1919 until 1923. Capital: Erevan.

Arménie (Fr.) Armenia.

ARMENWET (ovpt.) appears on 1899-1910 issue stamps of the Netherlands brought back into use in 1913-18 as official stamps to prepay mail regarding the poor laws.

armoiries (Fr.) coat of arms, more often blason.

armoured-car mail. See RISHON LE ZION ARMOURED-CAR MAIL.

armoury heraldry; armorial bearings.

arms type usually with some date and country name to specify the particular issues. Scores of countries have issued arms types with heraldic devices, coats-of-arms, or portions of such designs.

ARMY OFFICIAL (ovpt.) appears on regular issues of Sudan, 1898 and 1902-8, for use as army official stamps. Also appears on stamps of Great Britain, 1896-1903, for use as army official stamps.

Army Post Egypt (insc.) on 1936 stamps for use by British service men in Egypt. Replaced the former seals for similar use at reduced postal rates.

army postage stamps specific types for use by service men and women in wartime. Some countries have issued special envelopes for such use; Sweden prepared them with the addition of a printed stamp for return postage. British forces in Egypt in 1932 were provided with special labels providing reduced letter rates for mail to Great Britain. Canadian soldiers' and service persons' mail was microfilmed for transmission home during the Second World War.

ARMY SERVICE (ovpt.) appears on regular issues on Sudan, 1902-11, for use as army official stamps.

arrangement des timbres (Fr.) arrangement of stamps.

arrangement of postage stamps the art of mounting stamps on album pages made without pictures. The ultimate value of a stamp collection is greatly increased by good layouts of stamps and descriptive text (write-ups). *How to Arrange and Write Up a Stamp Collection* (Stanley Gibbons) is highly recommended as a guide. The late Stanley Phillips and C. P. Rang wrote the book, and it has been published since 1933 with five editions and seven reprints.

arrow block four or more postage stamps on the edge of a pane or sheet. The arrow resembling the letter V sometimes serves as a guide for guillotine operations on sheets or panes of stamps. Also facilitates counting parts of panes in post office. Many arrows point to the gutters dividing a sheet into panes of stamps.

arrow guide a marginal mark pointing to the centre of a sheet or pane either in vertical or horizontal position.

arruga (Sp.) crease.

Artcraft F.D.C., V.F. an abbreviation referring to first day covers on Artcraft brand envelopes, very fine.

artist's board high-grade drawing board used by artists for pen and ink drawings, wash drawings, watercolours.

Artmaster F.D.C. refers to Artmaster

art paper paper coated on both sides, with a glossy finish, for printing fine halftones.

art work in preparation of a printing plate, the art work includes not only the preliminary sketches, layout, and drawings, but also any retouching performed by the artists on the negatives or plates.

Arvizkárosultaknak (insc. on tab) 1913 semi-postal stamps of Hungary with a surtax for charity.

Arwad another name for Ile. Rouad. Stamps of the French offices in the Levant were overprinted ILE ROUAD vertically in the first issue of 1916 and horizontally in the second issue. France maintained a post office on the island during the French mandate period of the First World War. In ancient geography Arwad was a Phoenician city situated on a rocky island about three miles from the coast of what is now Syria. Mentioned in the Holy Bible in Ezekiel 27: 11.

ascender a lower-case letter that extends to the upper part of the body of the type, as b, d, k, l, t.

Ascension Island island of about 34 square miles in South Atlantic 2,000 miles west of Luanda, Angola, part of British Crown Colony of St. Helena. Issued stamps 1922.

Ascher, Dr. compiler of postal stationery catalogue *Grosser-Ganzsachen Katalog.*

A.S.D.A. American Stamp Dealers Association. Has sponsored annual postage stamp shows in New York City.

Ash, John In 1927 when the government of Australia established new printing equipment to produce paper money and stamps, John Ash, formerly with the De La Rue security printers, received the appointment of security printer to the Commonwealth Bank of Australia. The marginal imprint, John Ash, is well known to collectors of Australia and Papua stamps.

as is term in auction catalogue to describe doubtful material.

ASP (insc.) 1967 issue of Zanzibar and Tanzania to commemorate the "Tenth Anniversary of the Afro-Shirazi Party" – the inscription on each stamp.

asphaltum viscous, dark brown, liquid mineral pitch, used in photo-mechanical engraving processes, to protect certain parts of the plate against the action of the etching acid.

Aspinwall forwarding agent of New York City, partner in Howland & Aspinwall, importers and exporters who also forwarded mail. Also the former name of Colon, Colombia, where the British stamps were used between 1870 and 1881 with obliterator, E88. See BRITISH STAMPS USED ABROAD.

ASPP American Society of Polar Philatelists. Their announcement says they are "One of the leading organizations for collectors of cold-water philately."

ASSISTENCIA (ovpt.) appears on stamps of Azores and Portugal, postal tax stamps, 1911-12. Proceeds were for public charity.

Assistência D.L. No. 72 (sur.) appears with value changes on war-tax stamp of Portu-

guese India, Timor postal tax stamps of 1936-7.

ASSISTENCIA NACIONAL AOS TUBER-CULOSOS (insc. in oval frame with ANT insc. inside the oval) appears on Portugal franchise stamps of 1904 for use by the National Aid Society for Consumptives as free postage stamps.

Assistência Pública (insc.) appears on postal tax stamps of Portuguese India, 1960.

Astraea or Astrea, of classical mythology. Goddess of justice as a vignette on some U.S. 1875-95 newspaper stamps.

Asunción 1886 oval imprint on back of official stamps of Paraguay.

A & T initials plus denominations that are surcharged on stamps of French Colonies (1888) of Annam and Tonkin.

A.T.A. American Topical Association.

atado (Sp.) tied.

at betale or **a betale** (insc.) on stamps also inscribed NORGE at top and PORTOMAERKE in the bottom panel, postage-due stamps of Norway 1889-1923.

Athens, Ga. issued postmasters' provisional stamps for this town in Georgia in 1861, as part of the Confederate States of America.

Atlanta, Ga. issued postmasters' provisional envelopes for this town in Georgia in 1861, as part of the Confederate States of America.

att copper coin of Siam (Thailand). 64 atts equal one tical.

AUA (airline) Austrian Airlines, Vienna.

auction catalogues books or lists offering postage stamps and philatelic properties for sale by auction.

auctions, origin of J. Walter Scott, a young Englishman, introduced postage-stamp auction sales in New York City. In April 1872 the editor of the *Stamp Collector's Magazine,* an English stamp paper, stated in part, "Our chronicle of events this month would be incomplete if we omitted an account of the first sale by public auction of stamps held on this side of the Atlantic. It seems to have been inaugurated by J. W. Scott & Co. Early in the present year (1872) they opened a store in the English metropolis. . . ." With the publication of the first edition of the Second Series of the *American Philatelic Journal* in February 1888, Mr. Scott began a monthly account of his New York auction sales.

auf beiden Seiten bedruckt (Ger.) printed on both sides.

Aufdruck (Ger.) overprint, surcharge.

Aufdruckausgabe (Ger.) overprint issue.

aufgeklebt (Ger.) affixed, stuck on.

Auflage (Ger.) edition, issue.

Auflagezahlen (Ger.) copies printed.

auflegen (Ger.) to publish, to issue, to print.

Aufschrift (Ger.) inscription, legend.

Aufdruckfaelschung (Ger.) forged overprint.

Aufdruckfarbe (Ger.) colour of overprint.

Aufdrucktype (Ger.) overprint type.

Aufseher (Ger.) part of disinfected mark, supervisor, or inspector. (Courtesy of Herbert Dube)

Aufstellung (Ger.) list.

aufwaerts (Ger.) upward.

aufwerten (Ger.) to revalue.

Augusta, Ga. issued postmasters' provisional envelopes for this town in Georgia in 1861, as part of the Confederate States of America.

August issues (United States) The so-called August issues were proofs, sometimes called P.G.'s or *premières gravures*. Not to be confused with gravure printed stamps.

auksinas a coin of Lithuania. 100 skatiku equal 1 auksinas.

Auktion (Ger.) auction.

AUNUS (ovpt.) on stamps of Finland during occupation in 1919. Aunus is the Finnish name of Olenetz, a town in Russia. The stamps are listed with those of Russia in catalogues.

Au profit/de la/Croix Rouge/+ 50 Fr./ ten voordeele/van het/ Roode Kruis/ (7-line ovpt.) on 1942-3 stamps of Ruanda-Urundi. Semi-postal stamps of 1942 with surtaxes for the Red Cross.

aur a copper coin of Iceland. 100 aurar equal 1 krona. The coin is known as the ore in Norway, Sweden, and Greenland.

auserlesen (Ger.) exquisite, selected.

Ausfuehrung (Ger.) arrangement, execution, finish, quality.

Ausgabe (Ger.) issue.

Ausgabeort (Ger.) place of issue.

ausgebessert (Ger.) repaired.

ausgezeichnet (Ger.) excellent.

Aushilfsausgabe (Ger.) provisional issue.

Ausland (Ger.) foreign countries, foreign country.

Auslandsporto (Ger.) foreign postage.

ausser Kurs (Ger.) out of circulation, invalidated, obsolete.

Austin, Miss. issued postmasters' provisional envelopes for this town in Mississippi in 1861, as part of the Confederate States of America.

Austin, Texas issued postmasters' provisional envelopes in 1861, as part of the Confederate States of America.

Australasia the region of Oceania between the equator and latitude 47° south. Includes Australia, New Zealand, and other regional stamp-issuing authorities. Term not commonly used owing to its similarity to "Australia".

Australia self-governing dominion of the British Commonwealth of Nations of about 2,974,581 square miles, in Oceania south of Indonesia, with Indian Ocean on the west coast. Capital: Canberra. Six former British colonies confederated 1901 to form the Commonwealth of Australia: Tasmania, South Australia, Western Australia, Queensland, Victoria, New South Wales. Stamps inscribed Australia issued 1913.

Australian Antarctic Territories stamps issued since 1957 for the southern territory but also valid in Australia.

Australie (Fr.) Australia.

Australie du Sud (Fr.) South Australia.

Australie-Occidentale (Fr.) Western Australia.

Austria a federal republic of about 32,369 square miles in the southeastern part of Central Europe; formed in 1918, after the collapse of the Hapsburg Monarchy, out of the German-speaking provinces of the Alps and the Danube valley. Capital: Vienna. First stamps of the Austrian Monarchy issued in 1850. In 1867 the Austrian Empire split into a dual monarchy, and Hungary became an equal partner with Austria in the new Austro-Hungarian Monarchy. Mutual stamps of Austria and Hungary were issued in May 1867 for use by both countries, sometimes called neutral stamps. In May 1871 Hungary issued postage stamps.

Austrian-Italy Stamps for Lombardy and Venetia were first issued in 1850, with subsequent issues to 1864-5. See LOMBARDY-VENETIA.

Austrian Offices in Turkish Empire stamps of 1867-1914 consisted of various types similar to those of Austria. The only identifying feature is the word "soldi" (abbreviated "sld") and "para" or "piastre" on later surcharged and inscribed issues.

Austrian stamps In types of 1900-2 (Scott's) or 1901-2 (Gibbons), the obliterations consist of curved or straight bars, surcharges are in centimes or francs, and no country name appears. Used by the Austrian Offices in Crete.

ausverkauft (Ger.) sold out.

auswaehlen (Ger.) to choose, to select.

Auswahlsendung (Ger.) approval lot, approval shipment.

auswechseln (Ger.) to exchange.

Autaugaville, Ala. issued postmasters' provisional envelopes for this town in Alabama in 1861, as part of the Confederate States of America.

authentique (Fr.) genuine.

autogiro a type of aircraft with an huge overhead propeller turned by air pressure on a horizontal plane; should not be confused with helicopters. Many cachets have been used for both aircraft. Spain issued stamps in 1935-9 showing an autogiro flying over Seville and another series in 1939 portraying Juan de la Cierva with a picture of his autogiro invention over Madrid.

autographed cover any envelope, cover sheet, or aerogramme signed by a postmaster, a member of an airplane crew, and often by a person sending the letter.

autographed stamps individual stamps or blocks of stamps signed by the artist or a person in some way related to the theme of

*Autographed stamps
(designer Emanuel Hahn)*

the stamp. Example: the governor's signature on the Ohio commemorative stamp.

Automat (Ger.) vending machine.

automatic stamp affixing or vending machines dispensers used for the sale or use of postage stamps. Now the meter postage machines are more frequently used in offices.

autotype a collotype process in which the plate is coated with a light sensitive resin instead of gelatine. Some illustrations of stamps in books published around 1900 included autotype printing.

Autriche (Fr.) Austria.

Autriche-Hongrie (Fr.) Austria-Hungary.

avart (Swed.) variety or degenerate species.

avec gomme (Fr.) with gum.

avec oblitération portante sur (Fr.) tied.

(Cancel on both stamp and paper.)

Aviación y Comercio, S.A. (airline) point of origin, Madrid, Spain.

AVIACION (Sp. ovpt.) with a design of an airplane and three obliteration bars beside the tail of the aircraft. On Uruguay airmail stamp of June 9, 1948.

AVIACO (airline) Aviation y Comercio, S.A., Madrid, Spain.

A.V.I.A.N.C.A. (airline) Aerovias Nacionales de Colombia, S.A. Point of origin, Colombia. Formerly A.R.C.O.

Avião (sur.) appears with oriental text on regular-issue stamps for Macao airmail, 1936.

avion, aéroplane (Fr.) plane or airplane. Inscription on airmail labels of the world indicating the mail was sent by airmail ("Par Avion").

AVION NESSRE TAFARI (insc.) 1931 airmail stamps of Ethiopia (Abyssinia).

AVIONSKA POSTA (ovpt.) appears with design of an airplane on 1949 stamps for airmail postage, Jugoslavia in August 1949.

Aviso de Recepción (Sp. insc.) announcement of reception, appears on Salvador 1897 acknowledgment-of-receipt stamps.

avisporto maerke (insc.) on newspaper stamps of Denmark, 1907-15.

avos a coin of Macao and Timor. 100 avos equal 1 pataca. 78 avos equal 1 rupee.

A. W. Auner's Despatch Post in Philadelphia, Pennsylvania, issued U.S. local stamps in 1851.

Ayacucho name of Peruvian city overprinted on stamps of Peru. One of many provisional issues during Chilean-Peruvian War, 1879-82. Stamps issued 1881-4.

aytonomoe (insc.) on stamps of Epirus.

A.Z. (ovpt.) appears with a wreath design on 1927 stamps of Albania. Initials are those of Ahmed Zogu, president of Albania; subsequent issues portray him as King Zog I.

Azad Hind (insc.) on labels made to resemble stamps. Germany was reported to have prepared them for use in India in the event

that the German army conquered the country. After the Second World War, stamp dealers gave the labels as premiums to prospective buyers of approvals.

Azerbaidjan (Fr.) Azerbaijan.

Azerbaijan constituent republic of Union of Soviet Socialist Republics, of about 33,200 square miles. Capital: Baku. Issued stamps in 1919.

Azores nine Portuguese islands and some islets, of 888 square miles, in North Atlantic about 800 miles off coast of Portugal. Chief town: Ponta Delgada. Former colony but now a part of Portugal. First stamps issued in 1868 were Portuguese stamps overprinted "Açores".

Aztecs An early Mexican people who built roads for postal runners. Some Mexican stamps feature an Aztec birdman and other historical scenes.

azul (Sp.) blue.

azzurro (It.) blue.

B

B. abbreviation in auction catalogues, for "block".

B (in oval) (1) overprint on regular 1935-41 issues of Belgium, stamps used for official mail of the national railway management and for parcel post; (2) inscription on stamps without a country name, for issues

of Belgium in 1949 and subsequent years, used on parcel post and railway stamps.

B (ovpt.) on stamps of the Straits Settlements for use in Bangkok, Siam; Great Britain had permission by treaty since 1855 to use the post until mid 1885. Then Siam issued adhesive postage stamps. The use of B overprints ceased on July 1, 1885, the date that Siam joined the Universal Postal Union.

B (part of ovpt.) for Bluefields, a town and the capital of Zelaya. On stamps of Nicaragua for use in the province of Zelaya on the eastern coast.

B.A. (airline) British Airways Ltd. merged with Imperial Airways in 1939 to form British Overseas Airways Corporation (B.O.A.C.).

B.A. or **B.M.A.** (ovpt.) British Administration or British Military Administration. Appears as an abbreviation in the overprints "B.A. Eritrea", "B.A. Somalia", and "B.A. Tripolitania" with a surcharge on stamps of Great Britain in 1948 and subsequent years for use by the British military administrations in Eritrea, Italian Somaliland (Somalia), and Tripolitania.

Bache, Richard Benjamin Franklin's son-in-law, served as American colonial Postmaster General in Franklin's absence.

backbone in book-binding, the bound edge of a book.

background light flat tint, with or without designs, used as a decorative base for printing in a different colour or tone of the same colour. Brazil has used this technique.

backprinting any printing on the back of stamps, including advertisements, prayers, numerals, surcharges. See UNDERPRINTING.

backstamp an impression struck on the back of a letter at a receiving office or while mail is in transit. Backstamps usually indicate the city or town name or a sub-office name in conjunction with the time and the date mail arrived or passed through.

badge (her.) a distinctive mark or symbol worn by retainers or on possessions.

Bade (Fr.) Baden.

Baden former Grand Duchy in southwest Germany. Issued stamps 1851-68. In 1862, Baden issued Land Post, rural postage-due

stamps. From Jan. 1, 1872, used stamps of Germany.

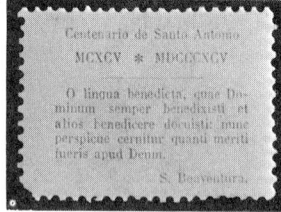

Backprinting: Latin prayer
on back of
Portuguese stamps (1895)

Baden (insc.) appears on stamps issued under French occupation of a zone in Germany, 1947-9. Listed with stamps of Germany in catalogues.

BAGHDAD (part of ovpt.) appears with "IN BRITISH" at the left side and "OCCUPATION" at the right, and with new values in annas at the bottom, on British occupation stamps for Mesopotamia in 1917. When the British mandate ended in 1932 Mesopotamia joined the League of Nations under the name Kingdom of Iraq. Stamps of Iraq are now used.

Bahawalpur (insc.) appears on stamps of Bahawalpur, a state (of about 17,494 square miles) in West Pakistan since 1947; prior to that an Indian state.

Bahamas More than 3,000 islands and rocks of about 4,404 square miles in West Indies off Florida coast; only a few are inhabited. Capital: Nassau. Stamps issued in 1859.

Bahamas SPECIAL DELIVERY (ovpt.) Canada and the Bahamas exchanged spe-

cial delivery stamps by an agreement of late 1915. Civilians in Canada could buy the Bahamas 5-penny stamps in May 1916 at Ottawa, Toronto, Westmount (part of Montreal), and Winnipeg. The stamps, made with three types of overprints, were on sale in Nassau in 1918, and for years later. Canada cancelled the arrangement. Contrary to some reports, these stamps were not made for the Canadian Armed Forces.

Bahnpoststempel (Ger.) railroad cancel.

Bahrain an archipelago of about 231 square miles in the Persian Gulf. Independent sultanate under British protection. Capital: Manama.

baht, bat silver coin of Siam (Thailand). 100 satangs equal 1 bat. It is the native name for the tical.

bailiwick a district under the jurisdiction of a bailiff or bailie.

baiocco, bajocco once a coin of base silver, later of copper or white metal, of Romagna and the Roman States. 100 bajocci equal 1 scudo. The coin is worth about a U.S. cent.

BAJAR PORTO (sur. and insc.) appeared since 1950 on Indonesia postage-due stamps.

Baker's City Express Post in Cincinnati, Ohio, issued U.S. local stamps in 1849.

bakgrund (Swed.) background.

Baku capital city of Azerbaijan (Azerbaidzhan). Baku Province issued stamps 1922-4, which are listed with those of Azerbaijan in catalogues.

Balasse, Willy a Belgian stamp dealer and publisher who produced the catalogue *Willy Balasse, Belgique, Congo Belge.*

Balbo airmails (nick.) set of two Italian stamps, both in three parts (triptych), used May 20, 1933, on the Rome-to-Chicago flight of General Italo Balbo. The return flight was cancelled.

balboa unit of gold standard in Panama. 100 centesimos equal 1 balboa. It is named after the explorer Vasco Nunez de Balboa.

balkenentwertung (Ger.) barred.

Balkenstempel (Ger.) bar cancellation.

balkstämpel (Swed.) bar cancellation.

Ballonpost (Ger.) balloon mail.

ballons montés (Fr.) refers to letters sent out of Paris by balloon during the Prussian siege of 1870-1. "Ballon non-monté" covers are those that were flown out of Paris by balloons without a balloonist.

balloon posts various mails carried by balloons, mainly in the United States. Examples of these mail services include the Jupiter Buffalo Balloon, the British Daily Graphic Service, and the French balloon post of 1870-1.

Baltimore, Md. This city in Maryland issued postmasters' provisional stamps and envelopes in 1845-6.

bamboo an arborescent grass that was one of the early sources of paper-making fibres.

Bamra (insc.) on stamps of Bamra, a feudatory state of 1,988 square miles in the central provinces of India. Issued stamps in 1888.

Banana stamps (nick.) a freak issue in 1969 from Tonga. Stamps are banana-shaped with matching cancels. Classified as gimmicks.

Banat issue Hungarian stamps overprinted "Bánát Bácska"; used in 1919 for less than a week, between the Serbian evacuation and Romanian occupation.

banco (skilling banco) a copper coin of Sweden. 48 banco equal 1 rixsdaler. This coin was last struck in 1858.

band, bande (Fr.) strip, as of stamps.

bandalette or **banderole** (Fr.) the Sunday labels (tabs) on certain Belgian postage stamps (1893-1913). Also called dominical

*Bandalette
(Sunday label)*

tablets because the bilingual words on them mean "Do not deliver on Sundays."

Bangkok capital of Thailand (Siam).

Bangla Desh new state formed in 1971 from the former East Pakistan. The name comes from a Bengali word meaning "Bengal nation". As a state, Bangla Desh is the seventh or eighth most populous country in the world, with more than 75 million people (specialists in geography do not agree on the exact population relative to that of other countries). Issued stamps in 1971 before the country broke away fully from Pakistan. Later the original eight values were overprinted "BANGLADESH LIBERATED".

bani coin of Romania; the word "bani" was overprinted on Austrian stamps while Romania was under Austrian occupation, 1917-18. Listed with stamps of Romania in catalogues.

BANK International Bank for Reconstruction and Development. Brazil (1955) and Iceland (1956) issued stamps featuring construction of power plants financed by BANK. In 1955 Turkey honoured the tenth meeting of the governors of the organization with a set of four stamps.

bank note engravers artists who engrave dies and plates for bank notes, stamps, and securities.

bank note paper a strong, durable, and pliable paper, made from cotton and linen rags and used for printing currency. Some of the 1919 regular issues and 1920 charity stamps of Latvia were printed on the back of unfinished bank notes. The backs of the stamps contain a pattern of the paper money.

bank note stamps U.S. issues printed by the various security printers in the United States: the National Bank Note Co., the Continental Bank Note Co., and the American Bank Note Co. All three printed certain stamps (1870-9) of the same or similar designs, some from the same plates. (See Scott's or Minkus U.S. Specialized catalogues.) Certain other commercial firms are not included among bank note stamp printers.

banner (her.) an armorial flag, vertically rectangular, in the Middle Ages.

bantams (nick.) describes the small stamps of South Africa issued to conserve paper

(1942-3), and the same stamps overprinted "S.W.A." for South-West Africa (1942-5). Victoria, a state in Australia, issued a similar miniature stamp in 1901.

banu a copper coin of Romania. 100 bani equal 1 leu. The coin was adopted in 1867 when Romania joined the Latin Monetary Union.

Baranya 1919 (ovpt. and sur.) appears on postage stamps of Hungary in 1919 during the Serbian occupation of Hungary. Baranya, one of the nineteen counties in Hungary, became a part of Jugoslavia when the Serbs, Croats, and Slovenes proclaimed

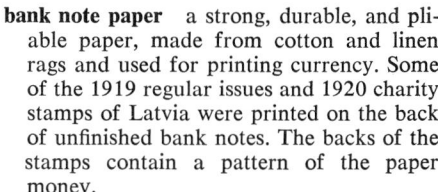

*Bank note paper
(used for stamps
of Latvia, 1920)*

their kingdom in 1918. The name of the kingdom was changed officially in 1929 to Jugoslavia, although postage stamps were inscribed "Jugoslavija" as early as 1926. Baranya stamps are listed with those of Hungary in stamp catalogues.

Barbade (Fr.) Barbados.

Barbacoas Issue postmasters' provisional stamps issued in 1903 for the municipality of Barbacoas in southwest Colombia in the former state of Cauca, which is now a department in the country. The type-set stamps have no identification, but bear the Spanish words "No hay estampillas", meaning no stamps available. Listed in catalogues with stamps of Colombia.

Barbados island of about 166 square miles in the West Indies, east of the Windward Islands. Former British colony. Became independent within the British Commonwealth on Nov. 30, 1966. Capital: Bridgetown. Issued stamps in 1852.

Barbuda coral island in West Indies, part of the Leeward Islands; British colony. Issued Leeward stamps overprinted "Barbuda", July 1922.

bar cancels cancellations formed of bars,

Bar cancel

often designed in ovals, circles, and rectangles, with or without numerals, letters, or symbols.

Barcelona a city state in northeastern Spain on the Mediterranean Sea. From 1930 to 1945, issued numerous postage stamps overprinted, surcharged, and inscribed, mainly locals. A set of six in 1929 for the international stamp show was called the Barcelona Issue. See *Catálogo Hevia de España* for details.

Barnard's Cariboo Express Francis J. Barnard, a native of Quebec, went to British Columbia in 1859 and established an express company in the next year. Through hard work and diligent management he became the leader in British Columbia, bought out Jeffray's Express, and won his tender to convey mails to the interior of British Columbia. Dietz and Nelson amalgamated with Barnard after 1862, and by 1866 Barnard controlled the group. Eventually the British Columbia Express Co. operated Barnard's company.

Barnard's City Letter Express in Boston, Massachusetts, issued U.S. local stamps 1845-7.

bar precancels an early type of precancellation on U.S., Canadian, and other postage stamps.

barre (Fr.) bar, as in a cancel or overprint.

barré (Fr.) barred.

Barre, Jean J. He and his son, D. A. Barre, were engravers at the French mint in Paris when the first stamps of France and Greece were being made. They became famous engravers of stamp dies. The father engraved the die for the first postage stamps of France, issued Jan. 1, 1849, and the son engraved the die of Hermes' head design for the first stamps of Greece, issued Oct. 1, 1861. Gibbons European catalogues give the details.

barred may refer to cancels made of parallel lines (bars), or to a type of remainder cancellation of bars, either plain or with enclosed decorations. Sometimes describes certain Canadian precancels on low-value stamps (1- to 5-cent) since the 1870 issue. Also refers to varnish bars, which are used to prevent the removal of cancels.

Barr's Penny Dispatch in Lancaster, Pennsylvania, issued U.S. local stamps in 1855.

Barwani (insc.) on stamps of Barwani, an Indian feudal state of about 1,332 square miles. Issued stamps in 1921.

bas (Fr.) bottom.

bas de casse (Fr.) lower case; refers to small letters, not capitals.

base (her.) lower part of shield.

base (1) wood or metal block on which printing plates are mounted; (2) paper that supports a coating material.

base colour the first colour printed, on which succeeding colours are laid; always an opaque colour.

Basel doves (nick.) 1845 stamps of Basel, a canton of Switzerland; named after the central motif of a dove in flight.

basic dyes or colours organic colouring agents in which the dye base takes the place of the basic or alkaline constituent of a salt. Basic colours are used for tinting paper stock in the beaters; they are not usually as fast to light as acid dyes, but are brighter hues.

B.A. Somalia (ovpt.) See B.A. OR B.M.A.

Basoutoland (Fr.) Basutoland.

basso (It.) bottom.

Basted Mills paper brand name of the paper

manufacturers, Basted Paper Company, who supplied thin wove paper for some New Zealand stamps. The Basted Mills are a subsidiary of Wiggins, Teape & Co. (1919), Limited.

Basutoland a former Crown colony of about 11,716 square miles in South Africa, southeast of Orange Free State, north of Cape Province. Became independent within the Commonwealth on Oct. 4, 1966, and the name was changed to Lesotho. Capital: Maseru. Issued stamps in 1933.

B.A.T. (airline) Bengal Air Transport Co., Ltd., India.

bateau à vapeur (Fr.) steamer.

bâtonné paper type of watermarked paper with lines or batons equally spaced in any one sheet but wider apart than laid lines.

Baton Rouge, La. issued postmasters' provisional stamps for this city in Louisiana in 1861, as part of the Confederate States of America.

Batoum (Fr.) Batum.

B.A. Tripolitania (ovpt.) See B.A. OR B.M.A.

battleships (nick.) 1898 proprietary and documentary (revenue) stamps of the United States featuring illustrations of battleships. These should not be mounted and mixed with postage stamps; they are revenue stamps.

Batum Russian city on Black Sea near Turkish border. British administration issued occupation stamps in 1919.

Batym (insc.) appears on stamps of Batum.

Bau de Poste (Fr.) postal bureau, post office. Appears as part of some French postmarks. (Courtesy of Hubert Dube)

Bavaria former kingdom of about 30,562 square miles, now part of the American zone in Germany. Principal city: Munich. Issued stamps from 1849 until 1920.

Bavaria 1862 6KR BL in auction catalogues, refers to 1862 stamp of Bavaria in the 6-kreuzer denomination, blue colour. Postage stamp catalogues provide the full, correct names of foreign currency and the periods of use.

Bavière (Fr.) Bavaria.

Bayern, or **Bayr** (Ger. insc.) appears on stamps of Bavaria.

Bayonne City Dispatch in Bayonne City, New Jersey, issued U.S. local stamps and envelopes in 1883.

B blank error (nick.) British 1841 1-penny red-brown stamps without the letter A in the lower right corner. The stamps should have had this letter, but the space was left blank. These errors come from sheets of stamps printed from Plate number 77.

British stamps at that time carried identifying letters in the lower corners of each stamp beginning with the top left-corner stamp, which was the first stamp in the sheet and had letters A-A. Stamps in the first horizontal row have letters A-L. The vertical row of stamps have numbers from A–A to A–T. The position of every stamp in the sheet can be identified by the letters.

B.C. (1) British Columbia, Canada; (2) British Colony; (3) before Christ; the abbreviation is placed after the figures of the year.

B.C.A. (ovpt.) British Central Africa. On stamps inscribed "British South Africa Company". They were the first postage stamps of Rhodesia. In 1907 the name was changed from British Central Africa to Nyasaland Protectorate.

B.C.M. (insc.) appears with the Arms of Great Britain on large stamps of the British Consulate mail of Madagascar.

B.C.O.F. Australian stamps of 1937-46 were overprinted "B.C.O.F./Japan/1946" in three lines for occupation use. Initials stand for "British Commonwealth Occupation Force".

B. Dpto. Zelaya (ovpt.) appearing on stamps of Zelaya, a province of Nicaragua, that were made to fill dealers' orders but were not regularly issued. Others with similar overprints were genuine. Refer to stamp catalogues for details on both types.

B. Dpto. Zelaya (ovpts. and sur.) on various issues of Nicaragua 1904-11, for use in the province of Zelaya on the east coast. Nicaraguan currency with two distinct values caused a need for special stamps for Zelaya. A similar example is the 12-pence inscription on stamps of the Province of Canada in 1851, when the shilling had different values in various parts of the country.

B.E.A. (airline) See BRITISH EUROPEAN AIRWAYS.

beaked (her.) having a beak of distinctive tincture.

bearers (1) wood or metal strips in the bed of a press or in a form; (2) strips of metal type-high placed around the type for protection in moulding; (3) excess metal or dead metal left around or on the surface of engravings type-high to protect the printing surface during electrotyping; (4) flat metal strips along the side of the press bed slightly less than type-high to prevent the cylinder from dropping too low during the passage of blank areas in the form. Bearers thus cause bars and rules to appear between panes of stamps and the results are sometimes seen in marginal paper of stamp panes. See JUBILEE LINES.

bear stamps (nick.) St. Louis, Missouri, postmasters' provisional stamps issued in November 1845 and used until 1847; featured heraldic bears as a portion of the arms of Missouri.

Beaumont, Texas issued postmasters' provisional stamps in 1861, as part of the Confederate States of America.

Bechuanaland (British Bechuanaland) a self-governing province of about 51,424 square miles in Union of South Africa comprising northern part of Cape of Good Hope Province. Capital: Mafeking. Not to be confused with Bechuanaland Protectorate. Issued stamps in 1885.

Bechuanaland Protectorate British protectorate of about 222,000 square miles in central South Africa, north of the Union of South Africa; not to be confused with Bechuanaland (British Bechuanaland). Became independent within the Commonwealth on Sept. 30, 1966, and the name was changed to Botswana. Bechuanaland Protectorate issued stamps in 1888 with the overprint "Protectorate" on the stamps of Bechuanaland. This overprint also appeared on stamps of Cape of Good Hope in 1889. Subsequent issues overprinted on British stamps from 1897; then the stamps were inscribed "Bechuanaland Protectorate" from 1932 to 1966.

bed part of a printing press on which the form is set for printing.

bedenken (Ger.) to consider.

Bedeutung (Ger.) meaning, importance.

befugt (Ger.) authorized.

Beiblatt (Ger.) supplement.

beifuegen (Ger.) to add, to enclose.

beigeben (Ger.) to attach.

Beilage (Ger.) enclosure.

Beispiel (Ger.) example.

Beitrag (Ger.) contribution.

Belge (Fr.) Belgian.

Belgian Airlines See SABENA.

Belgian East Africa See RUANDA-URUNDI.

Belgie (insc.) Belgium.

Belgien (Ger. sur.) Belgium. On German stamps issued in Belgium under German occupation, 1914-18.

Belgique (insc.) Belgium.

Belgisch Congo (insc.) Belgian Congo.

Belgium constitutional monarchy in northwest Europe, of about 11,774 square miles. Capital: Brussels. First stamps issued in 1849.

Belgium reduced postal rates 1946 stamps that were surcharged "—10%" by hand

and letterpress. Many varieties of little account resulted. These stamps are listed with regular issues in stamp catalogues.

BELIZE RELIEF FUND PLUS appears on 1932 semi-postal stamps of British Honduras, with a surtax to help the 1931 hurricane victims. "BELIZE" is on the top line; "RELIEF" is printed vertically on the left side, and "FUND" vertically on the right side. "PLUS" appears above new values at the bottom of the stamp.

Benadir (insc.) Italian Somaliland.

Ben Day a method of breaking down masses of tones in a photograph or other artwork into tints or mottled effects by dots of various sizes, and then transferring the images to metal printing plates by an engraving process. The background areas of stamps, the landscapes, and other illustrations on stamps by letterpress are frequently made by Ben Day (or Benday). The method was invented by Benjamin Day (1838-1916), an American printer and the son of Benjamin Harry Day, founder of the *New York Sun* newspaper.

Bengasi (sur.) on stamps of Italy used by the Italian offices in Africa in 1901. Listed with stamps of Italy in catalogues.

Benin French possession on Gulf of Guinea in west Africa, of about 8,627 square miles. Capital: Benin. Stamps issued 1892-4, overprinted on stamps of French colonies.

Benin town in Nigeria on western delta of Niger River. Used special postmarks in 1892. See Gibbons Part One catalogue.

BENTJANA ALAM (sur.) National disaster; appears with "1953" and "+10" on Indonesia semi-postal stamps of 1953.

Bentley's Dispatch in New York City, New York, issued U.S. local stamps in 1856.

benzine a liquid used to detect watermarks in stamps.

benzinempfindlich (Ger.) sensitive to benzine.

Berford & Co.'s Express in New York City, New York, issued U.S. local stamps in 1851.

Bergedorf section of Hamburg, Germany. Belonged to Lübeck and Hamburg 1420-1868; later part of Hamburg. Stamps issued in 1861.

Bericht (Ger.) report.

berichtigt (Ger.) corrected.

Berlin (ovpt.) on stamps of Germany issued for use in American, British, and French occupation sectors of Berlin.

Bermuda group of 360 small islands (about 21 square miles) twenty of which are inhabited, in the Atlantic about 580 miles southeast of Cape Hatteras; a British Crown Colony. Capital: Hamilton.

Bermudes, les (Fr.) Bermuda.

besa copper coin of Italian Somaliland. 100 besas equal 1 rupee. The coin is also used in Ethiopia (Abyssinia), where 100 besas equal 1 talari.

Besatzungsarmee (Ger.) army of occupation.

beschaedigt (Ger.) damaged.

Beschaffenheit (Ger.) condition.

beschraenkt (Ger.) limited.

beschreiben (Ger.) to describe.

Besetzungsgebiet (Ger.) occupied territory.

bestellen (Ger.) to order.

bestimmen (Ger.) to determine, to define.

Bestimmungsort (Ger.) destination.

betalt (Danish) paid; a marking on mail.

Betrag (Ger.) amount.

beurteilen (Ger.) to judge.

Beyrouth (Fr. sur.) Beirut; appears on postage stamps of French Offices in Beirut in the Turkish Empire issued in 1905.

Beyrouth (ovpt.) on stamps of Russia for use of Russian offices in Turkey in 1910.

bezahlen (Ger.) to pay.

bezahlt (Ger.) paid.

Bezirksmarken (Ger.) district overprint, district stamps.

B.G. Cen. 9 (insc.) appears without a country name on Modena newspaper tax stamps that were not used to pay postal charges, but which paid taxes on foreign newspapers.

Bhopal (insc.) appears on stamps of Bhopal, an Indian feudatory state of 6,902 square miles. Issued stamps in 1876.

Bhor State Postage (insc.) on stamps of Bhor, an Indian feudatory state of about 925 square miles, southeast of Bombay. Capital: Bhor. Stamps issued in 1879.

Bhutan semi-independent country on northeast border of India in Himalayas, of about 18,000 square miles. Capitals: Punakha in winter; Tashi Chho Dzong in summer. Stamps issued from 1962 to present.

BICENTENAIRE DE PORT AU PRINCE (insc.) on Haiti regular issue and airmail stamps, 1950, to mark 200th anniversary of Port-au-Prince in 1949. The stamps were issued about a year late.

bi-coloured postmarks postmarks or cancellations, usually decorative, in two colours. Some black postmarks bear manuscript dates indicating the delivery days of mail. These were used in some small communities in the United States.

bi-coloured stamps postage stamps printed in two colours. Some postal stationery has

been printed in two colours.

bi-coulore (Fr.) bi-coloured, a two-coloured stamp.

bicycle mail In 1894, in California, the Bicycle Mail Route issued U.S. local stamps and envelopes. In South Africa during the Boer War, a British officer, General Robert S. S. Baden-Powell, founder of the Boy Scouts, authorized a bicycle mail and issued two designs in photographic prints as postage stamps, April 9, 1900. One design features Sgt. Major Goodyear riding a bicycle; the other portrays Baden-Powell.

bienfaisance (Fr.) charity.

bieten (Ger.) to bid, to offer.

Bigelow's Express in Boston, Massachusetts, issued U.S. local stamps in 1848-51.

bight curve in a coast, or the bay formed by such a curve. Example: the bight of Biafra, a part of Spanish Guinea.

Bijawar (insc.) on stamps of Bijawar, a feudatory state of about 973 square miles in central India. Issued stamps in 1935.

bijzondere vluchten (Dutch insc.) special flight; appears on Netherlands airmail stamps, 1938-53 and 1966.

Bilderserie (Ger.) the face of a picture on a stamp; pictorial stamp, or pictorial series.

bilingual stamps issues printed in two languages; for example, stamps of Canada, Belgium, and South Africa, and those with

foreign-language surcharges and overprints, found among occupation stamps.

Billigung (Ger.) approval.

billon an alloy of silver and copper. Billon coins contain more than one-half copper. Some coins of Turkey were made from billon.

B.I.O.T. (ovpt.) British Indian Ocean Territories; on stamps of Seychelles issued Jan. 17, 1968.

birds on stamps Almost every country in the world has issued postage stamps with real, imaginary, or heraldic birds in the stamp designs.

Birmanie (Fr.) Burma.

bisected postage-due stamps In the United States, in October 1895, the postmaster at Jefferson, Iowa, bisected some 2-cent dues, cutting them vertically in half, and surcharged them "due 1 cent". See Scott's U.S. Specialized catalogue, or *The Postage Stamps of the United States* by John N. Luff.

bisects bisected stamps, stamps cut in half vertically, horizontally, or diagonally; usu-

ally cut to make stamps of values that postmasters did not have on hand. Stamps cut into any other portions are correctly called "split stamps" and should not be confused with bisected stamps.

Bishop marks The first post office stamps in the world were invented by Henry Bishop, British postmaster, who was appointed in 1660.

Bishop's City Post in Cleveland, Ohio, issued U.S. local stamps in 1854. These are classed as Carrier stamps in Scott's U.S. Specialized catalogue.

bistro (It.) bistre.

bit, bitt silver coin of Danish West Indies. 100 bits equal 1 franc. These bits were cut from the edge or centre of a Spanish piece of eight and countermarked for use in the West Indies. A bit equals one real, and the expression "two bits", meaning a quarter-dollar, may come from the division of an 8-reales piece into quarters.

BIT (Fr. insc.) Bureau International du Travail. Appears on various issues throughout the world.

BIT (U.N.) Bureau International du Travail (also known as the International Labor Organization, ILO, and the Organisation Internationale du Travail, OIT). The BIT has

been honoured by the United Nations in 1954 by stamps with marginal inscriptions "ILO 1954" on the 3-cent denominations and "OIT 1954" on the 8-cent stamps. The U.N. offices in Switzerland have special stamps for their use. The BIT held regional conferences in Uruguay in 1949 and in Brazil in 1952, and stamps were issued to honour these events. See INTERNATIONAL LABOR ORGANIZATION.

B.I.T. Oct. 1930 (Fr. ovpt.) Bureau International du Travail. On stamps of Belgium for the International Labor Organization. Also appears as "S.d.N. Bureau International du Travail" on Swiss stamps for the International Labor Organization in 1923 and subsequent years.

bite (1) in photo-engraving, the action of the etching acid on the metal plate; (2) a white spot in an impression due to a small piece of paper, or other foreign matter on the sheet, often found on postage stamps.

Bizone (Ger.) Anglo-American zone.

BKLT abbreviation for "booklet", used in auction catalogues, referring to a small book or to book postage depending on context.

BL black; often refers to the colour of surcharges or overprints. BL may indicate black or blue colour.

Blå (Swed.) blue.

black and white print monochrome illustration printed with black ink on white paper.

black cancellations The first cancellations on the penny black stamps of Great Britain, May 6, 1840, were black. Like Great Britain, many countries found black cancellations not clearly visible on black stamps.

Black Honduras (nick.) the world's rarest airmail stamp, issued in 1925. Named after the colour of the overprint "25¢ on 10¢", which is dark blue with a black overprint. This is the only known mint copy in existence. Before 1939 two copies were known – the mint copy of this lot, then part of the famous Dr. Cole collection, and a used copy. In the afternoon auction of February 27, 1961, the late F. W. Kessler sold this famous Black Honduras stamp for $24,500.

Black Jack (nick.) the 1863 2-cent black postage stamps of the United States. They portray a large head of Andrew Jackson, the seventh U.S. president. The name is also given to certain U.S. postal stationery printed in black in 1863-4.

black-out postmark a type of postmark that does not indicate the name of the originating office. Sometimes called "mute cancels." Not to be confused with A.P.O. (Army Post Office) or F.P.O. (Field Post Office) markings, which also show no place names.

black stamps the philatelist's name for proofs attached to the Austrian post office sheets announcing new issues. Also, postage stamps or postal stationery stamps printed in black.

blaeulichgrau (Ger.) bluish grey.

blanc, blanche (Fr.) white.

blanket (1) wool or rubber sheet covering the tympan of a cylinder press used in newspaper and poster work; (2) rubber sheet used on offset presses to transfer the impression from the plate onto the paper, used in printing stamps by offset lithography.

blass (Ger.) pale.

blassultramarin (Ger.) pale ultramarine.

Blatt (Ger.) page.

blau (Ger.) blue.

blaugrau (Ger.) blue-grey.

blaugruen (Ger.) blue-green.

blauschiefer (Ger.) blue-slate.

blauschwarz (Ger.) blue-black.

Blaustrichentwertung (Ger.) blue-pencil cancellation.

blauviolett (Ger.) blue-violet.

blazon the heraldic description of a coat of arms.

B L C I initials in the four corners of cer-

tain stamps to identify Bhopal issues of 1884-96 and 1902.

bleeding colour a colour that tends to spread or run when wet. Care should be taken with stamps printed with aniline inks, which bleed.

bleuâtre (Fr.) bluish.

bleu, bleue (Fr.) blue.

bleu de Prusse (Fr.) Prussian blue.

bleu-gris (Fr.) grey-blue.

bleuté (Fr.) blue-tinged; refers to bluish-toned paper. Some British penny blacks were made on this type of paper.

bleu-vert (Fr.) greenish blue or blue-green.

blind cancels those without information

about place of origin, date, and time. These are also known as obliterations or dumb postmarks.

blind embossing embossing without the use of printing ink or gold leaf.

Blindfeld (Ger.) blank space.

blind perforations impressions on stamp paper where the perforation pins did not puncture holes around stamp designs. The

stamps appear unperforated, but often a magnifier is needed to see these impressions.

blind rouletting Some postage stamps have attempted roulettes between the rows of stamps, which appear as mere surface impressions or skipped cuts that leave blank strips between two or more stamps. The resulting pairs of stamps seem imperforate between, but on close examination with a magnifier tiny impressions can be seen in the rows between stamps. These are scarce varieties found in the 1970-2 coil stamps of Canada. These coil stamps were made in ten-roll units of 100 stamps each in a single roll. Each roll in the larger rolls of ten had been perforated 10 horizontally and rouletted vertically with tiny nodes holding the rolls together. When two or more rolls of these postage stamps are unrolled together, some pairs or strips (three or more) show the blind rouletting, but appear imperforate. These are varieties, not errors, because faulty machine operations caused them. Other blind roulettes may have been made, especially before 1870, but they have not reached catalogue status. See BLIND PERFORATIONS; NODES.

Blindzaehnung (Ger.) missing perforation.

blitz perforations (nick.) refers to British colonial stamps produced originally by De La Rue until their plant was bombed on Dec. 29, 1940. Other printers in England continued the work, but they used perforating machines of different gauges.

BLKS blocks.

bloc (Fr.) block, miniature sheet, souvenir sheet.

blocco (It.) block.

bloc de hojas de papel (Sp.) souvenir sheet.

bloc de hojitas conmemorativas (Sp.) souvenir sheet.

bloc de hojitas en miniatura (Sp.) miniature sheet.

bloc de quatre (Fr.) block of four (stamps).

bloc-feuillet (Fr.) miniature sheet.

block solid piece of wood or metal on which a printing plate is mounted to make it type-high. In Great Britain, many stamp collectors refer to the entire unit of a printing plate plus the wood or metal mounting as a block.

block, block of stamps three or more adhesive postage stamps from two or more horizontal rows, not separated. Blocks other than those containing four stamps are usually specified as blocks of three, six, eight, and so on, but are in units smaller than a complete post office pane or post office sheet in the same design.

blockade mail During the Civil War in the United States, President Lincoln had the southern ports from South Carolina to Texas blockaded. Collectors seek blockade mail from this period, beginning in April 1861.

Blockstueck (Ger.) block of four, souvenir sheet.

bloco de sêlos (Port.) pad of stamps (the bundle as it comes from printers).

Blood, D. O., & Co. in Philadelphia, Pennsylvania, issued U.S. local stamps and envelopes in 1841-60.

blot out to cancel an engraved plate by scratching lines over it.

B.L.P. (It. ovpt.) Le buste lettere postali; on regular issue stamps of 1906-18. Issued from January to July 1921 and sold at a discount to a charitable organization to help returned, injured soldiers. The National Federation for Assisting War Invalids put the overprinted stamps on envelopes bearing advertisements and sold them at a profit with proceeds to the federation. The major part of the profits came from the advertisements on the special envelopes. "Busta" means envelope or case for papers.

Bluenose (nick.) denotes the 50-cent Canadian stamp of 1929 featuring the famous schooner *Bluenose* that won so many races for Canada.

blue paper, bluish paper Stamps of the 1909 regular issue of United States from 1 to 15 cents were printed on experimental greyish-blue paper. The colour is uniform in the paper stock. When Perkins Bacon printed some of the 1- and 2-penny stamps of Great Britain in 1841 and subsequent years, the ink contained prussiate of potash, which had an irregular bluing effect in the paper. Bluish papers have been used for some low-value and many high-value British colonial stamps, as a precaution against forgery.

Blumen (Ger.) flowers.

blur a slurred impression in printing or stamping by hand. Numerous postage stamps overprinted or surcharged appear with blurred impressions. These are varieties, not errors.

B.M.A. (ovpt.) British Military Administration 1945 ovpt. on Sarawak stamps of 1934-41 issue for use in Sarawak and British Borneo (consisting of Brunei, Labuan, and North Borneo).

B.M.A. Eritrea, B.M.A. Somalia, or B.M.A. Tripolitania See B.A. OR B.M.A.

B.N.A. British North America. Usually appears on stamps of British colonies in North America before Canadian Confederation in 1867. The colonies included the Province of Canada, Nova Scotia, New Brunswick, Prince Edward Island, Newfoundland, and British Columbia and Vancouver Island (separate colonies 1866).

B.N.A., F AVE British North America, fine

Block of three stamps

average; describes a lot containing various British North American colonial stamps issued before Canadian Confederation (1867).

B.N.A.P.S. British North America Philatelic Society.

B.N.F./CASTELLORIZO (2-line ovpt.) for "Base Navale Française", on stamps of French offices in Turkey during French occupation of Castellorizo in 1920.

BOAC See BRITISH OVERSEAS AIRWAYS CORPORATION.

Board of Education (ovpt.) on official stamps of Great Britain, 1902-4.

boardwalk margins (nick.) refers to postage stamps with wide margins on all sides.

body (1) shank or portion of type below the face; (2) main part of a book; (3) consistency and viscosity of a printing ink; (4) apparent weight of a sheet of paper.

Boehmen u. Maehren (Ger.) Bohemia and Moravia.

boekdrukken (Dutch) letterpress printing.

bogache a coin of Yemen. 40 bogaches equal 1 imadi.

Bogchan or **Bogaches** (1) coin of Yemen; (2) inscription on stamps of Yemen.

Bogen (Ger.) sheet, pane.

Bogenecke (Ger.) corner of sheet.

Bogenentwertung (Ger.) sheet cancellation.

bogenförmiger Durchstich (Ger.) This term has two meanings: arc roulette (percé en arc) and saw-tooth roulette (percé en scie). The French terms for rouletting, given here in parentheses, are often used in English. Rouletting, or percé, suggests piercing or cutting slits into the paper in various shapes: arc, saw-tooth, lines, and others.

Bogenmitte (Ger.) centre of sheet.

Bogenrand (Ger.) sheet margin.

Bogenwasserzeichen (Ger.) sheet watermark.

Bogenzahl (Ger.) sheet serial number.

Bogotá city in Colombia, issued local stamps 1889-1903.

bogus stamps labels made to deceive stamp collectors. Many bogus stamps were made prior to 1900. Some had names of imaginary countries such as "Sedang". "Bogus" as a term should not be used to describe faked or counterfeited postage stamps.

Bohemia and Moravia German protectorate comprising two western divisions of Czechoslovakia. The protectorate was dissolved in 1945. Issued stamps 1939-44; prior to that (1928-39), stamps of Czechoslovakia, overprinted in black, were used.

Böhmen und Mähren (insc.) Bohemia and Moravia; on the stamps of the German Protectorate of Bohemia and Moravia, 1939-41. Listed with stamps of Czechoslovakia in catalogues.

boiling method of cleaning stamps. Collectors take a risk in boiling stamps to clean them. Experiments with cheap stamps should precede any venture with scarce examples. Any person who boils stamps does so at his own risk.

bold-face type a heavy or thickened form of type face that gives a blacker effect.

bolívar silver coin of Venezuela. 100 centimos equal 1 bolivar. Named after Simón Bolívar, it is sometimes called the "venezolano".

Bolivar (insc.) appears on stamps of Bolívar, a former state but now a department of Colombia. The state issued postage stamps from 1863 to 1904.

Bolivar Sucre Miranda – Decreto de 27 de Abril de 1870 (ovpt.) or "Decreto de 27 de Junio de 1870", overprinted in small letters on Venezuelan stamps for postage and revenue, 1871-3. These were the only stamps available in Venezuela from March 1871 to August 1873.

Bolivia republic of about 416,000 square miles in central region of South America. Capital: Sucre; but the seat of government is La Paz. First stamps were used on mail delivered by a private carrier in 1863. Government issues followed in 1866.

boliviano a coin of Bolivia. 100 centavos equal 1 boliviano. 1,000 bolivianos equal 1 Bolivian escudo (1963).

Bolivie (Fr.) Bolivia.

Bolivien (Ger.) Bolivia.

bollo (It.) postmark.

BOLLO DELLA POSTA DI SICILLA (insc.) on stamps of Two Sicilies for use in Sicily, 1859.

BOLLO DELLA POSTA NAPOLETANA (insc.) on stamps of Two Sicilies for use in Naples, 1858.

BOLLO POSTALE (insc.) on San Marino special-delivery stamps.

BOLLO STRAORDINARIO PER LE POSTE (insc.) on Tuscany newspaper tax stamp of 1854.

bond paper originally glue-sized rag paper used for printing bonds and certificates; now denotes both rag and sulphite papers, sized for writing purposes, and used for letterheads and other commercial forms. Often used to produce modern first day covers with decorative cachets.

boners popular name for postage stamps with mistakes in the design. These are sometimes humorous, as on the 1934 stamps of Austria, which show a man with his ears backwards.

Bonny River postmark for Bonny, a seaport village at the mouth of the Niger River in Nigeria. Nigeria used special postmarks in 1892. See Gibbons Part One catalogues, British Empire and Commonwealth stamps section for details.

booklet panes small sheets of adhesive postage stamps bound in a booklet form. Collectors are warned not to remove the tabs at the binding edges of the booklet panes.

They are also advised to save all the parts of postage stamp booklets when these are taken apart or, as philatelists say, "exploded".

booklet stamps postage stamps that are removed from booklets or are in the booklet panes.

bootheel postmark an oval type of Barbados marking made from thick bars of about 5 millimetres in length placed around an oval opening that framed numerals from April 10, 1863, until 1882. Probably in 1886 the bootheels were recalled to the General Post Office in Bridgetown, and the numerals were removed. The name derives from the presence of marks resembling the metal studs sometimes found on men's shoes. Bootheel postmarks were also used in other parts of the world.

bord de feuille (Fr.) sheet margin, wing copy.

Bordeaux issue name given to the lithographed stamps of France made during the siege of Paris, 1870-1.

borde (Sp.) margin, border, outer edge, lip, verge.

border rule or ornament printed around a postage stamp design.

Boscawin, N.H. issued postmasters' provisional stamps for this town in New Hampshire sometime around 1846.

Bosnia and Herzegovina province of Jugoslavia; area variously quoted as 23,000 square miles, 19,904 square miles, and 19,-768 square miles. Stamps issued from 1879 until 1918.

Bosnian girl a design used on stamps of Bosnia and Herzegovina.

Bosnie (Fr.) Bosnia.

Bosnien-Herzegowina, or **Bosnien-Hercegovina** (insc.) Bosnia and Herzegovina.

Bothwell watermarked paper paper used for a limited quantity of 1868 postage stamps of Canada. The paper was horizontally watermarked "E & G Bothwell Clutha Mills" in the sheets. A letter or part of a letter appeared in each stamp.

Botswana British Commonwealth republic in central south Africa, north of Republic of South Africa, of about 224,000 square miles. Formerly British Bechuanaland Protectorate. Capital: Gaberones. First stamps issued Sept. 30, 1966.

Bouchir (Fr.) Bushire.

Bouton's City Dispatch Post in New York City, New York, issued U.S. local stamps in 1848.

Bouton's Manhattan Express in New York City, New York, issued U.S. local stamps in 1847. These are inscribed "Franklin City Free Despatch Post".

Bouvet Oya (ovpt.) on stamps of Norway. In 1934, the Milford Expedition visited Bouvet Island in the Antarctic and obtained permission from the Norwegian authorities in Cape Town, South Africa, to overprint some postage stamps. But Norway did not recognize the issue because official authorization had never been given to overprint the stamps. Denominations were 5-, 7-, 10-, 20-, and 30-ore. They are not listed in popular stamp catalogues.

box (1) rules that enclose type matter as a frame; (2) small rectangular space in type composition in which words or a short heading are set in different type.

boxed cancel a cancel that is framed, usually in a square or rectangular frame of one or more lines.

Boyaca once a state, now a department of the Republic of Colombia in South America. Issued stamps in 1902-4.

Boyce's City Express Post in New York City, New York, issued U.S. local stamps in 1852.

Boyd's City Dispatch (formerly Boyd's City Express) in New York City, New York, issued U.S. local stamps in 1867-77.

Boyd's City Express in New York City, New York, issued U.S. local stamps in 1844-67.

Boyd's City Post in New York City, New York, issued U.S. local stamped envelopes in 1864.

Boyd's Dispatch formerly Boyd's City Dispatch, in New York City, New York, issued local stamps in 1878-80.

Boy Scout stamps Virtually every major postal authority has issued stamps to honour Boy Scouts. Various books are devoted to this vast subject.

B.P.A. British Philatelic Association. An important organization for stamp dealers, but also open for membership to collectors and others. The Association bought the forgeries, materials, and business belonging to Sperati. This important move was extremely beneficial to collectors throughout the world. It stopped the possibility of spreading dangerous forgeries to collectors and dealers.

brackets typographical signs, [ ], used to enclose a note, reference, or explanation, and separate it from the context; not to be confused with parentheses, the semi-circular marks, ( ), that are also used in pairs.

Bradbury, Wilkinson & Co., Ltd. British security printers of postage stamps for many postal authorities.

Bradway's Despatch in Millville, New Jersey, issued U.S. local stamps in 1857.

Brady & Co. in New York City, New York, issued U.S. local stamps in 1857-8.

Brady & Co.'s Chicago Penny Post in Chicago, Illinois, issued U.S. local stamps sometime around 1860. Some doubt exists about the authenticity of the issue.

Brainard & Co. in Albany, New York, issued U.S. local stamps in 1844.

branch with reference to post offices, a station other than the main office in the community.

brandkastzegels (Dutch) safe, strongbox stamps. Appears as an inscription on marine insurance stamps.

Braniff International Airways (airline) point of origin: United States.

Brasil (Port. insc.) on stamps of Brazil.

Brasilien (Ger.) Brazil.

Brass River postmark of Brass, a town at the mouth of the Brass River in Nigeria. Used special postmarks in 1892. See Gibbons Part One catalogue.

Brattleboro, Vt. issued postmasters' provisional stamps for this town in Vermont in 1846.

brauchen (Ger.) to use, to need.

braun (Ger.) brown.

bräunlichrot or **braeunlichrot** (Ger.) brownish red.

braunrot (Ger.) brownish red.

Braunschweig (Ger. insc.) on stamps of Brunswick, in northern Germany.

Brazil a republic of about 3,275,510 square miles on north and east coasts of South America on the Atlantic. Capital: Brasília. Issued the famous Bulls' Eyes stamps on Aug. 1, 1843.

break tear in the web of a paper roll, occurs in coil or roll stamps.

break-up for colours to divide a type form that is to be printed in more than one colour into separate forms, one for each colour.

breitrandig (Ger.) having a wide margin.

Brême (Fr.) Bremen.

Bremen part of northwest Germany, about 99 square miles. Stamps were issued from 1855 to 1867. These were superseded by stamps of the North German Confederation in 1868.

Brésil (Fr.) Brazil.

brevstycke (Swed.) letter sheet; also a piece of a letter, or a cut square.

Bridgeville, Ala. issued postmasters' provisional stamps in 1861 for this town in Alabama, as part of the Confederate States of America.

Brief (Ger.) letter or cover.

Briefbewertung (Ger.) valuation of cover.

Briefgebuehr (Ger.) postage, letter rate.

Briefkopf (Ger.) letter head.

Briefmarke (Ger.) postage stamp.

Briefmarkenalbum (Ger.) stamp album.

Briefmarkenausstellung (Ger.) philatelic exhibition.

Briefmarke Wenden, or **Kreis Briefmarke Wendenschen** (insc.) on stamps of Wenden, a province of the Russian Empire, 1862-84.

Briefmarke WENDEN=schen Kreises (Ger. insc.) appears on the 1863 rectangular stamps of Wenden, listed by Gibbons as the first authorized postage stamps of the district. Stamps with a hyphen after "WENDEN" are said to be reprints. See WENDEN.

BRIEFPOST (insc.) on stamps of Germany issued under French occupation, 1945-6.

Briefrueckseite (Ger.) back of cover.

Briefsammlung (Ger.) letter collection.

Briefstueck (Ger.) fragment, piece of letter.

Brieftaube (Ger.) carrier pigeon.

Briefumschlag (Ger.) envelope.

Briefvorderseite (Ger.) face of cover.

Brigg's Despatch in Philadelphia, Pennsylvania, issued U.S. local stamps in 1847-8. Also issued envelopes and letter sheets in 1848.

brilliant mint in auction catalogues, describes an excellent postage stamp, as nearly perfect as can be.

Brinkerhoff Vending Machine Co. made machines to dispense U.S. postage stamps perforated by the company in various patterns of two and four holes. Refer to Scott's U.S. Specialized catalogue.

Britische Salomon Inseln (Ger.) British Solomon Islands.

British American Bank Note Company an organization of security printers in Canada. Printed the first postage stamps of the Dominion of Canada, 1868.

British Antarctic Territory British territory formerly part of the Falkland Islands Dependencies in the South Atlantic. Territory includes: Graham Land, later known as Graham Coast and now considered the western part of Palmer Peninsula; the South Shetland Islands; the South Orkneys; and other smaller or less-important islands. First stamps issued Feb. 1, 1963.

British army postal seals special labels at reduced rates that British servicemen used for their mail from Egypt. Sweden also issued special envelopes for their servicemen for similar use, but some of these had return postage stamps printed on the flaps.

British Central Africa A former British territory of about 37,800 square miles in central Africa west of Lake Nyassa, under charter to the British South Africa Company. Name was changed to Nyasaland Protectorate in 1907. Capital: Zomba. Issued stamps 1891 to July 22, 1908, when Nyasaland Protectorate stamps appeared.

British closed mail mail for foreign countries sent through British postal system.

British Colonial Post Office in America In 1707, the British Post Office took control of postal affairs in the North American colonies. The Post Office Act of 1710, in the reign of Queen Anne, drastically changed and improved mail service in the British colonies in North America.

British Columbia and Vancouver Island Canadian province of about 355,900 square

ONE PENNY

miles on the northwest coast of North America; formerly separate British colonies. Issued stamps jointly in 1860, and then separately from Nov. 1, 1865, to July 20, 1871.

British Consular Mail of Madagascar In 1884 the British consulate issued stamps of different designs printed by letterpress; they were used until 1886. Finally French authorities undertook administration of Madagascar in 1896. See BRITISH INLAND MAIL.

British East Africa Formerly referred to all of east African territory that was under British control.

British/East Africa/Company (4-line sur.) appears with new values on the Queen Victoria issue of Great Britain for 1890, for use in all the territory of East Africa under British control.

British European Airways (airline) point of origin – England.

British Forces in Egypt Letter Stamp (insc.) on special labels sold at reduced mail rates for British servicemen and their families for use from Egypt to the British Isles. They are also known as the Egyptian Military Concession Stamps. The service began on Nov. 1, 1932.

British Guiana former British Crown Colony of about 83,000 square miles, situated on the northeast coast of South America. Capital: Georgetown. Issued stamps from July 1, 1850 to May 26, 1966, when the colony became independent and changed its name to Guyana.

British Honduras British Crown Colony of about 8,867 square miles on the Caribbean Sea off Central America. Capital: Belmopan. Issued stamps in 1866.

British India the part of India under British control, as opposed to French and Portuguese India, both of which issued postage stamps.

British Inland Mail stamps issued in January 1895 under British authority for use in communities on Madagascar until the French authorities took administration of the island in 1896. Listed in Gibbons postage stamp catalogues.

British Levant broad name for the British offices in the Middle East. "Levant" suggests the land where the sun rises. Used British postage stamps with various surcharges or the name "Levant", 1885-1916. Listed in stamp catalogues.

British New Guinea a British colony on the eastern half of the island of New Guinea. First stamps were Queensland issues cancelled "NG" for New Guinea and later "BNG" for British New Guinea. The cancels served as overprints following the proclamation in 1884 of a protectorate known as British New Guinea. The first adhesive stamps were inscribed "BRITISH NEW GUINEA" in 1901-5, and in 1906 the name was changed to Papua. In 1949 the administrations of Papua and New Guinea were united under Australian control, and the stamps were inscribed "PAPUA AND NEW GUINEA". The word "and" was dropped in 1971, and the name inscribed was "PAPUA NEW GUINEA".

British North Borneo (insc.) on stamps of North Borneo issued in 1886 and subsequent years.

British Occupation (ovpt. and sur.) on stamps of Batum under British administration, 1918-20.

British Offices in Crete In 1898-9, the British authorities issued postage stamps during the joint administration of the island by Great Britain, Russia, France, and Italy following civil wars there. It was united with Greece in 1913.

British Overseas Airways Corporation (airline) point of origin: England. Often called BOAC.

British Post Offices were operated in Morocco, Siam, and the Turkish Empire. Refer to stamp catalogues for stamps of Morocco Agencies, Bangkok, and British Levant.

British / Protectorate / Oil Rivers (3-line ovpt.) on issues of Great Britain for the first stamps of Niger Coast Protectorate. The region formerly called Oil Rivers Protectorate was located on the west coast of Africa.

British Solomon Islands fifteen large islands and four groups of small islands, totalling about 12,400 square miles extending over an area of 375,000 square miles in the West Pacific Ocean; British protectorate. Issued stamps Feb. 14, 1907.

British Somaliland (ovpt.) on stamps of India for Somaliland Protectorate in 1903.

British South Africa Company (insc.) on stamps of Rhodesia under the administration of this company, 1890-1917.

British stamps used abroad Most of these are identified by various cancels of ovals formed of bars enclosing a letter (M for Malta), but mainly consisting of a letter plus a number (A25 Malta). There is a comprehensive list of over eleven pages and twenty illustrations in Gibbons Part One catalogue.

British West Indies (B.W.I.) numerous islands in the Atlantic Ocean and Caribbean Sea between North and South America.

Broadway Post Office in New York City, New York, issued U.S. local stamps in 1848.

broken circle (nick.) various postage stamps with broken frame lines around vignettes or denominations. Scott's U.S. Specialized catalogue lists and illustrates a broken circle variety in the $\frac{1}{2}$-cent stamp in the Washington Bicentennial issue of 1932.

broken hat (nick.) variety in the 2-cent stamp in Columbian Exposition issue, 1893. The third figure at the left of Columbus has a broken hat in certain stamps; listed in Scott's U.S. Specialized catalogue.

Bronson & Forbes in Chicago, Illinois, issued U.S. local stamps in 1855-8.

Brooklyn City Express Post in Brooklyn, New York, issued U.S. local stamps in 1851-64.

Brown, Mount a man of London, England, who published pioneer stamp catalogues in the 1860s. His 1870 edition, a pocket-size book, contained 204 pages with illustrations and descriptions, but no prices.

Brown, William a colourful figure in New York City in the late 1860s who sold postage stamps from a push-cart in lower Manhattan. He is said to have been responsible for hundreds of rare stamps with pinholes.

He strung his wares on threads or pinned stamps to a board at the back of his cart.

Browne & Co.'s City Post in Cincinnati, Ohio, issued U.S. local stamps in 1852-5.

Browne's Easton Despatch in Easton, Pennsylvania, issued U.S. local stamps in 1857.

Brown's City Post in New York City, New York, issued U.S. local stamps in 1876.

Bruch (in Marke) (Ger.) sharp crease (on stamp).

bruechig (Ger.) brittle, cracked; refers to cracked gum or adhesive on the back of a stamp.

brun (Fr. and Swed.) brown.

Brunei British Protectorate of about 2,226 square miles on northwest coast of Borneo. Capital: Brunei. Issued stamps in 1906.

Brunei (ovpt. and sur.) appearing on stamps of Labuan 1902-3, for use in Brunei.

brungul (Swed.) brownish yellow.

bruno (It.) brown.

brun-rouge (Fr.) red-brown.

Brunswick former duchy, now part of Germany; about 1,417 square miles. Capital: Brunswick. Stamps were issued from 1852 to 1865. Its stamps were superseded in 1868 by those of the North German Confederation.

Brunswick Star a type of duplex obliterator formed of a star-shaped array of 32 lines framing the number 131, and of a circular date stamp of Edinburgh to form the duplex marking, used between 1863-73. James Arnot wrote a sixteen-page brochure on Brunswick Stars, published by Ramsey Stewart, Edinburgh.

Brussels Treaty signed on March 17, 1948, by Belgium, France, Luxembourg, the Netherlands, and Great Britain. Apart from its economic, cultural, and social aspects, which later resulted in the creation of the Council of Europe, the treaty was the first West European military alliance made after the Second World War. On April 4, 1949, in Washington, D.C., the five member countries of the Brussels Treaty joined in a defensive pact with Canada, Italy, Norway, and the United States. The new pact became known as the North Atlantic Treaty Organization. Later Greece (February 1952), Turkey (April 1952), and West Germany (May 1955) joined the organization. According to the institutional treaty of NATO, member countries are bound to give mutual help in case of aggression, and the closest co-operation in peacetime in the economic, cultural, and social fields.

brutet (Swed.) broken.

Bruxelles 1929 Brussel (sur.) on precan-celled stamps of Belgium, 1929.

B/S backstamp, or backstamped.

B stamps (nick.) semi-postal stamps of the world. In Scott's catalogues numbers are preceded by the letter B.

Buccleugh Find discovery of forty-eight British mint 2-pence stamps of 1840 and fifty-five mint 1-penny reds of 1841; found in 1946 in a writing set owned by the Duke of Buccleugh about a hundred years earlier.

Buchanan (insc.) appears on Liberia registration stamps with no country name. Other 10-cent registration stamps were inscribed "Harper", "Grenville", "Monrovia", and "Robertsport".

Buchdruck (Ger.) typography.

Buenos Aires province of Argentina after 1862. It maintained its own postal services and issued stamps between 1858 and 1862. Cordoba and Corrientes were the two other stamp-issuing provinces of Argentina (1856-78).

Buffalo balloons refers to special adhesive labels of 1877 prepared for balloon flights by Samuel Archer King.

Buiten Bezit (Dutch ovpt.) on 1905-12 stamps of Dutch Indies, issued in 1908 for use outside of Java and Madura. "Buiten" means "outside (the town), out of, or without". "Bezit" means "possession, asset". Another issue of 1908 was overprinted "JAVA" for use there and in Madura.

Bulgaria republic in southeast Europe, of about 42,796 square miles. Capital: Sofia. Stamps have been issued from 1879.

Bulgarie (Fr.) Bulgaria.

Bulgarien (Ger.) Bulgaria.

Bullock Train a carrying agency managed by the India Post Office for the conveyance of goods only. Depicted on the 1937 India 2a 6p stamp. (Courtesy of *Indian Postal Guide*, January 1903, Special Coronation Edition)

bull's eyes (nick.) The first stamps of Brazil, issued on Aug. 1, 1843, were made by mechanical engraving in a complicated pattern with huge figures for denominations.

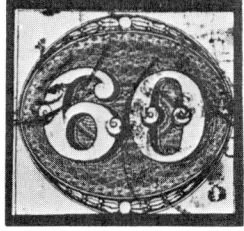

The large oval design without words but with a numeral resembled a huge eye; hence "bull's eyes". Smaller designs of 1844 are known as "goat's eyes".

Bundespost (Ger.) federal post, includes the whole operation of the post office department.

Bundesrepublik Deutschland (Ger.) German Federal Republic.

BUNDESREPUBLIK DEUTSCHLAND (insc.) German Federal Republic; on stamps of West Germany, issued Sept. 7, 1949.

Bundesstaat (Ger.) federal state.

Bundi State (insc.) on stamps of Bundi, a feudatory state of India of about 2,220 square miles. Issued stamps 1894-1947.

bunt (Swed.) bundle.

Burdell & Co.'s British and Australian Express (insc.) on local stamps for parcels, Australia, 1854.

bureau (Fr.) office.

bureau de poste (Fr.) post office.

bureau de poste ambulant (Fr.) travelling post office, railway post office.

bureau de poste auxiliaire (Fr.) sub–post office.

bureau de poste étranger (Fr.) foreign post office.

Bureau Imprints In 1894, when the Bureau of Engraving and Printing in Washington, D.C., was awarded the contract for postage stamp printing, the officers followed the custom of imprinting the name of the Bureau, plate numbers, and marginal impressions on postage stamp sheets.

BUREAU/INTERNATIONAL/DU TRA-VAIL (3-line ovpt.) International Labor Bureau. On stamps of Switzerland, 1950; also inscribed on issues of 1956 and subsequent years.

Bureau Issues postage stamps of the United States printed by the Bureau of Engraving and Printing in Washington, D.C. Most U.S. postage stamps from 1894 to the present, excepting the Overrun Countries issue of thirteen stamps in 1943-4, have been printed by the Bureau of Engraving and Printing.

Bureau of Engraving and Printing United States printers of postage stamps, revenue issues, paper money, bonds and securities. The bureau, located in Washington, D.C., is a division of the U.S. Treasury Department. Visitors are permitted to see certain manufacturing processes.

Bureau Precancels precancelled postage stamps of the United States bearing printed cancellations by the Bureau of Engraving

and Printing in Washington, D.C. Sometimes called Bureau prints, to distinguish them from locally made precancelled stamps.

bureaux à l'étranger (Fr.) offices abroad.

burelage certain patterns used in producing safety papers. Burelage impressions, formed of patterns in lines or dots, are printed on the surface of papers after they are manufactured. Many banks use burelage paper for checks. Sometimes the burelage shows more clearly than the printing on stamps.

burelé having a fine network of lines that form part of the design of the stamp or cover the front or strips of the back of an

Burelé band backprinting (Queensland stamp, 1882)

entire sheet. An example is the burelé band on the back of Queensland stamps.

burelly (her.) having a large number of bars.

burilagem (Port.) network, net, burelage.

burin cutting and engraving tool used by engravers of postal stamps, money, and other securities.

Burma republic of about 261,789 square miles, southeast of China and east of Pakistan and India on the Bay of Bengal. Capital: Rangoon. Part of British India before 1937; then part of the British Commonwealth until January 1948, when Burma became a republic. Used stamps of India overprinted in 1937; issued stamps 1938-40. Used surcharged stamps of Japan from 1937 to 1942 issued under Japanese occupation.

BURMA (insc.) on stamps of Burma issued 1938-40.

BURMA (ovpt.) on stamps of India 1926-34 issued for use in Burma on April 1, 1937.

burnishing (1) polishing of plates with a small steel hand-tool; (2) rubbing of a halftone plate with a hardened steel tool to spread the dots and increase their size, thereby darkening the tone of the plate.

Burundi kingdom in central Africa (area variously quoted as 10,374 square miles and 10,774 square miles). Capital: Usumbura (Bujumbura). Former U.N. trustee territory with Rwanda under Belgian administration. Kingdom of Burundi issued stamps 1962.

Burutu community operated in Nigeria by the Royal Niger Co. Chartered and Limited. Used special postmarks 1898-1900. Listed in Gibbons Part One catalogue.

Bury's City Post in New York City, New York, issued U.S. local stamps in 1857.

Bushire/Under British/Occupation (3-line ovpt.) on Persian stamps of 1911-13 for use in Bushire in 1915, during the British occupation of this Persian seaport.

Bush's Brooklyn City Express in Brooklyn, New York, issued U.S. local stamps in 1848.

Bussahir (insc.) on stamps of Bussahir, a state of India of about 3,320 square miles. Issued stamps 1895-1900.

busta (It.) cover.

busta giorno emissione (It.) first day cover.

B.W.I.A. (airline) British West Indian Airways Ltd. Point of origin: Trinidad.

By Authority imprint on lower left corner selvage of some stamp panes or sheets of Papua, New Guinea, and Australia.

Byrd, Richard Evelyn a U.S. naval officer and explorer. On his 1933 "Antarctic Expedition II" (the stamp inscription), mail was sent by ships of the expedition on payment of 50 cents plus the 3 cents U.S. postage, and cancelled in Little America in the Antarctic. Byrd stamps issued Oct. 9, 1933.

C

C used in Gibbons catalogues to indicate chalky paper in lists where ordinary paper also occurs.

C (ovpt.) for the Spanish word "campaña", meaning "level country"; on various stamps or types of stamps 1922-42 for local use in Paraguay, through rural areas but not in Asunción.

C A Crown Agents. Often used in watermarks of British Crown Colonies in gothic-type style or script letters.

C.A.B. (airline) Companhia Aeronautica Brasileira, Brazil.

Cabo (ovpt.) handstamped on issues of Nicaragua used in 1904-9. "Cabo" is a short form of "Cabo Gracias a Dios" used on the northeast coast of Nicaragua. It translates: "Cape Thanks to God", the

sailors' prayer of thanks when they arrived there safely. Different money values in Nicaragua created need for special postage stamps for a limited time.

Cabo Jubi, Cabo Juby (ovpts.) on stamps of Rio de Oro, Spain, and Spanish Morocco 1916-48 issued for use in Cape Juby under Spanish administration.

caboshed, cabossed (her.) full-face without neck showing.

CABO VERDE (insc.) on stamps of Cape Verde, Portuguese overseas territory off the west coast of Africa.

cache copper coin of French India on east coast of India, bordering on the Bay of Bengal. 24 cache equal 1 fanon, and 8 fanons equal 1 rupie. French settlements Chandernagor, Karikal, Mathé, Pondichéry, and Yanaon had stamps in various de-

nominations of this coinage, from 1923 until the unification of French India with India in 1949 and 1954.

cachet a decoration on an envelope, usually to commemorate some event such as an airport dedication, a first flight or sea voyage, or a postage stamp show. India, Poland, and South Africa are countries that have authorized the use of cachets (official cachets). Stamp shows, patriotic covers, and large advertising cards often provide exam-

ples of unofficial types of cachets. Cachets may be hand-painted, rubber-stamped, printed, or elaborately lithographed and engraved.

cachet à main (Fr.) handstamp.

cachet circulaire (Fr.) circular cancellation.

cachet d'arrivée (Fr.) arrival postmark.

cachet de la localité (Fr.) town postmark.

cachet faux (Fr.) forged cancel.

cadre (Fr.) border, frame, outline.

C.A.F.I.P. Canadian Association for Israel Philately.

Caisse d' Amortissement (Fr. sur.) appears with a change in value on French stamps for use as semi-postals in 1927-31. The French word "caisse" means "chest", "safe", or "strongbox", and "amortissement" means "redemption" or "buying up". Funds from the surtax on the postage stamps and from the government tobacco monopoly, plus voluntary contributions, were set aside to create a sinking fund for the stabilization of currency. The stamp issues were probably intended to boost the voluntary contributions, and were called Sinking Fund issues.

calcado (Sp.) offset, tracing.

Calchi, Khalke an Italian island of the Dodecanese group in the Aegean Sea, west of Rhodes; about 12 square miles. From 1912-22, Calchi used Italian stamps overprinted "Karki"; in 1930, overprinted "Calchi"; in 1932, overprinted "Carchi".

calcium sulphate a chemical used for coating papers; sometimes called "crown filler".

calcografía (Sp. and It.) copper engraving, copper-plate printing.

calender part of a paper machine, consisting of a stack of chilled iron rolls to smooth or iron out the surface of the paper.

calendering refers generally to the operation by which paper is smoothed at the end of the paper machine, but may also refer to a secondary operation on a different machine.

California City Letter Express Co. in San Francisco, California, issued U.S. local stamps in 1862-6.

California Penny Post Co. in numerous cities in California, issued U.S. local stamps and envelopes in 1855-9.

Calimno, Calino, Kalymnos an Italian island of the Dodecanese group in the Aegean Sea north of Kos Island; about 49 square miles.

Calimno, Calino (ovpts., also 1916 sur.) on stamps of Italy for use in Calino; from 1912 to 1921 stamps were overprinted "Calimno"; in 1930, they were overprinted "Calino". The 1916 issue was surcharged.

caliper a precision instrument to measure the thickness of paper to the microscopic measurements of a ten-thousandth of an inch. Most philatelists interested in paper thickness do not check their measurements beyond a one-thousandth of an inch. This is a highly technical branch of philately.

Callao used as a cancellation on stamps of Chile. Also used 1879-83 in certain cities in Peru under Chilean occupation.

C.A.M. Contract Air Mail. Letters carried by commercial airline carriers under contract with the U.S. Post Office Department.

cambio de color (Sp.) change of colour.

Cambodge (Fr.) Cambodia.

Cambodia See KHMER REPUBLIC.

Camden, S.C. issued postmasters' provisional envelopes in 1861 for this town in South Carolina, as part of the Confederate States of America.

camel mail Postage stamps of the Sudan displayed the Camel Post continuously from 1897 to the issues of 1940.

Cameroons former British mandate of about 34,081 square miles north of the equator on west coast of Africa; part of Republic of Cameroun since 1961. Capital: Buea.

Cameroun republic north of the equator in West Africa; area variously quoted as 166,489 square miles and 183,080 square miles. Capital: Yaounde. A German protectorate prior to the First World War, it was mandated to Great Britain and France, the two parts becoming independent in 1960 and 1961. Stamps issued before 1915 were German issues overprinted "Kamerun". Subsequent stamps were the 1900-15 issues of colonial key-types with the Kaiser's yacht as vignette. Cameroun·in 1915 was under British occupation. It was occupied by the French from 1915 until the permanent French Mandate in 1925. Cameroun issued stamps from 1960 as an independent state.

Cameroun (ovpts.) on 1915-25 stamps of Gabon, French Congo, and Middle Congo, issued under French occupation of the former German colony of Cameroun in West Africa.

camoscio (It.) buff.

campaign cover (1) a letter bearing data proving it went through the post during wartime; for example the Napoleon campaign in France-Switzerland when wartime mail (circa 1800) was marked; (2) the less important kind, mainly used in U.S. elections, to advertise a candidate's name and publicize him; sometimes mocking, for example, the "Gracie Allen for U.S. President" covers.

Campaña Contra el Paludismo (Sp. insc.) on labels for compulsory use on Mexican mail in 1939; it means "campaign against malaria". Proceeds of these postal-tax stamps went to a fund used to fight malaria.

Campeche a southern state in Mexico. Issued stamps in 1876 when Juárez was struggling to expel Emperor Maximilian.

Campionaria di Tripoli (It. insc.) this and similar Italian inscriptions appeared on stamps of Libya for 1934 and subsequent issues.

Campione d'Italia Italian enclave in Switzerland.

Canada self-governing Dominion in British Commonwealth of Nations; about 3,845,-144 square miles. It covers all of the north portion of North America except Alaska. Capital: Ottawa. Issued stamps in 1851.

Canada–United States Postal Convention In 1792, Canada and the United States concluded a postal agreement for the transportation of mail from Canada to Great Britain by way of New York.

Canadian Bank Note Company, Limited a division of the American Bank Note Company in New York City, New York; incorporated as a Canadian organization in November 1922.

Canadian locals bogus stamps bearing inscriptions of "Bancroft City Express", "Bell's Dispatch", "Ker's City Post", and others. These have no place in a legitimate collection of Canadian postage stamps, but some specialists save them as novelties, contrary to regulations in the Canadian Criminal Code.

Canadian Pacific Air Lines, Ltd. (airline) Point of origin: Canada.

Canadian Philatelic Society organization of stamp collectors formed in September 1919 in Winnipeg. In 1926, the society applied for a Dominion Charter of Incorporation and this was granted in the same year. In 1959, under the leadership of Dr. G. M. Geldert, the name was formally changed to the Royal Philatelic Society of Canada.

Canadian R.P.O. markings Canadian Railway Post Offices cancelled some mail with the name of the railway line and "R.P.O." Mail from the United States is sometimes postmarked with Canadian R.P.O. markings. See the handbook and catalogue of *Canadian Transportation Postmarks,* by T. P. G. Shaw, 195 pages, published by the Royal Philatelic Society of Canada.

Canal Maritime de Suez (insc.) on stamps issued by the Suez Canal Co. in July 1868 and discontinued in October. Many forgeries exist. Listed with stamps of Egypt in Gibbons catalogues.

Canal Zone U.S. Government reservation ten miles wide (about 553 square miles) through the republic of Panama from Atlantic to Pacific. Leased in perpetuity to the United States for a cash payment of $10,-000,000 in 1913; yearly rental is $250,000.

CANARIAS (part of sur.) on various stamps of Spain for use as airmail stamps in the Canary Islands 1936-7.

cancelacion (Sp.) cancellation.

cancelacion de la oficina postal del ferrocarril (Sp.) railroad cancel (travelling post office cancel).

cancelacion falsa (Sp.) forged cancel.

cancelado (Port. and Sp.) used, cancelled.

cancelado a pluma (Sp.) pen-cancelled.

cancelamento (Port.) cancellation.

cancellation impression used to obliterate a postage stamp to prevent its reuse. While cancellations are a form of postal markings for the destruction of stamps, they should not be confused with postal markings in the broader sense of the term.

cancellation devices Mainly prior to 1880, in the United States, Brazil, Canada, Austria, and other countries, postmasters could make their own cancelling devices. Some were highly decorative; others consisted of stars and crosses or were rough little designs of animals, symbols, emblems, and people.

cancelled by favour refers to stamps on mail that have been cancelled carefully at a patron's request. These are usually cancelled in small numbers, not in bulk quantities like stamps cancelled to the order of dealers and stamp wholesalers.

cancelled stamps postally used stamps or those cancelled to order or by favour. The

cancellations are intended to prevent reuse of postage stamps.

cancelled to order stamps postmarked or otherwise obliterated that have not been used for postal or fiscal purposes.

cancelling ink special ink used by post office personnel to deface postage stamps. The ink is composed of chemicals insoluble in common solvents.

candareen a small silver coin of China, spelled "candarin" on stamps of 1878-83. Foreigners in the Far East used this name for the Chinese coin "fen". 10 candareen equalled 1 mace.

Candia See HERAKLION.

cannelé (Fr.) rippled.

Canton (ovpt. and sur.) on stamps of Indo-China for use by the French offices in Canton, China, 1901-19.

Cantonals (nick.) adhesive postage stamps issued by the Swiss cantons of Zurich (1843), Geneva (1843), and Basel (1845). Also refers to Geneva envelope stamps used as adhesives in 1849.

CANTONAL TAXE (insc.) on 1843-6 stamps of the Swiss canton of Zurich. Listed with stamps of Switzerland in catalogues.

Canton, Miss. This town in Mississippi issued postmasters' provisional envelopes in 1861, as part of the Confederate States of America.

Cap de Bonne Espérance (Fr.) Cape of Good Hope.

Cape Juby Spanish administration in northwest Africa; about 12,700 square miles. Capital: Villa Bens (Cape Juby). Also called Cape Yubi, Cabo Juby. Stamps issued 1916-48. Stamps of Spain or Spanish Morocco were overprinted.

Cape of Good Hope former British colony of about 276,995 square miles at the most southerly part of Africa; became part of the Union of South Africa in 1910. Capital: Cape Town. Issued stamps Sept. 1, 1853.

Cape Thanks to God See CABO.

Cape triangles (nick.) for the triangular postage stamps of Cape of Good Hope, 1853-64.

Cape Verde group of volcanic islands (about 1,557 square miles) in the Atlantic Ocean about 500 miles west of Senegal; overseas territory of Portugal. Capital: Praia. First stamps issued in 1877; stamps are sometimes overprinted.

CAPEX Canadian Association for Philatelic Exhibitions. In September 1951, a century after Canada gained control of its post office, a massive international exhibition was staged in the Automotive Building in the Canadian National Exhibition grounds, Toronto, Ontario. Subscribers to the CAPEX fund were given a presentation booklet containing postage stamps of the 1951 postal centennial (these stamps are often called the CAPEX stamps).

Cap Juby (Fr.) Cape Juby.

CAPO Canadian Army Post Office.

capovolto (It.) inverted.

C.A.P.R.A. (airline) Compagnie Anonyme de Productions et Réalisations Aéronautiques, France.

caps printers' contraction for "capital letters".

caps and small caps term indicating that large and small capital letters are to be used in type composition.

caption (1) heading of chapter, section or page of a book; (2) title line underneath an illustration.

cap variety popular variety especially of the 2-cent carmine 1890 postage stamps of the United States. The variety occurred on the left "2" and on both figures "2" from certain plates. The so-called cap on the right "2" was said to be from imperfect inking, not a plate flaw.

Cap Vert (Fr.) Cape Verde.

Carbon tetrachloride (CCl₄) a colourless non-flammable liquid sometimes used as a solvent and to help the watermarks in stamps become visible when a few drops are added to the items in a watermark tray. This chemical has other valuable uses: it reveals hidden creases, small cuts, and tears in stamps that are not visible with high-power magnifiers (20x) or by means of black light. It does not show repairs or signs of removal of cancels, or altered overprints and surcharges that show up under black light. "Carbon-tet", as collectors refer to it, has become a priceless tool in detecting faulty stamps. (Courtesy of George Wegg, Toronto, Ontario stamp dealer)

carbon tissue paper coated with hardened dichromated gelatin containing carbon or other pigments in suspension; used for transfer work in the production of printing plates for gravure printing.

Carchi, Calchi, or Karki (ovpts.) on Italian stamps for use on the Italian Aegean island of Calchi, 1912-32.

cardboard postage stamp paper the stock employed for Russian postage stamps of 1915 that were used as coins. The 10-, 15-, and 20-kopeck stamps with printed backs were used for the equivalent values in currency.

Care of Mr. Waghorn a handstamp marking on letters from a postal link between Britain and India. In 1836, Thomas Waghorn, of Chatham, England, with help from the Bombay Steam Committee and others, established an overland route between Cairo and Suez in Egypt. He stamped mail with various impressions: for example "Care of Mr. Waghorn" for fast service to the Far East.

CARIFTA (insc.) Caribbean Free Trade Area. On 1969 stamps of Guyana, Barbados, Antigua, and Trinidad and Tobago. The Leeward and Windward Islands and

Jamaica were also members of the Caribbean Free Trade Area.

carimbado (Port.) cancelled, stamped.

carimbo ambulante ferroviário (Port.) railroad cancellation or travelling post office cancellation.

carimbo de favor (Port.) cancellation by favour.

carimbo falso (Port.) forged rubber stamp, forged cancel.

carimbo manual (Port.) handstamp.

Carinthia former province of Austria that became part of Jugoslavia in 1920. In 1920 postage stamps were Austrian, overprinted. In 1945 the Allied Military Government issue was used.

Carinthie (Fr.) Carinthia.

Caritas (Lat. ovpts. and inscs.) charity. On numerous semi-postal stamps of Luxembourg, 1924 and subsequent years.

Carlist issues postage stamps of Spain authorized by King Carlos VII during the Civil

*Carlist
postage stamp*

War and used in 1873-4. Listed with stamps of Spain in catalogues.

Carlos issues (nick.) for the stamps of Portugal and certain key-types of Portuguese colonial stamps. Stamps portray King Carlos, 1892 and subsequent years.

carmin (Fr.) carmine.

Carnes' City Letter Express in San Francisco, California, issued U.S. local stamps in 1864.

carnet (Fr.) booklet.

Caroline Islands extensive archipelago in western Pacific Ocean of about 550 square miles. Formerly a German colony; became a U.S. Trust Territory in 1949. In 1899 and 1900 stamps were German, overprinted. Stamps were issued until 1915.

Carpatho-Ukraine part of Czechoslovakia. A special stamp was issued in 1939.

Carranza overprint (nick.) Mexican stamp of 1915 named for a monogram of Venustiano Carranza on the stamp. He was proclaimed First Chief of Mexico, August to November 1914, and became provisional president of Mexico in 1915 and president

1917-20. He was murdered in May 1920.

carriage bed of the printing press, on which the form is laid and which runs under the cylinder.

carrier service system of mail delivery from post offices to homes or business addresses before the introduction of delivery by the post offices. A separate carrier fee was charged.

carrier stamps special stamps to pay the cost of delivering mail from a post office to the address on the mail and of picking up mail for delivery to the post office. Both private firms and the U.S. Post Office issued stamps for this service. Refer to United States Specialized catalogues.

carta (Port.) a sheet of paper; map, chart.

carta (Sp.) cover, letter.

carta aérea (Sp.) airmail letter.

carta con fili di seta (It.) granite paper.

carta del primer día (Sp.) first day cover.

carta de selos (Port.) sheet of stamps.

carta entera (Sp.) entire letter.

carta gessata (It.) chalk-surfaced paper.

carta tinto (It.) tinted paper.

carta unita (It.) wove paper.

carte-lettre (Fr.) letter-card.

carte postale (Fr.) postcard.

CARTILLA POSTAL DE ESPANA (Sp. insc.) on franchise stamps of Spain 1869, for use by Diego Castell in mailing his books on the postal history of Spain.

cartouche small design at the top of commercial letterheads, for example, representing a product of the firm, a monogram, or a trademark. Many stamp dealers use postage stamp designs.

Carúpano (part of insc.) on local stamps of 1902 issued for the Port of Carúpano, Venezuela. Forgeries exist.

casein a product of skimmed milk used for sizing and as adhesive in the manufacture of coated papers.

casement plate another name for duty plate, the plate that is changed in key-plate or key-type printing of colonial or other postage stamps.

cash a copper coin with a square hole in the centre, used in Shanghai and countries of the Far East. "Ch'ien" is the most common Chinese name for this coin. 16 cash equal 1 candareen. The design has remained the same for some 2,000 years, the hole in the centre being used to string the coin on a thread.

Cashmere See KASHMIR.

Caso, Kasos an Italian island of the Dodecanese group in the Aegean Sea, southwest of Karpathos; about 27 square miles.

Stamps were issued from 1912-32; Italian issues, overprinted "CASO".

CASO (It. ovpt.) on stamps of Italy 1812-32, for use in Caso (or Kasos), an island of the Dodecanese.

cassure de planche (Fr.) cracked plate.

castaño (Sp.) brown, maroon, hazel; chestnut tree.

Castellorizo, Castelrosso, or **Kastelorizon** island of the Dodecanese group in the eastern Mediterranean Sea; of about 4 square miles. Ceded by Turkey to Italy in 1923; retroceded to Greece in 1947. In 1920, the stamps issued were those of the French offices in the Levant, overprinted "CASTEL-LORIZO". From 1922 to 1932, Italian issues were used, overprinted "CASTELROSSO".

Castellorizo (ovpt.) appears on stamps of Castellorizo, handstamped with the letters BNF (Base Navale Française), ONF (Occupation Navale Française), or OF (Occupation Française). Castellorizo was under French occupation in 1920.

Castelrosso See CASTELLORIZO.

cat. catalogue, or catalogued at the amount shown.

Catacombs Restoration issues 1928 Spanish semi-postal or charity stamps.

catalogação (Port.) catalogue.

catalogues Postage-stamp catalogues illustrate, list, and price most authorized postage stamps. The first stamp catalogue, by Alfred Potiquet, appeared in 1861 in Paris, France. He boasted of his list, which included nearly 1,100 different adhesive stamps and more than 130 postal stationery items.

catalogue value the valuations listed in postage stamp catalogues. The prices are a guide, and not the actual retail or wholesale market values.

Catalonia historical section in the northwest region of Spain. Certain revolutionary stamps of the Carlist issues were used in 1874 in Catalonia.

catapult cover a type of airmail cover flown from a ship that used a catapult arrangement to start the plane on its flight. Mail from the ships *Europa* and *Bremen*, of the North German Lloyd Line, was sent in the early 1930s by catapult. Each cover bears an identification cachet.

catchword (1) a word given prominence by display or use of special type; (2) word placed at lower-right corner of a page and repeated on next page; (3) first word of an entry in a dictionary, glossary, or index; (4) word or words in the stub column of a table describing data in columns.

cathode in electroplating and electrotyping, the wax or lead mould that acts as the negative pole on which the copper or nickel is deposited.

Cauca once a state, now a department of the Republic of Colombia in South America. Issued stamps in 1879. Also had certain postmasters' provisionals listed in stamp catalogues.

C.A.U.S.A. (airline) Cia Aeronáutica Uruguaya, S.A. Point of origin: Uruguay.

Cavalla or **Kavalla** department and seaport of Greece. Stamps issued in 1913 were those of Bulgaria, surcharged.

Cavalle (ovpt. and sur.) on stamps of France for the use of French offices in Turkey, 1893, 1900.

Cayman Brac one of three islands in the Cayman Islands, about 200 miles northwest of Jamaica. The other two are Grand Cayman and Little Cayman.

Cayman Islands three islands in the Caribbean 200 miles northwest of Jamaica; about 93 square miles. Formerly dependency of Jamaica, a British Colony. Capital: Georgetown on Grand Cayman. Issued stamps Feb. 19, 1901.

C B R S One initial appears in each corner of the stamps of Sarawak issued Jan. 1, 1871. The letters stand for "[Sir] Charles Brooke Rajah [of] Sarawak". He lived from 1829 until 1917 and served as the second White Rajah of Sarawak; he was the nephew of Sir James Brooke (1803-68), the first White Rajah of the state.

CC Crown Colonies. Sometimes used as part of a watermark in British Crown Colonies postage stamps from 1863; gradually replaced by "CA" (Crown Agents) from 1882.

CCA (airline) Compañia Cubana de Aviación, S.A., Havana, Cuba.

C.C.C. Collectors Club of Chicago.

C.CH. (sur.) for Cochin China, appearing with new values on stamps of French colonies 1886-8, inscribed "Colonies Postes". Stamps of Indo-China used in 1892.

C.C.N.A. (airline) Cia Colombiana de Navigación Aérea, Colombia.

C.C. of N.Y. Collectors Club of New York (City).

C.C.T.A. Issue 1960 stamps of Gabon, Malagasy Republic, and some other south African countries, to commemorate the tenth anniversary of the Commission for Technical Co-operation in Africa south of the Sahara. The stamps are inscribed C.C.T.A.

c. de pesos coin of the Philippines.

C.D.S. circular date stamp or circular postmark with date and usually a town, state, province, or district name and the hour of the day.

C.E.A. (airline) Compañía Ecuatoriana de Aviación, or Ecuadorian Airlines, originating in Ecuador and Venezuela.

CECHY a MORAVA (insc. and similar ovpt.) on stamps of Czechoslovakia for use in Bohemia and Moravia.

C.E.F. China Expeditionary Force; overprinted on stamps of India that were used as military stamps, 1900-21.

C.E.F. (sur.) Cameroon Expeditionary Force; on stamps inscribed "Kamerun, Cameroons" under British occupation in 1915. New values in surcharges ranged from half a penny to five shillings.

cellophane trade name for a transparent sheet of cellulose produced by extruding a viscose solution through long, narrow slits into a settling bath; used for packaging and wrapping, but should not be used to cover postage stamps.

censored mail During wartime, governments delay some mail, and after censors read it, they apply censor markings before they forward it. During the Second World War the British retained tons of mail addressed to enemy countries and sold it for philatelic purposes at the end of hostilities.

censor marks rubber-stamp impressions or labels stuck to letters to show that censors opened the mail.

cent (1) copper coin of Canada. 100 cents equal 1 dollar. Dollars were introduced in 1859 for the Province of Canada. (2) copper coin of the United States. It has also been made of copper and nickel, a copper, tin, and zinc alloy, steel and zinc, and copper and zinc. 100 cents equal 1 dollar. There have been many varieties, large and small, and many have had special names (Indian Head; Lincoln Head).

cent (Fr.) hundred.

centai a coin of Lithuania. 100 centai equal 1 litas.

centavo a copper coin of Mexico and countries in Central and South America. 100 centavos equal 1 peso.

centenaire (Fr.) centenary.

Centenaire Algérie (insc.) appears on a 1929 French issue, without the name of the country, to mark the centennial of the French colony in Algeria.

Centenaire d l'Algérie (insc.) on Algeria centennial issue of 1930.

centesimi (coin) of Italy and the Italian colonies of Eritrea, Cyrenaica, Libia, Italian Somaliland, Oltre Giuba.

Centesimi (sur.) appears with new values on military stamps of Austria that bear the inscription "K.U.K. FELDPOST", for use in Italy during Austrian occupation in 1918; also appears on stamps of Bosnia for use in Italy during the Austrian occupation.

centesimi di corona (sur.) with new values on stamps of Italy 1921-2; issued for use in Dalmatia during the Italian occupation. Dalmatia eventually became Italian territory. These stamps listed under "Dalmatia".

centesimo a copper coin of Italy, Lombardy-Venetia, Uruguay, and Venezuela. 100 centesimi equal 1 litra or 1 peso.

centime a copper coin of France, the French colonies, Monaco, Belgium, Bulgaria, Luxembourg, Switzerland, and others. 100 centimes equal 1 franc. In Haiti 100 centimes equal 1 gourde.

CENTIMES (sur.) appears on stamps of Austria used by Austrian offices in Crete, 1903-7.

CENTIMES (sur.) appears on stamps of Germany for use by German offices in Turkey, 1908.

centimes (sur.) appears with the number 5 on stamps of Ethiopia in 1905, replacing "5¢/m" to make the surcharge easier to understand. (Courtesy of Roger Henry)

centimes à percevoir (insc.) postage-due stamps of Guadeloupe, with numeral but no country name.

centimetre (cm) the one-hundredth part of a metre, .3937 inch.

centimo coin of Spain, the Spanish possessions, Morocco, Venezuela, Costa Rica, the Dominican Republic, the Ivory Coast, and others. Countries that use this small coin, of either copper or nickel, have adopted the decimal system of currency. 100 centimos equal one peseta or peso.

centimos (insc.) on stamps of Spain, with name of country omitted.

centimos (sur.) on stamps of France for use by the French offices in Morocco, 1891-1910.

centrado (Sp.) centred.

centrage (Fr.) centring.

Central African Airways Corporation (airline). Point of origin: Southern Rhodesia.

Central African Republic formerly Ubangi-Shari. Republic north of the equator in West Africa; area 238,224 square miles. Capital: Bangui. Stamps have been issued since 1959.

Central Lithuania former duchy north of Poland and east of Lithuania; now part of Poland. Capital: Vilna. Stamps were issued 1920-2.

centrato (It.) centred.

centratura (It.) centring.

centré (Fr.) centred.

centre-line block of stamps a block from centre of a sheet with crossing centre lines. See GUIDE LINES.

centre lines vertical or horizontal lines in a stamp of the same colour as the stamp or of another colour in stamps of two or more colours. Centre lines extend partly or fully across the stamp panes or sheets, dividing the sheets in half in both directions. They help postal workers to speed counting of stocks of part sheets. Sometimes they serve as guides in perforating. A block of stamps with a centre line between them is called a "line block". A block from the centre of the sheet with crossing centre lines is called a "centre-line block". Some U.S. publications substitute the word "guide" for "centre", but this is less accurate. See GUIDE LINES.

centre spread centre or middle pages of a book, magazine, or folder on which the design covers the double-page area.

centring refers to the position of designs in adhesive postage stamps. Perfectly centred stamps have all margins of equal width.

CEPT Conference of European Postal and Telecommunications Administration. On June 22, 1959, in Montreux, Switzerland, a meeting was held by representatives of Finland and the eighteen member countries of the Organization for European Economic Co-operation (OEEC) – Austria, Belgium, Denmark, Finland, France, Germany, Great Britain, Greece, Iceland, Ireland, Italy, Luxembourg, the Netherlands, Norway, Portugal, Spain, Sweden, Switzerland, and Turkey. They agreed to establish the CEPT, and decided to issue simultaneously one or more stamps, according to a common motif, in honour of the first anniversary of the inauguration of CEPT in September 1960. The Finnish designer Pentti Rahikainen prepared the selected motif, the word "EUROPA" with the letter "O" consisting of a wheel with 19 spokes, one for each member country of CEPT. The stamps were issued simultaneously on Sept. 19, 1960, by the majority of the countries. Austria issued stamps on August 29; Portugal, September 16; Belgium and France, September 17. At the last moment, Liechtenstein joined in the release of the European stamps with a design of its own.

cercle (Fr.) circle.

Ceres type a key-type of Portuguese colonies based on the stamps of Portugal, 1912-31 and subsequent years. Ceres in ancient Italian mythology was goddess of the grain and harvest, and was later identified by the Romans with the Greek Demeter, who was goddess of vegetation and useful fruits.

cerotype form of wax engraving used for the reproduction of postage stamps, business cards, envelopes.

cerrado (Sp.) closed, full.

CERTIFICADA (insc.) on stamps of Bolivar 1879-85, for registration stamps.

certificado (Sp.) registered.

certificate (1) a statement regarding the status of a postage stamp, stamps, or any philatelic property whether or not the item described is genuine or forged. Usually photographs are stuck down on the certificates, which are then verified by the chairman of an expert committee that examined the property. (2) in limited editions of books, the statement usually printed on the page facing the title page, giving the number of books printed.

CERTIFIED MAIL (insc.) on U.S. stamps of 1955 for first-class mail, to provide delivery without indemnity. This service had a lower cost than registered mail service.

Ceskoslovenske Aerolinie (airline) Point of origin: Czechoslovakia.

CESKOSLOVENSKE VOJSKO NA RUSI (insc.) appears on stamps of Czechoslovak Legion Post, issued in 1919 for use by the Czechoslovak Legion in Siberia and by local people.

Cesko-Slovensko (insc.) on stamps of Czechoslovakia, a republic in central Europe of about 49,355 square miles. Capital: Prague. Issued stamps in 1918.

Ceylan (Fr.) Ceylon.

Ceylon island of about 25,332 square miles in Indian Ocean; self-governing Dominion of the British Commonwealth of Nations. Capital: Colombo. First stamps issued 1857.

CFA

CF abbreviation for Latin term "confer", meaning "compare".

CFA (sur.) Colonies Françaises d'Afrique. Appears with new values on stamps of France for use in the Reunion Islands. The monetary value is expressed in French African francs. (Illustration: p. 43)

C.G.H. Cape of Good Hope.

C.G.H.S. (ovpt.) Commission de Gouvernement Haute Silesie. On Prussian official stamps 1920-1, for use in Upper Silesia.

C.G.T. (airline) Compagnie Générale Transsaharienne, France.

C.H. Court House; appears as part of some early U.S. postmarks; used mainly after 1801 and for fifty years or more as part of community names.

Chachapoyas city in Peru, South America. Overprinted stamps of Peru were issued in 1884.

Chad, Tchad former French territory, now a republic in Africa; area variously quoted as 461,202 square miles, 495,752 square miles, and 496,000 square miles. Stamps of 1922 were overprinted on issues of the Middle Congo; in 1924-33 they were overprinted on issues of Afrique Equatoriale Française; from 1959 stamps of the republic have been issued.

chain breakers (nick.) stamps featuring a person breaking the chains of bondage. Examples include the stamps of Slovenia (region of Jugoslavia) in 1919 and the U.S. broken chain design stamps of Aug. 16, 1963.

chain lines in laid papers, the prominent, widely spaced lines parallel to the machine direction or grain of the paper. See LAID PAPER LINES.

Chala city in Peru, South America. Used overprinted Peru stamps in 1884.

chalcography the art of engraving on copper or brass.

chalking When the dry ink on a printed work can be rubbed off, the ink is said to be chalking. This chalking results from the use of too thin a vehicle on an absorbent paper, the pigment being left on the surface of the paper without sufficient varnish to bind it. It may also be caused by the use of a pigment not readily wetted by the ink vehicle, so that there is insufficient bond between pigment and vehicle.

chalky paper safety paper made with a chalky substance on the surface. Postage stamps have been printed on chalky paper to help prevent the removal of cancellations, so that the public could not re-use the stamps. The surface is so delicate that any attempt to remove the cancels destroys the surface of the stamp. Chalky paper also helps to prevent forgery.

Chalon, Alfred Edward a British portrait artist, born in 1781, who gained fame for his portrayal of Queen Victoria. The portrait became the basis for many postage stamp designs in the Province of Canada, New Brunswick, Natal, New Zealand, and others. These stamps became known as the "Chalon heads".

Chamba State (ovpt.) appears on stamps of India, 1886-1944, for use in Chamba, one of the Convention states of India.

chamois (Fr.) buff.

changelings Colours of postage stamps often change by exposure to gases, light, or chemical fumes. Such stamps are not rarities, nor are they desired in stamp collections. Specialists may display them to show that they do exist. Some colour changelings revert to their original colours after a few minutes in a weak solution of hydrogen peroxide. But collectors are warned to use great care in experiments carried out without experienced help.

changement de couleur (Fr.) often refers to the change made in the colour of a stamp when the rate changes.

changement du dessin (Fr.) change of design.

changes in colours On stamps, these may be the result of exposure to light, gases, or moisture. Various tones of colours occurred before 1900 when printers had little or no control of printing-ink colours used from one time (printing run) to another. Before 1952 when the Universal Postage Union withdrew colour requirements for low-value stamps, governments deliberately changed colours to conform with U.P.U. requests.

Channel Islands a British group of islands in the English Channel, ten to thirty miles off the coast of France, including Guernsey, Jersey, Alderney, Sark, and several other smaller islands; total area about 75 square miles. Guernsey issued provisional stamps under German occupation 1941-4, as did Jersey in 1941-2 under similar circumstances. Britain issued two stamps in 1948 with scenes of the islands and others, in the Regional series for Guernsey and Jersey in 1958-66. Listed in stamp catalogues.

Chapel Hill, N.C. This town in North Carolina issued postmasters' provisional envelopes in 1861, as part of the Confederate States of America.

charge (her.) anything borne on a shield.

charity labels stickers resembling postage stamps. They should not be mixed on the same pages with postage stamps, but should be kept separately.

charity stamps another name for semi-postal stamps. Some issues raise funds for charities. Others have been sold to collect money for research, or to repair or construct buildings. These stamps usually are inscribed with two denominations: one for postal service, the other for charity or other predetermined use.

Charkhari State (insc.) appears on stamps of Charkhari, a feudatory state in central India of about 703 square miles. Issued stamps 1894-1943.

Charleston, S.C. This town in South Carolina issued postmasters' provisional stamps and envelopes in 1861, as part of the Confederate States of America.

charnières (Fr.) hinges.

chase iron or steel frame in which type and illustrations are locked for printing or stereotyping.

Chattanooga, Tenn. This town in Tennessee issued postmasters' provisional envelopes in 1861, as part of the Confederate States of America.

check letters Early British stamps included letters in the corners to help prevent forgery.

Cheever & Towle in Boston, Massachusetts, issued U.S. local stamps in 1846-50.

chemical changeling name given to a postage stamp that has been changed in colour by chemicals. Hydrogen sulphide gas changes the colour of some green stamps to black.

chemical pulp wood pulp produced by any one of the chemical processes.

chemin de fer (Fr.) railway.

Chemins de fer Spoorwegen (insc.) on Belgian parcel post and railway stamps.

Cherifian Posts See SHERIFIAN POSTS.

Cherry Blossom stamps (nick.) Japanese issues from 1872 and certain stamps to 1874 showing the cherry blossoms as parts of the designs. (Courtesy of Harold Mayeda)

chevron (her.) charge shaped like two meeting rafters; the French "chevron" means "rafter".

Chiapas state in southeast Mexico; issued provisional stamps in 1866.

chiaro (It.) light.

Chicago forgeries (nick.) a group of stamps named after Chicago because they were advertised in a Chicago newspaper in 1895. The stamps were offered for sale by a company in Hamilton, Ontario, Canada. (Courtesy of John Luff)

Chicago Penny Post in Chicago, Illinois, issued U.S. local stamps in 1862-3.

Chiclayo city in Peru, South America. Overprinted stamps of Peru were issued in 1884.

chief (her.) the top part of a shield.

chiffre (Fr.) numeral, number.

chiffre taxe (insc.) appears without country name on imperforate and perforated postage-due stamps of France and the French colonies; also appears on stamps with a

Turkish crescent and star design or a toughra in separate squares or circles, without English or French words, on 1914 postage-due stamps of Turkey.

chignon the roll of hair worn by a woman at the back of her head.

children's stamps exist in three types: (1) postage stamps portraying children; (2) stamps designed by children – Canada and Great Britain have examples; and (3) the Royal Reprints of Great Britain. These were British stamps Queen Victoria ordered for her children.

Chile republic in southwest South America; a long narrow country on the Pacific Ocean west of the Andes Mountains, of about 286,400 square miles. Capital: Santiago. Issued stamps in 1853.

Chimborazo and other overprints on stamps of Ecuador (1902) involved so much forgery and faking that catalogue editors do not list them as they did years ago.

China republic in east Asia; area variously quoted as about 3,869,046 square miles, 3,691,502 square miles, and 2,903,475 square miles. First stamps issued in 1878.

China (ovpt.) on Hong Kong stamps used by British post offices in China, 1917-27. The stamps were discontinued in October 1930 when the British post offices closed.

China (ovpts. and surs.) on stamps of Germany, 1898-1913, for use by German offices in China.

china clay a fine grade of white clay used as a filler in paper and as a component of coating mixtures.

Chine (ovpt. and sur.) on stamps of France or Indo-China, 1894-1904, for use by French offices in China.

Chinese calendar often indicates the times for special issues of oriental postage stamps. The calendar was said to have originated in 2254 B.C. Astrologers compiled it as they worked under the instructions of Emperor Yao, who wanted it as a guide to crop planting for his largely agricultural peasantry. The years vary in length from 354 to 385 days, and the years run in cycles of twelve. The years are named after the following twelve animals: rat, ox, tiger, hare, dragon, serpent, horse, goat, monkey, cock, dog, and pig. Each year is divided into twenty-four sections based on observations of the weather and crop planting. Stamp designs often follow with animals of the years. All Chinese festivities and celebrations are based on the calendar. The New Year falls toward the end of January or early February by the English calendar, and the celebrations generally last between four and five days. (Courtesy of the Crown Agents Hong Kong bulletin)

Chinese paper The word "Chinese" used in reference to papers is a little confusing, since it is used loosely for some native papers, but not necessarily those made in China. According to the government-authorized book *Postage Stamp Catalogue of the Republic of China 1878-1957*, Chinese stamps were printed on French-made prelure paper (1878); and on thick paper with no other description (1902) by Waterlow and Sons Company, Limited, London. China used Canadian paper (1923) and De La Rue paper (1925). This book about Chinese postage stamps does not refer to any paper as Chinese.

Chinese stamps Some stamps of China, distinctly oriental in design, bear inscriptions in English: "China", "Chinese Empire", "Imperial Chinese", "Chinese Imperial Post", "Republic of China". Many Communist Chinese stamps have no English inscriptions.

Chios an island and department of Greece in the Aegean Sea off the west coast of Turkey; about 355 square miles. Stamps issued in 1913 were Greek stamps, overprinted.

Chi Rho See PX.

chocolat (Fr.) chocolate (the colour).

choix (Fr.) choice.

chops an official seal or stamp in India, China, or Japan. In China, chops are sometimes trademarks. The Japanese handstruck overprints on stamps of occupied countries during the Second World War are sometimes called "chops".

Chosen official Japanese name for Korea. Also spelled "Corea" and known as "Tyosen". A former kingdom on the east coast of Asia, from 1910 to 1945 it was a Japanese dependency. To people of the country, "Chosen" means "Land of Morning Calm". First stamps issued in 1884. Some stamps bear the inscriptions "Corean Post", "Imperial Korean Post", "Postes de Corée", and "Postes Imperiales de Corée".

Christiansburg, Va. This town in Virginia issued postmasters' provisional envelopes in 1861, as part of the Confederate States of America.

Christmas Island a territory of Australia (about 64 square miles) 230 miles south of Java in Indian Ocean; taken over from Singapore in 1958. Issued stamps Oct. 15, 1938.

Christmas stamp of Canada The map stamp of Canada bears the inscription "Xmas 1898". The 2-cent stamps paid for first-class mail to certain British colonies and Great Britain on December 25 for the first time. The stamps were issued for domestic use on Dec. 7, 1898.

chrome plating a technique of plating steel-engraved plates and possibly others for postage stamps and other security items to make plates last longer. Chromium hardness at nine compares to the diamond at ten. (Courtesy of Denis Coolican, Ottawa, Ontario)

chromium a metal used for plating postage stamp printing-plates. Plating hard-steel engraved printing-plates with chromium gives long-wearing qualities.

chromolithography colour printing by means of lithography. See OFFSET.

chrysanthemum designs In Japanese stamp designs, these were the emperors' crests. Most stamps of Japan from 1872 until 1947 had a chrysanthemum, resembling an open umbrella, in the design. (Courtesy of Harold Mayeda)

Ch. Taxe (part of Fr. sur.) Chiffre taxe; appears on the 1902-3 stamps of the French Offices in Turkey for use as postage-due stamps of Syria in 1920.

chun, chon a copper coin of Korea. 100 chun equal 1 won. Coin is circular with a square hole in centre. The modern Korean chun is the same as the Japanese sen and Chinese ch'ien.

Chypre (Fr.) Cyprus.

C.I.D.N.A. (airline) Cie. Internationale de Navigation Aerienne, France.

cijfer (Dutch) figure.

Cilicia a Turkish territory in southeast Asia Minor of about 6,238 square miles. Principal town: Seyhan. In 1919 stamps were Turkish, handstamped "CILICIE"; in 1920 stamps of France, surcharged, were used.

Cincinnati City Delivery in Cincinnati, Ohio, issued U.S. local stamps in 1883.

cinq (Fr.) five.

cinquante (Fr.) fifty.

cinquantenaire 24 Septembre (Fr. ovpt.) on stamps of New Caledonia, issued July 16, 1903, for fiftieth anniversary of French occupation.

cinta (Sp.) strip, ribbon, tape, band.

CIPEX Centenary International Philatelic Exhibition, held in New York City in May 1947.

cipher (1) a secret or disguised mode of writing; (2) a character formed by interweaving two or more initials such as "ER II" in British and colonial stamps and watermarks.

Circuit books usually small booklets of postage stamps owned by members who place them in the sales circuits of local stamp clubs or national philatelic societies. An estimated $1,000,000 in sales of these stamps took place in U.S. and Canadian stamp clubs in 1970. The sales-circuit managers send books to members and take them to local stamp-club meetings.

circulación (Sp.) current, circulation, currency, traffic, movement.

circulaire (Fr.) circular.

circular cancels plain, often without data

concerning time, place, or country. Some are mute or dumb cancels.

circular date stamps Sometimes called circle town postmarks, they consist of an outer circle or circles of various widths. These contain the town, city, or community name, date, and time of processing of the mail. Many other postmarks have data

enclosed in circles; H.P.O. (Highway Post Office) and R.P.O. (Railway Post Office) are examples.

circular delivery company stamps Owing to high rates of postage in Great Britain for circulars, various companies delivered circulars at much reduced rates and issued stamps to prepay the services. The Edinburgh and Leith Circular Delivery started business in 1865. Other companies followed in Glasgow, Liverpool, and London. See Robson Lowe, *Encyclopaedia of British Empire Stamps*, Vol. 1.

circulars (nick.) sometimes called the cotton reels of British Guiana. The first adhesive stamps (1850) of British Guiana had a circular design somewhat like labels on spools of thread, or reels of cotton thread.

círculo (Port.) circle.

Cirenaica, Cyrenaica former Italian colony; from 1951 a province of Libia on the Mediterranean Sea in North Africa; area variously quoted as 212,000 square miles, 330,173 square miles, and 75,340 square miles. Capital: Bengasi (Benghazi). Stamps from 1923-50 were Italian issues overprinted.

CIS (ovpt.) Commission Interalliée Slesvig; appears on stamps of Schleswig in 1920 that were used as official stamps during the plebiscite.

C.I.T.A.O. (airline) Compagnia Italiana Transporte Africa Orientale, Italy.

Cité du Vatican (Fr.) Vatican City.

Cito, Cito, Cito manuscript command on letters of Venice and probably those of other cities of Italy; (Lat.) "cito, citare", means "to put into violent motion". Hence, "deliver with utmost haste". Example on a parchment letter of 1536 from Venice.

City and Suburban Parcel Delivery Bryce Ltd. issued a 6-pence local-type stamp in Brisbane, Australia, about 1900. (Courtesy of Harold Gosney)

City Despatch Post in New York City, New York, issued U.S. local stamps in 1842-50.

CITY DESPATCH POST (insc.) on the 1842 stamps issued by the United States City Despatch Post, in New York City. These stamps portray George Washington.

City Dispatch in New York City, New York, issued U.S. local stamps in 1846.

City Dispatch in Philadelphia, Pennsylvania, issued U.S. local stamps in 1860.

City Dispatch in St. Louis, Missouri, issued U.S. local stamps in 1851.

City Dispatch Post Office in New Orleans, Louisiana, issued U.S. local stamps in 1847.

City Express Post in Philadelphia, Pennsylvania, issued U.S. local stamps in 1846-50.

City Letter Express Mail in Newark, New Jersey, issued U.S. local stamps in 1856.

City Mail Co. in New York City, New York, issued U.S. local stamps in 1845.

City One Cent Dispatch in Baltimore, Maryland, issued U.S. local stamps in 1851.

Civil Air Transport (airline). Point of origin: Taiwan (Formosa).

Civil War patriotic envelopes decorated U.S. envelopes illustrated with flags, slogans, and other propaganda. Some collectors specialize in these covers.

C.K.K.K.K. (airline) Chiu Ku Koku Kabushika Kaisha. Point of origin: Manchuria. During the Japanese occupation of China, the Japanese military forces managed this airline.

clair (Fr.) thin (referring to paper), clear, plain, bright.

Clamecy roulette type of separation prepared by a Frenchman named Clamecy. It resembles the serpentine roulettes of Finland with the teeth more pointed.

Clark & Co. in New York City, New York, issued U.S. local stamps in 1857.

Clark & Hall in St. Louis, Missouri, issued U.S. local stamps in 1851.

Clarke's Circular Express in New York City, New York, issued U.S. local stamps in 1863-8.

Clarksville, Texas issued postmasters' provisional envelopes in 1861, as part of the Confederate States of America.

claro (Sp.) light, clear.

classics rare and sometimes beautiful early issues, mainly the issues of a country prior to 1870.

clay a fine, powdery, silicious material, used as filler or coating pigment; also known as "China clay" or "kaolin".

clean-cut perforations perforations that are sharp, without ragged edges.

cleaned stamps postage stamps with obliterations removed. Collectors are warned about bargains in unused or mint stamps. They may be faked by cleaning. Such fakes are revealed under black light.

cleaning stamps Collectors are warned to use care when they clean stamps by any method. Experiments with common stamps should precede any attempt to clean scarce stamps.

Cl.H.S. (Ger. ovpt.) on 1906-20 German stamps for the correspondence of the Inter-Allied Commission. Used in Upper Silesia in 1920.

cliché (Fr.) (1) cliche or duplicate printing plate, stereotype or electrotype plate; (2) a common phrase or trite expression.

clipped corners See CUT CORNERS.

Clipperton Island a low coral atoll of about 6 square miles in the east part of the Pacific Ocean, about 730 miles off the coast of Mexico; populated by about thirty people. Sovereignty was disputed, but the island was awarded to France in 1931. Bogus stamps issued in 1895 feature an eagle or other bird with spread wings resting on the outline of a rough oval surrounding the date. "Clipperton Island" is at the top and "postage 5" at the bottom of the design.

clothes-line stamp (nick.) This and other, similar humorous nicknames were given at the time of issue, Nov. 2, 1939, to the U.S. commemorative 3-cent rose-violet stamp marking the fiftieth anniversary of statehood of North and South Dakota, Montana, and Washington. The light areas of the state maps look like sheets or towels hanging from the Canadian border line, which resembles a clothes-line.

clp in auction catalogues refers to clipped perforations.

C.L.S. (airline) merged with C.S.A. (Ceskoslovenske Aerolinie) when the air transport was nationalized after 1945.

C.M.T. and new values surcharged on Austrian stamps for use in the western Ukraine under Romanian occupation.

C.N.A.C. (airline) China National Aviation Corporation. Point of origin: China.

C.N.C. Chinese National Currency. See 1945 Chinese stamps.

CNPO Canadian Naval Post Office.

coach seal issue (nick.) 1914 stamps of Mexico in one Civil War issue for Sonora, a state in Mexico. Design includes a wagon and animals.

Coamo (nick.) name given to a provisional issue of Puerto Rico, 1898, that bears the inscription "Coamo". At that time the island was known as Porto Rico and was a conquered territory following the Spanish-American War.

coarse perforations refers to a small number of holes or perforations in two centimetres.

coarse screen half-tone screens of up to 100 lines to the inch, used for illustrations on rough-finished papers such as newsprint, and antique, eggshell, and M.F. (Machine Finished) papers.

coated paper any paper with a surface treated with clay, other pigment, an adhesive mixture, or other suitable material.

Lacquer or varnish are used sometimes to improve the printing or surface properties of the paper. Also used for stamps to help stop forgery.

coating machine machine on which coating slurry is applied to paper by means of rollers, the wet coating being evened on the paper surface by means of brushes; the wet coated paper is dried in festoon driers. In another type of machine, coating slurry is applied by means of a brush and evened out by a jet of air; the paper web is dried in a heated chamber.

Cochin China former French colony in south Indo-china incorporated into Viet Nam in 1949 (about 29,974 square miles). Capital: Saigon. From 1886 to 1888 stamps of French Colonies were used, surcharged in Black, "C. CH" and new values.

Cochinchine (Fr.) Cochin China.

Cochin or Cochin Anchal (inscs.) on stamps of Cochin (1892-1949), a feudatory state in southern India. In 1949, it united with Travancore to become the United State of Tranvancore-Cochin.

Co. Ci. (ovpt.) on stamps of Jugoslavia, for Jugoslavia-Ljubljana (Lubiana or Laibach) under Italian occupation.

Cocos Islands (Keeling Islands) territory of about 5 square miles administered by Australia, 1,330 miles northwest of Australia in the Indian Ocean. Issued stamps in 1963. These were replaced by Australian decimal-currency stamps on Feb. 14, 1966.

co-extensive lines printed lines in short lengths around sheets and panes of stamps.

C OF A Commonwealth of Australia; used as part of certain watermarks in stamps of Australia.

coffee-house mail During the colonial days in America, ship captains from overseas deposited mail at taverns and coffee houses in America, and picked up mail there for delivery in England.

cogwheel cancel type of cancel resembling waterwheel of a mill, used on early stamps of Bavaria, 1850-69. There are two official types: the wheels are shown both opened and closed, with paddles close together or

spaced more widely apart. Sometimes called a millwheel cancel. (Courtesy of Dr. Frank O. Theubert)

coil plate numbers sometimes found on U.S. roll or coil postage when these stamps were printed in sheets cut off-centre by mistake.

Roll postage stamps were processed in strips from individual sheets. The modern roll postage is now made in most countries from paper in continuous rolls, or web paper.

coil stamps, roll postage stamps made for use in vending or affixing machines (the latter have been largely replaced by metre postage machines in offices). Coils may be imperforate on the sides or ends, as in the United States, Canada, and Sweden, or perforated all around, as in Great Britain and parts of the Commonwealth.

coil stamp trailers paper at the beginning and end of each roll of coil stamps. The paper at the beginning (outer end) of a roll is called the "heads"; the inner end is known as the "tails". (Illustration: p. 50)

coil testing labels Some countries have made test labels in rolls for testing vending machines. The "poached-egg" labels of Britain are examples. The U.S. Post Office made test coil labels in the colour and size of the 4-cent, Lincoln-portrait stamps, issue of Nov. 19, 1954, in red-violet.

coin (Fr.) (1) corner or spandrel, often referring to pane or sheet of stamps; (2) a die for steel engraving.

coin daté (Fr.) dated corner.

coin de feuille (Fr.) corner copy.

coin envelope small open-end envelope, made from kraft or manila paper. Used as pay envelope and as container for small objects and postage stamps.

cold colours Blue, violet and green are said to be cold colours, as opposed to the psychologically warm effect of red, orange, and yellow.

Colis postal, Postcollo (ovpt. and insc.) on Belgium parcel post and railway stamps. "Postcollo" is on parcel post stamps 1928-30 and railway stamps 1945; "Postcolli" is on railway stamps 1947, 1957.

Colis Postaux (ovpt.) on parcel post stamps of French colonies; the 1960 Haiti stamp provides an example.

collateral data text, drawings, pictures, postmarks, and other materials used on stamp album pages to explain the stamps or covers.

Collectors Club philatelic organization established Oct. 5, 1896. The club building is at 22 East 35th Street, New York City.

college stamps Some colleges, mainly in Great Britain, have issued local stamps for their own delivery services.

collotype printing printing from a bichromated gelatine surface, that has been rendered non-uniformly ink-receptive by light transmitted through an unscreened negative. Some rare philatelic books have been printed by collotype or have had stamp illustrations reproduced by collotype printing.

Colombia (insc.) on the 1887-96 issues of the Republic of Panama. These stamps were issued while Panama was a department of the Republic of Colombia. Some Colombia stamps were also cancelled "Panama" at this time.

Colombia, United States of now a republic in the northern part of South America. Spanish explorers settled the country following Columbus's fourth and last voyage (1502-4). As the country developed, various states were formed; among them were the following nine states, which issued their own adhesive postage stamps at various times: Antioquia (1868); Bolivar (1863); Boyaca (1902), (Gibbons says 1899); Cauca (1879); Cundinamarca (1870); Magdalena (1901); Panama (1878); Santander (1884); Tolima (1870).

Colombie (Fr.) Colombia.

colon the unit of the gold standard in Costa Rica and El Salvador. 100 centimos equal 1 colon. There have been 2, 5, 10, and 20 colones since 1899.

Colon (Sp.) for Columbus, inscribed on early issues of Chile and on some Spanish-language stamps portraying Christopher Columbus.

Colonia de Rio de Oro (insc.) on stamps of Rio de Oro.

Colonia Eritrea (ovpt. and insc.) overprinted on stamps of Italy, 1892; inscribed on stamps of Italy, 1910.

Colonie Italiane, Coloniali Italiane (insc.) on stamps of Italian colonies.

Colonies de L'Empire Française This inscription appeared on an early general issue of stamps for all French colonies.

Colonies françaises (Fr.) French colonies.

Colonies italiennes (Fr.) Italian colonies.

Colonies Postes (insc.) on stamps of French colonies.

Coil stamp trailers: outer end and inner end

colonne (Fr.) pillar, sometimes a type of margin or gutter impression, or a vertical row or strip of stamps.

colophon (1) printer's signature at the end of a book, with date of completion of the work; (2) trademark of publisher on cover or on title page of book; (3) the modern colophon, at back of book, often includes technical data on book production such as typeface used, method of typesetting, illustrations, engravings, paper, method of printing, etc.

color (Sp.) colour.

colore (It.) colour.

coloré (Fr.) coloured, in colour.

coloreado (Sp.) tinted.

coloré au recto (Fr.) surface-coloured.

coloré dans la pâte (Fr.) coloured through, so that the colour is the same on both sides of the paper. Some stamps have colour on the surface but not on the back.

colorer (Fr.) to colour.

colorido (Sp.) coloured, in colour, colouration.

colour bath vat or tank in which surface-coloured papers are dipped.

colour changeling See CHANGELING.

coloured paper paper of uniform colour throughout. Stamps from all over the world have been printed on coloured paper in ink of a different colour. For example, the Mexico 1861 2-reales stamp was printed in jet-black ink on rose-coloured paper. It is described in Gibbons as "jet black/rose" and in Scott's as "pink" (in italics).

colour fading a gradual change in colour of paper, usually produced by exposure to light and acid present in the atmosphere.

colour filter coloured celluloid, gelatine film, or glass plate used for separating colours in the preparation of process-colour plates. These photographic filters often help to clarify postmarks and cancellations directly struck on stamps.

colour pigments pulverized, insoluble, coloured inorganic substances used in ink- and paper-making.

colour print print in more than one colour.

colour proofs test of colours for postage stamps, made from dies of steel engraving in any colour or from plates used in any printing process.

colours the pigments, lakes, or dyes used in the manufacture of coloured paper or ink. The shades of a given colour may vary widely in papers and inks made by different manufacturers and at different times by the same manufacturer.

colours of postage stamps The colour of low-value stamps (1-cent to 5-cent denominations) often indicated their specific classification according to an agreement among the members of the Universal Postal Union. In 1952 at Brussels, Belgium, the rules governing universal colours of postage stamps came to an end.

colour strength intensity of colour of a pigment or an ink.

colour trials Before postage stamps are completed, officials request proofs in various colours, or "colour trials". These stamps, in the unissued colours, may be called "colour essays", but they should not be confused with "essays", which are trial designs, which are changed or rejected, for postage stamps.

Columbia, S.C. This town in South Carolina issued postmasters' provisional envelopes in 1861, as part of the Confederate States of America.

Columbus, Christopher Also known as Cristoforo Colombo (It.), and Cristobal Colon (Sp.), he was born in or near Genoa, Italy (1451) and settled in Lisbon, Portugal. Columbus failed to convince the king of Portugal to supply funds for a voyage west on the theory that the world was round. King Ferdinand V of Castile and his wife Isabella financed the first voyages of Columbus, who discovered islands in the West Indies (1492) and eventually the South American coast. Columbus died in poverty in May 1506. Scores of postage stamps honour Christopher Columbus. The U.S. Columbian Exposition issue (1893) traced the life and work of Columbus on stamps from 1 cent to 5 dollars. Chile portrayed Columbus on every postage stamp from 1853 to 1903 and on many other issues.

Columbus, Ga. This city in Georgia issued postmasters' provisional envelopes in 1861, as part of the Confederate States of America.

comb-perforating machine strikes a line of perforations in one direction and another line in the other direction between each postage stamp. Modern comb-perforating machines strike more than one horizontal and vertical row at a time.

combinaison (Fr.) combination cover.

combinaison d'affranchissement (Fr.) mixed franking.

combinaison de piquage (Fr.) compound perforation.

combination cover probably the most debatable term in stamp collecting; "mixed franking". The process by which a cover bears the postage stamps of one country, paying the rate to the border of another, or to a foreign port, and also bears the stamps of the second country, is correctly called "mixed franking". Some specialists believe that the sender must have placed stamps of both countries on the letter in order for it to be correctly called a combination cover.

combination line and half-tone half-tone and line work combined in one plate.

COMITE FRANCAIS DE LA LIBERA-TION NATIONALE (insc.) on stamps of the French colonies. Listed with semi-postal stamps of French colonies, 1943. These stamps were used mainly in colonial post offices that had no stamps of their own.

commatology the study of postal markings of all kinds.

commémoratif, commémorative (Fr.) commemorative.

commemorative stamps issues overprinted, surcharged, or inscribed to mark some event of importance, not always of a national kind. While these issues usually sell for a limited time, the 15-cent stamp in the Canadian 1951 CAPEX commemorative set remained on sale until April 1954.

commems commemorative postage stamps.

Commerce type name of French colonial stamps of 1881-6.

COMMISSION D'ADMINISTRATION ET DE PLEBISCITE (part of ovpt.) on 1906-20 stamps of Germany for use in 1920 in Allenstein, East Prussia, during the 1920 plebiscite.

commission de controle provisoire (insc.) on temporary issues of the Albanian military authorities in 1949.

COMMISSION DE GOUVERNEMENT HAUTE SILESIE (insc.) on stamps of Upper Silesia, 1920.

COMMISSION SANITAIRE D'AGDE (Fr.) Sanitation Commission of Agde; an oval marking on the face of a letter, with the manuscript "Purifiée" or "Parfumée", meaning "purified" or "fumigated". (Courtesy of Herbert Dube)

commonwealth the people of a state or the state itself; a republic or state in which the people rule; for example, the British Commonwealth of Nations or the Commonwealth of Australia.

Commonwealth issues postage stamps of the British dominions, members of the British Commonwealth of Nations.

Comores (insc.) short form of Archipel des Comores (Grand Comoro Island), on stamps of the Comoro Islands.

Comoro Islands French overseas territory. Volcanic islands in Mozambique Channel northwest of Madagascar (about 790 square miles). Capital: Dzaoudzi, Mayotte. First stamps as a separate French territory issued in 1950.

COMPAC (nick.) Commonwealth Pacific. On Dec. 3, 1963, Britain issued a commemorative stamp, 1-shilling 6-pence value, to mark the opening of the Trans-Pacific telephone cable. The stamp is inscribed "COMMONWEALTH CABLE".

Compagnie Générale de Transports Aériens Air Algérie (airline). Point of origin: Algeria.

Companhia de Moçambique. (insc.) Mozambique Company. Appears as an overprint on stamps of Mozambique 1892. Inscribed on issues from 1918 to 1941. Stamps were superceded by those of Mozambique.

Companhia do Nyassa Nyassa Company. Nyassa is a region of Mozambique formerly governed under royal charter by the Nyassa Company.

compartment lines irregular lines outside the normal printed area of the stamp. This type of flaw occurs in plates made for letterpress printing (described as "typographed" in U.S. catalogues and "surface printed" in British ones). When the plates, either originals or duplicates, are not carefully finished in the margins, a ridge of metal remains, high enough to receive ink and print irregular border lines. The flaws may occur in any stamps produced by letterpress; they are common in 1-penny stamps of Australia 1914-23, and also occur in the New Zealand stamps in the Dominion issue. These flaws appear almost daily in newspaper pictures and advertisements. (Courtesy of D.M. Neil)

COMPLEMENTARIO (insc.) appears with large denominations in centre oval, on Mexico postage-due stamps, 1908.

complementary colours (1) those pairs of coloured lights that, when mixed together, produce white or grey light; (2) Complementary colours in colour printing, result in harmony by contrast, provided they are well balanced, but when mixed together produce a dark-brown, almost black, colour.

composition des feuilles (Fr.) composition of sheets or panes with regard to the number of postage stamps in one unit.

compound perforation refers to stamps with more than one size of perforations. When stamp catalogues describe perforation gauges as "perf 12" that means the stamp has 12-gauge perforation on all four sides. "Size 12 x 8" on the 3-cent stamps of Canada, June 24, 1931, means that the top and bottom of each stamp are 12-gauge and the sides are 8-gauge. Perforations are described in clockwise order: top, right, bottom, and left sides. Some stamps of Bosnia and Herzegovina, 1906 issue, have four different sizes on one stamp.

común (Sp.) common.

comune (It.) common.

COMUNICACIONES (insc.) appears, sometimes with no country name, on stamps of Spain 1872-99.

concentric ring cancellations cancels with two or more rings having a common centre.

condensed type tall, narrow type, or type that is thin in proportion to its height.

condition of stamps refers to the quality of stamps in all their aspects: gum, perforations, margins (to judge centring), degree of cancellation defacement of used stamps, thin spots, over-hinged stamps. All these factors must be considered in judging the condition of stamps and postal stationery.

condominium a territory under joint rule of two authorities, for example, New Hebrides, a group of islands in the southwest Pacific, under the joint administration of France and Britain.

Confederate patriotic covers Many colourful envelopes exist with propaganda pictures and slogans intended to inspire Southerners during the U.S. Civil War.

Confederate Postmasters' Provisionals postage stamps issued by Confederate postmasters before the Confederate issues went on sale. While these stamps were made for local use in their original communities, many paid postage throughout the Confederate States.

Confederate stamp engravers and printers These included Thomas de la Rue & Company, London; Hoyer & Ludwig and also Archer & Daly, Richmond, Virginia; J. T. Paterson, Augusta, Georgia; and Keating & Ball, Columbia, South Carolina, who also printed stamps but did not engrave plates. See *Confederate States Catalog and Handbook* (1959), Dietz Press, Richmond, Virginia.

Confederate State forgeries Many counterfeits of the provisional and regular-issue stamps exist. See Dietz, *Confederate States Catalog and Handbook* (1959), Dietz Press, Richmond, Virginia.

Confederate States of America Various

postmasters in cities and towns in the southern United States issued stamps and stamped envelopes in the period between June 1, 1861, when the use of U.S. stamps was forbidden in the South, and October 1861, when stamps were authorized by the Confederate Government. For details about these provisionals see the U.S. Specialized catalogues.

Confédération du Nord (Fr.) North German Confederation.

Confed. Granadina (insc.) Granada Confederation; appears on stamps of Colombia 1859-60.

CONFEᵒⁿ ARGENTINA (insc.) on the first stamps of the Argentine Confederation, 1858-60. Subsequent stamps issued were for the Argentine Republic.

Confoederatio Helvetica (insc.) on 1941 semi-postal stamps that marked the 650th anniversary of Swiss independence, and again in subsequent years.

Congo an independent state founded by Belgium, now a republic in central Africa. The area is variously quoted as 804,757 square miles, 904,757 square miles, and 893,000 square miles. Capital: Kinshasa (Leopoldville). It has issued stamps since 1886, first as an independent state, then from 1908 to 1959 as the Belgian Congo, and from 1960 as the Congo Democratic Republic.

Congo the name of various countries, all in Africa and listed in stamp catalogues: (1) Congo Democratic Republic in Central Africa, formerly an independent state founded by King Leopold II of Belgium. Known as the Belgian Congo; (2) French Congo, originally a separate colony, but in 1888 joined to Gabon. Ceased to exist in 1906; (3) Congo Republic in West Africa at the equator, issued stamps in 1959; (4) Middle Congo in Western Africa on the Atlantic coast at the equator. In 1907 Middle Congo issued stamps inscribed "Moyen Congo". Declared a separate colony. Stamps issued until 1933. See catalogues for complicated details; (5) Portuguese Congo, in northern region of Portuguese Angola. Issued stamps 1894-1915. Angola stamps replaced them.

Congo belge (Fr.) Belgian Congo.

Congo français (Fr.) French Congo.

Congo portugais (Fr.) Portuguese Congo.

Congo, Republic of declared in November 1958; formerly Middle Congo; issued stamps in the following year. See MIDDLE CONGO, FRENCH EQUATORIAL AFRICA, and stamp catalogues for details.

CONGRATULATIONS/FALL OF/BA-TAAN AND/CORREGIDOR/1942 (5-line sur.) appears with new value on stamps of the Philippine Islands in 1942 issued under Japanese occupation to commemorate the Japanese capture of the peninsular province of Bataan in the Philippines and the rocky Corregidor Island that guards the entrance to Manila Bay.

Congreso de los Diputados (insc.) on Spanish official stamps, 1896-8.

conio (It.) die.

Connell Stamp In 1860 Charles Connell of Woodstock, New Brunswick (Canada), postmaster of the British province of New Brunswick, ordered brown 5-cent stamps bearing his portrait in place of the likeness of Queen Victoria. Mr. Connell resigned as a result of public reaction. This stamp was never placed on sale.

Conseil de l'Europe (Fr. insc.) Council of Europe on commemorative stamps issued May 31, 1952. The Council of Europe was created by a statute signed in London on May 5, 1949, on behalf of Great Britain, Belgium, Denmark, France, Ireland, Italy, Luxembourg, the Netherlands, Norway, and Sweden. It came into force on Aug. 3, 1949. The idea behind it was that the sovereign states of Europe should develop closer association if they were to recover their prosperity and reassert their influence in the post-war world. Comprehensive details of the Council of Europe are found in *The Council of Europe* by A. H. Robertson, B.C.L., S.J.D., (New York: Frederick A. Praeger Inc.)

Constantinople former name of Istanbul, Turkey.

Constantinopoli (sur.) appears with new values on stamps of Italy 1909-23 for use in Italian offices in Constantinople, Turkey.

CONSTANTINOPOL – POSTA ROMANA (ovpt.) on 1908-18 stamps of Romania for Romanian Post Offices in Turkey 1919. A similar overprint is on Romania postal tax stamps in 1919 for use by the same offices.

constitution stamps issued to mark new constitutions: Ceylon 1947, Malta 1948, India 1950, Ghana 1957, and others. Many former British colonial issues marked the introduction of self-government involving new constitutions.

CONSUMPTIVES HOME (insc.) on New South Wales semi-postal stamps of 1897 to mark Queen Victoria's diamond jubilee and to provide funds from the surtax to help consumptives.

contents table printed at the beginning of a book listing the chapter numbers, titles, and subtitles of chapters with their page numbers.

Continentals, Continental issues (nick.) U.S. postage stamps printed by the Continental Bank Note Co.

continente (insc.) appears on some early stamps of Portugal, suggests mainland Portugal.

continuous overprint type of overprint repeated on the stamps, not limited to one on each stamp as is the usual case with overprints.

contour (Fr.) border of lines.

Contract Air Mail (C.A.M.) These are U.S. flights authorized by the government. The post office contracted for private carriers to fly the mail.

Contraseña – Estampilla de Correos (Sp. ovpt.) means "countersign – post office engraving"; also appears as "Estampilla de Correos – Contraseña". On stamps of Venezuela 1873-6.

contrefaire (Fr.) (to) counterfeit.

contre remboursement (Fr.) cash on delivery.

control (1) the regulation of machinery or processes; (2) the testing of products to determine their quality. In paper and ink manufacturing, technical control of the different steps of production plays an important part in maintaining the quality of the products.

contrôle (Fr.) (1) plate marking, usually on marginal papers; (2) control censure.

controlled mail Collectors and dealers often buy special postage stamps, commemoratives, high-value stamps, or kinds of stamps seldom used (airmail and special delivery) and have business houses use them. Then the philatelists procure the used stamps. In some cities controlled mail is big business.

control numbers and letters common in the marginal paper of many British stamps and on some Canadian stamp margins, along with plate numbers. The control numbers are usually made for the printers' records. Letters in margins of some U.S. stamps were a type of control over the plates that workmen had received from the security vaults. Controls also appear on margins of stamp sheets of other countries.

controuver (Fr.) to forge, to invent, to counterfeit.

Convention states of British India stamps Stamps of India were overprinted for use in the individual states or throughout India. Chamba issued stamps 1886-1946, a 14-

anna stamp was issued in 1948; Faridkot issued stamps 1887-1900; Gwalior, 1885-1949; Jind, Jeend, or Jhind, 1885-1943; Nabha, 1885-1946; Patiala, 1884-1947.

Coo, Kos an Italian island of the Dodecanese group in the Aegean Sea, southwest of Turkey; about 111 square miles. From 1912-32 stamps issued were Italian, overprinted. On 1912 stamps the overprint is "Cos"; on 1930 stamp overprint is "Coo".

Coo (It. ovpt.) on stamps of Italy for use in Coo, an island of the Dodecanese, 1912-32. Also known as Kos or Cos, the modern Greek names.

cooking liquor chemical solution used in cooking rags or wood to remove the impurities and produce cellulose fibres suitable for papermaking.

Cook Islands, Rarotonga archipelago of nine large islands and many small ones (about 89 square miles) in South Pacific, northeast of New Zealand; a dependency of New Zealand. Capital: Avarua, Rarotonga Island. Issued stamps in 1892.

Cook's Dispatch in Baltimore, Maryland, issued U.S. local stamps in 1853.

Coolgardie Cycle Express Company operated a local mail and telegram delivery service (1894-6) in western Australia where the gold rush drew hundreds of fortune-seekers.

copie (Fr.) copy.

copper Copper plays an important part in the graphic arts. It is used in the making of intaglio plates, photo-engravings, electrotypes, gravure cylinders, and flat plates.

copper-line etching (1) intaglio printing plate produced by drawing a design with an etching needle or tool on a wax-coated copper plate, the exposed metal being subsequently etched by acid; (2) a line etching on copper, instead of zinc, for reproduction of fine lines or details.

copper-plate engraving line engraving. The only engraving correctly called "line engraving" is the work done on copper plates. The engraving may be done by hand or machine, or it may be etched in part to save the engraver's time. "Taille-douce" is French for engraving on copper but not steel. Engraving in lines on steel is correctly called "steel engraving", not "line engraving" as some stamp catalogues state.

copper sulphate also known as "blue vitriol"; used as the electroplating solution in making copper electrotypes and in building up the shell of rotogravure cylinders.

coppia (It.) pair.

copyright The copyright is the exclusive right, secured by law, for authors and artists to publish and control their works during specified periods. Usually printed in capitals or small capitals on back of title page.

cor (Port.) colour.

Córbould Henry, and his son Edward H., prominent British artists who contributed to the artistic beauty of early stamps of Great Britain and her colonies.

Córdoba a province of Argentina. Issued stamps in 1858.

cordoba a silver coin of Nicaragua. 100 centavos equal 1 cordoba. The coin was introduced in 1913.

Corée (Fr.) Corea or Korea.

cores diferentes (Port.) different colours.

Corfou (Fr.) Corfu.

Corfu an island and department of Greece, in Ionian Sea; about 227 square miles. Capital: Corfu. In 1923, under Italian occupation, overprinted Italian stamps were used; in 1941, overprinted stamps of Greece were used.

cork cancellations obliterations, often decorative: leaves, symbols, petals, or other simple designs. As cork is a difficult substance to carve, whittle, or engrave, many of the so-called "cork" cancellation devices must have been made of wood or soft metal. The United States, Brazil, and Guatemala employed similar designs in these

crude but effective obliterations, which are so common on Canadian stamps from 1870 to 1900.

corne de poste (Fr.) post-horn.

corner block a block of four or more postage stamps from any of the four corners of a sheet or pane of stamps. Similar blocks with plate-number inscriptions are called "plate-number blocks" or "plate blocks". See PLATE BLOCK.

corner card the printing in the upper left corner of envelopes. Some collectors seek hotel advertisements, machinery, textile, or automotive corner cards. One collector in Jamestown, New York, saved corner cards of funeral directors, casket makers, anything with a hearse or other subject relevant to the undertakers' business.

cornice (It.) frame.

Cornwell's Madison Square P.O. in New York City, New York, issued U.S. local stamps in 1856.

Coronation Durbar Postmarks circular postmarks and cancellations of India to commemorate the durbars of King Edward VII and King George V. "Durbar" is a term used in India for a formal state ceremony. The durbar for King Edward VII was commemorated by postmarks "1 Ja. 1903" cancelling stamps portraying Queen Victoria. A major durbar honoured King George V and Queen Mary in 1911 when they went to India for their Imperial Coronation. Elaborate folders with stamps and cancels mark the event, dated Dec. 1, 1911.

coronation issues postage stamps issued to commemorate the coronation of a royal couple or a monarch.

Coronations (nick.) stamps of Great Britain and the British Commonwealth issued to commemorate the coronations of King George VI and his wife, Queen Elizabeth, in 1937 and later issues for Queen Elizabeth II in 1953.

Coronation Silver Jubilee issue Spanish charity or semi-postal stamps of May 1927.

COROS Collectors of Religion on Stamps Society.

Corps Expéditionnaire Franco-Anglais Cameroun (ovpt.) on stamps of Gabon 1915; issued under French occupation of the former German protectorate on the west coast of Africa.

correio (Port. insc.) mail, postal service; appears on stamps of Portugal.

correio (sur.) appears with new values in reis, on stamps of Portugal.

correio aereo (insc.) on airmail stamps of Portugal, 1936-41.

corrente (It.) current.

correo (Sp.) mail, correspondence, post office, postal services, postman, and other related meanings.

correo aéreo (Sp. ovpts. and inscs.) airmail; on 1920 and subsequent issues of Spain and Spanish-language postal authorities.

correo oficial (Sp.) official mail.

correos (insc.) appears above portraits of women, with the values given in reales plata, on stamps of Cuba 1855-64.

CORREOS DE COLOMBIA (insc.) on stamps of Colombia.

CORREOS DE ESPANA (insc.) on stamps of Spain.

Correos Fonopostal (Sp. insc.) on Argentine stamps. Argentine issued three stamps on Dec. 11, 1939, for the recording and mailing of special, flexible phonograph letters.

CORREOS FRANCO or FRANCO CORREOS (insc.) appears without country name on stamps of Spain 1850 and subsequent years.

CORREOS INTERIOR (insc.) appears without country name on stamps of Philippines 1856 and Spain 1853.

COR/REOS. ME/XICO (insc.) "COR" appears vertically on the left, "REOS. ME" at the top, and "XICO" vertically on the right side (for "Correos Mexico") on provisional stamps for the Mexican state of Chiapas in 1866. The various states in Mexico continued to use the provisional stamps until the regular issues of the Republic of Mexico were brought into use.

CORREOS NACIONALES (ovpt. and sur.) appears, sometimes with new values, on Guatemala revenue stamps used for postage in 1898.

CORREOS SMP URBANOS MEDELLIN (insc.) on stamps for the City of Medellin. Listed with stamps of Colombia.

CORREOS Y TELEGRAFOS (Sp. insc.) Posts and Telegraphs; on 1890 and subsequent issues of Argentina.

CORREO URBANO DE BOGOTA (insc.) on 1889 and later issues of Colombia local stamps, listed in catalogues.

correo urgente (Sp. insc.) special delivery service; on 20-centimos stamps of Spain in 1930.

CORREO URGENTE URBANO (insc.) on special delivery stamps of Colombia, 1917.

CORRESPONDENCIA A DEBE (Sp. insc.) postage due; on stamps of Panama.

CORRESPONDENCIA URGENTE (Sp. insc.) appears on special-delivery stamps of Spain since 1905. Some issues have overprints.

Corrientes province of Argentina; issued stamps from 1856-78.

corrigé (Fr.) corrected.

cortada en dos (Sp.) bisect.

cortado ao meio (Port.) bisected.

cortado de envelope (Port.) cut square.

Correos:
on stamp
of Cuba

COSTA ATLANTICA/B (ovpt.) "costa" means coast, "Atlantica" means Atlantic, and B is for Bluefields, a town and capital of Zelaya Department in Nicaragua on the southeast coast. In 1907, regular-issue stamps were overprinted thus for use in the Department.

Costa Rica republic of about 23,000 square miles between Nicaragua and Panama in Central America. Capital: San José. Issued stamps 1863.

cote (Fr.) catalogue prices.

côté (Fr.) side.

Côte des Somalis (Fr.) French Somaliland.

Côte d'Ivoire (Fr.) Ivory Coast.

Côte d'Or (Fr.) Gold Coast.

Côte du Niger (Fr.) Niger Coast.

Côte Française des Somalis (insc.) on stamps of Somali Coast, a French overseas territory on the Gulf of Aden. Issued stamps in 1894.

cotelé (Fr.) ribbed (paper).

cotton a plant producing seed hairs, which are used in the manufacture of textiles. In the paper industry, cotton fibres are used, in the form of new and old rags. Cotton is the purest form of cellulose fibres.

cotton reels (nick.) See CIRCULARS.

couchant (her.) lying down.

couché (Fr.) (1) side, sideways; (2) chalky (paper).

couleur (Fr.) colour.

couleur de surcharge (Fr.) colour of overprint.

counter-etching In offset lithography, the grained plate is subjected to the action of dilute acids to remove metallic oxide and dirt from the surface.

counterfeit cancellation sometimes called "forged postmarks" or "forged cancels"; made to change genuine postage stamps to increase their philatelic value. Famous counterfeiters like Sperati have forged stamps, postmarks, and envelopes to simulate rarities.

counterfeit stamps forged stamps, imitation or spurious stamps made to deceive post offices and philatelists. Not to be confused with fakes, which are genuine stamps that have been altered in some way to increase their philatelic value.

coupé au carré (Fr.) cut square.

coupé en deux (Fr.) bisected.

coupé tout autour (Fr.) cut to shape.

courbé (Fr.) curved.

coureurs-de-bois adventurous traders in New France (mainly Quebec) prior to the final British conquest of French Canada in 1763. The coureurs-de-bois took to the woods as unlicensed traders with the Indians. Contrary to the common belief that these men were postal couriers, they never transported mail in New France.

Courland See KURLAND.

couronne (Fr.) crown, coronet, wreath – all common parts of stamp designs.

Cour Permanente de Justice Internationale (ovpt.) on 1934-40 stamps of the Netherlands for use by the International Court of Justice.

courrier de l'étranger (Fr.) foreign mail.

courrier de service (Fr.) official mail.

Courtland, Ala. This town in Alabama issued postmasters' provisional envelopes in 1861, as part of the Confederate States of America.

couvert (Dutch) envelope, cover.

cover an envelope, letter sheet, or postal stationery item with or without adhesive postage stamps. Collectors save these for their postal markings, stamps, or both. Before the popular use of envelopes (1840), people wrote letters, then folded the paper and wrote the addresses on the outside; other people covered their letters with an extra piece of paper; hence the word "cover". Today collectors also refer to modern, used letter sheets (aerograms) or envelopes as "covers".

cover collecting the branch of stamp collecting dealing with covers of all kinds.

covered wagons popular motifs on U.S. postage stamps, drawing attention to the westward expansion of the country.

cover service a service offered by dealers, who prepare first day covers for collectors.

Cowan paper paper produced by Alexander Cowan and Sons, Limited. They have plants in southern Scotland, South Africa, New Zealand, and Australia. The firm provided distinctive hard wove paper with or without the watermarks NZ and a star for New Zealand postage stamps. (This watermark alone does not distinguish Cowan papers.)

cowrie a small sea-shell, which is still used as currency in certain parts of the East and on the African coast. 50 cowries equal 1 penny. Much labour is involved in polishing and threading them. The Chinese name is "pei". First stamps of Uganda in 1895 were in values of cowries.

CP (ovpt. and sur.) Colis Postaux; appears on the parcel post stamps of the Ivory Coast 1904, while it was a colony of France.

cpl or **comp** complete.

cpl sets complete sets.

C.P.S.G.B. Canadian Philatelic Society of Great Britain.

cr in auction catalogues, crease.

C.R. (insc.) on the second issue of stamps of Fiji; initials for King Cakobau. R stands for "Rex", Latin for king; hence "Cakobau Rex".

cracked plate a term to be used with great care. There are some stamps with microscopic lines from fissures in a steelengraved plate. An example is the Canada 1908 1-cent stamp in the Quebec historical set known as the Tercentenary issue.

Cracow issues Austrian stamps of 1916 overprinted "Poczta Polska" in 1919.

crash cover often referred to as "interrupted mail". Crash covers are those retrieved from aircraft that met some kind of disaster. The first came from the French balloon *LeJacquard*. It ascended on Nov. 28, 1870, from Paris and crashed into the sea near Plymouth, England. Most covers have no stamps.

Crawford Medal After the death of Lord Crawford there was a widely felt desire to perpetuate his memory in some way, possibly by the award from time to time of a medal bearing his name. A committee set up in March 1914 reported on May 7, 1914. There were to be three medals, named after Lord Crawford, Tapling, and Tilleard; and these would be awarded annually by the Council of the Royal Philatelic Society, London, each in respect of a period of two years preceding the date of the award. The Crawford Medal was to be of silver-gilt for the most valuable and original contribution to the study and knowledge of philately; open for world wide competition. The other two medals of silver were open to Fellows, Members and associates of the Royal Philatelic Society only. (From *The Royal Philatelic Society, London, 1869-1969*, page 51) See TAPLING MEDAL; TILLEARD MEDAL,

cream-white paper a white paper with a cream cast, as opposed to a blue-white one.

creased (1) refers to some freak stamps, not errors. During any printing process – en-

graving, letterpress, lithography, or gravure – paper can accidentally become creased and then printed. When the stamps are soaked, the unprinted area, which may be from a hair-width to an eighth-inch, unfolds, showing the colour of the paper. (2) an adjective describing stamps that have been handled carelessly and thus have become creased. Avoid stamps of this poor quality.

creeping flowing of ink beyond limits of the design. This occurs with inks that are not viscous enough.

Crescent and Star (1) design on most stamps of Turkey, a symbol of the Turkish Caliphate; (2) design with crescent enclosing star, overprinted on stamps of Straits Settlements of 1876 for use in Johore, a state in the Federation of Malya; (3) design in oval frame with "S", for stamps of Selangor in 1878, thought by some specialists to have a doubtful origin; (4) design in oval frame with "SU", for stamps of Sungei Ujong, a former nonfederated native state on the Malay Peninsula.

Cressman & Co.'s Penny Post in Philadelphia, Pennsylvania, issued U.S. local stamps in 1856.

crest (her.) a figure fixed to the helmet as a distinctive sign in battle; often confused with badge.

Crete island and department of Greece, in Mediterranean Sea; about 3,199 square miles. Capital: Canea. First stamps in 1898 issued under joint administration by France, Great Britain, Italy, and Russia. Austria, France, and Italy had post offices on Crete and issued overprinted stamps from 1902-8, the year Crete united with Greece.

Crimea peninsula in south Soviet Russia. Scene of the Crimean War (1854-6), involving Great Britain, France, and Sardinia against Russia. The British Army Field post offices used special cancels composed of two types of ovals of three bars top and bottom enclosing (1) a crown with one star on each side, or (2) a star between two circles. The latter has been nicknamed the oxo cancel.

Croatia federated republic of about 44,453 square miles in southeast Europe that joined with Jugoslavia in 1945. Capital: Zagreb. From 1941 to 1945 stamps were Jugoslavian, overprinted "Nezavisna Drzava Hrvatska"; this appeared as a surcharge and overprinted on stamps of Jugoslavia 1941 and as an inscription on later issues for Croatia.

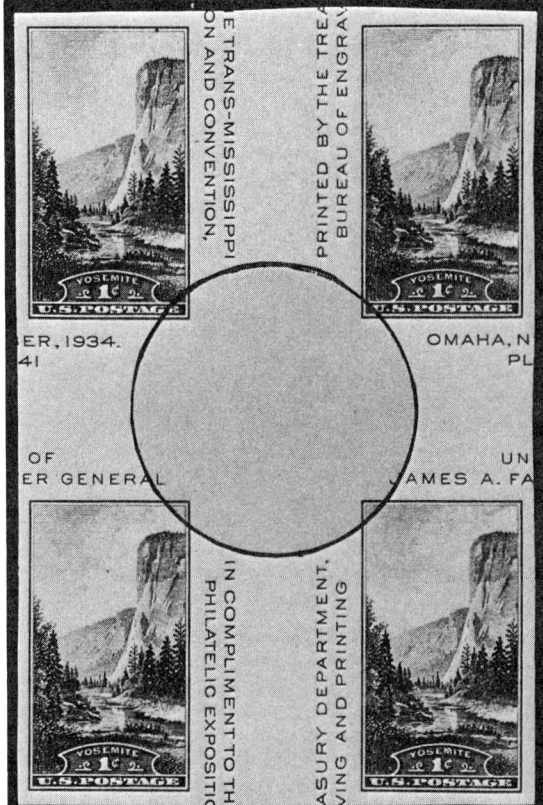

Cross-gutter block of four stamps

croix (Fr.) cross.

Croix de Lorraine (Fr.) a cross with two bars used as an anti-tuberculosis symbol on postage stamps and on many Christmas seals. In the design, the top bar is smaller. The English term is "Cross of Lorraine".

croix de Malte (Fr.) Maltese cross.

croix encadrée (Fr.) framed cross as a postmark or part of a stamp design.

croix gammée (Fr.) Maltese cross.

Croix Rouge (insc.) Red Cross; on Ethiopia stamps surcharged with a red cross and new values on former stamps made but never issued.

Crosby's City Post in New York City, New York, issued U.S. local stamps in 1870-1.

crosses widely used as motifs and cancellation designs.

cross-gutter blk of 4 cross-gutter blocks of four stamps occur with two stamps on each side of horizontal and vertical gutters.

cross in circle design overprinted on stamps of Siam 1912-17, sold with a surtax for the Siamese Red Cross Society, 1918. (The country name was changed in 1939 officially from Siam to Thailand, back to Siam in 1946, and again to Thailand in 1949.)

Cross of Lorraine See CROIX DE LORRAINE.

cross-reference reference, in text of a book, to another part of the same book.

crown design appearing with value in cents surcharged on stamps of India and the Straits Settlements, on the first issue of 1867.

Crown Agents a British organization in London that supplies postage stamps to the British Crown Colonies.

Crown Agents for the Colonies a watermark inscription on the selvage of British colonial stamps with a single crown and the letters "CA". The inscription reads upwards on the left selvage, downwards on the right selvage. Some sheets of 240 (four panes) have these watermarks in the horizontal gutter.

Crown CA watermark design in many British Crown Colonies stamps issued through the Crown Agents (CA) in London.

crown cancellations Many of the early Canadian stamps, especially those issued 1868-1900, are found with a variety of decorative crowns engraved for use in defacing the stamps. Portions of these crown cancellations have been erroneously called "geometric postmarks" by collectors and stamp dealers who did not recognize them as parts of crown cancellations.

Crown CC a watermark design similar to the Crown CA. "CC" stands for Crown Colonies.

crown circle postmark British consular offices employed these in some cities in the United States in the 1840s; also familiar on numerous letters mailed in Great Britain.

Crown Key-types Portuguese colonial stamps featuring the Portuguese crown. Examples can be found among the stamps of Portuguese India (1877) and Angola (1870-7).

crown of St. Stephen and post-horn design on newspaper stamps of Hungary 1871-2. These stamps have no lettering.

crown paper paper watermarked with a crown and used by Great Britain for making postage stamps.

crown watermarks types of watermarks used by postal authorities since the penny black of 1840 in Great Britain. Catalogues illustrate the numerous crown watermarks.

Crusades a series of religious military expeditions to the Holy Land covering the years 1095-1291, which probably had much influence on the development of heraldry.

cruzeiro a coin of Brazil. Since 1942, 100 centavos equal 1 cruzeiro.

CRUZ ROJA (insc.) on 1941 postal tax stamps of Honduras, with funds for the Red Cross; also appears on 1966 semipostal stamp of Colombia, with proceeds for the Colombian Red Cross.

CRUZ VERMELHA (part of insc.) on Brazil 1935 semi-postal stamp marking the Third Pan-American Conference of the Red Cross.

Cs, or **Csomag** (sur.) appears with new values on 1946 Hungary parcel post stamps.

C.S.A. Confederate States of America. Also C.S.

C.S.D.A. Canadian Stamp Dealers' Association.

C.S.S.A. (airline) Corporación Sud-Americana de Servicios Aéreos, Argentina.

ct in auction catalogues, abbreviation for "cut into".

C.T.O. cancelled to order.

ctr an abbreviation used in auction catalogues for "centred to right".

ctt an abbreviation used in auction catalogues for "centred to top".

cuadernillo (Sp.) booklet.

cuadriculado (Sp.) quadrille.

cuadro (Sp.) frame, square, picture.

cuarto (Sp.) one quarter; a room.

cuarto, quarto a copper coin of Spain and the Philippines. 8 cuartos equal 1 real. The coin dates from the reign of King Ferdinand and Queen Isabella.

Cuba island republic in the Greater Antilles south of Florida; about 44,164 square miles. Capital: Havana. From 1855 to 1898 stamps were issued under Spanish dominion; from 1898 to 1902 under administration of the United States. Cuban regular issues of 1896 and 1898 are surcharged. From 1902 issues are of the Republic of Cuba.

Cucuta city in Colombia; issued provisional stamps 1900-4.

CUERNAVACA CORREOS (insc.) appears on handstamped postage stamps issued in 1867 for the city of Cuernavaca, Mexico, located about 45 miles south of Mexico City. It is the capital of Morelos State, and was an ancient Indian town captured by Cortés before the siege of Mexico.

Cumming's City Post in New York City, New York, issued U.S. local stamps in 1845.

Cunard Line British shipping company originally named the "British & North American Royal Mail Steam Facket Company"; carried passengers, freight, and mail between England and the United States. The first ship, named *Britannia*, sailed from Liverpool to Halifax and Boston, July 4-19, 1840. Sir Samuel Cunard, the founder, was born at Halifax, Nova Scotia, in 1787.

Cundinamarca formerly a state in Colombia, now a department. Issued stamps 1870-1904.

cuño (Sp.) a die, stamp, impression.

Curaçao name for Netherlands Antilles prior to 1949.

Curly Heads (nick.) Spanish and Spanish Colonial stamps featuring King Alfonso XIII (1889-99).

currency the term applied to money with specified values.

currency paper paper made from flax pulp, new linen, and cotton rags for printing banknotes.

current issue or **current stamps** postage stamps in use at the present time.

current number consecutive number of a plate, irrespective of the denomination of the stamp.

curved plate   reinforced plate that has been curved to fit the cylinder of a rotary press.

cut   plate for printing postage stamps.

cut cancellations   obliterations that cut the paper fibres in a postage stamp.

Cut cancellation

cut corners   on U.S. stamp sheets, an old printers' trick to detect reversed sheets. This precautionary step was taken after the Dag Hammarskjold inverts. Cut corners have been used on paper for all stamps printed on sheet-fed Giori presses. When some of the four corners in a pile of sheets are stacked differently from the others, the uncut corners stick out. The Giori stamp-printing presses are equipped with an electronic finger that runs along the cut corners before the sheets enter the presses. Any interruption, such as a reversed sheet, trips the finger and stops the presses. (Courtesy of Belmont Faries, Editor, *S.P.A. Journal*)

Cuthbert, Ga.   This town in Georgia issued postmasters' provisional envelopes in 1861, as part of the Confederate States of America.

cut-outs   term used to denote impressions originally part of envelopes, postcards, or from postal stationery or wrappers that were cut off for use as ordinary stamps.

cut square   an adhesive or postal stationery stamp not cut to shape.

Cut square stamp

cutter   (1) a machine for cutting the web of paper into sheets of desired length; (2) operator of a cutting-machine.

Cutting's Despatch Post   in Buffalo, New York, issued U.S. local stamps in 1847.

cut to shape   stamp of any kind cut out around the design, in contrast to those cut with paper around the stamp design.

Cut to shape stamp

Cuzco   city in Peru, South America. Used overprinted stamps of the Peruvian city of Arequipa (1881-5) during the occupation by Chile of Lima and Callao.

cv   in auction catalogues or dealers' advertisements, means "catalogue value".

cylinder machine   a type of paper machine with a rotating cylinder covered with wire-cloth and partially immersed in a vat containing the pulp suspension; the paper web is formed around the cylinder. There may be a series of such cylinders, with vats filled with the same pulp or with different pulps. Thus solid or filled boards may be built to various thicknesses by combining or laminating the webs formed on each cylinder.

cylinder numbers   appear in margins of British and some colonial postage stamps printed by gravure. Cylinder numbers from gravure printing cylinders are equivalent to plate numbers from steel engraving plates.

cylinder press   a press consisting of an oscillating flatbed, passing alternately under inking rollers, and a rotating cylinder, which holds the paper against the moving type.

Cypern   (Ger.) Cyprus.

Cyprus   island republic of about 3,572 square miles off Turkey in the Mediterranean; British Crown Colony until 1960. Capital: Nicosia.

CYPRUS   (ovpt.) on postage stamps of Great Britain 1880 to July 1881 for use in Cyprus. Some interesting forgeries on the British 1-penny reds are known, overprinted on used stamps. The overprint covers the cancellations. Inscribed stamps were issued in 1881.

Cyrenaica See CIRENAICA.

Cyrénaïque (Fr.) Cirenaica.

Cyrillic alphabet (or Slav alphabet) an alphabet named after St. Cyril, the Apostle of the Slavs, and used by Russians, Bulgarians, and people of the states that united to form Jugoslavia after the First World War, with certain differences among some of the characters. On postage stamps printed in the Cyrillic alphabet, the characters are not sufficiently like those of the Latin alphabet to enable English-speaking people to read them and understand their meanings. See the appendix.

Czech exile stamps During the Second World War, the Czechoslovakian government-in-exile in London issued commemorative stamps to mark the twenty-fifth anniversary of the Republic of Czechoslovakia. These stamps are not listed in the popular stamp catalogues.

Czechoslovak Legion Post 1919-20 issues for use from Siberia by the Czechs and local people.

Czechoslovakia republic in central Europe; about 49,373 square miles. Capital: Prague. First stamps were issued in 1918-19.

D

D (insc.) appears in each corner of the 50-haleru personal delivery stamp of Czechoslovakia issued in 1937; the stamp is triangular and carmine in colour.

D (ovpt.) appears as a colourless open letter within a black circle, on 1892-4 stamps of the Dutch Indies for use as official stamps in 1911. The colour of the stamp shows through the open letter D on the overprint.

Daenemark (Ger.) Denmark.

Dahomey republic on the Gulf of Guinea in west Africa; area variously quoted as 43,232 square miles, 44,749 square miles, and 45,900 square miles. Stamps issued from 1899 had the inscription "Afrique Occidentale Française" and the name of the colony, as part of the colonial administration of French West Africa. Issues from 1960 were those of the Republic of Dahomey.

DAI NIPPON / 2602 / MALAYA (3-line ovpt.) on stamps of the Malayan States and Straits Settlements during the Second World War; issues of the Japanese invasion and occupation.

Dalmatia former Austrian crownland on the Adriatic coast, included in the federated republics of Bosnia and Herzegovina in Jugoslavia since 1945; about 4,915 square miles. Capital: Zara. Stamps were issued in 1921-2 under Italian occupation.

Dalton, Ga. This town in Georgia issued postmasters' provisional envelopes in 1861, as part of the Confederate States of America.

dancing roller a roller mounted on springs to even the tension on the paper machines and on web presses.

dandy roll skeleton roll covered with woven wire, riding on top of the wet sheet to give the upper surface of the paper the same wire markings as the lower surface of the paper, which rests on the wire of the paper machine. It also compresses the wet sheet and breaks up the foam or air bubbles on the surface of the sheet. The dandy may carry laid markings and watermark designs.

Danemark (Fr.) Denmark.

Danmark (insc.) on stamps of Denmark.

Danish West Indies In 1917 the United States purchased these islands in the West Indies, east of Puerto Rico. The islands are now the U.S. Virgin Islands. Area is about 132 square miles. Capital: Charlotte Amalie. From 1855 to 1917, postage stamps were issued by Danish West Indies; since 1917, stamps and currency of the United States have been used.

Dansk-Vestindien (insc.) on stamps of the Danish West Indies.

Dantzig (Fr.) Danzig.

Danube Steam Navigation Co. issued local stamps of Austria, listed in catalogues prior to 1900 and again after 1960.

Danville, Va. This town in Virginia issued postmasters' provisional stamps and envelopes in 1861, as part of the Confederate States of America.

Danzig or **Dantzig** formerly Free City, now a Polish province; about 754 square miles. Capital: Danzig. From 1920 to 1923, German stamps overprinted "DANZIG" were used. For 1925-38, stamps were printed "FREIE STADT DANZIG". For 1925-38, Polish offices in Danzig issued stamps of Poland with the overprint "PORT GDANSK". In 1939, under German administration, surcharged stamps of Danzig were issued.

Dardanelles (ovpt.) on stamps of Russia for use in the Russian offices in the Turkish Empire at the Dardanelles, 1909-10.

dashes plain or ornamental pieces of rule used to separate parts of printed matter.

data (It.) date.

date cuts King Edward VII stamps of Great Britain printed at Somerset House have vertical cuts in the jubilee line. Two cuts under the last stamp of the bottom row of the sheet or pane indicate the 1912 printing. One cut under the last stamp indicates the 1911 printing. (Courtesy of Stanley Phillips)

Datia or **Duttia** a feudatory state in central India. Issued stamps 1893-1920. Stamps became obsolete in 1921.

datierte Ecke (Ger.) dated corner.

Datum (Ger. and Swed.) date.

Dauerausgabe (Ger.) permanent issue, regular issue, definitive issue.

Davis' Penny Post in Baltimore, Maryland, issued U.S. local stamps in 1856.

day of issue refers to the day postage stamps or postal stationery were issued. Sometimes it appears in postal markings and other cancels.

dc abbreviation in auction catalogues, meaning "discoloured".

D.D.L. (airline) Det Danske Luftfartselskep. Amalgamated with the Swedish airline A.B.A. (A.B. Aerotransport), and the Norwegian airline D.N.L. (Det Norske Luftfartselskep) to form S.A.S. (Scandinavian Airlines System).

DDR (insc.) Deutsche Demokratische Republik; German Democratic Republic, on stamps of East Germany.

dead horse refers to the illustration on 10-cent stamps in the Trans-Mississippi issue of U.S. postage, 1898.

Dead Letter Office, or **D.L.O.** name of a bureau within post office departments of the English-speaking world where letters are sent when they cannot be delivered in normal circumstances by the local postmen. In Canada, the office is now called the "Undeliverable Mail Office".

death mask (nick.) a series of stamps that depict a weird image or mask on the five low-value stamps of Serbia, 1904. The image may be seen when the stamps are turned so that the top edge is nearest the viewer. The issue commemorated the 100th anniversary of the Karageorgevitch dynasty and the coronation of King Peter I. The death mask appears between the two profiles on the stamp. These stamps gained universal popularity when collectors discovered that the mask resembled the murdered King Alexander. The stamps have been cleverly forged, despite their penny values.

de bas en haut (Fr.) upward.

Debrecen autonomous city in east Hungary; after the First World War Romania issued occupation stamps (1919) by overprinting stamps of Hungary. In 1920, a second issue

consisted of stamps inscribed "Magyar Posta".

decalco (It.) offset.

decalque (Port.) offset.

déchiré (Fr.) torn.

deckle in hand papermaking, the removable frame that determines the size of the sheet.

deckle-edged paper paper with feathery edges produced by leaking of the pulp underneath the deckle, or by squirting small water jets at specified intervals on the wet web.

deckle straps the endless rubber straps on a paper machine that prevent the pulp suspension from overflowing at the side of machine wire, and thus determine the width of the sheet.

decorative postmarks of Austria Many small post offices in Austria had no uniform postmarks. Postmasters made their own, because each office required identification. When postmasters became tired of writing the town names, they acquired decorative postmarks to stamp mail.

découpé (Fr.) cut square.

Decreto de 27 Junio, 1879 (double ovpt., 1 line inverted) appears on stamps of Venezuela 1879. "Decreto" is Spanish for "decree"; these stamps were authorized by official decree.

Dede Agach See ALEXANDROUPOLIS.

dedication covers those with cachets dedicated to some event. These items are collected with covers bearing cachets of other types, especially airmail first flights.

deep etching in photo-engraving, additional etching to secure proper printing depth, where dense black lines are used or in combination line and half-tone cuts; it is also employed in long runs to compensate for wear and in printing on rough paper to reduce fill-in.

deep-etch offset offset printing with plates on which the printing areas are etched below the surface to compensate for wear of long runs and to allow for the transfer of a thicker film of ink.

défaut (Fr.) flaw.

défaut de la planche (Fr.) plate flaw.

défectueux (Fr.) defective, imperfect.

defeituoso (Port.) insufficient, defective (describing a stamp variety).

defekt (Ger.) defective.

DEFENSA NACIONAL (insc.) appears on the 1937-42 postal tax stamp of Ecuador, a national defence issue.

DEFICIENTE (insc.) appears on postage-due stamps of Nicaragua and Paraguay.

déficit (insc. and ovpt.) on postage-due

stamps of Peru.

définitif   (Fr.) definite.

definitives   collectors' word for regular-issue postage stamps as opposed to commemoratives or special issues. The definitives remain in continuous use, while others have a limited period of validity or use.

de haut en bas   (Fr.) downward.

deitado   (Port.) horizontal.

Delacryl   name devised by De La Rue security printers to describe their invention of the only process specially designed to produce postage stamps. The invention combined all the distinctive features of the four major printing processes: lithography, gravure, steel engraving, and letterpress.

De la Ferté, J. F. J.   a man who gained fame as a postage stamp engraver with De La Rue, the British security printers.

De La Rue postage stamp papers   refers to numerous types of paper the company used in printing postage stamps for Great Britain, the British colonies, and other stamp-issuing authorities. De La Rue introduced, for example, a handmade wove safety paper watermarked and treated with prussiate of potash for the 1855 postage stamps of Great Britain. The chemical application prevented ink penetration, resulting in a protective measure against the erasing of postmarks. This paper has a distinct bluish colour. De La Rue also patented the chalky wove paper used for some postage stamps of Great Britain in the first issues of King Edward VII, 1905-10. These are merely two of the many papers De La Rue manufactured.

delayed mail   Various reasons have been given for delaying mail. Usually, markings indicate the cause of delay. One example is "Delay Regretted – Found in Unused Mailbag".

DELEGACOES   (insc.) appears on Red Cross franchise stamps of Portugal, 1926.

delgado   (Sp.) thin.

deliberate errors   In order to prevent certain stamps from remaining rarities, some governments printed more errors to reduce the values. In 1909, Canada issued 100,000 King Edward 2-cent imperforate stamps to force down the high prices of imperforates on sale to stamp collectors. The Post Office of Canada sold the stamps at face value to applicants through the postmaster in Ottawa. In 1937, Greece issued postal-tax stamps with the overprints inverted. To prevent speculation additional stamps were issued with deliberately inverted overprints. The Dag Hammarskjold stamps of the

United States, Oct. 23, 1962, were also discovered with an error; the yellow colour was inverted. Millions of errors were specially printed to prevent speculation. Other examples, such as the special printings of U.S. stamps of March 15, 1935, are known.

delivery-tax stamps   Spanish stamps of 1931 issued as postage due, then used later in the year as regular postage stamps.

Delta Air Lines, Inc.   (airline) point of origin: United States.

Democratic People's Republic of Korea or **North Korea**   the region of Korea north of the 38th parallel of latitude. Prior to 1945 this region was a part of Korea, a nation occupying a large peninsula on the east coast of Asia. Following the Second World War, Russia occupied North Korea and issued postage stamps in 1946. In September 1948 the Democratic People's Republic of Korea was established under Russian auspices. Capital: Pyongyang. On Sept. 19, 1948, the new government began issuing stamps that have become propaganda issues. See: KOREA; REPUBLIC OF KOREA.

demi, demie   (Fr.) half.

demi-cercle   (Fr.) semi-circle.

Deming's Penny Post   in Frankford, Pennsylvania, issued U.S. local stamps in 1854.

démonetisé   (Fr.) demonetized.

demonetized   stamps declared no longer valid for postal service. For example, all stamps of the provinces of Canada, New Brunswick, and Nova Scotia issued prior to July 1, 1867, were demonetized on April 1, 1868, the day the Dominion of Canada issued postage stamps for the confederated provinces.

Demopolis, Ala.   This town in Alabama issued postmasters' provisional envelopes in 1861, as part of the Confederate States of America.

Denmark   northwest European kingdom of about 16,576 square miles. Capital: Copenhagen. First stamps were issued in 1851.

denomination   in postage stamp collecting, the face value printed on stamps.

dentado   (Sp.) perforated.

dentado de peine   (Sp.) comb perforation.

dentado en línea   (Sp.) line perforation.

denteação   (Port.) comb perforation.

denteação em linha   (Port.) line perforation.

denteação por folha   (Port.) harrow perforation.

dentelé   (Fr.) perforated.

dentelé en ligne   (Fr.) line perforation.

dentelé à la herse   (Fr.) harrow perforation.

dentellato   (It.) perforated.

dentellatura   (It.) perforation.

dentellatura a pettine   (It.) comb perforation.

dentellatura lineare   (It.) line perforation.

dentelure en lignes   (Fr.) line perforation.

dentelure en peigne   (Fr.) comb perforation.

dentelure incomplète   (Fr.) interrupted perforation (for example, on some Netherlands stamps).

dentelure irregulière   (Fr.) rough perforation.

dentelure nette   (Fr.) clean-cut perforation.

dentelure partielle   (Fr.) part perforation.

dentelure piquage   (Fr.) perforation.

Denver issue   (nick.) 1914 stamps of Mexico printed in Denver, Colorado.

De of A   (insc.) Departmento de Antioquia; appears on 1890 provisional stamps of Antioquia, a former state of Colombia.

DE OFICIO   (ovpt.) appears on official stamps of El Salvador.

department stamps   issues made especially for various government departments. South Australia issued over thirty-five different department stamps with department names overprinted on regular issues. The United States, Great Britain, and Argentina have also issued such stamps.

dependencies   regions in various parts of the world operating under the authority of another government. For example, Aitutaki is a dependency of New Zealand and has often used New Zealand stamps with an overprint. Also, in 1946, Falkland Islands issued special stamps for its dependencies.

déplacé   (Fr.) misplaced.

deposit   (1) a substance that settles down from a solution or a suspension; (2) in electrotyping, the copper that is formed or deposited on the wax mould.

Dept. of State   (insc.) Department of State; on United States official stamps of 1873 for this department.

Dept. of the Interior   (insc.) Department of the Interior; on United States official stamps of 1873 for this department.

derecha, a la derecha   (Sp.) right, to the right.

dernier jour   (Fr.) last day.

des.   design or designed.

desenho dos selos   (Port.) design of stamps.

design   preliminary sketch or plan for work to be done; also an outline plan, drawing, or the finished work.

design printing   a process in which the paper web is put through a colour bath and then pressed between engraved rolls, which leave a design on paper; used for safety paper.

DESINFIZIERT   (Ger.) disinfected marking; appears in modern type, 1915 and subsequent years. (Courtesy of Herbert Dube)

DESMIT RBL   (sur.) appears with new values on 1920 stamps of Latvia issued in 1921.

dessin   (Fr.) design, drawing, plan, pattern.

destro   (It.) right.

de tous côtés   (Fr.) on all sides.

Detroit River Postal Service   a unique postal service in the United States that delivers mail to, and receives mail from, ships sailing the Detroit River.

deutlich   (Ger.) clear, plain.

DEUTSCHE BUNDESPOST   (insc.) appears on German stamps of the Federal Republic. "Bundespost" is equivalent to "Royal Mail". (Courtesy of D. Hecken)

DEUTSCHE FELDPOST DURCH U-BOOT   (Ger. insc.) appears on German military stamps of 1945 for the use by German troops stationed on the Hela peninsula of Danzig. By conforming to an arrangement, their mail was delivered home by U-boat. The postage stamps were blue with no postal charge indicated. The period of use was short, and forgeries exist. See UNTERSEEBOOT-POST.

Deutsche Lufthansa Aktiengesellschaft   (airline) point of origin: West Germany.

Deutsche Mark, DM   (Ger.) German mark, currency in West Germany.

Deutsche / Militaer- / Verwaltung / Montenegro   (sur.) appears with new values on stamps of Jugoslavia for use in Montenegro in 1943, issued under German occupation.

Deutsch Neu-Guinea   (insc.) on stamps of German New Guinea, 1901.

Deutsch Neu-Guinea   (ovpt.) on stamps of Germany for use in German New Guinea, 1898.

Deutsch-Oesterreichischer Postverein   (Ger.) German-Austrian Postal Union.

DEUTSCH-OSTAFRIKA   (insc. and sur.) German East Africa; appears as a surcharge with various denominations in pesa on stamps of Germany for use in German East Africa in 1896; also appears as an inscription on the Kaiser's Yacht key-types of 1900-16 for German East Africa.

DEUTSCHE POST   (insc.) on stamps of Germany for use in the Allied occupation sectors following the Second World War. Sometimes called Deutsche Bundespost.

Deutsche Post in der Tuerkei   (Ger.) German post offices in Turkey.

Deutsche Post in Marokko   (Ger.) German post offices in Morocco.

Deutsche Post/OSTEN   (2-line sur.) appears

on German stamps of 1934-6 for use in Poland, 1939, under German occupation.

Deutsches Reich (insc.) German Empire; on stamps of Germany, 1872-1944.

DEUTSCHOSTERREICH (Ger. ovpt.) on regular issue 1916-18 Austrian stamps, the first issue of the Republic of Austria.

Deutsch-/Südwest-Afrika (2-line diagonal Ger. ovpt.) German Southwest Africa. The 1897-8 overprints on 1889 German stamps were the first stamps of the colony. In 1898, the surcharge was changed to no hyphen between Südwest and Afrika. In 1900, colonial stamps had the former inscription, with a hyphen on the German colonial key-types 1900-19.

DEUTSCHE VERSICHERUNGSBANK BERLIN WERTBRIEF BEFORDERUNG DEUTSCHLAND – AMERIKA (Ger. insc.) appears on the German postage stamps used for mail sent by U-boat to the United States in the early years of the First World War, before the United States entered the conflict. See UNTERSEEBOOT-POST.

deux (Fr.) two.

De Valayer a Frenchman who got permission from King Louis XIV to establish a postal system in 1653. He put up mail boxes on street corners and advertised that he would deliver all letters enclosed in his envelopes placed in his letter boxes. He sold the envelopes that resemble modern wrappers. People destroyed his business by putting garbage and live rats in his mail boxes.

Devastación de la Ciudad (partial insc.) on postal tax stamps of Dominican Republic 1930, issued following a hurricane that devastated the city of Santo Domingo on Sept. 3, 1930.

device (1) a fanciful design; (2) an invention or contrivance fitted to a special use or purpose; (3) heraldic emblem.

devise (Fr.) slogan.

dexter (her.) the right hand of the wearer, or the spectator's left.

D.F.U./FRIM-UDST/19 38 (3-line ovpt.) Danmarks Filatelist Union; on stamps of Denmark 1938, issued to mark the stamp exhibition held at Slagelse in connection with the Tenth Stamp Day, Sept. 2, 1938.

Dhar a feudatory state in central India. Issued postage stamps 1897-1900. The stamps became obsolete in 1901.

diadems crowns or decorative bands used to signify royalty and worn by queens and other royal women. Queen Victoria wears a diadem in the first British stamps, the 1-

and 2-penny values of 1840.

diagonale (It.) oblique.

diagonal half provisional stamps cut in half from one corner to the other, creating triangular stamps. Guatemala, Falkland Islands, and St. Vincent issued such stamps. See postage stamp catalogues for other authorized examples.

diagonal stroke or **diagonal dash** a short slanted line (/); used in stamp literature to indicate where the lines in overprints and surcharges begin and end; for example, "10 cents 10/China" is a 2-line surcharge for German stamps used in China. Also used between the names of colours in price lists and stamp catalogues to mean "on"; the first colour mentioned is the colour of the ink and the second is the colour of the paper used for the stamps.

diamond roulette or **lozenge roulette** a type of roulette consisting of small crosses that slit the paper between rows of stamps. This is probably the rarest type of rouletting employed by any government. It is also known by the French name of "percé en croix". The first issue of Madeira in 1868, overprinted on stamps of Portugal, were diamond- or lozenge-rouletted.

dibujo (Sp.) design.

dicitura (It.) inscription.

dick (Ger.) thick.

Dickinson or silk-thread paper Named after its inventor, John Dickinson, this was a patented paper made with imbedded continuous silk threads in the paper substance. The threads were placed in the paper so as to have one or more pass through each bank note, postage stamp, or letter sheet. The Dickinson silk-thread paper was a security measure against forgery of British paper money, the 1-shilling and 10-penny adhesive postage stamps of 1847 and 1848, and the Mulready covers of 1840. Silk-thread paper was made in Pasing, Upper Bavaria, for the postage stamps of Bavaria for the 1849, 1850, and other issues. For over a century Pasing has been famous as a paper-manufacturing city – hence the name "Pasing" for Bavarian silk-thread paper.

die (intaglio) A die is a steel plate, frequently the size of a man's palm or smaller. Engravers inscribe lines, dashes, and dots to form postage-stamp designs for steel-engraved stamps. These are intaglio dies (with lines below the surface).

die (letterpress) De La Rue, security printers of London, England, developed a method of engraving dies with the design standing in relief. The printers used these dies as moulds to cast duplicate printing plates for the British issue of 4d stamps of 1855, and certain subsequent issues of Great Britain and other authorities.

die-cutting cutting paper by means of variously shaped dies on a percussion press; many envelopes are die-cut.

Diego-Suarez town near north end of Madagascar. From 1890 to 1894, the stamps issued were those of the French Colonies, surcharged or overprinted; after 1896, stamps of Madagascar were used.

dienst (Ger.) service, good turn, post.

DIENST (ovpt.) on regular issues of the Dutch Indies 1883-1909 used in 1911 as official stamps; some were inscribed "NED INDIE".

Dienstbrief (Ger.) official letter.

Dienstbriefumschlag (Ger.) official envelope.

Dienstmarke (Ger.) official stamp.

Dienstpost (Ger.) official mail.

Dienststelle Feldpostnummer (Ger.) a military unit with fieldpost number.

Dienststempel (Ger.) official cancellation.

dienstzegels (Dutch) official stamps.

die proof a trial printing of a postage stamp from an engraved die. Engravers make proofs of the dies they are working on to study their own progress.

die-sunk in stamp collecting, refers to the depressed area in paper or cardboard. Engravers frequently make proofs from the dies they have engraved. The steel die presses a recessed area the size of the die. A similar depressed area occurs when printers use letterpress plates and achieve die-sunk depressions. Wedding invitations and greeting cards are often die-sunk.

difetto (It.) defect, blemish, flaw; hence a variety or error in philately.

diligencia (Sp. insc.) care, haste; appears on the first stamps of Uruguay in 1856.

dinar a gold coin of Persia (now Iran). 100 dinars equal 1 rial. Names "dinar", "dirhem", and "dirhan" are used for gold and silver coins in other countries as well. In modern Iran 1,000 dinars equal 1 kran silver, 100 dinars equal 1 senar silver, 50 dinars equal 1 shahi copper, and 25 dinars equal 1 pul copper.

dinar a silver coin of Jugoslavia, and Tunisia. 100 paras equal 1 dinar. It has the same value as the franc and lira. The coin was adopted when Jugoslavia joined the Latin Union monetary system.

dinero a silver coin of Peru. 10 centavos equal 1 dinero.

DIOS PATRIA LIBERTAD (Sp. insc.) appears on 1879 stamps of the Dominican Republic.

DIOS PATRIA REY (insc.) appears on the Carlist stamps – stamps of Spain portraying the Spanish King Carlos VII and used in the provinces under Carlist rule, 1874-5.

diplomatic frank special postmark granted to members of diplomatic corps.

directory markings post office stamps struck on mail by postal workers on dead-letter or undeliverable-mail offices, who often use city or regional directories to help locate the person in the address. An example is "Moved – No Forwarding Address".

dirhan, dirhem, dirham a silver coin of Morocco. 100 francs equal 1 dirhan. Many varieties of this Arabian coin have been used since the seventh century. The name comes from Greek "drachma", a silver coin.

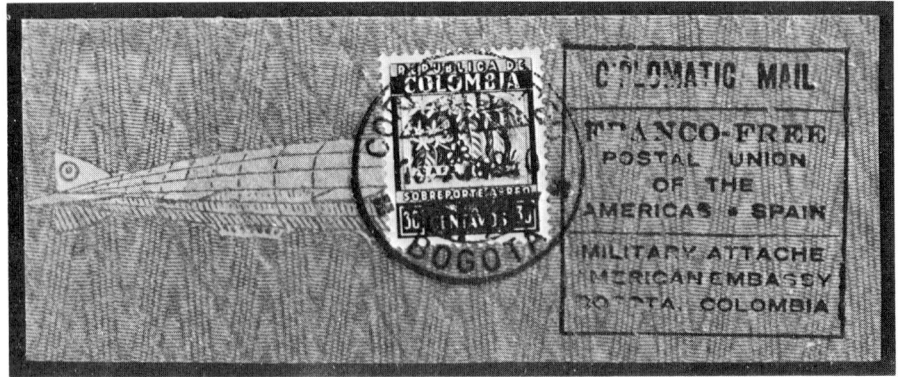

Diplomatic frank

discards   soiled or defective printed sheets of stamps, set aside or destroyed.

Disctd. P.O.   Discontinued Post Office, refers to covers mailed from post offices that have closed for some reason, for example when business does not warrant the expenses of maintaining the office.

disegno   (It.) design.

diseño   (Sp.) design.

disinfected mail   The fumigation of papers and letters to prevent contagion of epidemic diseases was introduced in 1537, according to S. Romanin (1853). The act of detaining people who were coming from an infected region began in 1377 at Ragusa in Dalmatia, on the eastern shore of the Adriatic. Travellers were detained at a point distant from the city for thirty days (trentina) and later for forty days (quaranta giorni), hence the word "quarantine". Beginning in Venice in the sixteenth century, officials disinfected letters from infected areas. This procedure lessened after 1850, and by 1884 was discontinued by most European countries. Mail has been disinfected as late as 1947 in North Africa (refer to *Disinfected Mail* by K. F. Mayer, M.D., Gossip Printery, Inc., Holton, Kansas).

disinfected mail folly   the foolish and unnecessary act of disinfecting mail. According to the Official Records of the World Health Organization, No. 37, in Geneva, April 1952: "Mail, newspapers, books, and other printed matter shall not be subject to any sanitary measure."

displayed   (her.) spread out (applied chiefly to the wings of an eagle).

display type   large or bold type used to make certain words or areas more conspicuous.

disposição dos selos   (Port.) arrangement of stamps.

district   in the United States, a region without elective or representative government, such as the District of Columbia.

disturbed gum   gum that is not distributed evenly on a stamp, as mint-stamp gum should be.

dix   (Fr.) ten.

dix-huit   (Fr.) eighteen.

dix mille   (Fr.) ten thousand.

dix-sept   (Fr.) seventeen.

D.J.   (ovpt.) Djibouti; on 1893 stamps of Somali Coast, a French overseas territory on the Gulf of Aden. Stamps were inscribed "Djibouti" in 1894.

D.L.H.   (airline) Deutsche Lufthansa A.G. Point of origin: Germany.

D. L. O.   Dead Letter Office.

DM   (ovpt.) Dienstmark; on regular issues of Danzig 1921-3 for use as official stamps.

D.N.K.K.   (airline) Dai Nippon Koku Kaisha, Japan.

D.N.L.   (airline) Det Norske Luftfartselstep. Point of origin: Norway. See D.D.L.

doble   (Sp.) double.

doble impresión   (Sp.) double impression.

Dockwra, William   a merchant of London, England, who established his own postal service in 1680. He employed the handstamp "Penny Post Paid" on letters as a means of control.

doctor blade or knife   the device on a gravure printing press that scrapes the ink from the surface of the plate and leaves the remaining ink in the microscopic pockets to be picked up by the paper in contact with the plate.

documentary stamp   a kind of U.S. revenue stamp.

Dodecanese, Dodecanesus   a group of Greek islands in the southeast Aegean Sea; about 486 square miles. From 1912 to 1940, under Italian occupation, Italian stamps were overprinted with the name of the island; from 1947, Greek stamps were overprinted.

dog team mail   the delivering of mail by dog team to outpost communities in parts of Canada and Alaska. The U.S. Post Office guide publishes Alaskan routes.

dollar   (1) a British silver coin used in Hong Kong, the Straits Settlements, and other places. First struck for circulation in 1896, it is based on a metric system, and 100 cents equal 1 dollar. (2) a unit of American currency, either paper or coin; 100 cents equal 1 dollar.

domestic mail   mail posted in a country for delivery within the country.

Dominica   largest island (about 305 square miles) in the Windward group of West Indies, southeast of Puerto Rico. Joined West Indies Federation in 1958, after being a Presidency of the Leeward Islands and then a colony under the Governor of Windward Islands. Capital: Roseau. Issued stamps in 1874.

Dominicaine, République   (Fr.) Dominican Republic.

dominical labels or tabs   See BANDALETTE OR BANDEROLE.

Dominican Republic   the eastern two-thirds of Hispaniola, in the West Indies. The Republic of Haiti occupies the western third of the island. Capital: Santo Domingo. Columbus visited the island in 1492, and it was settled in 1493. It became the centre of Spanish rule in the West Indies. Colourful events followed until 1844, when the republic was formed. Dominican Republic issued stamps in 1865.

Dominique (Fr.) Dominica.

Dom Pedros (nick.) stamps of Brazil, 1866 and subsequent issues, portraying the Emperor Dom Pedro II.

DOPLATIT or DOPLANTE (insc. and ovpt.) on postage-due stamps of Czechoslovakia.

DOPLATA (insc. and sur.) on postage-due stamps of Poland.

doppel (Ger.) double.

Doppeldruck (Ger.) double impression or double print.

Doppellinie (Ger.) double line.

Doppelringstempel (Ger.) double-ring cancel.

doppelter Aufdruck (Ger.) double overprint.

doppia incisione (It.) re-entry.

doppio (It.) double.

doppio stampa (It.) double print.

dormant (her.) sleeping; with the head upon the forepaws (when speaking of animals).

Dorpat (Ger.) Tartu, a province of Estonia and a city on the Ema River. Variously under Russia (1704), Poland, and Sweden. Occupied by Germans February to December 1918; they issued stamps in March 1918. Later occupied by the Bolsheviks. Peace was signed between Estonia and Russia in February 1920. Russian stamps of 1909-12 were surcharged 20 and 40 pfg. Stamps are listed in Gibbons.

dot-and-dash hunters (nick.) derogatory term describing those who magnify the importance of microscopic dots, dashes, and other unimportant variations in stamp printing that have no major significance to the stamps or to stamp collecting as a hobby.

double-coated paper paper heavily coated on one or two sides, used for fine illustrations on some postage stamps.

double deficiency post-office term for the double charge made on letters that were not prepaid with enough postage. The balance not paid (short paid) is doubled when the postman delivers the letter.

double eagle heraldic design, without country name, on stamps of Bosnia and Herzegovina, 1879-1906.

Double Geneva (nick.) first issue of the Swiss canton of Geneva produced in two parts in 1843. The stamps were imperforate, printed in pairs with a coat of arms on each one and inscribed "10/Port Cantonal/cent" across the two stamps. Vertical

halves as 5-centimes stamps were also used. A rare form reads "Cantonal Port".

double grill two grills in one postage stamp. Grills are embossing devices resembling miniature pancake griddles, which are used to punch tiny depressions in postage stamps to enable them to absorb cancelling ink. This helps prevent the use of stamps for a second time.

double impression two impressions, one usually lighter in colour, of a postage stamp design, by any printing process. These should not be confused with double transfers, which are restricted to steel-engraved postage stamps. Double overprints or surcharges are also classified as double impressions.

double impression (Fr.) double print.

double letter See SINGLE, DOUBLE, AND TREBLE LETTERS.

double-lined letters those formed of outlines sometimes used in watermarks. Printers' term is "outline letters". Examples include some war-tax stamps of Canada inscribed "War Tax 1T¢" (1-cent tax).

double overprint an error or an intentional double printing to attract collectors. Beware of bargains and buy with an expert certificate.

double papers (1) postage stamps printed on papers intentionally stuck together. The Douglas patent paper is one type. (2) The joined ends of web paper used on rotary presses make an unintentional double paper. When the rolls of paper come near the end, the printers glue the end paper to the starting point of the new roll. This saves time in feeding the paper through the press. As a result, the stamps printed on the joint are produced on two thicknesses of paper, or on double paper.

double perforations frequently occur in postage stamps. These are varieties with no value, examples of printers' waste.

double-pointed tooth roulette See RHOMBOID ROULETTE.

double print repeated impression on the same stamp.

double surcharge a type of double impression consisting of two surcharges on one stamp; believed to have sometimes been made intentionally to please tyro stamp collectors.

double transfer Operators of transfer presses working in the steel-engraving process have by mistake rocked in an impression of a stamp in the wrong place on the steel plate. Without removing the first impression entirely, both transferred lines appear in some postage stamps.

Douglas' City Despatch in New York City, New York, issued U.S. local stamps in 1879.

Douglas Patent paper a type of safety paper made from two sheets, a thick sheet on the bottom with thin paper mounted on it. Before mounting, the top paper was punched with eight small holes arranged in a circle. These circles of holes were arranged so that one circle would appear in the area of each stamp when it was printed. Scott's U.S. Specialized catalogue lists the 1-cent grey-blue of August 1881 and the 3-cent blue-green of July 1881 as varieties punched with eight small holes in a circle.

douze (Fr.) twelve.

DO-X designation mark on famous German aircraft that flew west to east across the Atlantic Ocean in 1932. Newfoundland issued special stamps for the service on May 20, 1932, with "Dornier DO-X" as part of the surcharge.

drachma a silver coin of Corfu, Greece, and Crete. 100 lepta equal 1 drachma or 1 franc. The drachma goes back to the early days of Greek history, when it was a handful of obeliskoi, or currency bars.

dragon mythical four-legged beast, part serpent, with wings.

dragon issues (nick.) Japanese stamps of 1871-2 issued in values of mon and sen with designs representing male and female dragons. (Courtesy of Harold Mayeda)

dragon's blood a resinous powder used as an acid resist in zinc line etchings, to prevent under-etching of the printing areas when the plates are etched.

drei (Ger.) three.

Dreifarbendruck (Ger.) three-colour print, three-colour printing.

Dreiringstempel (Ger.) three-ring cancel.

dreissig (Ger.) thirty.

dreizeilig (Ger.) of three lines.

drier any substance added to printing ink that increases its drying rate.

driers on a paper machine, steam-heated cylinders on which the paper web is dried.

DRIJVENDE BRANDKAST (insc.) appears on Netherlands 1921 marine insurance stamps.

droit (Fr.) right (as in "to the right side").

drop letter one posted in the office controlling the area in which the address is located.

Druck (Ger.) printing.

Druckart (Ger.) kind of printing.

Druckauflage (Ger.) number printed.

Druckdatum (Ger.) date of printing.

Druckfehler (Ger.) printing error.

Druckmangel (Ger.) imperfection in printing.

Druckplatte (Ger.) printing plate.

Druckprobe (Ger.) trial printing, proof.

Drucksache (Ger.) printed matter.

Druckvermerk (Ger.) printer's remark.

drukfout (Dutch) typographical error, misprint, printer's error.

drukwerk (Dutch) a printed paper.

dry end the part of the paper machine where the paper reaches a dry state.

dry printing printing on dry paper as opposed to that done on paper made wet by water or a chemical solution.

dry proofing paper a light, absorbent paper used for pulling a proof of a postage stamp.

Drzava (insc.) on stamps of Jugoslavia from 1919. Also overprinted on stamps of Bosnia in 1918.

Dubai sheikdom under British protection on Qatar Peninsula in Persian Gulf. Chief town: Dubai. Issued stamps in 1963.

dubbelprägling (Swed.) double impression.

dubbeltryck (Swed.) double print.

Dublette (Ger.) duplicate.

ducat This is probably the best known of all gold coins, but it has also been struck in silver for the Two Sicilies and Italy. 200 tornesi equal 100 grana, which equal 1 ducat. It is believed to have been first struck by Roger II of Sicily about 1150. The coin had the figure of Christ and the motto SIT.T.XTE.D.Q.T.V.REG.ISTE.DUCAT., for "Sit tibi, Christe, datus, quem Tu regis, iste ducatus". This translates as "Unto Thee, O Christ, be dedicated this duchy which Thou rulest". The name of the coin comes from the last Latin word.

Duc. di Parma (insc.) on 1857-9 stamps of Parma, a former independent duchy. Issued stamps 1852-9, before annexation to Sardinia in 1860.

Due Grana (insc.) appears without a country name on stamps of the Neapolitan Provinces 1861, which bear the portrait of King Victor Emmanuel II. The grana was a coin; 100 grana equalled 1 ducat. The stamps are listed with those of the Two Sicilies in Scott's stamp catalogues.

duenn (Ger.) thin.

dues (1) postage-due stamps; (2) fees paid for membership in a club or society.

Duitsch Oost Afrika / Belgische Bezetting (part of ovpt.) Belgian occupation of German East Africa; on 1915 stamps of Congo, 1916.

Dulac, Edmond a British artist and designer of the 1937 Coronation issue and certain other subsequent issues, listed in the Stanley Gibbons Part One stamp catalogue.

dumb postmarks those without information about place of origin, date, and time. Also known as "obliterations", "blind cancels".

d'une autre couleur (Fr.) of a different colour.

dunkelblau (Ger.) dark blue.

dunkelblaugrau (Ger.) dark blue-grey.

dunkelblaugruen (Ger.) dark blue-green.

dunkelbraun (Ger.) dark brown.

dunkelbraunkarmin (Ger.) dark brown-carmine.

dunkelgelbgruen (Ger.) dark yellow-green.

dunkelgrau (Ger.) dark grey.

dunkelgraublau (Ger.) dark grey-blue.

dunkelgruen (Ger.) dark green.

dunkelkarmin (Ger.) dark carmine.

dunkelorange (Ger.) deep orange.

dunkelviolett (Ger.) dark violet.

dupla impressão (Port.) double impression.

Dupl., Dup. duplicate or duplicates.

duplex handstamp also called a duplex cancellation. A cancel device in two parts: one part is a date stamp, either circular or some other shape, and the other is an obliteration to cancel the stamps. Both parts were originally made on one hammer or cancel device. The duplex cancels are now made by machines.

duplex paper paper having different colours on each side of the sheet.

duplicate more than one copy of the same stamp, collection, or accumulation.

Dupuy & Schenck in New York City, New York, issued U.S. local stamps in 1846-8.

Durazzo See DURRËS OR DURAZZO.

DURAZZO (sur.) appears with new values on stamps of Italy for postal service (1909-11) in Durazzo, a city seaport in Albania, a part of the Turkish Empire until 1912.

Durchschnitt (Ger.) average.

durchsichtig (Ger.) transparent.

Durchstich (Ger) roulette.

durchstochen (Ger.) rouletted.

durchlocht (Ger.) punched, perforated.

Durrës or **Durazzo** prefecture in west Albania; about 616 square miles. Stamps

issued from 1909-16 were those of Italy, surcharged.

Dutch Guiana also known as Surinam; a former Dutch colony on the northeast coast of South America. First stamps issued in 1873.

Dutch Indies former Netherlands possession in the Malay Archipelago of the East Indies; now part of Indonesia. About 735,-268 square miles. Capital: Jakarta (Djakarta), formerly Batavia. Stamps were first issued in 1864; some were stamps of The Netherlands, surcharged or overprinted. Since 1950, stamps of the United States of Indonesia have been issued. Postage-due stamps were issued in 1845-6.

Dutch New Guinea (West New Guinea, West Irian) western half of the island of New Guinea; about 159,334 square miles. A former Netherlands possession, it came under Indonesian administration in 1963. Capital: Hollandia. New Guinea stamps were issued from 1950 to 1962. In 1962 under temporary United Nations administration, New Guinea stamps were overprinted "UN-TEA". In 1963, Indonesian stamps were used, overprinted "IRIAN BARAT".

Duttia alternative name for Datia.

duty plate one of two plates used in printing two-colour postage stamps. The duty plate prints the country or postal-authority name and value, or the value (denomination) only. The head plate prints the rest of the stamp. Also used for stamps printed in one colour by De La Rue for many British stamps. A faulty alignment of the duty plate shows when the country name and value overlap the proper areas in the key plates. Examples are Leeward Islands ¼ penny (d) King George V brown-colour stamps; and the ¼ d brown and 1-shilling emerald-colour stamps in the King George VI issue.

dyes artificial colouring substances, usually derived from organic products. Examples include coal-tar derivatives and aniline dyes.

E

E essay, in auction catalogues.

E (ovpt.) Eisenbahn; appears on regular issues of Bavaria for railway officials, 1908.

E.A.F. (ovpt.) on stamps of Great Britain for use by East Africa Forces in Italian Somaliland, 1943.

Eagle City Post in Philadelphia, Pennsylvania, issued U.S. local stamps in 1847-50.

E.A.P.&T. Administration East African Posts & Telecommunications Administration. Tanganyika, formerly part of German East Africa, became a trust territory under the United Nations in 1948. From 1935, Tanganyika as a British-mandated territory was grouped with Kenya and Uganda under the E.A.P.&T. Administration. Tanganyika was included in the inscription on stamps from 1935 to 1963 (Scott's catalogue) that reads: "Kenya, Uganda, Tanganyika". On April 26, 1964, Zanzibar joined with Tanganyika to form the United Republic of Tanganyika and Zanzibar. Later the name was changed to Tanzania.

early impression term describing postage stamps produced in the first part of a printing run, before the plates show any indication of wear.

East Africa and Uganda Protectorates territory of about 350,000 square miles on the Indian Ocean in central east Africa. Issued stamps from 1903 until 1919. These stamps, overprinted "G.E.A.", were used in 1917 during the British occupation of German East Africa.

Eastern Air Lines (airline) point of origin: United States.

Eastern Karelia a former autonomous territory in the eastern part of what is now the Karelo-Finnish Soviet Socialist Republic, known as "Karelia". A dispute arose between Finland and Russia over the territory, but Finland occupied the area in 1941-4 and issued stamps overprinted "ITA-KARJALA" on Finnish stamps, and later inscribed this on the 1943 issue.

Eastern Rumelia Balkan region, formerly an autonomous unit of the Turkish Empire, now part of Bulgaria; about 12,585 square miles. Capital: Plovdiv (Philippopolis). Stamps issued 1880-4 were those of Tur-

key, overprinted; in 1885, those of South Bulgaria; from 1886, those of Bulgaria. See SOUTH BULGARIA.

Eastern Silesia former duchy in north Austria-Hungary between Prussian Silesia and Moravia. After the First World War, it became the Czech province of Slezsko (Silesia). The region was eventually divided between Poland and Czechoslovakia. During a plebiscite in 1920 Czech stamps were overprinted "SO/1920" on two lines. "SO" stood for "Silesie Orientale", meaning East Silesia. Eventually the regions used stamps of either Poland or Czechoslovakia.

East India Postage (insc.) appears on postage stamps of India indicating general issues under the authority of the East India Company, 1855-64.

East River Post Office in New York City, New York, issued U.S. local stamps in 1852-65.

Eatonton, Ga. This town in Georgia issued postmasters' provisional envelopes in 1861, as part of the Confederate States of America.

E.C.A. Economic Commission for Africa. On United Nations 4-cent and 11-cent stamps, 1961.

ECAFE Economic Commission for Asia and the Far East. On Nov. 24, 1947, the Philippines issued three stamps to commemorate the conference of ECAFE held at Baguio. The United Nations emblem, the inscription "ECAFE", and the denominations complete the stamp designs.

écarlate (Fr.) scarlet.

echt (Ger.) genuine.

echt gelaufen (Ger.) genuine, postally used.

Eckbuchstabe (Ger.) corner letter.

Ecke (Ger.) corner.

Eckverzierung (Ger.) corner ornamentation.

E.C.L.A. (insc.) Economic Commission for Latin America. Appears on United Nations 4- and 11-cent stamps, 1961.

ECSC European Coal and Steel Community.

Ecuador a republic of about 275,936 square miles on the Pacific on the northwest coast of South America. Capital: Quito. Issued stamps in 1865.

Ecuador control marks Thieves stole large

quantities of stamps from the government stores in Guayaquil in 1902 during a fire. Most of the stolen stocks were revenue stamps. The government, hoping to prevent the stamps from being used, instructed the provincial authorities to handstamp their stocks with special control marks to distinguish them from the stolen stamps.

Ecuadorian Airlines See C.E.A.

Ecuador provisionals temporary postage stamps of Ecuador. Many were prepared locally in provinces by hand stamps. But confusion between genuine stamps and forgeries caused some catalogues, Scott's for instance, to delete them.

edging, stamp edging term used by non-collectors for perforations or marginal paper.

EDIFICIOS POSTALES (sur.) appears with new values on 1931 postal tax stamps of El Salvador.

EDUCACION NACIONAL (insc.) appears on 1950 postal tax stamps of Peru.

Edwardian refers to many objects, including postage stamps, of the time of King Edward VII of Great Britain, 1901-10.

EEC European Economic Community.

EEF (insc.) appears on first issue of Palestine stamps under British military occupation in 1918. The stamps were used in Palestine, Trans-Jordan, Lebanon, and other nearby states. See catalogues for details.

EESTI OHUPOST (insc.) appears on 1924-5 Estonia airmail stamps.

EESTI POST (insc.) appears on stamps of Estonia.

E.E.U.U. DE COLOMBIA (insc.) appears on stamps of 1879 for the former state of Tolima, now a department of Colombia. A similar inscription is on stamps of Colombia for 1871 and later years.

E.E.U.U. DE VENEZUELA (insc.) appears on 1905 stamps of Venezuela for interior postal use.

EFIMEX (insc.) appears on airmail stamps of Mexico 1968, issued to mark the International Philatelic Exhibition held in Mexico City, Nov. 1-9, 1968. The stamp resembles a postage stamp of Uruguay issued in April 1969.

E.F.O. (ovpt.) French Oceanic Establishments; on stamps of French Polynesia.

E.F.O. material errors, freaks, and oddities.

EFTA (insc.) European Free Trade Association; appears on stamps of Great Britain, 1967.

EFTERPORTO (insc.) appears on postage-due stamps of the Danish West Indies, 1905-13.

Egée (Îles de la mer) (Fr.) Aegean Islands.

EGEO (ovpt.) appears on 1906-8 stamps of Italy for use in Egeo in 1912. Egeo, or Isole Italiane Dell Egeo, is one of the Aegean Islands. Stamps were among the general issues for the Aegean Islands. Inscribed stamps issued 1933-40. Stamps of Egeo follow those of Italy in catalogues.

Egypt a republic of about 386,198 square miles in north Africa on the Mediterranean and Red seas. Once part of Turkey, later a British Protectorate, and then a monarchy. Became a republic in 1953. Merged with Syria in 1958 to form the United Arab Republic. Capital: Cairo. The earliest stamps, those of 1866, were of Arabesque design, watermarked with pyramid and star, and with the values expressed in para or PE (piastre) with a Turkish overprint in black. The Sphinx appears on later issues, 1867-1906. Subsequent issues were inscribed "Égypte" or "Egypt".

Egypte (Fr.) Egypt.

Egyptian Military Concession Stamps See BRITISH FORCES IN EGYPT LETTER STAMP.

Eighteen Forty-Seven (nick.) the first postage stamps issued in the United States.

Eighth Avenue Post Office in New York City, New York, issued U.S. local stamps in 1852.

Eilmarke (Ger.) express-letter stamp, special-delivery stamp.

Eilzustellung (Ger.) special delivery.

einfaches Papier (Ger.) wove paper.

einfarbig (Ger.) monochrome.

Einfassung (Ger.) frame, border.

Einfuehrung in den Katalog (Ger.) introduction to the catalogue.

Einheit (Ger.) unit.

Einheitsmuster (Ger.) unity design.

eins (Ger.) one.

Einschreibebrief (Ger.) registered letter.

Einschreibemarke (Ger.) registration stamp.

Einsteckbuch (Ger.) stock book.

Einzelmarke (Ger.) single stamp.

Eire (insc.) appears on stamps of the Irish Free State, and later on those of the Republic of Ireland.

Eisenbahn (Ger.) train, railway.

Eisenbahnmarken (Ger.) railway stamps.

EJERCITO CONSTITUCIONALISTA TRANSITORIA MEXICO (insc.) appears on 1913 stamps of Sonora, provisionals issued in 1913 during the Civil War. Tabs at bottom show revenue use, but with the tabs removed they were postage stamps. The entire stamp was used at first.

EJERCITO RENOVADOR (insc.) appears on stamps prepared for use in 1923, but never used, in Sinaloa, a state in northern Mexico.

EL a designation on certain U.S. stamp plates for "Electrolytic Iron", indicating plates made by the electrolytic process.

EL AL (airline) Israel Airlines. Point of origin: Jerusalem, Israel. "EL AL", loosely transliterated from Hebrew, means "to the skies".

ELDO European Space Vehicle Launcher Development Organization, which launched the Eldo Europa 1 rocket at Woomera, South Australia, on May 24, 1966. The event was commemorated by a postal marking in Australia.

electric car service mail service by street cars or electric trolley cars between certain communities and within cities of the United States. Also known as street-car service.

electric-eye booklets booklets made from special plates bearing heavy dashes in the margins of the plates. These plates print sheets of stamps for booklet panes. Some panes bear the heavy "electric-eye" dashes.

electric-eye device a device controlled electronically to help the perforating equipment perforate U.S. stamps accurately in the margins between rows of stamps. Electric-eye perforated stamps bear horizontal or vertical bars in the marginal paper and gutters between panes of stamps. For details refer to Scott's U.S. Specialized catalogue.

electric eyes (nick.) U.S. postage stamps with marginal markings used as electronic guides in perforating the sheets.

electrotype Electrotyping is a method of duplicating relief printing forms by pressing the form into wax or soft lead and then depositing copper on the matrix. The thin copper shell is later backed with lead.

elf (Ger.) eleven.

elfenbein (Ger.) ivory.

Elobey, Annobon, and Corisco a group of islands off the west coast of Africa near Guinea, attached administratively to Spanish Guinea; about fourteen square miles. Capital: Santa Isabel. Stamps were issued 1903-10.

El Parlamento Español Cervantes (insc.) appears on 1916 official stamps of Spain, marking the 300th anniversary of the death of Miguel de Cervantes Saavedra, who lived 1547-1616.

El Salvador a republic on the Pacific coast of Central America bordered by Guatemala, Honduras, and the Gulf of Fonseca. Capital: San Salvador. First stamps issued 1867.

Elsass (Ger.) Alsace.

Elsass-Lothringen (Ger.) Alsace-Lorraine.

Elua Keneta (insc.) on stamps of Hawaiian Islands.

emblazon to depict according to the rules of heraldry.

emblems symbols or designs used to represent ideas; a badge, sign, picture, or design with some allegorical significance. Emblems may appear in watermarks or stamp designs; the maple leaf for Canada, the eagle for the United States, the rose for England, and others are examples of emblems.

embossed issue (nick.) any postal issue produced entirely or in part by embossing. The country name and date of issue should be included in a write-up. Great Britain, 1847, The Gambia, 1869-87, and Sardinia, 1853-63 are examples.

embossed stamp envelopes a type of printing that creates a design in part, or entirely, in relief. Many early postal stationery envelopes were printed with embossed stamps in Canada and the United States, for example.

embossing the raised surface obtained by stamping or tooling. Some early issues of Great Britain, The Gambia, and certain European countries consisted of embossed stamps. Many government-authorized stamped envelopes were printed by embossing.

em circulação (Port.) current.

emergency handstamp any kind of cancelling device used as a temporary measure for cancelling postage stamps.

émis, émise (Fr.) issued.

emisión (Sp.) issue, emission.

emisión conmemorativa (Sp.) commemorative issue.

emisión local (Sp.) local issue.

emisión provisional (Sp.) emergency issue, provisional issue.

emissão (Port.) issue.

emissão comemorativa (Port.) commemorative issue.

emissão local (Port.) local issue.

emissão provisória (Port.) provisional issue.

emission issue.

émission (Fr.) issue.

emission (Swed.) issue.

émission commémorative (Fr.) commemorative issue.

emissione (It.) issue.

emissione locale (It.) local issue.

émission provisoire (Fr.) provisional issue.

émissions locales (Fr.) locals; postage stamps used to prepay local delivery in a city or community but not for use to distant places.

émissions spéculatives (Fr.) speculative issues.

Emory, Va. This town in Virginia issued postmasters' provisional stamps and envelopes in 1861, as part of the Confederate States of America.

emoussé (Fr.) blunted, referring to short perforations.

Empire City Dispatch in New York City, New York, issued U.S. local stamps in 1881.

Empire issues (nick.) early issues of France inscribed "Empire Franc", 1853 and subsequent issues.

emplacement (Fr.) setting.

employé dans les bureaux français à l'étranger (Fr.) used in French offices abroad.

Emp. Ottoman (insc.) appears on stamps of Turkey.

en alto (Sp.) on top.

en bas (Fr.) below, at the bottom.

encadré (Fr.) boxed, framed; usually describing postmarks with frames.

encased postage stamps stamps used as money, sometimes called "stamp currency" when the postage stamps were not enclosed in small protective cases. These have been issued during shortage of coins. For example, in 1915 Russia issued paper money printed to resemble postage stamps with the Russian words meaning "Having circulation on a par with silver subsidiary coins". During the American Civil War period, John Gault of New York patented small metal cases to hold a postage stamp on one side and an embossed advertisement on the other side. These were used instead of small change (listed in U.S. specialized stamp catalogues). Stamps of Great Britain were sometimes used in lieu of change during the First World War,

while Belgium and France used encased stamps as coins. In 1900, the British South Africa Co. stamps, and, at a later date, Rhodesia stamps, were stuck on cardboard and authorized for use as coins. France and Austria encased stamps and used them for small coins of the values shown on the stamps. Germany encased stamps of 1921 for use as coins. See POSTAL CURRENCY; FRACTIONAL CURRENCY NOTES.

ENCOMENDAS POSTAIS (Port. insc.) appears on parcel post stamps of Portugal.

ENCOMIENDA, ENCOMIENDAS (Sp. insc.) appears on parcel post stamps of 1929 and later years for Uruguay.

encre (Fr.) ink.

endgueltig (Ger.) definitive, final.

en dos colores (Sp.) bi-coloured, bi-colour.

endwise coils coil postage stamps with perforations across the top and bottom of each stamp (horizontal perforations). "Coil stamps" is another name for roll postage stamps. The endwise roll or coil postage stamps are imperforate on both sides.

en forma de arco (Sp.) arc, a type of roulette.

engine turning the machine-engraving of intricate, symmetrical patterns on metal. The Canadian Post Office uses the term to describe the interlacing, engraved designs on the bottom margins of certain Canadian stamps in the King George V issues, portraying His Majesty in an admiral's uniform; these stamps are called "Admirals" or "admiral issues". See GEOMETRICAL ENGRAVING.

engraved refers to postage stamps produced by steel engraving. Modern postage stamps are not made from copper plates because copper is too soft.

engraver's proofs As an engraver progresses with his work of engraving a die (not a

Encased postage stamps

Engine turning

plate), he makes his own proofs (trial hand-printings) to check on his work.

engraving hand work of inscribing a postage stamp design on a die. Steel-engraved stamps are retouched by engraving but are often erroneously called "re-entries" (which are done by machine).

en haut (Fr.) top.

enkel (Swed.) single.

en kvart (Swed.) one quarter, such as one quarter of a sheet of stamps. (Courtesy of B. Clemens, Swedish Consulate, Toronto, Ontario)

enquadrado em linhas (Port.) border of lines.

ensaio (Port.) essay.

ensayo (Sp.) essay, test, assay, try, proof.

Enschedé, J., & Sons security printers of Haarlem, The Netherlands.

en scie (Fr.) serrated (perforated).

entier (Fr.) entire, cover.

entièrs postaux (Fr.) postal stationery.

entire a complete letter, cover, envelope, or postal stationery item with adhesive postage or printed stamps that passed through the mail. The description "entire" should not be used in reference to pre-stamp covers, mail sent before adhesive stamps were introduced. (Courtesy of Bernard Harmer, New York)

ENTREGA ESPECIAL (Sp. insc.) delivery special; appears on special-delivery stamps of Cuba and other Spanish-language countries.

ENTREGA IMMEDIATA (Sp. insc.) appears on special-delivery stamps of Cuba, 1899, with incorrect spelling of the Spanish word for "immediate". In 1902 the spelling was corrected to "inmediata".

ENTREGA INMEDIATA (Sp. insc.) immediate delivery; appears on special-delivery stamps of Mexico, Cuba, and other Spanish-language countries.

Entwertung (Ger.) cancellation, devaluation, invalidation.

Entwertungsstempel (Ger.) cancel or cancellation.

Entwurf (Ger.) design.

envelopes flat paper containers for letters; they came into common use following the introduction of penny post in Great Britain in May 1840.

enveloppe (Fr.) envelope.

enveloppe patriotique (Fr.) patriotic cover.

enveloppes premier jour (Fr.) first day covers.

épais, épaisse (Fr.) thick.

epaulettes (nick.) the first issue of Belgium, 1849; it portrays King Leopold I wearing a uniform with epaulettes on the shoulders.

Epire (Fr.) Epirus.

Epirus an ancient country in northwest Greece, now divided between Greece and Albania; about 3,611 square miles. A provisional government issued stamps in 1914. Epirus was occupied by Greece in 1916.

épreuve (Fr.) proof.

épreuve d'artiste (Fr.) artist's proof.

E.P.S. Essay-Proof Society, a philatelic organization that specializes in essays and proofs.

Equateur (Fr.) Ecuador.

Erfahrung (Ger.) experience.

ergaenzen (Ger.) to complete.

Ergaenzung (Ger.) completion, supplement.

Ergaenzungswert (Ger.) supplementary value.

Erhaltungszustand (Ger.) condition.

E.R.I. (Latin ovpt.) Edward Rex Imperator; appears on stamps of South African Republic (Transvaal).

Erinnerungsausgabe (Ger.) commemorative issue.

Eritrea a former Italian colony in northeast Africa on the Red Sea, federated with Ethiopia in 1952; about 45,754 square miles. Capital: Asmara. Stamps issued 1892-1934 were stamps of Italy, overprinted; in 1910 and subsequent years stamps were inscribed "Eritrea" for the Italian colony; from 1938 to 1941 stamps of Italian East Africa were issued.

Erklaerung (Ger.) explanation.

Erneuerung (Ger.) renewal.

EROPA Organization of Public Administrators. The organization has been honoured by stamp issues, including that of Persia (Iran) on Dec. 4, 1966.

E.R.P. European Recovery Program.

errata a list of author's or printer's errors, usually inserted at the beginning of a book between the title page and the preface.

erreur (Fr.) error.

erreur de couleur (Fr.) colour error.

erreur d'impression (Fr.) printing error.

erro de cor (Port.) colour error.

erro de impressaõ (Port.) printing error.

error de color (Sp.) colour error.

error de impresión (Sp.) printing error.

errore (It.) error.

errors mistakes in the production of postage stamps. These are not to be confused with varieties. Men make errors, while machines cause varieties. Errors include inverted centres, surcharges, overprints, and frames, and mistakes in colours, papers, and watermarks. See VARIETIES.

Erse language of the people of the Republic of Ireland.

Erstdruck (Ger.) first printing; first edition.

Erste k.k. pr. Donau (partial insc.) appears on Danube local stamp issued by the Danu-

bian Steam Navigation Co. (1866-71). Listed in some European catalogues.

Erstflug (Ger.) first flight.

erstklassig (Ger.) first class.

Ersttagsbrief (Ger.) first day cover.

Ersttagsstempel (Ger.) first day cancel.

Erythrée (Fr.) Eritrea.

ES (script ovpt.) Estado Sonora; appears on stamps of Mexico in 1914 during the Mexican Civil War for use in Estado Sonora, the state of Sonora.

ESC or **E** escudo, high-value coins; the letters are inscribed on some Portuguese and colonial stamps.

escaso (Sp.) scarce.

escudo a coin struck in both silver and gold. It is used in Portugal, Chile, Bolivia, Cuba, Angola, and other countries. The escudo equals 10 reales silver, or 5 pesos gold, or 1,000 bolivianos. "Escudo" means

"shield", and is the Spanish equivalent of the French "ecu" and Italian "scudo".

Escuelas (Sp. insc.) school, normal school, or training college for teachers. Appears on stamps of Venezuela, 1871 and subsequent years, with no country name. These stamps, usually for revenue, were used provisionally for postage. See notes in catalogues.

escutcheon (her.) a shield bearing arms.

E.S. DE ANTIOQUIA (insc.) appears on 1868 stamps of Antioquia, then a state and now a department of Colombia.

E.S. DE PANAMA (insc.) appears on 1878 issue of Panama, when it was a department of Colombia.

espace blanc (Fr.) blank space.

espacio blanco entre dos grupos (Sp.) gutter, paper between panes of stamps.

Espagne (Fr.) Spain.

España (Sp.) Spain.

ESPANA (Sp. insc.) Spain; appears on stamps of Spain for 1860-1 and later years.

ESPANA FRANQUEO (Sp. insc.) appears on 1873 Carlist stamps of Spain.

ESPANA VALENCIA (Sp. insc.) appears with portrait of King Carlos VII on 1874 Carlist stamps of Spain.

Esparto paper book or printing paper made in England and Europe. The name derives from Esparto grass, which is grown in North Africa and used to make paper pulp. Esparto paper has been used for various postage stamps of New Zealand.

especial, especiales (Sp.) special.

ESPERIMENTO POSTA AEREA/MAGGIO 1917/TORINO-ROMA ROMA-TO-RINO (3-line ovpt.) appears on special-delivery stamps of Italy for use as the country's first airmail stamps.

espesso (Port.) thick.

espresso (It. insc.) express or special deliv-

ery; appears on special-delivery stamps of Italy.

essai (Fr.) essay.

Essai (Ger.) èssay.

essai de couleur (Fr.) colour trial.

essai incomplet (Fr.) progressive proof.

essay from the French "essai", "an attempt". Essays are postage-stamp designs submitted but rejected. They may be of the entire stamp design or any part (vignette, frame, portrait), but they are not designs of the finished stamps sold to the public. Essays may be artwork, engravings, or impressions from printing plates.

essay plate a plate with one subject, used for proofing a design.

Essex Letter Express in New York City, New York, issued U.S. local stamps in 1856.

est. estimated, in auction catalogues.

Estado da India (insc.) appears on stamps of Portuguese India.

ESTADO DE NICARAGUA (Sp. insc.) appears on stamps of Nicaragua.

Estado Guayana (Sp. insc.) State of Guayana; appears on local stamps for Guayana, with the inscription "Venezuela" sometimes occurring. Revolutionaries issued twenty different stamps in 1903.

ESTADO. S. DEL. TOLIMA (insc.) appears on stamps of Tolima, 1870 and subsequent years. Tolima was originally a state, and is now a department, of the Republic of Colombia.

Estados Unidos de Colombia United States of Colombia; issued postage stamps 1862-86. Then stamps of the Republic of Colombia were issued.

Estaf. (Fr.) estafette, a vehicle that carried only mail and not passengers. The abbreviation appears in some Paris postmarks. (Courtesy of Herbert Dube)

Est Africain Allemand Occupation Belge (part of ovpt.) appears on 1915 stamps of the Congo, German East Africa, under Belgian occupation.

Estampilla de Correo (ovpt.) See CONTRASEÑA.

estampille (Fr.) postal marking, handstamp.

Estensi (It. insc.) appears on stamps of Modena, in northern Italy.

ESTERO (ovpt.) on stamps of Italy 1874-81 for Italian Offices abroad in South America, Africa, Turkey and other countries.

Estland (Ger.) Estonia.

Estonia a former republic on the Baltic Sea in north Europe, now incorporated into the Soviet Union as Estonian Soviet Socialist Republic; about 18,361 square miles. Capital: Tallin. Stamps were issued for Estonia as an independent state from 1918 to 1940.

Estonie (Fr.) Estonia.

estrecho (Sp.) narrow, close.

estreito (Port.) narrow, close.

estucado papel (Sp.) chalky paper.

ETA (airline) Empresa de Transportes Aéreos, Brazil. On June 19, 1929, Brazil issued a series of five stamps for use on mail carried on the Rio de Janeiro–Camposet–São Paulo route in Brazil. These were local airmail stamps. The company ceased operations in 1929, according to the Sanabria Airpost catalogue.

Etablissements de l'Oceanie (insc.) appears on stamps of French Oceania.

ETABLISSEMENTS FRANCAIS dans L'INDE (insc.) appears on stamps of French India.

ETAT FRANCAIS (insc.) appears on the June 7, 1943, semi-postal stamps of France. They mark the 87th birthday of Philippe Pétain (1856-1951), Marshall of France. The surtax went to the national relief. Pétain, successful defender of Verdun in 1916, became the premier of France in June 1940, when he arranged for an armistice with Germany on the basis of capitulation. After his arrest and trial for treason in 1945 he was imprisoned on the Island of Yeu off the coast of Brittany. He has been portrayed on many postage stamps.

ETAT IND. DU CONGO (insc.) Free State of Congo. Appears on stamps of the Belgian Congo, 1886-98.

Etats confédérés d'Amérique (Fr.) Confederate States of America.

Etats de l'Eglise (Fr.) Roman States.

Etats Malais fédérés (Fr.) Federated Malay States.

Etats-Unis d'Amérique (Fr.) United States of America.

Ethiopia (Abyssinia) a monarchy in northeast Africa west of the Red Sea; area variously quoted as 305,731 square miles and 350,000 square miles. First stamps, issued in 1894, had inscriptions in Amheric only, and bore a portrait of Menelik II or else a lion with a crown and a banner in the left forepaw. Later issues have the overprint "Ethiopie" or inscription "Postes Ethiopiennes" and value expressed in guerches. Modern issues include pictorials, many with portraits of Emperor Haile Selassie.

Ethiopian Air Lines, Inc. (airline) point of origin: Ethiopia.

Ethiopie (Fr.) Ethiopia.

ETIOPIA (insc.) appears on stamps of Ethiopia under Italian occupation, 1936.

etiquette (Fr.) ticket or label; describes airmail stickers of a standard blue colour with the French words "par avion" and an inscription in the language of the country of origin.

etiquette pour adresse (Fr.) address label.

étoile (Fr.) star.

étoile muette (Fr.) dumb or mute; a type of

cancellation without words or figures. Called "silent" in some English handbooks.

étranger, étrangère (Fr.) foreign.

étroit (Fr.) narrow, close.

E.U. or EE. UU. Estados Unidos, Spanish for "United States". The abbreviation appears frequently in inscriptions on certain South American stamps. For example, "EE. UU. de Venezuela" means "the United States of Venezuela", the official name of the country.

E.U. DE COLOMBIA (insc.) appears on various issues of Colombia 1862 and others later.

EU DO BRAZIL (insc.) appears on 1890-1 stamps of Brazil.

Eupen a commune in east Belgium about twenty-one miles east of Liege. Formerly in Germany, transferred with Malmedy and Moresnet to Belgium by the Treaty of Versailles in 1919. Taken in the Second World War by an Allied advance in September 1944. Belgium issued occupation stamps, 1919-21, overprinted "ALLEMAGNE DUITSCHLAND" on two lines on Belgian stamps of 1915-20. In 1920, overprints read "Eupen" or "Malmédy" and Belgian stamps were surcharged "EUPEN & MALMEDY" with new values in German money.

EURATOM European Community for Atomic Energy.

Europa (insc.) appears on stamps of the Common Market countries of Europe: Belgium, Federal Republic of Germany, France, Italy, Luxembourg, and The Netherlands. Since 1951 these countries have been members of the European Coal and Steel Community. They have issued stamps each year in common designs beginning in 1956.

Europa stamps On Dec. 5, 1951, the Consultative Assembly of the Council of Europe made a recommendation for the creation of a postal union among the member countries. More than two years earlier, on Sept. 5, 1949, the assembly had suggested issuing postage stamps in the various countries for the purpose of declaring unity. The special commission proposed by the Messina Conference met in July 1955 to examine the possibilities of European co-operation in posts and telecommunications. The commission recommended the introduction of postage stamps with a common design symbolizing the European idea. The Ministers of Posts of Belgium, France, Germany, Italy, Luxembourg, and The Netherlands decided on the simultaneous issue of these stamps during their meeting

in Paris on Jan. 20, 1956. Twenty-two artists entered sketches in a contest of stamp designs. In its meeting of March 20, the international jury selected the motif of the French designer Daniel Gonzague, which represented a metal construction consisting of the letters EUROPA with the green flag of the European movement waving behind it. The six postal administrations issued their stamps simultaneously on Sept. 15, 1956.

European Coal and Steel Community On May 9, 1950, the Premier of France, Robert Schuman, on behalf of his government, proposed the creation of a European economic community. He submitted the proposal to the consultative assembly of the Council of Europe in August 1950. After prolonged talks during several meetings, six countries decided to join the community: Belgium, France, the German Federal Republic, Italy, Luxembourg, and The Netherlands. The organization remains open to all other member countries of the Council of Europe. The Treaty of the European Coal and Steel Community was signed on April 18, 1951, effective on July 25, 1952. The objectives of the community were to sponsor and help the development of the economy and to improve the standard of living in the member countries by a more rational distribution of coal and steel production. From February to May 1953 all restrictions and customs formalities among the member countries of this organization were abolished. The first European Common Market became a reality.

European Recovery Plan The tremendous destruction in Europe during the Second World War brought an absolute need for economic aid. The United States offered help. Twenty-four billion dollars was allotted for the European Recovery Program, usually referred to as the "Marshall Plan" after Gen. George C. Marshall, who promoted it. On April 16, 1948, the Treaty of the Organization for European Economic Co-operation (O.E.E.C.) was signed by Austria, Belgium, Denmark, France, the German Federal Republic, Great Britain, Greece, Iceland, Ireland, Italy, Luxembourg, Norway, The Netherlands, Portugal, Sweden, Switzerland and Turkey. One major task of the organization was the administration and distribution in member countries of the allotted funds. This common activity of Western European countries for their mutual economic and social restoration stressed the need for and benefit of a closer co-operation. The work later

brought about the creation of the Council of Europe and of the European Economic Community.

évaluation (Fr.) pricing.

exchange clubs stamp collecting groups that trade stamps, usually by mail. Collectors are warned to investigate such clubs and their activities. Individuals, not national societies, often operate them for profit.

exchange markings Canadian exchange markings were handstruck impressions on mail addressed to the United States. They appeared in a variety of straight lines: "Canada" or "Canada/paid 10 cts.", and some oval or circular markings. The United States Post Office employed a great variety of exchange markings, some in arcs, straight lines, ovals, or circles, all used on mail addressed to Canada. Exchange markings on mail between Canada and the United States came into use after the first postal convention of 1792 between the two countries.

Executive (insc.) appears on official stamps for use by the United States executive branch of the government, 1873.

exhibition labels often small seals resembling adhesive postage stamps used to advertise stamp shows. Numerous types exist, perforated or imperforate, some in small units resembling souvenir sheets, but without postal value.

exhibition sheets postage stamps issued to commemorate postage stamp shows in the United States, Europe, and Israel. These have postal validity.

ex libris (Latin) out of the library; bookplate bearing the name of the owner, his coat of arms, or some symbolic design or motto.

experimental labels The various security printers make labels as experiments before they prepare postage stamps of the same types for printing or production. The "poached-egg" labels of Britain and similar blank U.S. coils and the floral label of Canada are examples.

Experimental label (Canada)

expertize describes the act of examining postage stamps and philatelic items to determine their status: genuine, forgery, or fake.

explode to take postage stamp booklets apart. All parts of the booklet should be saved: the covers, staples, instruction pages, and the interleaves with or without advertising.

exploded postage stamp booklets that have been taken apart.

EXPOSICION DE BARCELONA (insc.) appears on stamps of Spain 1930 to commemorate the Barcelona Philatelic Congress and Exposition.

EXPOSICION GENERAL ESPANOLA (insc.) appears on stamps of Spain 1929.

EXPOSICION GRAL SEVILLA-BARCE-LONA (insc.) appears on the Exhibition issue of Spain 1929.

exposition (Fr.) exhibition.

EXPOSITION (sur.) appears with native text on regular-issue stamps of Ethiopia for use as semi-postal stamps in 1949.

Exposition Coloniale Internationale Paris 1931 (insc.) colonial exposition issue; appears without colony name on stamps of France.

Exposition industrielle Damas 1929 (ovpt.) Damascus Industrial Exhibition; appears on stamps of Syria.

exprès (Fr.) express.

EXPRES (insc.) appears on special-delivery stamps of Italy, Canada, Egypt, and other countries. Appears as "Exprès" with a grave accent on stamps of Canada, except for the 1946 stamps, which have a circumflex accent – "Exprês"; this was corrected to a grave accent in 1947.

Expres or **Espresso** (insc.) on special-delivery stamps of Italy. Similar words appear on special-delivery stamps of other countries.

Express Company labels These served as government postage stamps but were sold by commercial firms for mail and parcel delivery, mainly in the United States, but also to some extent in the Australian states.

Express Delivery 15¢ (3-line sur.) on special-delivery stamps of Mauritius, 1903.

Express Delivery Inland 15¢ (4-line sur.) on stamps of Mauritius for inland special-delivery service, 1904.

express delivery stamps, express letter stamps a type used for the prepayment of individual delivery of mail. Virtually the same as special-delivery stamps.

expressfrimärken (Swed.) express or special-delivery stamps.

Expressmarke (Ger.) special-delivery stamp.

EXTERIOR (vertical insc.) appears on 1922-6 parcel post stamps of Ecuador.

Extrême-Orient (Fr.) Far Eastern Republic.

extranjero (Sp.) foreign country.

EXTRA-RAPIDO (ovpt., insc., or sur.) appears on stamps of Colombia; used on domestic mail carried by airlines other than A.V.I.A.N.C.A., the national airline of Colombia.

F

F an abbreviation used in auction catalogues to indicate that a stamp is in average condition; for example, the perforation may touch the design, so that the stamp is fair rather than excellent.

F a marking that appears in margins of certain U.S. stamps. The letter was engraved on the soft steel plate to indicate that it was ready to be hardened and then used in printing stamps. It occurs on flat plates, not curved ones.

F plate ready for hardening

F (ovpt.) for "Fugitives"; appears on French franchise stamps of 1939 issued for use by the Spanish refugee soldiers who fled to France.

face the front of an adhesive postage stamp, postcard, envelope, or aerogram. The name and address are on the face.

face or **face value** the denominations expressed on postage stamps to show their original cost. Sometimes the original face values are changed by surcharging.

facing slips authorized printed forms or plain pieces of paper bearing the address of mail for local or distant post offices. The slips bearing dates are wrapped on top of bundles of letters. Metered mail is wrapped

and presorted by city, state, province, or other region, and each bundle has a facing slip on the top of a bundle held with string. Bags of mail have labels serving the same purpose of destination, date, and sometimes other data to help the post office speed mail to its destination, but these labels are not called facing slips.

facsimile a copy intended to be an exact reproduction of a postage stamp or valuable cover with or without adhesive postage stamps. Prior to 1900, facsimiles were made by fakers or forgers as space fillers in stamp albums. Facsimiles are forgeries or altered stamps made to deceive stamp collectors.

FACTAJ (sur.) appears with new value on parcel post stamps of Romania, 1928.

facteur (Fr.) postman, letter carrier.

faded colour colour of ink or paper that has lost its brightness due to exposure to light, heat, or chemical agents.

fading Certain stamps of the world fade under any kind of light. Some fade in a few days, while others may be exposed for months before fading.

Faelschung (Ger.) forgery.

fahl (Ger.) pale.

fahlblau (Ger.) pale blue.

fahlbraun (Ger.) pale brown.

Fahne (Ger.) flag.

Fahrendes Postamt (Ger.) Travelling Post Office.

Faidherbé (nick.) French colonial key-type stamps portraying General Louis Faidherbé. The stamps of French Guinea, 1906-7, are an example.

fakes, faked stamps genuine postage stamps altered in some way to increase their values. Faked stamps include those repaired, with perforations removed or altered, margins added, gum added, or surcharges or overprints added, removed, or altered. Fakes should not be confused with forgeries, which are counterfeits.

Faksimile (Ger.) facsimile.

F.A.L. (airline) Fiji Airways, Ltd. Point of origin, Fiji.

fale a Samoan house shown on the 1968 Christmas stamp of Western Samoa.

Falkland Island Dependencies include the South Georgia and South Sandwich islands. Postage stamps were issued in February 1946 for these outposts with inscriptions until 1954. Overprinted stamps of Falkland Islands in 1944 were made for the separate islands of Graham Land, South Georgia, and South Orkneys. Eventually, in March 1962, the widely scattered islands became a colony of the British Antarctic Territory.

Falkland Islands a British Crown Colony of about 4,618 square miles, 300 miles east of the Straits of Magellan at the southern point of South America. South Georgia, South Shetland Islands, South Orkneys, Sandwich Islands, and Graham Land are dependencies. Capital: Stanley. First issued stamps in 1878.

falsch (Ger.) wrong, forged.

Falschstempel (Ger.) forged cancel.

falsificação (Port.) forgery.

falsificación (Sp.) forgery.

falsificazione (It.) forgery.

falso (It.) forgery.

falso, falsificado (Sp.) wrong, forged.

falta (Sp.) fault.

F.A.M. Foreign Air Mail.

Famous Americans, Famous American Series seven different series, each of five stamps, issued in 1940 to honour American authors, poets, educators, scientists, composers, artists, and inventors.

famous people on stamps Explorers, musicians, royal families, and other groups of famous people have been portrayed on stamps of the world. The subject is so great that a collection of them could fill fifty or more albums. Collections can be made of individual groups.

fancy cancellations a name often applied to decorative postmarks used in the early years of adhesive stamps. Many so-called cork cancellations are among these.

fanon, fanam gold and silver coins of French India and India. 8 fanons equal 1 rupee. The name was probably a corruption of "panam", from the Sanskrit "pana", meaning wealth. "Fanon" is the French term.

fantasy a bogus label made to resemble an authorized postage stamp.

FAO Food and Agriculture Organization. The United Nations issued two stamps to honour the FAO in 1954. Also, the Philippines marked the occasion of a conference held in 1948 in Baguio by issuing a stamp.

FAPA (insc.) Federation of Asian Pharmaceutical Associations; appears on Korean stamps of Sept. 16, 1968, to mark the opening of the third general assembly of the federation, held in Seoul, South Korea, in September 1968.

Farbaenderung (Ger.) change of colour.

Farbe (Ger.) colour.

Farbenabart (Ger.) colour variety.

Farbendruck (Ger.) colour print, colour printing.

Farbenprobedruck (Ger.) colour trial, colour test.

Farbentabelle (Ger.) colour guide.

Farbenwechsel (Ger.) change of colours.

farbiger Durchstich (Ger.) rouletted in coloured lines.

farblos (Ger.) colourless.

Farbschwankung (Ger.) colour variation.

Farbstoff (Ger.) dye, pigment.

FARDOS POSTALES (insc.) appears on parcel post stamps of El Salvador, 1895.

Far Eastern Republic or **Far Eastern Region** former division of Soviet Russia in Asia, including Pacific Coast and borders of Manchuria; about 900,745 square miles. Capital: Chita. Stamps issued under short-term, independent government 1920-2 were Russian, surcharged or overprinted.

farg (Swed.) colour.

Faridkot a feudatory state in India, issued stamps 1879-86. They became obsolete on Dec. 31, 1886. Later stamps were issued under Faridcot as a Convention state.

Faridkot State (ovpt.) on stamps of India for Faridkot, a Convention state in India, 1887-93. Also valid throughout India. Gibbons says the overprinted stamps were used until March 31, 1901.

Farley issues (nick.) U.S. postage stamps issued while Postmaster General James A. Farley served during the early years of President Franklin D. Roosevelt's administration. The name is often applied to special printings in 1935 of certain issues resulting from complaints over the distribution of imperforate sheets to certain government officials and others. Sometimes referred to as "Farley's follies", a disrespectful term now seldom used.

Faröe Islands or Faeroes or Faeroerne, a group of islands in the north Atlantic north of British Isles. Consist of twenty-two islands, seventeen of which are inhabited. A Danish possession since 1380. Its people failed to get independence in 1946. In 1940-1, while the British occupied the Faröe Islands, five Danish overprinted stamps were issued, listed under Denmark in catalogues.

farthing a copper coin of the United Kingdom and some British possessions. It is one-fourth of a penny. Half-, third- and quarter-farthings have been struck. The farthing is now obsolete in Great Britain.

Farwell (nick.) U.S. stamps privately perforated by the Farwell Co., a wholesale dry-goods company in Chicago, Illinois. The company perforated their own roll postage for private use. Scott's U.S. Specialized catalogue lists two types, perforated vertically.

fasces a design of a bundle of wooden rods with an axe in the middle, the symbol of a king's authority in ancient Rome. It became the emblem of the Italian Fascists and appears with a wavy line on certain stamps of Italy for the Italian Social Republic, a puppet government proclaimed by Mussolini in 1943. Authorized-delivery stamps and postage-due stamps of Italy were overprinted in this way without words. See REPUBBLICA SOCIALE ITALIANA.

Faserpapier (Ger.) granite paper.

fast colours Modern postage stamps are printed with inks that have been made as fade-proof as possible.

Faunce's Penny Post in Atlantic City, New Jersey, issued U.S. local stamps in 1885.

faux (Fr.) counterfeit or forgery – not a fake. Collectors should distinguish between a fake and a forgery.

faux pour collectioneurs (Fr.) a forgery made to defraud stamp collectors, not a counterfeit made to cheat the post office.

faux pour servir (Fr.) a forgery made to defraud the post office.

F.C. in auction catalogues, a fiscal cancel.

FCO BOLLO (insc.) Franco Bollo; appears on the 1865 issue of postage stamps of Italy.

F.D.C. first day cover. Envelope, postcard, or aerogram stamp cancelled on the first day of the issue.

F.D.C. collection first-day-cover collection.

FDR 1 & II the auction catalogues numbered I and II of the Franklin D. Roosevelt stamp collections.

fecha (Sp.) date.

Federated Malay States See FEDERATION OF MALAYA.

Federated Malay States (insc.) on stamps of these states issued 1900.

Federated Malay States (ovpt.) appears on stamps of Negri Sembilan and Perak, 1900.

Federation of Malaya Sovereign State of British Commonwealth of Nations, of about 50,700 square miles, in southeast Asia. Federation includes the states of Johore, Pahang, Negri Sembilan, Selangor,

Perak, Kedah, Perlis, Kelantan, and Trengganu, and the settlements of Penang and Malacca. Capital: Kuala Lumpur.

Federation of South Arabia a British Dependency formed of fourteen states and regions of Aden Colony and part of the Aden Protectorate. Issued stamps in 1963. The federation did not include the eastern part of the Aden Protectorate with the states of Kathiri and Qu'aiti.

Federstrich (Ger.) pen stroke.

Federstrichentwertung (Ger.) pen-stroke cancellation.

federzugentwertung (Ger.) pen-cancelled.

Fehldruck (Ger.) printing error.

Fehler (Ger.) error.

Fehlliste (Ger.) want list.

Fehlzeichnung (Ger.) design error.

fein (Ger.) fine.

feiner Druck (Ger.) fine print, fine printing.

fel (Swed.) fault.

Feldpost (insc. and ovpt.) appears on military parcel-post stamps of Germany, 1942-4; also appears on various military stamps of Austria, 1915-18.

Feldpoststempel (Ger.) field-post cancel.

fêle (Fr.) cracked, referring to a damaged printing plate.

feltryck (Swed.) misprint.

FEN. (ovpt.) abbreviation for "fenigi", a coin; appears on the 1918 Polish local stamps of Warsaw for use in Poland under German occupation.

fen, fun (1) a silver coin of China. 100 fen equal 1 yuan, or Chinese dollar. The name given to this coin by foreigners is "candareen"; (2) a coin of Manchukuo, used 1932-45.

Fenian labels items of doubtful use made over 100 years ago. Inscribed "Republic of Ireland", the labels were produced for or by the Fenian Brotherhood, a revolutionary group in Ireland. (Courtesy of the *American Philatelist*, the A.P.S. monthly journal, March 1971 issue, and of a 1971 A.P.S. press release.)

fente (Fr.) crack, split, gap, as a crack in a plate or in gum.

Fernando Po, Fernando Poo Spanish island in Bight of Biafra, a part of Spanish Guinea, south of Nigeria; about 800 square miles. Capital: Santa Isabel. From 1868 to 1960 stamps of Spanish Guinea were used, at times surcharged or overprinted; from 1960, stamps of Fernando Po were issued. Stamps inscribed "Fernando Poo" were issued in 1868 and are still in use. Spanish Guinea did not issue stamps until 1902.

Ferrari, Philippe la Rénotière von (1848-

1917) a German philatelist who lived in Paris. Following the First World War, the French government seized his world-famous collection and sold it by public auction as part of the German post-war indemnity. It sold for more than £400,000. His last name may also be spelled "Ferrary".

ferriage refers to the action or business of conveyance by a ferry, or to the fare or charge for this service. Ferriage markings were applied to mail between Canada and the United States before many bridges were built across rivers separating the countries.

FERROCARRIL ORIENTAL (ovpt.) appears with new values on Dec. 28, 1929, stamp of Guatemala issued to mark the inauguration of the Eastern Railroad between Guatemala and El Salvador.

fess (her.) the middle part of a shield.

FESTAS DA CIDADE (insc.) appears below "LISBOA" on postal tax stamps of Portugal, 1913. Funds from the stamps were devoted to works of public charity. The inscription means "Lisbon, Festival of the City". (Courtesy of the Consul of Portugal, in Toronto, Ontario)

fett gestempelt (Ger.) heavily cancelled.

fetter Druck (Ger.) bold type.

FEZZAN or **FEZZAN GHADAMES** (insc.) appears on stamps of Libya issued under French occupation, 1946-51.

F.F. first flight.

F.I.A.F. (Sp.) la Federación Interamericana de Filatelia; Inter-American Federation of Philately, an organization working to benefit stamp collecting in South America and parts of North America.

Fidji (Fr.) Fiji.

feudatory states of India some 33 of the 562 Indian states. Many issued their own adhesive postage stamps. See stamp catalogues for these issues, also for those of India, Pakistan, and the Convention states of India.

feuille (Fr.) sheet.

feuillet (Fr.) miniature sheet.

Fezzan a region of desert and oases in southwest Libia; about 150,000 square miles. Capital: Sebha. Stamps were issued during French occupation, 1946-51; Italian and Libian stamps overprinted "FEZZAN Occupation Française" and "R.F. FEZZAN" were French occupation issues.

Fidschi-Inseln (Ger.) Fiji Islands.

field (her.) the surface of a shield.

Field Post Office (F.P.O.) the postal depots to handle mail of servicemen and women, mainly in wartime. F.P.O.s may be located on land or sea. Austria, for example, issued stamps 1915-17 inscribed "Feldpost" for military use. Handstruck markings like circular date stamps often served to indicate military use by British, Commonwealth, and U.S. personnel.

Figueroa Flight Stamp a special, semi-official stamp issued for use on January 1, 1919, between Valparaiso and Santiago, Chile. The Aero clubs of Chile sponsored the flight by an aviator named Figueroa.

figure (1) small illustration or diagram used in a postage stamp design; (2) an Arabic numeral.

figures (nick.) various groups of stamps of the world: for example, the early issues of the German states, which are inscribed with huge figures of denominations. Certain French colonial postage dues and Portuguese colonial stamps are called the figures key-types.

Fiji a British Crown Colony consisting of 250 islands (about 7,083 square miles) east of New Hebrides in South Pacific. Capital: Suva. Issued stamps in 1870.

Fiji Times Express (insc.) appears on the first stamps of Fiji, issued in 1870, which were type-set and printed at the office of the Fiji *Times*.

fil a coin of Jordan and Kuwait. 1,000 fils equal 1 dinar.

fil de soie (Fr.) silk thread.

filigrana (Sp., Port., and It.) watermark.

filigrana acostado (Sp.) sideways watermark.

filigrana coricata (It.) sideways watermark.

filigrana de fabricante (Port.) papermaker's watermark.

filigrana de fôlha (Port.) sheet watermark.

filigrana de la hoja (Sp.) sheet watermark.

filigrana del fabricante (Sp.) papermarker's watermark.

filigrane (Fr.) watermark.

filigrane couché (Fr.) sideways watermark.

filigrane de brochage (Fr.) stitch watermark.

filigrana del fabricante (Sp.) papermaker's watermark.

filigrane de feuille (Fr.) sheet watermark.

filigrane du fabricant (Fr.) papermaker's watermark.

filigrane individuel (Fr.) individual watermark.

filigrane inversé (Fr.) inverted watermark.

filigrane renversé (Fr.) reversed watermark.

Filipinas (insc.) on stamps of the Philippines.

filler a copper coin of Hungary, Fiume, and Jugoslavia. 100 filler equal 1 krone (korona), 1 pengo, or 1 forint. The coin was introduced in 1892.

fillers cards or papers used in envelopes to

hold them upright as they pass through cancelling machines. Sometimes describes any stamps used to fill space in an album; these are better known as "space-fillers".

Finanzstempel (Ger.) revenue cancellation.

Fincastle, Va. This town in Virginia issued postmasters' envelopes in 1861, as part of the Confederate States of America.

fine app. in auction catalogues or advertisements, means "fine appearance". Usually the stamps so described have some faults – thin spots, short perforations, narrow margins on stamps – but look good from the front. Collectors should inspect stamps with this description.

fine aver. in auction catalogues, means "fine average". Collectors should inspect stamps with this description.

fine perforations refers to postage stamps with many holes in a length of two centimetres; sixteen perforations, for example, are classified as fine, as opposed to eight perforations, which would be classified as coarse.

fine screen (1) in paper-making, a type of sieve to remove the fibre knots, shives and coarse particles from the diluted pulp; (2) in photo-engraving, a screen with more than 100 lines to the inch.

fingers (on a press) grippers that hold a sheet of paper in place on the printing cylinder or remove the paper from the cylinder.

Finland (Suomi) from 1809 to 1917 a Grand Duchy of Russia, then a north European republic; about 130,165 square miles. Capital: Helsinki. Stamp issues from 1856 to 1917 under Russian Empire; from 1917, issues of republic.

Finlande (Fr.) Finland.

fino (Port.) thin or fine.

F.I.P. (Fr.) Fédération Internationale de Philatelie; International Federation of Philately.

Fipex Souv. Sh. Fifth International Philatelic Exhibition Souvenir Sheet; a souvenir sheet of two U.S. stamps issued in 1956 to commemorate the exhibition held in New York, April 28 to May 6, 1956, at the new Coliseum Building.

first day the day when a new issue is authorized for sale.

first day cover envelope or postal stationery item posted with adhesive postage stamps cancelled on the day the stamps were issued. Certain events – the introduction of postal service by the United Nations, for example – have been commemorated by first day covers mailed with meter postage stamps.

first $1.00 postage stamps The first $1.00 postage stamps of the world were issued in 1867 by British Columbia, which produced them by surcharging the 3-pence denomination. But these were not placed on sale. In 1869 a $1.00 surcharged issue went on sale, but these are not Canadian stamps, since the authorities of British Columbia operated an independent postal service until the province joined Canada in 1871.

first flight cover an envelope posted for delivery by airmail on the initial flight of an authorized route specified by the post office department. Very often, cachets have provided the basic information about the first flights along an authorized route or between two specified places. India authorized the first airmail flight in February 1911.

first flight mail mail on the initial flight of an airplane, dirigible, rocket, or balloon.

first U.S. adhesive postage stamps The first government-authorized adhesive postage stamps for general use in the United States consisted of 5-cent and 10-cent denominations, for use beginning July 1, 1847.

fiscal pertaining to revenue and financial affairs; in philately, a revenue stamp or a postage stamp cancelled with some kind of revenue marking by hand stamp or manuscript.

fiscale (It.) revenue tax.

fiscale postale (It.) fiscal-postal.

fiscals postally used From time to time revenue stamps have been authorized for postal use. Victoria, a former British colony and now a state in Australia, authorized revenue or fiscal stamps in January 1884 for postal use as well as for revenue. These are called "postal-fiscal stamps". Many other countries have used postal-fiscals.

fiscal stamp a revenue stamp. Fiscal stamps authorized for postal use are called "postal-fiscals". Revenue or fiscal cancels on postage stamps convert them to fiscal stamps.

fiscaux (Fr.) fiscals.

fiscaux-postaux (Fr.) postal-fiscals.

fiskalisch (Ger.) fiscal, revenue.

Fiske & Rice in New England, issued U.S. local stamps in 1851-4.

fita (Port.) strip (three or more stamps attached).

Fiume also known as Rieka or Rijeka; a seaport capital of the former Carnaro province in northeast Italy. In 1947 Fiume became a seaport of Croatia. Its history began in the ninth century; as part of the Byzantine Empire, it was held by Austria, France, and Hungary at various times. Italy occupied the city and issued overprinted stamps of Hungary in 1918. It was annexed to Italy in 1924 and Italian stamps were used. Transferred to Jugoslavia by treaty in 1947.

five-cent error (nick.) the 5-cent U.S. stamps issued in 1917 in which the 5-cent value was inserted in the printing plate of 2-cent rose-colour stamps. The errors appear in auction sales in blocks of nine 2-cent stamps with the centre stamp the 5-cent error or in blocks of twelve with two 5-cent stamps in the middle. The same arrangements of the errors occur in imperforate panes.

five-cent rate refers to the international postal rate established by the U.P.U. (Universal Postal Union) in 1875. Five cents was equivalent to the 20-centime charge; blue-colour postage stamps indicated this rate until the Thirteenth Congress of the U.P.U. in 1952, when colours indicating rates were discontinued.

fjärdedel (Swed.) fourth. (Courtesy of B. Clemens, Swedish Consulate, Toronto, Ontario)

flag a general term covering pennons, ensigns, standards. Hundreds of flags are shown on stamps.

flag cancellations cancels resembling flags flying in a breeze. The designs often contain words announcing special events.

flag cover envelope with flag design.

flag-of-truce letters civilian letters mailed during the American Civil War; not to be confused with prisoner-of-war letters of the same period.

flags issues (nick.) postage stamps of any country featuring flags as the central design. Often refers to the U.S. wartime issues of 1943-4 to honour thirteen overrun countries during the Second World War.

flag stamp Flags are a popular motif on stamps of the world. Topical collectors form collections confined to this subject.

flap the loose end of an envelope.

flappers (nick.) refers to wing margins on British and some colonial stamps, those of Bermuda for example.

flat plate a printing plate for stamp production on a flatbed press, in any kind of printing, as compared to curved plates from rotary presses.

flaw a variation of any kind in stamps or postal stationery.

flèche (Fr.) arrow of the kind used to point to something, on stamps or covers.

Fleming, Sir Sandford (1827-1915) designer of the Province of Canada 3-pence beaver stamp of 1851. The Scottish-born Canadian

engineer became chief railway engineer of the Canadian Pacific Railway. He invented the method of dividing Canada into time zones, and his plans became universal. Russia and other countries paid tribute to him. One plaque in mid-town Toronto, Ontario, commemorates his time-zoning achievement, and another smaller bronze plaque marks the Yonge Street location in Toronto of his office, where he designed his famous beaver.

fleur (Fr.) flower.

fleur-de-lis (her.) a flower design used in heraldry, a device of the French Bourbons; an iris.

fleurette (Fr.) little flowers used in postmarks; those on postmarks of Bermuda are examples.

fleuron (Fr.) a floret, a carved or painted flower; little flowers in postmarks and cancels.

flip file album to hold covers.

floating-safe stamps issued in 1921 by The Netherlands. As a safety measure against shipwrecks, insured mail was placed in floating safes kept on deck to preserve the mail if a ship sank. These stamps were used for this purpose for one year.

floating stamps off paper Certain stamps should not be totally submerged in water because the printing ink may be soluble in water and run or even disappear from the stamp. Some Dutch Indies and Indian feudatory states stamps were printed with water-colour inks. Other stamps, many from Central and South America, were cancelled in inks made intentionally to run when they are soaked or even submerged in water for a short time (twenty minutes or more). These cancels are called "fugitive cancels". These stamps can be removed from envelopes or other paper by placing them, design up, on a soaking-wet blotter, paper, or fine cloth. When the paper bearing the stamps becomes soaked, the stamps can be lifted off without damage.

flora and fauna name of a popular topical subject dealing with the plants of any district and the animal life of a region or period.

floreated decorated with ornaments representing flowers, or with a reasonable likeness to real flowers. This floreated decoration sometimes occurs in stamp frames and borders.

Florida (insc.) appears on Uruguay airmail stamps used for one day in 1925.

flown covers envelopes or letter sheets (airgraphs) carried by any aircraft. It must be possible to adduce proof of flight from back stamps or other postal markings. For example, a letter from Lima, Peru, dated Nov. 3, 1937, with a New York back stamp of Nov. 7, 1937, is sufficient proof of flight. Seapost could not be that fast.

Floyd's Penny Post in Chicago, Illinois, issued U.S. local stamps in 1860.

Flug (Ger.) flight.

Flugfelag Islands H.F. (airline) point of origin: Iceland.

FLUGFRIMERKI (insc.) appears on airmail stamps of Iceland.

Flugplatz (Ger.) airfield, airport.

Flugpost (Ger. insc.) airmail; appears on stamps of Danzig, Germany, and Austria.

Flugpostmarke (Ger.) air stamp.

Flugzeug (Ger.) airplane.

fluorescent a stamp printed on paper with an optical brightener content that glows an intense whitish-violet when activated by either short- or long-wave ultra-violet light. These papers are commonly referred to as "britc" or "hi-brite". There is some attempt to further subclassify as "medium-brite" and "lo-brite". (Courtesy of Alfred G. Boerger)

Fluoreszenz (Ger.) fluorescence.

flyspeck philately (nick.) that branch of stamp collecting dealing with minor varieties. The term is derogatory, but this need not deter collectors interested in plating stamps printed by processes other than steel engraving. Varieties in certain steel-engraved stamps are often of major importance, for example the various re-entries in the British penny-blacks of 1840.

F.M. (ovpt.) Franchise Militaire; appears on regular-issue stamps of France, 1901-39, for use as military stamps.

FMO Fleet Mail Office.

FNR JUGOSLAVIJA (insc.) on stamps of Jugoslavia.

foglietto (It.) souvenir sheet, small sheet.

foglio (It.) sheet.

F. O.G. N.H. indicates fine-quality stamps with original gum and never hinged (mounted with a hinge).

foil stamps Postage stamps printed on metallic foil are novelties, and are not practical for postage use. They attract younger collectors, but advanced collectors do not buy these metal-foil issues. Burundi, Russia, and Tonga are among the countries that have issued these freak stamps, but Tonga became over-ambitious with continual issues on foil since 1963.

fôlha (Port.) sheet.

fôlha comemorativa (Port.) souvenir sheet.

FOMENTO-AERO- / COMUNICACIONES (2-line sur.) appears with new value on airmail postal tax stamps of Ecuador, 1945.

fond (Fr.) background, ground.

fondo (Sp. and It.) background, ground, rear, bottom.

FONDUL AVIATIEI (insc.) appears on the 1937 postal tax stamps of Romania.

Fono Fou (insc.) on Western Samoa stamps introduced March 31, 1958; refers to the new parliament of Samoa I Sisifo, or Western Samoa.

Fonopost a development in Argentina to record a person's voice and provide postal delivery of the records. The Argentine delegation held demonstrations of the Fonopost during the Eleventh Congress of the U.P.U. in 1939. Later in 1939 Argentina issued a series of three stamps for mailing the records.

football or **soccer** a popular sport portrayed on stamps of the world. Hungary issued an unusual stamp on Dec. 3, 1959, to mark the victory of Hungary's soccer team over the British team at Wembley, England, with a score of 6 to 3 on Nov. 25, 1953.

forato (It.) rouletted.

foratura a sega (It.) saw-tooth roulette.

Forcados River the main navigable channel of the Niger River. A postmark bearing the name "Forcados River" and a date in a

Foil stamps
(Russia)

circle was used to cancel British stamps in 1892. The cancels are listed in the British Commonwealth sections of Gibbons catalogues.

FORCES FRANCAISE LIBRES/LEVANT (sur.) appears on stamps of Lebanon and Syria for use as military stamps by the Free French Administration in 1942.

FOREIGN AFFAIRS (part of insc.) appears on the 1896 official stamps of Hawaii.

(Foreign)/Express/Delivery (3-line sur.) appears with new value on stamps of Mauritius, 18-cent value, for the foreign special-delivery service, 1904.

foreign stamps term referring to issues of any country apart from stamps of the collector's own country.

forerunners stamps or labels, usually provisionals, used before authorized issues are made for public use. Many unofficial airmail labels of Canada, Colombia, and Uruguay, for example, are forerunners. The Jewish National Fund labels (J.N.F.) of Israel, with a Hebrew overprint, are popular forerunners of Israeli stamps.

forgery an imitation of a genuine postage stamp made intentionally to defraud the postal authorities or collectors. Forgeries should not be confused with bogus stamps or fakes.

Genuine   *Forged*
stamp   *stamp*

forint a silver coin of Hungary. 100 filler equal 1 forint. "Forint" is the Hungarian word for "florin".

format refers to the layout of postage stamps: panes, sheets, coils, booklets, or souvenir or miniature sheets. Horizontal or vertical designs are also formats of stamps.

Format (Ger. and Fr.) size.

formato (It.) size.

form, forme all set-up matter locked up in a stet ready to go to press in letterpress printing. (A stet is a metal frame in which type and illustrations are locked for printing or stereotyping.)

Formosa island in the China Sea, formerly in south part of Japanese Empire (1895). Japanese made it a strong military base during the Second World War; later it was returned to China after the defeat of Japan. When the Communists overran mainland China, the Chinese government moved to Formosa. In 1945 Japan issued stamps for Formosa, and in 1949 the Republic of China began to issue stamps for use there. By 1968 the island was better known as Taiwan. "Formosa" is the Portuguese word for "pretty".

Formose (Fr.) Formosa.

forty-sevens (nick.) the first two U.S. government-authorized adhesive postage stamps, issued July 1, 1847.

forwarding agents businessmen who take care of forwarding or shipping merchandise from one seaport to another. They also forwarded mail before 1875. If the company name and address on the cover of a letter differ from the name and address on the letter, the cover was likely handled by a forwarding agent. (Courtesy of Kenneth Rowe, specialist and author)

fotograbado (Sp.) photogravure.

fount a set of type of a particular size and face.

four-colour process printing done with a set of four colour plates, usually yellow, blue, red, and black. The half-tone screens for different colours are set at different angles, such as 90° for yellow, 45° or 135° for black, 75° for red, and 15° for blue. The colour separation is obtained by use of colour filters.

Fourdrinier paper machine a modern paper machine named after the Fourdrinier brothers, who financed the development of the machine. Nicolas Louis Robert invented it at the beginning of the nineteenth century. It consists of an endless, moving web of wire cloth on which a sheet of paper is formed from pulp suspension.

Fournier, François a stamp forger of Geneva, Switzerland, who also "repaired" defective stamps. Mail censorship during the First World War ended his mail-order business.

Four S's See SOCIETY FOR THE SUPPRESSION OF SPECULATIVE STAMPS.

fox to discolour postage stamps, leaves in books, and other paper articles.

foxed paper spotted or stained paper, found in some postage stamps issued by tropical countries; foxing is the result of mildew or other organic agents.

F.P.O. Field Post Office.

fractional currency notes paper money bearing reproductions of postage stamps of the United States. Five different issues of fractional currency notes were used between 1862 and 1876. The notes helped to stop the shortage of small denominations in metal coins; they measured about 3 by 3½ inches and were printed on security paper like bank notes. See ENCASED STAMPS; POSTAL CURRENCY.

fractional stamps split or bisected stamps, cut to render service at a portion of the original value expressed on the complete postage stamp. Used fractional stamps should be on an original envelope or letter sheet with a cancel tying the stamp to the paper. See BISECT.

fragment (Fr.) piece (of a cover).

fragmento (Sp.) piece (of cover), fragment.

frame the printed border around a part of a postage stamp design.

frame plate the printing plate used to print the borders or frames in stamps made with two or more colours. Frame plates often include the country name, designs, lines, or words. The impressions from the frame plate may be parts of the outer designs, or they may surround the entire designs like frames on pictures.

franc a gold coin in the fourteenth century, later a silver coin, and now aluminum. It has been used in France, the Danish West Indies, Switzerland, Belgium, Monaco, the French colonies, and elsewhere. 100 centimes equal 1 franc. In the currency reorganization during the French Revolution (1795), the silver (now aluminum) franc was adopted as the unit of currency of France.

FRANC (sur.) appears on stamps of Austria used by Austrian offices in Crete, 1903-7.

FRANCA (Sp. ovpt.) appears on the 1884 provisional stamps of Chiclayo and Ancachs in Peru. The Spanish word "franco", or "franca", means free or exempt. Therefore, mail bearing these stamps arrived free of charge.

France republic in west central Europe, of about 212,655 square miles. Capital: Paris. First stamps were issued in 1849-50.

France d'outre-mer (insc.) appears on stamps of the French Colonies general issue, 1943.

France Libre (insc., ovpt., or part of sur.) Free France; appears on stamps of French possessions during the Second World War.

FRANCE LIBRE F.N.F.L. (ovpt. and sur.) appears on stamps of St. Pierre and Miquelon, 1941-2, issued under the Free French

Administration. These are believed by some authorities to be speculations. A 1941 issue included the overprint "Noël 1941". The letters F.N.F.L. stand for "Forces Navales Françaises Libres" – Free French Naval Forces.

franchise stamps special issues granted to persons for free postal services. For example, in 1869 Spain granted a franchise to an author for the distribution of his work on postal history, and again in 1881 to another author to distribute his book on philately. Refer in Scott's catalogue to Spain, Numbers S1 and S2. Portugal also issued similar special stamps.

Francis paper security paper patented by Dr. S. W. Francis of New York City. The paper turned brown when it was soaked in an alkaline liquid. Cancellations of an acid solution applied by a sponge turned the paper a deep blue. The U.S. 2-cent Andrew Jackson and 3-cent Washington stamps (1863) of the National Bank Note issues were ordered on the Francis paper and sent to Newport, Rhode Island, for experimental use. (Courtesy of John N. Luff.)

franco a silver coin of the Dominican Republic. 100 centavos equal 1 franco.

franco (Danish) postage paid; a marking on mail.

franco (insc.) free; on stamps of Switzerland, indicating that postage stamps were prepaid delivery and that the mail arrived free at the address.

FRANCO (insc.) appears on stamps of Philippines 1854-63, issued under Spanish Dominion.

Francobolli Pubblicitari (It.) See PUBLICITY POSTAGE STAMPS OF ITALY.

Franco Bollo (It. insc.) appears with "Poste Italiane" on stamps of Italy; occurs on imperforate stamps of Sardinia 1851-61, on regular issues and newspaper stamps; appears on stamps of Italy 1862-3, Sardinia 1851-63, and Two Sicilies 1859-61, all bearing the portrait of King Victor Emmanuel II and no country name; also appears on stamps of the Roman States 1852-68, having various designs.

francobollo commemorativo (It.) commemorative stamp.

francobollo di beneficenza (It.) charity stamp.

FRANCOBOLLO DI STATO (It. insc.) Italian official stamp; appears with large numerals in an oval, but no country name. (Illustration: p. 92)

francobollo fiscale (It.) fiscal stamp.

francobollo per espressi (It.) special-delivery

*Francobollo
di Stato*

stamp.

francobollo per espresso (It.) express letter stamp.

francobollo per giornali (It.) newspaper stamp.

francobollo per le lettere in ritardo (It.) a too-late stamp.

francobollo per lettere raccomandate (It.) registration stamp.

francobollo per pacchi postali (It.) parcel post stamp.

francobollo per posta aerea (It.) airmail stamp.

francobollo postale (It.) postage stamp.

Franco Bollo Postale (insc.) on stamps of the Roman States, with denominations in "Baj" for "bajocchi" or in centesimi.

FRANCOBOLLO TOSCANO (insc.) appears on postage stamps of Tuscany, 1851-2, 1857-60.

Franco Marke (insc.) appears with coat-of-arms and no country name on a Bremen issue of 1856-60.

Franco Scrisorei (insc.) appears with values in par, or parale, on first stamps of Moldavia-Walachia, 1862. These principalities formed the Kingdom of Romania in 1859. Stamps for Romania were issued on Jan. 23, 1865.

FRANCO 6Cˢ CORREOS (insc.) This and similar inscriptions appear with no country name on early stamps of Spain.

frank also called "free frank"; the signature of a person entitled to send letters post-free. Modern franks are usually made by handstruck impressions or meter postage stamps.

frank, diplomatic an impression on mail from a diplomatic office in a foreign country to indicate free postal service.

franked a common word in stamp-collecting language, meaning "postage paid". Hence, "franco", "franqueo", and other foreign spellings, inscribed or in overprints and surcharges. Also used as a handstamp on early mail.

Frankeerzegel (part of sur.) appears on 1926 Netherlands postage-due stamps for use as 1926-7 issues of Surinam and on 1927 Surinam stamps; a similar surcharge appears on Curaçao stamps, of the Netherlands marine insurance type, for regular use in Curaçao, a former Dutch colony now known as Netherlands Antilles.

frankering (Dutch) prepayment, postage.

Frankiermaschine (Ger.) postage meter.

frankiert (Ger.) postage paid, franked.

Franklin, Benjamin appointed postmaster of Philadelphia in 1737. In 1753 he became Deputy Postmaster General of the British colonies in America, but lost his appointment in 1774, before the American Revolution.

Franklin City Despatch Post in New York City, operated by Bouton's Manhattan Express, issued U.S. local stamps in 1849.

Franklin, N.C. This town in North Carolina issued postmasters' provisional envelopes in 1861, as part of the Confederate States of America.

franqueo (Sp. insc. and ovpt.) appears on various issues of Peru.

FRANQUEO DEFICIENTE (Sp. insc.) appears on postage-due stamps of Ecuador, Nicaragua, Paraguay, and Salvador.

Franqueo Impresos (insc.) appears on stamps of Spain in 1872-3.

Franqueo Oficial (Sp. ovpt.) appears on official stamps of various Spanish-language countries.

FRANQUICIA POSTAL (Sp. insc.) appears on franchise stamps of Spain in 1881.

Franzoesisch-Guiana (Ger.) French Guiana.

Franzoesisch-Hinterindien (Ger) French Indo-China.

Franzoesische Kolonien (Ger.) French Colonies.

Franzoesisch-Kongo (Ger.) French Congo.

Franzoesisch-Sudan (Ger.) French Sudan.

Frazer & Co. in Cincinnati, Ohio, issued U.S. local stamps 1845-51.

frazionato (It.) bisected.

freaks any kind of abnormal postage stamps or postal stationery items. The freaks include creased paper varieties, faulty perforations, incorrect folds in postal stationery, misplaced stamps on stationery items, and many other faults. Since most of these items are caused by machinery, they are not errors – merely varieties. See ERRORS.

Fredericksburg, Va. This town in Virginia issued postmasters' provisional stamps in 1861 as part of the Confederate States of America.

free refers to postal markings on mail to indicate it was carried free of charge. Some government officials or other persons have been authorized to use this frank.

free frank See FRANK.

free franked covers letters sent free of postal

charge, usually by government officials, royalty, or members of the armed services. The word "franked" here is redundant. But in the bilingual marks or meters of Canada, the words "Free – Franco" appear; "franco" is the French word for "free".

Free India See AZAD HIND.

FREI DURCH ABLOSUNG (insc.) free under special exemption; appears with "Nr. 16" on German local official stamps for use in Baden, 1905; appears with "Nr. 21" on German local official stamps for use in Prussia, 1903.

Freimarke (insc.) appears on stamps of Württemberg, some without a country name, 1851-68; also on stamps of Thurn and Taxis, 1852-67.

FREIMARKE (insc.) appears with no country name on stamps of Prussia 1850-60, and on stamps of Württemberg 1857-68, 1873.

Freistaat Bayern (Ger. ovpt. and sur.) overprinted on 1906-19 stamps of Germany for use in Bavaria in 1919; also overprinted on regular issues of Bavaria for use in 1919-20; surcharged on regular issues of Bavaria for use as semi-postals in 1919.

FREIE STADT DANZIG (insc.) appears on various stamps of 1921-39 of Danzig, a former free city and state.

fremd (Ger.) foreign, strange.

Fremdsprache (Ger.) foreign language.

French Congo See FRENCH EQUATORIAL AFRICA.

French crisp paper French colonial authorities purposely introduced a type of brittle paper known as crisp paper for many French colonial postage stamps in the 19th century. For example, the postage stamps of St. Pierre and Miquelon were printed on this paper. (Courtesy of Dr. R. Maresch)

French Equatorial Africa formerly the French Congo; a French overseas territory in northwest Africa of about 959,256 square miles. Capital: Brazzaville. Stamps issued 1936-57 were overprinted and inscribed "Afrique Equatoriale Française". In 1958 French Equatorial Africa became four separate republics: Central African Republic (which had been Ubangi-Chari), Chad, Middle Congo, and Gabon.

French 40 Diff. from 6 col In auction catalogues, this note means that forty different stamps from six French colonies compose the lot in a postage-stamp auction.

French Gabon See GABON.

French Guiana a French overseas department on the northeast coast of South America; about 34,740 square miles. Capital: Cayenne. Stamps issued from 1886 to 1947 were those of the French Colonies, surcharged, overprinted, or inscribed.

French Guinea a former French territory in West Africa, became a republic in 1958. Area variously quoted as about 96,886 square miles, 108,455 square miles, and 89,436 square miles. Stamps from 1892 to 1941 were printed "Afrique Occidentale Française" with the name of the colony; these were followed by issues of French West Africa in about 1944, and from 1958 by issues of Republic of Guinea.

French India a former French territory now restored to India; about 197 square miles. Capital: Pondichéry. From 1892 to 1952 stamps issued were those of the French Colonies, with the name of the colony.

French offices in China The French maintained post offices in China prior to 1923.

French Morocco a former protectorate in northwest Africa, now independent; about 153,870 square miles. Capital: Rabat. From 1891 to 1911, stamps of France were used, surcharged or overprinted; in 1912-13 stamps were issued by Cherifien posts; as a French protectorate 1914-56, some stamps issued were overprinted "Protectorat Français", some "TANGER"; from 1956 stamps of Republic of Morocco were issued.

French offices in Crete The French maintained post offices in Crete when it was an autonomous state.

French offices in Egypt France maintained post offices in Alexandria and Port Said from 1899 to 1929, and issued stamps inscribed "Alexandrie" and other issues for Port Said.

French offices in Turkish Empire The French maintained post offices in the Turkish Empire prior to 1923.

French offices in Zanzibar The French maintained post offices in Zanzibar until 1906. French stamps were surcharged, overprinted, or inscribed for use in Zanzibar, 1894-1904.

French Polynesia a French overseas territory comprised of islands in central Pacific Ocean; about 1,544 square miles. Capital: Papeete. Sometimes called "French Oceania". The territory issued its first stamps in 1892.

French Southern and Antarctic Territories French territories in the Antarctic; about 9,000 square miles. Stamps issued from 1955 were those of Madagascar, overprinted "TERRES AUSTRALES ET ANTARCTIQUES FRANÇAISES".

French Sudan a French territory in west Africa of about 590,966 square miles. Capital: Bamako. Stamps issued from 1894 were those of French Colonies, overprinted. Stamps of French Sudan were superseded by those of French West Africa.

French West Africa a former French overseas territory in West Africa, became a republic in 1958; about 1,815,768 square miles. Capital: Dakar. Stamps issued from 1943 were those of the French Colonies surcharged; after 1958 stamps were issues of the republic.

Friendly Islands See TONGA.

Friend's Boarding School in Barnesville, Ohio, issued U.S. local stamps in 1877.

Frimaerke KGL Post (insc.) on stamps of Denmark 1851, without country name. By 1854 the inscription was shortened to "F.R.M. K.G.L. POST".

frimarke or **Frimaerke** (insc.) appears on stamps of Denmark, Norway, and Sweden.

frit (Danish) free (appears as a marking on mail).

frontispiece illustration or picture facing the title page in a book.

F.R.P.S.L. Fellow of the Royal Philatelic Society, London.

F.U. in auction catalogues and advertisements, indicates that a stamp is in "fine used" condition.

Fuchs, Emil an Austrian artist who moved to England in 1897. One of his etchings portraying King Edward VII was the model used for many postage stamps of the British Commonwealth.

Fuehrungslinie (Ger.) guide line.

fuenf (Ger.) five.

fuenfundzwanzig (Ger.) twenty-five.

fuenfzehn (Ger.) fifteen.

fuenfzig (Ger.) fifty.

fuera de curso (Sp.) obsolete.

Fuerstentum (Ger.) principality.

Fuerstentum Liechtenstein or **Fürstentum Liechtenstein** (insc.) appears on stamps of the principality of Liechtenstein. First stamps were issued in 1912 under the Austrian post office administration.

fugitive cancels a type of security cancel made purposely in soluble ink, so that the ink will run and destroy the postage stamp when any attempt is made to remove the cancel for the purpose of using the stamp a second time. These cancels, usually in red, violet, blue, or tones of these colours,

should be handled carefully when a batch of stamps is being soaked in water, since the colours will run and destroy other stamps in the water bath.

fugitive colours colours that are not fast to light, water, or other liquids such as carbon tetrachloride or benzine, which is often used in detecting postage stamp watermarks.

Fujaira See FUJEIRA.

Fujeira or **Fujaira** a trucial state on the Persian Gulf. Issued stamps first in 1964. These labels are not allowed in many stamp exhibitions, and are mainly for beginners in stamp collecting.

full-length Victorias (nick.) stamps of Victoria, Australia, of 1852-6 portraying Queen Victoria on a throne in a full-length illustration as opposed to the half-length portrait of 1850, and other portraits showing the Queen's head.

Full O.G. in auction catalogues and advertisements, indicates that there is original gum on the entire stamp.

fumigated mail See DISINFECTED MAIL.

Funchal a Portuguese district on the southeast coast of Madeira. Postage stamps were issued 1892-1905, then superseded by those of the Azores 1905-1931, as well as by those of Madeira, and then those of Portugal.

fundo (Port.) background.

fuori corso (It.) obsolete.

FUR BERLINER WAHRUNGSGESCHA-DIGTE (insc.) appears on German semipostal stamps of 1949 issued under the occupation forces of the United States, Great Britain, and France.

FUR KRIEGS/BESCHADIGTE (sur) appears with new values on stamps of Germany for use as semi-postal stamps of the German Republic in 1919. A similar surcharge appears on 1914-16 stamps of Bavaria for use as semi-postal stamps in 1919.

fusée (Fr.) rocket.

Fussnote (Ger.) footmark, footnote.

Futuna part of the French overseas territory of Wallis and Futuna Islands.

F.V. meter machine fixed-value meter postage stamp machine, limited to one denomination.

Fwd. forwarded.

G

G. an abbreviation used in dealers' advertisements or auction catalogues to mean "good". However, beware of the quality of a stamp described as "G.", because often such a stamp is really of poor quality.

G or **G.W.** (ovpt.) on stamps of Cape of Good Hope for use in Griqualand West.

G. or **GR.** or **GN** green colour.

GAB (sur.) Gabon; appears with additional values on stamps of Gabon inscribed "COLONIES POSTES".

Gabon, Gabun, or **Gaboon** former French territory in southwest Africa, now a republic; area variously quoted as about 93,218 square miles and 103,089 square miles. Stamps issued from 1886 were those of French Colonies, surcharged or overprinted; from 1958 stamps were issues of the republic. In 1910, Gabon issued inscribed stamps featuring an African warrior and a woman in a native costume, which became popular with junior collectors.

Gadames or **Ghadames** oasis and town in northwest Libia near Algerian border. In 1943 stamps of Italy and Libia were overprinted "FEZZAN Occupation Française" and "R.F.FEZZAN" for "Fezzan-Ghadames". Stamps issued 1948-51.

Gahagan & Howe City Express in San Francisco, California, issued U.S. local stamps 1864-70.

Gainesville, Ala. This town in Alabama issued postmasters' provisional envelopes in 1861 as part of the Confederate States of America.

Galveston, Texas issued postmasters' provisional envelopes in 1861 as part of the Confederate States of America.

Gambia a former British Crown Colony and Protectorate of about 4,068 square miles extending inland on west coast of Africa from the mouth of the Gambia River. Capital: Bathurst. Issued the famous embossed-head stamps portraying Queen Victoria, 1869-87. These stamps are sometimes called the "Cameos of Gambia". Gambia became independent in 1965 as a state in the British Commonwealth.

Gambie (Fr.) Gambia.

G. A. Mill's Despatch Post in New York City, New York, issued U.S. local stamps in 1847.

Gandon, Pierre a prominent French postage stamp designer.

Ganzsache (Ger.) entire; postal stationery.

gaps the untagged areas across web direction that were not covered by the mats for Type I tagging; found on U.S. sheet-stamp margins and coil stamps. (Courtesy of Alfred G. Boerger)

Garantiezeichen (Ger.) mark of guarantee.

gare (Fr.) railway station.

garter type of watermark developed from the design of the Order of the Garter. Used in British stamps, 1855-7. Refer to catalogues for examples.

Garzon issue an 1894 type-set issue of postmasters' provisional stamps of Colombia. Listed in stamp catalogues.

gasto (Port.) worn.

gauche (Fr.) left.

gauge a device for measuring sizes of perforations and roulettes.

GBNO (Sp. ovpt.) abbreviation for the Spanish word "gobierno", meaning "government". Appears on Mexican stamps in 1914 for use in Salamanca during the Mexican revolution of 1913-16.

G. Carter's Despatch in Philadelphia, Pennsylvania, issued U.S. local stamps and envelopes in 1849-51.

GCM (cipher ovpt.) appears on various stamps of Mexico for use in Oaxaca in 1914-15, during the civil war period.

G & D (sur.) appears with various values on stamps of Guadeloupe and Dependencies, 1903-4.

G & D or **G et D** (sur.) appears with new values on former stamps of Guadeloupe,

Gambia:
embossed
stamp

95

for use in Guadeloupe and the Dependencies that formed part of the colony in 1903.

Gdańsk From 1925 to 1937, stamps of Poland were overprinted "Port Gdańsk" for the Polish offices in Danzig. "Gdańsk" is Polish for "Danzig". The city was made a part of Poland after the Second World War.

GD-OT (ovpt.) appears on newspaper stamps of Bohemia and Moravia of 1939 for use by commercial firms.

G.E.A. German East Africa. A former German dependency in Africa, acquired in the period 1885-90 and administered by Germany until 1916 when Great Britain captured the colony. The territory was divided among Great Britain, Portugal, and Belgium. In 1917 Great Britain issued stamps overprinted "G.E.A." on the British colonial stamps of East Africa and Uganda Protectorates, the 1912-14 issue. In 1921, Britain overprinted "G.E.A." on stamps of the Kenya and Uganda issue of 1921 (Scott); stamps were also inscribed "East Africa and Uganda". The first issue is on paper watermarked with a multiple crown and "CA". The 1921 stamps are on paper watermarked multiple crown and script CA".

geaendert (Ger.) changed, modified.

geaetzt (Ger.) etched.

Gebaeude (Ger.) building.

gebogen (Ger.) bent, curved.

gebraucht (Ger.) used (cancelled).

gebrochen (Ger.) creased, broken.

Gebuehr bezahlt (Ger.) postage paid.

Gebuehrenstempel (Ger.) fee stamp.

Gebuehrenzettel (Ger.) fee label.

GEBYR (ovpt.) appears on tax stamps of Denmark used as late-fee stamps in 1923. At first it indicated a charge for completing postal forms and addressing mail.

Gebyrmaerke (insc.) appears on late-fee stamps of Denmark, 1926-34.

Gedenkblock (Ger.) souvenir sheet.

Gedenkmarke (Ger.) commemorative stamp.

Gedenkzahlen (Ger.) memorable dates.

geeinigt (Ger.) united.

Gefaelligkeitsabstempelung (Ger.) cancellation on request, cancelled to order.

gefaelscht (Ger.) forged.

gefaerbt (Ger.) coloured, dyed.

gefasertes Papier (Ger.) fibrous paper.

gegittert (Ger.) quadrille.

Geheimzeichen (Ger.) secret mark.

geklebt (Ger.) affixed, pasted.

gekreuzt (Ger.) crossed.

gekuerzt (Ger.) abbreviated, shortened.

gelb (Ger.) yellow.

gelbbraun (Ger.) yellow-brown.

gelbgruen (Ger.) yellow-green.

gelblichgruen (Ger.) yellowish-green.

gelboliv (Ger.) yellow-olive.

gelborange (Ger.) yellow-orange.

Geld (Ger.) money.

geldigheidsduur (Dutch) period of validity.

Geldueberweisung (Ger.) money order.

gelegenheidszegels (Dutch) stamps issued occasionally.

Gelegenheit (Ger.) opportunity, occasion.

gelocht (Ger.) punched.

gemischt (Ger.) mixed, compound.

gemischte Zaehnung (Ger.) compound perforation.

Gen.-Gouv. Warschau (ovpt.) appears on stamps of Germany for use in Poland under German occupation, 1916-17.

genau (Ger.) accurate(ly).

Genehmigung (Ger.) authorization.

general collector one who collects postage stamps of the world at random, in contrast to a specialized collector, who limits his hobby to a concentrated subject in philately.

General Gouvernement (sur. and insc.) appears as part of a decorative surcharge on stamps of Poland issued in 1940 under German occupation; also appears as an inscription on stamps of Poland 1940-4, under German occupation.

generalizing collecting all postage stamps of the world, rather than specializing in one country or subject.

General Postal Union See UNIVERSAL POSTAL UNION.

General Post Office usually refers to the main post office in a city or country. If no country name is given, it is assumed that the reference is to the British Post Office in London. Frequently shortened to G.P.O.

Generalstabskarte (Ger.) general ordnance map.

Genève (partial insc.) Geneva; appears on stamps of Geneva, a canton of Switzerland, 1843-50.

genomskinlig (Swed.) transparent.

genuine stamp one known to be authentic, not a fake or forgery.

geometric engraving the intricate and precise combination of curved, oval, and straight lines criss-crossing on a steel or copper printing plate incised by a special lathe. The lathe engraves interlacing patterns to a uniform depth, a feat that no man can accomplish by hand. The patterns, used as a measure to help combat forgery, were part of the 1-penny black stamps and 2-penny blues of Great Britain in 1840 and subsequent issues in the same design, and on many other stamps. Other names for this technique of engraving include engine turning, rose engraving, and lathe work. See ROSE ENGINE.

Geo-philately a name coined by the Geology Unit of the American Topical Association for stamp collecting that specializes in rocks and geology.

Georgetown, S.C. This town in South Carolina issued postmasters' provisional envelopes in 1861 as part of the Confederate States of America.

Georgia an ancient kingdom bordering on the Black Sea, now a constituent republic with Armenia and Azerbaijan of the U.S.S.R.; about 26,875 square miles. Capital: Tiflis. Stamps were issued 1919-23 by Georgia, then replaced by those of the Transcaucasian Federated Republics.

Georgian refers to the era of the reign of King George V and King George VI of Great Britain and the Commonwealth.

Georgian key-types British colonial stamps designed by De La Rue from two different dies portraying George V. Used mainly in 1912-39. Examples are: Ceylon 1935; Fiji 1938; Gilbert 1939; Leeward 1938; Mauritius 1938; Nigeria 1936; St. Lucia 1936; Seychelles 1938; Sierra Leone 1932; and Straits 1936. See illustrations in stamp catalogues.

gerade (Ger.) straight.

geriffelt (Ger.) rippled.

gerippt (Ger.) ribbed.

German East Africa former German territory of about 360,000 square miles bordering on the Indian Ocean. The greater part of it became Tanganyika Territory. Capital: Dar-es Salaam. First stamps were German issues of 1893, surcharged in pesas; then German colonial key-types (portraying the Kaiser's yacht) were used. In 1916 Belgium issued occupation stamps of Congo handstamped "RUANDA" and another series handstamped "URUNDI"; subsequent issues were overprinted and surcharged. See catalogues for details.

Germaniaausgabe (Ger.) Germania issue.

German offices in China Germany maintained post offices in China prior to 1923, and issued stamps for use in China in 1898.

German offices in Morocco Germany maintained post offices in Morocco and issued stamps for use in Morocco 1899-1911.

German offices in Turkish Empire Germany maintained post offices in the Turkish Empire. German stamps were surcharged for use in the Turkish Empire, 1884-9. Later issues were of Germany, surcharged, and

used until 1908.

German Southwest Africa former German territory mandated to Union of South Africa in 1920 by League of Nations; about 317,725 square miles. Capital: Windhoek. Stamps issued 1897-1913 were those of Germany, overprinted. When the territory was mandated to Union of South Africa in 1920, stamps of South Africa, overprinted in English or Afrikaans alternately, were used.

Germany a former federal republic in central Europe. In 1949 the United States, Britain, and France formed the West German Federal Republic and Russia set up the East German Democratic Republic. The present combined area is about 137,593 square miles. Capitals: Bonn in the West German Federal Republic and East Berlin in the East German Democratic Republic. First stamps of the German Empire were issued in 1852.

Gerusalemme (ovpt.) Jerusalem; appears on stamps of Italy for use by Italian offices in Jerusalem when it was part of the Turkish Empire, 1909-11.

Geschichte (Ger.) history.

geschlossen (Ger.) closed, full.

geschnitten (Ger.) cut rather than perforated.

Gesetz (Ger.) law.

gesprungene Platte (Ger.) cracked plate.

gessata carta (It.) chalky paper.

gestempelt (Ger.) cancelled, used.

gestochen (Ger.) engraved.

gestreift (Ger.) laid.

gestreiftes Papier (Ger.) laid paper.

gestrichenes Papier (Ger.) coated paper.

getoent (Ger.) tinted, toned.

gevlogen brief (Dutch) flown cover.

gewellt (Ger.) wavy.

gewoehnlich (Ger.) ordinary, common.

gezaehnt (Ger.) perforated.

G.F.B. (ovpt.) Gaue Faka Buleaga, meaning "on government service"; appears on official stamps of Tonga, 1893.

G-F Lot in auction catalogues, means "good to fine lot". This note is a warning that all stamps in the lot being described are not of top quality.

Ghadames (partial insc.) Gadames; appears on 1946 stamps of Libya issued under French occupation.

Ghana since 1957, a republic of about 91,-843 square miles between the Ivory Coast and Dahomey on the west coast of Africa. Formerly the British Crown Colony of the Gold Coast; includes the former British Togoland. Capital: Accra. Issued stamps in

1875.

ghost plate numbers faint impressions of numbers appearing on certain U.S. stamps caused by the offset of the numbers from the printed paper to the tagging surface to the next impression of the intaglio plate. They are found primarily in the experimental Type I tagging. (Courtesy of Alfred G. Boerger)

ghurush, ghrush a silver coin of Turkey. 40 paras equal 1 ghurush. Later issues of the coin are made of billon.

giallo (It.) yellow.

Gibbons, Stanley an Englishman who founded a stamp business in 1856; today his name is probably the most famous in the world of stamps. Stanley Gibbons Ltd. does business virtually everywhere, publishing stamp catalogues, albums, and books. They also operate a famous stamp shop at 391 Strand in London, England, and conduct postage stamp auction sales there.

Gibbons catalogues postage stamp catalogues published by Stanley Gibbons Limited, of London, England. These books price the stamps in sterling. (The short-lived Gibbons-Whitman catalogues priced stamps in dollars and cents.) Gibbons catalogues provide the day and year of issue of stamps and the printers' names. The books include simplified lists of stamps to suggest a representative collection for most countries.

Gibraltar a British Crown Colony of about 2 square miles. It includes the Rock of Gibraltar, a promontory that commands entrance to the Mediterranean on the south coast of Spain. Capital: Gibraltar. Issued stamps in 1886.

Gibraltar (ovpt.) appears on stamps of Bermuda for use in Gibraltar, 1886.

Gilbert and Ellice Islands Colony consists of the Gilbert, Ellice, and Phoenix groups, the Line Islands (Christmas, Fanning, and Washington), and Ocean Island. In all, there are about thirty-seven small islands lying between 4°N. and 11°S. of the equator in the Central Pacific Ocean, roughly mid-way between Honolulu, Hawaii, and Brisbane, Australia. The sea area is over 2 million square miles and the land area is about 375 square miles. First stamps were Fiji overprints; then the colony issued its own stamps in 1911. The islands became a British Crown Colony on Jan. 12, 1916.

Gilbert and Ellice Protectorate (ovpt.) on stamps of Fiji for use in the Gilbert and Ellice Islands.

Giori press U.S. issues are printed by Giori presses, which are capable of using various plates. Some engraved types are inked in different colours, all of which are printed in one impression.

giornali (It.) newspapers or journals.

GIORNALI (It. insc.) appears on newspaper stamps of Italy 1862 and Sardinia in 1861.

Gitterstempel (Ger.) grid cancel.

Gitterstruktur (Ger.) quadrille texture.

Gladstone roulette, Treasury roulette Archer-rouletted postage stamps of Great Britain. The rouletting was done at the British Treasury while William Ewart Gladstone served as Chancellor of the Exchequer.

glanspapper (Swed.) glossy paper.

Glanzdruck (Ger.) glossy printing.

glanzlos (Ger.) without gloss.

Glanzpapier (Ger.) glossy paper.

glatt (Ger.) smooth.

gleich (Ger.) equal, identical, same, similar, immediately.

gleichlaufend (Ger.) parallel.

gleichwertig (Ger.) equal value.

gleichmaessig (Ger.) uniform(ly).

Glen Haven Daily Mail in Glen Haven, New York, issued U.S. local stamps 1854-8.

G.N.R. (It. ovpt.) Guardia Nazionale Repubblicana. In December 1943 and February 1944, Italy overprinted the 1929-42 issues with these letters. Overprinted stamps were primarily issued by the National Republican Guards in Brescia for ordinary postal use. (Courtesy of *I Francolsolli Dello Stato Italiano*, an Italian government book)

goat's eyes (nick.) the second issue of Brazil stamps of 1844-6, similar to the huge so-called bull's eyes of 1843. Since the designs

on these stamps also looked like eyes, collectors named them "goat's eyes". This issue is also called the "slanting figures of Brazil".

GOBIERNO (Sp. ovpt.) government; appears on regular issues of Peru, 1890-1914, for use as official stamps.

GOBIERNO V CONSTITUCIONALISTA (Sp. ovpt.) appears on stamps for the constitutional government of Oaxaca, a state in southeast Mexico. During the Civil War,

1914-16, the overprints were made on various issues of Mexico for use in Oaxaca.

gold-beater's skin (nick.) a thin, strong, translucent paper used for the 1866 stamps of Prussia.

Gold-beater's skin (back of stamp)

Gold Coast See GHANA.

Goldkueste (Ger.) Gold Coast.

GOLFE DE BENIN (insc.) appears on 1893 stamps of Benin, a former French possession now part of Dahomey.

Goliad, Texas issued postmasters' provisional stamps in 1861 as part of the Confederate States of America.

gom (Dutch) gum.

goma (Sp.) gum, rubber.

goma canelada (Port.) ribbed gum.

goma original (Sp.) original gum.

gomma (It.) gum.

gomma originale (It.) original gum.

gomme (Fr.) gum.

gommé (Fr.) gummed.

Gonzales, Texas issued postmasters' provisional stamps in 1861 as part of the Confederate States of America.

Gordon's City Express in New York City, New York, issued U.S. local stamps in 1848-52.

Gordon stamps (nick.) series of stamps issued in 1935 by Sudan to honour General Charles George Gordon, who was Governor of Sudan 1877-80. Gordon had a colourful life in China, Egypt, and Mauritius.

GORNY SLASK (insc.) appears on labels of a dubious nature for Upper Silesia under Polish occupation following the First World War.

gothique (Fr.) gothic.

gotico (Port.) gothic.

gouge a scratch or long mark on a printing plate. In steel engraving or gravure the incised line picks up ink and prints an impression on postage stamps. On stamps printed by lithography or letterpress, the gouge may cause a line in the colour of the paper owing to an absence of printing ink.

gourde a silver coin of Haiti. 100 centimes equal 1 gourde. This is a French colonial term, equivalent to the Spanish word "gordo", for "thick".

Governatorato del Montenegro (ovpt.) on stamps of Jugoslavia for use in Montenegro under Italian administration, 1941-2.

government imitations or **government reprints** Sometimes when a government desired to reprint an obsolete issue, the original dies or plates were not available. In these circumstances new plates were officially made; the resulting labels are called government imitations or reprints. They are authorized forgeries.

government issues postage stamps issued by governments or authorized countries, colonies, or states, but not by individual postmasters or other persons.

GOVERNO MILITARE ALLEATO (ovpt.) appears on stamps of Italy for use in Italy under the Allied Military Government occupation, 1943.

GOVT PARCELS (ovpt.) appears on official stamps of Great Britain, 1883-6, for mailing of government parcels.

Goya, Francisco Jose de a famous Spanish artist honoured by Spain in 1930 by a set of stamps that includes his famous painting *La Maja*, a reclining nude female.

G.P. DE M (ovpt. and sur.) appears on stamps of Mexico in 1916-18. Owing to the depreciation of Mexican paper currency, overprints were printed and some in 1916 were surcharged to increase their values to par with the newly introduced paper money.

G.P.E. (sur.) appears with new values on stamps of French Colonies for use in 1884 as a general issue in Guadeloupe, a French colony in the West Indies at the time.

G.P.O. General Post Office.

grá (Swed.) grey.

grabado (Sp.) engraving.

gradazione di colore (It.) shade.

Grafflin's Baltimore Despatch in Baltimore, Maryland, issued U.S. local stamps in 1856.

grafting a kind of faking of postage stamps to enhance their values. Refers to adding margins and repairing holes and thin spots in stamps. Such repairs can be seen under black light.

Graf Zeppelin a German dirigible named after its inventor, Count Ferdinand von Zeppelin, a German soldier and aeronaut. The *Graf Zeppelin* made its first flight carrying mail from the United States to Germany in October 1928. Cachets and cancels bear the dates Oct. 27 and 28, 1928. The first *Graf Zeppelin* flight carrying mail from Germany to the United States began on May 15, 1929, but the backstamps on letters read "New York, Aug. 5, 1929". Engine trouble forced the *Graf Zeppelin* to come down at Cuers, France. As a result, a single-line, red-coloured German cachet appears on the letters meaning "Delivery postponed owing to a mishap on the first American flight". This dirigible remained in service for nine years and made 650 flights, 144 of them over the Atlantic Ocean. It flew over one million miles before it was grounded.

Graf Zeppelin covers mail carried on the *Graf Zeppelin* that bears cachets to prove such flights.

Graf Zeppelin issues airmail stamps issued by the United States, Argentina, Germany, and other countries that issued stamps for mail carried on the *Graf Zeppelin.*

Graham Land part of the Falkland Islands Dependencies, later named the Graham Coast; in Antarctica due south of Tierra del Fuego. Explorations proved that North and South Graham Islands were part of the mainland of the western region of Palmer Peninsula. Annexed to Great Britain by John Briscoe. In 1963 stamps were issued inscribed "British Antarctic Territories"; Graham Land was included in these territories.

GRAHAM LAND/DEPENDENCY OF (2-line ovpt.) appears on stamps of Falkland 1938-41 for use in Graham Land in 1944.

grain On the paper machine, the fibres tend to align themselves lengthwise with the flow or machine direction; this preferred orientation of the fibres, the grain, affects certain characteristics of the paper, such as tearing strength, rigidity, and folding quality.

Granadine Confederation a former Spanish vice-royalty that occupied what is now Colombia, Panama, Venezuela, and Ecuador. Spaniards conquered the region in 1537-8, and named it Nueva Granada. The area was reorganized into the Granadine Confederation. It issued postage stamps in 1859 under this name and then under the name "United States of New Granada" in 1861. Finally, in 1862, stamps were issued for the United States of Colombia.

Grand Comore (insc.) on stamps of Grand Comoro Island.

Grand Comoro largest island in Comoro group in north Mozambique Channel; about 456 square miles. Chief town: Moroni. As a former French colony, issued stamps from 1897 to 1912. These were superseded by stamps of Madagascar and in 1950 by those of Comoro Islands.

grand consommation paper a poor-quality stock that often contained foreign matter, fibres, and specks as a low grade of granite paper. G.C. paper (*papier de grande consommation* or just "G.C." paper) was used in some French stamps of 1917, for the French offices in the Levant and Ile Rouad. (Courtesy of Dr. R. Maresch)

Grand Duchy of Luxembourg See LUXEMBOURG.

Grande-Bretagne (Fr.) Great Britain.

Grande-Comore (Fr.) Grand Comoro.

grand format (Fr.) large size.

grand, grande (Fr.) great, large.

Grand Liban See LEBANON.

GRAND LIBAN (Fr. sur. and insc.) appears as a surcharge on stamps of France for use in Lebanon in 1924 under French mandate; also is inscribed on stamps of Lebanon in 1925.

Grand Liban or **Gd Liban** (sur.) appears on stamps of France, 1924-5, for use in Lebanon under the French mandate.

granite paper postage-stamp or security paper made with coloured fibres in the paper substance. When the fibres turn the paper bluish in colour, as in some writing papers, it is called "silurian paper".

Graphik (Ger.) graphic, work of graphic art.

grasgruen (Ger.) grass-green.

grau (Ger.) grey.

graublau (Ger.) grey-blue.

graubraun (Ger.) grey-brown.

graugruen (Ger.) grey-green.

grauschiefer (Ger.) grey-slate.

gravado (Port.) engraved.

gravé (Fr.) engraved.

graver burin, a steel cutting-tool used by engravers in cutting designs in plates.

gravering (Swed.) engraving.

graveur (Fr.) engraver.

graviert (Ger.) engraved.

Gravierung (Ger.) engraving.

gravure ink thin, non-tacky ink with volatile solvent or vehicle, which dries by penetration and by evaporation.

gravure paper thin, light-weight, smooth-feeling paper used for printing catalogues, magazines, and newspaper picture sections, and billions of postage stamps.

gravure sur acier (Fr.) steel-plate printing.

gravure sur bois (Fr.) woodblock printing.

Gravurmangel (Ger.) faulty engraving.

grease in stamps This may be removed by submerging the stamps in benzine or gasoline without additives. Care should be taken not to submerge gravure-printed stamps in these solvents. Pressing a warm iron against stamps between pieces of clean paper may also remove grease.

Great Britain a constitutional monarchy of about 94,279 square miles northwest of the mainland of Europe. Capital: London. Issued the first adhesive postage stamps in the world on May 6, 1840.

Great Lebanon See LEBANON.

Great Seal of Bahamas design appearing on the 1930-1 stamps of the Bahamas.

Great Seal of Barbados design appearing on the 1950-3 stamps of Barbados.

Great Seal of the Province of New Brunswick design featured on Canadian commemorative stamps of 1934. An early example is still preserved in the new parliament building library in Fredericton, the capital of New Brunswick.

Great Seal of the United States a design on the 1934 U.S. airmail special-delivery stamp in the dark-blue colour and on the red and blue stamps of 1936.

Grèce (Fr.) Greece.

Greece a kingdom in the southwest part of Balkan Peninsula in southeast Europe; about 50,147 square miles. Capital: Athens. First stamps were issued in 1861.

Green, Colonel E. H. a famous accumulator of postage stamps, one-time owner of the 24-cent U.S. inverted-centre sheet. He was the son of the well-known miser Hetty Green. H. R. Harmer, Inc. sold the Green collection by auction.

green backs (nick.) postage stamps of some countries printed in green with aniline ink that penetrates the paper and shows as a green tint on the back of the stamps. Some Papua stamps issued 1916-31 with green borders, and the 1929 stamps overprinted "AIRMAIL" on former issues, provide excellent examples of green backs.

Greene, Vincent G. one of the five most prominent philatelists of Canada. He was president of the Canadian International Philatelic Exhibition (CAPEX), held Sept. 21-9, 1951, the biggest international philatelic exhibition ever held in Canada. He was also co-author (with Dr. C. M. Jephcott and John H. M. Young) of *The Postal History of Nova Scotia and New Brunswick*, is a Fellow of the Royal Philatelic Society, London, and has signed the Roll of Distinguished Philatelists.

Greenland an island northeast of North America; about 839,800 square miles. Capitals: Godthaab, Godhavn. A Danish colony, and from 1953 an integral part of Denmark, Greenland has issued stamps since 1938.

Greensboro, Ala. This town in Alabama issued postmasters' provisional envelopes in 1861 as part of the Confederate States of America.

Greensboro, N.C. This town in North Carolina issued postmasters' provisional envelopes in 1861 as part of the Confederate States of America.

Greenville, Ala. This town in Alabama issued postmasters' provisional stamps and envelopes in 1861 as part of the Confederate States of America.

Greenville Court House, S.C. issued postmasters' provisional envelopes in 1861 for Greenville, South Carolina, as part of the Confederate States of America.

Greenwood Depot, Va. This town in Virginia issued postmasters' provisional stamps in 1861 as part of the Confederate States of America.

Grenada a British colony of about 133 square miles in Windward Islands, British West Indies. Capital: St. George's. Issued stamps in 1861.

Grenade (Fr.) Granada.

Grenville (insc.) appears on Liberia registration stamps with no country name or value. Other registration stamps, with 10-cent value, were inscribed: "Harper", "Buchanan", "Monrovia", and "Robertsport".

G.R.I. (sur.) Georgius Rex Imperator; appears with new values on stamps of German New Guinea and Marshall Islands, New Britain; also appears on stamps of German Samoa for use in Samoa under British Dominion, 1914.

grid cancellation a type of cancel, sometimes called a "gridiron cancel" because the parallel bars resemble the markings on a football field.

Griechenland (Ger.) Greece.

griffe (Fr.) a canceller or signature stamp (in philately).

griffe à chiffres (Fr.) numeral canceller.

griffe avec cachet (Fr.) duplex canceller.

Griffin, Ga. This town in Georgia issued postmasters' provisional envelopes in 1861 as part of the Confederate States of America.

grigio (It.) grey.

grilled gum a term, seldom used, that describes the ribbed gum found on some Canadian stamps. See GUM IN BARS.

grill cancellation or **grille cancellation** a type of obliteration formed of small squares, dots, or other small designs within a square, oval, rectangle, or other figure. Generally grill cancels do not have a frame or border.

grill or **grille** In philately, this word has three

meanings: (1) the pattern caused by an embossing device, as is used in stamps of the United States (1867-70) and Peru to impress a design of small pyramids into the

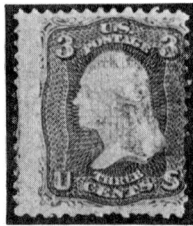

Grill stamp

stamp paper to prevent anyone from removing cancels to use the stamps a second time; (2) the pattern of small, light-coloured lines on album pages; and (3) a type of cancel made of small squares or rectangles in a pattern, usually in rows.

grill pages   stamp album pages printed with tiny squares approximately one-eighth inch on a side.

grill postmark   cancelling device designed with little squares to obliterate postage stamps. Many countries have used grilled postmarks, the United States, Canada, and France among them.

grill types   Lester G. Brookman discussed numerous grills in *The 19th Century Postage Stamps of the United States*. Among these are ten grills beginning with A and continuing through the alphabet to J. Another is called the "Z grill". He also lists and describes experimental, marginal, and essay grills (pp. 239-314). This subject is extremely complicated for the novice and is a highly specialized one in philately.

gripper margin   margin on the side of a sheet of paper that is held by the grippers on a printing cylinder.

grippers   mechanical fingers that hold the paper in place on the printing cylinder of a press while the paper is being printed.

Griqualand West   a former British Crown Colony of about 15,197 square miles north of the Orange River and west of Orange Free State in South Africa; annexed to Cape Colony in 1880. Chief town: Kimberley. Issued stamps in 1877.

gris   (Fr. and Sp.) grey.

gris-brun   (Fr.) brownish grey.

gris-lilas   (Fr.) grey-lilac.

gris-olive   (Fr.) olive-grey.

G.R./MAFIA   (2-line ovpt.) appears on stamps of German East Africa for use in Mafia Island, 1915-16, while it was under British occupation.

groat   thick, silver coin. This word and its equivalents such as the German "groschen", Italian "grosso", French "gros", Polish "grosz", and others are from the Latin words "denarii grossi", large pennies. The old English groat was worth 4 pennies. In 1888 a groat was issued for British Guiana.

grob   (Ger.) coarse.

grober Druck   (Ger.) coarse printing.

grobe Zaehnung   (Ger.) coarse perforation.

Groënland   (Fr.) Greenland.

grön   (Swed.) green.

Grönland   (Ger.) Greenland.

Grønland   (insc.) appears on stamps of Greenland.

groschen   silver coin of Austria and Germany, sometimes called "silbergroschen". 100 groschen equal 1 schilling. In Germany 30 silbergroschen or groschen equal 1 thaler. First struck in Bohemia in 1300, this coin, under many variations of the name, has been popular all over Europe.

Grossbuchstabe   (Ger.) capital letter.

GROSSDEUTSCHES REICH   (insc.) Great Germany; appears with the additional inscription "BÖHMEN UND MÁHREN" on stamps of the German protectorate of Bohemia and Moravia in 1943-4. Listed stamps of Czechoslovakia in catalogues.

GROSSDEUTSCHES REICH GENERAL GOUVERNEMENT   (insc.) appears on stamps of Poland in 1943-4, issued under German occupation.

grosse barbe   (Fr. nick.) the 1905 postage stamps of Belgium portraying King Leopold II with a large beard. Earlier stamps, 1869-1900, featured the King with a smaller, more pointed beard. (Courtesy: Willy Balasse, Brussels, Belgium)

Grossformat   (Ger.) large-size format.

Grosshandel   (Ger.) wholesale.

grossion   silver coin of Albania. 1 grossion equals 40 paras or 1 piastre.

grosz   a thick, silver coin (sometimes copper) of Poland. 100 groszy equal 1 zloty. This is the Polish term for the French "gros", Italian "grosso", German "groschen", and others. The name means "thick pennies".

Grove Hill, Ala.   This town in Alabama issued postmasters' provisional stamps in 1861 as part of the Confederate States of America.

G.R./POST/MAFIA   (3-line ovpt.) appears on stamps of German East Africa in 1915 for use in Mafia Island while it was under British occupation; also appears on stamps of India overprinted "I.E.F." (Indian Expeditionary Force) for use in Mafia Island in 1915-16 under British occupation.

gruen (Ger.) green.

gruenblau (Ger.) green-blue.

grueso (Sp.) thick.

grumpap or pap British name for a stamp issued solely for sale to collectors and not to meet a postal requirement. Thousands of stamps of African and Qatar peninsula countries and states are examples.

grupo (Sp.) pane.

Gruppe (Ger.) pane.

gruppo (It.) pane.

G. S. Harris City Despatch Post in Philadelphia, Pennsylvania, issued U.S. local stamps sometime about 1847.

Guadalajara the third largest city in Mexico, and capital of Jalisco State. In 1867, during the struggle by Juarez to free Mexico of Emperor Maximilian, Guadalajara issued provisional stamps that resembled circular date cancels. Maximilian had been installed in 1864 by Napoleon III, who also sent French troops to Mexico. When towns were set free of the French intruders, they issued provisional stamps. These provisionals are now listed in stamp catalogues following or combined with Mexican listings.

Guadeloupe the two islands of Basse-Terre and Grande Terre in eastern West Indies, an overseas department of France; about 583 square miles. Capital: Basse-Terre. From 1884 until 1947, stamps issued were those of the French Colonies. In 1947 the islands became an integral part of France.

Guam a former Spanish island in the West Pacific, about 1,450 miles east of the Philippines. Occupied by Spain in 1565; captured in June 1898 by the United States and ceded to them by Spain in December 1898. U.S. stamps overprinted "Guam" were used from 1899 until 1901, while the post office was under U.S. Navy control. U.S. stamps are now valid in Guam. See GUARD MAIL (GUAM).

Guanacaste a province of Costa Rica, of about 4,000 square miles, on northwest coast of Central America. Overprinted stamps of Costa Rica were used in the provinces, 1885-90.

guarani a coin of Paraguay. 100 centimos equal 1 guarani.

guardant (her.) having the face in a heraldic device turned towards the viewer.

guard mail (Guam) Guam guard mail was a local post inaugurated in 1930 by Commander Willis W. Bradley, Jr., of the U.S. Navy, Commandant of Guam, the largest and southernmost of the Mariana Islands in the West Pacific Ocean, about 1,450 miles east of the Philippines.

Guatemala a republic of about 45,452 square miles south of Mexico in Central America. Capital: Guatemala. Issued stamps in 1871.

Guyana the former British Crown Colony of British Guiana on the northeast coast of South America. Capital: Georgetown. On May 26, 1966, British Guiana became an independent member of the British Commonwealth and changed its name to Guyana. On Feb. 23, 1970, Republic Day, Guyana became a republic with a president elected for six years by the National Assembly, in secret ballot. The new constitution, instituted on Republic Day, provided that the president must be a Guyanese over the age of forty. The President of the Republic of Guyana will be the Head of State and Commander in Chief of the Armed Forces. Guyana remained a republic in the British Commonwealth and issued postage stamps inscribed "Guyana".

GUAYANA (insc.) appears on stamps of Venezuela, 1903, for local use in the Venezuelan state of Guayana.

GUYANA / INDEPENDENCE / 1966 (3-line ovpt.) appears on 1954 stamps of British Guiana on May 26, 1966, when the former British Crown Colony became an independent member of the British Commonwealth, and changed its name to Guyana. Nearly four years later Guyana became a republic but remained in the British Commonwealth, and on Republic Day, Feb. 23, 1970, issued four stamps. The lowest value portrayed Prime Minister L. Forbes S. Burnham and a map locating Guyana in South America.

gueltig (Ger.) valid.

guerche a silver coin of Ethiopia (Abyssinia). 16 guerche equal 1 menelik dollar or talari.

Guernsey stamps one of the regional issues by Great Britain in 1958, for use in Guernsey. Other regionals include: Northern Ireland, Jersey, Isle of Man, Scotland, and the combined region of Wales and Monmouthshire. These stamps resemble other British issues but have their own heraldic emblems.

guerre (Fr.) war.

Guete (Ger.) quality.

guide arrow a marginal mark pointing to the centre of a sheet or pane, either in vertical or horizontal position.

GUERNSEY (insc.) appears on stamps issued in 1941-4 for use in Guernsey in the Channel Islands while they were under German occupation. British 1940 stamps bisected were also used and regional stamps were introduced in 1958. See CHANNEL ISLANDS.

guide dots microscopic dots made on printing plates to help the make-up men in printing shops or at platemakers' shops to get the postage stamp designs in their correct positions. Many guide dots may be seen on Canada 1868 stamps ("large Queens") made by steel engraving. These should not command premiums. Usually the guide dots are removed before printing.

guide-line block any block of stamps with a guide line through it. Sometimes the name is shortened to "line block".

guide lines (1) lines on steel-engraved printing plates to assist the operator in lining up rows of subjects. Faint impressions often appear on stamps; (2) printed lines of various widths to guide the operation of cutting stamp sheets into post office panes or units for booklet postage.

guilder gold coin of The Netherlands. 100 cents equal 1 guilder. The guilder is also known as a "gulden" and "florin".

guild marks usually pen and ink marks, sometimes designs, made on stamps in Venice or Genoa. As early as 1305 men in Venice formed the Compagnia dei Correri della Illustrissima Signoria, an organization of guild carriers like modern postmen. They applied guild marks to show they had carried the messages. They operated until 1797.

guillochage (Fr.) engine turning.

guilloché (Fr.) engine-turned.

guillotine machine used to cut paper, book edges, and sheets of stamps into panes.

Guiné (ovpt.) appears on stamps of Cape Verde for use in Portuguese Guinea, 1881-5.

Guinea republic of the coast region in West Africa between the Gambia and Gabon rivers; area variously quoted as about 96,-865 square miles, 96,886 square miles, and 108,455 square miles. Stamps before 1959 were those of French Guinea (1892-1944) and French West Africa (1944-59), and from 1959 stamps were those of the republic.

Guinée espagnole (Fr.) Spanish Guinea.

Guinée française (Fr.) French Guinea.

Guinée portugaise (Fr.) Portuguese Guinea.

gul (Swed.) yellow.

gulden also called "florin" or "forint"; formerly a gold coin, later made of silver. It was used in Germany, Austria, Hungary, Turkey, the United Kingdom, and other countries. The first gold florin was struck in Florence, Italy, in 1252, with a lily on the reverse side. In 1344, Great Britain struck a gold florin, and in 1849, a silver florin. In Austria, 60 kreuzers equal 1 gulen, and 100 neu-kreuzers equal 1 gulden. In Hungary, 100 filler equal 1 forint.

Gültig 9. Armee (ovpt.) appears in a framed box on German stamps of 1906-17 overprinted in 1918 for the German occupation of Romania.

gum the adhesive on postage stamps; it was called "cement" on the first stamps of Great Britain. The adhesives on stamps vary in colour from white to light brown. While gum is applied mainly to the back of stamps, some have been gummed on the printed side.

gum arabic a gum obtained from either of two species of acacia, used as an adhesive on postage stamps. Also used on flaps of envelopes and aerograms. Some stamp hinges are made with this gum.

gumatelist a collector who is more interested in the gum on a stamp than in the stamp itself. (Courtesy of Donald Sinclair)

gumately a term for the quest for postage stamps in the exact immaculate condition in which they left the post office of origin. The term ridicules the emphasis placed on the importance of undisturbed gum. Continental European collectors allegedly instituted the "mint-never-hinged" classification of postage stamps after the Second World War. Postage stamps often represent better investments than do currency, stocks, bonds, or real estate. But the advanced philatelist is not usually concerned about whether a stamp is pristine or whether it bears the faint trace left by a proper stamp hinge having been carefully applied to the original gum. (Courtesy of Donald Sinclair)

gum-breaker bars lines on the gummed side of postage stamps made purposely to stop the stamps from curling.

gum in bars gum appearing in parallel ridges on the back of stamps. Horizontal bar lines appear in the gum on most of the mint stamps of the Canadian King George V regular issue of 1930. On the stamps of this issue printed during the first few months, horizontal bar lines appearing in the gum on most of the mint stamps were quite marked. Later they were not so prominent, scarcely showing on some of the stamps. The lines were produced by certain rollers in the fracturing machine, intended to break the crystals of gum to make the sheets remain flat.

gummed paper paper coated on one side

with gum arabic or dextrin and used for printing stamps. Gumming is the process by which stamp paper is coated on one side with adhesive.

gummed paper tape generally kraft paper coated on one side with fish or other glue, cut in narrow rolls, and used for sealing or reinforcing purposes.

Gummi (Ger. and Swed.) gum.

Gummiarten (Ger.) kinds of gum.

Gummibruch (Ger.) gum crack.

Gummidruck (Ger.) offset printing.

Gummifehler (Ger.) gum defect.

gumming (1) process by which labels, stamps, envelopes, and gummed tapes are coated with adhesive; (2) coating of offset plates with a film of gum arabic to preserve them from dust and humidity.

gumming machine machine for the application of gum or adhesive on back of stamps, labels, gummed paper tapes, or envelope flaps.

Gummiriffelung (Ger.) gum ribbing.

Gummistempel (Ger.) rubber stamp.

gumpaps (British nick.) labels made to represent postage stamps.

gum stains stains sometimes caused by chemical actions among the gum, printing inks, and papers. Attempts to remove stains may be destructive. Use great care, or leave stamps as they are.

gum watermarks designs in the gum, not true watermarks. Czechoslovakia issued a series of stamps in 1925 with a quadrille pattern in the gum and "C.S.P.", the initials of the republic, on the back of the stamp.

gut gerandet (Ger.) with full margin.

Gutschein (Ger.) credit note, voucher.

gutter (1) the marginal paper between two unsevered panes of stamps printed side by side or one above the other; blocks with this paper are called "gutter blocks"; (2) space formed by inner margins of two facing pages.

Gutter Blks of 4 Gutter blocks of four stamps; these consist of two stamps on each side of the gutter paper that divides panes in a sheet of stamps. The gutters may be vertical or horizontal, depending on the direction of the gutter paper, thus resulting in two types of gutter blocks.

gutter pair two stamps, one on each side of a gutter, either vertical or horizontal.

guttersnipes (U.S. nick.) faulty postage stamps, often made when the guillotine cuts the stamps in the designs rather than in the gutters. These distorted items have gained popularity.

Guyane anglaise (Fr.) British Guiana.

Guyane française (Fr.) French Guiana.

GUY. FRANC. (sur.) appears with dates and new values on stamps of the French Colonies for use in French Guiana, 1886-8.

Guy's City Despatch in Philadelphia, Pennsylvania, issued U.S. local stamps in 1879.

G.W. (ovpt.) appears on Cape of Good Hope stamps for the 1877 issue of Griqualand West, a former British Crown Colony in South Africa.

GWALIOR (ovpt.) appears on stamps of India for use in Gwalior, a Convention state of British India, 1885-1949.

Gutter block of four stamps

Gutter pair

H

habilitado (Sp.) authorized. The word is often overprinted, surcharged, or hand-stamped on former postal issues of Spanish-speaking countries to make them valid again.

HABILITADO PARA CORREOS or HA-BILITADO CORREOS (sur.) appears on stamps inscribed "Derechos" or "Telegra-phos", the revenue or telegraph stamps for the Philippines 1881-97, under Spanish Dominion.

Hackney & Bolte Penny Post in Atlantic City, New Jersey, issued U.S. local stamps in 1886.

Haga Patria (insc.) appears on 1929 postal tax stamps of Mexico. The people were obligated to use the labels which did not pay postal services. "Haga" is a form of the irregular Spanish verb "hacer", to make, create, do. "Patria" is Spanish for "mother-land, native country".

hagiology a catalogue of saints; a history of saints or sacred literature. Can provide ideas for stamp collections on the lives and legends of saints. This is a popular topic among collectors of religious subjects on stamps.

Haiderabad (Fr.) Hyderabad.

hair-lines term originally used to indicate the fine lines crossing the corners of some British stamps; inserted to distinguish impressions from certain plates. This term is often used now to denote any fine lines in white or in colour made intentionally or accidentally on a stamp.

Haiti a republic of about 10,714 square miles in west Hispaniola in the West Indies. Capital: Port-au-Prince. Issued stamps in 1881.

Hakenkreuz (Ger.) swastika.

halbamtlich (Ger.) semi-official.

halbamtliche Flugmarken (Ger.) semi-official airmail stamps.

halbamtliche Marken (Ger.) semi-official stamps.

halbiert (Ger.) bisected.

Halbkreisstempel (Ger.) semi-circle cancellation. Scores of semi-circular postal markings and cancels are known.

Hale & Co. in New York City, New York, issued U.S. local stamps in 1844.

haleru a coin of Czechoslovakia. 100 haleru equal 1 korona.

Half-length Victorias (nick.) stamps of Victoria, Australia, of 1850 with a half-length illustration of Queen Victoria, as opposed to the full-length portrait of 1852-6.

Halfpenny (ovpt.) appears on diagonally cut half-stamps inscribed "ONE PENNY", of St. Christopher in 1885.

half-tone reproduction of an image or illustration obtained by means of a half-tone engraving.

half-tone plate photo-engraved plate in which the image is broken up into fine dots by introduction of a ruled screen between the original and the photographic plate.

half-tone screen usually a cross-lined mesh engraved on glass, the lines being opaque and the spaces between transparent. It is those spaces that produce the dots on the half-tone plate; the number of lines per inch varies from 50 to 200 or more, screens up to 100 lines being known as "coarse screens" and those from 100 lines and up as "fine screens".

Hall & Mills' Despatch Post in New York City, New York, issued U.S. local stamps in 1847.

Hallettsville, Texas issued postmasters' provisional stamps in 1861 as part of the Confederate States of America.

halv (Swed.) half.

halverat (Swed.) bisected or halved.

Hambourg (Fr.) Hamburg.

Hamburg a former German state in north Germany; area variously quoted as about 288 square miles and 160 square miles. Stamps were issued 1859-67, to be superseded in 1868 by those of the North German Confederation.

Hamburgh, S.C. This town in South Carolina issued postmasters' provisional envelopes in 1861 as part of the Confederate States of America.

Hamilton Bank Note Company security printers in New York City. N.F. Seebeck, an executive of the company, produced stamps for certain Central American countries and Ecuador. The stamps were sold to dealers after the issues were discontinued, and became known as Seebecks.

handbook a reference book of convenient size; in philately, a handy guidebook, not to be confused with a stamp catalogue.

hand cancel cancellation applied by hand to deface a stamp.

hand-chopped term referring to handmade overprint or surcharge of Japanese characters on occupation stamps made by Japan mainly during the Second World War. The term appears in philatelic literature; usually noted as handstamped in catalogues.

handgestempelt (Ger.) handstamped, hand-cancelled.

handmade paper Handmade paper is too expensive to compete with machine-made paper. The art of making paper by hand is fast disappearing; some drawing and water-colour papers are still made by hand. Many classical stamps were made on handmade paper.

handstamp (1) the forerunner of postage stamps. Such impressions are often correctly classified as postage stamps, called "handstruck postage stamps"; (2) a manual device made of metal or other substance to cancel adhesive stamps, or impress postal markings such as "registered", "way let-

ters", "too late".

handstamped, handstruck refers to an impression stamped or struck by hand.

handstämpel (Swed.) handstamp.

Handstempel (Ger.) handstamp, hand cancel.

handstruck often refers to postal markings made by hand as compared to machine-made impressions. Handstruck postage stamps formed an important phase in the postal histories of countries that used them. They indicated payment of postage, or free postage on mail from persons granted the privilege. These markings should not be confused with post office stamps such as the Bishop marks of England in 1661 and subsequent years, handstruck postage-due stamps, or instruction or information marks.

handstruck postage-due stamps markings on mail to indicate the amount of postage that the postman is required to collect on delivery of mail. The marks on international mail are divided into two parts of a circle. The top part contains handwritten numerals showing the amount of postage due in the country of origin. The bottom figures show the "going rate of postage" in the country to another country. The postman

Handstruck postage stamp: tombstone postmark

then divides the bottom figure into the top and that is the amount of postage due that he collects. Other methods of calculations may exist. (Courtesy of the postmaster at Buffalo, New York)

handstruck postage stamps markings on mail like postal cancellations, but having the words "paid" or "post paid" in the language of the country where the letters originated. Such markings in rectangles with circular tops are called "tombstone postmarks" or "paid stamps". (Illustration: p. 107)

Hanford's Pony Express in New York City, New York, issued U.S. local stamps, envelopes, and letter sheets in 1845.

Hanover, Hannover formerly a province of Prussia in north Germany; about 14,944 square miles. Stamps were issued 1850-64, to be superseded by those of Prussia in 1866.

Hanseatic League a trading confederacy embracing most of the commercial Germanic cities during the Renaissance.

Harding memorial U.S. stamps These were issued Sept. 1, 1923, and were printed from flat plates, with perf. 11 or imperforate. Eleven days later the same design stamps were printed by rotary press, perforated 10 and 11. The rotary-printed stamps are a half-millimetre higher than the flat-plate stamps. The perf. 11 stamps are exceedingly rare.

hard paper a type of paper with a surface that repels ink. Because of this surface, printers use a special ink. Any attempt to remove cancellations from hard papers usually destroys the stamp design.

harp (her.) a rare charge, chiefly associated with Ireland.

Harper (insc.) appears on Liberia registration stamps showing no country name and no value. Other 10-cent registration stamps were inscribed: "Buchanan", "Grenville", "Monrovia", and "Robertsport".

Harrison stamp printers Harrison & Sons, Limited, of London began printing British postage stamps in 1911. This company has printed many stamps for Great Britain and the Commonwealth. They are noted as pioneers in gravure printing of stamps.

harrow kind of perforations made by a machine capable of operating on an entire sheet of stamps at each descent of the needles or perforating pins.

harsh lines heavy lines in an engraving or etching.

Hartford, Conn., Mail Route issued U.S. local stamps in 1844 for Hartford, Connecticut.

has-been stamps (nick.) the Canadian Imperial Penny Post stamps of 1898. The stamps bear the inscription "We hold a vaster Empire than has been."

HASHEMITE KINGDOM OF JORDAN (insc.) appears on stamps of the independent Kingdom of Jordan, which became an independent state in 1946.

"Haste, Haste, Post Haste" an instruction written by royalty, usually prior to 1800, on some pre-stamp covers to indicate rush delivery. For couriers who could not read, kings and mediaeval dignitaries sometimes added a sketch of a man dangling from a gallows. Swedish royalty used one to three feathers to indicate the demands for speed.

Hatay formerly Alexandretta; located on the Mediterranean coast. A former autonomous unit among Levant States, now part of Turkish Republic; area about 9,997 square miles. Capital: Antioch. Chief towns: Antioch and Alexandretta (Iskenderun). Stamps issued in 1939 were those of Turkey surcharged.

Hatay Devleti (sur.) Hatay Post; appears on Turkey stamps of 1931-8 for use in Hatay, formerly known as Alexandretta.

hatching more commonly known as "crosshatching", a method of creating shadows and dark areas with crossed lines, mainly incised in steel dies for engraving or drawn in the original artwork used in other printing processes.

Hauptstadt (Ger.) capital city.

Haupttype (Ger.) principal type, main type.

Hauptwerte (Ger.) principal values, main values.

haut de casse (Fr.) upper case; refers to capital letters.

Haute-Silésie (Fr.) Upper Silesia.

Haute-Volta (Fr.) Upper Volta.

haut, haute (Fr.) high, upper. The French words form part of inscriptions on postage stamps. For example, Haute-Silésie (Upper Silesia) and Haut-Sénégal Niger (Upper Senegal and Niger).

Haut-Sénégal et Niger (Fr.) Upper Senegal and Niger.

HAUT-SENEGAL NIGER (insc.) appears on stamps of Upper Senegal and Niger, a former French colony in northwest Africa, 1914-17.

Hawaii (Sandwich Islands) twenty islands about 2,100 miles southwest of San Francisco, California, formerly a kingdom and republic. The first stamps, in 1851, called "missionaries", are among the world's great rarities. Most of the used stamps came from missionaries writing to the mainland.

In 1959 Hawaii became the fiftieth state of the United States, an event commemorated by a U.S. airmail stamp issued on Aug. 21, 1959.

Hawker (nick.) the first airmail stamps of Newfoundland (1919) overprinted in five lines: "First/Trans-/Atlantic/Air Post/ April, 1919". Harry George Hawker and his co-pilot, Kenneth Mackenzie Grieve, hoping to win the £10,000 prize offered to the first airman to fly across the Atlantic in seventy-five hours or less, left Newfoundland on May 18, 1919. They crashed less than 1,000 miles out, and were picked up by a Danish freighter. The mail was retrieved and taken aboard for eventual delivery.

hc in auction catalogues, means "heavy cancel".

heading brief summary of text set at the beginning of an article or chapter; often used to describe titles on postage stamp album pages.

head plate another name for the key plate that prints the portrait or central design of all the stamps in any number of series for different colonies or postal authorities.

heads (nick.) the first stamps from roll postage. The paper attached to the first stamps (top or left side) distinguishes these from the tails, which have paper attached to the right or bottom.

health stamps usually semi-postal stamps with the surtax funds intended for use in health-promoting plans and activities. New Zealand has issued the best-known health stamps since December 1929. Since 1930 most of these issues have included the word HEALTH in the designs. Other countries, mainly in Europe, have issued stamps with surtaxes for health and medical research.

Heath, Charles He and his son Frederick gained fame as British engravers of postage stamp dies.

heavily hinged refers to stamps that have been hinged more than once; sometimes these have parts of hinges remaining on the stamp.

Hechler, Henry a former Halifax, Nova Scotia, stamp dealer and faker of Canadian stamps and postal stationery envelopes. He bisected Canadian stamps of the 1870 designs and placed them on envelopes with extra postage to pay the charges. He then removed the excess postage, leaving covers mailed with bisects. He overprinted Canadian postal stationery envelopes with military markings of the 63rd Rifles, a volunteer group from Halifax.

Heft (Ger.) booklet.

Heftchenbogen (Ger.) booklet pane.

Heftchenmarken (Ger.) booklet stamps.

H.E.H. THE NIZAM'S GOVERNMENT (insc.) appears on stamps of Hyderabad, a feudatory state in central India, in 1927.

H.E.H. THE NIZAM'S SILVER JUBILEE (insc.) appears on stamps of Hyderabad, a feudatory state in central India, in 1937.

Heilung Kiang See KIRIN AND HEILUNGKIANG.

HEJAZ & NEJD, HEDIAZ & NEDJDE, or **HEDJAZ & NEDJDE** (inscs.) appear on 1929-32 issues of Hejaz-Nejd. Ibn Saud governed the two countries as king after he captured Hejaz in 1926. The two countries were finally united in 1932, and named Saudi Arabia.

helbrev (Swed.) entire, full or whole letter.

Helena, Texas issued postmasters' provisional stamps in 1861 as part of the Confederate States of America.

Helft den Kindern/Mecklenburg Vorpommern (insc.) on German local charity stamps.

Helgoland (Ger.) Heligoland.

Helguera, Leon a Mexican artist and designer of the United Nations 1½-cent and 50-cent stamps in the first issue of 1951. He also designed United States stamps: the 1943 Allied Nations stamps, the 1947 Postal Centenary stamp, the 15-cent airmail stamp of 1947, and the United States-Canada Friendship issue of 1948.

helicopter mail For the local delivery of mail, helicopters ("copters") were introduced in July 1946 in the United States.

Heligoland island of about ¼ square mile near the north coast of Germany in the North Sea. Former British possession ceded to Germany in 1890. Issued stamps in 1867.

heliogravura (Port.) intaglio engraving.

Heliogravuere (Ger.) intaglio engraving.

héliogravure (Fr.) photogravure. The word should not be used in English text to describe the printing method.

HELLAS (insc.) appears on bilingual stamps of Greece, 1966 and subsequent years. In ancient geography, Hellas was a district and town in Thessaly, and was known as the region inhabited by the Hellenes in central Greece. See the appendix for Greek philatelic words.

heller coin of silver, and later of copper, used in German East Africa, Austria, Jugoslavia, Liechtenstein, and other countries. 100 heller equal 1 krone or 1 rupee. This coin was first struck at Hall in Würtemburg in the thirteenth century.

hellgrau (Ger.) pale grey.

hellrot (Ger.) light red, bright red.

HELVETIA (insc.) Latin name for the region that is now Switzerland; appears on stamps of Switzerland.

Henzada issue stamps of Burma issued under Japanese occupation, 1942. Henzada is a district in the Irrawaddy division of Lower Burma. A town of the same name is the capital.

Heraklion or **Candia** a district in the British section of administration in Crete where stamps were issued 1898-9.

heraldic colours (her.) These include gules (red), azure (blue), sable (black), vert (green) and purpure (purple).

herdenkingszegel (Dutch) commemorative stamp.

herdruk (Dutch) reprint.

Herkunftsstempel (Ger.) postmark of origin.

Hermes in Greek mythology, the messenger of the gods. Identified with the Roman mythological figure Mercury. Both have been featured on postage stamps: Hermes on the first issues of Greece, 1861-95, and Mercury on the 1851-73 newspaper stamps of Austria and on subsequent issues to 1922.

Herm Island one of the Channel Islands that issued local stamps. They were not valid for international mail.

Herstellung (Ger.) production.

Herzegovina See BOSNIA AND HERZEGOVINA.

HERZOGTH or **HERZOGTHUM** (insc.) appears on stamps of Holstein, 1864-6.

HERZOGTH SCHLESWIG (insc.) appears on stamps of Schleswig, 1864-5.

hexagone (Fr.) hexagon.

hexagones (Fr.) honeycombs.

H.H. NAWAB SHAH JAHAN BEGAM (insc.) appears on stamps of Bhopal, a feudatory state of India.

H.I. & U.S. Postage (insc.) Hawaiian Islands and United States postage; appears on stamps of Hawaii, 1851-2.

Hickok, James Butler ("Wild Bill") (1837-76) an American scout and U.S. marshal; also a stage-coach driver, and scout in the Union Army during the U.S. Civil War. He won fame as a daring rider with the Pony Express, a mail service in the American West, 1860-1.

Hidalgos (nick.) certain stamps of Mexico bearing portraits of Miguel Hidalgo y Costilla.

hidden dates These appear on stamps of Canada. Beginning with the regular issue of June 1, 1935, many dies used for Canadian stamps bore a date to indicate the year of manufacture. The dates did not appear on certain stamps, for example, the Winston Churchill commemorative. Others did not have these dates when a date was part of the stamp designs, as in the Pauline Johnson stamps of 1961 and the Red River Settlement stamps of 1962. By error, hidden dates are sometimes called "secret dates", but they are not secret, as some identifying marks on early U.S. stamps are.

Highway Post Offices (H.P.O.) a U.S. system of mail delivery by truck; mail is sorted, picked up, and left enroute. This postal service was instituted by the U.S. government in 1941 between Washington, D.C., and Harrisonburg, Virginia.

Hilfspostamt (Ger.) temporary post office, auxiliary postal substation.

Hilfspostmarken (Ger.) provisional stamps.

Hill, Edwin brother of Rowland Hill; became chief of the stamp office at Somerset House in Great Britain.

Hill, Frederic brother of Rowland Hill; became assistant secretary of the British Post Office Department.

Hill, Pearson son of Rowland Hill; is credited with inventing a machine cancelling device some years after he was appointed to work in the British Secretarial Department in 1850.

Hill, Rowland an English postal reformer responsible for the introduction of the penny post throughout Great Britain, and for the famous 1-penny black, 2-pence blue adhesive postage stamps of May 6, 1840, and the same denominations and colours of the Mulready covers and letter sheets. Queen Victoria knighted him for his work. His postal reforms led the way for the rest of the world.

Hillsboro, N.C. This town in North Carolina issued postmasters' provisional stamps in 1861 as part of the Confederate States of America.

Hill's Post in Boston, Massachusetts, issued U.S. local stamps in 1849.

himmelblau (Ger.) sky blue.

Hind, Arthur a world-famous philatelist of Utica, New York. He owned the British Guiana 1-cent magenta postage stamp error.

hinges small pieces of strong paper gummed on one side and used for mounting stamps. Collectors are warned to buy good-quality, peelable hinges. Cheap hinges may damage stamps if they are not easy to remove.

Hintergrund (Ger.) background.

HIRLAPJEGY (insc.) appears on 1900 newspaper stamps of Hungary.

Hispania ancient spelling of "Spain"; also refers to the Iberian peninsula.

historical flight cover   letter carried on a pioneer flight. Many bear cachets and postmarks noting facts, fliers, engineers, and the purpose of the flight.

H. M. Ships   wording on some cancels applied on board naval ships, mainly on British ships. "H. M." may be short for "His Majesty's" or "Her Majesty's".

Hochdruck   (Ger.) typography.

Hochwasser 1920   (Ger. ovpt.) high water, flooding; appears on the regular issues of the Republic of Austria, 1919-21, issued for use as semi-postal stamps on March 1, 1921. They were sold at three times face value to help flood victims.

Hoechstwert   (Ger.) top value.

Hoehe   (Ger.) height.

höger   (Swed.) right.

Hohenzollern   the name of the family that ruled Germany until the end of the First World War. A ship of this name is featured on many German colonial stamps, known as the "yacht key-types".

HOI HAO   (part of sur. and ovpt.) on stamps of Indo-China of 1892-1906 for use by the French post office in Hoi Hao, China. Stamps issued 1901-19.

hoja   (Sp.) sheet, leaf.

hoja de bloc   (Sp.) souvenir sheet.

hojitas   (Sp.) small sheets.

hold-down strips   technical name for a band of elaborate engravings and interlacing designs on the bottom margins of certain Canadian stamps in the King George V issues portraying His Majesty in an admiral's uniform (the "Admirals" or "admiral issues"). The recesses, or engraved lines in the hold-down strips, held ink that served as an adhesive to make the paper stay on the plate before the first row of stamps was printed. See GEOMETRIC ENGRAVING.

hole cancel   Some old Spanish and British colonial stamps were cancelled by a punched hole when they were used as revenue stamps. Fakers replaced some punched circles in the Spanish stamps and sold them as mint stamps.

Holland   See NETHERLANDS.

Hollandshjálp 1953   (sur.) appears with a surtax on Iceland stamps of 1953 to raise funds for Netherlands flood relief.

Holmes' Catalogue   a one-time popular catalogue of Canada and British North America. Many editions were compiled by the late Dr. L. Seale Holmes of London, Ontario, Canada.

Holstein   a former Grand Duchy, and historical region in northwest Germany. Became a member of the German Confedera-tion in 1815. Occupied by Prussia and incorporated by Prussia as a part of Schleswig-Holstein. Issued its own stamps in 1864-6; these were superseded by issues of the North German Confederation on Jan. 1, 1868.

Holzschnitt   (Ger.) wood engraving.

Homan's Empire Express   in New York City, New York, issued U.S. local stamps in 1852.

homolosine maps   maps in which each continent has a central meridian from which other meridians are laid out.

Honduras   republic of about 44,275 square miles south of Guatemala in Central America. Capital: Tegucigalpa. Issued stamps in 1866.

Honduras britannique   (Fr.) British Honduras.

Hong Kong   a British Crown Colony; a peninsula and island of about 391 square miles near the mouth of the Canton River in southeast China. Capital: Victoria. Issued stamps in 1862.

Hongrie   (Fr.) Hungary.

hongs   in China, a series of rooms used as warehouses, maintained by Chinese businessmen and merchants who before 1842 had a monopoly of trade with foreigners. Some hongs were used as postal depots in China prior to the government-controlled postal services.

Hopedale Penny Post   in Milford, Massachusetts, issued U.S. local stamps in 1849-54.

Hópflug Itala/1933   (2-line ovpt.) on regular-issue stamps of Iceland for airmail use in June 1933, to mark the flight of Italian General Italo Balbo from Rome to Chicago. A squadron of 24 Italian seaplanes made a good-will flight and stopped at Iceland, where special overprinted stamps were applied to mail bound for the United States.

horadado con alfileres   (Sp.) pin perforation.

horisontell   (Swed.) horizontal.

horizontal bisect   a postage stamp cut in half horizontally, each half being used as a single postage stamp at half the value of the original stamp. Sometimes these are surcharged with denominations confirming the value of the postage stamps.

hors (de) cours   (Fr.) obsolete.

horseshoe cancellation   (nick.) a type of cancel with an open end. Examples may be seen on stamps of Sicily, 1859 issue, purposely made so that the obliteration did not mark the head of the portrait of King Ferdinand II.

hor. strip   horizontal strip of stamps, usually with a number to denote quantity in the strip.

Horta   a district of Portugal in the Azores on the southeast coast of Fayal Island; about 305 square miles. Capital: Horta. Horta issued stamps 1892-1905; now uses stamps of Portugal.

hotel corner cards   Envelopes printed with the names of hotels have become a specialized branch of philately.

hotel stamps   special issues made by hotels in various parts of the world to pay for mail delivery from the hotels to the nearest post offices when pick-up and delivery services were not provided. These services were provided in the Imperial Hotel in Tokyo, Raffles Hotel in Singapore, and in the world-famous Shepherd's Hotel in Cairo. Probably the best-known labels came from Switzerland, Austria, and Hungary. The landlords of Rigi Kaltbad, Swit-

Hotel stamps (Switzerland)

zerland, issued the first hotel stamps. Rigi Kulm and Hotel Belalp followed the lead. Many other hotel stamps have been issued.

house organ   small magazine or newspaper, sometimes a single sheet of printed paper, issued by stamp dealers for clients or prospective customers.

Houston, Texas   issued postmasters' provisional envelopes in 1861 as part of the Confederate States of America.

Howard & Jones, London   the name of a papermaker appearing in watermarked

paper. In 1916 Afghanistan issued 2-paisas postage stamps with this watermark.

howler   a slang expression that refers to a gross error in some statement in philatelic literature.

Hoyt's Letter Express   in Rochester, New York, issued U.S. local stamps in 1844.

HRVATSKA   (ovpt. and insc.) appears on stamps of Hungary in 1918 for use in Croatia-Slavonia; appears as part of overprints and inscriptions with "S H S", and other words, dots, and obliteration lines to signify Croatia, Serbs, Croats, and Slovenes. These were issued prior to the complete unification of the states to form the Kingdom of Jugoslavia. In 1921 postage stamps for the entire Kingdom went on sale, replacing former issues of the individual states.

HRZGL FRM or **HRZGL FRMRK**   (insc.) appears on stamps of Holstein 1864, a former province of Prussia.

H/S   often appears in stamp auction catalogues to indicate a handstruck postal marking or a handstruck postage stamp.

HT. SENEGAL-NIGER   (insc.) appears on stamps of Upper Senegal and Niger, a former French colony in northwest Africa, 1906-7.

Huacho   a city in Peru. Issued postage stamps in 1884.

hue   colour, tint; variety of colour caused by admixture of another.

huit   (Fr.) eight.

hulpe-uitgifte   (Dutch) provisional issue.

Humboldt Express   in Nevada, issued U.S. local stamps in 1863.

humidor   often called a "sweatbox", an airtight container of plastic or other material containing a sponge or cloth under a protective cover, used to remove stamps from paper.

Humphreys, William   British engraver with Perkins, Bacon & Co. of London, England, who worked on some early dies of British stamps. He died in 1865.

Hungary   a state in Central Europe north of Czechoslovakia, sometimes called the Land of the Magyars. Capital: Budapest. The former dual monarchy formed in 1867 included Austria and other smaller states; it collapsed after the First World War, and Hungary proclaimed itself an independent republic in 1918. A soviet government was formed under Béla Kun in 1919; in 1920 a monarchy was formed, which was dissolved in favour of a republic in 1946. Stamp issues marked these changes. Some postage stamp inscriptions read "Magyarorszag".

Huntsville, Texas issued postmasters' provisional envelopes in 1861 as part of the Confederate States of America.

Hussey's Post in New York City, New York, issued U.S. local stamps and wrappers in 1854-82.

hybrid a stamp printed on fluorescent paper and tagged with a phosphor overprint. Examples are some U.S. city mail delivery and 1964 Christmas stamps. (Courtesy of Alfred G. Boerger)

hybrid proof proof of a postage stamp on India or other paper mounted on a die-sunk card.

Hyderabad known as the "Nizam's Dominions"; a former state in British India that became a part of Andhra Pradesh in central Deccan in 1956. First stamps issued in 1869-71; others were in use until 1950, then Indian stamps were used. Refused to enter the Indian Union in 1947, but yielded in 1948 after warnings of force.

hydrogen peroxide (H_2O_2) a chemical often used to restore the original colours to postage stamps affected by gases, chemicals, and exposure. Collectors are warned to use great care in applying hydrogen peroxide to stamps, since the chemical is known to have bleached all colour from some postage stamps.

hyphen-hole a type of perforation formed of rectangular holes; sometimes called a "roulette".

I

I.A.L. (airline) International Air Lines, Ltd., Great Britain. Also Imperial Airways Limited, which merged in 1939 with British Airways, Limited, to form the British Overseas Airways Corporation, known as B.O.A.C.

IAO (Dutch insc.) Internationale Arbeidsorganisatie; International Labour Organization.

I.A.T.A. International Air Transport Association.

ibidem, ibid., or **ib.** (Latin) in the same place.

ICAO International Civil Aviation Organization. The United Nations issued ICAO stamps in 1955, as did Canada in the same year. OACI is the abbreviation for the French and Spanish names of this organization.

Icaria (also Ikaria, Nikaria, Kariot) an island in the Aegean Islands, part of Samos department of Greece; about 99 square miles. Special issues in 1912-13 under Greek occupation were stamps of Greece, overprinted.

I.C.C. (ovpt.) International Control Comission; appears on stamps of India, 1965, for use in Laos and Viet Nam.

Iceland an island republic between North Atlantic and Arctic oceans; about 39,709 square miles. Capital: Reykjavík. Stamps have been issued since 1873.

ICEM (insc.) Intergovernmental Committee for European Migration. Stamps of the Netherlands Antilles honoured this organization with a semi-postal stamp Jan. 31, 1966.

ICFTU 1949-1959 (insc.) appears on stamps of the Chinese National Republic on Formosa, issued on Dec. 7, 1959, to commemorate the tenth anniversary of the International Confederation of Free Trade Unions.

Idar (insc.) on stamps of Idar, a feudatory state in India of about 1,669 square miles. Capital: Himmatnagar. Issued stamps in 1939.

idem or **id.** (Latin) same, same as above.

identifying stamps Study the illustrations on stamps and attempt to decide on a country of origin. Then refer to a stamp catalogue for stamps of similar designs and lettering. This often requires time and patience.

IDROVOLANTE / NAPOLI - PALERMO - NAPOLI (sur.) appears with new values on 1917 airmail stamps of Italy for the June 27, 1917, flight from Naples to Palermo and return.

i.e. or **id est** (Latin) that is.

I.E.F. Indian Expeditionary Force. The abbreviation is overprinted on 1914 stamps of India.

I.E.F. "D" (sur.) appears on stamps of Turkey, with values in annas, for use in Mesopotamia under British occupation, 1919.

Ierusalem (ovpt.) appears on stamps of Russia in 1909-10 for use by the Russian offices in the Turkish Empire.

Ifni a Spanish coastal district of southwest Morocco in Africa; about 741 square miles. Capital: Sidi Ifni, which is also the administrative capital of Spanish West Africa. Stamps issued since 1941 are those of Spain, overprinted.

I GILDI '02-'03 (ovpt.) appears on regular issues of Iceland for 1902-3 and on regular issues for official use 1902-3.

I.G.Y. International Geophysical Year, July 1957-December 1958; a period of scientific investigation by about 70 countries, 25 of which issued stamps to mark the event.

IHD International Hydrological Decade, 1965-74. The abbreviation is inscribed on stamps of China for June 1968.

Ikaria See ICARIA.

Ile de France provisionals (nick.) provisional airmail stamps of France surcharged "10 FR.", issued in August 1928 for catapult mail from the *Ile de France*, crossing the Atlantic Ocean to France. Forgeries exist.

Ile de la Réunion (insc.) appears on stamps of Réunion, a former French colony in the Indian Ocean.

Ile du Prince Edouard (Fr.) Prince Edward Island.

Ile Rouad (Fr.) Arwad.

ILE ROUAD (ovpt.) appears on stamps of the French offices in the Levant, for use in Ile Rouad, or Arwad, 1916.

Iles Caimanes (Fr.) Cayman Islands.

Iles Comores (Fr.) Comoro Islands.

Iles Vierges (Fr.) Virgin Islands.

ILES WALLIS et FORTUNA (ovpt. and

insc.) overprinted on stamps of New Caledonia for use in Wallis and Futuna Islands; inscribed on stamps of Wallis and Futuna Islands.

I.L.O. (insc.) International Labor Organization. Appears on many issues of the world.

imadi a coin of Yemen. 40 bogaches equal 1 imadi.

imitation officielle (Fr.) government imitation.

impale (her.) a method of arranging or marshalling by placing two coats side by side on one shield. This type of heraldry is known on stamps.

imperfección en la impresión (Sp.) printing imperfection, variety.

imperforates (nick.) any postage stamps without perforations or roulettes. Mainly

refers to the first stamps of countries, prior to 1860.

imperforate, unperforated terms used to describe postage stamps without perforations.

Imperial British East Africa Company (insc.) appears on stamps of British East Africa, 1890-5.

IMPERIAL CHINESE POST (insc.) appears on stamps of China for 1897 and subsequent years.

Imperial crest of Japan a design of a chrysanthemum with sixteen petals; appears on the early stamps of Japan except the first issue, which features a dragon. The value in sen (Sn), rin (Rn), or yen (Yn) is also a guide to identifying stamps of Japan.

Imperial Crown name of a type of British watermark introduced in 1880-3; noted in stamp catalogues.

Imperial Journal stamps a type of Austrian revenue stamps, not for postal service. The post office collected the revenue by stamps inscribed "ZEITUNGS STEMPEL" – "Zeitung" is German for "newspaper" and "Stempel" is German for "stamp". Used 1853-90.

IMPERIAL KOREAN POST (insc.) appears on stamps of Korea, 1900-1.

IMPERIO COLONIAL/PORTUGUES (2-line insc.) appears on postage-due stamps of Portuguese Africa, 1945.

IMPERIO MEXICANO (insc.) appears on

1866 stamps of Mexico with the portrait of Emperor Maximilian.

Imper. reg. posta austr. (insc.) Imperial and Royal Austrian Post; appears on the 1883 issue of Austria for use in Austrian offices in the Turkish Empire.

impresion (Sp.) print, printing.

impresion de fondo (Sp.) burelage.

impresion doble (Sp.) double print.

impresion en relieve (Sp.) embossing.

IMPRESOS (Sp. insc.) printed matter; appears on newspaper stamps of Cuba 1888 and of the Philippine Islands 1886-96.

impressed watermark imitation of a watermark, produced by engraved rubber rings in the moist web as it passes through the wet presses of the paper machine.

impression mark made by a stamp or a mould, as a motif in embossing or the printing of cancellations, cachets, forwarding agents' marks, and others.

impression (Fr.) printing.

impressióne a rilievo (It.) embossing.

impression en relief (Fr.) embossing.

impression en taille douce (Fr.) copper-plate engraving, not an engraving in steel or other metals.

imprimatur (Lat.) let it be printed. Sometimes found in conjunction with "sheet", to indicate the first impression from a plate endorsed with an official certificate to that effect, and a direction that the plate be used for printing stamps.

imprimatur stamps and sheets Early British stamps were produced in proof sheets with the correct watermarks, colours, and denominations for registration at Somerset House on the Strand, London, the headquarters of the British Inland Revenue.

IMPRIME (handstamped) appears on 1891 newspaper stamps of Persia.

Imprime's (ovpt.) appears with Persian text on 1908 newspaper stamps of Persia.

imprint (1) The name of the printing company that produced the stamps, often with details about the stamps, as for example on tabs of Israel or margins of Canada stamps, is a printer's imprint. Collectors save these imprints, usually attached to the four adjacent postage stamps (sometimes more) and call them "plate-number blocks" or "imprint blocks". (2) The name of the distributor of goods advertised, printed on the cover or elsewhere on a stamp catalogue, booklet, or price list is an imprint.

imprint to mark by pressure; to stamp letters, words, or designs on paper by means of a printing press of any kind.

imprint block block of stamps with the printer's name on the marginal paper.

IMP^{TO} DE GUERRA (insc.) appears on war-tax stamps of Spain, 1874 and subsequent years. The stamps, like postal tax is-

sues, did not pay postal charges, but were obligatory.

IMPUESTO DE ENCOMIENDAS (insc.) appears on Uruguay parcel post stamps, 1938 and later issues.

IMPUESTO DE GUERRA (insc., ovpt., and sur.) appears as an inscription on war-tax stamps of Spain, 1874-98; also is an overprint and a surcharge on Puerto Rico war-tax stamps, 1898.

I.N.A.E.C. (airline) Iloilo-Negros Air Express Co., Philippines.

in basso (It.) downward.

incidental grill See ACCIDENTAL GRILL.

incisione (It.) steel engraving.

inciso (It.) engraved.

incl. includes, included.

Inde Française (insc.) appears on stamps of French India. Most stamps of this former French territory were inscribed "ETABLISSE-MENTS FRANÇAIS DANS L'INDE". The five settlements of this territory united with India between 1949 and 1954.

Independence, Texas issued postmasters' provisional stamps in 1861 as part of the Confederate States of America.

India a republic of about 1,221,880 square miles in south central Asia, divided in 1947 into the two self-governing dominions of Pakistan and India. Capital: New Delhi. Issued stamps in 1852.

India (insc.) on Portugal Ceres type of stamps of Portuguese India, 1913-21.

India experimental post offices These used special cancellations as the postal service increased in new post offices and substations. The newly created offices were provided with special cancellers in specific designs in 1873. Three types appeared: (1) a small rectangle of thirteen to eighteen horizontal lines measuring 17 by 15 millimetres; (2) a diamond shape of bars 30 millimetres high and 25 millimetres wide; (3) a cancellation formed of six crescents measuring 30 millimetres high and 17 millimetres wide with two crescents, one above

the other top and bottom, and two other crescents, one at each side. These are rare cancellations that can be found among the common India postage stamps of 1882-7. After 1900 ordinary circular date stamps in two-ring circles were used with the words "EXPERIMENT P. O." around the circle and the dates in horizontal lines across the circle. The postmarks measure 33 millimetres wide. All measurements are from individual stamps and may vary a millimetre or so on other stamps.

Indian feudatory state inscriptions The stamps of the feudatory states of India have inscriptions in various native characters; in many cases there are no English inscriptions.

India paper, India proof paper a thin, opaque paper sometimes used for proofing the engravers' dies and the finished postage stamp printing plates before commercial printing begins.

INDIA PORTUGUESA or INDIA PORTU-GUEZA (insc.) appears on stamps of Portuguese India.

Indien (Ger.) India.

Indo-China a southeast peninsula of Asia; former French colony (Indochine) and protectorate divided into Cambodia, Laos, and Viet Nam in 1949; about 280,849 square miles. Capital: Hanoi. From 1889 stamps issued were those of the French Colonies, surcharged; after 1949 stamps of the individual countries were issued.

Indochine (Fr.) Indo-China.

INDOCHINE (insc.) appears on stamps for use in Indo-China.

Indonesia a republic in the East Indies of about 735,865 square miles; a former Netherlands colony. Capital: Jakarta, a seaport known as Batavia prior to 1949, when the territory was named Netherlands Indies. Stamps of the Republic of the United States of Indonesia were issued from 1950.

Indore State Postage (insc.) on stamps of Indore, a feudatory state in central India of 9,902 square miles. Capital: Indore. Issued stamps in 1886.

Industrielle/Kriegs-/wirtschaft (3-line ovpt.) War Board of Trade; appears on 1918 official stamps of Switzerland.

Infancia (Sp. insc.) infancy, childhood; on 1929 postal tax stamps of Mexico. Stamps were compulsory, but paid no postal service; the funds were intended for child welfare work.

Inflationsmarken (Ger.) inflation stamps.

Ingermanland See INGRIA.

Ingria, Ingermanland, or **North Ingermanland** a district of early Russia southeast of the Gulf of Finland. Stamps were issued in 1920 under the short-lived provisional government.

Inhaltsverzeichnis (Ger.) index.

Inhambane a district in southeast Mozambique of about 21,000 square miles. Capital: Inhambane. Stamp issues from 1895 to 1917 were those of Mozambique, overprinted; they were replaced by stamps of Mozambique.

Inini an inland section of French Guiana in northeast South America of about 30,130 square miles. Capital: St. Elie. In 1930 Inini was separated from French Guiana; during separation, stamp issues 1932-41 were of French Guiana, overprinted; the two were reunited in 1946 when the colony became an overseas department of France.

initial letter a large capital or ornamental letter, used at the beginning of a chapter or important paragraph. Many watermarks have been formed from initial letters: A for Australia, for example, or USIR for United States Internal Revenue.

initials in margins of U.S. stamps These occur because initials were stuck in the plates to identify the Department of Engraving and Printing employees who handled the plates. Some two-colour stamps, the Pan-American issue for example, have been known to have eight or more initials in the margins.

ink See PRINTING INK.

Inkeri (insc.) appears on stamps of North Ingermanland.

Inland (part of sur.) appears with price changes on stamps of Liberia, 1909-12.

Inland Revenue (insc. and ovpt.) overprinted on stamps of Mauritius in 1889; inscribed on Mauritius stamps 1896-8.

Inland Revenue of Great Britain the department in Great Britain that handles matters of revenue. Headquarters are at Somerset House in London where some British postage stamps were printed.

in Punkten durchstochen (Ger.) pin-perforated.

Inschrift (Ger.) inscription.

inscrição (Port.) inscription.

inscripción (Sp.) inscription.

inscriptions Words or numerals, and sometimes both, are referred to as inscriptions if they were originally printed on the stamps, rather than appearing as overprints or surcharges.

Inselpost (Ger.) island mail.

inskription (Swed.) inscription.

INSTRUCCION (insc.) on stamps of Venezuela, 1893-5; stamps were so inscribed for domestic mail; discontinued in 1895.

instructional markings post office stamps that give any instruction, such as: "Return to sender", 'Do not use this cover again", "More to pay".

Insufficiently prepaid./Postage due. (insc.) appears printed on two lines on orange, green, or other coloured labels, with values in cents on Zanzibar postage-due stamps of 1931-3.

intaglio printing The term derives from an Italian word meaning "in recess". It refers to any kind of printing with lines, dots, or both, below the surface of the printing plate: engraving in steel or copper, and gravure. The ink applied to the plate is wiped off and the ink below the surface of the plate is picked up and transferred to the paper. Thus the stamps are printed.

integral stamps U.S. pre-cancels with extra overprinting on values over 6 cents. People using those pre-cancels were required to show their initials, and the month and year the stamps were used. These stamps have been mechanically overprinted and hand-stamped.

INTERINSULAR POSTAGE (insc.) appears on Bahamas 1-penny stamp of 1859. This stamp was valid only on mail between New Providence and the out-islands, until the use of British stamps in the Bahamas ceased in May 1860.

INTERIOR (insc.) appears on the 1922-6 parcel post stamps of Uruguay.

Interior Office issues Paraguay stamps,

Initials in margin of U.S. stamps

1922 and subsequent issues, for sale in rural or country areas for local use. Not for use in the capital (Asunción) or for foreign mail. Stamps have the overprint "C" for "Campana", meaning rural.

interleave to insert an extra leaf, usually a blank or ruled one, between regular leaves of a book or stamp album.

Internationale Fluechtlingsorganisation (Ger.) International Refugee Organization.

International Institute for Nuclear Research (CERN) an institution operated by thirteen European nations at Meyrin in the Swiss canton of Geneva to encourage and discover peaceful uses for atomic energy. (Courtesy of Swiss PTT notice)

International Labor Organization The I.L.O. was set up during the negotiations leading to the Treaty of Peace between the Allied nations and Germany at Versailles, June 28, 1919. Originally it was an autonomous part of the League of Nations, but when this organization was dissolved in 1946, the I.L.O. became the first specialized agency of the United Nations. It consists of the International Conference, the governing body, and the International Labor Office. The office serves as secretariat and is established at Geneva, Switzerland. Today the I.L.O., which has more than one hundred member countries, goes on seeking to improve labour conditions and raise living standards throughout the world. Approximately eighty-eight countries planned special stamps on the occasion of the fiftieth anniversary of the I.L.O. in 1969. (Courtesy of Netherlands PTT)

International Postal Convention Before

1863, postal officials throughout the world noticed the increasing confusion in dispatching mail to foreign countries. When U.S. Postmaster General Blair suggested that postal officials hold a convention to help solve the problem, twelve European nations and the United States met in Paris in 1863. Owing to world unrest, activities came to a standstill until 1874, when Dr. von Stephen of Germany convened the first conference of the General Postal Union (the first name given to the Universal Postal Union).

international reply coupons small pieces of paper sold by post offices everywhere that can be exchanged in any member country of the U.P.U. for a postage stamp or stamps representing the amount of postage for an ordinary single-rate letter destined for a foreign country.

International Vending Machine Co. in Baltimore, Maryland, issued coil stamps resembling the government issue of 1908, vertical perf. 12. The International coils of 1906-9 were perforated 12½ to 13.

interpanneau (Fr.) gutter.

inter-panneau bloc or pair British stamp dealers use this term to describe gutter blocks or pairs. The stamps have a gutter to divide them. "Inter" is Latin for "between, among"; and "panneau" is French for "panel or a pane of stamps". Hence an inter-panneau block is two or more stamps printed one directly above and the other below the marginal paper or gutter dividing the two panes of stamps. A similar arrangement between two horizontal panes of stamps with two or more stamps from

Interrupted perforations: four different types

each pane and the gutter between them is a gutter pair or block. The blocks must be less than a full pane. They are often called cross-gutter pairs of blocks.

interrumpido (Sp.) broken.

interrupted perforations sometimes called "syncopated perforations"; best known among the 1924-31 issues of The Netherlands intended for use in vending machines. Three popular types and one scarce kind existed. One type had groups of four holes with blank spaces equal to two or three holes between the groups on the short ends or sides of each stamp. A second type had the same arrangement of holes and spaces on all four sides. A third variety had a missing perforation on each top and bottom corner. The fourth kind, used on the 7½-cent stamps of 1927, had two groups of three holes on the horizontal sides of each stamp. The United States permitted vending-machine manufacturers to perforate stamps for their own machines. These may be included with interrupted perforations. These stamps are illustrated and listed in Scott's U.S. Specialized catalogues.

intersheet gutters These divide sheets of stamps printed on continuous paper, called "web paper", instead of on sheets of paper.

interspazio (It.) gutter.

in Umlauf setzen (Ger.) to put into circulation.

invalidated stamps demonetized issues; stamps that no longer pay for postal services.

inverted refers to a portion of a postage stamp design printed upside down in relation to another portion. These may be one-colour stamps, for example those of Western Australia, or two-colour, or even multi-colour stamps. The Canadian St. Lawrence Seaway stamp with the error in the printing, however, is not correctly called an inverted centre, because the Canada Post Office Department is not sure which was

inverted – the lettering or the centre. Surcharges and overprints have also been inverted.

inverted watermarks those upside down in relation to normal ones. See WATERMARK POSITIONS.

invertido (Sp. and Port.) inverted.

invt. ovpt. inverted overprint.

inv. sur. inverted surcharge.

Ionian Islands seven Greek islands in the Ionian Sea; about 853 square miles. Stamps issued for Cephalonia and Ithaca under Italian occupation in 1941 were those of Greece overprinted; another issue of 1941 were stamps of Italy overprinted "Isole Jonie"; under German occupation in 1943 the Zante issue had an additional overprint in Greek.

Ionikon (insc.) appears on stamps for use in the Ionian Islands.

Ionische Inseln (Ger.) Ionian Islands.

I.O.V.R. (insc.) appears on the 1948 postal tax stamps of Romania.

I.P.O. These letters appear in a rectangular frame known as a tieprint, part on the stamp and the balance on the envelope to tie one to the other. The letters stand for Imperial Post Office, that is, the Chinese post office, and are found on letters to foreign countries posted in China with Chinese and Hong Kong stamps. Chinese stamps prior to 1914 were not valid outside of the country because China did not belong to the Universal Postal Union until 1914.

I/POLSKA/WYSTWA/MAREK (sur.) appears with new values and a cross in outline on the regular issue of 1919 to mark the first stamp exhibition in Poland. The semi-postal stamps helped to raise money for the Polish White Cross Society.

IPOSTA 1930 (Ger. wmk.) appears in a souvenir sheet of four stamps featuring buildings, on the German semi-postal issue of 1930 with 59 pfennigs for charity. Each person who paid for admission to the International Philatelic Exhibition, Sept. 12-21, 1930, could buy one sheet for 1 mark, 70 pfennigs. Face value of stamps in the sheet was 98 pfennigs. (Courtesy of Paula Lischka)

ipsa stamps independent postal system stamps. The U.S. Postal Service press release No. 124, dated Nov. 29, 1971, stated in part: "Referring to reports that 'ipsa stamps' with denominations of 1 to 50 cents are to be issued by a private firm on Nov. 30, the Postal Service noted that putting such stamps on envelopes or packages would disqualify such envelopes or pack-

Inverted centre

Inverted surcharge

ages for mailing in the U.S. mails."

I.Q.S.Y. International Quiet Sun Year, a sequel to the International Geophysical Year. In 1965 Nigeria issued two stamps showing the satellites Telstar and Explorer XII over a map of Africa, and the I.Q.S.Y. emblem.

I.R. (ovpt.) Internal Revenue; appears on U.S. postage stamps of 1895-8 for revenue use.

Iran formerly Persia; a kingdom in western Asia of about 628,000 square miles. Capital: Tehran. The first stamps were issued in 1870. Earliest issues feature a lion holding a sabre in its right paw, and with its tail half encircling the sun in the background. Later issues show the portraits of the Shahs and are generally inscribed "Persanes", or "Postes Persanes". Modern stamps include pictorials.

Iran (insc.) appears on stamps of Persia in 1935, when Persia adopted "Iran" as its official name.

Iraq a republic of about 116,600 square miles in west Asia, bounded by Syria, Turkey, Persia, Saudi Arabia, and Jordan. Formerly the Turkish province of Mesopotamia, mandated to Great Britain from 1920 to 1932. Capital: Baghdad.

Iraq (sur.) appears with values in annas and rupees on stamps of Turkey, 1918, for use in Mesopotamia under British occupation.

Ireland (Eire) an island of about 26,601 square miles in the Atlantic west of England. A republic except for six counties in the north. Capital: Dublin. Issued stamps in 1922.

Irland (Ger.) Ireland.

I.R. LAZZARETTO SAN CARLO IN TRIESTE a disinfected marking that appears on letters that were disinfected in Trieste, for the Imperial Royal Lazaret in Trieste. (Courtesy of Herbert Dube)

I.R.O. International Refugee Organization. The I.R.O. is represented by two 1953 stamps of the United Nations.

I.R. Official (ovpt.) on stamps of Great Britain, 1882-1904, for official use of the Inland Revenue Department.

iscrizione (It.) inscription.

Iskenderon (Turk.) Alexandretta.

Island (Dan. and Ger.) Iceland.

Island (insc.) on stamps of Iceland.

ISLAS DE JUAN DE FERNANDEZ (part of sur.) appears on Chile 1905 issue for use as the 1910 stamps of the Juan Fernandez Islands. Stamps were valid in Chile.

ISLAS GALAPAGOS (insc.) appears on 1957 stamps for Galapagos Islands. Listed with stamps of Ecuador in catalogues.

Isle of Man stamps one of the regional issues by Great Britain in 1958. Other regionals include: Northern Ireland, Guernsey, Jersey, Scotland, and the combined region of Wales and Monmouthshire. Stamps resemble other British issues but have their own heraldic emblems.

ISOLE ITALIANE DELL'EGEO (ovpt.) appears on stamps of Italy for use in the Aegean Islands.

ISOLE JONIE (ovpt.) appears on stamps of Italy in 1941 issued during the Italian Occupation of the Ionian Islands in the Ionian Sea. Used by six of the islands, but the seventh island, Cerigo in the Mediterranean Sea south of Greece, used Greek regular stamps.

Israel a republic on the southeast Mediterranean Sea; about 7,993 square miles. Capital: Jerusalem. First stamps were issued in 1948.

Israel postage-due stamps first issued in 1948 by overprinting the first coin-design stamps in denominations of from 3 to 50 mils, often called 3 to 50 prutas. Subsequent postage-due stamps of Israel in 1949 and 1952 have no English or French inscriptions to indicate their use.

issue the name applied to a stamp or a series of stamps sold at post offices during some stated period of time. The word usually has some prefix like "pictorial" issue or "Coronation" issue, or the stamp may be designated as an issue of a certain year.

Istanbul formerly Constantinople; a vilayet (province) in northwest Turkey; about 2,149 square miles. Capital: Istanbul.

Istria a former province of Italy, now part of Jugoslavia. There were stamp issues for Istria and the Slovene Coast under Italian occupation 1945-7, some surcharged.

ISTRIA/LITTORALE SLOVEN (2-line insc.) appears on 1945 stamps for Istria and the Slovene Coast. Listed with stamps of Jugoslavia.

ITA-KARJALA (ovpt.) appears as an overprint, or as an inscription with "Suomi-Finland", on stamps of Finland issued under Finnish military administration of Karelia.

Italia, Italiane (insc.) appears on stamps of Italy.

Italian East Africa, Africa Orientale Italiana former Italian colony in east Africa on Red Sea of about 665,970 square miles. Capital: Asmara. Stamps were issued 1938-41; prior to 1936, stamps of Ethiopia, Eritrea, and Italian Somaliland were used.

Italian offices in China Italy maintained post offices in China. Stamps were issued for use there in 1917.

Italian offices in Crete Italy maintained post offices in Crete, and issued stamps for use there in 1900.

Italian offices in Turkish Empire Italy maintained post offices in the Turkish Empire. General issues of stamps began in 1908.

Italian Somaliland, Somalia Italiana former Italian colony in east Africa, now a republic, of about 194,000 square miles. Capital: Mogadiscio (Mogadishu). Stamps issued 1903-37 were surcharged, overprinted, and inscribed "BENADIR" or "SOMALIA ITALI-ANA". In 1936 it became part of Italian East Africa; under British administration 1941-9, then an Italian trust until the republic was formed in 1960. Somalia issued stamps from 1950.

Italian stamps with ovals in red and green In 1956 Italy issued two stamps showing identical globes in lines, one set in red, and the other in green. When these are viewed with suitable glasses made with coloured acetate, the two globes combine into one stereoscopic picture: a globe that is a symbol of the United Nations. This process was discovered by Köhler, Graf, and Calov. The glasses have a red-orange lens at the left and a blue or bluish-green lens at right. Under these, the globe has three dimensions. Glasses are supplied with the book *I Francobolli Dello Stato Italiano*, the Italian government book that is the source of this data.

Italia Occupazione Militare Italiana isole Cefalonia e Itaca (ovpt.) appears on stamps of Greece for the Ionian Islands under Italian occupation.

italics sloping characters, distinct from Roman type, used to emphasize a word or a sentence.

Italien (Ger.) Italy.

Italienische Kolonien (Ger.) Italian Colonies.

Italienisch-Ostafrika (Ger.) Italian East Africa.

Italy a republic in southern Europe of about 119,764 square miles. Capital: Rome. First stamps were issued in 1862.

I. T. U. International Telecommunications Union. The United Nations (1956) and Viet Nam (1952) have honoured the I.T.U. with stamps. "U.I.T." is the French equivalent.

Iuka, Miss. This town in Mississippi issued postmasters' provisional envelopes in 1861 as part of the Confederate States of America.

Ivory Coast, or **Côte d'Ivoire** a republic, formerly a colony of French West Africa; area variously quoted as about 129,807 square miles, 123,200 square miles, and 127,520 square miles. From 1892 to 1944 stamps were used inscribed "Cote d'Ivoire"; 1945-58, stamps of French West Africa were used; stamps of the republic were issued in 1959.

ivory heads varieties of the 1841-57 British stamps. Owing to a peculiar chemical reaction between the printing inks and paper of the 1-penny and 2-pence stamps a cameo

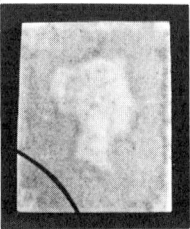

design appears on the back of some stamps in these issues. Where the ink was thin over Queen Victoria's likeness the paper appears nearly white against a blue background. Listed as varieties.

IX CONGRESSO/FILATELICO/ITALI-ANO/TRIESTE/1922 (5-line It. ovpt.) appears on four regular-issue stamps of Italy 1907-8 to commemorate the Ninth Italian Philatelic Congress at Trieste, June 4, 1922, and valid until Sept. 30, 1922. Philatelic societies promoted periodic reunions for the study of postage stamps and problems concerning philately; of a great value for the dissemination of philatelic knowledge. See *I Francobolli Dello Stato Italiano*, an Italian government book.

izquierdo (Sp.) left, left-hand.

J

Jabez Fearey & Co.'s Mustang Express in Newark, New Jersey, issued U.S. local stamps in 1870.

Jackson, Miss. This city in Mississippi issued postmasters' provisional envelopes in 1861 as part of the Confederate States of America.

Jacksonville, Ala. This town in Alabama issued postmasters' provisional envelopes in 1861 as part of the Confederate States of America.

Jaffa (ovpt.) appears on stamps of Russia, for use in Russian offices in Turkey.

Jahr, jaehrlich (Ger.) year, annual.

Jahrestag (Ger.) anniversary.

Jahreszahl (Ger.) calendar year.

Jai Hind free or liberated India. See AZAD HIND.

Jaipur State (insc.) on stamps of Jaipur State, a feudatory state in India. About 15,610 square miles. Capital: Jaipur. Issued postage stamps in 1904.

Jamaica a former British colony; an independent state since 1962; about 4,411 square miles. South of Cuba in the Caribbean. Capital: Kingston. Issued stamps in 1860.

Jamaique (Fr.) Jamaica.

JAMHURI 1964 (ovpt.) handstamped on Oct. 17, 1961, stamps of Zanzibar for use on Jan. 17, 1964. "Jamhuri" means "republic". Bradbury Wilkinson & Co., Ltd., British security printers, overprint the same 1961 issue in one and two lines. The later issue of June 21, 1964, was inscribed "JAMHURI ZANZIBAR". Refer to stamp catalogues listing Zanzibar.

Jammu and Kashmir a state in northern India. Jammu, formerly a province in Kashmir, issued stamps 1867-77, Kashmir issued stamps in 1866, and Jammu and Kashmir issued stamps together as a feudatory state in 1878-94. Listed with stamps of India.

Janina (sur.) appears on stamps of Italy 1902-11 for use in the Italian offices in the Turkish Empire. Janina (also Joannina or Ioannina) is a department of Greece.

Japan a constitutional monarchy, island chain off eastern coast of Asia in western Pacific Ocean; about 142,007 square miles. Capital: Tokyo. First stamps were issued in 1871.

Japanese chops official seal or stamp used in various Far Eastern countries, mainly India, China, and Japan. The Japanese occupation forces used chops as cancels and overprints on stamps of the occupied countries.

Japanese offices in China Japan maintained post offices in China, where overprinted stamps were used in 1900-22.

Japanese offices in Korea Japan maintained post offices in Korea, where overprinted stamps were used 1900-1.

Japanese paper originally made of mulberry fibres. Referred to as native laid or wove paper, Japanese papers were used for many classical stamps of Japan 1871-3 and again for the 1874 issue.

Japan occupation stamps issued for use during the Second World War in these colonies and states: Brunei, Burma, Dutch Indies for Java and Sumatra, Hong Kong, Malaya, North Borneo, Philippines, and Sarawak.

Japon (Fr.) Japan.

Jasdan a feudatory state of India; issued one denomination of stamps in 1942.

JATO Jet Assisted Take-Off. An airmail collector's term for mail planned for transmission aboard aircraft sent aloft with the help of rockets. This was a visionary idea superseded by the jet-propelled aircraft.

jaune (Fr.) yellow.

jaune-bistre (Fr.) bistre-yellow.

jaune foncé (Fr.) dark yellow.

Java an island in Malay Archipelago, formerly part of Dutch Indies, now part of Republic of Indonesia; about 48,830 square miles. Dutch Indies used stamps of The Netherlands, surcharged or overprinted, 1864-1950; then stamps of the republic were issued.

J B R S initials in the corners of 1869 stamps of Sarawak, for "(Sir) James Brooke Rajah (of) Sarawak". Sarawak was placed under British protection in 1888 and was ceded to Great Britain on July 1, 1946. It became a state in the Federation

122

of Malaysia on Sept. 16, 1963. Sir James lived from 1803 until 1868. His nephew, Sir Charles Brooke, followed him and became the second White Rajah.

JEEND STATE (part of ovpt.) appears with "SERVICE" on stamps of India for official use in 1885 in Jind, a state in India in the North Punjab.

Jefferson Market P.O. in New York City, New York, issued U.S. local stamps in 1850.

Jemen (Ger.) Yemen.

Jenkins' Camden Dispatch in Camden, New Jersey, issued U.S. local stamps and envelopes in 1853.

Jersey one of the Channel Islands. Issued provisional stamps 1941-3. Great Britain included Jersey in the regional issues of 1958-66. As an independent postal authority, Jersey issued stamps in 1969. Refer to stamp catalogues.

Jersey stamps one of the regional issues by Great Britain in 1958. Other regionals include: Northern Ireland, Guernsey, Isle of Man, Scotland, and the combined region of Wales and Monmouthshire. Stamps resemble other British issues but have their own heraldic emblems.

Jerusalem a district in south-central Palestine of about 1,650 square miles. From 1909 to 1911, stamps of Italy, surcharged, were issued by the Italian offices in the Turkish Empire, as were Russian stamps, overprinted, from the Russian offices in Turkey, for use in Jerusalem.

Jetersville, Va. This town in Virginia issued postmasters' provisional stamps in 1861 as part of the Confederate States of America.

jet mail airmail flown by jets. The first government-authorized mail flown by jet plane was from Toronto, Ontario, to New York City, New York, in 1950. Unofficial jet flights took place in the United States in 1946 (Schenectady, New York, to Washington, D.C., on June 22, 1946).

Jhalawar an Indian feudatory state in north-central Union of India. Issued stamps 1887-90. Since 1949 it has been a part of Rajasthan.

JIND or **JHIND STATE** (ovpt.) appears on stamps of India for use in Jind, a state in India in the North Punjab.

JIPEX/1936 (2-line ovpt.) appears on South Africa booklet panes of six stamps issued in 1933, made to mark the Johannesburg International Philatelic Exhibition in 1936.

job printer a printer doing mostly contract or casual work as opposed to one publishing material for resale.

Johnson & Co.'s City Despatch Post in Baltimore, Maryland, issued U.S. local stamps in 1848.

Johore a state on the southern tip of Malay Peninsula of about 7,330 square miles in Southeast Asia. Capital: Johore Bahru.

Johore or **Johor** (ovpt., sur., and insc.) surcharged and overprinted on stamps of Straits Settlements, 1876-92, for use in Johore, 1892-1965.

joined paper Joined paper occurs when pressmen repair or connect rolls of continuous paper. Stamp collectors classify joined paper as double paper when stamps are printed over the double thickness.

joint line the coloured line that often appears between coil stamps where the curved plates on a rotary press meet. The microscopic line between the plates picks up enough ink to print a line resembling a guide line in the colour of the stamps.

joint line pair Coils printed from curved plates sometimes show a line of colour (not a guide line) between the stamps where the rotary plates meet or join on the press. Many Canadian coils show this line.

joint pair, joined stamps two postage stamps stuck together to form a continuous strip for roll postage. For example, Canadian stamps were at first printed in sheets that were cut up and pasted together in vertical or horizontal strips to form rolls. Later developments in printing stamps involved printing the roll from a continuous web of paper. But when stamps from these strips were torn or separated, employees carefully repaired them to make complete rolls for vending-machine and dispenser use. Joined pairs or strips with joined stamps should not be separated.

Jonesboro, Tenn. This town in Tennessee issued postmasters' provisional envelopes in 1861 as part of the Confederate States of America.

Jones' City Express in Brooklyn, New York, issued U.S. local stamps in 1845.

Jones's paper named after the producers, consisted of various types, found especially among the postage stamps of New Zealand: chalk surface paper for stamps of 1924-5 and the unsurfaced coarse paper for the Coronation stamps of 1937 and health stamps of 1938.

Jordan or **Trans-Jordan** a kingdom since 1946 of about 37,500 square miles in the Middle East east of Israel; former Turkish territory, mandated to Great Britain after the First World War. Capital: Amman. Issued stamps in 1920.

Jordan & Co. formerly Squier & Co.'s City Letter Dispatch; in St. Louis, Missouri, issued U.S. local stamps in 1860.

JORNAES (insc.) appears on newspaper stamps of Portugal, Portuguese colonies, and Brazil.

jour d'emission (Fr.) day of issue.

journal (Fr.) newspaper.

journal stamps See NEWSPAPER STAMPS.

JOURNAUX/DAGBLADEN/1928 (3-line bilingual ovpt.) appears on Belgium newspaper stamps overprinted on former parcel-post stamps. The issues of 1929-31 were made without the date in the overprint.

J.R.G./AEREO (part of sur.) Junta Revolucionaria de Gobierno; appears on 1947 airmail stamps of Venezuela.

Juan Fernandez Islands See ISLAS DE JUAN DE FERNANDEZ.

Jubaland, Trans-Juba, or **Oltre Giuba** a former Italian protectorate, now part of Italian East Africa; about 33,000 square miles. Chief town: Kismayu. As a separate colony 1924-6, Jubaland used Italian stamps, overprinted "OLTRE GIUBA".

Jubilaeum (Ger.) jubilee.

JUBILE DE L'UPU (partial insc.) appears on 1924 issue of Switzerland to mark the fiftieth anniversary of the founding of the Universal Postal Union.

jubilee lines coloured lines around the panes or sheets of stamps of Great Britain, British colonies, and certain other states. De La Rue, the security printers, added type rules around the letterpress forms to protect the edges of the printing plates from excessive wear as an economy measure in 1887 in the fiftieth anniversary of Queen Victoria's reign – jubilee year, and hence the name of the lines. The same type of line appears on some lithographed stamps of Palestine. The lines are of two major types: continuous or with breaks

with short lengths known as co-extensive lines.

jubilees (nick.) any postage stamps issued to mark some jubilee celebration. Especially applied to British and Commonwealth postage stamps for Queen Victoria's Jubilee (Canada, 1897) and for the Silver Jubilee of King George V and Queen Mary's twenty-fifth anniversary of their reign in 1935.

Judenpost (Ger.) Jewish post.

JUEGOS OLIMPICOS (Sp. insc.) appears on 1924 semi-postal stamps of Costa Rica to pay expenses of athletic games.

Jugoslavia, Yugoslavia federal republic in southeastern Europe of about 96,201 square miles. Capital: Belgrade. First stamps of the republic were issued in 1918.

Jugoslavija (insc.) appears on stamps of Jugoslavia.

Jummo et Cachemire (Fr.) Jammu and Kashmir.

jump coils two adjacent coil stamps appearing on different levels. These occur where the end of the curved printing plate makes its latest impression from the same plate as the plate turns on a rotary press.

Junagarh, Junagadh a feudatory state in India near Bombay. First stamps were issued in 1864. Refer to Soruth in stamp catalogues.

June 8, 1946 (insc.) appears on British Colonial omnibus issue of June 1946. On June 8 the British staged a victory parade in London, England. The stamps are listed in some catalogues as the Peace issue.

Jungferninseln (Ger.) Virgin Islands.

junior collectors Beginning stamp collectors of all ages are referred to as junior collectors.

Junior Philatelic Society British stamp collectors' group with headquarters in London.

Justice (insc.) appears on U.S. official stamps of 1873 for the Justice Department.

K

K. (insc.) for "krone", a coin; appears on stamps of Bosnia and Herzegovina with no country name, 1900.

Kabinettstueck (Ger.) very fine to excellent copy; word occurs in descriptions of quality of stamps in auction catalogues.

Kaiman-Inseln (Ger.) Cayman Islands.

Kaiser (Ger.) emperor.

Kaiserkrone (Ger.) imperial crown.

Kaiserliche und Konigliche (insc.) Kaiser's and King's; appears on stamps of Austria.

Kais. Königl Oesterr Post (insc.) appears on 1883 issue of Austria. From 1890 "Königl" was spelled "Koenigl".

Kalayaan Nang Pilipinas (insc.) appears on 1943 stamps for the Philippines under Japanese occupation.

Kamerun (Ger. insc.) on stamps of Cameroon.

Kammzaehnung (Ger.) comb perforation.

kamtanding (Dutch) comb perforation.

Kanada (Ger.) Canada.

kangaroos (nick.) Australian stamps featuring a kangaroo on a map of the country. These stamps were issued in 1913 for the first time, and subsequently 1914-35.

Kans. (ovpt.) Kansas; appears on 1926-7 U.S. stamps. Issued officially May 1, 1929, to help prevent losses from post office burglaries. Used about a year. Similar stamps were overprinted "Nebr." for the same use.

Kans. and Neb. (control ovpt.) Kansas and Nebraska; appears on a special issue prepared in 1929 by overprinting these abbreviations on the 1926-7 U.S. regular-issue stamps. Authorized as a means of preventing post-office burglaries.

Kansas City roulettes These provisional U.S. stamps were imperforate sheets rouletted and sold with official approval in 1914. See Scott's U.S. Specialized catalogue for details.

Kap der Guten Hoffnung (Ger.) Cape of Good Hope.

Kapverdische Inseln (Ger.) Cape Verde Islands.

Karelia a constituent republic of the U.S.S.R.; area variously quoted as about 77,720 square miles, 55,198 square miles, and 68,900 square miles. Capital: Petrozavodsk (Kalinisk). Set of stamps was issued in 1922 during brief period of independence; stamps of Finland, overprinted, were issued under Finnish administration 1941-3.

Kariot See ICARIA.

Karjala (insc. and part of ovpt.) Karelia. The inscription was in 1922 on stamps issued for the region when the Karelians rebelled against Russia. The overprints were on stamps of Finland, 1941, indicating Karelia was under Finnish occupation.

Karki (ovpt.) appears on stamps of Italy, 1912-23, for use in Calchi, one of the Aegean Islands.

Karlfonds (insc.) appears on 1918 semipostal stamps of Bosnia and Herzegovina. The premium from these stamps went to a charity fund known as "Karl's Fund" (King Karl I).

karmin (Ger.) carmine.

Kärnten Abstimmung (Ger. ovpt.) Carinthian Plebiscite; appears on stamps of Austria for use in 1920 in Carinthia.

Karolinen (Ger.) Caroline Islands.

Karpathos or **Scarpanto** an Italian island of the Dodecanese group in the Aegean Sea, between Rhodes and Crete; about 118 square miles. From 1912 to 1932, Karpathos issued Italian stamps overprinted "SCARPANTO".

Kartonpapier (Ger.) carton paper.

Kashmir or **Cashmere** part of the Indian feudatory state of Jammu and Kashmir, two regions governed by the same ruler. Issued stamps 1866-70, entirely in native text.

Kastenzaehnung (Ger.) harrow perforation.

katalogisieren (Ger.) to enter in a catalogue.

Katalognummer (Ger.) catalogue number.

Katanga a province that separated from the Republic of Congo in 1960. Issued Congo stamps overprinted "KATANGA" and a set of stamps tolerated in the international mails although the government that authorized them had not been recognized by the long-established nations of the world. The United Nations declared the secession ended in September 1961.

Kathiri State of Seiyun a state in Aden Pro-

125

tectorate. Issued stamps in July 1942, along with those of the Qu'aiti state of Shihr and Mukalla. A member of the Aden Postal Union.

Kavalla See CAVALLA.

Kedah a state in the Federation of Malay on the west coast of Malay Peninsula; about 3,660 square miles. Capital: Alor Star. Issued stamps in 1912.

Kedah (insc.) appears on 1912-62 stamps for use in Kedah, one of the states in the Federation of Malay.

keerdruk (Dutch) turned printing – tête-bêche.

kehrdruck (Ger.) tête-bêche.

Kelantan a state in the Federation of Malay on the east coast of Malay Peninsula; about 5,750 square miles. Capital: Kota Bahru. Issued stamps in 1911.

Kellogg's Penny Post & City Despatch in Cleveland, Ohio, issued U.S. local stamps in 1853.

Kemahkotaan or **Ketahkotaan 1892-4** (ovpt.) appears on stamps of Johore for the Coronation issue of Johore, 1896. Johore is one of the states in the Federation of Malaya.

Kennedy find an accumulation of envelopes and correspondence filed by the Bank of Montreal between 1840 and 1853, bearing the name of Mr. Kennedy, who was the New York City agent for the Province of Canada Post Office. Some 10,000 rare covers had U.S. and Canadian stamps on them, as well as adhesive stamps of New Brunswick and Nova Scotia. John F. Negreen, a New York stamp dealer, purchased the lot. A beautiful example of a Kennedy letter is in the Canada collection of the Royal Ontario Museum in Toronto, Ontario.

Kenttä-Posti (ovpt.) appears on military stamps of Finland, 1941-63.

Kenttapostiä (insc.) appears on military stamps of Finland, 1941-63.

Kenya a British Commonwealth state since 1963 of about 224,960 square miles on Indian Ocean in East Africa; a former British colony. Capital: Nairobi.

Kenya et Ouganda (Fr.) Kenya and Uganda.

KENYA/TANGANYIKA/UGANDA (sur.) appears with new values on stamps of South Africa issued 1941-2.

Kerassunde (ovpt.) appears on stamps of Russia, 1909-10, for use in Russian offices in Turkey.

key plate In printing colonial and some other stamps with millions of identical central designs, the key plates print the por-

tions never changed throughout the issues. Also called the head plate.

key-types refers to stamps of a basic design with spaces for colonial names and denominations printed by separate printing plates. The central designs are printed by the key plates. If the designs feature a monarch or other person they are sometimes called the "head plates". Since the other plates perform the duty of providing information regarding country names and values, they are called the "duty plates".

K.G.C.A. (sur.) Carinthian Government Commission, Zone A; appears with changes in values on stamps of Jugoslavia for use as the 1920 plebiscite issue for Carinthia.

KGL/POST/FRM (insc.) appears with values in cents, on stamps of the Danish West Indies, 1855-73.

Khmer Republic formerly the kingdom of Cambodia in southeast Indo-China; about 69,866 square miles. Capital: Pnompenh. At one time a French protectorate; in 1970 the monarchy was abolished. First stamps issued in 1951. Stamps of March 18, 1970, were inscribed "REPUBLIQUE KHMERE".

Kiao-Tchéou (Fr.) Kiautschou.

Kiauchau (also Kiaohsien, Kiautschou, or other spellings) city and seaport in eastern China in the province of Shantung. Occupied by Germany in 1897, and, with an additional 200 square miles, became a German protectorate in 1898. Seized by Japan in 1914, and returned to China in 1922. In 1900 Germany issued the German offices in China stamps, surcharged, and from 1900-9 issued German colonial yacht key-types inscribed "KIAUTSCHOU".

kicking-mule cancellation a design originating in Port Townsend, Washington, in 1877, that shows a mule with its hind legs in a kicking action.

Kidder's City Express Post in Brooklyn, New York, issued U.S. local stamps in 1847.

killer bars horizontal lines forming part of an obliteration.

killers types of cancellations usually without details. Many collectors call the decorative cancels of Canada, the United States, and Brazil by this name. Smudged cancels that blot out the stamp designs and degrade the stamps for philatelic use are often classified as killers.

kiloware refers to mixed packages or boxes of stamps. Government offices sometimes offer kiloware for sale. Such stamps are usually on pieces of paper from a variety of mail – letters, parcels, and papers – and are not sorted.

Kinderstempel (Ger.) Loosely translated, it means "stamp for a child". In Europe years ago, manufacturers made kits for little children to play at stamp collecting. The

stamps were extremely small, about half size or slightly larger than half.

Kinderwohlfahrt, Kinderfuersorge (Ger.) children's welfare.

KING EDWARD VII LAND (ovpt.) appears on 1-penny 1906 stamps of New Zealand, used in 1908 on the Shackleton Antarctic Expedition. Listed in Gibbons Part One stamp catalogues.

king's heads (nick.) stamps portraying kings of a country as opposed to portrait stamps of queens issued by the same postal authorities; term is frequently used in connection with British and Commonwealth stamps of King Edward VII, King George V, and his sons Edward VIII and George VI.

Kingston, Ga. This city in Georgia issued postmasters' provisional envelopes in 1861 as part of the Confederate States of America.

Kingston/Relief/Fund./1d. (4-line sur.) appears on Barbados semi-postal stamps issued Jan. 25, 1907. The stamps sold for 2 pence each, with 1 penny for postage and 1 penny for relief of earthquake victims in Kingston, Jamaica.

Kionga part of Mozambique in southeast Africa, formerly part of German East Africa; about 400 square miles. In 1916 Kionga used stamps of Lourenço Marques, surcharged.

Kionga (sur.) on stamps of Lourenço Marques in 1916, for use in Kionga, after Portugal occupied this part of a German colony in East Africa.

kip a coin of Laos. 100 ats equal 1 kip.

Kirin and Heilungkiang issues postage stamp issues of 1927-9 for use in these two provinces in Manchuria. Kirin is a province in northeast China in Manchuria, bordering Russia and Korea; its capital is Kirin. Heilungkiang is the northernmost province in China in North Manchuria. In 1927-9 Chinese stamps were overprinted for use in these two provinces, which became part

of the Chinese communist territory. The communists organized Manchuria into six provinces, including Kirin and Heilungkiang.

Kishangarh a feudatory state in India. Stamps inscribed "KISHENGARH" were issued 1899-1929, and again 1945-7. From 1913 the stamps were inscribed "KISHANGARH".

K.K.L. stamps Keren Kayemeth L'Israel, name of the Jewish National Fund labels often sold at synagogues of the world to raise money towards the purchase and redemption of land in Palestine. J.N.F. labels were authorized at the Fifth Zionist Congress in Basle, Switzerland, in 1901. The first K.K.L. or J.N.F. labels were distributed in 1902 from the main office of the organization in Vienna. Some Jewish people used the charity labels on their letters by sticking them beside the postage stamps, an act contrary to law since the J.N.F. stamps did not pay for postage according to the Universal Postal Union regulations. In 1948 the labels were used as stamps in the area that became Israel.

K.K. OESTERR POST (insc.) appears on stamps issued for use in Liechtenstein under Austrian postal administration, 1912-18.

K. K. Osterreichische Post or **Kaiserliche Königliche Osterreichische Post** Imperial and Royal Post, Austria.

K.K. Post-stempel (insc.) appears on newspaper stamps for use in Austria or Lombardy-Venetia, 1851-63.

KLAIPEDA (insc.) appears on 1923 stamps of Memel issued under Lithuanian occupation.

klassisch (Ger.) classical.

Klebefalz (Ger.) hinge.

klein (Ger.) small, little.

Kleinbogen (Ger.) miniature sheet.

Kleinbuchstabe (Ger.) small letter.

kleur (Dutch) colour.

Klischee (Ger.) cliché.

KLM (airline) Koninklijke Luchtvaart Maatschappij, Royal Dutch Airlines. Point of origin: The Netherlands.

knife the device or tool employed to die-cut envelope blanks; not an envelope-maker's term.

K.N.I.L.M. (airline) K.Nederlandsch-Indische Luchtvaart Mij., Netherlands.

Knoxville, Tenn. This city in Tennessee issued postmasters' provisional stamps and envelopes in 1861 as part of the Confederate States of America.

kolom (Dutch) column.

Kolonialaufdruck (Ger.) colonial overprint.

Kolonne (Ger.) column.

Kolumbien (Ger.) Columbia.

kombiniert (Ger.) combined.

KONGELIGT POST FRIMAERKE (insc.) appears on 1851 stamps of Denmark. "KONGELIGT" is vertically on the left side, "FRIMAERKE" is vertically on the right, and "POST" appears at the top of the stamp.

Kongo (Ger.) Congo.

KONGRESI K.K.SH. (part of sur.) appears with a red cross on Albania 1946 semipostal stamps, with the surtax for the Albanian Red Cross.

Kontrollbuchstaben (Ger.) control letters.

Kontrollnummer (Ger.) control number.

kopeck a copper coin of Russia, Armenia, and Finland. 100 kopecks equal 1 ruble. Named from "kopiejka", a spear; the coin has the design of a horseman armed with that weapon. Until 1704, the coin was of silver.

Kopf (Ger.) head.

kopfstehend (Ger.) inverted.

kopparstickstryck (Swed.) copper-plate gravure.

Korana a crown, former coin of Hungary.

KORCA or **KORCE** (insc.) appears on 1914-17 issues of Korce, the former name of Korrcë, a prefecture in southeastern Albania. Listed with stamps of Albania.

Korea (Corea, Chosen, or Tyosen) a former kingdom declared in 1895, and later a dependency of Japan (1910-45), located on the east coast of Asia. Area 85,248 square miles. Capital: Seoul. Korea issued stamps from 1884 until June 1905, when the Korean postal service was amalgamated with postal services of Japan. The people of Korea used Japanese stamps until 1945, the time of the U.S. occupation of southern Korea and the Russian occupation of northern Korea. Both countries issued occupation stamps. See REPUBLIC OF KOREA; DEMOCRATIC PEOPLE'S REPUBLIC OF KOREA.

Korfu (Ger.) Corfu.

Korkstempel (Ger.) cork postmark, cork cancel.

Kouang-Tcheou (sur.) appears with new values on stamps of Indo-China or Cameroun 1906-41, for use in French offices in Kwangchowan, China.

Koztarsasag (ovpt.) appears on Hungarian special delivery stamps of 1916, for use as special delivery stamps by the Hungarian Republic in 1919.

K.P.K./17-26 SEPT./19 37 (3-line ovpt.) appears on 1937 stamps of Denmark to mark the fiftieth anniversary of the founding of the oldest philatelic society, the Kobenhavns Philatelist Klub (K.P.K.) in Denmark.

Kr. kreuzer; coin name appearing on stamps of Austria, Baden, and Hungary.

krajczar Hungarian name for kreuzer, a copper coin. 100 krajczar equal 1 forint. The Bohemian name for this coin is "krejcar".

kran silver coin of Persia (Iran). 1 kran equals 20 shahis or 1,000 dinars. When introduced by Fath Ali Shah in 1826, it weighed 108 grains.

Kreideaufdruck (Ger.) chalk coating.

Kreidepapier (Ger.) chalk-surfaced paper.

Kreis (Ger.) circle.

KREIS (part of insc.) appears on stamp made for Wenden in 1862 but not issued. A similar inscription appears on 1878-80 stamps for Wenden. Listed with stamps of Russia.

Kreta (Ger.) Crete.

kreuzer also spelled "kreutzer"; a copper coin of Austria, Hungary, and Germany. 60 kreuzer equal 1 gulden. The name is derived from the German "kreuz", meaning "cross". The old German coin, of silver or copper, had a cross stamped on it, but the modern coin usually has a double eagle on the obverse side.

Kriegsausgabe (Ger.) war issue.

Kriegsdruck (Ger.) war-time printing.

Kriegssteuer (Ger.) war tax.

Kriegssteuermarke (Ger.) war-tax stamp.

Kriegswinterhilfswerk (Ger.) war-time winter relief.

Kriegszuschlagsausgabe (Ger.) war-surtax issue.

krijtachtig (Dutch) chalky.

kritpapper (Swed.) chalky paper.

Kroenung (Ger.) coronation.

krona a silver denomination used in Sweden and Iceland. The krona of Sweden is divided into 100 öre, and the coin of Iceland into 100 aurur (shortened to aur in stamp inscriptions). In Czechoslovakia, a similar coin called the "koruna" is divided into 100 haleru.

krone a silver denomination of Norway and Denmark; also used in Greenland, which is an integral part of Denmark. 100 öre equal 1 krone. Sweden and Iceland have a similar coin called a "krona". Austria also used a krone that was divided into 100 heller. Bosnia and Herzegovina introduced the heller and krone in 1900.

K. u. K. Imperial and Royal; on stamps of Austria, and of Bosnia and Herzegovina.

K u K FELDPOST (ovpt.) appears with values in bani on stamps of Romania under

Austrian occupation.

K.u.K. FELDPOST (insc.) appears on Austrian occupation stamps used in Italy, 1918.

The stamps bear no country name and are surcharged in centesimi or lire (lira).

K.u.K. MILITAR POST (insc.) on stamps of Bosnia and Herzegovina, 1912-18.

KUPA (part of ovpt.) on Jugoslavia stamps 1941-2 issued under Italian occupation of the Fiume Kupa zone. See stamps of Jugoslavia in catalogues (spelled "Yugoslavia" in some books). "Jugo Slavia", in two words, is the regular inscription on the stamps.

Kupferdruck (Ger.) copper-plate printing.

kupferrot (Ger.) copper-red.

Kupferstich (Ger.) copper engraving.

Kurland or **Courland** on east shore of Baltic Sea, now Kurzeme and Zemgale, provinces of Latvia. In 1916-17, under German occupation, overprinted German stamps were used; in 1919 under Russian occupation, stamps of Latvia were overprinted.

Kurs (Ger.) rate of exchange.

kursierend (Ger.) current.

Kurtz Union Despatch Post in New York City, New York, issued U.S. local stamps in 1851-3.

kuvert (Swed.) envelope.

Kuvertausschnitt (Ger.) cut square.

Kuwait a sheikdom of about 5,800 square miles on northwest coast of Persian Gulf. British Protectorate until 1961. Capital: Kuwait. First issued stamps in 1923, which were overprinted stamps of India.

Kuwait (ovpt.) appears on stamps of India, 1923-45, for use in Kuwait under British protection. In 1948, stamps of Great Britain, surcharged in annas and rupees, were used. Pictorial stamps issued since 1959.

Kwangchowan a French-leased region in China. Used Indo-China stamps surcharged "Kouang/Tcheou-Wan" and with Chinese characters, 1906. Similar overprints were used until 1941; some stamps were inscribed, 1937-9.

Kwidzyn See MARIENWERDER.

K Württ. Post (insc.) appears on stamps of Württemberg.

kyat a coin of Burma. 100 pyas equal 1 kyat.

L

L (ovpt.) for "Lansa", appears on airmail stamps of Colombia, 1950.

La Agüera (ovpt.) appears on stamps of Rio de Oro, 1920. The 1922 issue was inscribed in this way for this Spanish possession in northwest Africa. Subsequently, Spanish Sahara stamps were used.

L.A.B. (airline) Lloyd Aero Boliviano, Bolivia. Formerly controlled by German interests, but expropriated in 1941; operated by PANAGRA (Pan American Grace Airways Inc. of New York).

label (1) a piece of paper resembling a stamp, but without value in postal service. These were often made to imitate postage stamps for collectors, as in the case of those of Lundy Island, Herm, Sedang, and many others. (2) The first British stamps of May 6, 1840, bore a marginal inscription reading: "Price 1d Per Label. 1/-per Row of 12. £1 Per Sheet". Some British collectors regard postage-due stamps as labels.

Labrador labels bogus items made to resemble postage stamps. In 1908 the labels were issued by an American company that was said to have a charter from Canada and Newfoundland to develop the natural resources of Labrador, since 1949 a part of Canada. Apparently the company did not have a charter (if such an organization did exist). Labels were inscribed "LABRADOR" on each side and "U.S.A. Post Office U.S.A." across the bottom. The promoters were seized and their labels were destroyed by the Canadian authorities.

Labuan a British possession of about 35 square miles in the East Indies six miles northwest of Borneo; part of North Borneo Colony administration. Capital: Victoria. Issued postage stamps in 1879.

Labuan (ovpt.) appears on stamps of North Borneo with various overprints, 1894-1905, for use in Labuan.

L.A.C. (airline) Lineas Aéreas Del Cauca, Colombia.

La Canea (ovpt. and sur.) appears on stamps of Italy for the use by the Italian offices in Crete, 1901-6.

Lachs (Ger.) salmon.

Lackstreifen (Ger.) bar of varnish.

La Croce Rossa (It.) the Red Cross.

L.A.C.T. (airline) Lineas de Aviación Condor Tampa, Peru.

Lady McLeod (nick.) stamps inscribed "L McL.", for local use in Trinidad. See L MCL.

Lady Minto Fete stamps (also known as the Viceroy's stamps) a series of three labels issued at the time of the popular Lady Minto's feat in Calcutta, a festival from December 1906 to January 1907. The issue was restricted by the government because private individuals cannot issue stamps in competition with the postal service. The labels portrayed Lord and Lady Minto on each of two 4-anna labels and a map of India on the 1-rupee value. The sale of the labels was for public benefit, but the 1-rupee was held back. Lord Minto, the fourth Earl of Minto, was viceroy of India in 1905-10 and worked for Indian self-government.

LA GEORGIE (insc.) appears on stamps of Georgia, 1919.

Lagos a former British Crown Colony and protectorate of about 3,460 square miles in West Africa. Purchased by Great Britain in 1861, became part of protectorate and colony of Southern Nigeria in 1906. Capital: Lagos. Issued stamps in 1874.

La Grange, Texas issued postmasters' provisional envelopes in 1861 as part of the Confederate States of America.

Laibach (Ger.) Ljubljana.

laid bâtonné similar to bâtonné paper, but with the spaces between the distinct lines filled in with laid lines close together. See BÂTONNÉ PAPER.

laid dandy roll dandy roll with wires set in relief on its surface producing their imprint on the wet web of paper. The resulting appearance of watermarks in parallel lines may be detected in horizontal or vertical translucent lines.

laid paper shows light and dark adjacent lines in the substance when a finished sheet is held to the light. The thickness of the alternate light and dark lines remains the same in one sheet of paper but may vary in different papers.

laid paper lines appear in paper in vertical and horizontal directions. The widely

spaced lines (about one inch apart) are impressed in the wet web of paper parallel to the direction of the machine, often referred to as the grain. These heavy lines, the chain lines, are made by wires called chains on the dandy roll. The chains support the transversal (thin) laid wires on the same dandy roll. The fine lines close together are known as the laid lines. They run across the grain of the paper. "Vergeures", French for the laid lines, means the wire used in paper-making or the wire mark.

Lake City, Florida issued postmasters' provisional envelopes in 1861 as part of the Confederate States of America.

L.A.L. (airline) Linea Aerea Levante, Italy.

laminated paper paper made of several plies of paper pasted together or combined with cellophane, metallic foil, cloth, or other substance.

LAN (airline) Linea Aérea Nacional. Point of origin: Chile.

Landesname (Ger.) name of country.

Landkarte (Ger.) map.

LAND-POST (insc.) appears with "PORTO-MARKE", on rural postage-due stamps of Baden, 1862.

Landstormen (part of ovpt.) appears on 1916 Sweden charity stamps with an extra charge for a clothing fund for mobilized reservists known as the "Landstorm".

LANSA (insc.) appears on 1950 Colombia airmail stamps.

Laos a kingdom in northern Indo-China of about 91,428 square miles. Capital: Vientiane. Before 1951 Laos used stamps of Indo-China; from 1951, stamps of Laos as an associated state of the French Union, then as a kingdom, were used.

L.A.R.E.S. (airline) Point of origin: Romania. Ceased operations in 1945 and merged with Aeroflot, the chief administration of the Civil Air Fleet under the Council of Ministers of the U.S.S.R.

large cents issue (nick.) the first stamps issued by the Dominion of Canada in 1868. After the public complained about the large size, the post office ordered smaller stamps in 1870, excepting the 15-cent value. It remained in use until the turn of the century. These stamps in large format are also called "the large Queens", "large Queen's heads", in comparison with small cents, "Queens" or "Queen's heads".

largo (Port.) wide, broad.

L. Arrow Blk. a block of four stamps from the left side of a pane with marginal paper bearing an arrow to indicate the centre line in the pane.

Las Bela (insc.) on stamps of Las Bela, 1897-1904, a feudatory state in India.

L.A.S.O. (airline) Linea Agrea Sud Oeste, Argentina.

last day cancellations dated postmarks used on mail from post offices, states, colonies, or countries on the last day of official use of stamps. Example: Newfoundland ceased issuing postage stamps when the colony joined Canada on April 1, 1949.

last day covers letters mailed on the last day of postal service from a single post office or from an entire state. An example is Newfoundland letters on the day before the colony joined Canada in 1949.

lastra (It.) plate.

Latakia a former republic, now part of

Late Fee postmark and cancel

Syria; about 2,310 square miles. Capital: Latakia. Latakia was known as Alaouites until 1930. Stamps issued 1931-3 were of Syria, overprinted "LATTAQUIE"; superseded in 1937 by stamps of Syria.

Late Fee cancels and postmarks applied to mail that arrived late, but that was accepted on payment of an additional fee. (Illustration: p. 131)

late fee stamps the kind used to denote an extra charge paid on mail left at the post office after the normal closing hours of the office. In Victoria, Australia, these are inscribed "too late stamps", and in other places a postal marking indicates the same thing.

L.A.T.I. (airline) Linee Aeree Transcontinental Italiana, Italy.

Latin Monetary Union With the depreciation in the value of silver in the nineteenth century, France, Belgium, Switzerland, and Italy in 1865 (joined by Greece in 1868) devised a standard system of currency, based on the decimal system of the French franc. The gold standard was adopted, and each country agreed to accept coins of all other countries of the union.

Lattaquie (ovpt.) appears on stamps of Syria for use in Latakia, 1931-3.

Latvia, Latvija since 1940, a republic of the U.S.S.R. in northern Europe at the eastern end of the Baltic Sea; about 25,399 square miles. Capital: Riga. Stamps were issued for Latvia, 1918-40, as an independent republic. In 1919 Germany occupied Latvia and German stamps were issued overprinted "Libau". Latvia was also occupied by Russia, in 1919 and again in 1940.

Latvia stamps with maps Because of a paper shortage in 1918, when the first issue of Latvia stamps went on sale, the authorities at the mint used German map paper and lithographed the stamps on the back.

laureated issues (nick.) stamps portraying rulers with crowns or wreaths of laurel. Stamps of New South Wales 1851-6 and France 1862-70 provide examples.

LAV (airline) Linea Aeropostal Venezolana. Point of origin: Venezuela.

lay-out lines similar to guide lines inscribed in steel-engraved plates for postage stamp printing. When not erased, they print faint lines near stamp designs; prevalent among the 1868 Canadian stamps and early stamps of Great Britain.

lazaretto (1) believed to be the name of a hospital in Rome in the twelfth century built by King Rotharo II; (2) a building or ship used as a hospital for the care of persons with loathsome or contagious diseases; (3) quarantine station or place where mail was fumigated or disinfected. (Courtesy of Herbert Dube)

L.C. refers to the large crown watermarks of Great Britain.

LE/1 (2-line insc.) appears on 1937 1-pound stamp of Egypt to show that the value was in terms of the money of Egypt, not of Britain or a colony.

League of Nations stamps postage stamps of Switzerland specially overprinted "Société des Nations". These stamps were used in the offices of the League of Nations and are listed in postage stamp catalogues.

Lebanon a republic at the eastern end of the Mediterranean Sea; about 3,470 square miles. Capital: Beirut. Under French mandate 1920-41, Lebanon stamps were those of France, surcharged or overprinted; from 1941 stamps of the republic were used.

Lecocq press an unusual machine used to print stamps in horizontal strips. The 1868-72 issues of Peru were printed this way, and were embossed.

Ledger Dispatch in Brooklyn, New York, issued U.S. local stamps in 1882.

Leerfield (Ger.) blank field.

Leeward Islands former name for a group of islands of about 423 square miles in West Indies southeast of Puerto Rico; former British colony. Capital: St. John. Consists of five presidencies: (1) Antigua, including the dependencies of Barbuda and Redonda; (2) British Virgin Islands; (3) St. Kitts-Nevis, including St. Christopher, Nevis, and Anguilla; (4) Montserrat; and (5) Dominica (until 1940). These five presidencies became British colonies in 1956. Postage stamps of the Leeward Islands were used 1890-1956.

legato (It.) tied.

LEGI POSTA (sur.) appears on 1920 airmail stamps of the Monarchy of Hungary.

Leipziger Messe (Ger.) Leipzig Fair.

Lemnos an island province in the Greek department of Lesbos, in the northern Aegean Sea off west coast of Turkey; about 175 square miles. Capital: Kastron. Stamps issued in 1912 were regular issues of Greece, overprinted.

lempira a coin of Honduras. 100 centavos equal 1 lempira (1933).

Lenoir, N.C. This town in North Carolina issued postmasters' provisional stamps and envelopes in 1861 as part of the Confederate States of America.

leopards (nick.) eight 1934 stamps of Nyasaland featuring a leopard against a sun and rays.

lepton a copper coin of Corfu, Greece, and Crete. 100 lepta equal 1 drachma. Literally "a tiny coin", the lepton is the equivalent of the centime in decimal currency.

Leros or **Lero** (ovpt. and sur.) appears on stamps of Italy for use in Lero, one of the Aegean Islands, 1912-32.

Lesbos or **Mytilene** an island in the eastern Aegean Sea off the northwest coast of Turkey; part of Greek department of Lesbos; about 623 square miles. Chief town: Mytilene. Stamps issued in 1912 were those of Turkey, overprinted.

Lesotho the former British Crown Colony of Basutoland; became independent Oct. 4, 1966. Capital: Maseru. Issued stamps in 1966.

letra (Port. and Sp.) letter (meaning both correspondence and a letter of the alphabet).

letra redonda (Port.) Roman (refers to a style of type face).

lettera intera (It.) entire letter.

letter boxes receptacles for mail from the public; postal employees clear the boxes at specified intervals.

letter carrier a postman.

Letter Express issued U.S. local stamps in 1844.

letterpress printing a relief printing process by means of type, original plates, stereos, electrotypes, wood, rubber, or composition plates. This process is also called surface printing or typography, but both of these terms lack accuracy.

letter sheet a type of early letter, folded, with a space for the name and address. Modern letter sheets may be private products or productions of post office departments. This is a type of postal stationery similar to aerograms.

letter-tax stamps postal-tax stamps.

Lettland (Ger.) Latvia.

Lettonie (Fr.) Latvia.

lev, leu a silver coin of Bulgaria, Thrace, and Romania. In Bulgaria and Thrace 100 stotinki equal 1 lev. In Romania 100 bani equal 1 leu. Adopted in 1867, when the Latin monetary system was adopted; the name parallels "lira" and "livre".

Levant (insc. and ovpt.) inscribed on stamps of France for use by French offices in Turkey; overprinted on stamps of Great Britain for use by British offices in Turkey in 1905 and on stamps of Poland in 1919 for use by Polish offices in the Turkish Empire.

Lexington the county seat of Holmes County, in west-central Mississippi. The post-master at Lexington, Miss., issued 1- and 10-cent envelopes with stamped impressions known as postal stationery during the U.S. Civil War.

"Ley 8310" (Sp. ovpt.) Law 8310; appears on Peru 1935 postal tax stamps for postal tax use in 1936. Funds raised were for the construction of St. Rosa de Lima Cathedral in Peru.

leyenda (Sp.) inscription.

L.F.F./1¢ (2-line sur.) Liberian Frontier Forces; appears on stamps of Liberia, 1916, a type of military stamp for use by the armed forces away from home.

Libau (ovpt.) appears on stamps of Germany 1919 for use in Latvia.

Liberia a republic in West Africa along the southeast border of Sierra Leone; about 43,000 square miles. Capital: Monrovia. Stamps have been issued since 1860.

Liberty, Va. This town in Virginia issued postmasters' provisional stamps in 1861 as part of the Confederate States of America.

Libia, Libya a kingdom in North Africa on the south coast of Mediterranean Sea; a former Italian colony; about 679,358 square miles. Capitals: Tripoli and Bengazi. As a colony 1912-51, Libia issued stamps of Italy, overprinted; from 1951 United Kingdom of Libia (Libia, Cyrenaica, and Tripolitania) issued stamps.

libretto (It.) booklet.

Libyen (Ger.) Libya.

lichtblau (Ger.) light blue.

Lichtenstein, Alfred F. founder of the Philatelic Foundation, New York; died in 1947.

Liebhaberpreis (Ger.) connoisseur's valuation.

Liechtenstein an independent principality on the east bank of the Rhine River between St. Gallen and Graubunden, cantons of Switzerland; about 62 square miles. Capi-

Lietuva: on stamp of Lithuania

tal: Vaduz. Stamps have been issued since 1912, first under Austrian administration of the post office, then under independent administration, and since 1921 by Swiss authority.

liegend (Ger.) horizontal.

Lietuva or **Lietuvos** (insc. and sur.) appears inscribed on stamps of Lithuania; also appears as part of a surcharge on Russian stamps for use in South Lithuania, 1919. (Illustration: p. 133)

Life Insurance Stamps New Zealand official stamps for the Life Insurance Department in the New Zealand government, in use since 1891.

ligature a single piece of type on which two or more letters are cast, such as ff, ffi.

Lignes Aeriennes F.A.F.L. (sur.) appears on stamps of Syria under Free French administration.

Lignes Aerienne de la France Libre (insc.) appears on stamps of Syria under Free French administration.

lijntanding (Dutch) line perforation.

lila (Ger.) lilac.

Lima Principal (cancel) appears on stamps of Chile, 1879-83, for use in Peru under occupation by Chile.

Limbagan 1593-1943 (sur.) appears on stamps of the Philippines for use under Japanese occupation in 1943. "Limbagan" is the Tagalog word for printing press. (Tagalog is one of the Malayo-Polynesian languages.) The stamps were issued to commemorate the 350th anniversary of printing in the Philippines.

LINDBERGH ENERO 1928 (decorative sur.) appears with design of airplane on 1928 stamps of Costa Rica to honour Charles Lindbergh during his good-will tour of Central America.

LINEA AEREA NACIONAL (Sp. insc.) appears on airmail stamps of Chile, 1931.

linea di separazione (It.) line of separation.

line block British name for any letterpress printing plate in lines, that is, without the dots that occur in half-tones.

line cancellations obliterations consisting of one or more words made on one or more lines to deface postage stamps or postal stationery; more frequently used prior to 1900.

line-engraved issues often applied erroneously to stamps printed by steel engraving. In North America at least, line engraving is done in copper only and no other metal. This mistake referring to line engraving has been made for more than a century; attempts to correct it seem futile.

line engraving engraving in which the effect is obtained by lines or combination of lines by direct incision of the graver on a copper plate and no other metal. A letterpress line engraving is a reproduction of a line drawing, in which the lines or printing areas are in relief, the non-printing areas being etched or routed away. The use of the term "line engraving", when referring to steel-engraved stamps, is incorrect, but the mistake has been made for over a hundred years.

line perforations This term has two meanings depending on the process of manufacture. Canadian postage stamps are perforated in lines when the sheets travel along a table and pass under wheels so arranged that they perforate the gutter paper between each row of postage stamps in one direction; at the end of this, at a right angle, the sheets travel in the other direction and are perforated on a similar machine in the opposite direction. The other type of line perforation is made by a direct strike of one row of perforations at one time, horizontal or vertical.

line pair term used mainly in the United States to indicate two unsevered stamps with the guide line between them.

line roulette straight cuts pierced in postage stamp paper between rows of stamps. This

method of rouletting has been used for economy, speed, and emergency. The first three denominations of Israel in the 1948 issue were line-rouletted in a limited quantity as an emergency measure.

line roulette in colour line roulette made with coloured lines showing the rouletting was produced in one printing operation, to lower costs. Printers' notched rules slit the paper as the stamps were being printed. When printers used this method, the notched rules and the surface of the printing plates were inked at the same time, producing coloured lines.

Linieneinfassung (Ger.) border of lines.

linienfoermig (Ger.) linear, in a straight line.

Linienzaehnung (Ger.) line perforation.

links (Ger.) left.

linotype trademark name of an automatic composing machine, which casts a line of type from a line of matrices assembled by an operator or a computer device.

lion the most heraldic of beasts, represented as lean and fierce.

lion passant, regardant (her.) design of a lion holding a sword in its right forepaw with the sun behind it; central design in a coat of arms printed on the 1868 first issue of Persia (Iran).

lion rampant and crowned (her.) design on stamps of Bulgaria, 1879 and subsequent issues, that have Russian inscriptions.

Lipso or **Lisso** (ovpt.) appears on stamps of Italy for Lipso, one of the Aegean Islands, 1912-22.

lira formerly a silver coin of Italy, Vatican City, and Corfu; it is now made of aluminum. 100 centesimi equal 1 lira or 1 franc. From Latin "libra", a pound; this was at first money of account, but is now a standard unit. In Turkey, 100 kurush equal 1 lira.

lire (sur.) name of a coin; appears on Austrian stamps of 1917-18 inscribed "KuK Feldpost", for Italy under Austrian occupation in 1918.

Lire di Corona (ovpt.) name of a coin; appears on Italian special delivery stamps for use in Dalmatia.

lisse (Fr.) smooth.

Lisso, Lipsos an Italian island of the Dodecanese group in the Aegean Sea, north of Leros; about seven square miles. Stamps issued 1912-32 were of Italy, surcharged or overprinted.

listado (Sp.) laid (paper), listed, striped.

litas a coin of Lithuania and Memel. 100 centai equal 1 litas in Lithuania, and in Memel 100 centu equal 1 litas.

Litauen (Ger.) Lithuania.

lithographed stamps those printed by any of the lithographic processes.

lithographie (Fr.) lithography.

lithography process of planographic printing from a stone or metallic plate on which a design has been suitably prepared.

Lithuania a republic in northern Europe at east end of Baltic Sea, incorporated into U.S.S.R. in 1940; about 21,330 square miles. Capital: Vilnyus. Lithuania (Lietuva) issued stamps from 1918 until 1940, when it became a republic in the U.S.S.R.

litografia (It.) lithography.

litografía (Sp.) lithography.

littoral the coast or shore. For example,
Venezuela is on the northern littoral of South America.

Litwa Srodkowa (ovpt. and insc.) Central Lithuania; appears on stamps of Central Lithuania, 1920-1.

Livingston, Ala. This town in Alabama issued postmasters' provisional stamps in 1861 as part of the Confederate States of America.

Ljubljana, Lubiana, Laibach a city of Slovenia in northwest Jugoslavia. Stamps issued in 1941 under Italian occupation were those of Jugoslavia, overprinted; under German occupation, 1944, stamps were those of Italy surcharged.

Ljubljanska, Ljubljana, or **Laibach** (sur.) German occupation surcharges on stamps of Italy for use in Jugoslavia, 1944, during the German occupation.

ljus (Swed.) light.

L.K.I.S. (part of sur.) appears in the inner corners of a Maltese cross where the spokes converge, and above "KARA/INVALIDIEM/SIOS", for charity stamps of Latvia, 1923. The extra charge of 10 santims went to the Latvian War Invalids Society.

l.l. (1) loose leaf (album) or loose leaves; (2) lower left.

L MARQUES (part of ovpt.) appears on Mozambique newspaper stamps used as newspaper stamps of Lourenço Marques.

L McL (insc.) appears on famous local stamps of Trinidad in 1847, known as "The Lady McLeod" stamps, issued by David Bryce, owner of the steamship with that name. He sold the stamps at five cents each to prepay the mail he carried aboard between Port of Spain and San Fernando, Trinidad.

L.M.C.S.S. Letter Mail Code Sort System, a U.S. experimental operation in 1970 in Cincinnati, Ohio, to speed sorting mail automatically by coding the envelopes. This stage follows the segregating, facing, and cancelling stages in automatic mail handling. This topic becomes part of the tagged-stamps branch of philately.

localized watermarks watermarks so distributed in the paper web that they will appear at a specified place in the cut sheets.

local, locals postage stamps valid for use within a defined region, as opposed to those used in international service. For example, the Lady McLeod local stamps of Trinidad paid carrying charges between Port of Spain and San Fernando.

local mail any kind for local delivery within the area of the post office where the mail was deposited.

Look-alike stamps

Local-Taxe (insc.) appears on 1843-6 stamps of the canton of Zurich in Switzerland.

l'Oceanie (insc.) on stamps of French Polynesia (French Oceania).

Loch (Ger.) hole.

Lochentwertung (Ger.) cancellation by punching.

Lochung (Ger.) punching, perfins (perforated initials).

Lockport, N.Y. This city in New York issued postmasters' provisional stamps in 1846.

Locomotive Express Post issued U.S. local stamps in 1854.

LOCUST CAMPAIGN (ovpt.) appears on regular issues of Jordan for use as semipostals in 1930 to help combat a locust plague.

L.O.F./1928 (ovpt.) appears with design of airplane on Philippines regular-issue stamps of 1917-25 issued Nov. 9, 1928, for the London-Orient flight from London to Manila.

Loja Franca (control ovpt.) used in 1902 for Province of Loja in Ecuador after a fire in Guayaquil. Some specialists believe these overprints are not authorized on postage stamps, just on revenue stamps. Some catalogues do not list them.

Lokalaufdruck (Ger.) local overprint.

Lokalausgabe (Ger.) local issue.

Lokalbref (insc.) appears on local stamps of Sweden issued by the government for use in Stockholm in 1856.

lokalpostmarke (Ger.) a local.

Lokoja a town in Nigeria on the Niger River; used special postmarks 1899-1900. Lokoja was formerly the capital of Northern Nigeria. See Gibbons Part One catalogue.

L.O.L. (airline) Lieutuvos Oro Linijos, Luthuania.

Lombardy-Venetia issued adhesive postage stamps from 1850 to 1865. The history of Lombardy begins in the sixth century A.D. Following their invasion of Italy, the Lombards, a German people, founded a kingdom in the Po Valley. Over 1,000 years

later, Lombardy was ceded to Austria in 1713, became part of Napoleon's Cisalpine Republic in 1797, and part of the Kingdom of Italy in 1805. It was restored to Austria as part of the Lombardo-Venetian kingdom of 1815, but with other states threw off Austrian rule and was annexed to the kingdom of Sardinia in 1859; Venetia was annexed to the kingdom of Italy in 1866.

London Gang (nick.) a group of forgers: A. Benjamin, J. Sarpy, and G. K. Jefferies (alias Kirke) of London. They were indicted and sent to jail; their trial was reported in London newspapers, Jan. 2, 1892.

London prints Postage stamps printed in London, England, as compared with stamps of the same design and value printed elsewhere.

Long Island in the Aegean Sea. Occupied by the British in May 1916. The British issued stamps by overprinting Turkish revenue stamps "G.R.I. POSTAGE", and later issued typewritten stamps. Listed in Gibbons Part One catalogue.

look-alikes (nick.) stamps of nearly identical designs.

loop rounded part of a character, such as the lower part of "g":

loose-leaf albums those made for ring binders or spring-back covers, as opposed to bound albums with permanently bound pages. One type is the peg-fitting albums, with small metal posts that go through punched holes in the album pages.

loose ship letter, loose ship, or **packet-ship letter** markings of Australia and Tasmania, equivalent to paquebot markings struck in other parts of the world. The mail was placed on ships but not cancelled aboard. When the ships arrived in ports of Australia or Tasmania the mail was removed and stamped "loose ship letter" or other similar mark. (Courtesy of M. A. Studd)

Lord Howe Island provisionals The Lord Howe Island post office had no 2-penny stamps when postage was increased in 1930. The postmaster had instructions by cable to use the 1½-penny Sturt design stamps (of Australia) with the endorsement in manuscript "2 d paid P.M. L.H.I." (Postmaster, Lord Howe Island). The postal authorities from Australia had intended that he endorse the envelopes, but he wrote on the stamps. The original Australian stamps were inscribed "CENTENARY" to mark the 100th anniversary of Capt. Charles Sturt's exploration of the Murray River.

Lorraine See ALSACE AND LORRAINE.

lose Marken (Ger.) loose stamps.

Lösen (insc.) appears without country name on 1874-7 postage-due stamps of Sweden (Gibbons states 1874-82).

lot in a stamp auction, one stamp set, cover, or accumulation. Anything given a number in a stamp auction is called a lot.

LOT (airline) Polskie Linie Lotnicze. Point of origin: Poland.

Lothringen (Ger.) Lorraine (Alsace and Lorraine).

Lothringen (ovpt.) on stamps of Germany, 1940, for the German occupation of Lorraine.

LOTNICZA (part of sur.) appears on former stamps of Poland for use in 1947 as airmail stamps.

Lourenço Marques southernmost district of Mozambique in southeast Africa; about 28,800 square miles. Capital: Lourenço Marques. Stamps issued from 1895 to 1922 were inscribed; others were stamps of Mozambique or the Portuguese colonies, overprinted or surcharged; finally stamps of Mozambique were used.

Lowden forgery British 1-pound type of the King Edward VII issue of July 16, 1902. The counterfeits were printed by lithography and cancelled by a Channel Islands marking. Listed in Gibbons Great Britain Specialized catalogue.

lozenge roulette See DIAMOND ROULETTE.

lozenge stamps or **diamond stamps** a stamp that is diamond-shaped. These have been issued by many countries.

L.P. (sur.) appears with new values, and a design similar to the Cross of Lorraine, on

stamps of Russia for use in Latvia under Russian occupation in 1919.

l.r. lower right.

L. & S. Post (ovpt.) appears with two bars each side, on 1931 airmail stamps of Newfoundland for use in 1933 for land and sea postage. The bars obliterated the inscription "Air Mail".

LTSR/1940 VII 21 (ovpt.) appears on stamps of Lithuania issued under Russian occupation in 1940. The overprints were in red on some stamps and blue on others.

Lübeck former autonomous free state on Baltic Sea, now part of Germany; about 116 square miles. Capital: Lübeck. Stamps issued 1859-68; then stamps of the North German Confederation were used.

Lublin issue overprinted Austrian stamps used in Poland. See POLSKA POCZTA.

luchtpost (Dutch) airmail.

LUCHTPOSTDIENST (insc.) appears on airmail stamps of Belgian Congo, 1930.

LUCHTPOSTZEGEL (insc.) appears on 1933 Netherlands airmail stamps.

luchtrecht (Dutch) airmail fee.

Luebeck (Ger.) Lübeck.

Luff, John famous American philatelic writer, author of *The Postage Stamps of the United States* (1902); former editor of Scott's stamp catalogues.

Luftfeldpost (insc.) appears on German military air post stamps.

Luftpost (Ger. and Swed.) airmail.

LUFTPOST (Ger. insc.) appears on etiquettes sent by airmail from German-language countries.

Luftpostausstellung (Ger.) airmail exhibition.

Luftpostdienst (Ger.) airmail service.

Lugpost (Africaans insc.) appears on South Africa airmail stamps.

luminescent describes a stamp that emits light, i.e. glows, when activated by either short- or long-wave ultra-violet (UV) light. (Courtesy of Alfred G. Boerger)

luminescent paper Paper that is luminescent is sometimes used to print stamps for use in automatic mail-handling machinery. Examples are found in Australia issues of 1961; other such issues are noted in stamp catalogues.

Lundy Island an island in the Bristol Channel, England. Issued private labels as local stamps not listed in the popular catalogues.

Lupe (Ger.) magnifying glass.

Luxembourg, Luxemburg a grand duchy of western Europe between Belgium and Germany; about 999 square miles. Capital: Luxembourg. First postage stamps of 1852 portrayed Grand Duke William III in oval

frame with "POSTES" above and values in words and numerals in upper corners, but no country name.

Luxusstueck (Ger.) gem, fine copy, superb object in every respect.

L.V. meter machine limited-value meter postage stamp machine, used for a restricted number of denominations of postage stamp impressions.

Lydenburg town in Transvaal; had stamps of 1900 of the first British occupation overprinted "VRI" *(Victoria Regina et Imperatrix)* and used during the second British occupation. Issued under military authority.

Lyman's British North America Retail Postage Stamp Catalogue a yearly production of the Robert W. Lyman (Canada) Co., Toronto, Ontario, now owned and operated by Jack MacRory. It lists postage stamps of Canada, and of the former British colonies that confederated to become the Dominion of Canada.

Lynchburg, Va. This town in Virginia issued postmasters' provisional stamps and envelopes in 1861 as part of the Confederate States of America.

M

M for the German "Mark der National-bank"; East German currency since 1969.

M (sur. and insc.) appears on the Belgium military parcel-post stamps of 1939 and the 1967 military stamps portraying King Baudouin.

M.A. (ovpt.) Ministerio de Agricultura; appears on official stamps of Argentina, for departmental use by the Ministry of Agriculture, 1913-38.

Macao a Portuguese colony on a peninsula in the southeast part of Macao Island; about 6 square miles. Capital: Macao. Stamps have been issued since 1884.

Macau (ovpt. and insc.) on stamps of Macao.

Macav (insc.) on stamps of Macao, 1930-66.

mace a heavy staff or club, once a weapon of war, but later a symbol of authority or office. As a staff of office, it is carried by an official in parliament in Canada and parts of the British Commonwealth. Shown on stamps of Barbados, 1939, and Canada in 1958.

mace silver coin of China. 10 mace equal 1 tael. "Mace" is the name given by foreigners to the Chinese tsien.

Machin definitives (nick.) British stamps introduced in March 1969, designed after a plaster cast of Queen Elizabeth II by Arnold Machin.

machine calender calender stack located at the end of the paper machine, between the driers and the winder, on which the paper is smoothed out.

machine cancellations the kind applied to mail by machinery, sometimes distinguished by a message enclosed in a rectangular frame. The impressions are usually clear as compared to handstruck cancels.

machine-made describes a product made by means of a machine, in opposition to one made by hand.

machine-made paper paper produced on a paper machine, in contrast to paper made by hand. Even paper experts sometimes have difficulty distinguishing between the two.

machine wire endless woven wire cloth on which the diluted paper stock flows and on which the paper web is formed. The water drains through the wire, depositing the fibres as a felted mass.

Macon, Ga. This city in Georgia issued postmasters' provisional stamps and envelopes in 1861 as part of the Confederate States of America.

Madagascar See MALAGASY REPUBLIC.

Madagaskar (Ger.) Madagascar.

Madeira a Portuguese island group in eastern Atlantic Ocean off coast of Morocco; about 302 square miles. Capital: Funchal. Stamps 1868-98 were those of Portugal, overprinted; since 1898, stamps of Portugal have been used, but in 1928 an inscribed series was issued for obligatory use on certain days in 1928-9. Funds from sales went to help build a museum.

Madère (Fr.) Madeira.

Madrid the capital of Spain. The League of Nations commemoration issue of 1929 included the name "Madrid" in an overprint. Revolutionary stamps were issued in Madrid in 1931; these were stamps of 1920-30 overprinted "Republica".

Mafeking Besieged (sur.) appears with values changed on stamps of Cape of Good Hope and Bechuanaland, 1900, during the Boer War.

Mafekings (nick.) provisional stamps issued in 1900 at Mafeking by order of Major-General Baden-Powell. The first issues listed in catalogues were stamps of Cape of Good Hope, then of Bechuanaland, surcharged. The unusual issue of three stamps in 1900 consisted of photographic prints featuring a bust of the major-general on two different 3-pence stamps and 1-penny stamps showing Sgt. Major Goodyear riding a bicycle.

Mafia a former German island in the Indian Ocean off the coast of Tanzania opposite the mouth of the Rufiji River. Captured by British forces in December 1914. Stamps issued in 1915-16; eventually used stamps of Tanganyika under British mandate. See Gibbons Part One catalogue.

Magdalena once a state, now a department of the Republic of Colombia in South America. Issued postmasters' provisional stamps in 1901.

Magic Letter Express in Richmond, Virginia, issued U.S. local stamps in 1865.

magnifying glass convex lens, which enlarges objects seen through it.

MAGYAR KIR. POSTA (insc.) on stamps of Hungary.

MAGYAR NEPKOZTARSASAG (insc.) appears on 1949 series of three Hungarian stamps to commemorate adoption of the Hungarian People's Republic constitution.

MAGYARORSZAG (insc.) appears on stamps of Hungary.

MAGYAR TANACSKOZTARSASAG (insc. and ovpt.) appears on Hungary 1919 issues of the Soviet Republic, listed with stamps of Hungary. The words mean "Hungarian Soviet Republic".

maiden voyage covers letters posted on board ships on their first voyages.

mail The old French word "malle" was used to designate a leather-, cotton-, or baize-lined saddle-bag in which letters were carried by postal messengers. Later it was anglicized to "male", then "maile", and finally "mail". "Royal mail", therefore, originally meant "royal letterbag". "Royal mail" now is a term embracing the whole postal system. To post or mail a letter originally meant to hand the letter to the postmaster at the post house or in his post office. The mail was then placed in the official postage saddle-bag and conveyed to the next destination by the authorized post-rider, who was either a postman or a postboy depending on his age. (Historical data from a radio broadcast by the late Dr. James Goodwin)

mail boat obliterations obliterations applied to sailors' mail that is carried on a mail ship. Gibbons describes these obliterations this way: "For many years it was supposed that obliterations numbered A80 to A99, B03, B12, B56, B57 and C79 were used at Naval Stations abroad (the whereabouts of which were not known) owing to the fact that these are almost invariably found on sailors' letters. It is definitely known that these obliterations were allotted to mail boats and they are therefore omitted from this catalogue." See BRITISH STAMPS USED ABROAD; also refer to the list under the section on British stamps used abroad in Gibbons Part One catalogue.

mailomat a Pitney-Bowes machine operating as a coin device to provide postage by metered impressions according to the money deposited. These were installed for public use in the United States.

Mailometers (nick.) the U.S. coil stamps privately perforated by the Mailometer Company of Detroit, Michigan. This company operated under various names: The Shermack Mailing Machine Co., Mail-om-eter Co., and Mail-O-Meter Co. The company perforated U.S. stamps from the 1906-8 to the 1916-17 issues. Scott's U.S. Specialized catalogue lists four types of vertical perforations in these issues made for sale in the company vending machines.

mail-tube service See PNEUMATIC POST.

main stroke heavy line or principal stroke of a letter.

maître de poste (Fr.) postmaster (French-Canadian term).

major varieties stamps with some obvious difference in colours, perforations, or paper that is easily seen without a magnifier. May also include obviously different designs.

Majunga issue stamps issued for use in Madagascar, 1895-6. These were French stamps of 1876-84 with manuscript and handstruck surcharges.

make up to set off type matter from galleys into pages, inserting cuts, running heads, and folios.

Makulatur (Ger.) printers' waste.

Malacca a state of about 640 square miles in the Federation of Malay, on the west coast of Malay Peninsula in Southeast Asia. Capital: Malacca. Issued stamps in 1948.

Malagasy Republic formerly known as Madagascar; an island republic in the Indian Ocean off the east coast of South Africa; 227,678 square miles. Capital: Tananarive. From 1884 to 1886, stamps issued by the British consulate in Madagascar were in use; stamps issued since 1889 were general issues of the French Colonies or stamps of the colonies or France surcharged or overprinted; from 1958, stamps of the Malagasy Republic have been issued.

Malawi a republic in the British Commonwealth, independent since July 1964; formerly Nyasaland. Area is 36,100 square miles. Capital: Zomba. Issued stamps 1964.

Malaya (insc.) appears with portrait of a man in oval frame flanked with a palm tree on each side and no other English inscriptions on 1950-61 issues for Perak. There are issues for: Kelantan, 1951; Pahang, 1950; Perak, 1950; Selangor, 1949; and Trengganu, 1949; all have portraits of the respective sultans.

MALAYA appears with no additional name on stamps of Selangor, various issues of 1935-55. Selangor was one of the nine states in the Federation of Malaya, and joined the Federation of Malaysia in 1963.

Malaya, Federated Malay States   a peninsula of about 27,585 square miles in Southeast Asia. Former British Protectorate; joined Federation of Malaysia in 1963. Capital: Kuala Lumpur.

Malayan Federation   also known as Federation of Malaya. Consists of nine states: Johore, Kedah, Kelantan, Negri Sembilan, Pahang, Perak, Perlis, Selangor, and Trengganu, along with the settlements of Penang and Malacca. Stamps bear these inscriptions.

Malayan Postal Union   (insc.) appears on postage-due stamps of the Federated States of Malaya, 1938-65.

Malaysia or **Federation of Malasia**   a federation of fourteen states on the Malay Peninsula in Northwest Borneo in Southeast Asia; part of the British Commonwealth; about 180,417 square miles. Capital: Kuala Lumpur.

mal-burin   an unrepaired mark in a steel-engraved plate showing the place where an engraver's burin slipped and gouged the plate. An excellent example of this appears in one stamp in the sheet of half-cent stamps in the Quebec issue of Canada 1908. This is not a re-entry, as some collectors believe it to be.

Maldive Islands   an independent sultanate comprised of 2,000 islands, totalling about 115 square miles 400 miles southwest of Ceylon in Indian Ocean. Capital: Malé. In 1906, it issued stamps overprinted "MALDIVES" on stamps of Ceylon; in 1909 the first stamps were inscribed for the sultanate.

Maldiven   (Ger.) Maldive Islands.

Maldives Iles   (Fr.) Maldive Islands.

M.A.L.E.R.T.   (airline) point of origin: Hungary; after nationalization in 1946 it became M.A.L.E.V. (Magyar Legikozlegedesi Vallalat), the Hungarian Air Transport.

Mali, Federation of   a temporary republic established Jan. 17, 1959, consisting of the Republic of Senegal and the Sudanese Republic. The two states separated in 1960, becoming the republics of Senegal and Mali.

Mali, Republic of   a republic on the west coast of Africa; had been the Sudanese Republic when that state was federated with the Republic of Senegal. The Republic of Mali declared independence in June 1960, following the termination of the federation, and began to issue postage stamps in 1961. Senegal resumed postal issues in 1960.

Malmédy   (ovpt.) appears on stamps of Belgium, for use in Germany under Belgian occupation, 1919-21.

malo oficial   (Port.) official mail.

Malta   a British Commonwealth island state of about 122 square miles south of Sicily in the Mediterranean. Capital: Valletta. British stamps used 1857-85. From 1860 to 1885 Malta used a half-penny stamp for local mail exclusively.

Malta forerunner   in auction catalogues, postmark or cover struck with some identification from Malta before the colony had postage stamps for international use in 1885. The postmarks of bars and "A 25" that cancelled stamps of Great Britain or were struck on covers are examples of Malta forerunners.

Malte   (Fr.) Malta.

Maltese cross   (1) various designs used as cancellers of British stamps, 1840 and sub-

sequent years. See Gibbons British Specialized catalogue for designs used in different post offices. (2) designs or small decorations used on postage stamps, mainly for issues of Malta; (3) designs of watermarks in British stamps of 1867 and others.

Malteserkreuz   (Ger.) Maltese cross.

Manchukuo, Manchutikuo, or **Manchoukuo** a former state, sometimes referred to as an empire, in eastern Asia. From 1932 to 1945, organized as Japanese territory consisting of three provinces of old Manchuria and Jehol. Became an independent republic early in 1932 after the Japanese occupation in 1931, and an empire in 1934. Capital: Hsinking (Changchun). Issued stamps 1932-45; then Manchukuo returned to China after the Second World War.

Manchuria, Manchow   a territory in northeastern China; issued overprinted stamps in 1927 to defeat speculators who were procuring stamps there and selling them at a profit elsewhere. See MANCHUKUO.

mancoliste   (Fr.) want-list.

MANDATED TERRITORY OF TANGAN-YIKA   (insc.) on stamps of Tanganyika, 1927-31.

mandate stamps often temporary issues of an occupation force in a territory mandated to a country other than the original country that had controlled the land. Many territories were mandated after the First World War. Palestine, a former part of Turkey, for example, was mandated to Great Britain in 1923. Stamps issued after that time were the mandate issues. Previous issues of Palestine were occupation stamps issued under British military occupation forces.

mandat-poste (Fr.) money order.

Mandchoukouo (Fr.) Manchukuo.

Mandchourie (Fr.) Manchuria.

Mandschurei (Ger.) Manchuria.

mangelhaft (Ger.) insufficient, defective.

manila a strong, brownish-coloured, coarse paper, used for wrappers and large envelopes; usually smooth on one side and rough on the other. Paper dealers often spell it "manilla".

Manizales (insc.) appears on local stamps of a private post in Antioquia, a former state of Colombia.

manuel (Fr.) handbook.

Manuel key-types or **Manoel key-types** stamps of Portugal 1910, and for colonial use as in Angola 1912, and Azores 1910.

manuscript cancellations defacing marks made by writing in ink over the postage stamps to prevent their re-use. The writing may include numerals, dates, and names. Manuscript postal obliterations should not be confused with revenue cancels in ink. "Pen cancellations" refer to the oblitera-

tions in lines or crosses only, without writing.

manuscript surcharge or overprint a change made on a stamp by handwriting.

manuscrit (Fr.) manuscript.

Maple leaves issue (nick.) the Canadian postage stamps of 1897 portraying Queen Victoria. One maple leaf appears in each corner, with the denominations printed in English words only around the frame enclosing the Queen's portrait. In the following year the department altered the design to have numerals in the two lower corners of the stamp design. This second issue is known as the "numerals issue".

map paper a strong, well-sized paper, with good folding quality, made from bleached chemical pulp, a mixture of rags and pulp, or all rags, suitable for lithography. Some stamps and envelopes were printed on discarded maps.

map stamps So many hundreds of stamps featuring maps have been issued that some collectors specialize in the subject of map stamps, and call themselves carto-philatelists. The American Topical Association has a Map Stamps Unit for these collectors.

maravedis a copper coin of Spain. 32 maravedis equal 8 cuartos or 1 real. A Moorish gold coin in the eleventh and twelfth centuries, it is now a standard copper coin.

marca de garantía (Sp.) mark of guarantee.

marca de revisão (Port.) control mark.

marco (Sp.) frame.

marge (Fr.) margin.

marge d'intervalle (Fr.) gutter margin.

*Manuscript
surcharge*

Marginal inscription

margem de selo (Port.) margin of stamp.

marges entières (Fr.) full margins.

margin blank space around the edges of postage stamp designs. Not to be confused with the border.

marginal (Swed.) margin.

marginal inscription anything printed on the margins of postage stamp sheets – descriptions, numbers, designs, or printers' names.

marginal marking types There are four main types, to serve these purposes: (1) act as decorations; (2) convey information; (3) give instructions; (4) serve as protection. Some marginal markings decorated the sheets of stamps and served a second purpose as well. For example, the British issue of 1887-92 was printed with panes of stamps divided by coloured bars in the gutters. This helped in the letterpress printing because the bars prevented air from causing vibrations in the paper between the sections of the form that printed the panes. Information in gutters includes security printers' names, their code numbers and letters, and plate number blocks. Instruction marks may be arrows pointing to centre lines, text reading "Mail early in the day", warning notices on pre-cancelled panes of stamps, and registration marks to guide printers in the exact registration of one colour with another. Protection marks used to fill gutters and margins often decorate stamp panes and sheets and also prevent forgers from getting genuine paper for counterfeits. Jubilee lines of all types also protect the plates from wear around the edges. Scores of marginal markings exist.

marginal pair two stamps, vertical or horizontal, with attached marginal paper showing that the stamps adjoined the margin.

marginal watermarks the type in margins of stamp sheets or panes. Examples are often found in Australia, New Zealand, and Papua stamps.

margin copies the sheet stamps with electric-eye (EE) plate number and similar markings. In the United States tagged issues, these copies often show visibly the varying types. (Courtesy of Alfred Boerger)

margin copy in auction catalogues, a stamp adjoining the margin (with some paper attached) from a sheet or pane.

margine (It.) margin.

margin imprint in auction catalogues, refers to blocks, pairs, or strips with some kind of inscription; the inscription is usually described in the catalogue.

Marginal pair

Maria Theresa thaler or dollar a silver coin dated 1780, with the head of Maria Theresa. Known also as the Levant dollar, it is always struck with the date 1780, and its original fineness is retained. It is used in Ethiopia, Zanzibar, and other countries. 16 guerche equal 1 Maria Theresa dollar or 1 menelik dollar.

Mariana Islands, Marianas formerly the Ladrone Islands, an island group in west Pacific Ocean east of Philippine Islands; ceded from Spain to Germany in 1899; about 246 square miles. Capital: Saipan. Stamps issued in 1899 under Spanish dominion were Philippines overprinted issues; in 1899 German stamps overprinted "Marianen" were used. Later, in 1901, German yacht key-types were issued and used until 1919.

MARIANAS ESPANOLAS (Sp. ovpt.) appears on stamps of the Philippines for the Mariana Islands under Spanish administration, 1899.

Marianen (ovpt. and insc.) overprinted on stamps of Germany for the Mariana Islands in 1900 under German administration; in the same year German colonial key-types were inscribed, and these were used until 1916. Gibbons gives the date of the overprints as Nov. 18, 1899, and for the key-types, Jan. 1901.

Marienwerder or **Kwidzyn** a district of northeast Germany bordering on Poland. The 1920 plebiscite resulted in favour of Germany. The plebiscite issue of stamps of that year were stamps of Germany overprinted "Commission Interalliée Marienwerder".

Marietta, Ga. This city in Georgia issued

postmasters' provisional envelopes in 1861 as part of the Confederate States of America.

Marineschiffspost (Ger.) naval post.

Marion, Va. This town in Virginia issued postmasters' provisional stamps in 1861 as part of the Confederate States of America.

maritime mail mail carried by ships; often distinguished by postmarks, cancels, or handstruck stamps, reading "ship letter", "posted at sea", or "paquetbot".

mark a silver coin of Germany, German New Guinea, the Mariana and Marshall Islands, Saar, Samoa, and others. 100 pfennig equal 1 mark. 16 schillings equal 1 mark. The mark was originally a standard weight of precious metal, and was frequently used as money of account. It is now the standard coin of Germany.

Mark der Nationalbank, M (Ger.) East German currency from 1969.

Mark Deutscher Noterbank, MDN (Ger.) East German currency, 1965-9.

Markenanordnung (Ger.) arrangement of stamps.

Markenbild (Ger.) design.

Markenhaendler (Ger.) stamp dealer.

Markenheftchen (Ger.) stamp booklet.

Markenoberrand (Ger.) top margin of stamp.

Markenpreis (Ger.) price of stamp(s).

Markenrand (Ger.) stamp margin.

Markenrolle (Ger.) coil of stamps.

Markensammler (Ger.) stamp collector.

Markensammlung (Ger.) stamp collection.

markka a silver coin of Finland and Karelia. 100 pennia equal 1 markka. Finland's coins are based on the Latin monetary system. The markka was issued in 1865.

Maroc (Fr.) Morocco.

Maroc (insc.) appears on stamps of Morocco as a French protectorate.

Marocco (sur.) appears with values changed on stamps of Germany for use in German offices in Morocco.

Marokko (Ger.) Morocco.

marque de franchise (Fr.) frank.

marque de l'imprimeur (Fr.) imprint.

MARQUEZ DE POMBAL (insc.) appears on postal-tax stamps of Portugal and Azores, 1925. The Marquis was a Portuguese statesman who helped rebuild Lisbon after an earthquake in 1755. The funds were used to erect a monument to him in Lisbon.

marron (Fr.) brown.

Marruecos (Sp.) Morocco.

Marruecos (ovpt. and insc.) on stamps for use in Spanish Morocco.

Marschall-Inseln (ovpt.) appears on 1897 stamps of Germany for use in the Marshall Islands in the west Pacific Ocean. The 1899 overprints read "Marshall-Inseln".

Marshall Iles (Fr.) Marshall Islands.

Marshall Islands a group of atolls and reefs in western Pacific Ocean. Former German possession, mandated to Japan 1920-45; a United States Trust Territory since 1947; about 176 square miles. Capital: Jaluit. Stamps of Germany, overprinted "Marschall-Inseln", were used 1897-9, then inscribed German colonial yacht key-types were used, 1900-16. These colonial stamps of Marshall Islands were surcharged "G.R.I." with new values in British currency and used in 1914-15 in New Britain.

Martinique an island overseas department of France in the Windward Island group of West Indies, of about 385 square miles. Capital: Fort-de-France. From 1886 the island used stamps of the French Colonies, surcharged. Inscribed issues were used 1908-47 with no break. Martinique became a department of France in 1947.

Masaryk, Thomas Garrigue (1850-1937) first president of Czechoslovakia, portrayed on the 1920 issue and on various subsequent postal issues. A statesman and philosopher, he married an American, Charlotte Garrigue, and took her surname as his middle name. He was a professor at Prague, a member of parliament 1891-3, and a critic of Austrian policy. He escaped from Austria in 1914, headed a revolutionary group, and obtained recognition for Czechoslovakia government.

Maschinenpapier (Ger.) machine-made paper.

Masonic cancellations Crude impressions resembling the Masonic symbol of a compass and square were employed by some Canadian and U.S. postmasters who engraved their own postmarking devices or had them made from wood or metal. This was one of the many decorative cancellations used in North America, mainly before 1900.

Mason's New Orleans City Express in New Orleans, Louisiana, issued U.S. local stamps in 1850-7.

Massachusetts one of the thirteen original colonies of the British Commonwealth in North America. The British North American postal system had its origin in Massachusetts.

master plate the printing plate made to be duplicated, but not necessarily used to print stamps.

matasellado (Sp.) cancellation, postmark, letter stamp.

matasello de barras (Sp.) bar cancellation, postmark, letter stamp, cancel formed of bars.

matasello de complacencia (Sp.) cancellation on request.

matasello de mano (Sp.) handstamp.

matched pairs usually refers to the British 1-penny blacks (1840) and penny red stamps (1841) bearing the same corner letters printed by the same plates.

matrice (Fr. and It.) printing term referring to a matrix or mould; in French, also can mean "type".

matrices the paper substance or metal used to cast stereotypes; commonly called "mats", which is the abbreviation.

matrix (1) a brass mould used in type founding and in machine composition; (2) paper or plastic-coated board, bearing the imprint of a form, used for casting a stereotype; (3) a device used for impressing a seal on wax.

mats See MATRICES.

Mauretanien (Ger.) Mauritania.

Maurice Ile (Fr.) Mauritius.

Mauritania a republic in west Africa, former French territory; area variously quoted as 415,900 or 323,310 square miles. Capital: Nouakchott (formerly St. Louis). From 1906-41 French colonial inscribed issues were used, then stamps of French West Africa were used; from 1960 stamps of Islamic Republic have been used.

Mauritanie (Fr.) Mauritania.

Mauritius a British island in a group with Rodriquez (a dependency) and Réunion (a French island). The group is located in the Indian Ocean 400-500 miles east of Madagascar. Its area is about 720 square miles. Capital: Port Louis. Mauritius was the first British colony to issue adhesive postage stamps with government authority, on Sept. 21, 1847; these are among the great rare stamps of the world. Two of the 1-penny, red-orange stamps on a neat folded letter sold for $380,000 on Oct. 21, 1968, in an H. R. Harmer, Inc., auction sale in New York City.

maximum card postcard depicting the illustration used on a stamp, or a similar one. The stamps are usually stuck to the face of the postcard and sometimes cancelled on the first day of the issue. This stamp does not prepay postage in accordance with the U.P.U. regulations, but many exceptions are known.

Mayfair find name given to the discovery of numerous rare stamps bought from British colonial postmasters 1850-60 and discovered sixty to seventy years later in London.

Mayotte a French island in the southeast part of the Comoro group nearest to Madagascar; about 140 square miles. Chief town: Dzaoudzi. Issued inscribed stamps, and some surcharged, from 1892 to 1912. Superseded by stamps of Madagascar, and in 1950 by stamps of the Comoro Islands.

M.B.D. (ovpt.) appears on 1893-4 official stamps of Nandgaon, a feudatory state in central India.

Mbledhja/Kushtetuëse/12-IV-39/XVII (4-line ovpt.) appears on regular issues of Albania 1930, and on airmail stamps of 1939 for Albania under Italian dominion. The same stamps had an additional surcharge in 1939 for airmail use.

M.C. Maltese Cross.

M.C.C. Tour of West Indies (insc.) appears on stamps of Guyana issued Jan. 8, 1968, and of Jamaica, Feb. 8, 1968, to mark the visits of the Marylebone Cricket Club of London to these places. Nine stamps formed small sheets of three identical rows showing a cricket field with a wicketkeeper, batsman, and bowler on separate stamps framed by a decorative border.

McGreely's Express, Alaska issued U.S. local stamps in 1898.

McIntire's City Express Post in New York City, New York, issued U.S. local stamps in 1859.

McMillan's City Despatch Post in Chicago, Illinois, issued U.S. local stamps in 1855.

MDN for the German "Mark Deutscher Noterbank"; East German currency, 1965-9.

MEA (airline) Middle East Airlines Company, S.A. Point of origin: Lebanon.

Mearis' City Despatch Post in Baltimore, Maryland, issued U.S. local stamps in 1846.

Mecklenb. Schwerin (insc.) appears on stamps of Mecklenburg-Schwerin.

Mecklenb. Strelitz (insc.) appears on stamps of Mecklenburg-Strelitz.

Mecklenburg-Schwerin a former grand duchy bordering on Baltic Sea in northern Germany; now part of Germany; about 5,050 square miles. Capital: Schwerin. Stamps issued 1856-67 were superseded by North German Confederation issues in 1868-70.

Mecklenburg-Strelitz a former grand duchy of about 1,131 square miles and then a state of the German empire since 1870. Comprised of two areas, Stargard and Ratzeburg, divided by Mecklenburg-Schwerin. Capital: Neustrelitz. Issued stamps in

1864, but they were superseded by those of the North German Confederation in 1868.

MECKLENBURG VORPOMMERN (insc.) appears on stamps issued in 1945-6 for use in the Russian zone of Germany during the Allied Occupation.

medallions (nick.) stamps featuring portraits in oval frames; popular name mainly of issues from Belgium (1849-50), Canada (1932), and South Africa (1913-22). Not all stamps with oval portraits are known as medallions.

medals on stamps These are featured or included in stamp designs of Victoria (British colony) in 1900. The entire central design features the Victoria Cross. Subsequent issues of Russia, Malta, and other places include medals.

Medellin a city in Colombia; name appears on postage stamp issues of Colombia, 1902.

MEDIA ONZA (Sp. insc.) appears on official stamps of Spain, 1854-63. The Spanish words mean "half ounce", to show weight of the mail.

medio (Sp.) half.

meergruen (Ger.) sea-green.

M.E.F. (ovpt.) Middle East Forces; appears on stamps of Great Britain 1937-42, for use by British offices in Africa.

mehalek an Ethiopian coin, of which 16 equal 1 thaler or talari, used 1928-36.

mehrere (Ger.) several.

mehrfach (Ger.) multiple.

mehrfarbig (Ger.) multicoloured.

Meiji stamps of Japan issues from the first stamps of 1871 to 1913. The Meiji era was named after Emperor Mutsuhito, who opened Japanese ports to the world. A free translation of Meiji might be "the enlightened world". In this period the New Japan began. (Courtesy of Harold Mayeda)

Méjico (Sp. insc.) appears on certain early postage stamps of Mexico.

mellanrum (Swed.) space; hence, a gutter.

Melville, Fred J. (1883-1940) a famous British philatelic writer, author of numerous books about postage stamps of individual states.

Memel a former autonomous state on Baltic Sea, became semi-autonomous under Lithuania; about 1,092 square miles. Capital: Memel. Stamps issued in 1920 were those of Germany, overprinted, and in 1920-3, French stamps surcharged. In 1923-4 occupation stamps were issued under Lithuanian authority.

Memelgebiet (ovpt.) Memel Territory; appears on stamps of Germany for use in Memel.

memorial stamps the type issued to honour some important person after death; those stamps issued immediately after death, however, are known as "mourning stamps".

Memphis, Tenn. This city in Tennessee issued postmasters' provisional stamps and envelopes in 1861 as part of the Confederate States of America.

Menant & Co.'s Express in New Orleans, Louisiana, issued U.S. local stamps in 1853-5.

Mensajerias (ovpt. and insc.) appears on stamps of Uruguay, 1921-59, used as special delivery stamps.

Mercantile Library Association in New York City, New York, issued U.S. local stamps in 1869-75.

Mercator's projection a method of projection in making maps with the meridians and parallels of latitude drawn at right angles throughout.

Mercuries (nick.) stamps featuring the god Mercury, in Roman mythology the son of Jupiter and messenger of the gods. Often identified with the Greek Hermes. The term usually refers to the Austrian newspaper stamps of 1851-6 and 1867-73. A design of the head of Mercury and lightning occurs on special handling stamps of Austria of 1916-21.

Merkur (Ger.) Mercury, the messenger of the gods in Roman mythology.

merone another spelling of "maroon", a brown-red colour.

merry widows (nick.) U.S. 1908 special delivery stamps featuring a helmet of Mercury that could be mistaken for a woman's hat.

Merson key-types French stamps of 1900-27 with a design symbolizing liberty and peace. The designer was Luc-Olivier Merson. The design was used as a colonial key-type, in French Morocco for example.

Mesopotamia a former Turkish province of about 143,250 square miles in western Asia. Capital: Baghdad. See IRAQ.

Messenkope's Union Square Post Office in New York City, New York, issued U.S. local stamps in 1849.

meta (It.) half.

metallic inks Scores of stamps are printed in gold, silver, and copper colours. Some metallic inks were used on certain early stamps of Persia (Iran). Numerous modern stamps are printed with gold-colour inks. Examples: Great Britain 1966 stamps with gold impressed head of Queen Elizabeth II.

metallik a low-grade silver coin of Crete. 4 metallik equal 1 grosion. The coin varied greatly in value, in accordance with the percentage of silver it contained, until it was standardized in 1911.

Metelin (ovpt.) appears on stamps of Russia for use in 1910 by Russian offices in the Turkish Empire. Other overprints include: Constantinople", "Jaffa", "Ierusalem", and "Kerassunde". They are listed in stamp catalogues following stamps of Russia.

meter the detachable, portable part of some meter postage stamp machines. The meter contains the printing dies for words and numerals.

meter advertisement the unofficial portion of meter impression that may carry slogans or advertisements. Meter stamp collectors do not distinguish between slogans and advertisements as do collectors of postally used adhesive postage stamps.

meter borders the lines on meter postage stamps that enclose town marks, and sometimes resemble perforations. These are not the frames.

meter combination cover a cover with meter postage stamps from two machines or with a combination of meter stamps and adhesive postage stamps.

meter denomination or **meter value** the figure on a meter postage stamp showing the amount of postage.

meter design the entire meter postage stamp impression.

meter device a complete meter postage stamp machine.

metered mail letters, parcels, or any mail prepaid by meter postage stamps.

meter frame the outline of the meter postage stamp portion of the meter stamp. This is not the border.

meter frank the denomination part of a meter postage stamp, often with the country name of the place where the meter stamp originated.

meter identification number a meter, license, machine, or permit number appearing in a meter postage stamp impression.

meter impression the entire printed area of a meter postage stamp.

meter indicia the denomination part of a meter postage stamp.

meter key letter sometimes called a prefix; an indication of the make or series of a meter postage stamp machine.

meter postage stamps impressions made by meter machines. Accepted as authorized postage throughout the world.

meter provisional dies the printing plates for stamp portions (franks), values, town names, or country names in meter postage stamps.

meter replacement dies printing plates for a meter postage stamp machine that are changed to replace worn dies. They are sometimes changed for a new owner or for use in another city or town.

Meters, 50 Foreign in U.S. auction catalogues, refers to meter postage stamps from countries other than the United States.

meter tape paper used for meter stamps that are to be pasted on mail. It is used mainly for large parcels or bundles that cannot be put through the machine.

meter town cancel or mark the part of a meter postage stamp showing the place of origin of mail: city, state, province, or country.

Metropolitan Errand and Carrier Express Co. in New York City, New York, issued U.S. local stamps and envelopes 1855-9.

Metropolitan Post Office in New York City, New York, issued U.S. local stamps in 1852-3.

Mexican revolutionary provisionals stamps overprinted 1914-15 for use in various states and towns of Mexico. The following cities or states issued stamps during the Civil War: Acambro, Acaponeta, Aguascalientes, Allende, Baja California, Chihuahua, Ciudad Jaurez, Colima, Hermosillo, León, Matehuala, Mazatlán, Monterrey, Queretaro, Salamanca, San Luis Potosi, San Pedro de Las Colonias, Sonora, Torreon, Viezca, Zacatecas. Most places overprinted their stamps "GOBIERNO CONSTITUCIONALISTA" or abbreviations of it, meaning "constitutional government". Other overprints include monograms and "E.C. TRANSITORIO", Spanish for "Constitutional Army Provisional of Colima". San Luis Potosi used the overprint "E.C. DE M." on three lines meaning "Constitutional Army of Mexico". Refer to Minkus or Gibbons catalogues for details.

Mexico a republic of about 763,944 square miles occupying most of the southern part of North America. Capital: Mexico. Issued stamps in 1856 and for the Empire from April 1864 to May 1867.

Mexico perforation varieties in gauges These occur on stamps of Mexico, 1886-94, caused by breakdown of perforating machines. Started with 11- or 12-gauge perforations and finally came down to 5½ and 6. The gauge means the number of holes in two centimetres. (Courtesy of Dr. R. Maresch)

Mexiko (Ger.) Mexico.

Mexique (Fr.) Mexico.

mezzo (It.) half.

M.F. papers machine-finished papers.

M.G. (Sp. ovpt.) Ministerio de Guerra, the Ministry of War. Appears on stamps of Argentina for official use, 1913-38. (Courtesy of Catálogo de los Sellos Postales de la República Argentina)

M.H. (Sp. ovpt.) Ministerio de Hacienda, the Ministry of Finance. Appears on stamps of Argentina for official use, 1913-38. (Courtesy of Catálogo de los Sellos Postales de la República Argentina.)

MI Michel catalogue.

M.I. (Sp. ovpt.) Ministerio del Interior, the Ministry of the Interior. Appears on stamps of Argentina for official use 1913-38. (Courtesy of Catálogo de los Sellos Postales de la República Argentina.)

M.I. blocks a common term to describe United Nations stamps in blocks with marginal inscriptions, frequently on the sides of the panes or sheets as opposed to the corner blocks of Canada and the United States. Many U.S. postage stamps in blocks also have had marginal inscriptions of the security printers. M.I. blocks should not be confused with Israel blocks, which have tabs bearing marginal inscriptions.

Micanopy, Florida issued postmasters' provisional envelopes in 1861 as part of the Confederate States of America.

Michel catalogues stamp catalogues published in German, and popular throughout the German-speaking areas of Europe.

microfilm mail used during the siege of Paris, 1870. Pigeons carried microfilmed letters, which are now rarities. Microfilm process became popular during the Second World War to reduce bulk in the mail of the armed services.

microphotography art of reducing objects photographically to a microscopic or very small size; used in recording letters, stamps, documents, or books on film for filing and storing purposes. An aid in helping to identify an entire stamp collection.

microscope optical instrument consisting of a lens or combination of lenses, which magnifies minute objects and makes possible the examination of their texture or structure. Its use sometimes helps to detect a forged postage stamp.

Middle Congo a former French colony on the Atlantic coast of Africa at the equator; about 139,000 square miles. Capital: Brazzaville. First stamps were inscribed "Moyen Congo", 1907-22. From 1924 former

Middle Congo stamps were overprinted "Afrique/Equatoriale/Française"; then new designs inscribed "Moyen-Congo" were issued in 1933. Finally, in 1959, the Republic of Congo issued postage stamps with this name inscribed. See FRENCH EQUATORIAL AFRICA; also refer to stamp catalogues and encyclopaedias for historical details.

Middle East Forces stamps British postage stamps overprinted "M.E.F." and used between 1942 and 1947 in Ethiopia, Cyrenaica, Eritrea, some of the Dodecanese islands, and Somalia. The stamps were overprinted in both Cairo and London. In 1950 these stamps became valid for postage in Great Britain. Used copies with local postmarks are much scarcer than stamps used in Britain. See postage stamp catalogues for details about the stamps and their use by British Occupation Forces in the former Italian colonies.

mil (sur.) million; appears on German official stamps 1920-3.

milesimo a copper coin of Uruguay, Cuba, and other countries. 1,000 milesimos equal 1 peso.

Militaerausgabe (Ger.) military issue.

Militaerpostmarke (Ger.) military postage stamp.

MILITARPOST (insc.) appears on stamps of Bosnia and Herzegovina.

military parcel post stamps issues made for military authorities to prepay the postage on parcels. There is a German 1942 issue of this type.

M.P.E.S. Military Postal Express Service. The initials have been used by the U.S. Army Post Office in circular date stamps. These duplex markings are not cancels.

military special delivery stamps Germany and Italy have issued military special delivery and military airmail special delivery stamps. See catalogues for details.

military stamps These are usually issued by occupation forces that have taken control of a country or region. Airmail and parcel post military stamps have been issued, in addition to regular military stamps.

Mill. or **Millièmes** (sur.) appears with numerals of values on stamps of Alexandria for use by the French offices in Egypt.

Millbury, Mass. This town in Massachusetts issued postmasters' provisional stamps in 1846.

mille (Fr.) thousand.

Milledgeville, Ga. This town in Georgia issued postmasters' provisional envelopes in 1861 as part of the Confederate States of

America.

millésime (Fr.) refers to a date, usually on a coin or monument. In philately the word refers to the figures for years or dates of printing in the gutters of certain French regular issues and some French colonial stamps. Similar dates appeared on margins of the Belgian issue of 1849-50 called "Medallions".

millieme a nickel coin of Egypt, Palestine, Cyprus, Cyrenaica, and other countries. 1,000 milliemes equal 1 pound. 10 milliemes equal 1 piastre. The coin is also called "ochr-el-guerche". There are coins representing 2 and 5 milliemes, also of nickel.

millime a nickel coin of Tunisia. 1,000 millimes equal 1 dinar.

millimetre (mm.) the thousandth part of a metre. A French measure used by philatelists everywhere to measure anything on postage stamps; sizes of overprints, surcharges, the distances between lines, the widths or heights of stamp designs, etc. It is not used to measure the thickness of paper, however.

mill wheel cancel type resembling the water wheel of a mill; used on early stamps of Bavaria, 1850 and following years to 1869. Also two official types: closed and open, showing the paddles close and some spaced wider apart. Sometimes called a cogwheel cancel. (Courtesy of Dr. Frank O. Theubert)

milreis a silver coin of Portugal, Brazil, Angola, Azores, Portuguese India, and others. 1,000 reis equal 1 milreis. The milreis of Brazil is one-half the value of the milreis of Portugal. There are gold coins of 2 and 5 milreis.

mils a coin of Israel, Cyprus, Jordan, and others. 1,000 mils equal 1 pound.

MILY ADMN (ovpt.) appears on stamps of Burma, 1945, under British military administration.

Min. Cat. minimum catalogue price.

Mindestpreis (Ger.) the lowest price, minimum price.

mineral pigments pulverized inorganic substances, natural or artificial, such as ochres or prussian blue, which are used in the manufacture of coloured papers and inks.

Min-Hsin-Chu privately owned postal services in China; served the public before 1878. Some of these organizations were established as early as the fifteenth century, in the period of the Mings.

miniature sheet a sheet of stamps of the same denomination and colour as other, larger sheets issued by the same country; should not be confused with souvenir sheets, which are usually a type of commemorative. Reference to U.S.-published catalogues helps to distinguish the exact type. British collectors and publishers often group the two as one classification.

miniatyrblock (Swed.) miniature sheet.

Minkus catalogues postage stamp catalogues published by Minkus Publications, Incorporated, of New York City. These books introduced price lists with totals for complete sets, extensive notes about postal issues, and more illustrations than some catalogues.

minnesblock (Swed.) souvenir sheet.

minor thinnings in auction catalogues, a description indicating that the stamps are thin in some parts and therefore are of a lower quality.

minor varieties stamps differing from the normal in some small way: faulty printing, perforations, papers; the differences, however, are not important enough to gain listings in the popular catalogues.

Min Sheet miniature sheet, in auction catalogues.

mint term used to denote that a stamp or envelope is in the exact condition as it was when issued, with all the original gum if the stamp was made with an adhesive substance. Some stamps, modern Chinese ones, for example, are made without gum. People apply the gum at post office wickets.

mirror print A proof from a die made in relief for stereotypes is a mirror print, a negative. The term also refers to any other kind of proof or impression that can be read in a mirror held in front of it. It will then appear as a positive and can be seen or read.

Mischung (Ger.) mixture.

Mischzaehnung (Ger.) compound perforation.

misplaced overprint a variety in overprinting.

misplaced perforations Sometimes, because of faulty conditions, the perforations do

not appear in the margins. Stamps so perforated are varieties, not errors, and should not command high prices.

missionaries (nick.) the first issue of stamps of Hawaii, so named because many were found on mail from missionaries located in the islands.

mission mixture postage stamps sold in bags or other containers, but with duplication. The name derives from the fact that some religious organizations gather stamps in great quantities for sale to dealers who retail them to collectors.

Missionsmischung (Ger.) mission mixture.

mis-strike a freak in envelope production.

mitad (Sp.) half.

MIT FLUGPOST (Ger. insc.) appears on etiquettes sent by airmail from German-language countries.

Mitte (Ger.) centre.

Mitteilung (Ger.) communication, information.

mittelstark (Ger.) of medium thickness.

Mittelstueck (Ger.) centre piece.

mixed franking mail with stamps of two or more countries. Prior to the formation of the U.P.U., stamps of both the country of origin and the country of delivery, and occasionally countries in transit, were required for mail sent to a foreign land. Loosely refers to stamps of different issues on one cover, postcard, or item of postal stationery.

mixed perforations On some of the 1901-7 stamps of New Zealand, the original perforation was to some extent defective; portions of the sheet having this perforation were patched with strips of paper on the back and reperforated, usually in a different gauge.

mixer a small tank provided with an agitator in which the vehicle and pigment of printing inks are stirred and mixed prior to being processed in the ink mill.

mixture unsorted stamps, often on paper. Mixtures frequently include duplicates.

M.J.I. (Sp. ovpt.) Ministerio de Justicia e Instrucción Pública, the Ministry of Justice and Instruction; on stamps of Argentina for official use 1913-38. (Courtesy of Catálogo de los Sellos Postales de la República Argentina)

mlrd. (sur.) Milliarde, a billion; on German official stamps 1920-3.

M.M. (Sp. ovpt.) Ministerio de Marina, the Ministry of Marine; on stamps of Argentina for official use, 1913-38. (Courtesy of Catálogo de los Sellos Postales de la República Argentina)

M.O.B. money order business; part of handstamps, usually for post office money orders. See M.O.O.N.

Mobile, Ala. This city in Alabama issued postmasters' provisional stamps in 1861 as part of the Confederate States of America.

mobile post offices moving post offices, usually on trucks or vans equipped to handle, sort, and process mail while travelling from one place to another to deliver and pick up mail in communities along highways. Also known as highway post offices (H.P.O.) and travelling post offices (T.P.O.). "Post ambulante" in France and Belgium refers to a post office on a truck or train.

Moçambique (Port. insc.) appears on stamps of Mozambique, also known as Portuguese East Africa (although this name did not appear on the stamps).

model the drawing, photograph, art work, or any other item the engravers use as a guide when they engrave a postage stamp die.

Modène (Fr.) Modena.

Modonesi (insc.) appears on stamps of Modena, a former duchy in northern Italy. Made a duchy in 1452, and annexed to the Cispadane Republic in 1796. Eventually the duchy was united to the dominions of King Victor Emmanuel I in 1860. Stamps were issued in 1852, and by a provisional government in 1859. These stamps were superseded by stamps of Sardinia in 1860, and by those of Italy in 1862.

Moheli an island of the Comoro group in the Mozambique Channel; about 89 square miles. Former French colony. Chief town: Fomboni. Stamps were issued 1906-12; superseded by Madagascar issues, and in 1950 by Comoro Islands postage stamps.

moiré (Fr.) of a watered appearance; a pattern of lines overprinted or underprinted on postage stamps as a security measure.

The 1915 stamps of British Honduras provide examples of the overprints. Some 1872 Mexican stamps imperf. have moiré printing on the backs; this is an example of underprinting.

moitié (Fr.) half; in philately, a stamp cut in two to fill a specified postal rate.

Moldavia a former principality; it included Bessarabia and Bucovina. The United Principalities of Moldavia and Walachia had separate and identical administrations 1858-61, and united in 1861 as Romania. Moldavia issued postage stamps 1858-9, Moldavia and Walachia issued stamps 1862-3, and Romania issued stamps in 1865.

mon, mun a copper coin of Korea and Japan. 100 mon equal 1 tempo or 1 sen. The word means crest or badge. Copper coins representing 5 and 10 mon are issued.

Monaco an independent principality on the Mediterranean Sea near French-Italian border; about 370 acres. Capital: Monaco. First stamps were issued in 1885.

Monarchie-Ausgaben (Ger.) issues of the monarchy.

money letter A variety of handstruck impressions were the forerunners of registered stamps. Mail stamped "money letter" was frequently charged at an increase of one postal rate above its normal rate.

money made from stamps The Russian stamps of 1915-17, printed on the back, served as currency. The printing translates as "Having circulation on par with silver subsidiary coins". See catalogues for details. Other stamps were also encased to use as money.

Mongolei (Ger.) Mongolia.

Mongolia a republic in east central Asia of about 625,783 square miles. Capital: Urga (Ulan Bator). Stamps were issued 1924-45. These are Scott's dates; laws prohibited further data in the United States. Gibbons gives dates of inscribed stamps in use to 1966.

Mongolie (Fr.) Mongolia.

Mongtze, Mong-Tseu, or Mongtseu (surs.) on stamps of Indo-China with values in Chinese currency 1903-8, and in 1919 surcharged in piastres and cents, for use by the French offices in China.

monk white spot on a printed sheet due to poor ink distribution or to the presence of a small piece of paper or other foreign matter. Causes some stamp varieties.

Monmouthshire and Wales combined region stamps one of the regional issues by Great Britain in 1958. Other regionals include: Northern Ireland, Guernsey, Isle of Man, Jersey, and Scotland. Stamps resemble other British issues, but have their own heraldic emblems.

monnaie (Fr.) money, change, mint.

monochrome print stamp printed in one colour.

Monrovia (insc.) appears on Liberia registration stamps with no country name. Other 10-cent registration stamps were inscribed "Harper", "Grenville", "Buchanan", and "Robertsport", all with no country name and no value shown.

monster (Dutch) as a business term, it means "sample" or "pattern"; its philatelic meaning would be "specimen".

Mont-Athos (ovpt.) appears on stamps of Russia for use by the Russian offices in Turkey.

Monte Cassino / 18 v 1944 / Gr 55 (3-line sur.) on Polish stamps of the government in exile in Great Britain. The stamps marked the capture of Monte Cassino, Italy, May 18, 1944, by Polish forces.

Montenegro a former kingdom in southwest Europe, now part of Jugoslavia; about 5,333 square miles. Capital: Cetinje. Stamps were issued from 1874. In 1918 Montenegro united with other countries, and became part of Jugoslavia in 1929. The stamps of Montenegro have no inscriptions in English; all wording is in Cyrillic.

Monténégro (Fr.) Montenegro.

Monterey (partial insc.) Monterrey; appears on stamps of this city in Mexico that issued one value in 1867.

Montevideo (insc.) appears on carrier issues of Uruguay, 1858.

Montgomery, Ala. This city in Alabama issued postmasters' provisional envelopes in 1861 as part of the Confederate States of America.

Montreal prints stamps of Canada, mainly the designs of small queens of 1870 and following years. These were printed in Montreal and called "Montreal prints" to distinguish them from others printed in Ottawa.

Montserrat a British colony since 1956 of about 33 square miles in the West Indies southeast of Puerto Rico. A Leeward Island presidency until 1956. Capital: Plymouth. Issued stamps in 1876. From 1890 to 1903 the key-types of the Leeward Islands were used exclusively.

Montserrat (ovpt.) appears on stamps of Antigua.

M.O.O. Money Order Office; a small impression for money orders in Great Britain and many Commonwealth countries, sometimes used to cancel postage stamps.

Moody's Penny Dispatch in Chicago, Illi-

M.O.O.N. cancellation

nois, issued U.S. local stamps in 1856.

M.O.O.N. Money Order Office Number; a Canadian stamped impression carelessly used to cancel postage stamps, contrary to Canadian post office regulations.

M.O.P. (Sp. ovpt.) Ministerio de Obras Públicas, the Ministry of Public Works; appears on stamps of Argentina for official use, 1913-38. (Courtesy of Catálogo de los Sellos Postales de la República Argentina)

Moque/gua (2-line ovpt.) appears on provisional issues of Arequipa, 1881-5, for Moquegua during the war between Chile and Peru. Also overprinted "Moquea" on stamps of Peru, 1885.

Morelia (insc.) appears on stamps of Morelia, one of the Mexican towns that issued provisional stamps in 1867 during the struggle of Juarez to free Mexico.

mörk (Swed.) dark.

Mormon stamps bogus labels portraying Brigham Young. Fraudulent issue in the United States to deceive stamp collectors. The fraud occurred in the mid 1860s.

Morocco a sultanate of northwest Africa; about 172,104 square miles. Capital: Rabat. Prior to 1956, stamps of French Morocco and Spanish Morocco were used; from 1956 stamps of the independent nation were issued.

Morocco Agencies (ovpt.) appears on Gi-

braltar stamps, 1898 and subsequent years. Then British stamps, surcharged in French, Spanish, and British currency, were used until 1937; also appears with new denominations on stamps of Great Britain for use by British offices in Morocco.

Morvi (insc.) appears on stamps of Morvi, a feudatory state in India. Issued postage stamps 1931-48.

Mosul issue Turkish stamps surcharged on three lines: "Postage/I.E.F. 'D'" and values in annas on third line for use in 1919 in Mesopotamia. Mosul is the name of a province and city, now in Iraq.

MOTHER SALLY TROUPE (insc.) appears on the 1969 Christmas stamps of Guyana. One of the traditions at Christmastime in Guyana is the Masquerade Bands. The appearance of the bands decked in their gay costumes in towns and villages a week before Christmas signifies that the Christmas festivities have begun in Guyana. The long-legged lady shown on the two stamps is a popular masquerade character. The dancer's skill on sixteen-foot high stilts never fails to amaze and amuse the people who watch the progressive festivities. (Courtesy of Crown Agents Stamp Bureau)

Motivsammlung (Ger.) topical collection.

mottle a unique pattern caused by tagging offsetting onto a minimum-contact roll used to reverse web travel on tagging press prior to gumming operation. The 5-cent, 1966 Washington coils most frequently display this condition. (Courtesy of Alfred G. Boerger)

mottled print spotty print due to poor distribution of the ink; certain coloured inks, such as browns and greens, have a tendency to mottle, especially on solids. Stamps with this type of printing are varieties.

motto (her.) word or phrase adopted by choice, not hereditary or part of the achievement, unless so stated.

Mouchon type French stamp design named after Eugene Louis Mouchon, the designer and engraver. The stamp features a seated

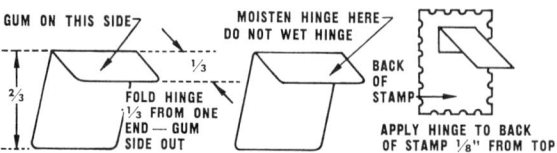

Mount: How to apply to a stamp

woman with a plaque reading "Droits de l'Homme". Stamps were issued in 1900.

Moulin balls metal containers filled with mail. During the siege of Paris, some French people placed mail in the containers, then dropped them into the Seine River, which flows through Paris and on to the English Channel. A small number of the Moulin balls were found as they floated through Paris.

mount (1) a hinge or acetate container for mounting postage stamps; (2) to place any philatelic item on a page or exhibition display; also used to describe the assembling process of exhibits in a stamp show.

Mount Brown catalogues British postage stamp lists in book form, published in 1863 and subsequent years. The 1870 illustrated edition with pages 4″ x 6″ has 204 pages, listing stamps from Austria to Würtemburg, but none are priced. This edition is full of errors.

mounted an old English term usually applied to indicate that a stamp trimmed close to the design had had new margins added.

mourning stamps postage stamps issued as a tribute to a person who has just died. While the United States, Russia, Belgium, and some other countries have issued

Mourning stamp (Greece: F.D. Roosevelt)

stamps to honour their national leaders, rulers, or presidents, Canada has never issued a mourning stamp. Some collectors consider the Canadian Queen Victoria postage stamps of 1893 mourning stamps because they portray the Queen wearing a garment that resembles "widow's weeds".

moveable types term used to distinguish single types from slugs or blocks. Used to print some classical stamps, for example, some of Hawaii, Uganda, British Guiana, and Fiji.

Moyen Congo (insc.) appears on stamps of Middle Congo.

Moyen-Congo (ovpt.) appears at top of

stamps, with "A.E.F." at bottom, on postage-due stamps of France, 1928. A.E.F. stands for "Afrique Equatoriale Française".

Mozambique a Portuguese possession in Southeast Africa of about 297,654 square miles. Capital: Lourenço Marques. Stamps have been issued since 1877.

Mozambique Company a company chartered by Portugal in 1891, which administered the territory of Mozambique Company. First stamps were those of Mozambique, overprinted "COMP A DE MOCAMBIQUE".

Mozambique Company a territory of about 51,881 square miles including Manica and Sofala districts in Mozambique. When the charter expired in 1941, the territory reverted to Mozambique. Capital: Beira. Stamps issued 1892-1918 were those of Mozambique, overprinted or surcharged. Later issues were inscribed "Companhia de Mocambique".

M.Q.E. (sur.) appears with new values on stamps of French Colonies for Martinique, 1887 issue.

M.R.C. (Sp. ovpt.) Ministerio de Relaciones Exteriores y Culto, the Ministry of Foreign Affairs and Religion. Appears on stamps of Argentina for official use, 1913-38. (Courtesy of Catálogo de los Sellos Postales de la República Argentina)

M. SH miniature sheet, in auction catalogues.

mss. manuscript. May refer to a town name, cancel, postal marking, direction for route, or postage rate written on letters or other mail showing amount of postage paid or postage due.

Mt. Everest label a blue sticker resembling a postage stamp; issued in 1924, the label shows the mountain and has the inscription "Mt. Everest Expedition". A swastika is in each corner. Used on postcards and letters with a circular double ring cachet to cancel the labels. It reads "Mt. Everest Expedition 1924" around the circle and "Rongbuk-Glacier Base Camp" inside. The mail was dispatched by postal runners from the camp in Tibet to India, and forwarded by Indian postage stamps. The labels did not pay the postage.

Mt. Lebanon, La. This town in Louisiana issued postmasters' provisional stamps in 1861 as part of the Confederate States of America.

MUBA Swiss Industrial Fair, Basel. A 20-centime stamp honouring this fair features the helmet of Mercury and laurel leaves in a stylized design. Since its modest beginnings in 1916, the fair has become the great industrial and commercial show of Switzerland (Courtesy of the Swiss PTT *Gazette*, 1966)

mudanca de cor (Port.) change of colour.

muddy print stamps in which details are lost due to poor quality of ink, excessive use of ink, causing fill-in of the small non-printing areas, and hence producing stamp varieties.

Muehlradstempel (Ger.) millwheel cancel, cogwheeel cancel.

muestra (Sp.) pattern or specimen.

Mukalla city and capital of the Qu'aiti State of Shihr and Mukalla in Eastern Aden.

Mulready, William the artist who designed the famous letter sheets and envelopes bearing his name for the British post office; authorized in black for 1-penny and blue for 2-pence rates beginning May 6, 1840.

MULTA (insc.) appears on postage-due stamps of Chile, Costa Rica, Ecuador, and other Spanish-language countries.

MULTADA (insc.) appears on postage-due stamps of Chile, 1894-6.

MULTAS (ovpt.) appears on postage-due stamps of Ecuador, 1929.

multicolores (Sp.) multicoloured.

multicolour stamps colour reproductions in which three or more colours are used. Many of the modern stamps are printed in four or more colours.

multiple any number of unsevered stamps in blocks or strips, but not pairs or full panes or sheets.

mültiple (Port.) multiple.

multiple watermark more than one watermark design in a single stamp.

mung a coin of Mongolia. 100 mung equal 1 tugrik.

Muscat and Oman an independent sulta-nate of about 82,000 square miles under British protection, on the southeast Arabian Peninsula on Arabian Sea. Capital: Muscat. Issued stamps in 1944.

Muster (Ger.) type, design, sample, specimen.

Musterdruck (Ger.) specimen.

mute cancellation obliteration without words or numerals; one giving no details.

Mutter und Kind (Ger.) mother and child.

Mutualidad de Correos (Sp. insc.) mutuality for postal services (interchange of mail); hence, postal union. (Courtesy of Dr. R. Maresch)

M. V.i.R. (Ger.) Militar Verwaltung in Rumanien, Military Administration in Romania. Various overprints and surcharges on German and Romanian stamps 1917-18, for use in Romania under German occupation.

M.V. meter machine multi-value meter postage stamp machine, capable of impressing any value of postage on mail or on tapes.

M.V.S.N. (It.) 1926 and 1928 Milizia Volontaria Sicurezza Nazionale; means Valuntary Militia for National Defense.

MX Maltese cross; usually refers to cancels.

Myaungmya issue stamps of Burma issued under Japanese occupation in 1942. Myaungmya is a district in the Irrawaddy division of Lower Burma. Town of the same name is the capital.

Mytilene alternate name for Lesbos, island in east Aegean Sea off northwest coast of Turkey, part of Greek department of Lesbos; about 623 square miles. Chief town: Mytilene. Stamps issued in 1912 were those of Turkey, overprinted.

N

N.A.A.F.I. (insc.) Navy, Army, Air Force Institutes; from an emblem on some British Forces in Egypt postal labels of 1932.

Naba souvenir sheet sheet inscribed "NABA 1934 ZURICH" and issued Sept. 29, 1934, for the Swiss National Philatelic Exhibition at Zurich.

Nabha a state in the Punjab region of India; 966 square miles. Issued stamps in 1885. Capital: Nabha.

NABHA STATE (ovpt.) appears on stamps of India for use in Nabha, 1942-6.

N.A.B.S.A. (airline) Navegacão Aérea Brasileira, S.A., Brazil.

NAC (airline) New Zealand National Airways Corporation. Point of origin: New Zealand.

Nachahmung (Ger.) imitation.

Nachdruck (Ger.) reprint.

nachgraviert (Ger.) re-engraved, retouched.

nachgummiert (Ger.) regummed.

Nachkriegsausgabe (Ger.) post-war issue.

NACHMARKE 7½ (Ger. sur.) signifies new value surcharged on Austrian regular-issue stamp for use as postage-due stamps in 1921.

NACH PORTO (insc.) appears on postage-due stamps of Liechtenstein issued under Swiss administration of the post office.

nadelstichartig durchstochen (Ger.) pin-perforated.

Naffy seals or labels (nick.) British Forces in Egypt letter stamps for use by the men and their families for personal mail from Egypt to Great Britain. Naffy stands for "Navy, Army, Airforce Institutes".

name blocks four or more stamps in blocks of flag stamps of the United States, 1943-4. They bear names of countries overrun by German forces during the Second World War, but no plate numbers.

Nandgam (insc.) on stamps of Nandgaon, a feudatory state in central India of 871 square miles. Issued stamps 1891 (Scott's) or 1892 (Gibbons). Capital: Rajnandgaon.

Nandgame (Fr.) Nandgaon.

Nansei Islands See RYUKYU ISLANDS.

não denteado (Port.) unperforated.

NA O'SWIATE (insc.) for public instruction; appears on semi-postal stamps of Poland, 1927. The surtax was for educational work.

naphthadag stamps special British issues for use in electronic machinery produced to handle mail. On Nov. 19, 1957, the innovation of electronic post office machinery and electronic stamps with graphite lines on the back began at Southampton, England. Black lines distinguish the naphthadag stamps.

Napier perforating machines These were made by David Napier and Son of Lambeth, a metropolitan borough of London, England. The Napier machines were used when Britain introduced perforated stamps in 1854.

Naples a seaport and industrial commune, founded about 600 B.C. United with Sicily at various times in history. Naples issued stamps in 1858, Sicily in 1859, and the Neapolitan Provinces in 1861. These stamps were superseded by stamps of Italy in 1862.

Napoletana (insc.) on stamps of Naples, 1858. See TWO SICILIES.

naranja (Sp.) orange.

Nashville, Tenn. This city in Tennessee issued postmasters' provisional stamps and envelopes in 1861 as part of the Confederate States of America.

NA SKARB (insc.) National Funds; appears on semi-postal stamps of Poland, 1924. Stamps were sold at a premium of 50 groszy each for charity.

NA/SLASK/2 M. (sur.) appears on the 1920 regular issue of Central Lithuania, for use as a semi-postal stamp in 1921. The surcharge means "2 marks for Silesia".

Natal a former British Crown Colony on the southeast coast of South Africa on the Indian Ocean. Zululand province was annexed to Natal in 1897. Total area is 35,-285 square miles including Zululand. In 1910 Natal united with other British colonies: Cape of Good Hope, Transvaal and Orange Free State to form the Union of South Africa. It is now a province in the Republic of South Africa. Natal capital: Pietermaritzburg.

Natal (insc.) appears on stamps of Natal,

1857-1909.

National Airlines, Inc. (airline) Point of origin: United States.

Nationaler Verwaltungsausschuss (ovpt.) appears on stamps of Montenegro under German occupation in 1943.

National issue National Bank Note Company printings of U.S. stamps 1870-1.

NATIONALSOZIAL DEUTSCHE ARBEI-TERPARTEI (insc.) appears on 1938 German franchise stamps for use by the National Socialist German Workers' Party. "NATIONALSOZIAL" is located vertically on the left of the stamp, "ARBEITERPARTEI" is on the right, and "DEUTSCHE" is at the top.

NATIONS UNIES/OFFICE EUROPEEN (2-line ovpt.) appears on Switzerland stamps for the United Nations European office. Listed with stamps of Switzerland in catalogues.

native paper often yellowish or greyish in wove or laid types. The early issues of Kashmir and some of the stamps and cards of Nepal were printed on native paper. It was handmade.

Native States (1) the states of Straits Settlements; (2) the states of India.

NATO North Atlantic Treaty Organization.

Nauru a former German island possession of about 8½ square miles on the equator between Solomon and Marshall islands in the western Pacific. Mandated to British Empire after First World War; since 1947 a United Nations Trusteeship Territory, administered by Australia. Issued stamps in 1916.

naval cancellations postmarks applied to mail on board naval ships.

naval covers envelopes with impressions to show that a member of some naval attachment or in some branch of the navy posted the letters.

naval philatelists collectors of stamps, postal stationery, or postmarks related to navies of the world, especially those from ships. Sometimes called "navophilatelists".

navidad (Sp.) Christmas (day), nativity.

Navy Dept. (insc.) on U.S. official stamps of 1873 for the Navy Department.

naye paise a copper coin of India, Bahrain, and other countries, mainly in the Middle East. 100 naye paise equal 1 rupee.

NCE (sur.) appears on stamps of French Colonies, 1881-1915, for use in New Caledonia.

N.D. HRVATSKA (insc.) appears on stamps of Croatia 1943-4, an independent state 1941-5 that later became a part of Jugoslavia.

Neapolitan Provinces a temporary administration that included Naples. Issued stamps in 1861; superseded by stamps of Italy in 1862.

near airs (nick.) stamps in denominations of airmail rates, but without the words "air mail" or "airmail" printed on them.

Nebr. (ovpt.) Nebraska; appears on 1926-7 U.S. stamps, issued officially May 1, 1929, to help prevent losses from post office burglaries. Used about a year. Similar stamps were overprinted "Kans." for the same use.

Ned. Antillen, or **Nederlandse Antillen** (insc.) appears on stamps of The Netherlands Antilles, formerly Curaçao.

Nederland (insc.) on stamps of The Netherlands.

Nederlandsch-Indie (insc.) on stamps of the Dutch Indies.

Ned-Indie or **Ned. Indie** (insc.) on stamps of the Dutch Indies.

Nederl-Indie (insc.) appears on stamps of the Dutch Indies.

nedtill (Swed.) bottom.

negative in photography and in photoengraving, the plate or film made from an image or a positive and just the reverse of it; dark areas become light and light areas become dark.

negligible thin spot in auction catalogues, describes a fault in a stamp.

négociant en timbres (Fr.) stamp dealer.

NEGOUS TEFERI (ovpt.) appears with crown, cross, and Ethiopian characters handstamped in red, violet, or black, on commemorative issue of Ethiopia, Oct. 7, 1928, to mark the coronation of Regent Tafari Makonen as Negus (king). He was proclaimed King of Kings of Abyssinia under the name Haile Selassie I, and an overprinted series in 1930 commemorated this.

Negreen find See KENNEDY FIND.

Negri Sembilan a state of the Federation of Malaysia, on west coast of Malay Peninsula, of about 2,580 square miles. Capital: Seremban. First stamps in 1891 for Negri Sembilan were overprinted on stamps of Straits Settlements.

negro (Sp.) black.

Nejd or **Najd** a former kingdom in central Arabia, now part of Saudi Arabia; about 447,000 square miles. Capital: Riyadh. First stamps, issued in 1925, were overprints handstamped on stamps of Turkey or Hejaz; in 1932 Nejd and Hejaz united as Saudi Arabia and stamps were issued with the inscribed name.

NEMZETI MAGYAR KORMANY Szeget,

1919 (ovpt.) appears on 1919 semi-postal stamps of Hungary. "NEMZETI" is located at the top of the stamp, "MAGYAR" is located vertically at left, "KORMANY" vertically at right, and "Szeged, 1919" at the bottom.

Nennwert (Ger.) face value.

Nepal a kingdom of about 54,000 square miles between Tibet and India in Himalaya Mountains. Capital: Kathmandu. Issued stamps in 1881.

Ne Pas Livrer le Dimanche (insc.) appears on certain labels attached to Belgian stamps, meaning "Do not deliver on Sunday." These are called "dominical labels".

nero (It.) black.

Nesbitt envelopes postal stationery with stamps of the United States printed on them. George F. Nesbitt & Co. made the post office envelopes, 1853-70. "Nesbitt types" refers to post office envelopes made by the Nesbitt company, as opposed to those made by Plimpton Manufacturing, Morgan Envelope Co., and others. See Scott's U.S. Specialized catalogue for details.

Netherlands a kingdom of about 13,433 square miles in northwest Europe on the North Sea. It includes the area that was the former autonomous country of Holland, which was divided in 1840 into the two provinces of North and South Holland. Capitals: Amsterday and The Hague. First stamps were issued in 1852. The postage stamps are inscribed "Nederland", not "Holland".

Netherlands Antilles or **Curaçao** a territory of The Netherlands in West Indies; about 403 square miles. Capital: Willemstad. First stamps were issued in 1873. Scott's U.S. Specialized catalogue for de-

NETTA FUORI E SPORCA DENTRO (It.) a disinfected mark used on letters about 1780, meaning "clean inside and dirty outside." (Courtesy of Herbert Dube, from mail in his collection of fumigated letters)

NETTO DI FUORA E DI DENTRO (It.) a disinfecting marking on letters about 1883, meaning "clean outside and inside". (Courtesy of Herbert Dube, from mail in his collection of fumigated letters)

NETTO TUTTO (It.) a disinfected mark known on mail in Europe about 1831. The handstruck impression means "completely purified". Mail was fumigated at stations located near borders of two countries because people believed that the letters carried germs that would cause plagues.

(Courtesy of Herbert Dube)

Netz (Ger.) network, net.

Neuauflage (Ger.) new edition.

Neudruck (Ger.) reprint.

Neue Hebriden (Ger.) New Hebrides.

neuf (Fr.) (1) mint or new, referring to postage stamps; (2) nine.

neuf avec gomme (Fr.) mint.

neuf sans gomme (Fr.) unused, no gum.

Neufundland (Ger.) Newfoundland.

neukreuzer a coin of Austria. 100 neukreuzer equal 1 gulden.

Neuschottland (Ger.) Nova Scotia.

Neuseeland (Ger.) New Zealand.

Neusuedwales (Ger.) New South Wales.

nuevo (Sp.) new.

never-issued stamps those prepared but never placed in use.

Nevis a former presidency of about 50 square miles in British Leeward Island colony, southeast of Puerto Rico in the West Indies. Issued stamps 1861-90; from 1890-1903 Leeward Island key-type stamps were used; from 1903 stamps of St. Kitts-Nevis and stamps of the Leeward Islands were used; and from 1952 stamps of Saint Christopher-Nevis-Anguilla were used.

New Britain an Australian military government island territory of about 13,000 square miles northeast of New Guinea in the South Pacific. Prior to First World War was part of German New Guinea, called "Neu-Pommern". German stamps were overprinted "Deutsch-Neu-Guinea" in 1898; German colonial yacht key-types of 1901 were inscribed "Deutsch-Neu-Guinea" and "Deutsch-Neuguinea". Capital: Rabaul.

New Brunswick an eastern Canadian province of about 27,985 square miles on the Gulf of St. Lawrence and Bay of Fundy; once part of the British province of Nova Scotia. Capital: Fredericton. Issued its own adhesive postage stamps in 1851 and used them until Confederation in 1867, then used Dominion of Canada postage from 1868 to the present.

New Caledonia a French territory in the southwestern Pacific Ocean, east of Queensland; variously quoted as about 6,531 square miles and 8,548 square miles. Capital: Noumea. First stamp, portraying Napoleon, was used Jan. 1, 1860, to Sept. 17, 1862. From then French colonial stamps were used until 1881, when the issue of French stamps was surcharged in various type faces. In 1905 the first regular issue of pictorial stamps was introduced.

Newfoundland an eastern Canadian island

province of about 42,734 square miles in the Atlantic; a self-governing British Empire dominion until 1933, and a British Crown Colony until union with Canada in 1949. Capital: St John's. Issued first adhesive stamps in 1857. Now uses Canadian postage stamps and postal facilities, as the tenth province of Canada.

New Granada a Spanish vice-royalty on the northwest coast of South America, conquered and named by Spaniards 1537-8. Part of Peru until 1718; freed from Spanish rule in 1819; reorganized into Granadine Confederation in 1858, the United States of New Granada in 1861, and the United States of Colombia in 1886. The Granadine Confederation issued stamps in 1859-60, the United States of New Granada in 1861, and the United States of Colombia in 1862.

New Guinea, Territory of a territory of about 93,000 square miles on the northeast part of the island of New Guinea. This former German possession was a mandate administered by Australia and included several nearby islands. Capital: Rabaul. Issued stamps in 1914. See PAPUA AND NEW GUINEA.

New Haven, Conn. This city in Connecticut issued postmasters' provisional envelopes in 1845.

New Hebrides a group of islands in the southwestern Pacific Ocean; a condominium under Britain and France; about 5,700 square miles. Capital: Vila. Stamps were issued by both countries; French issues date from 1908, with the early issues being those of New Caledonia overprinted "Nouvelles Hébrides"; early British issues date from 1908, and were those of Fiji overprinted "New Hebrides Condominium".

new issues stamps or postal stationery items as they appear for sale to the public. Many collectors subscribe to new issue services from dealers.

new issue service Some stamp dealers provide their customers with the new stamps of their choice as soon as possible after the day of issue.

New Orleans, La. This city in Louisiana issued postmasters' provisional stamps and envelopes in 1861 as part of the Confederate States of America.

New Republic a temporary state formerly part of Zululand. In January 1903, the territory joined with Natal, the British colony in South Africa. Later it was annexed to South African Republic as a district. First stamps, in 1886, were printed "Nieuwe Re-

publiek".

New Smyrna, Florida issued postmasters' provisional stamps in 1861 as part of the Confederate States of America.

New South Wales a former British Crown Colony of about 309,432 square miles in southeast Australia; united with five other British colonies in 1901 to form the Commonwealth of Australia. Capital: Sydney. Issued stamps in 1850.

newspaper key-types term sometimes used to describe some Portuguese colonial designs of newspaper or journal stamps.

newspaper stamps postage stamps specially made for mailing newspapers. Some newspaper stamps have been printed on the newspapers, usually on the front page; oth-

Newspaper stamp (France)

ers have been made by the United States, Belgium, and Austria specifically for mailing newspapers.

newspaper-tax stamps stamps printed or impressed on newspapers. The British newspaper-tax stamps, printed on the front

pages of newspapers, also covered transportation charges. They are not listed in the popular stamp catalogues.

New York City This city in New York had postmasters' provisional stamps in 1845, carriers in 1842 and following years, and locals during the same general period.

New York City Express Post in New York City, New York, issued U.S. local stamps in 1847.

New Zealand a group of islands in the Pacific Ocean about 1,200 miles southeast of Australia. Self-governing dominion in British Commonwealth of Nations. Capital: Wellington. First stamps issued July 1855.

NEZAVISNA DRZAVA HRVATSKA (ovpt. and insc.) appears overprinted on various issues of Jugoslavia for use in Croatia in 1941; also inscribed on stamps of Croatia 1943.

N.F. (ovpt.) Nyasaland Force; appears on stamps of Nyasaland Protectorate in 1916, issued under British occupation of German East Africa.

N.G. no gum.

ngultrum a coin of Bhutan. 100 chetrum equal 1 ngultrum or rupee.

Niassa See NYASSA.

nibs an uncommon term for the teeth parts of perforations. "Teeth" is a more accurate word.

Nicaragua a republic of about 57,145 square miles between Honduras and Costa Rica in Central America. Capital: Managua. Stamps first issued in 1862.

nichtamtlich (Ger.) unofficial.

nichtamtliche Lochungen (Ger.) unofficial perforations.

nickel-faced stereo a duplicate printing plate coated with nickel to increase its wearability and life.

Niederlaendisch-Indien (Ger.) Dutch Indies.

Niederlande (Ger.) The Netherlands.

Nieuw Guinea (insc.) on stamps of Dutch New Guinea.

Nieuwe Republiek (insc.) on stamps of the New Republic.

Niger a republic in northern Africa; formerly a French territory; about 493,822 square miles. Capital: Niamey. First stamps of the colony, issued in 1921-2, were those of Upper Senegal and Niger, overprinted or surcharged; from 1959 stamps of the republic were issued.

Niger Coast and River postmarks "Lokoja", "Abutshi", "Benin", "Bonny River", "Brass River", "Forcados River", and "Old Calabar River" were among postmarks or cancels on British stamps used 1889-92 from the Niger Coast and River communities.

Niger Coast Protectorate formerly called the Oil Rivers Protectorate. A British Protectorate in western Africa; organized as Oil Rivers Protectorate in 1892 and enlarged in 1893, then renamed Niger Coast Protectorate. With another enlargement in 1900 the area became the Protectorate of Southern Nigeria. Niger Coast Protectorate, located on the Gulf of Guinea, issued stamps overprinted "Oil Rivers/British/ Protectorate" in 1892, surcharged and overprinted issues in 1892-3, and inscribed stamps in 1894-8. In January 1900, stamps were superseded by Northern and Southern Nigerian issues. Details are given in catalogues.

Nigeria a republic since 1963 of about 372,-674 square miles on Gulf of Guinea on African west coast, formerly a British colony and protectorate. Capital: Lagos. Issued stamps in 1914.

Nigérie (Fr.) Nigeria.

Nigérie du Nord (Fr.) Northern Nigeria.

Nigérie du Sud (Fr.) Southern Nigeria.

Nigerkueste (Ger.) Niger Coast.

Niger Territory a territory in eastern region of French West Africa. Originally (1904) a part of Upper Senegal Niger colony. Made a military territory in 1912 and a civil colony in 1922. First stamps were those of Upper Senegal and Niger overprinted "Territoire/du Niger", 1921-6. Became Republic of the Niger on Dec. 19, 1958, but stamps of the republic were not issued until 1960. For about two years Niger used stamps of French West Africa, until republican stamps came into use.

Nikaria or **Nicaria** See ICARIA.

Nippon (insc.) meaning "place where the sun rises"; appears on modern stamps of Japan.

Nisiro or **Nisyros** an Italian island of the Dodecanese group in the Aegean Sea, south of Kos; about 18 square miles. Stamps issued 1912-32 were Italian stamps overprinted "Nisiro".

Niuafoou Island an island in the extreme northern part of the Tonga Archipelago in the southwest central Pacific Ocean. Owing to steep shores and difficult landing, mail was delivered in metal cans. Because of this, it became known as the Tin Can Island.

Niue (ovpt.) appears on stamps of New Zealand for use in Niue, 1902. It was annexed to New Zealand with Cook Islands in 1901.

Niue or **Savage Island** a New Zealand dependency since 1901 of about 100 square miles, northeast of New Zealand in the South Pacific. Capital: Alofi. Issued stamps in 1902.

NIWIN (sur.) appears with new values on 1923 regular-issue stamps for use in 1947 as semi-postal stamps for the Netherlands Indies relief organization, National Inspanning Welzijnszorg in Nederlandsch Indie.

nk in auction catalogues, indicates a nick in margin.

Nlle. Calédonie (ovpt. and insc.) appears on stamps of New Caledonia.

nodes a Canadian term developed from the Latin "nodus", meaning "knot"; small points of paper on the edges of roll postage stamps (coils). Rolls of 100 stamps are packed in longer rolls, ten to a package. Postal clerks break off the number of single rolls customers require. The nodes hold the ten-roll pack together, but are easy to break apart in single rolls or more. Nodes exist on the coil stamps portraying Queen Elizabeth II and on stamps of 100 to a roll, but not on the larger rolls.

NO HAY ESTAMPILLAS (Sp. insc.) no stamps available; appears on certain postmasters' provisional stamps of Cauca when it was a state in Colombia.

noir, noire (Fr.) black.

nom du district (Fr.) district name.

Nominalwert (Ger.) face value.

non-curling gummed paper To prevent curling of stamps, the dried gum film is broken or cracked. Many modern stamps are printed on paper treated this way.

non-dentelé (Fr.) imperforate.

non dentellato (It.) imperforate, not perforated.

Nordamerikafahrt (Ger.) North America flight.

Nordborneo (Ger.) North Borneo.

Norddeutscher Bund (Ger.) North German Federation.

NORDDEUTSCHER POSTBEZIRK (insc.) North German Postal District; appears on stamps of North German Confederation, 1868. The official stamps of 1870 are inscribed "NORD-DEUTSCHE-POST".

Nordnigerien (Ger.) North Nigeria.

Nord-Ouest Pacifique, Iles du (Fr.) North West Pacific Islands.

Nord-Rhodesien (Ger.) Northern Rhodesia.

NOREG (insc.) appears on a 1951 commemorative set of three stamps to mark the centenary of the birth of Arne Garborg (1851-1924), Norwegian poet, novelist, and speech reformer. He urged the people of Norway to use the ancient spelling "Noreg"

for the Norwegian country name, instead of "Norge".

Norfolk Island an Australian dependency of about 13½ square miles, 800 miles east of Australia in the South Pacific. Issued stamps in 1947.

Norfolk Island (sur.) appears with new value on an Australia provisional stamp for a revised postal rate in Norfolk Island, Dec. 7, 1959.

Norge (insc.) appears on stamps of Norway.

normal in general reference to the tagged stamps of the United States, any postage stamp that was not printed on luminescent paper. (Courtesy of Alfred G. Boerger)

normal watermarks ones that can be viewed in their correct positions from the front of the stamps. See WATERMARK POSITIONS.

North Borneo a British Crown Colony of about 29,500 square miles in the northeast part of Borneo in the Malay Archipelago; joined the Federation of Malaysia in 1963. Capital: Jesselton. Issued stamps in 1883.

North China stamps issues from June 1941 until 1945 made for the Japanese-controlled areas of North China; mainly overprinted issues until Feb. 7 and Aug. 15, 1945, when pictorial stamps in ten designs went on sale. Stamps of North China were discontinued after the defeat of Japan in the Second World War. See catalogues for details.

North Epirus formerly part of Greece, now in Southern Albania. Stamps of Greece overprinted, were used during the Greek occupation of Northern Epirus, 1914-16, and also in 1940-1.

Northern Council Four member countries of the Council of Europe (Denmark, Iceland, Norway, and Sweden) made an alliance with Finland, called "Nordisk Rad" (Northern Council). This pact of the five Scandinavian countries brought them into closest co-operation in their economies, culture, and social welfare. On Oct. 30, 1956, the postal administration of the five countries decided to issue special stamps in honour of the Day of Northern Countries. Printed in the same colours and with a common motif, the stamps differ only in the name of the issuing country. The motif represents five flying swans from a poem by Hans Hartvig Seedorff Pedersen, "Svanerne fra Norden" ("The Swans of the North").

Northern Ireland stamps one of the regional issues by Great Britain in 1958. Other regionals are for Guernsey, Jersey, Isle of Man, Scotland, and the combined region of

Wales and Monmouthshire. Stamps resemble other British issues but have their own heraldic emblems.

Northern Nigeria a former British Protectorate of about 281,703 square miles in West Africa adjoining Southern Nigeria. Capital: Zungeru. Issued stamps 1900-12; in 1914 stamps of Nigeria were used.

Northern Rhodesia a former British Protectorate separated from Southern Rhodesia almost entirely by the Zambesi River; area variously quoted as 287,640 square miles and 290,320 square miles. The British South Africa Company administered Northern Rhodesia and most of the country that became Nyasaland in southern Africa. In 1924 Northern Rhodesia became a British Protectorate and in 1925-53 issued stamps inscribed "Northern Rhodesia". The Federation of Southern Rhodesia, Northern Rhodesia, and Nyasaland was created in 1953, and issued stamps in 1954-63 inscribed "Rhodesia & Nyasaland". The Federation was dissolved at the end of 1963. Stamps inscribed "Northern Rhodesia" reappeared for less than one year, and were replaced by stamps inscribed "Zambia", the name Northern Rhodesia took when it became an independent republic on Oct. 24, 1964.

North German Confederation formed 1815-66. By 1866 most German states were included in the customs union. Prussia became leader of the German unification, accomplished in 1871. The North German Confederation issued stamps 1868-70, then used stamps of the German Empire from Jan. 1, 1872.

North Ingermanland a former autonomous state in northern Russia, now part of the U.S.S.R. Capital: Kirjasalo. Stamps inscribed "Inkeri" were issued in 1920, during a brief period of independence.

North Korea See KOREA. Russian occupation stamps were issued in 1946 and stamps of the Korean People's Republic were issued in 1948.

North Viet Nam or **Democratic Republic of Viet Nam** a republic in Southeast Asia; formerly the northern portion of the kingdom of Viet Nam; about 57,900 square miles. Capital: Hanoi. Issued postage stamps since 1945, but these are not listed in stamp catalogues published in the United States.

North West Pacific Islands or **Northwestern Islands** a widely scattered group of islands north of New Guinea, including part of New Guinea and islands of the Bismarck Archipelago. Stamps issued 1915-22 were Australian issues overprinted "N.W./Pacific/Islands" and used in former German Pacific islands. Refer to stamp catalogues for various issues.

Norvège (Fr.) Norway.

Norway a kingdom in northwest Europe on the western part of the Scandinavian peninsula; about 119,085 square miles. Capital: Oslo. The first stamps were issued in 1855.

Norwegen (Ger.) Norway.

Nossi-Bé or **Nosy-Be** an island of about 113 square miles in the northeast Mozambique Channel off the northwest coast of Madagascar; former French Protectorate. Chief town: Hellville. From 1889 to 1893, stamps of French Colonies were used, overprinted and surcharged; in 1894 they were inscribed; after that Madagascar stamps were used.

Notausgabe (Ger.) emergency issue.

note brief explanation or statement, such as a footnote or sidenote, usually set in smaller type than the main text. Stamp catalogues contain valuable notes for collectors and dealers.

Nothilfemarken (Ger.) relief stamps.

Notopfer / 2   Berlin / Steuermarke (3-line insc.) appears on compulsory tax labels not valid for postal services, but similar to

postal tax stamps, for use in German occupation zones to help defray costs of blockaded mail in 1948.

Nouveau-Brunswick (Fr.) New Brunswick.

Nouvelle-Calédonie (insc.) on stamps of New Caledonia.

Nouvelle-Ecosse (Fr.) Nova Scotia.

Nouvelle-Galles du Sud (Fr.) New South Wales.

Nouvelle-Guinée (Fr.) New Guinea.

Nouvelle-République, Afrique du Sud (Fr.) New Republic, South Africa.

Nouvelles-Hébrides (Fr. insc.) appears on stamps of the New Hebrides.

nouvelle valeur (Fr.) new value.

Nouvelle-Zélande (Fr.) New Zealand.

Nova Scotia since 1867, a province of about 21,428 square miles in eastern Canada. Capital: Halifax. Issued its own adhesive postage stamps in 1851 and used them until Confederation in 1867, then used Dominion of Canada postage from 1868 to the present.

nova tiragem (Port.) new printing.

novcic a copper coin of Bosnia, Herzegovina, and Jugoslavia. 100 novcica (neukreuzer) equal 1 florin.

NOVINY (ovpt.) newspaper; appears on special-delivery stamps of Czechoslovakia for use as newspaper stamps in 1926.

Nowanuggur or **Navanagar** an Indian feudatory state on the Gulf of Clutch in western India. Issued stamps 1877-93, which became obsolete in 1895 when stamps of India began to be used. Stamps are listed in Gibbons under an alternate spelling: "Nawanagar". They show a coat of arms in a circle and inscriptions in the Indian language.

N.R.A. (insc.) National Recovery Act; appears on U.S. stamps of Aug. 15, 1933, issued to draw attention to and support for the N.R.A.

N.S.B. (sur.) appears with new values on stamps of the French Colonies, 1890 and subsequent years, for use by Nossi-Bé, a former French Protectorate in the Indian Ocean.

N. Sembilan (insc.) on stamps of Negri Sembilan, one of the federated Malay states. Issued stamps in 1891; issued stamps in 1965 as part of Malaysia.

N.S.W. Postage (insc.) appears on 1897 semi-postal and 1891-2 postage-due stamps of New South Wales.

nuance (Fr.) shade.

Nueva Granada (insc.) appears on stamps of Colombia. The complete form of the inscription is "Estados Unidos de Nueva Granada".

numbered copy Some copies of limited or deluxe editions of books have notations giving the total quantity printed and the number of the individual book.

numbering (1) the printing of numbers in the marginal paper of sheets or panes of stamps, used by some governments as a security measure and to facilitate handling; (2) the procedure of counting stamps in a sheet or pane to indicate the exact location of a variety or error; the top left stamp in the pane or sheet is number one. Counting proceeds horizontally row by row to the end of the unit.

number one the first adhesive postage stamp of a country listed in stamp catalogues.

numeral cancels or **postmarks** any obliterator including a numeral as the central motif.

numeral cancels on British postage stamps

Numeral cancel

These often indicate that the stamps were used from British consular offices in foreign countries, but the numerals are not a positive proof of such use. For example, stamps with a C88 cancel were used from Santiago de Cuba, sometimes called St. Jago de Cuba. But those with C89 cancels originated from Dudley, Northumberland. Gibbons British Commonwealth stamp catalogues have excellent lists of the British stamps used abroad. One cannot find the place of origin of the numerals without a guide such as the Gibbons lists. (Courtesy of the late Grant Glassco, a specialist in British stamps used abroad)

numéro (Fr.) number.

numéro de la planche (Fr.) plate number.

numéro do catálogo (Port.) catalogue number.

Nummer (Ger.) number.

Nummernstempel (Ger.) numeral cancel.

nuovo con gomma (It.) mint.

nuovo senza gomma (It.) unused.

nur fuer Drucksachen (Ger.) printed matter only.

N. W. Pacific Islands (ovpt.) appears on stamps of Australia for use in the North West Pacific Islands.

Nyassa or **Niassa** a province in northern Mozambique, part of Portuguese East Africa; about 73,290 square miles. Capital: Porto Amelia. In 1897 Nyassa used Mozambique stamps, overprinted; used inscribed issues from 1901 until 1925; then used Mozambique stamps.

Nyassaland (Fr.) Nyasaland.

Nyasaland Protectorate a former British Protectorate of about 49,000 square miles on Lake Nyasa in South Africa; since July 6, 1963, the independent state of Malawi in British Commonwealth. Issued stamps in 1891 overprinted "B.C.A." on stamps of Rhodesia, in 1897 with the inscription "British Central Africa", in 1908 with the inscription "Nyasaland Protectorate", and in 1934 with the inscription "Nyasaland".

N.Y.F.M. New York Foreign Mail. Mail originating in New York City (1870-6) for foreign addresses had special authorized cancellations that collectors call "geometrics". Designs include decorated circles, snowflake types, stars, and combined dashes. These markings were also found on mail of other dates. (Courtesy of David Lidman)

N.Y.R.B.A. (airline) New York Rio Buenos Aires Line. Point of origin: United States.

nytryck (Swed.) reprint.

N.Z. New Zealand.

O

O in Gibbons catalogues, indicates ordinary paper in lists where chalky paper also occurs.

O.A.C.I. abbreviation for the Spanish and French names of the International Civil Aviation Organization. The United Nations issued O.A.C.I. stamps in 1955; Canada issued some in 1955.

oanvänd utan gummi (Swed.) unused, without gum.

O.A.T. a handstruck mark on airmail during the Second World War and subsequent years. Airmail specialists say the letters mean "Onward Air Transmission". Others disagree and believe the letters stand for "Onward Air Transport".

Oaxaca a Mexican city and the capital of Oaxaca State in southern Mexico. Issued stamps during the 1913-16 Civil War.

O.B. (ovpt.) Official Business; appears on certain stamps of the Philippines, 1931-48.

oben (Ger.) above, at the top.

oberhalb (Ger.) above.

Oberrand (Ger.) upper margin.

Oberrandaufdruck (Ger.) overprint on upper margin.

Oberrandstueck (Ger.) upper margin copy.

Oberrandzahlen (Ger.) upper margin numbers.

Oberschlesien (Ger.) Upper Silesia.

oblicuo (Sp.) oblique.

obligatory stamps usually special issues that the public must use at specified times. The 1928 issue of Madeira is an example.

oblique roulette the type with parallel slits that slant between the stamps in rows in sheets or panes.

oblit. obliterated, obliteration.

obliteração (Port.) cancellation, postmark.

obliteração de barras (Port.) bar cancellation.

obliteração por perfuração (Port.) cancellation by punching holes (in stamps).

obliterado (Port.) used, cancelled.

obliteration (1) a postmark without indication of town, country, or time; may appear to be anything from a smudge to an artistic decorative postmark, such as the early Austrian postmarks and cancellations used to prevent stamps or postal stationery from being used a second time – these are known as "killers"; (2) an overprint to deface a

Obliteration overprint

former value or part of a stamp design.

oblitération (Fr.) obliteration, cancellation.

oblitération à la plume (Fr.) pen cancellation.

oblitération à la roulette (Fr.) roller cancellation.

oblitération complète (Fr.) a complete cancellation.

oblitération de chemin de fer (Fr.) railroad cancel (R.P.O.), or travelling post office (T.P.O.) cancellations.

oblitération de complaisance (Fr.) cancellation done to order.

oblitération en barres (Fr.) bar cancel.

oblitération en ligne (Fr.) straight-line cancel or postmark.

oblitération lavée (Fr.) cancellation removed.

oblitération mécanique (Fr.) meter mark, meter postage.

oblitération muette (Fr.) silent cancellation or obliteration, mute cancel.

oblitération portante (Fr.) tied by a cancellation or tied on a cover.

oblitération postale (Fr.) postmark.

oblitéré (Fr.) cancelled.

oblitéré à plume (Fr.) pen-cancelled.

Obock or **Obok** a seaport village in French Somaliland, East Africa. Used stamps of French Colonies, handstamped "ОВОСК", in 1892; then used handstamped, surcharged stamps until inscribed stamps were issued in the same year. Obock stamps were replaced in 1901 by stamps of the Somali Coast.

Ob Ost (partial Ger. ovpt.) appears on

stamps of Germany in 1916-17, as an occupation issue by Germany for use in Lithuania.

obsolescent postage stamps those about to
become obsolete. For example, stamps
portraying King George VI of England
that were issued prior to his death and remained in use after he died were called
obsolescent until all stamps of the issue had
been sold. Once they were no longer in use,
they were called obsolete.

obsolete postage stamps (1) those that are no
longer available or valid for postal use; (2)
postage stamps no longer sold by a postal
authority; these should not be confused
with obsolescent postage stamps.

oc in auction catalogues, means off centre.

OCCUPATION AZIRBAYEDJAN (ovpt.)
appears on privately overprinted stamps of
Russia, for use in Azerbaijan.

Occupation française (ovpt.) appears on
newspaper stamps of Hungary, for use under French occupation, 1919.

Occupation Francaise du Cameroun (ovpt.)
appears on 1907 stamps of Middle Congo
for use in Cameroun in 1916. A similar
overprint with the spelling "Française" was
issued during the French occupation of the
former German colony, 1916-17.

occupation stamps issues authorized by an
invading commission or government army
that has taken control of a country or region. Many examples exist and are listed
in stamp catalogues.

Oceanic Settlements See FRENCH POLYNESIA.

Oceanie or **L'Oceanie** (insc.) appears on
stamps of French Polynesia, formerly Etablissements de l'Oceanie.

ocean mail letters or parcel post materials
sent by ship, as opposed to airmail. Postmarks such as "paquebot", "posted at sea",
and "ship letter" all indicate ocean mail.

ocker (Ger) ochre.

octogonal (Port.) octagonal.

octogone (Fr.) octagon.

OCUPACION DE PASCUA (insc.) appears
on Chile 1940 semi-postal stamps marking
the fiftieth anniversary of the occupation
of Easter Island by Chile. The surtax was
for charity work.

odontomètre (Fr.) perforation gauge.

O.E.E.C. Organization for European Economic Co-operation.

Oesterreich (Ger.) Austria.

Oesterr-Post or **Osterreichische Post** (insc.)
on stamps of Austria.

OEUVRES DE SOLIDARITE FRANCAISE
(insc.) on 1943-4 semi-postal stamps of the
French Colonies. The surtax was for the

Solidarity Fund.

OEUVRES SOCIALES F.O.M. (insc.) appears on Cameroun semi-postal stamps of
1950, for charity. The same text, plus a
cross and new values, appears as a surcharge on 1942 St. Pierre & Miquelon
semi-postal stamps.

O F CASTELLORISO (ovpt.) appears on
stamps of France issued in 1920 under
French occupation of Castellorizo.

off centre refers to a stamp with uneven
margins on one or more sides.

offen (Ger.) open.

Offentlig Sak (insc.) appears on official

stamps of Norway.

Office International des Chemins de Fer (Fr.
insc.) Central Office for International Railway Transport. Appears on stamps of
Switzerland 1967. (Courtesy of Switzerland PTT notice)

official city a city or town designated by a
post office department as the place where a
stamp will be issued.

officially sealed labels Officially sealed labels
are not postage stamps, since they do not
pay for postal service of delivering mail;
similarly they cannot be classified as postage-due stamps. Postal employees in the

Dead Letter Office or the Undeliverable
Mail Office were sometimes forced to open
letters incorrectly addressed in order to
find the correct return address. Other times
they erroneously opened letters with return
addresses on them. In either case, they

Offsetting: normal and reverse

sealed the letters with these official seals to indicate that an authorized person had opened the mail. The United States and Canada used these labels.

official stamps   adhesive or postal stationery stamps made purposely for use by government personnel or departments. Many official stamps were provisional issues with perforated initials. Some of Canada, for example, had "OHMS" in them.

Official stamps of Argentina   From 1913 to 1938 Argentina issued postage stamps overprinted with various initials for the names of ministries that used them (Scott's catalogue gives the dates 1913-37). See these listings for the Spanish names: M.A.; M.G.; M.H.; M.I.; M.J.I.; M.M.; M.O.P.; and M.R.C.

Offisieel   (Africaans ovpt.) appears on southwest Africa stamps inscribed in the same language. These were official stamps, used 1927-52, with various designs. The English word "Official" was overprinted on the stamps inscribed in English. The stamps were made in alternate languages in the sheets.

offiziell   (Ger.) official(ly).

offizieller Ersttagstempel   (Ger.) official first-day-cover cancel, first day cancellation.

off-loaded   post office term for "unloaded", when mail is taken off any carrier – train, aircraft, or ship.

off paper   description in stamp advertisements indicating that used stamps had been soaked off paper.

offset   one kind of lithography in which the printing is offset from the plate to a blanket that lays down the impression on the paper or substance being printed.

offset, set-off   the impressions on the back of postage stamps that have been piled on other stamps while the ink was still wet. The design is therefore transferred or set off in this way.

Offsetdruck   (Ger.) offset print, offset printing.

offsetdruk   (Dutch) lithographed.

offset ink   short, tacky, water-repellent ink

made with strong, acid-resistant pigments.

offset issues   postage stamps of the world printed by offset lithography. Sometimes the term specifies U.S. regular-issue stamps of 1918-20 printed by this method.

offset paper   a type of hard-sized paper for use on offset presses.

offset press   a press that consists of a plate cylinder, a transfer or blanket cylinder, and a printing cylinder. The inked image is transferred from the plate onto the rubber blanket and from there to the paper held on the printing cylinder.

offsetting   in philately refers to the transference of impressions or pictures to the back of stamps in a pile while the stamps are still wet. The offsets are reversed.

offsettryck   (Swed.) offset.

oficial   (Sp. and Port.) official.

Oflag II C-D-E or **Oflag VIIA**   names of Polish officers' prisons used during the Second World War. "Oflag" is the abbreviation for the German words "Offizieren Lager", officers' camp. During the war, officers organized a postal system among the camps and issued stamps for use from one camp to another.

O.G.   original gum, previously mounted.

O.G. N.H.   original gum, never hinged.

O.H.E.M.S.   (ovpt.) On His Exalted Majesty's Service; appears on official stamps of Egypt, 1922.

O.H.H.S.   (ovpt.) On His Highness's Service; appears on official stamps of Egypt, 1907-22.

O.H.M.S.   (ovpt.) On His (or Her) Majesty's Service; appears on official stamps of India, 1874-1909. Also overprinted on stamps of Canada 1949-50. Canadian stamps also have the perforated initials "OHMS".

ohne   (Ger.) without.

ohne Gummi   (Ger.) without gum.

ohne Wasserzeichen   (Ger.) without watermark.

oil in stamps   This may be removed by the submersion of stamps in benzine or gasoline without additives. Pressure with a warm iron against the stamps between pieces of clean paper may also remove oil. Care should be taken not to submerge gravure-printed stamps in these solvents.

OIL RIVERS (ovpt.) appears at the bottom of British stamps, also bearing the overprint "BRITISH PROTECTORATE", used in 1892, for the Niger Coast Protectorate on the west coast of Africa.

OIT See BIT and INTERNATIONAL LABOR ORGANIZATION.

Old Calabar River postmark of Nigeria, used in 1891. See Gibbons Part One catalogue.

Oldenburg a former German state in northwest Germany; about 2,083 square miles. Capital: Oldenburg. Stamps were issued by Oldenburg 1852-67; then stamps of North German Confederation were used. The spelling in French is "Oldenbourg".

Old English type characters similar to those used by the early printers.

oliv (Ger.) olive.

olivbraun (Ger.) olive-brown.

olive tagging a peculiar dull-green shade of tagging found on the U.S. 5-cent Washington stamps, 1966. The standard colour for this issue was a bright yellow-green. (Courtesy of Alfred G. Boerger)

olivgelb (Ger.) olive-yellow.

olivgruen (Ger.) olive-green.

Oltre Giuba (insc. and ovpt.) meaning "beyond the Juba River"; inscribed on stamps of Italian Jubaland; also overprinted on Italian stamps of 1925.

OLYMPIC GAMES 1948 (insc.) on stamps of Great Britain issued July 29, 1948.

Olympische Spiele (Ger.) Olympic games.

Omahas (nick.) stamps of the United States commemorating an exposition at Omaha, Nebraska, June 1 to Nov. 1, 1898.

O.M.F. abbreviation for the French words "Occupation Militaire Française", which mean "French Military Occupation".

O.M.F./Cilicie (2-line sur.) appears with new values on French stamps of 1900-17 for use in Cilicia, in southeastern Asia Minor. Stamps were issued under French occupation. Similar surcharged stamps were issued in 1920.

O.M.F. Syrie (sur.) appears on various French stamps for use as regular-issue and postage-due stamps of Syria under French mandate, 1920-2.

omission de couleur (Fr.) albino; refers to impressions of stamp designs without colours or to postmarks stamped without ink.

Omnibus issues of the British Commonwealth

The number of stamps in each issue is given in brackets: 1935 Silver Jubilee (249); 1937 Coronation (202); 1945-46 Victory (164); 1948-49 Silver Wedding (138); 1949 U.P.U. (315); 1951 B.W.I. University College (28); 1953 Coronation (106); 1953-54 Royal Visit to Australia-New Zealand, West Indies, etc. (13); 1958 British Caribbean Federation (30); 1963 Freedom from Hunger (37); 1963 Red Cross Centenary (70); 1964 Shakespeare (12); 1965 I.T.U. (66); 1965 I.C.Y. (62); 1966 Churchill (132); 1966 Royal Visit (26); 1966 World Football Cup Championships (40); 1966 W.H.O. Headquarters, Geneva (44); 1966 UNESCO (81). (Courtesy of Stanley Gibbons catalogues)

omvänt (Swed.) inverted.

On/C G/S (3-line ovpt.) On Cochin Government Service; appears on 1913-48 official stamps of Cochin, an Indian feudatory state.

on cover refers to stamps on their original letters or envelopes. Stamps on wrappers may be included.

One Cent Despatch in Baltimore, Maryland, and also in Washington, D.C., and Georgetown, D.C., issued U.S. local stamps in 1856.

ONE HUNDRED YEARS (insc.) appears on stamps of New South Wales 1888-9, to mark the centenary of the colony.

one-penny black British postage stamps that were the first adhesive stamps in the world; used May 6, 1840, for the first time. (The penny black is known cancelled before May 6.)

one-penny red British postage stamps introduced in 1841 to replace the first stamps, printed in black. The black stamps were difficult to cancel in black or red.

O.N.F. Castellorizo (ovpt.) appears on stamps of French Offices in Turkey in 1920 for use in Castellorizo, an island in the Dodecanese group in the Mediterranean Sea near Asia Minor. Castellorizo was formerly a Turkish island occupied by the French and ceded to Italy in 1923, then retroceded to Greece in 1947. The entire population was Greek.

ongetande (Dutch) imperforate.

On H.M.S. or **O.H.M.S.** (ovpt. or punched initials) on His (or Her) Majesty's Service; usually appears on British colonial stamps.

ON/K S/D (3-line ovpt.) appears on 1918 official stamps of Kishangarh, a feudatory state of India.

on paper dealers' note in advertisements, usually describes mixtures not soaked off paper.

on piece stamps on an envelope or a piece of the original paper, as opposed to mint stamps or stamps removed from paper.

ON/SS (2-line ovpt.) appears on stamps of Travancore 1911-33, for official use.

On/S. S./S. (3-line ovpt.) On Sirmoor State Service; appears on official stamps of Sirmoor, 1890-6 issues.

on the nose, or **socked on the nose** The late Theodore Steinway, a prominent stamp collector of New York City, popularized the idea of collecting postage stamps that have the entire postmark within the printed area of the stamps, "socked on the nose".

ontwerp (Dutch) design.

O.N.U. abbreviation for the French, Spanish, and Italian names for United Nations Organization (U.N.O.). A number of countries have honoured various anniversaries of the United Nations and inscribed "O.N.U." or "U.N.O." on their stamps: Lebanon (1956), Italy (1956), and Indonesia (1951), for example.

onze (Fr.) eleven.

O O a cancel with a sunray or star design between the letters, appearing on British stamps of early issues such as the penny reds and other stamps, 1841-57. These were used mainly during the Crimean War (1853-56) and the following year. These cancels, with three bars top and bottom and two at each side, are often called "OXO cancels". (Courtesy of the late Grant Glassco, specialist in British stamps used abroad)

opaque ink The opacity of inks depends on the refractive index and the fineness of the pigment used.

opdruk (Dutch) overprint, surcharge.

open bootheel postmark one without numerals or data within the oval. See BOOT-HEEL POSTMARK.

O.P.S.O. (ovpt.) On Public Service Only; appears on 1892-1901 New Zealand official stamps for post office departmental use.

O.R. Origine Rurale; a French postmark struck on mail posted in small communities that had not been assigned a post office number.

orangebraun (Ger.) orange-brown.

Orangeburg coils the U.S. 3-cent deep-violet stamps of Jan. 24, 1911, used in Orangeburg, New York. The rare perforations 12 and the small quantity used combine to make these the rarest U.S. coils or roll postage.

Orange Etat libre (Fr.) Orange Free State (River Colony).

Orange Free State a republic in south Africa; formerly the Orange River Colony, a British Crown Colony of about 49,647 square miles between the Orange and Vaal rivers. Part of the Union of South Africa since 1910. Issued Cape of Good Hope stamps, overprinted, in 1900. Capital: Bloemfontein.

orangegelb (Ger.) orange-yellow.

orangerot (Ger.) orange-red.

Oranje-Freistaat (Ger.) Orange Free State.

Oranje Vrij Staat (Dutch) Orange Free State.

orb ball, spherical body. The British orb with a cross above it is an emblem of royalty, used in simple form as a watermark in some British stamps.

Orcha (insc.) appears on stamps of Orcha, a native feudatory state of India of about 2,080 square miles. Capital: Tikamgarh. Issued stamps in 1912. The 1939 issue is inscribed "Orchha State".

ordinaire (Fr.) regular.

ordinario (Sp.) ordinary.

ORDINARY (ovpt.) handstamped on Liberia official stamps of 1901-2 for regular postage.

ordinary paper Collectors usually refer to plain wove papers as ordinary, as opposed to watermarked, tinted, coloured, chalk-surfaced, or other types.

ore a copper coin of Greenland, Norway, Sweden, and Denmark. 100 ore equal 1 rixsdaler (1858-74). 100 ore equal 1 krone since 1874. The name of the coin may have been derived from "eyrir", a Norse word for ounce. It is called "aur" in Iceland. It was of silver until about 1626.

ORGANISATION ETATS RIVERAINS DU SENEGAL (insc.) appears on 1970 stamps of Guinea for the Organisation of Riparian States of the Senegal River. Representatives from the States of Guinea, Mali, Mauritania, and Senegal met in 1968 and formed the regional West African organization. (Courtesy of Republic of Guinea bulletin)

ORGANISATION / INTERNATIONALE / POUR/LES REFUGIES (4-line ovpt.) appears on stamps of Switzerland for use by the International Organization of Refugees in 1950.

original cover a letter with or without adhesive postage stamps, as it was posted.

original gum Virtually all stamps are gummed on the back by the printers. This gum is known as original gum (O.G.). The expression "mint" implies that a stamp still has its original gum.

Originalgummi (Ger. and Swed.) original

gum.

Originalwert (Ger.) original value.

orizzontale (It.) horizontal.

ORO PASTAS (insc.) appears on airmail stamps of Lithuania.

ORTS-POST (insc.) appears on the first issue of the Federal Administration of Switzerland, 1850.

Ortspost (Ger.) local post.

Ortspostmarke (Ger.) local stamp.

Ortsringstempel (Ger.) town-ring cancel.

O.S. (insc.) appears with design of heraldic shield on Norway official stamps of 1951-2.

OS (ovpt.) On Service; appears on various stamps of the world for official use; the official stamps of Liberia are an example.

OS a postmark in a double-line circle, struck on some British covers shortly after the 1-penny black was issued in May 1840; means "Old Stamp", one that had been used for postal service.

oscuro (Sp.) dark.

O.S.E. (ovpt.) for the French "Oeuvres Sociales de l'Enfance", child social welfare; appears on air post stamps of French Morocco, for use as air post semi-postal stamps in 1938.

O.S./G.R.I./1d (3-line sur.) appears on German New Guinea stamps in 1915, for use as the official stamps of New Britain under the Australian military government. The island Neu-Pommern, a former part of German New Guinea, fell to Australian invaders, who renamed it New Britain. It became part of New Guinea under Australian mandate after the First World War.

O.S.G.S. (ovpt.) On Sudan Government Service; appears on official stamps of Sudan.

Osterreich (Ger. insc.) Austria; appears in a panel below a post-horn, with no other words, on stamps issued during the 1945 occupation of Austria by the Allied Military Government of Great Britain and the United States, for civilian use in the regions of Austria under British, French, and American occupation.

Osterr-post (insc.) This and similar spellings occur on stamps of Austria.

OSTLAND (Ger. ovpt.) Eastland; appears on stamps of Germany, for use in Russia under German occupation, 1941-3.

OSTROPA 1935 (insc.) appears on a German souvenir sheet with a clear watermark showing the name above four stamps and the date below them. The sheets, with 46-pfennigs worth of stamps, sold for 1 Mark 70 pfennigs, the entrance charge in June 1935 to the East European Philatelic Exhibition at Konigsberg in East Prussia. The

sulphuric acid in the gum of the stamp attacks the paper, especially in the watermarks.

OTAN abbreviation for the French, German, and Italian names of the North Atlantic Treaty Organization.

otandat (Swed.) imperforate.

Ottawa printings Canadian issues of 1870 and subsequent years. Some were printed in Ottawa, Ontario, and others in Montreal, Quebec. They are distinguished by the colours and gums in identical designs.

Otvorenle slovenského/snemu (2-line sur.) appears with date and new value on Czech stamps of 1936 for use in Slovakia in 1939.

OUBANGUI-CHARI (ovpt. and insc.) appears as an overprint on stamps of Middle Congo in 1922 and on postage-due stamps of France in 1928 for use in Ubangi-Shari, a former French colony in West Africa; also inscribed on stamps of Ubangi-Shari.

OUBANGUI-CHARI-TCHAD (ovpt.) appears on stamps of Middle Congo for use in Ubangi-Shari, a former French colony in West Africa, in 1915-22. Later the colony used stamps of French Equatorial Africa.

Ouganda (Fr.) Uganda.

O.U.S. (ovpt.) Oxford Union Society; appears on certain British stamps of 1858 and subsequent years, withdrawn in 1870.

outline letters types that comprise only the outline of the letter, as contrasted to solid types, which print in full face.

out of register out of position. For example, when a colour in a stamp design fails to coincide with the other colours, the design is out of register.

Outre-Djouba (Fr.) Jubaland.

outre-mer (Fr.) overseas.

outremer (Fr.) ultramarine.

ouvert, ouverte (Fr.) open.

överföring (Swed.) transfer.

övergäende (Swed.) transitory, passing over. The term is used for a postage stamp tied to the paper by a cancellation.

overissues copies of postage stamps that have not been sold. Some old issues have been sold as remainders.

overland mail mail service on land, not by water routes. The pony express in the United States and the first Canadian mail route in 1763 (between Quebec City and Montreal with a stop at Three Rivers, Quebec) are examples of overland mail. Another example was the mail delivery overland across Egypt between Suez and Alexandria, a service introduced in 1836 by Thomas Waghorn. Formerly the mail to India went by way of Cape of Good Hope, but Mr. Waghorn saved many days' time in delivering mail from Britain to India. Many letters he carried bear cachets: "care of Mr. Waghorn, Alexandria".

overprint, overprinting any printing added to the face side of postage stamps after the stamps have been printed. Overprinting may alter the stamps to suit them for some purpose other than that of the original issue. Overprinted stamps may be pre-cancels. Not to be confused with surcharged stamps, which are overprinted issues with changes of prices.

overrun nations stamps (nick.) the 1943-4 issue of thirteen U.S. stamps featuring the flags of countries overrun by Germany during the Second World War.

överst (Swed.) top.

Overton & Co. of New York City, Boston, Massachusetts, and Albany, New York, is-sued U.S. local stamps in 1844.

övertryck (Swed.) overprint.

ovpt. or o'pt. overprint.

O. W. Official (ovpt.) Office of Works; appears on official stamps of Great Britain, 1896-1902; discontinued.

Oxford, N.C. This town in North Carolina issued postmasters' provisional envelopes in 1861 as part of the Confederate States of America.

oxidized stamps stamps printed with inks that change in colour by contact with oxygen in air. Similarly, some printing inks are reduced, resulting in a change of colour that sometimes may be oxidized back to the original colour. Collectors are advised to consult experienced chemists to determine whether a stamp has been reduced or oxidized to cause a change in colour.

OXO cancels See o o.

oxydé (Fr.) oxidized.

P

P (ovpt.) appears with design of crescent and star in an oval on stamps of Straits Settlements in 1878 from Perak, one of the Federated Malay States. Became part of Malaysia and issued stamps in 1965.

P poor, referring to the poor quality of an item in an auction catalogue.

P 1 (sur.) appears with Arabic writing on stamps of Turkey for use in Thrace, 1913.

P.A.A. (airline) Pan American Airways Incorporated. Point of origin: United States.

Paar (Ger.) pair.

pacchetto (It.) bundle.

pacchi (It.) parcel post.

PACCHI POSTALI (It. insc.) appears on parcel post stamps of Italy and San Marino. The Italian stamps have been in two parts since 1914; those of San Marino have been

in two parts since 1928. Half the stamp was stuck to a way-bill and cancelled. The other half was stuck to a receipt given to the sender.

Pacific Steam Navigation Company printed stamps for trial use in 1857 in Peru. The stamps feature a sail-and-steam ship and initials "P.S.N.C.", one in each corner of the stamp. Peru issued these stamps in February 1857.

Pack, Charles Lathrop a famous American philatelist and authority on stamps and postmarks of many countries, especially of Canada and Brazil.

Packenmarke Wenden (insc.) appears on 1863 stamps of Wenden, a district of the province of Livonia, now part of Latvia.

·Packenmarke WENDEN=schen Kreises (Ger. insc.) appears on 1863 stamps of Wenden issued for parcels exclusively. See WENDEN.

packet Subsequent to the Ship Letter Act of 1815 in Great Britain, the post office was authorized to establish packets to India and

the Cape of Good Hope to be despatched once a month by any vessel the post office selected for the purpose. The term "packet" included any ship, even a private vessel. Packet postage on a single letter was three shillings, six pence. By any ship, but not a packet boat, the outward postage was one shilling, two pence and inward postage was eight pence. Private owners were compelled to carry mail as ship letters when the post office required the services. Mail for India and the Cape was carried on H.M. (His Majesty) ships by East India Company merchant men, but more frequently by privately owned vessels. No special port of departure or arrival was established. The letters in many instances bore special postmarks.

packet cancellation ship cancellation on stamps or postal stationery; packet postmarks on pre-stamp or stampless covers.

packet postage stamps those sold in envelopes, bags, or packages for stamp collectors.

Packhoi or Pak-Hoi (ovpt.) appears with oriental characters on stamps of Indo-China 1903-19 for use by the French offices in China.

padpost (nick.) contraction of "pictorial advertising on postal stationery". Refers to advertising printed usually in upper left corners of postcards and envelopes, popular mainly between 1870 and 1920. (Courtesy of Edward Richardson)

PADROES DA GRANDE GUERRA (insc.) appears on postal-tax stamps and postal tax-due stamps of Portugal, 1925.

P.A.G.A.C. (airline) Pan American Grace Airways Company; also known as Pan American Grace Airways Incorporated (P.A.G.A.I.). Point of origin: United States. See PANAGRA.

P.A.G.A.I. See P.A.G.A.C.

Pahang a state of about 13,820 square miles in the Federation of Malaysia, on the east coast of Malay Peninsula. Capital: Kuala Lipis. Stamps of Straits Settlements were overprinted or surcharged "Pahang", 1889-99. As a sultanate on the Malay Peninsula, Pahang introduced inscribed stamps in

1965 as a part of Malaysia.

pahlavi a coin of Persia (Iran). 20 rials equal 1 pahlavi.

PAID usually a handstruck mark on early mail before the use of adhesive stamps was compulsory in Canada, Britain, the United States, and other countries; sometimes combined with denominations, "ship letter", or other markings. These are cancels if they cancel stamps; otherwise they are postal markings.

paid permit See POSTAL PERMIT.

paio (It.) pair.

pair two stamps attached vertically or horizontally, known as a vertical or horizontal pair.

paire (Fr.) pair.

paire d'intervalle (Fr.) gutter pair.

paisa a copper coin of Afghanistan, parts of India, and other places. The value has varied, from 40 to 80 paisa equalling a rupee. In German East Africa and some other parts of Africa, it is called "pysa" or "pesa", and 64 pesa equal 1 rupee.

Paita (ovpt.) appears on stamps of Peru in 1884 following the war between Chile and Peru, 1879-82 for use in the city of Paita.

Paketmarke (Ger.) parcel post stamp.

Pakistan since 1956, a republic of about 364,737 square miles in south-central Asia. Formed in 1947 when India was divided into the Dominions of India and Pakistan. Capital: Rawalpindi (formerly Karachi). Issued stamps overprinted on India stamps in 1947.

PALACIO DE COMUNICACIONES (insc.) appears on postal-tax stamps of Colombia.

Palaestina (Ger.) Palestine.

Palatinate a territory in Germany that came under French occupation after the Second World War. Occupation stamps were issued first in 1947, and are listed with German issues in catalogues.

pâle (Fr.) pale.

pale refers to a lighter tone than the pure colour printed on a postage stamp.

paleography science of deciphering and reading ancient scriptures and hieroglyphic writings.

Palestine a former British mandate of about 10,429 square miles on the Mediterranean in western Asia. Was a part of the Ottoman Empire until mandated to Great Britain. Occupied by British forces in First World War. Capital: Jerusalem. Issued stamps in 1918.

pálido (Sp.) pale.

pallido (It.) pale.

Palmer, Ralph an early British theatre manager in Bath, England, a city about 105 miles from London. He became a pioneer stagecoach operator with help from William Pitt, the Prime Minister. Ralph Palmer studied mail transportation and stagecoach operations. He got a government contract after he proved his service was superior in August 1784. Stagecoaches in Britain carried mail for nearly 150 years, until railways began to provide speedier mail service.

palms (nick.) the 1941 Sudan issue featuring a landscape with palms, in contrast to the 1960 series depicting a Sudanese forest. Hundreds of other stamps show palms.

PANAGRA an impression on certain airmail letters from Peru, and probably other countries, carried by Pan American Grace Airways. Juan Terry Trippe, head of Pan Am, bought an airline in Peru. The wealthy W. R. Grace steamship line, not wishing to lose a virtual trading monopoly on the west coast, joined in partnership with Mr. Trippe to form the Pan American Grace Airways, known as PANAGRA. For details see C. R. Roseberry, *The Challenging Skies.*

Panama a republic of about 28,576 square miles between Colombia and Costa Rica in Central America. Capital: Panama. Formerly one of the nine states of Colombia that issued stamps, 1878-96. Panama became an independent republic in 1903 and introduced its own stamps that year.

Pan-American Postal Union In 1920 all the countries in North, Central, and South America, except Canada and British, French, and Dutch Guiana, agreed to carry mail at their domestic rates, and to transport mail without charging member countries.

Pan-Am Expo cover envelopes specially printed with cachets or corner cards of the Pan-American Exposition held in Buffalo, New York, from May 1 to November 1, 1901.

pane a half, quarter, or other portion of a sheet of stamps in various numbers printed with gutters to separate them, or made purposely for booklet postage.

panel printed matter enclosed by rules or borders at the head of a chapter or column or in an advertisement to give prominence to part of the composition.

pango a coin of Hungary, in use from 1926. 100 fillers equal 1 pango.

panneau (Fr.) pane (of stamps).

pantograph an instrument for mechanically copying drawings, engravings, designs, and plans, either on the same scale as the original, or on a reduced or enlarged scale. Used to produce plates for meter postage stamps.

Papal States See ROMAN STATES.

papel (Sp. and Port.) paper.

papel avitelado (Sp.) wove paper.

papel coloreado (Sp.) tinted paper.

papel con filamentos (Sp.) granite paper.

papel da máquina (Port.) machine-made paper.

papel estucado (Sp.) chalk-surfaced paper.

papel fibroso (Port.) granite paper.

papel gessado (Port.) coated paper, chalky paper.

papel listado en la pasta (Sp.) coated paper.

papel lustro giace (Port.) glossy-coated paper.

papel manual (Port.) handmade paper.

papel tizado (Sp.) glossy paper.

paper a sheet of felted cellulose fibres, used for writing, printing, or wrapping purposes. The invention of paper dates back to A.D. 105, when a Chinese man, Tsai Lun, made paper from vegetable fibres and old rags to replace the more expensive silk and other textile fabrics that were then used for recording writings. Two main divisions of paper are handmade, which are produced sheet by sheet, and machine-made, produced entirely by machinery, generally in long continuous rolls, afterwards cut into sheets.

paper cement adhesive made from rubber latex and a volatile solvent or vehicle.

paper drill rotating machine for making holes in paper, especially used in ring pages for stamp albums.

paper gauges a variety of instruments for measuring thickness of paper.

paper machine machine on which cellulose fibres and other constituents of paper are formed into a sheet, which is pressed, dried, calendered, and wound into rolls or cut into sheets. The paper machine was invented by Nicolas Louis Robert, a Frenchman, in 1798, but was commercially developed by the Fourdrinier brothers, with the help of Bryan Donkin. The Fourdrinier brothers gave their name to this type of paper machine, the first one being put into commercial use in 1803. The cylinder type of paper machine was invented by John Dickinson in 1808.

papermaker (1) skilled workman employed on a paper machine; (2) executive of a paper manufacturer.

papermakers' watermarks watermarks with names of the producers or their trade names in the postage stamp papers. Pirie

and Bothwell watermarks are examples.

paper mill plant in which paper is manufactured from raw materials.

Papier (Fr. and Ger.) paper.

Papierabart (Ger.) paper variety.

papier avec fragments de fils de soie (Fr.) granite paper.

papier bâtouné (Fr.) ribbed paper.

papier bleuté (Fr.) blued paper. In English sometimes called "bleuté paper".

papier côtelé (Fr.) ribbed paper.

papier couché (Fr.) chalky paper.

papier fait à la machine (Fr.) machine-made paper.

papier fait à la main (Fr.) handmade paper.

Papierfalte (Ger.) paper crease, paper fold.

Papierfalz (Ger.) paper hinge.

Papierfarbton (Ger.) shade of paper.

papier filigrané (Fr.) watermarked paper.

papier glacé (Fr.) glossy-coated paper.

papier granit (Fr.) granite paper.

papier mélange de fils de soie (Fr.) granite paper.

papier ordinaire (Fr.) wove paper.

papier pelure (Fr.) onion skin, pelure.

papier teinté (Fr.) tinted paper.

papier vélin (Fr.) wove paper.

papier vergé (Fr.) laid paper.

Papua and New Guinea mandated territories of Australia north of Australia, on the eastern half of the island of New Guinea; about 183,540 square miles. Capital: Port Moresby. Issued stamps inscribed "British New Guinea" in 1901, overprinted "Papua" in 1906, inscribed "Papua" in 1907, and inscribed "Papua and New Guinea" in 1952. As of July 1, 1971, the country acquired a flag, coat of arms, and a new name – Papua New Guinea. (Courtesy of Mr. Sinake Giregire, Minister of Posts and Telegraphs, Port Moresby, Papua New Guinea)

Papua oddities Papua first stamps were Queensland issues cancelled N.G. for New Guinea. Later stamps were cancelled B.N.G. Therefore no mint stamps of the first two issues exist because they were Queensland stamps. In 1901 the first adhesive stamps were inscribed "British New Guinea" with a native craft called the Lakatoi as the feature design. Every postage stamp of Papua from 1901 until the pictorial issue of 1932 carried the same illustration. Papua is the only country in the world that has issued a stamp listing all the post offices in its territory (the shilling stamp of 1932).

papyrus a type of matted sheet made by the Egyptians from the layers of papyrus, a

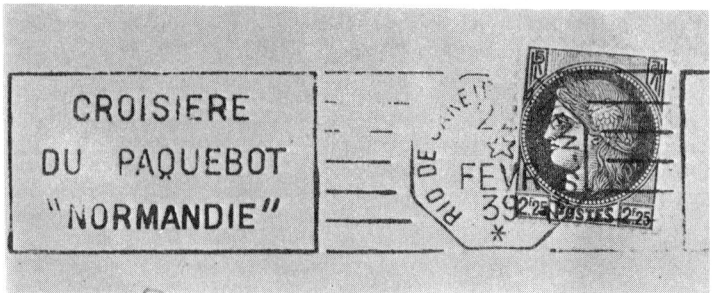

Paquebot cancellation

species of rush growing in North Africa. Papyrus was an ancestor of paper; paper derived its name from it.

paquebot (Fr.) mailboat. A postal marking and cancellation used throughout the world, often with stamps of one country cancelled by another. Great Britain used the word "Paquebot" as a handstamp in 1894, although the U.P.U. did not adopt universal use of the word until the 1897 U.P.U. Congress in Washington, D.C.

paquetes (Sp.) parcel post.

paquetito (Sp.) bundle.

par (Swed.) pair.

para (1) a copper coin of Jugoslavia. 100 paras equal 1 dinar. Adopted in 1867 when the country joined the Latin monetary union; pieces with values of 5 and 10 paras in nickel were also struck. Russia issued a copper para equal to 3 dengi in 1771 and 1772 for Moldavia and Walachia. (2) various silver or copper·coins used in the Ottoman Empire about 1,000 years ago, but in Serbia, Montenegro, Egypt, Turkey, and Russia in modern times.

PARA (insc.) coin name, appears on stamps of Egypt as a Turkish suzerainty.

para (sur.) appears on various foreign stamps (of Austria, France, Germany, Great Britain, Italy, Romania) for use in their offices in Turkey.

Paraguay a republic of about 157,006 square miles bordering on Bolivia, Brazil, and Argentina in South America. Capital: Asunción. Issued stamps in 1870.

PARA os POBRES (insc.) appears on 1915 Portugal postal tax stamps for public charity. Some are overprinted "Açores" for use in the Azores.

paraph the flourish that is sometimes added at the end of a signature; examples on stamps are found in the 1873-6 issues of Porto Rico (now spelled Puerto Rico).

par avion (Fr.) by airmail. "By airplane" is

a literal translation.

parcel post a classification of mail devoted to conveying merchandise. Some countries issued stamps for use on parcels: the United States (1912), Belgium (1879), San Marino (1928), and Italy (1884) are examples. The U.P.U. established international parcel post service in 1878.

parcel post, postage-due stamps The U.S. Post Office issued this type of postage-due stamp in 1912 when parcel post stamps were issued.

parcel post stamps specially printed postage stamps intended for use in mailing parcels. In 1912-13 the United States Post Office issued parcel post stamps: twelve denominations, from 1 cent to 1 dollar, all in carmine or carmine-rose colour.

pardo (Sp.) brown.

parecido (Port.) similar.

pareja (Sp.) pair.

parenthesis semi-circular mark, generally used in pairs, ( ), to indicate the beginning and end of an incidental or explanatory phrase or clause inserted in the main sentence.

Parisot issue stamps of the Dominican Republic 1879-80, surcharged "U.P.U." and new values. These were considered speculations, not authorized by Dominican Republic. They were named after H. K. Parisot, the Paris dealer who sold them.

Park, Bertram a British photographer whose portraits of British royalty were used on certain colonial stamps.

Parma a former duchy and now a province of Italy; about 2,745 square miles. Capital: Parma. Stamps were issued from 1852 until Parma was annexed to Sardinia in 1860.

Parme (Fr.) Parma.

partially perforated refers to stamps with one to three sides without perforations; the term is often shortened to "part-perforate".

"Particular" (ovpt.) appears above a horizontal design of heavy crosses, on official stamps of Nicaragua for use in 1921 as regular postage stamps in Nicaragua.

partido en dos (Sp.) bisected.

part O.G. in auction catalogues, indicates that there is original gum on part of the stamps.

part-perforated refers to an error or variety in a postage stamp that normally is perforated completely. Coil stamps of the United States, Sweden, and Canada that are made so that opposite sides or ends are without perforations, and stamps in panes with one side or an end not perforated, may be classified as part-perforated issues, but they are printed and finished in that way intentionally, not by mistake.

PASCO (ovpt.) appears on stamps of Peru, 1884, for use in Cerro de Pasco, a city in Peru that had provisional stamps after the war between Chile and Peru, 1879-82.

passant (her.) walking (of an animal), with one forepaw off the ground.

paste-ups adjacent coil stamps pasted together to form a continuous strip. Sometimes called "joined stamps" or "joined pair" when one stamp is pasted to an adjacent one.

PATA 1970 (insc.) appears on French Polynesia issue of April 7, 1970, to publicize the Pacific Area Travel Association Congress.

pataca a silver coin of Macao and Timor. 100 avos equal 1 pataca. First struck in reign of King John IV of Portugal (1640-56); the pataca had a value of 320 reis then.

P.A.T.C.O. (airline) Philippine Aerial Taxi Co. Point of origin: the Philippines.

Patiala a state of India in the Central Punjab; 5,942 square miles. Capital: Patiala. Issued stamps in 1884.

PATIALA STATE (ovpt.) appears on stamps of India for use in the state of Patiala. Also appears with the additional overprint "SERVICE" on stamps of India for use as official stamps in Patiala.

patinata carta (It.) glossy paper.

Patmo or **Patmos** an Italian island of the Dodecanese group in the Aegean Sea, south-southwest of Samos; about 22 square miles. Stamps issued 1912-32 were those of Italy, overprinted.

patriotic covers or cards usually envelopes, but sometimes postcards, with decorative national themes to inspire the public. Patriotics are a popular branch of stamp collecting. U.S. wartime covers since the Civil War and Queen Victoria anniversaries are examples of patriotic covers.

PATRIOTIC FUND (insc.) appears on 1900 Queensland semi-postal stamps sold for 1 and 2 shillings for 1-penny and 2-pence stamps. The surtax went to a Boer War patriotic fund.

patriotisches Kuvert (Ger.) patriotic cover.

patte (Fr.) flap of envelope.

PATZCUARO FRANCO (insc.) appears on a doubtful provisional issue of 1868 for Patzcuaro, a city of Mexico.

payé (Fr.) paid.

Pays-Bas (Fr.) The Netherlands.

P.D. (Fr.) port destinataire. French postal marking indicating mail sent collect.

P.D. (sur.) appears with numeral on stamps of French Colonies, for use by St. Pierre & Miquelon, 1886.

P.E. (insc.) appears on 1866 stamps of Egypt; the letters are an abbreviation for the French words meaning "Egyptian post".

peace and commerce types French and French colonial stamps introduced in 1876 in France. These key-type stamps were designed by J. A. Sage and engraved by E. L. Mouchon. They are sometimes called the "Sage type".

peace and navigation type French key-type design of colonial postage stamps, 1892 and subsequent years; sometimes called the "tablet key-type".

peace issues (nick.) postage stamps issued to mark the return to peace after a war. Japan

Partially perforated stamps

issued four peace stamps in 1919. Following the Second World War, British and Commonwealth victory stamps commemorated the victory of the Allies. Peace stamps and victory stamps are similar in their purpose and ideals.

peacocks (nick.) elaborate overprints of Burma on former issues made during the Japanese occupation of Burma in 1942.

pearl decorations a handy device of stamp designers to frame portraits or fill spaces. Some have tiny marks enclosed: the Canada 1932 Types I and II, for example. The size of the inside marks distinguishes the types. Great Britain, the United States, and other countries have used pearls on stamps.

peça de luxo (Port.) very fine copy.

Pechino (sur. and ovpt.) appears with new denominations on stamps of Italy for use by the Italian offices in Peking, China.

peelable label address labels used to address first day covers so they may be removed after the first day cover is serviced and readdressed.

PELITA (sur.) appears on Dutch Indies regular-issue stamps with new value and the design of a biblical lamp for use as 1948 semi-postal stamps of Indonesia. The surtax was for war victims and charity.

pelure a thin, hard paper, sometimes greyish in colour, almost transparent, with the designs showing through to the back of stamps. Some Australian stamps provide good examples; other examples are found in stamps of Indian feudatory states.

PEN. (insc.) penni, a coin; the abbreviation appears on stamps of Finland.

penalty envelopes or stamps government-stamped impressions or envelopes stating that a penalty will be imposed for private or personal use. Issues of the United States, Norway, and South Africa provide examples.

Penang an island of about 400 square miles off the west coast of Malay Peninsula in Southeast Asia. Capital: Georgetown. Issued stamps in 1948; these are listed with Malaya stamps in catalogues.

pen cancellation an obliteration made by pen and ink in lines or crosses to prevent stamps from being used a second time. Not to be confused with manuscript cancels made of letters, figures, or words.

pence issues postage stamps issued in the sterling values of pence. Often used to describe stamps of the Province of Canada used between 1851 and 1859.

pengo a coin of Hungary, in use from 1926. 100 fillers equal 1 pengo.

penni a copper coin of Finland and Karelia. 100 pennia equal 1 markha.

PENNI or **PENNIA** (insc.) name of a coin, appearing on stamps of Finland.

penny originally a small silver coin, then a copper, and now a bronze coin of the United Kingdom and some British possessions. 12 pence equal 1 shilling. English pounds, shillings, and pence are abbreviated £, s., and d., from Latin terms "librae", "solidi", and "denarii". The solidus is also known as "schilling" and "shilling" in old records.

penny black The first adhesive postage stamps in the world, made by Perkins, Bacon & Co. in London and issued by Great Britain on May 6, 1840. Production was neither simple nor easy, but the printers planned to make the steel engraved dies

Penalty stamp

in parts employing both mechanical engraving and hand engraving. The late Frank Godden explained how the engravers developed the dies, and gave his permission to reproduce the stages of production: Fig. 1: The engravers used a stock roller to impress the elaborate machine-engraved background in order to prevent forgery. Then an artist outlined the area for Queen Victoria's head. He burnished out the area, but the steel was too rough on the die to engrave the head, so engravers transferred the impression to a new die and engraved it. Fig. 2: This is the transferred engraving on the new die. Fig. 3: Frederick Heath engraved the likeness of Queen Victoria from a drawing by Henry Corbould. The original artwork was a medal designed by William Wyon to mark the Queen's first visit to Guildhall, on Lord Mayor's Day in 1837. Fig. 4: The words "POSTAGE" and "ONE PENNY" were inscribed on the die, and small rays were added in the upper corners. The engravers transferred 240 impressions on each plate. Fig. 5: The letters were struck in the lower corners by hand punches on 240 stamps on the plate, with letters AA at the top left and TL in the bottom right corner.

Penny Blue Trial colour trial of 1-penny 1840 stamp of Great Britain.

Penny Express Co. issued U.S. local stamps in 1866.

penny-in-the-slot machines British term for stamp vending machines.

penny post The penny post was a postal service in various parts of the world, operated by charging one penny in British money, or its equivalent in other countries, for the delivery of letters or small packets. In some offices in the United States the charge was just one cent, a coin often referred to as a penny. The following is a brief chronological account of the penny post.

De Valayer (or La Petite Poste de Paris): Monsieur de Valayer tried to organize a penny post in Paris in 1653, under a royal decree of King Louis XIV. He sold labels to attach to mail, and charged one sol (about one English penny) each for them. His post failed because of a lack of patrons and because people dumped garbage into his street mail boxes, thus destroying the mail. His name is also spelled "de Villayer".

London: A mail delivery service was founded in London by Robert Murray and William Dockwra. In 1680 they introduced

Penny black

Fig. 1
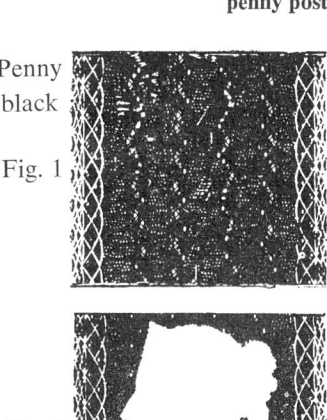

Fig. 2

Fig. 3

Fig. 4
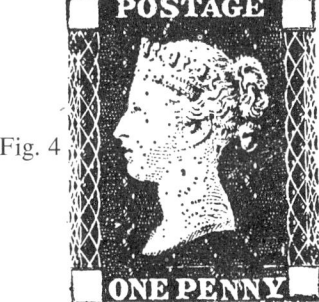

Fig. 5

the first paid (postage) stamps in the world. These were handstruck impressions in a triangular design of two lines framing the words "Penny Post Paid". An initial in the centre of the impression indicated the post office in the city. The men operated their post until 1682, when the government suppressed it. The service became a government penny post, but still used the Dockwra-type handstruck stamps.

England: The first penny post in the English towns and cities outside of London was authorized by an Act of Parliament in 1765. The postal services began in 1793 in Birmingham, Manchester, and Liverpool, and some years later the penny posts exceeded 2,000. As a result of the widespread service, hundreds of handstamped impressions appeared on mail with the town name, date, and "PY POST" or "Penny Post". Most had no dates; but the marks were struck at the receiving offices, not where the mail was delivered in another office. Many towns had numerous offices. For example, Bristol had no less than sixty-three penny posts.

Scotland: In 1765, Peter Williamson established the first Scottish penny post in Edinburgh, where he kept a coffee shop in the Parliament House. Men attending the courts used the Williamson shop to forward letters by porters (or caddies) to different parts of the city and suburbs. Business increased so much that Williamson started a penny post with hourly deliveries. His men wore uniforms and rang bells to announce their deliveries. If Williamson used any markings on the letters and mail, they are not known, but he did have some official recognition.

Ireland: The first penny post outside of England and Scotland was established in Dublin, Ireland, in 1773. Postal services came under control of a deputy for Ireland who was responsible to the postal authorities in London, although control changed from time to time. No "Penny Post Paid" handstamps of Ireland are known before 1782, when the Dockwra type is known to have been used. The real Irish activity in penny posts took place between 1805 and 1850. Over 200 places in Ireland adopted penny posts.

British soldiers and sailors: By an act of the British legislature in 1795, soldiers and sailors in any part of the British Dominions could send or receive single letters (those written on one piece of paper without enclosures) for one penny each. The service-

men's letters had to be prepaid and then countersigned by their superior officers. Because servicemen, mainly the officers, abused the penny post, a new act was passed to penalize any person who used the service to avoid postal charges.

New York: Various U.S. organizations established their own private postal services in New York, Albany, and Philadelphia. The owners of the New York Penny Post announced that they would commence business in December 1839, as the first penny post in America.

Great Britain: In 1840 Great Britain introduced the first penny post that used adhesive postage stamps, prepaid letter sheets, and envelopes. Values of the three items were one penny in black and two pence for the blue-coloured postal items. The use of the letter sheets and envelopes indicated the prepayment of postal services. Rowland Hill was credited with the innovation since he had urged the government to reduce postal charges and to reform the post office operations. For years he tried to convince the authorities that lower postage would increase the volume of mail and offset the increased expenses that could take place. Queen Victoria knighted him for his work, which some postal historians have claimed to be the greatest step forward ever taken in post office operations. See PENNY BLACK.

Canada: In July 1898 an Imperial Conference on postal rates was held in London, England. At the proposal of Postmaster General the Hon. William Mulock of Canada (later Sir William), they decided to introduce a penny post for Great Britain, Canada, Newfoundland, and Cape Colony as well as Natal in South Africa. Sir William stimulated interest in the penny post by introducing the service at Christmas, 1898, and by the issue of the famous map stamp of Canada, which features the British areas in the world that took part in the new penny post.

Penrhyn Island   a New Zealand dependency of about 3 square miles in South Pacific; part of the Cook Islands. The native name is Tongareva. First stamps of Penrhyn Island were stamps of New Zealand 1902, surcharged with new values.

Pensacola, Florida   issued postmasters' provisional envelopes in 1861 as part of the Confederate States of America.

Perak   a state in the Federation of Malaya since February 1948; formerly one of the Federated Malay States. Located on the west coast of the Malay Peninsula; about 7,980 square miles. Capital: Taiping. Refer to Malaya in stamp catalogues.

PERAK (insc.) appears on stamps of Perak. Some authorities say these stamps were issued in 1891, while others quote 1892.

Perak (ovpt.) on Straits Settlements stamps in 1880.

perçage (Fr.) roulette.

perçagem (Port.) roulette.

perce (Port.) rouletted.

percé (Fr.) denotes slits or pricks, with no part of the paper being removed, in contrast to "perforated", in which small discs of paper are punched out.

percé en lignes (Fr.) rouletted in lines.

percé en losanges (Fr.) pierced in lozenges, refers to a lozenge roulette.

percé en points (Fr.) pierced by pins, refers to a pin perforation.

percé en scie (Fr.) saw-tooth rouletted, refers to a saw-tooth roulette.

percé en serpentin (Fr.) serpentine rouletted.

percé en zigzag (Fr.) pierced in zig-zags, refers to zigzag roulette.

percevoir (Fr.) to collect.

Perçue (Fr.) from the French word "percevoir", to gather or collect taxes; hence, the tax (postage) was prepaid on letters bearing this postmark.

perf. perforation.

perforated implies the removal of small discs of paper, not simply slits or cuts in the paper.

perforated horizontally refers to stamps perforated along top and bottom and imperforate on the sides.

perforated initials or **perfins** refers to the letters punched in adhesive postage stamps to help prevent theft of the stamps. Ones that read "OS" (Official Service), "OHMS" (On His Majesty's Service), or similar initials were made for official use. Other stamps may be perforated with a company's or organization's initials.

perforated vertically refers to postage stamps perforated on the sides and imperforate top and bottom.

perforating machine machine equipped with needles mounted on a blade or rotating disc used to perforate sheets of paper.

perforation gauge a device to measure perforations; it has rows of dots made in the exact sizes of the perforations (holes) in postage stamps. Gauges have been made of cardboard, metal, or plastic. The plastic gauges sold by Stanley Gibbons have lines from top to bottom so arranged that they run in an angle and cross various sizes of

perforations, even to the fractions.

perforations the holes punched in the margins of stamps to facilitate separating them. Perforation 12 means that twelve holes appear in a space of two centimetres (often referred to as twenty millimetres in the United States). Mixed perforations, an arbitrary term, applies to a single stamp with perforations of more than one gauge.

perforato a punti (It.) pin perforation.

perforazione ad arco (It.) percé en arc.

perforazione a losanghe (It.) lozenge roulette.

perforazione a serpentina (It.) serpentine roulette.

perforazione a zigzag (It.) zigzag roulette.

Perfs close R.F. in auction catalogues, indicates that the perforations are close to the right side, but the stamps are fine quality.

Perfs nibbed in auction catalogues, indicates perforations that are not full length.

perfuração (Port.) perforation.

Pergamentpapier (Ger.) parchment paper.

Perkins, Bacon & Co. British security printers who made the first adhesive postage stamps in the world, the 1-penny blacks and 2-pence blues. The company started in business in 1819 under the name of Perkins and Firman. In May 1829, Joshua B. Bacon, a brother-in-law of Mr. Perkins, became a partner, and the company name was changed to Perkins and Bacon. The company printed numerous classical stamps. (Refer to the two-volume work *Perkins Bacon Records* by Percy de Worms with a foreword by Sir John Wilson, Bart., C.V.O, published by D. Van Nostrand Company, Inc., Princeton, New Jersey, Toronto, Ontario, and London.)

Perlis a state in the Federation of Malaysia, on west coast of Malay Peninsula; about 310 square miles. Capital: Kangar. Issued stamps in 1948.

Per Luchtpost (Dutch) by airmail.

Per Lugpost (Africaans) by airmail.

permanence the property of paper that causes it to resist changes in one or more of its characteristics, when submitted to natural or artificial aging conditions.

permit stamps See POSTAL PERMIT.

per Nachnahme (Ger.) cash on delivery (C.O.D.).

Perot stamps the locals made by W. B. Perot, postmaster of Hamilton, Bermuda. He made them from 1848 to 1861 to prevent personal losses when some people left their letters in his post box but did not deposit their coins to pay his delivery fee. These stamps are the Bermuda or Perot postmaster's provisionals.

Pérou (Fr.) Peru.

peroxide Hydrogen peroxide in weak solutions with water may be used to revive the colours of postage stamps and stamp paper, providing these are not injured by water. Collectors are warned to use great care and not to use full-strength peroxide.

PER PACCHI (ovpt.) appears on 1929 regular issues of the Vatican for use as 1931 parcel post stamps of Vatican City.

perper the gold standard of Montenegro (Jugoslavia). 100 paras equal 1 perper or 1 kruna. It has the same value as the krone of Austria.

Persane (insc.) appears on stamps of Persia (Iran).

Persia See IRAN.

Persien (Ger.) Persia.

personal-delivery stamps a type of Czechoslovakia stamps 1937-46 and Bohemia and Moravia 1939, to prepay special personal-delivery service to the persons named on the letters.

Peru a republic of about 482,258 square miles on the west coast of South America. Capital: Lima. Issued stamps in 1857.

Peru provisional issues In 1878 difficulties arose between Chile and Bolivia when Chile laid claim to part of the nitrate districts that Bolivia operated. Peru supported Bolivia; then Chile declared war on both countries on Feb. 5, 1879. Finally, in 1873, Peru was defeated. While Chile occupied Peru, various provisional stamps were issued for Ancachs (1884), Apurimac (1885), Arequipa (1881), Ayacucho (1881), Chachapoyas (1884), Chala (1884), Chiclayo 1884), Cuzco (1881-5), Huacho (1884), Moquegua (1881-3), Paita (1884), Pasco (1884), Pisco (1884), Fiura (1884), Puno (1882-3), and Yca (1884).

Pesa (ovpt.) name of a coin, appearing on stamps of Germany, for use in German East Africa, 1893.

peseta a silver coin of Spain, Andorra, and other countries. 100 centimos equal 1 peseta. Originally part of the peso (8 reales), the peseta equalled 2 reales. It replaced the escudo in 1868.

PESETA (insc.) name of a coin, appearing with no country name on early stamps of Spain.

peso a silver coin of Mexico, Canal Zone, Uruguay, El Salvador, and other South American countries. 100 centavos or 8 reales equal 1 peso. It is the Spanish equivalent of the dollar. The value "VIII" or "8 reales" is often found on the shield on the reverse side, from which the term "piece of eight" derives. The peso in use today is based on the decimal system, and is equal to 100 centimos, centavos, or centisimos.

Pétain, Henri Philippe (1856-1951) a former French commander and politician. See ÉTAT FRANÇAIS.

Petersburg, Va. This town in Virginia issued postmasters' provisional stamps in 1861 as part of the Confederate States of America.

petit cachet (Fr.) small cancellation.

petit, petite (Fr.) small, little.

petroglyphy rock carving. An example of rock carvings can be seen on 1963 stamps of Norway.

P.F. Philatelic Foundation.

Pfalz (Ger.) Palatinate.

pfenning or **pfennig** a copper coin of Germany, certain former German colonies, and other places. 100 pfennigs equal 1 mark. The word may be related to "penny"; the pfennig was the silver denarius of the Middle Ages.

PF or **PFG** (sur.) for "phennig", a coin; the letters appear on stamps of Germany for use by German offices in China.

Pfg. (sur.) for "pfennig", a coin; appears on Russian stamps of 1909-12, for use in Estonia under German occupation, 1918.

P.G. part gum.

P.G.'s (nick.) for "premières gravures", proposed designs of certain U.S. classical postage stamps of 1861. The modern experts in U.S. stamps have concluded that the P.G.'s were essays or sample stamps, completely produced with gum and perforations. Some nineteenth-century specialists, including John Luff, considered them to be the issued stamps that became known as the August issue. They are all believed to have been printed in August 1861. The P.G.'s are not to be confused with gravure-printed postage stamps.

P.G.S. (ovpt.) Perak Government Service; appears on stamps of Straits Settlements for use as official stamps of Perak in 1890. Listed after stamps of Malaya in catalogues. Some specialists say the stamps were issued in 1889.

ph in auction catalogues, means "pinhole".

PH in auction catalogues, means "photo".

Phagwah Festival (insc.) appears on Guyana stamps of Feb. 26, 1969. Phagwah (or Holi) is one of the gayest of Hindu festivals. Its significance is partly social and partly religious. It marks the destruction of an evil society by God and its replacement by a righteous one. It is also a great social occasion because it heralds the arrival of spring and the gathering of the winter crops. In celebrating the festival, it is customary for those participating to sprinkle each other lavishly with sweet-smelling powders and to spray liquid of magenta crystals. (Courtesy of Crown Agents Stamp Bureau)

Pharmacopoeia Philatelica (Lat.) Drugs on Stamps; appears as a heading for Chapter 1 in the American Topical Association handbook number 55, which lists the stamps of the world on this varied topic.

philancier a derogatory name for those whose main interest in stamps is not collecting but making money. It is not used to describe dealers, whose business is selling postage stamps to collectors.

philatective or **philatelective** a person who concentrates on microscopic faults in postage stamps. The term is sometimes used sarcastically.

philatelic pertaining to philately.

philatelic agencies government post office departments authorized to sell postage stamps and often postal stationery at face value directly to stamp collectors and dealers. Collectors are warned about the problem of getting fine-quality stamps from foreign agencies, which will not replace poor stamps as promptly as they fill orders.

philatelic cancels special postmarks not used for normal mail; often they are decorative postmarks commemorating an event.

Philatelic Congress of Great Britain an organization established in 1909 in England; meets annually for philatelic interests and social events.

Philatelic Foundation a chartered non-profit organization founded by the late Alfred F. Lichtenstein, and devoted entirely to the advancement of philately. It is located at 99 Park Avenue in New York City.

philatelic literature stamp magazines, catalogues, books, handbooks, radio or television scripts, or any other kind of regular or specific publications devoted to postage stamp collecting.

philatelic magazines and papers These are devoted to a wide variety of stamp collectors' subjects. Stamp dealers can tell collectors where the papers originate and give the proper names of numerous publications both privately printed and prepared for philatelic societies.

philatelic plagiarism the use on a stamp of a design that resembles the design on a stamp previously issued. Some examples are: the Mauritius 1847 imitation of the British penny blacks and blues; the 1856

Corrientes, Argentina, stamps intended to resemble the French 1849 issue; the Canadian 1959 Country Women stamps similar to a Polish 1958 issue flopped (turned left to right) and also resembling a 1946 German coin of similar design.

Philatelic Protection Association formed in May 1891 in London to prevent the dissemination of forgeries. The members succeeded in taking some British forgers to court and obtaining conviction.

philatelic station cancels special cancellations struck on mail posted at temporary post offices at stamp exhibitions. Some collectors save these items.

philatelic terms words and phrases having meanings particular to stamp collecting.

philatélie (Fr.) philately.

Philatelie (Ger.) philately.

philatélique (Fr.) philatelic.

philatelist from Greek words "philos", meaning fond of, and "ateleia", exemption from payment. The term "philatelist" originally meant "a person fond of exemption from payments". The word has developed to describe the real students of postage stamps and other related subjects (postal history or covers stamped or pre-stamp periods, for example), as distinguished from mere collectors of stamps.

philatéliste (Fr.) philatelist.

philatologist a stamp collector interested more in the history portrayed by postage stamps than in the stamps themselves.

Philippinen (Ger.) Philippine Islands.

Philippines a former Spanish colony, now a republic; a group of 7,100 islands southeast of Asia, of about 115,600 square miles. Capital: Quezon City. Stamps were issued under Spanish dominion 1854-98; under American dominion, stamps of the United States were overprinted in 1899-1904 and then inscribed "PHILIPPINE ISLANDS" with the addition of "UNITED STATES OF AMERICA", 1906-35. From 1935 to 1946 stamps of the Commonwealth were issued; then issues of the republic were used.

phoenix a legendary bird, often used as feature design on stamps.

Phonopost Service a service of the Chinese armed forces. On June 27, 1960, a single stamp was issued by the Republic of China publicizing this service. The $2-value stamp depicted a young man recording a message and a mother listening to the recording. The design of a reel of tape with wings divides the two pictures diagonally. See FONOPOST.

phonopost stamps also called "recorded

stamps". Argentina issued three stamps on Dec. 11, 1939, for the recording and mailing of special flexible phonograph letters. Formosa (Taiwan) issued stamps on June 27, 1960, to publicize the Phonopost Service of the Chinese army. The first postal congress of the U.P.U. regulated the transmission of recorded messages, among seven other types of ordinary mail.

phosphorescent refers to a stamp overprinted (tagged) with luminescent substances that glow either orange-red or yellow-green when activated by short-wave ultra-violet light. (Courtesy of Alfred G. Boerger)

photo in auction catalogues, indicates that a lot or item is illustrated with its lot number for easy identification.

photo-engraving a process for producing a design on a sensitized metal plate by placing a transparent negative between the plate and the source of light. Coated areas, which are not rendered water-insoluble by light, are washed off and etched with acid solutions.

photographic-sensitized paper paper made for photographic use. The first Boy Scout issue in April 1900 during the Boer War was photographically produced on this type of paper.

photogravure (1) a process for making prints from photo-mechanically prepared intaglio plates; (2) the stamps from such a plate.

photogravure paper a highly finished paper suitable for printing by photogravure process.

photogravure printings stamps made by gravure printing as opposed to those printed by other processes.

photolithography a lithographic printing process in which the image or design is reproduced on a zinc plate by photographic means, instead of being drawn by hand. See OFFSET.

photomicrography the art of photographing minute particles through a microscope to produce a magnified record. This method is used to detect forged postage stamps.

Phrygian Bonnet (1) name of a small postmark with "P.P." meaning "carried prepaid". It is a popular, scarce Paris postmark. Its name derives from the fact that it resembled a type of bonnet worn by people of Phrygia, an ancient country in Asia Minor. (Courtesy of Herbert Dube) (2) the classical name for the Cap of Liberty that appears in the coat of arms of various postage stamps, for example, the

Pigeon Post: local stamp

early issues of Colombia and other stamps of South and Central American countries.

PIASTRA (sur.) appears on stamps of Italy for use by Italian offices in Crete, 1900-1.

piastre a silver coin of Turkey, Syria, Egypt, Indo-China, and others. 40 paras equal 1 piastre. 100 centimes equal 1 piastre. 100 piastres equal a Turkish lira or pound. The name may come from "plastra", meaning a small metal plate. The Spanish dollar, or peso, is also called a piastre.

picado (Sp.) rouletted.

picado a serpentina (Sp.) serpentine rouletted.

picado en sierra (Sp.) saw-tooth rouletted, refers to a saw-tooth roulette.

picado en zigzag (Sp.) pierced in zigzags, refers to zig-zag roulette.

picadura (Sp.) roulette.

picadura en forma de arco (Sp.) percé en arc.

picadura en rombos (Sp.) lozenge roulette.

pictorial FD cancel first day cancellation with an illustration.

pictorial postmarks impressions including a picture or design of any kind, such as a flag, Santa Claus, or airplane, with or without words.

pictorials stamps with designs featuring landscapes, seascapes, buildings, or other scenes.

picture stamps variously called "view stamps", "pictorials", or "landscape stamps". So many picture stamps exist that specialized topical collections can be formed.

pie copper coin of India and Aden. 12 pies equal 1 anna. It is not to be confused with a pice, which is divided into 3 pies.

piega (It.) crease.

Pietersburg issue stamps for the town of Pietersburg in Transvaal, 1901, which was for a time the headquarters of the Dutch forces during the Boer War. These are type-set stamps listed with those of Transvaal in catalogues.

pig a moulded bar or cake of typographic or stereotype metal, which is melted and used for casting types or stereos.

Pigeon Post of Great Barrier Island This was a carrier pigeon postal service established in 1896 between Great Barrier Island and New Zealand. Local stamps issued for the service were inscribed "Great Barrier – Pigeon Gram – Auckland". The pigeon post ended Sept. 26, 1908, after twelve years of service.

pigment an insoluble mineral colouring substance, used in ink or paper manufacture.

Pilgrim Tercentenary (insc.) appears on the U.S. set of three commemorative stamps issued Dec. 21, 1920, to mark the 300th anniversary of the landing of the Pilgrims at Plymouth, Massachusetts.

PILIPANAS (insc. and part of sur.) on various stamps of Philippines, 1962 to the present.

pillars on British stamp margins De La Rue, British security printers, encountered difficulties in January 1888 in producing 4- and 9-pence British stamps. The printers made stamps in panes with gutters between them.

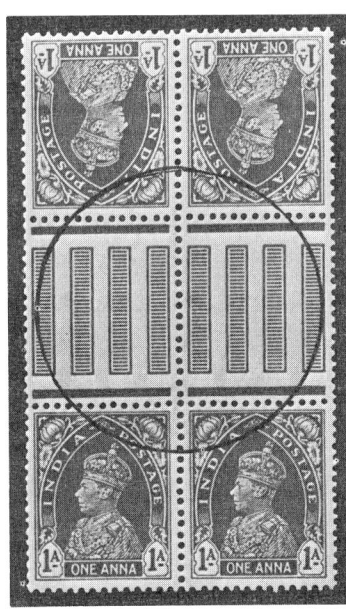

The letterpress plates consisted of type slightly raised above the shoulders of metal. Air passed between the metal and paper causing the paper to flutter. To stop

this, De La Rue introduced pillars typehigh to receive ink and hold down the gutter paper so that two colours would register perfectly, that is, each colour would be in its right place without overlapping.

Pim & Co. publishers of New Zealand stamp catalogues and other books in New Zealand.

pince (Fr.) tweezers, stamp collectors' tongs used to handle postage stamps.

pin-holes small holes in the body of a sheet of paper or in the coating, caused by sand and other gritty materials or by air bubbles and froth. Some classical stamps have pinholes from being strung on threads for display.

pink backs (nick.) postage stamps printed in red, rose, or similar colours in aniline inks that penetrate the paper and show as a pink glow on the back of the stamps. Pink backs are common among certain U.S. stamps printed in about 1894, and again during the First World War. See GREEN BACKS.

Pinkney's Express Post in New York City, New York, issued U.S. local stamps in 1851.

pin perforation an inaccurate term for pin roulette.

pin roulette also called a zigzag roulette; a series of pin-holes to separate stamps.

These are sometimes mistakenly called pin perforations (a perforation has the paper removed).

pinsin or **pinsine** (insc.) appears on stamps of Ireland.

pintado (Port.) coloured, in colour.

P.I.-U.S. INITIAL FLIGHT December-1935 (ovpt.) appears on regular-issue stamps of Philippines in 1935 for the first trans-Pacific flight of the China Clipper from Manila in the Philippines to San Francisco, California.

Pinzette (Ger.) tweezers.

pioneer flights experimental airmail flights from temporary post offices, frequently authorized by post office departments prior

Pneumatic post stamp (Italy)

Plate block

to established air post service.

Pips Daily Mail in Brooklyn, New York, issued U.S. local stamps in 1862.

piquage non officiel (Fr.) private perforation on stamp.

piquage (Fr.) perforation, especially perfin.

piqué (Fr.) perforated.

piqûre d'épingle (Fr.) pin-hole.

Pirie watermark a papermaker's watermark reading "Alexr Pirie & Sons", for a papermaking firm in the village of Stoneywood, near Aberdeen, Scotland. The Pirie company sold paper to dealers in Montreal, Quebec, and then to the security printers The British American Bank Note Co. Ltd. This Pirie watermark appeared in a small number of 15-cent Canadian stamps in 1876. Only a portion appears in any single stamp.

Pirie watermarked paper paper used for a limited quantity of 1876 postage stamps in Canada. The company name, Alexr Pirie & Sons, was watermarked diagonally across the sheet, with the result that most stamps from the Pirie paper have no watermarks.

Pisco city in Peru, issued overprinted stamps in 1884.

Piscopi (It.) Telos.

Pitcairn Islands a British colony of about 2 square miles halfway between Australia and South America in the South Pacific. Issued stamps in 1940.

Pittsylvania Court House, Va. issued postmasters' provisional stamps in 1861 in Virginia, as part of the Confederate States of America.

Piura (ovpt.) appears on Peru regular issues in 1884 after the war between Chile and

Peru. Piura, a city on the Piura River in Peru, issued provisional stamps.

Pjónustumerki (ovpt.) appears on Iceland official stamps of 1930. The initial letter is actually the Runic letter thorn, not the letter P, and has the sound of "th".

PL or **PL. No. Blks.** plate-number blocks.

pl # in auction catalogues, means "plate number".

plaatgravure (Dutch) engraving.

plancha (Sp.) plate.

planche (Fr.) plate.

planche de cuivre (Fr.) copper plate.

planche défectueuse (Fr.) worn plate.

planche nettoyée (Fr.) cleaned plate.

planography printing processes, such as lithography and pantone, in which areas not to be printed are made ink-repellent, while areas to be printed are made ink-receptive.

P.L. & R. *Postal Laws and Regulations,* a book published by the United States Post Office as a guide, and an information and instruction manual.

plåt (Swed.) plate.

plate (1) a glass or metal plate sensitized for photographic reproduction; (2) any metal plate carrying reproductions used in printing; (3) a printed illustration.

plate block or **plate-number block** This is usually considered to consist of four or more stamps from two or more horizontal rows, unsevered and with marginal inscriptions including a plate number. It may be three stamps unsevered from two horizontal rows with marginal paper and inscriptions intact with a plate number.

plate curving a process by which steel-engraved plates, electrotypes, and stereotypes are curved to fit on the plate cylinder.

plate cylinder cylinder of a rotary press on which the curved plates are attached.

plate flaws any kind of damage done to a plate that shows on stamps. Some flaws pick up ink and print the impressions on the plates. Some plate flaws have been so extensive that the plates were rejected and never used.

plate-making all operations involved in the preparation and making of printing plates.

platen perforating the operation of perforating postage stamps as they are printed. Many rouletted stamps were processed in the same way.

platen press press in which both form and paper are on flat surfaces that are brought against one another to form the impression.

plate number impression that records details or the exact number of a printing plate. Certain early issues of Great Britain included plate numbers within the stamp designs. In any modern issues the plate numbers are on the marginal paper.

plate-number block See PLATE BLOCK.

plate proofs proofs from a finished printing plate from any method of printing. Proofs are made from a portion of a plate, or from a full plate made for one, two, or more colours.

plate-wiping paper lightweight tagboard, used for wiping intaglio-engraved plates between impressions.

plate variety a stamp printed from a plate that included one or more subjects different from the others in the plate. The term is used in philatelic literature to distinguish these varieties from die alterations, usually mentioned in stamp catalogues. So many plate varieties of stamps are known that the popular stamp catalogues can not list all of them, but the specialized books often show the most popular examples.

plating the act of placing each stamp back in its original position in a pane or sheet. This is an advanced form of philately requiring numerous stamps, even thousands at times.

Platte (Ger.) die, plate.

Plattendruck (Ger.) plate printing.

Plattennummer (Ger.) plate number.

Plattenschaden (Ger.) plate defect.

Pleasant Shade, Va. This town in Virginia issued postmasters' provisional stamps in 1861 as part of the Confederate States of America.

PLEBISCITE OLSZTYN ALLENSTEIN (ovpt.) appears on stamps of Germany for use in Allenstein, East Prussia, in 1920.

PLEBISCIT SLESVIG (insc.) appears on stamps of Schleswig, 1851.

plebiscite stamps stamps issued by authorities representing international commissions or committees appointed to supervise plebiscites in various parts of the world. Plebiscite is a direct vote of all the people in a region on a measure to determine a form of government. On conclusion the region adopts stamps of the country that was the choice of the people. They are temporary issues, and not to be confused with occupation stamps.

pli (Fr.) crease.

plié (Fr.) creased.

Plimpton name used to describe certain U.S. postal stationery envelopes. Plimpton Manufacturing Co. of Hartford, Connecticut, printed U.S. official postal stationery in 1874-5.

PL. PR. plate proof.

P.L.U.N.A. (airline) Primeras Lineas Uruguayas de Navegación Aérea. Point of origin: Uruguay.

P.M. (1) post meridiem, or afternoon, appearing after the figures of the hour; (2) postmaster.

P.M. (It. ovpt.) Posta Militaire; appears on stamps of Italy 1943 for use as military stamps for regular mail.

P.M. autographs postmasters' autographs

P.M.G. Postmaster General.

PMKD postmarked.

PMKS postmarks.

pneumatic post (mail tube service) Italy, France, New York City, and other centres have operated local transmission of mail by underground tube. Italy issued special postage stamps for pneumatic service.

poached-egg labels (nick.) test labels made in Great Britain for coil-stamp vending machines. Some were accidentally used as postage stamps. The design resembles a

poached egg, and the label is the same size as the 1937 British stamp.

POBLACT (part of Erse insc.) appears on so-called forerunners of July 1922, the Irish Republican Army issue. These are not listed in the popular catalogues.

pochette a type of envelope of any of various crystal-clear materials for stamp protection; a stamp mount. Such accessories now available for the protection of stamps and gum may prove harmful. Care must be exercised to ensure that air can circulate around the stamps, which might otherwise adhere to the pochette.

Poczta (insc.) postage; appears on stamps of Poland.

Poczta Polska (sur.) Polish postage; appears on stamps of Germany in 1919 for Poznan (Posen), a Polish department in the west-central region. From 1814 to 1914 Poznan was occupied by Germans and became the centre of German life and culture in Poland. On Aug. 5, 1919, the first Poznan occupation stamps were issued, and the second issue of German surcharged stamps went on sale for a limited time in 1923. See POLSKA POCZTA.

POHJOIS INKERI (insc.) appears on stamps of North Ingermanland, now a part of Russia. See NORTH INGERMANLAND.

POINTE du RAZ Finistere (Fr. insc.) Cape Finistere, a department in northwest France; the name appears on a 20-franc stamp of France in 1946.

points up or **points down**   refers to the direction of points in grills.

point system   term applied to modern system of type sizes and spacing material used in the British Commonwealth and the United States.

POLAIRE INTERNATIONALE 1932-33 (Fr. insc.) appears with "2ME ANNEE" on airmail stamps of Russia 1932, to mark the second International Polar Year in connection with the flight to Franz-Josef Land in the Arctic Ocean.

Poland   a former kingdom, now a republic in Europe on the Baltic Sea; about 150,459 square miles. Capital: Warsaw. Stamps issued 1860-5 under Russian dominion; stamps of Russia were used until the republic was formed in 1918.

Poland exile stamps   postage stamps issued by the Polish government-in-exile in London, England, 1941-4. Four series of stamps were listed by Scott's, Gibbons, and Minkus catalogue editors.

POLE DU NORD 1931 (Fr. insc.) appears on the airmail stamps of Russia in 1931.

Polarflug (Ger.) polar flight.

Polen (Ger.) Poland.

policromo (It.) multicoloured.

Polish locals   stamps issued following the First World War for use in various parts of Poland. They include the Warsaw issues (1918), Lublin issue, Cracow issues, and Poznan (Posen) issue. Refer to stamp catalogues for details of these stamps.

Polish offices in Danzig   Poland maintained post offices in Danzig 1925-38, and issued Polish stamps overprinted "PORT GDANSK".

Polish offices in Turkish Empire   Poland maintained post offices in the Turkish Empire; stamps were issued overprinted "Levant", 1919-21.

Pologne (Fr.) Poland.

Polska (insc.) appears on stamps of Poland.

Polska Poczta (ovpt.) appears on Austrian military semi-postal stamps in 1918 for Lublin, a Polish city southeast of Warsaw captured by the Austrians in August 1914 and July 1915. Between 1772 and 1795 the area of Poland was divided among Russia, Austria, and Prussia – hence the Austrian interest in Poland.

polychrome (Fr.) multicoloured.

Pomeroy's Letter Express   in New York, issued U.S. local stamps in 1844.

Ponce issue   the first provisional stamps of Porto Rico (spelled "Puerto Rico" since 1932), 1898. These are listed in the specialized books.

pont (Fr.) gutter.

Ponta Delgada   capital of Azores and a district of Portugal. Stamps were issued 1892-1905, superseded by stamps of the Azores, and in 1931 by Portugal stamps.

ponte (It.) gutter.

Pony Express   a mail service originating on April 3, 1860, between St. Joseph, Missouri, and Sacramento, California. The service ended in 1861 with the opening of a transcontinental railroad.

Poonch (Punch)   a feudatory state in the Jammu province of Jammu and Kashmir State in northern India. Capital: Poonch. Issued stamps 1876-90.

P.O. Paid   in Philadelphia, Pennsylvania, issued U.S. local stamps in 1852.

Pope and King (nick.) the Spanish semi-postal or charity stamps issued as the Santiago issue and the Toledo issue. These stamps replaced the regular-issue stamps from Dec. 23, 1928, to Jan. 6, 1929. The proceeds went to restore catacombs in Rome. Each stamp portrays Pope Pius XI and King Alfonso of Spain.

Popper, Julius   a daring Romanian mining engineer and legendary figure who set himself up as a dictator of Tierra del Fuego. He issued a local stamp in 1891. In his catalogues, Victor Kneitschel illustrates one on a cover with two stamps of Argentina, cancelled "San Sebastian", for a cape on the island. The letter was addressed to Argentina. The Popper story appears in

Catálogo de los Sellos Postales de la República Argentina, published in Buenos Aires, Argentina.

porosity the ability of paper to absorb fluids; this is an important factor in developing printing and writing inks. Porosity is adequately determined by measuring the rate of flow of air through the paper.

porous paper paper that is absorbent, and usually has a soft, open weave. It is difficult to remove the cancellations from stamps made on porous paper without destroying the stamp designs.

Port Cantonal (insc.) appears on 1843 stamps of Geneva, a canton of Switzerland.

Porteado (insc.) appears on stamps of Portugal and its colonies.

PORTEADO RECEBER (insc.) postage due; appears on stamps of Portugal and the Portuguese colonies.

Porte de Conducción (insc.) appears with values in large figures on 1897 parcel-post stamps of Peru.

Porte de Mar stamps These were used on foreign mail leaving Mexico in 1875. The denominations indicated the sum of money

paid to sea captains who carried the mail to a foreign port.

Porte Franco (Port. insc.) postage paid; appears on Portuguese stamps supplied to various charitable, scientific, and military associations for postage. These are franchise stamps. Portugal lists include the Red Cross, civilian rifle clubs, the Geographical Society of Lisbon, and the National Aid Society for Consumptives. Stamps used 1889-1938.

Porte Franco (insc.) on regular-issue stamps of Peru, 1852-72, with heraldic designs but no country name.

Port Fouad (ovpt.) appears on the issue of four stamps of Egypt in 1926 to mark the inauguration of Port Fuad, a city opposite Port Said.

PORT GDANSK (ovpt.) appears on stamps of Poland for use by Polish offices in Danzig, 1925-37.

Port Hood provisionals makeshift postage stamps made by a boy in Port Hood, Nova Scotia, in 1899. He cut 3-cent stamps into one-third and two-third parts and stamped the figure 1 on the small parts and 2 on the larger portions; he had no authority to do this surcharging. Leslie Davenport, a Toronto stamp dealer, said, "I doubt if there are ten copies of the stamps that this 10-year-old boy made with his rubber type stamps which every boy owned at that time, including myself. Unfortunately he sent some to Gibbons in London, and as a consequence they fell for it, and the stamps have been in the catalogues ever since. We (certain Canadians) have been trying to get them out of the catalogues for the last 40 years, but they continue to list them. The late Donald King of Halifax investigated the procedure and found the above statements correct."

Port-Lagos (ovpt. or sur.) appears on stamps of France for use by French offices in Port Lagos in the Turkish Empire.

Portland Vase, Wedgwood reproduction of the featured illustration on the cachet of the Wedgwood first day cover for the 1-pound booklet of British stamps, containing the story of Joseph Wedgwood and issued May 24, 1972. See WEDGWOOD £1 BOOKLET.

Port Lavaca, Texas issued postmasters' provisional stamps in 1861 as part of the Confederate States of America.

Porto (Ger.) postage.

Porto (insc. and sur.) appears without country name on Austria postage-due stamps, 1908-17. Also appears with word "piastre" on stamps of Austria for use by Austrian offices in Turkey.

Porto Betalt; P.O., Norge (inscs.) on official mail from Norway, indicates the postage on the mail was paid.

Portoerhoehung (Ger.) increase in postage.

portofrei (Ger.) free of postage.

Portofreiheitsmarke (Ger.) franchise stamp.

PORTOMAERKE (insc.) appears on postage-due stamps of Danish West Indies in 1902.

PORTO-MARKE (insc.) appears with "LAND-POST" on rural postage-due stamps of Baden, 1862.

PORTOMARKE (Ger. insc.) appears on postage-due stamps of Austria, Bosnia and Herzegovina, and Norway.

PORTO PFLICHTIGE DIENST SACHE

(Ger. insc.) appears on stamps of Württemberg, 1875-1921, for use as official stamps for the Communal Authorities.

Porto Rico See PUERTO RICO.

Portosatz (Ger.) rate of postage.

Portovorauszahlung (Ger.) prepayment of postage.

port payé (Fr.) post paid; the term is frequently struck as "PP" in a frame or on envelopes or letter sheets.

portraits Apart from monarchs or rulers of states, many countries refrain from using portraits of living people on stamps. A noted exception was the U.S. "Iwo Jima" stamp of July 11, 1945, which portrayed servicemen. Also contrary to this procedure, some smaller countries honour the major powers by portraying living persons of these countries.

PORT-SAID (ovpt. and insc.) appears on stamps of France for use by French offices in Port Said, Egypt.

Port Said cancels cancellations on British stamps issued after 1877; may be found with an Egyptian cancellation. Such cancels on stamps or postmarks and cancels on letters are from mail posted from British ships. (Courtesy of the late Grant Glassco, specialist in British stamps used abroad)

Portugal a republic on the Atlantic Ocean occupying the west side of Iberian Peninsula; about 34,240 square miles. Capital: Lisbon. First stamps were issued in 1853.

Portugiesisch-Afrika (Ger.) Portuguese Africa.

Portugiesisch-Guinea (Ger.) Portuguese Guinea.

Portugiesisch-Indien (Ger.) Portuguese India.

Portugiesisch-Kongo (Ger.) Portuguese Congo.

Portuguese Congo an exclave of Angola on the southwest coast of Africa. Capital: Cabinda. Stamps were issued 1894-1915; and were replaced by those of Angola in 1920.

Portuguese East Africa name sometimes given to the Portuguese colony of Mozambique. See MOZAMBIQUE.

Portuguese Guinea a Portuguese colony in West Africa of about 13,994 square miles. Capital: Bissau. Stamps have been issued since 1881, the first issues being those of Cape Verde overprinted "Guiné".

Portuguese India now part of Indian Republic; formerly a Portuguese colony on west coast of India; about 1,537 square miles. Capital: Pangim. Stamps were issued 1871-1961; in 1961 it was annexed by India.

PORTZEGEL (sur.) appears on Netherlands commemoratives of 1907 for use as postage-due stamps in the same year.

Posen (Poznan) issue See POCZTA POLSKA.

POSESIONES ESPANOLAS DEL SAHARA OCCIDENTAL (insc.) appears on 1924 stamps of Spanish Sahara, on the northwest coast of Africa.

posição na folha (Port.) sheet position.

posición en la hoja (Sp.) sheet position.

position blocks blocks of stamps from the same positions in sheets or panes, and often made into stamp collections. The position blocks most popular with collectors in the United States and Canada are plate number blocks and tab blocks of Israel.

position dans la feuille (Fr.) sheet position.

position dans la planche (Fr.) plate position.

position dots microscopic dots printed from plates, usually steel-engraved, that were not carefully finished before printing. These dots on the plates helped the transfer-press operator (siderographer) to align the subjects on the plate.

positioning of colours a non-technical term for the registration of two or more colours in postage stamp printing by any process, from two or more colour plates. Giori presses can print two or more colours from one engraved plate.

position sets sets of postage stamps from the same positions in sheets or panes. Often position sets come from margins that contain data, sheet numbers, or illustrations (like "Mr. Zip" in margins of many U.S. postage stamps). Arrows in margins of stamps of Great Britain, the United States, or other countries may be found in collections of position sets. Single stamps are probably the most popular stamps in collections of position sets.

positive A positive film, plate, or print reproduces the lights and shadows of the original. See NEGATIVE.

POSSEEL (Africaans insc.) postage: appears on alternate stamps of South Africa and South-West Africa.

post This is a word with various related meanings, from the Latin "ponere", to place. The word developed from the practice of placing riders at fixed stations on a route or road. Each rider took turns in carrying the mail from one post station or post house to the next one. Out of this such words developed as post stage, which came to mean the charge for sending letters (postage) and postal, postboy, postcard, posthaste, post horse, postman, postmark, postmaster, post office, post paid; all have common origin with the word post.

POSTA (insc.) appears above the design of a bird with spread wings, and "CESKO" at left and "SLOVENSKO" at right, on the first newspaper stamps of Czechoslovakia, 1918-20.

posta aerea (It.) airmail.

POSTA CESKOSLOVENSKE ARMADY SIBIRSKE (insc.) Appears on stamps issued by Czechoslovakia for use by the army in Siberia, 1919-20; Siberian Czechoslovak Legion Post.

Posta 15 or **Posta 35** (sur.) appears on revenue stamps of Tannu Tuva, 1933.

postage a word developed from "post" and "stage". Originally it meant the money paid to a postmaster to have his post riders carry letters over one or more stages (according to the late Dr. James Goodwin, postal historian, in a radio broadcast). The meaning of "postage" has not changed; it still means a prepayment of charges to carry mail from one place to another through a postal system. Since 1840 the postage stamps on mail indicate the same prepayment of services.

Postage (ovpt.) appears on the diagonal half of a stamp portraying a queen's head, on an issue of Grenada.

POSTAGE (insc.) appears with a scenic postage design and native lettering on stamps of Hyderabad.

POSTAGE AND REVENUE (ovpt. and sur.) appears overprinted on early stamps of British Guiana, Malta, Mauritius, and Sierra Leone; also appears surcharged on early issues of Grenada.

Postage Due (insc.) appears with denominations in pence or shillings on stamps of Great Britain and Australia.

postage-due stamps adhesive or handstruck impressions on mail to show the amount of postage owing or the total short-paid on foreign mail.

postage-due stamps of Switzerland From 1878 to 1924 these had no inscriptions and no words suggesting postage due. In 1924 Swiss postage dues were inscribed "Helvetia" (Switzerland), but gave no indication of their purpose.

postage-due stamps of Turkey Regular-issue stamps were used 1863-1913. The 1914 and subsequent issues to 1926 included the French words "Chiffre Taxe". In 1936 postage dues of Turkey were inscribed "Postalar Takse Pulu".

POSTAGE I.E.F. "D" (ovpt.) appears on stamps of Turkey for use in Mesopotamia, 1919.

Postagentur (Ger.) postal agency.

POSTAGE & REVENUE (insc.) appears on early stamps of Great Britain without a country name, but with the denominations in pence, shillings, or pounds, and portraits of a king or a queen.

postage stamp an authorized document (stamp) in use since 1840 that is affixed to mail of any kind that governments accept for transmission to indicate the prepayment of postal charges.

POSTAGE TAX (insc.) appears on postage-due stamps of Sudan.

POSTALARI (insc.) appears, sometimes with "TURKIYE", on stamps of Turkey.

POSTALAR TAKSE PULU (insc.) appears on postage-due stamps of Turkey, 1936.

postal cards postal stationery cards authorized by post office departments.

POSTAL CHARGES (sur.) appears with new value on stamps Papua and New Guinea, 1960. These stamps paid postage due, airmail surcharges, and storage charges. They were replaced in 1960 by postage-due stamps.

postal concession labels These were introduced on Nov. 1, 1932, by Great Britain for use by members of the army, navy, and air force and their families to send letters from Egypt to their homes in the British Isles and Ireland. The labels sold at reduced postal rates; for example, the new rate was 10 mills, while the old rate was 15 mills for mail weighing to 20 grams. Letters had to be posted in regimental or unit post boxes.

postal currency postage stamps used as money. In 1915-17 Russia issued postage stamps printed on thin cardboard with printing on the back. The text appears with a coat of arms, and means "Having circulation on par with silver subsidiary coins." At about the same time European countries put stamps in small cases. See EN-CASED STAMPS; FRACTIONAL CURRENCY NOTES.

postal-fiscal an authorized fiscal stamp used for postal purposes. Not to be confused with a fiscal stamp postally used, as is permitted in many countries.

postal-fiscals of Great Britain These were authorized for postal use on June 1, 1881. Details and lists are given in Gibbons Part One catalogue.

postal history the study of every facet of post office operations from the earliest days to the present. Postal history may be studied from various viewpoints: by country, state, or postal authority in terms of postal markings, or postage stamps, for example.

postalisch (Ger.) postal.

postally used describes a stamp or postal stationery item that has passed through the regular post office procedure, not cancelled to order or by favour.

postal markings or **postmarks** any kind of impressions, marks, or manuscript notations applied to mail as it passes through the post office or made by an authorized postal employee. Postmarks are impressions that may obliterate postage stamps or postal stationery to prevent the items from being used a second time. Postmarks include many classifications: date stamps, registration marks used as cancellers, and obliterations without dates in designs.

postal meters machine-made impressions called meter postage stamps. A. H. Pitney invented the postal meter machine, first used in 1914 in Chicago, Illinois. By 1958 meter postage stamps replaced half of all adhesive stamps used in the United States.

postal-note stamps stamps that were sold at post offices for small denominations. They were used in conjunction with former postal money orders in Canada. These stamps were issued in amounts to $10 in the United States from Feb. 1, 1945, until they were discontinued on March 31, 1951. Postal-note stamps did not prepay postal services and are not postage stamps. In both countries the postal-note stamps were exchanged for cash at post offices.

postal permit printed notices on postcards and envelopes by post office permission used on mail intended to be returned to the sender, so that the person returning the mail does not need to pay postage. Permitholders receive a greater return of mail this way, even though they must pay a slight increase over the normal postal rates for the specific items. These permits are especially popular with businessmen in Canada, the United States, and some other countries.

postal rates the various amounts of postage required to send mail anywhere. Rates are set by each postal authority and are sent to the Universal Postal Union in Switzerland.

postal stationery envelopes, aerograms, postcards, and wrappers, with postage stamps printed on them and sold by the post office department. Postal stationery items are official issues of the department in contrast to various items or cards privately printed.

postal tax-due stamps stamps used to collect money in cases in which people did not

apply the postal-tax stamps to their mail. Romania used them 1915-31.

postal-tax semi-postals a combination of tax stamps that did not prepay any postal charges. For one week, Nov. 15-22, 1947, Brazil issued these stamps, for 40 centavos plus 10 centavos. Use was obligatory.

postal-tax stamps Various countries have issued labels that must be used on every piece of mail when decrees order them used. These labels, which are known as obligatory tax stamps in Britain, do not pay any part of the postal charges; they raise money for some predetermined plan. An example is the issue of Colombia 1935-7 and subsequent labels for the Red Cross.

Postal-tax stamp (Colombia)

Colombia also raised money for a new communications building in this way. Cuba, Ecuador, and the Dominican Republic are others that have issued postal-tax stamps.

Postal Union See UNIVERSAL POSTAL UNION.

POSTAL UNION CONGRESS LONDON 1929 (insc.) appears on stamps of Great Britain, May 10, 1929.

postal unions various postal unions exist throughout the world. These are agreements to control and set rates and to supervise postal services. The Pan-American Postal Union is an example. The Universal Postal Union is the world-wide organization.

POST & RECEIPT (insc.) appears with values in annas on stamps of Hyderabad.

Postanweisung (Ger.) money order.

Postanweisungsmarke (Ger.) money-order stamp.

posta pneumatica (It.) pneumatic post.

POSTA PNEUMATICA (insc.) appears with "REGNO D'ITALIA" on pneumatic post stamps of Italy, first issued in 1913.

POSTA ROMANA CONSTANTINOPOL (ovpt.) appears on stamps of Romania for use by Romanian offices in Turkey, 1919.

postas le nioc (insc.) appears on postage-due stamps of Ireland.

Postat e Qeverriës së Përkohëshme (ovpt.) appears on stamps of Turkey for use from June 16, 1913, in Albania. Similar stamps, surcharged in the circle of the overprint, were issued in 1913. Refer to catalogues for details.

Postauto (Ger.) postal motor coach.

postbestelling (Dutch) postal delivery.

postbewijszegels (Dutch) postal-order stamps.

postblad (Dutch) letter card.

postbode (Dutch) postman.

postboot (Dutch) mail boat.

postcard bristol a type of cardboard about 6/1000 inch or more in thickness. The smooth-finished postcard bristols are used by governments to produce postal stationery cards imprinted with postage stamps.

postcards (1) cards printed with postage stamps as authorized issues by post office departments; (2) privately printed cards bearing pictures or greetings on one side with space for address and message on the back.

post de campagne (Fr.) field-post.

poste (Fr.) post.

poste aérienne (Fr.) airmail.

Poste Aèrieo or **Poste Aérienne** (ovpt. and insc.) appears on Persia airmail stamps bearing no country name.

poste ambulante (Fr.) railway post.

poste aux lettres (Fr.) letter mail.

POSTE COLONIALI ITALIANE (3-line insc.) appears on stamps of Ethiopia under Italian occupation, 1936.

Posted at Sea a postal marking. Mail may be posted on board ship providing that the country of registration of the ship is a member of the Universal Postal Union. Such mail may or may not be postmarked "Paquebot", an impression applied on shore.

poste-restante (Fr.) often a handstamp on mail indicating a department in a post office where letters may be left until they are picked up. Often this kind of mail is sent to general delivery at the post office named in the address.

Post Estensi (insc.) appears on stamps of Modena, a former duchy in northern Italy.

Poste Italiane (insc.) appears on stamps of Italy.

poste locale (Fr.) city mail.

Poste Locale (insc.) appears with no country name, but a cross in heraldic shield, on 1850 stamps of the Switzerland federal administration.

poste militaire (Fr.) field-post stamp.

poste rurale (Fr.) rural mail.

poster stamps labels without postage stamp values, not good for postal service; advertising labels or charity labels. Some collectors consider Christmas and Easter seals as poster stamps.

Postes (insc.) postage; appears on stamps of Belgium, France, French Colonies, Canada, Luxembourg, and other countries.

Postes (insc.) appears above an oval portrait with values in words and numerals in upper corners, but no country name, on stamps of Luxembourg. The first postage stamps of 1852 portrayed Grand Duke William III.

Postes (insc.) appears on top line with value on bottom line and an oval portrait of a man but no country name, on stamps of Belgium 1849-66.

Postes (insc.) appears with a numeral of value and "Centime" or "Centimes" printed on a network of coloured lines, on stamps of Alsace and Lorraine issued under German occupation, 1870.

Postes de Corée (insc.) appears on stamps of Korea.

POSTES ETHIOPIENNES (insc.) appears on stamps of Ethiopia.

POSTES IMPERALES DE COREE (insc.) appears on stamps of Korea, 1903.

Postes Ottomanes (insc.) appears on stamps of Turkey.

Postes Persanes (insc.) appears on stamps of Persia (Iran).

POSTES SERBES (ovpt.) appears on 1900-7 stamps of France for use in Serbia, 1916-18, during a stamp shortage at Corfu.

Poste Vaticane (insc.) appears on stamps of Vatican City.

post fiscals revenue stamps used as postage stamps.

postfrisch (Ger.) mint.

postfrisk (Swed.) just printed.

Postgebiet (Ger.) postal district.

Postgebiet/Ob. Ost (2-line ovpt.) appears in German script on German stamps for use during the German occupation of Lithuania, 1916-17.

Postgebuehren (Ger.) postal rates or postal fees.

Postgeschichte (Ger.) postal history.

Posthornmuster (Ger.) post-horn design.

post-horns popular designs used as the central portions, or as parts, of numerous postmarks. Horns existed in many ancient cultures, and over the years they acquired properties that made them useful instruments. Post riders were required on many roads to blow their horns at mile or so intervals to let postmasters know all was well. Designs of post-horns were used as watermarks, small fillers to complete designs, and in overprints.

post horse a horse ridden by a post rider, in a pony express.

Postkutsche (Ger.) mail coach.

POSTLUCHTDIENST (insc.) appears on

airmail stamps of Belgian Congo, 1920.

postman   formerly called a postal courier; a man or woman who delivers mail to the public at their homes, mail boxes, or places of business. A postman is an outside worker, not a worker at the counters in post offices, but in small rural offices postmen may also work indoors to serve the people.

Postmarke   (Ger. insc.) postage; appears on

stamps of Brunswick.

postmarks   the markings applied to mail as the mail passes through some authorized post office. If the postmark defaces postal stationery or cancels a stamp it is then called a cancellation. The postmarks are any markings, either back or front, providing they are authorized post office marking. Postmarks may be struck on the back of mail. They are then "backstamps", indicating arrival or transit, whichever the case may be. Other markings on the mail determine the type of postmarks they are. For example, registered mail from San Francisco, California, to Australia by Fiji will have a San Francisco handstamp on the back of the letter, a Fiji arrival mark which is also a transit mark, and then the arrival mark in the post office in Australia. Those are all postmarks, and unless they cancel stamps on the back or front of letters they are not cancellations.

postmaster   the keeper of the post house. He had charge of the post horses and postmen in the early days of mail delivery. (Courtesy of a radio broadcast by the late Dr. James Goodwin)

postmasters' provisionals   various postage stamps and postal stationery items issued by postmasters of, for example, the United States, the Confederate States of America, Peru, Mexico, Bermuda, and Canada.

Postmasters' provisional stamps of the United States   Postmasters in the following communities issued their own stamps: Alexandria, Virginia; Annapolis, Maryland; Baltimore, Maryland; Boscawen, New Hamp-

shire; Brattleboro, Vermont; Lockport, New York; Millbury, Massachusetts; New Haven, Connecticut; New York, New York; Providence, Rhode Island; St. Louis, Missouri; Tuscumbia, Alabama.

Postminister   (Ger.) Postmaster General.

Post Obitum   (Lat.) after death. The words have been inscribed many times on U.S. Post Office seals. They were printed repeatedly in the background in the January 1887 issue of brown-colour seals. Some specialists say that the first issue was used exclusively by the Dead Letter Office, and when a change involved the widespread use of the seals, mainly by the postmasters, the design with "Post Obitum" was no longer appropriate and was changed to a background of interlacing circles.

post office   a room in the post house or inn of the postmaster where he kept his records; hence a place set aside to receive and hand out letters. (Courtesy of a radio broadcast by the late Dr. James Goodwin)

post office bulletin   a notice about new issues or other post office data.

post office department   a department found in all governments; the post is not private enterprise.

POST OFFICE DEPT.   (insc.) appears with the inscription "OFFICIAL STAMP" in an oval, on 1873 U.S. official stamps for use by the U.S. Post Office Department.

post office Mauritius stamps   (nick.) a classical issue of 1847 inscribed "Post Office" instead of "Post Paid". The mistake was corrected in the next year. These 1- and 2-penny stamps are among the ten most famous rarities.

post office monopoly   Postal service is a universal monopoly of governments, and is not a private enterprise. Governments frequently contract private companies to transport mail under supervision.

post office savings-bank stamps   Three commemorative stamps in 1961 marked the centenary of British post office banks, which William Ewart Gladstone, Chancellor of the Exchequer, had opened in September 1861.

post office sheet   a pane of stamps or sometimes a full sheet, as the stamps were printed in large units and later guillotined into panes or post office sheets.

post office stamps   labels or stamped impressions giving information, instructions to postal employees and the public. Examples: the letter T without a frame or in a circle, standing for tax. It means postage shortpaid or money due owing to insufficient postage prepaid. Registration labels or handstamps, return to sender labels, dead letter office stamps or undeliverable mail office stamps are all post office stamps. Scores of others in the world are used daily.

Postpaketmarke (Ger.) parcel post stamp.

postpakket verrekenzegels (Dutch) parcel postage-due stamps.

POST & RECEIPT appears with values in annas, on stamps of Hyderabad, 1937, a feudatory state in Central India.

Postreiter (Ger.) post rider.

post road a road on land or a route at sea over which authorized carriers transport mail.

Post Schilling (insc.) appears with no country name on the Schleswig-Holstein 1850 issue.

Post Stamp (insc.) appears with oriental let-

tering on stamps of Hyderabad.

poststämpel (Swed.) postmark.

Poststempel (Ger.) postmark, postal cancellation.

Postverkehr (Ger.) postal communications, movement of mail.

Postvertrag (Ger.) postal agreement, postal treaty.

Postverwaltung (Ger.) postal administration.

Postvorschrift (Ger.) postal regulations.

Post Waggon (Ger.) mail coach, postal railroad car.

postzegel (Dutch) postage stamp.

Postzegel (insc.) appears with a man's portrait in oval frame, without country name, on stamps of The Netherlands, 1852-67. The portrait is of King William III.

Postzegel (sur.) appears with values on Netherlands 1907 issue for use as postage-due stamps.

Postzustellung (Ger.) mail delivery.

P.O.T.S. Post Office Training School, Great Britain.

pound (decimal currency) On Monday Feb. 15, 1971, Great Britain officially changed its currency from the sterling of pounds, shillings, and pence to the decimal system of 100 pence equal to 1 pound. Britain had

been undergoing the transition carefully and slowly, and had even issued metal coins ahead of the official date of change. On June 17, 1970, about eight months before the formal date, Britain issued 10-, 20-, and 50-pence stamps in the popular Machin bas-relief portrait design of Queen Elizabeth II that had been used for the sterling denominations. On the official day of change, Britain issued thirteen new denomination stamps, ½- to 9-pence. (Courtesy of the British Government Office)

pound (Israeli) The Israeli pound is equal to 100 agorot or 1,000 protot.

pound (sterling) highest monetary value expressed on British and many British colonial postage stamps. One pound equals 20 shillings. It originally meant a pound in weight of silver, and was the amount of silver that could be coined into 240 silver pennies. In Troy measure, which is still used by jewellers, 20 pennyweights make one ounce and 12 ounces, one pound.

pound (Turkish) or **lira** a gold coin of Turkey. 100 piastres or kurush equal 1 pound or lira. After the adoption of the gold standard in 1885, the pound Egyptian was similarly divided, and is equal to 100 piastres or 1000 millièmes.

pourpre (Fr.) purple.

pour remplir (Fr.) a filler.

P.O.W. prisoner of war.

P.P. (ovpt.) for the French "port payé"; appears in a rectangular frame on postage-due stamps of France for use by French offices in French Morocco. Used just one day, on Oct. 10, 1903.

P.P.P.P. (Fr.) postal marking used on mail in France to indicate an address beyond Paris. The first two P.'s stand for "port payé" (carried paid) and the third P. for "passer", meaning to pass, to go, to pass on. The fourth P. stands for Paris. Hence "postage prepaid for delivery of mail beyond Paris". (Courtesy of Herbert Dube)

prachtstueck (Ger.) fine to very fine condition.

Praegedruck (Ger.) embossing.

praegen (Ger.) to emboss.

pràglingstryck (Swed.) embossing, impression.

prairie dog a popular flaw or minor variety of a dog on the wing of the 5-cent blue U.S. 1928 Aeronautics Conference issue. Listed in Scott's Specialized U.S. catalogue, Plate 19658, lower left pane, stamp number 50.

pre-cancel any stamp or postal stationery item cancelled before use. Pre-cancelled

items are sold by some kind of permit to prevent their use a second time.

precancel (Swed.) pre-cancel.

precursor (Sp.) forerunner.

precursore (It.) forerunner.

Preis (Ger.) price.

Preiskorrektur (Ger.) price correction.

premier choix (Fr.) superb, sound.

premières gravures proposed designs of some U.S. classical stamps, which were essays or sample stamps, complete with perforations and gum, but not postage stamps. Believed to have been printed in August 1861; some specialists called them the August issues. Not to be confused with gravure printing.

premier tirage (Fr.) early print.

premier vol (Fr.) first flight.

PRENSA (Sp. sur.) printing press; appears in different type styles with new values on newspaper stamps of Uruguay, 1922-6.

préoblitération (Fr.) pre-cancellation.

pre-obliterazione (It.) pre-cancel.

préoblitéré (Fr.) pre-cancelled.

préos (Fr.) pre-cancelled stamps.

presentation books or **booklets** books containing displays of postage stamps; they originated with the various security printers, whose salesmen carried examples of their work in these books. Since the formation of the Universal Postal Union, member countries submit to it presentation books of sample postage stamps in current use.

press-proof final proof passed by the postal authorities.

pre-stamp covers pre-adhesive covers, letters, letter sheets, or envelopes posted before adhesive postage stamps were issued.

Preussen (Ger.) Prussia.

preussischblau (Ger.) Prussian blue.

prexies (nick.) a shortened form of "presidents"; popular terms for the U.S. 1938-54 issues portraying the presidents in order of their terms in office, from George Washington on the 1-cent stamps to Calvin Coolidge on the 5-dollar value.

price list an index of stamps for sale with

prices; may be in leaflet brochure, or booklet form.

Price's City Express in New York City, New York, issued U.S. local stamps in 1857-8.

Price's Eighth Avenue Post Office in New York City, New York, issued U.S. local stamps in 1854.

Priest's Despatch in Philadelphia, Pennsylvania, issued U.S. local stamps in 1851.

PRIMA RACHETA COSMICA IN LUNA (sur.) appears with change in value on stamps of Romania 1959, to mark the first Russian rocket to reach the moon, Sept. 14, 1959.

primary colours Yellow, red, and blue are the three basic colours from which all other colours may be derived by mixing of the primary colours with one another, in different proportions. In photo-engraving, a green filter is used to produce the red plate, a red filter to prepare the blue plate, and a blue-violet filter to obtain the yellow plate.

primer vuelo (Sp.) first flight; appears in some cachets of Spanish-language countries.

primitives British term sometimes used to describe early stamps of the world, mainly those before 1860.

PRIMO VALORES DECLARADOS SERVICIO INTERIOR (sur.) appears with new values on 1933 commemorative stamps of Dominican Republic for domestic use as insured letter stamps. A similar inscription is on these stamps for 1940-68.

primo volo (It.) first flight; appears in cachets with other words describing events.

Prince Consort essay a trial design for British stamps portraying Prince Albert of Saxe-Coburg-Gotha, husband of Queen Victoria. In 1850, under the promotion of Henry Archer, inventor of the British perforating machines, a letterpress design of the Prince was made into essays for presentation to the British Post Office. Listed and shown in Gibbons Great Britain Specialized catalogue, and dated 1851. Great Britain did not change to letterpress at that time, but continued to issue steel-engraved stamps, which is inaccurately called recess printing.

Prince Edward Island an eastern Canadian island of about 2,184 square miles in the Gulf of St. Lawrence off east coast of New Brunswick and Nova Scotia; formerly a British Crown Colony, and a Canadian province since 1873. Capital: Charlottetown. Issued its own adhesive postage stamps in 1861 and used various issues until Confederation with the Dominion of Canada in 1873. Then used Canadian postage, 1873 to present.

Prince's Letter Dispatch   in Portland, Maine, issued U.S. local stamps in 1861.

PRINCIPAUTE DE MONACO   (insc.) appears on early stamps of the Principality of Monaco.

print   (1) anything that is reproduced by one of the printing processes; (2) an impression from an engraving or plate.

print and turn   a method of printing a portion of a postage stamp sheet or pane, then turning the sheet to print the remaining part. They are finished in tête-bêche units. The U.S. Buffalo balloon stamps of 1877 are a well-known example.

printing on both sides   By error some stamps have been printed clearly on both sides. These should not be confused with designs set off from wet sheets below, which show the designs and lettering flopped (the left side appears at the right as a negative print).

printer   (1) owner or manager of a printing business; (2) a compositor or one working in a mechanical department of a printing plant.

printer's imprint   name of the security printer below each stamp or on the margin of the sheet or pane.

printer's mark   name, address, or place of printing.

printers' waste   spoiled printed material usually discarded as waste paper. In stamp collecting, many rarities, including errors in overprinting and surcharging or in perforating varieties or other faults, are examples of spoiled stamps known as printers' waste. Many times this material finds its way to dealers, who sell it although it often never went through post offices of the world.

printing   the art of making reproductions by impressions from dies, plates for any printing process. The five basic kinds of reproductions used to make postage stamps include: (1) steel engraving, printing from flat or curved plates with the designs set below the surface, and made by the transfer process from steel dies. Collectors often refer to this process as line engraving, which is an inaccurate term unless the work was done on copper. Called intaglio printing. (2) Gravure printing, also intaglio, meaning that the designs are all set (by etching) below the surface. (3) Lithography, formerly printing from special stone plates, but now from metal. The designs are produced with a substance that attracts ink but repels water. The plates are kept wet as the ink is transferred to the paper or other stamp items from the plates. (4) Embossing is the least used process for postage stamps and postal stationery. The designs are impressed in the paper from relief plates with designs projecting upwards. (5) Letterpress printing (known as "surface printing" in Great Britain and referred to as "typographed" in U.S. catalogues) is a relief process by means of types, rubber plates, electrotypes, or stereotypes.

printing area   extent of surface to be printed.

printing cylinder   cylinder that carries the sheet to be printed to the form.

printing flaws   damage showing on postage stamps as a result of some lack of quality control; not usually constant varieties. These are mere varieties and not errors. Collectors are warned against paying high prices for such material.

printing ink   Printing inks are intimate mixtures of pigments, oils, varnishes, driers, toners, and, frequently, waxy compounds. The working properties of the inks are adjusted to the printing process, the kind of press, the grade and kind of paper, and the type of work to be reproduced.

Prinz-Eduard-Inseln   (Ger.) Prince Edward Island.

prisoner-of-war markings   These are not post office marks. There are two basic types: (1) those that identify prisons by name and give their locations, and (2) those consisting of censor stamps or labels.

prisoners' letters or **prisoner-of-war mail**   letters from prisoners captured in any war. Civil War mail in the United States and Boer War prisoners' letters are in wide demand by specialists. Prisoners' mail from the First and Second World Wars still exists.

privat   (Ger.) private.

Private Coil Pairs 320 BR. IIA   refers to U.S. coil stamps processed by the Brinkerhoff Co. of Sedalia, Missouri. "320" is Scott's catalogue number and "IIa" is the type of perforation shown in Scott's U.S. Specialized catalogue.

private overprints   Some postage stamps have been overprinted with company names, initials, or both as a security measure to help prevent any stolen stamps from being used.

private perforations   sometimes called "commercial perforations"; occur on postage stamps of any country. Many U.S. coil stamps were privately perforated for company-owned vending machines. France,

Spain, and Canada are a few other countries where privately perforated stamps have originated.

Private Post Office   in San Francisco, California, issued U.S. local envelopes in 1864.

private separations   any type of perforations or roulettes made by individual persons or groups, but not authorized or made by post offices.

private stamps   those issued by companies (hotel stamps) or individuals. Usually classified as "phantoms" or "cinderellas". Spain and Portugal issued special stamps for private use, known as "franchise issues". Sometimes companies overprinted regular

stamps with company names or abbreviations to prevent stolen stamps from being used.

Privat Post   (insc.) appears on many German local stamps that are not listed in stamp catalogues.

Privatzaehnung   (Ger.) private perforation.

prix   (Fr.) price.

prix de base   (Fr.) basic price.

pro   (Sp.) benefit, advantage.

PRO AERO   (insc., ovpt., and part of sur.) appears on airmail stamps of Switzerland.

Probebogen   (Ger.) proof sheet.

Probedruck   (Ger.) essay. Also means proof, but the English word "proof" is sometimes spelled "Druckprobe" in German.

Probezaehnung   (Ger.) trial perforation.

PRO CARTERO   (insc.) appears on 1944 semi-postal stamps of Argentina, with a surtax on each stamp. Funds were for the Postal Employees Benefit fund.

procédé d'impression   (Fr.) any type of printing used for stamp production: engraving, gravure, and letterpress are examples.

process printing   method of printing in the three primary colours from half-tone plates; sometimes a black plate or other colour plates are added.

PROFUMATA AL/ CONFINE DI MET/ KOVICH   (It.) a handstruck disinfected marking on letters in about 1841 at Metkovich, a disinfecting station on the Dalmatian frontier near Bosnia. The three-line

marking means "Fumigated at the frontier in Metkovich". (Courtesy of the fumigated mail collection of Herbert Dube)

PROFUMATA AL CONFINE DI SIGN   (It.) a disinfected marking meaning "Fumigated at the frontier of Sign"; used about 1843. Sign, Sinj, or Signo designates a locality northeast of Spalato in Dalmatia. (Courtesy of the fumigated mail collection of Herbert Dube)

progressive proof   single proofs of each plate of a set of colour plates and combined proofs, showing the result of each successive colour printed and assembled in proper sequence.

Pro Juventute   (insc.) appears on Switzerland charity stamps or semi-postals with proceeds for child welfare and other charities.

Pro Natura   (insc.) appears on Swiss stamps of Feb. 21, 1966, issued to publicize the international congress of the Union for the Preservation of Natural Beauty. Delegates from sixty countries met in Lucerne in June 1966. (Courtesy of a Swiss PTT notice)

proof   a trial printing of a sheet of stamps for inspection and correction if necessary. Proofs may be of postage stamps being prepared for coils, booklets, or post office sheets or panes. Die proofs are examples made from dies.

proof paper   special paper, often extremely thin like strong tissue paper, for pulling the proofs from both dies and printing plates. When the proofs on these papers are mounted on die-sunk cards, the resulting items are called hybrid proofs.

PRO OPERA PREVIDENZA M.V.S.N.   (It. insc.) appears on set of four semi-postal stamps issued Oct. 26, 1926, and again on March 1, 1928, in different values and colours. Surtax proceeds were for the M.V.S.N. (Milizia Volontaria Sicurezza Nazionale – Voluntary Militia for National Defense).

PRO/PLEBISCITO/TACNA y ARICA/ 1925   (4-line insc.) appears on Peru plebiscite issues used 1925-9 as postal tax stamps, intended to defray plebiscite costs.

PROTECCION AL ANCIANO   (Sp. insc.) appears on semi-postal stamps of Uruguay 1930, with surtax in aid of the elderly people.

Protectorat Français   (ovpt.) appears on stamps inscribed "Maroc", for the French protectorate of Morocco, 1914-21.

PROTEJA A LA INFANCIA   (Sp. insc.) appears on Mexico postal-tax stamps for child welfare, 1929.

PRO UNION IBEROAMERICANA (Sp. insc.) For the Spanish American Union; appears on Spain 1930 issues, Spain pictorial stamps and airmails.

prova (It.) essay. Also used in Italian for the English word "proof".

Providence Despatch in Providence, Rhode Island, issued U.S. local stamps in 1849.

Providence, R.I. This city in Rhode Island issued postmaster's provisional stamps in 1846.

Provincia de Macau (insc.) appears on stamps of Macao.

provincial stamps of Canada Prior to the Canadian Confederation of 1867, Nova Scotia, New Brunswick, and the Province of Canada (Ontario and Quebec) used their own stamps, 1851 to March 1868. Then the Dominion of Canada issued stamps on April 1, 1868. British Columbia and Vancouver issued stamps in 1860, Vancouver Island in 1865, and British Columbia 1865-9. Prince Edward Island issued stamps 1861-72, and Newfoundland, 1857-1949. All use stamps of Canada now.

Provincie Modonesi (insc.) appears on stamps of the provisional government of Modena (in northern Italy), 1859.

PROVINZ LAIBACH (part of ovpt. and sur.) appears on stamps of Italy issued during the German occupation of Jugoslavia for use in Laibach (Ljubljana), a city and capital of Slovenia in northwest Jugoslavia.

provisional booklet a makeshift type of postage stamp book made for temporary use in much the same way as provisional stamps on stationery. Few exist, but the Canada booklet with beaver-design stamp instead of Queen Elizabeth stamps issued April 1, 1954, is one example made when a revised increased postal rate came into effect and no Queen Elizabeth 5-cent stamps were available.

Provisional/Govt./1893 (ovpt.) appears on issues of Hawaii for use in 1893.

provisionals postage stamps or postal stationery intended to fill a temporary need for postage.

provisoire (Fr.) provisional.

Provisorien (Ger.) provisionals.

Provisorio (Sp. ovpt. and sur.) appears on Spanish-language provisional stamps.

provisorische Marken (Ger.) provisionals.

provisorisk emission (Swed.) temporary issue.

Provisorium (Ger.) provisional (stamp).

provisorium (Swed.) temporary system.

Swedish collectors use the term to describe a provisional issue of stamps or postal stationery or a provisional stamp – that is, one introduced as a makeshift item for use until the regular item becomes available.

provtryck (Swed.) essay.

provvisori (It.) provisionals.

prueba de impresión (Sp.) trial printing, proof.

Pruefung (Ger.) examination, expertizing.

Pruefungszeichen (Ger.) examiner's mark, expertizer's mark.

Pruefungszeugnis (Ger.) examiner's certificate.

Prusse (Fr.) Prussia.

Prussia formerly a kingdom, now part of Germany; about 113,545 square miles. Capital: Berlin. Stamps issued 1850-67 were superseded by North German Confederation issues.

pruta, prutot former coins of Israel, replaced by agora and agorot.

PRZESYLKA URZEDOWA (insc.) appears on official stamps of Poland, 1933-5.

P.S. (insc.) appears as an elaborate monogram design on stamps issued 1882-3 by Cauca, a former state and now a department of the Republic of Colombia.

P.S.N.C. (insc.) Pacific Steam Navigation Company; the letters appear on the first stamps of Peru, 1857, with one letter placed in each corner of the stamp.

P.S.S. Philatelic Specialists Society.

P.T.A. (insc.) appears with the inscription "Parent Teacher Association 1897-1972 U.S." on 8-cent stamps of the United States issued in September 1972. The association, first known as the National Congress of Mothers, was founded in 1897 by Mrs. Phoebe Hearst and Mrs. Alice Birney. Its goal was to improve the quality of education. Current membership is about ten million in the United States. There is a similar organization in Canada.

Pto Rico or **Puerto Rico** (insc.) appears on stamps of Puerto Rico.

P. T. S. Postal Transportation Service; the letters appear as part of obliterations on some mail carried by the U.S. highway post office vehicles.

PTT Post, Telephone, Telegraph. These are the initials of the departments of governments, mainly in Europe, that administer the postal services, telephone operations, and telegraphs. The exact designations may vary from one country to another.

pu in auction catalogues, means "punched initials".

publicity overprints overprinting to publi-

Publicity overprint (Hungary, 1953)

cize some thing or event. Hungary produced an outstanding example in 1953, with a stamp of the same year featuring soccer players and overprinted "London-Wembley 1953, XI, 25. 6:3." The stamps were issued to announce the defeat of the British soccer players on Nov. 25, 1953, by the Hungarians by a score of 6 to 3. Many overprints, while resembling commemoratives, are in reality publicity overprints. Other examples exist among stamps overprinted for the *Graf Zeppelin*, for instance of Paraguay in 1931 and Argentine in 1930.

publicity postage stamps of Italy or Franco-bolli Pubblicitari. These were issued in November 1924 and again in February 1925, as a set of twenty postage stamps with advertising labels attached, including one 60-centime special-delivery stamp. Two of the international firms among the twelve advertising on these labels were Singer Sewing Machines and Columbia phonographs, the latter the forerunners of modern record players. The advertisers paid a fee to advertise their products. Neither the public nor the collectors welcomed the idea. The stamps with labels were not valid after Aug. 27, 1925.

Public Letter Office in San Francisco, California, issued U.S. local envelopes in 1864.

Puerto Rico (Porto Rico) an American commonwealth island of the West Indies in the Atlantic Ocean; about 3,435 square miles. Capital: San Juan. From 1855 to 1871, stamps were issued under Spanish dominion for Cuba and Puerto Rico; 1877-98 there were inscribed issues; 1873-5 stamps of Cuba were used, overprinted; 1898-1900 stamps were issued under U.S. authority; then U.S. postage was used.

pul, poul a copper coin of Persia (Iran) and Afghanistan. 40 puls equal 1 kran. 100 pouls equal 1 rupee Afghani.

pulp any disintegrated cellulose fibres, in sheets or slush form, used in papermaking. After beating and diluting, the pulp is known as "stuff".

punched cancellations circular or oval holes punched in stamps to cancel them.

punch-perforated stamps stamps with perforated initials.

punctured stamps (1) stamps cancelled by a punched hole; (2) stamps damaged by an early method of displaying them, on strings like clothes on a line; (3) stamps with punched figures, designs, or letters (perfins). Some Canadian stamps of revenue types and Spanish stamps for telegraph service were cancelled with a punched hole.

punktartiger Durchstich (Ger.) pin perforation.

Puno a city in Peru, had overprinted stamps 1882-5 that were used during the war between Chile and Peru. Gibbons gives dates of use as 1881-5.

PUOLUSTUSVOIMAT (insc.) appears on 1943-4 military stamps of Finland.

pup (nick.) in England means a "scarce stamp", one often worth considerably more than catalogues indicate; sometimes called "sleepers" in North America.

purpur (Ger.) purple.

purpurlila (Ger.) purple-lilac.

purpurviolett (Ger.) purple-violet.

PUTTIALLA STATE (ovpt.) appears on stamps of India, first issued in 1884, for use in Patiala, a Convention state of India. Later issues have the overprint "PATIALA STATE" or "PATIALA SERVICE" for the official stamps.

PVA gum polyvinyl alcohol gum, a type introduced in Great Britain by Harrison &

Sons, security printers. The adhesive replaced gum arabic in 1968. It is thin and dull, and has a slight yellow tone to show that stamps have been gummed. Gum arabic has a shine easily seen on mint stamps, but neither PVA nor arabic gum is of any account on used stamps. Sometimes the PVA gum may shine in a certain type of light.

P.W.P.W. Polska Wytwornia Papierow Wartosciowych (State Printing Office), printers of certain Polish postage stamps.

PX a sacred monogram known as the Chi Rho, formed by various designs of combined letters P and X. The sign is on the 1959 commemorative stamps of Finland marking the centenary of the Missionary Society of Finland. The letters originate from the Greek word meaning Christ.

Pyapon issue stamps of Burma issued under Japanese occupation, May 1942. Pyapon is a district in the Irrawaddy division of Lower Burma. A town of the same name is the capital.

Q

Q.A.N.T.A.S. (airline) Queensland and Northern Territories Aerial Services Limited. Point of origin: Australia.

Qarku Korces (sur.) appears with new value on stamps of Albania for use in 1918 as local postage stamps of Korce.

Qatar a peninsula in east Arabia of about 8,000 square miles; a sheikdom under British protection. Capital: Dotia. Issued British stamps surcharged with new values in 1957, then inscribed stamps since 1961.

QEA (airline) Qantas Empire Airways Ltd. Point of origin: Australia.

qintar a coin of Albania. 100 qintars equal 1 franc or 1 lek.

Quadratformat (Ger.) square type, square size.

quadriculado (Port.) quadrille.

quadrillé (Fr.) quadrille.

quadrille (1) a watermark design in small squares; (2) stamp album pages with squares for the arrangement of stamps.

Qu'aiti State of Shihr and Mukalla a state in Aden Protectorate and a member of the Aden Postal Union. Issued stamps in July 1942, along with those of the Kathiri State of Seiyun.

qualities of stamps These are described by stamp dealers and auctioneers as: superb, very fine, fine quality, and good. Superb is top quality; very fine is next to superb, but may have heavier cancels, a wider margin, or other minor faults; fine quality means the stamp is still intact but may be off centre or have a slightly heavy cancel or other faults, like a crease or fine cut not visible on the front. A stamp described as good quality usually fails to find a place in a selected collection.

quarante (Fr.) forty.

quart (Fr.) quarter.

Quadrille: watermark design

quarter-stamps four small stamps in a unit. Any portion of the four parts could be used. Stamps of Spain and Brunswick provide examples of these.

quarto (It.) quarter.

quartz lamp a type of ultra-violet-ray lamp used to examine postage stamps. The rays immediately show whether a stamp has been repaired or whether pen and similar marks have been removed. This is a valuable instrument in helping a collector detect faked postage stamps.

Quarzlampe (Ger.) quartz lamp.

quatorze (Fr.) fourteen.

quatre (Fr.) four.

quatre-vingt-dix (Fr.) ninety.

quatre-vingts (Fr.) eighty.

quattrino a coin of copper or billon, used in Tuscany and other Italian states. 60 quattrini equal 20 solidi equal 1 lira. The coin, which is mentioned in a ballad in 1415, may have a special name, as the Quattrino Penterino (1684-1733) on which there is a figure of a panther.

Quebec Airways Ltd. See CANADIAN PACIFIC AIR LINES, LTD.

Queen's heads See LARGE CENTS ISSUE.

Queensland a former British Crown Colony of about 670,000 square miles in northeast Australia; one of the six colonies that united to form the Commonwealth of Australia in 1901. Capital: Brisbane. Issued stamps in 1860.

Quelimane or **Quilimane** part of Portuguese East Africa colony in Mozambique; about 39,800 square miles. Capital: Quelimane. Stamps of 1913-14 were the Vasco da Gama issue of Portuguese Colonies surcharged; they were replaced by those of Mozambique. Stamps of 1914-16 were Ceres-design key-types inscribed for use in Portuguese colonies and similar to the stamps of Portugal issued in 1912-31.

quetzal a coin of Guatemala. 100 centavos equal 1 quetzal.

Quetzals (nick.) stamps of Guatemala, 1879 and subsequent years, featuring the quetzal, a colourful Central American bird.

quinze (Fr.) fifteen.

Q.V. Queen Victoria, ruler of Great Britain 1837-1901.

R

R in some catalogues indicates the degree of rarity of an item by the number of letters used; for example, RR indicates an item more rare than one marked R.

R (insc.) for the Spanish word "Registro", meaning "registered"; appears on some Spanish-language stamps, for example the registration stamps of Colombia, 1883-1904.

R (insc.) appears on stamp covered with design and oriental script, issued for use in Jhind, a feudatory state in north India. The letter R is the initial of Raghbar Singh, at one time a Rajah.

R (sur.) appears with new value on Panama regular issues for use as registration stamps of the Republic of Panama, 1916-17.

R (sur.) appears with new value on stamps of French Colonies, for use in Réunion in 1885.

R.B.S. (insc.) appears on 1851 stamps of Denmark. Rigsbank-Daler, the basic Danish coin, was divided into 96 Rigsbank-Skilling (R.B.S.). The term Skilling was often used instead of Rigsbank-Skilling.

rabais (Fr.) reduction in price, discount.

raccomandato (It.) registered.

rag content paper any paper, but usually bond or ledger paper, containing from 25% to 75% rag fibres; used for stamp album pages.

Rahmen (Ger.) frame.

Rahmenmuster (Ger.) frame design, border design.

railroad mail in Great Britain a mail service established in 1833 between Liverpool and Manchester. On July 1, 1837, the first British travelling post office operated between Liverpool and Birmingham.

railroad postmarks postal markings to indicate the transportation of mail by railroads. Many of these markings include the letters "R.P.O." for Railroad Post Office. In the United States, these are called railway postmarks, and are duplex markings with letters of various sizes and positions.

railway air stamps labels used in 1933 by the Great Western Railway on mail to be carried by British domestic airlines; unauthorized by the British post office. These stamps and other similar ones were with-

Railroad postmark

drawn. Great Britain never authorized stamps inscribed "airmail".

railway stamps Belgium issued railway parcel stamps beginning in 1879 and continuing through the next century. These stamps bear the inscriptions "CHEMIN DE FER" (French) and "SPOORWEGEN" (Flemish). Later issues were inscribed "COLIS POSTAUX" and "POSTCOLLI". Designs of most railway parcel stamps of Belgium featured railway scenes after 1934, for example, trains, scenes at the railroad, and railway stations. In Belgium the parcel transportation services are mainly operated by the Belgian Railways, a private company somewhat like the privately owned express companies in the United States and the Canadian Pacific Railway. The railway parcel stamps of Belgium were issued for the company.

Rainbow proofs Great Britain made experimental proofs for colour, cancellations, ink, and paper trials, possibly from May to December, 1840.

Rajasthan (the Greater Rajasthan Union) a state in northwest India composed of former states; originally organized in 1947 as the Union of Rajasthan and reorganized in 1956. Capital: Jaipur. Issued Bundi stamps overprinted in 1948-9, and Jaipur stamps of 1931-47, overprinted "Rajasthan" in 1949.

Rajpeela or **Rajpipla** an Indian feudatory state near Bombay. Issued three stamps in

1880.

Raleigh, N.C. This town in North Carolina issued postmasters' provisional envelopes in 1861, as part of the Confederate States of America.

ram (Swed.) frame.

ramie plant of the nettle family, found in India and China and used in papermaking.

rampant (her.) reared up on the hind legs (referring to an animal).

R.A.N.A. (airline) Rhodesia and Nyasaland Airways, Ltd. Point of origin: Southern Rhodesia.

rand a coin of Basutoland, Bechuanaland, Tristan da Cunha, South Africa, and other countries. 100 cents equal 1 rand.

rand (Dutch) margin, edge.

Rand (Ger.) margin (for example, of a postage stamp or pane of stamps).

Randaufdruck (Ger.) This word has various meanings according to the context. In philately it usually means "printing on the margins", hence "marginal print" or "marginal inscription." (Courtesy of William Maresch)

Randblock (Ger.) margin block.

Randnummer (Ger.) marginal number.

Randpaar (Ger.) margin pair.

Randwasserzeichen (Ger.) margin watermark.

rappen a copper coin of Switzerland and Liechtenstein. 100 rappen equal 1 franc. The rappen is equal to the centime. The word derives from the German word "Rabe", meaning raven, and is used for coins depicting this bird.

rareté (Fr.) rarity.

rarissime (Fr.) very rare.

rarity Rare stamps and covers are the result of limited numbers of the items that were issued or saved. Some rarities exist because most of the stamps of covers were destroyed or lost. For example, collectors made thousands of covers rare by removing stamps from letter sheets and envelopes. The public made rarities by cutting stamps to the shape of the designs. Rarities also result from printing errors.

raro (It.) scarce.

raro (Sp.) rare, unusual.

Rarotonga chief island of the Cook Islands. Discovered in 1820, claimed by Germany 1880-9, but formally annexed by Great Britain in 1889 and transferred to New Zealand in 1901. Issued first stamps in 1892, inscribed "Cook Islands Federation". "RARATONGA" was surcharged on stamps in 1919 and inscribed 1920-31.

Ras Al Khaima an Arab sheikdom in Arabia on the Persian Gulf. Has treaty relations with Great Britain, but operates an independent postal administration. First stamps issued on Dec. 21, 1964.

Rastertiefdruck (Ger.) photogravure.

rate the amount of postage required to carry mail from one post office to another.

RATNI DOPRINOS (insc.) appears on 1943-4 postal tax stamps of Croatia.

R A U (Fr. ovpt.) Republique Arbe Unie. Appears with Arabic text on 1957 stamps of Syria issued on Oct. 6, 1958, for International Children's Day. Syria issued postage stamps as a member of the United Arab Republic from 1958, when Syria and Egypt merged to form the United Arab Republic; but Syria seceded from the union in September 1961 and declared its independence.

Rautendurchstich (Ger.) lozenge rouletting, lozenge perforation.

Rawdon, Wright Hatch & Edson printers of the first adhesive postage stamps for the Province of Canada and the United States.

Rayons (nick.) 1850-2 postage stamps of the Federal Administration of Switzerland. "Rayon" inscribed on the stamps means "district" or "area".

R. Colon (ovpt. and cancel) appears on Colombia registration stamps of 1905 and on provisional registration stamps of the Republic of Panama.

R. Commissariato/ Civile/ Territori Sloveni/ occupati/ LUBIANA (5-line ovpt.) appears on various stamps of Jugoslavia during the Italian occupation of the western region of Slovenia in 1941. This part was known as the Province of Ljubljana. The Italians produced regular-issue, semipostal, airmail, and postage-due stamps by overprints and surcharges with the name spelled "Lubiana" (the Italian translation). These are listed with stamps of Jugoslavia in catalogues.

R. de C. (Sp. sur.) Reconstrucción de Comunicacions; appears on Nicaragua postal tax stamps of 1921 and subsequent years. One stamp, plus regular postage, was required on each piece of mail to help pay for a new post office building. Not valid as postage.

R. de C. Garzon (insc.) appears on 1894 stamps of Tolima. These were postmaster's provisional stamps with the added Spanish words, "No hay estampillas", meaning "There are no stamps". Tolima, a department of Colombia, was originally a state.

R.D.P. Roll of Distinguished Philatelists.

real a silver coin of Spain, Portuguese India, Costa Rica, Cuba, Ecuador, and other countries. 8 reales equal 1 peso. The 8-real piece is the Spanish dollar, or piece of eight. When first struck, it was called "nummus realis", or money of the king. First denominations of Cuba and Puerto Rico stamps were issued in values of reales plata, inscribed "RL PLATA". The plural of "real" is "reales" or "reis".

Real-Aerovias-Nacional (airline) Point of origin: São Paula, Brazil.

Reays (nick.) U.S. postal stationery items printed in 1870-1 by George H. Reay of Brooklyn, New York.

rebuts (Fr.) returns; the word appears in a postmark stamped on mail from Paris by the French office for undeliverable mail.

Recapito Autorizzato (insc.) appears on Italian authorized-delivery stamps, issued first in 1928 for private delivery of correspondence, and not for delivery through the post office. A type of tax stamps authorized by Italy. Valid until Dec. 31, 1948.

RECARGO (Sp. insc.) surcharge or additional load; appears on war-tax stamps of Spain.

recarimbado (Port.) overprint.

RECEBER (insc.) appears on 1904 postage-due stamps of Angola, a Portuguese territory in southwestern Africa on the Atlantic Ocean.

receiving mark a postmark stamped on an envelope by the receiving office. Collectors often call these "backstamps" when they appear on the back of covers. Today the application of receiving stamps (postmarks) is almost entirely limited to registered mail and letters forwarded to other·offices.

recess printing an inaccurate term, used especially by English catalogue editors, to describe the steel engraving process. The confusion arises because gravure printing plates are also recess plates. The recess printing plates, gravure and engraved, are made with pockets below the surface of the plates to hold ink. The excess ink is removed from the surface of the plates, and the paper under pressure pulls the ink out of the recesses to print postage stamp designs.

rechteckig (Ger.) rectangular.

rechts (Ger.) right.

recommandation (Fr.) registration.

Recommande (Fr. insc.) appears on labels on envelopes in French-language countries to show registration.

reconstruction another name of plating, the act of replacing stamps in their original positions in sheets or panes.

recorded message stamps See PHONOPOST STAMPS.

recorte de sobre entero (Sp.) cut square.

RECOUVREMENTS (insc.) appears on 1910-32 postage-due stamps of Monaco.

rectangulaire (Fr.) rectangular.

rectificado (Sp.) corrected.

recut refers to extra minor hand repairs on plates or dies. Usually just a portion of the plates or dies were recut, especially before 1900.

recutting (1) a term used by the Japanese to refer to the production of a copy of the original printing. (2) the repairs made on original printing plates to strengthen the lines in designs.

Red Cross (insc.) appears with a design of a dancer on 1953 semi-postal stamps of Siam (Thailand).

Red Cross stamps special issues to honour the organization of some accomplishments. Nearly every country has issued some type of stamp to honour the Red Cross or its equivalent societies.

Red Grid Canc. a red-colour cancellation of horizontal or vertical bars of any thickness.

Red Honduras (nick.) provisional airmail stamp of Honduras used in 1925 when the regular-issue stamps were overprinted "AERO CORREO". The Red Honduras was a 5-centavo stamp overprinted in red on the light-blue stamps of 1915. About ten of these rarities have been known.

redrawn a revised stamp.

redrawn stamp designs designs changed for one reason or another. Example: the Austrian 6-groschen stamps of 1935 portrayed a man with his ears appearing backwards. The redrawn design corrected this.

Reed's City Despatch Post in San Francisco, California, issued U.S. local stamps in 1853-4.

re-engraved refers to engraving a second or third time on a postage stamp die. Also the production of a new die may be different in some respect so there may be a difference in the finished postage stamps. Re-engraving should not be confused with re-

Red Cross stamp (Denmark)

touching, which alters merely a portion of
the stamp design.

re-entry   (1) When a printing plate is being
repaired by a re-entry – a second attempt
to rock in the stamp design on a steel plate
for engraving postage stamps – the transfer-press operator sometimes fails to register the new impression with the old one. A
perfect re-entry leaves no second line on
the stamps because the projecting lines
from the transfer roller fit the original impression perfectly. When the operator fails
to make his registration microscopically
perfect, the result is a visible doubling of a
line or lines. (2) a visible line or lines on a
postage stamp, resulting from an imperfect
re-entering of the plate. These re-entries
may have been caused when an old plate
was burnished in part, but not entirely. Portions of the first series of impressions, or
lines on the printed stamps, may be visible.
In contrast, some postage stamps of the
world are known with an entire duplication
of lines throughout the design, indicating
that the second attempt to rock in the design was made on a new plate, not a repaired one. Little lines caused by an engraver who repaired the plate by hand are
not re-entries, such lines are retouched.
Double transfers are made in much the
same way, but they are made in new plates
as compared to re-entries made in plates
that have been on presses.

reg.   registered.

reg. cover   in auction catalogues, refers to a
registered cover.

Regence de Tunis   (insc.) appears on postage-
due stamps of Tunisia, 1901-3.

Regierungs/Dienstsache   (ovpt.) appears with
the design of a crown on regular issues of
1930-41 for use as official stamps of Liechtenstein, 1932-41.

regionals   British postage stamps printed in
1958 with designs for Scotland, Northern
Ireland, England, Wales and Monmouthshire, Jersey, Guernsey, and the Isle of
Man. Each design was sold in the designated region, but the stamps were valid
anywhere in Great Britain.

registration marks   These appear in marginal
paper, often as crosses in the colours of the
plates. The markings help guide the printers in putting the various colours in their
correct positions.

registration stamp   a type of stamp used for
mailing registered letters. Many countries
throughout the world have issued special
stamps for registration purposes.

REGISTRY   (insc.) appears on U.S. regis-

tration stamps of Dec. 1, 1911. The stamps
were discontinued in May 1913.

REGNO D'Italia   (It. ovpt.) Kingdom of
Italy; appears in various overprints on
stamps of Fiume in 1924. By the Treaty of
Rome, Jan. 27, 1924, Fiume became an
Italian city.

regomado   (Port.) regummed.

regommé   (Fr.) regummed.

regrabado   (Sp.) re-entry.

regravado   (Port.) re-engraved, retouched.

regravé   (Fr.) re-engraved.

regular issues   postage stamps in use for any
length of time, often re-ordered year after
year. Regular issues are sold while commemoratives are available.

regular perforations   normal perforations, in
contrast to rough, ragged, or other types.

regumming   a type of faking by putting gum
on faulty stamps that had little or no gum.
This kind of faking is increasing because of
the growing fad of collecting mint stamps
never hinged. Few stamp collectors can tell
whether stamps issued prior to 1900 have
original gum or were regummed.

Reichspost   (Ger. insc.) state post; appears on
early stamps of Germany.

reihenweise   (Ger.) in rows.

reihenzähnung   (Ger.) comb-perforation.

reimpresión   (Sp.) reprint.

reimpressão   (Port.) reprint.

réimpression   (Fr.) reprint.

Reis   (insc.) the name of a coin; appears with
no country name on stamps of Portugal.

reissue   a stamp or series brought into use
again after being obsolete or out of use for
some time. Stamps of Central and South

*Regular
perforations
on a stamp*

America overprinted or surcharged with the word "HABILITADO" are examples of re-issued stamps.

REJISTRO (insc.) appears on registered stamps of Colombia, 1870-7.

Reklame-Eindrucke (Ger.) advertising label. Some postage stamps of Germany had se-tenant labels advertising stamp collectors' supplies. These are not listed in the popular catalogues.

rekommenderat (Swed.) registered.

relief printing printing done from raised surfaces, such as from type, woodcuts, and line and halftone plates.

remainders stamps printed during the period of issue and left on hand when that issue has gone out of use. These are often can-celled and sold to stamp dealers. Cancels are often quite distinctive and differ from the normal cancellations of the country.

Remainder cancellation of North Borneo

The remainder cancellations of North Bor-neo and Mauritius are examples.

removing stamps The most common method of removing stamps from paper is by soak-ing them in clean water and drying them between clean papers. Some people, mainly new collectors, try to steam postage stamps off paper. Great care should be taken in submerging certain stamps in water; those printed in water-soluble inks may run in water. Steam may cause the same prob-lems. Collectors can use the boxes: stamp lifter, sweatbox, stripeasy, or any similar box. See STAMP-REMOVING BOX.

renversé (Fr.) inverted.

rep in auction catalogues, means "repair".

rep a type of wove paper that has been passed between ridged cylinders on rollers on a paper machine, resulting in corriga-tions in the paper substance.

repaired stamps usually these are genuine stamps that have been treated to replace thin spots, perforations, or cuts or to make them look better. Some famous world rari-ties have been repaired.

réparation (Fr.) repair.

réparé (Fr.) repaired.

repariert (Ger.) repaired.

re-perforating a kind of faking in which per-forations are added to postage stamps made with square edges, and sometimes to those with wide margins, so as to enhance their value.

replicas imitation labels to represent postage stamps, used as space fillers in albums mainly before 1900.

reprint the reproduction from the original plate of a postage stamp that had been printed at an earlier time. Sometimes gov-ernments (those of Austria and the United States, for example) have made their own reprints of former issues of postage stamps. These are called "government reprints" or sometimes "government imitations". How-ever, when new plates were used, these were not really reprints, but instead were government-authorized forgeries.

Rep S. Marino (insc.) appears on 2- and 5-cent stamps of San Marino for internal use in 1899.

REPUBBLICA SOCIALE ITALIANA (ovpt. and insc.) Italian Social Republic; appears overprinted with a design of fasces on Italian stamps issued in 1944 by the Italian Social Republic, a government established briefly in Northern Italy by Mussolini dur-ing the German occupation. Some of the issues are overprinted with the design only and not the text. The words appear in-scribed on later issues.

Repub. Franc. (insc.) appears on early stamps of France and on some stamps of French Colonies.

república (Sp.) republic; the Spanish word often appears with "de" or "del" followed by a name (usually of a place of origin).

Republica Dominicana (Sp. insc.) appears on stamps of the Dominican Republic.

República Española (Sp. insc.) appears on stamps of Spain.

REPUBLICA MOCAMBIQUE (sur.) ap-pears on various Portuguese colonial stamps for use in Mozambique in 1913.

República Oriental (insc.) appears printed

Reprint: original stamp and a reproduction of it

around an oval enclosing the coat of arms, on 1864 stamps of Uruguay.

REPUBLICA PERUANA (insc.) appears on stamps of Peru.

REPUBLICA PORTUGUESA (insc.) appears on stamps of Portugal.

REPUBLIC OF/BOTSWANA (ovpt.) appears on stamps of Bechuanaland Protectorate issued Sept. 30, 1966, the day Bechuanaland Protectorate became the independent Republic of Botswana. See BOTSWANA.

Republic of Congo See CONGO, REPUBLIC OF.

Republic of Korea or **South Korea** the region of Korea occupied by the United States following the Second World War. Since 1945 the 38th north parallel of latitude has formed the boundary between North and South Korea. Capital: Seoul. The U.S. occupation forces issued postage stamps under military rule in February 1946 and other issues until April 1948. First stamps of the Republic of Korea went on sale on May 10, 1948. See: DEMOCRATIC PEOPLE'S REPUBLIC OF KOREA; KOREA.

REPUBLIEK STELLALAND POSTZEGEL (insc.) appears with values printed in words on stamps of Stellaland Republic, 1884-5. The six stamps feature a coat of arms consisting of a shield with four quarters surmounted by a five-pointed star. The star represents a comet seen by some of the founders of the republic; it also accounts for the name Stellaland, which comes from the Latin word for "star". See STELLALAND.

REPUBLIKA NG PILIPINAS (ovpt. and sur.) appears on stamps issued May 7, 1944, for use in the Philippines under Japanese occupation.

REPUBLIK OSTERREICH (Ger. insc.) appears on stamps of Austria, from 1945.

République Centrafricaine (Fr.) Central African Republic, formerly the French Colony of Ubangi-Shari, part of French Equatorial Africa.

République Française (insc.) appears on stamps of France, sometimes with the letters "RF"; also appears on general issues of French Colonies.

REPUBLIQUE GEORGIENNE (insc.) appears on stamps of Georgia, 1920.

République Libanaise (Fr. insc., ovpt., and sur.) appears inscribed on stamps of Lebanon; appears overprinted on 1925 issues of Lebanon for use in 1927; also appears as a surcharge in 1928 on stamps of Lebanon.

République Syrienne (insc.) appears on stamps of Syria.

REPULO POSTA (sur.) appears in 1918 on the first issue of Hungary airmail stamps.

RESELLADA (Sp.) re-authorized. Appears in decorative overprints on 1900 postage issues of Venezuela. Also appears as an overprint with "POSTAL" on 1925-9 and later postal-tax, revenue, and telegraph stamps of Ecuador to convert them to postal use.

reserve plates plates for the Queen Victoria steel-engraved stamps of Great Britain that were held in reserve at Somerset House in London in case of an emergency, such as a fire at the printer's plant. Britain used steel-engraved plates in 1840-41, and occasionally until 1864.

resetting refers to any re-arrangement of units made for stamp printing, especially those made by letterpress printing.

Résistance (sur.) appears in 1943 with new values on military stamps of Syria, 1943, issued under Free French Administration.

RESMI (ovpt. and insc.) appears overprinted below the design of a crescent and star on official stamps of Turkey, 1951-7. Also inscribed on official stamps of Turkey, 1947-62.

RETARDO (Sp. insc.) appears on late-fee stamps of Colombia for use by the Republic of Panama, overprinted "REPÚBLICA DE PANAMA" by handstamp. The 1904 stamps were inscribed; then overprints and some surcharges were used until 1921.

retiré (Fr.) withdrawn.

retouché (Fr.) retouch.

retouching refers to repair work on plates, dies, or individual stamp designs within a plate.

RETOURBRIEF (partial insc.) appears on the return letter labels of Bavaria. In his *Philatelic Handbook (1885)*, Major Edward B. Evans wrote: "A large number of so-called Return Letter Stamps of Bavaria have been chronicled and collected in the first instance because the earliest types were attractive in appearance. They are hardly worthy of the name postage stamps as they did not pay for postage, postage due or even freedom of charge" (like some franks). These labels are not listed in stamp catalogues, but they do appear in old stamp collections offered for sale to dealers.

Retourmarke (Ger.) return stamp.

retourné (Fr.) reversed.

Retta a postal cancellation in the shape of a diamond formed by diamond-shaped dots. When Egypt introduced adhesive postage stamps in 1866, the post office used obliterators in the form of an unframed diamond with nine diamond-shaped dots in each row. A dated postmark struck on the letters indicated the office of origin. The Retta subsequently took slightly different forms in Egypt. The diamond-shaped or lozenge cancels are not exclusive to Egypt. Stamps on the first maritime mail from Cyprus were known cancelled by a Retta-type marking.

return letter stamps   special issues for free or reduced postage, supplied to army, navy, or airforce men and women. For example, Sweden authorized envelopes with return stamps printed on the flaps.

retuschiert   (Ger.) retouched.

Retymno   (insc.) appears on 1899 stamps of the district of Rethymnon in Crete, which was in the Russian sphere of administration. Listed with stamps of Crete.

Réunion   a French island department of the Mascarene group in the Indian Ocean, of about 970 square miles. Capital: St. Denis. Stamps have been issued since 1852, with two rarities inscribed "Ile de la Réunion". Issues of 1885-91 were those of French colonies surcharged or overprinted; subsequent issues were inscribed, overprinted, and surcharged when the island became a department of France.

Réunion   (ovpt. and insc.) overprinted on stamps of French Colonies for use in Réunion in 1885, 1891; also inscribed on stamps of Réunion.

revalidado   (Port.) authorized re-use of a former stamp issue. In 1928 Portugal overprinted stamps of 1912-26 and sold them.

revalidated stamps   former issues brought back into use, often by overprinting or surcharging; not to be confused with revalued stamp issues, which are mainly postal stationery envelopes surcharged with the word "revalued".

revalued postal stationery   postcards or envelopes surcharged with the word "revalued" and new values.

revenue   refers to stamps for fiscal use, as distinguished from those for postal use. A stamp may be available for both purposes, or for one only; the use is almost invariably indicated by the inscription. Some revenues have been accepted for postage: stamps of Victoria, Australia, are an example.

reversed   turned around or put in an opposite direction.

reversed watermarks   watermarks that can be read or seen in a normal position when viewed from the back. This is one of the five common positions of watermarks.

Revenue stamp for postal use

revised die   any die originally engraved for a postage stamp design, then changed in some way. Stamps printed from revised dies are usually listed in stamp catalogues as being from Die I, Die II, and so on.

R.F.   République Française. Appears with no country name on some stamps of France. Also appears with a country name on stamps of France and various French colonies and departments.

R. H.   (insc.) Republic of Haiti; appears in the corners of postage-due stamps of Haiti.

Rheatown, Tenn.   This town in Tennessee issued postmasters' provisional stamps in 1861 as part of the Confederate States of America.

Rheinland-Pfalz   (insc.) appears on stamps of Germany for use in the Rhine Palatine 1947-9, while under Allied occupation.

Rhein-Ruhr-Hilse   (sur.) appears with new values on regular issues of Germany, for use as semi-postal stamps, Feb. 19, 1923.

Rhodes   an Italian island of the southern Sporades group in the Aegean Sea off the southwest coast of Turkey; about 545 square miles. Stamps issued 1912-44 were inscribed; those of Italy were overprinted or surcharged.

Rhodesia   a region in southeastern Africa of 440,664 square miles. Capital: Salisbury. Cecil Rhodes (1853-1902), by a treaty with King Lobengula of the Matabele, obtained a great area north of Bechuanaland and the mineral rights in the area, and in 1889 founded the British South Africa Company and also received a charter from London to promote civilization and good government. The country was named Rhodesia in 1895, but the British South Africa Company continued to administer the postal services; it issued postage stamps from 1890 that were used until the colony was provided with stamps from Southern Rhodesia in 1924 and others for Northern Rhodesia in 1925. See NORTHERN RHODESIA; SOUTHERN RHODESIA; RHODESIA (SELF-GOVERNING STATE OF).

Rhodesia (ovpt. and sur.) appears overprinted on stamps of British South Africa Company in 1909; also surcharged with values on stamps of British South Africa Company in 1909.

Rhodesia (Self-Governing State of) the former Southern Rhodesia; the country was renamed in October 1964. On Nov. 11, 1965, Ian Smith, Prime Minister of Rhodesia, made his famous Unilateral Declaration of Independence (U.I.D.). Great Britain declared the action illegal and refused to recognize the new postage stamp issues, printed in Salisbury, as valid prepayment of postage on incoming mail. Sanctions were imposed on Rhodesia and the importation of Rhodesian stamps was not permitted in Britain, the United States, and certain other countries. Stamp catalogues list the stamps for the convenience of collectors.

Rhodesia and Nyasaland a British federal state of the Commonwealth of Nations comprising Southern Rhodesia, Northern Rhodesia, and Nyasaland. They were three distinct political units or territories with varying degrees of self-government. Capital: Salisbury. Rhodesia and Nyasaland issued postage stamps from 1954 until the Federation was dissolved at the end of 1963. See SOUTHERN RHODESIA; RHODESIA; NORTHERN RHODESIA.

Rhodésie (Fr.) Rhodesia.

Rhodésie du Nord (Fr.) Northern Rhodesia.

Rhodésie du Sud (Fr.) Southern Rhodesia.

Rhodesien (Ger.) Rhodesia.

R.H. OFFICIAL (ovpt.) appears on official stamps of Great Britain in 1902 for use by members of the Royal Household.

rhomboid roulette or **double-pointed tooth roulette** consists of diamond-shaped microscopic slits. It is a rare type, with no French name, listed by the editors of Senf catalogues, published in Germany. Mexico employed the rhomboid roulette on issues from 1868 to 1870.

Rialtar Sealadac na hErieann 1922 (Irish ovpt.) appears on 1912-19 stamps of Great Britain, for use by the Provisional Government of Ireland.

RIAU (ovpt.) appears on stamps of Indonesia for use in the Riouw Archipelago, 1945-60. Listed with stamps of Indonesia.

ribbed paper or repped paper; paper with a ribbed surface obtained by embossing between engraved steel rolls. See REP.

Richmond, Texas issued postmasters' provisional envelopes or letter sheets in 1861 as part of the Confederate States of America.

richtig (Ger.) correct, right.

Rickett's & Hall in Baltimore, Maryland, issued U.S. local stamps in 1857.

Rieka See FIUME.

riel coin of Cambodia. 100 sen or cents equal 1 riel.

RIGSBANK SKILLING (insc.) coin name, appears on stamps of Denmark, 1851.

rilievo (It.) embossing.

rin a small copper coin of Japan, one-tenth of a sen.

Ringgold, Ga. This town in Georgia issued postmasters' provisional envelopes in 1861 as part of the Confederate States of America.

Ringstempel (Ger.) ring cancel.

Rio de Oro a Spanish colony of about 71,600 square miles in northwest Africa on Atlantic coast. Capital: Villa Cisneros. Stamps of the colony were issued 1905-20; then issues of Spanish Sahara were used.

Rio Muni a Spanish province in West Africa of about 10,040 square miles. Chief town: Bata. Stamps have been issued since 1960.

Rios 19 See LOJA FRANCO.

Riouw Archipelago a group of islands in the Netherlands Indies, of about 2,279 square miles. Overprinted stamps of Indonesia have been issued since 1954.

riparian pertaining to the banks of a river; riparian states are those located on rivers.

riporto (It.) transfer.

RIS (ovpt.) appears on stamps of Dutch Indies (formerly the Netherlands Indies) for use in the United States of Indonesia, 1950-1.

Rishon Le Zion armoured-car mail an emergency mail service in Palestine between Rishon Le Zion and Tel Aviv during the Arab-Jewish riots in 1948. Special stamps were issued for the service; they are not listed in the popular catalogues.

ristampa (It.) reprint.

ritaglio (It.) cut square.

Rivadavias (nick.) the 1864-72 postage stamps of Argentina, portraying Bernardino Rivadavia, an Argentine statesman (1780-1845) who took an active part in the Argentine struggle for independence from Spain. The United States recognized the Argentine independence in 1823, as did Great Britain in 1825.

RIVERS (ovpt.) appears on lower right part

of a half stamp of Great Britain that was bisected for use in Niger Coast Protectorate in 1892; sometimes appears with the surcharge "½ d" in 1893.

rixdaler or **rigsdaler**   a silver coin of Sweden, Iceland, Denmark, and other countries. In Sweden, 100 ore equal 1 rixdaler; in Iceland, 96 skillings equal 1 rigsdaler; and in Denmark 96 skillings equal 1 rigsbank daler. This coin is the equivalent of the reichsthaler.

Riyal   new coinage of 1967 for Qatar-Dubai on the Qatar Peninsula. 1 riyal equals 100 dirhams.

Rizeh   (ovpt.) appears on stamps of Russia for use by Russian offices in the Turkish Empire, 1909-10. Rizeh (or Rizé or Coruh) was a Turkish seaport on the Black Sea.

R.M.S.   Railway Mail Service; appears in cancels for the Railway Post Office in the United States.

R.O.   (ovpt.) Roumelia (or Rumelia) Oriental, Eastern Rumelia. Appears on stamps of Turkey for use in Eastern Rumelia, 1880.

Robertsport   (insc.) appears on Liberia registration stamps with no value or country name. Other 10-cent registration stamps were inscribed "Harper", "Buchanan", "Grenville" and "Monrovia".

Robison & Co.   in Brooklyn, New York, issued U.S. local stamps in 1855-6.

Roche's City Dispatch   in Wilmington, Delaware, issued U.S. local stamps and envelopes in 1850.

rocket mail   experiments in sending mail from one place to another in rockets. The experiments began in 1931 in Austria by Friederich Schmidt. Pioneers in Germany, India, Britain, and the United States tried rockets for mail transmission. Jet airplanes virtually stopped further experiments; rockets were impractical vehicles for mail transportation.

rocking in   the stage in making steel-engraved printing plates when the transfer roll is guided back and forth by the siderographer (or sideographist, the operator of a transfer press used to transfer impressions onto a steel printing plate from a transfer roll).

röd   (Swed.) red.

rode kruis   (Dutch) red cross.

Rodi   (insc. and ovpt.) appears on Italian stamps used in Rhodes, 1912-24.

Rodrigues   an island in the Indian Ocean 365 miles northeast of Mauritius. Mauritius stamps were used from 1861, cancelled "B 65".

Rogers' labels   labels named after Cal Rog-

ers, an American pioneer flyer who left Sheepshead Bay, New York, on Sept. 17, 1911, for California. In his plane, Vin Fiz, named after his sponsor's soft drink, he carried special mail bearing ordinary stamps and the Rogers' labels. He took 49 days to fly the 4,331 miles to Long Beach, California.

rojo   (Sp.) red.

Rollenmarken   (Ger.) coil stamps.

roller cancellations   continuous cancellations struck by a device with the printing words, lines, and sometimes dates made on a wheel. The postal employees roll the canceller over stamps or postal stationery to cancel them.

Roll of Distinguished Philatelists   (R.D.P.) a British honourary group founded in 1921 by the Philatelic Congress of Great Britain. King George V was first to sign the Roll.

roll paper   paper which is made into rolls of any specified width or diameter.

roll stamps   See COIL STAMPS.

Rollstempel   (Ger.) roller postmark, roller cancellation.

Romagna   Italian province of about 5,626 square miles; formerly a province of the States of the Church. Capital: Ravenna. Stamps were issued in 1859. Romagna was annexed to Sardinia in 1860, and has used stamps of Italy since 1862.

Romagne   (insc.) appears on stamps of Romagna.

Romagnes   (Fr.) Romagna.

romain   (Fr.) Roman.

romaines   (Fr.) serifed letters.

Romana, Romania, or **Romina**   (insc.) appears on stamps of Romania.

Romania   (Roumania or Rumania) a republic in east Europe of about 91,671 square miles. Capital: Bucharest. First stamps were issued by Moldavia in 1858, and in 1859 Moldavia united with Walachia to form Romania. First stamps of Romania were issued in 1865.

Roman numerals   numerals composed of certain letters of the alphabet: I, V, X, L, C, and M, for 1, 5, 10, 50, 100, and 1000. These are used in some stamp designs.

Roman States   (States of the Church or

Roman States stamp

Papal States) the former temporal domain of the Pope in central Italy; about 16,000 square miles. Capital: Rome. Stamps were issued 1852-70; these were superseded by stamps of Italy.

Roman type normal upright type used for printing, as distinguished from such styles as italic, gothic, and Old English.

Roosevelt, Franklin Delano (1882-1945) the 32nd president of the United States; the best-known U.S. stamp collector, joined the Collectors Club of New York. After Mr. Roosevelt died, the late George B. Sloane of New York appraised the Roosevelt collection at $80,000. It was finally sold for $228,075 by H. R. Harmer Inc., the foremost stamp auctioneers in the world. The auction prices realized probably exceeded expectations because of post-war inflation and the Roosevelt connection.

rosa (Ger.) pink.

rosace a design suggesting a rose; a rosette sometimes used as a decoration in stamp designs, in postal markings, and on the flaps of envelopes. Used mainly in the 1840-75 period.

Rose Engine an invention of Jacob Perkins that, according to his specifications, was an engine lathe for engraving circular or oval lines of an even depth in metal or on other substances. This was one of many inventions of Jacob Perkins, who also developed the first machinery to transfer designs engraved on steel to steel or copper plates for printing banknotes, postage stamps, bonds, and stock certificates. Through the past century and a half, various geometric engraving machines have been developed. Virtually every security printer who engraves on steel or copper uses some form of the original geometric engraver. For details consult the book *Postage Stamps in the Making*, by John Easton, who finished the work that Fred J. Melville started. Faber and Faber of London published the book. See ENGINE TURNING; GEOMETRIC ENGRAVING.

rose-terne (Fr.) dull rose.

Rosettenmuster (Ger.) rosette design.

Ross Dependency a sector of Antarctica proclaimed British on July 30, 1923, and placed under New Zealand administration. Issued first stamps in 1957.

Ross-Smith issue Australia issued a special stamp affixed to mail at the conclusion of the Ross-Smith flight from England to Australia. Stamps are inscribed in four lines: "First / Aerial Post / England / Australia". The flight started November 10, 1919, from England. Twenty-nine days later, Ross-Smith, his brother, and two companions concluded their flight of 11,500 miles.

rosso (It.) red.

Roststempel (Ger.) grill cancel.

rot (Ger.) red.

rotary plates special curved plates made to fit cylinders used on rotary-type presses. Stamps printed by rotary presses are longer or wider than the same designs printed by flat plates. Certain U.S. stamps from both types of plates differ in rarity. The U.S. flat-plate stamps have plate numbers at the bottom of each pane.

rotary press a high-speed press on which paper in a continuous web is printed by passage between the printing cylinder and the plate cylinder.

rotary press booklets any postage stamp booklets printed by rotary presses, as compared to those made by flat plates. The rotary-printed stamps are higher or wider than the same designs printed from flat plates. Canada and the United States have issued both kinds of booklet stamps.

Rotationsdruck (Ger.) rotary printing.

rotbraun (Ger.) red-brown.

rotocalco (It.) photogravure.

rotogravuredruk (Dutch) gravure, photogravure printing.

rotogravure printing a form of intaglio printing carried out on a rotary press; the designs are etched directly into the surface of a copper cylinder.

rotorange (Ger.) reddish-orange.

rotto (It.) broken.

roue à dents (Fr.) cogwheel; may refer to a type of cancellation or cogwheels in stamp designs.

rouge (Fr.) red.

rough perforations the varieties that are not clear cut. Rough perforations sometimes resemble roulettes when no definition of

punched holes exist. They are common in some issues of Mexico 1882-92, and in New Zealand stamps of 1901-2.

roulette or **rouletting** short lines punched

in paper or cardboard to make separation of the parts easy and quick. The roulettes do not remove any of the paper substance as do perforations. On Oct. 1, 1847, Henry Archer submitted a plan to the British Post Office officials to make machinery for stamp separation. During his experiments, Mr. Archer developed rouletting with the production of the serpentine roulettes that resembled the movements of a snake. These are sometimes called the Treasury roulettes, a rare type of British stamp separation. The most common roulettes are lines and lines made with colours of the stamps with straight lines between rows of postage stamps. See DIAMOND ROULETTE; OBLIQUE ROULETTE; PIN ROULETTE; SAW-TOOTH ROULETTE; SERPENTINE ROULETTE.

Roumania   See ROMANIA.

Roumanie   (Fr.) Romania.

Roumelie Orientale   (ovpt.) appears vertically on stamps of Turkey for use in 1880 in Eastern Roumelia (or Rumelia).

rovesciato   (It.) reversed.

Royal Cypher   initials of a sovereign in script type to resemble handwriting. Sometimes used as part of stamp designs (for example, Fiji 1871), as overprints (for example, Sarawak 1946), and as watermarks (for example, various issues of Great Britain, 1912-8).

Royal Niger Company   a commercial organization formed in 1882 as the National African Company. Received its charter in 1886. Postal markings for some offices read: "The Royal Niger Company Chartered and Limited". The company purchased British postage stamps and sent them to the territories they controlled. These stamps were used from June 1, 1895, until Dec. 31, 1899, when the company charter was revoked and its territories were incorporated with Northern and Southern Nigeria. While the British stamps were in use, large cancellations were made for and used by Akassa, Burutu, Lokoja, and Abutshi. In Gibbons stamp catalogues, the British Empire section lists Bonny River, Brass River, Forcados River, and Old Calibar River as examples. Collectors are urged not to remove stamps from envelopes with these scarce coloured cancels. They are not revenue cancellations, although they resemble some revenue markings. Many specialists in Nigeria and Oil Rivers stamps seek these markings of the Royal Niger Company.

Royal Niger Company, Chartered and Limited   appears in postmarks of various

shapes and sizes, used 1888-1900 on mail from towns on the Niger Coast and River. These postmarks are illustrated and priced in Gibbons Part One catalogue.

Royal Philatelic Society of Canada   See CANADIAN PHILATELIC SOCIETY.

Royal Reprints   In the true sense, these were neither royal nor reprints. They were special postage stamps Queen Victoria ordered for her children. They were made from

Plate 66 of the 1854-7 1-penny red stamps. Reprints were in black and carmine-rose.

royal visits   (nick.) stamps issued to commemorate visits by royalty to other countries or colonies.

Royaume d' or **Royaume de** or **Royaume du**   (Fr.) Kingdom of. This phrase, with the name of the postal authority that follows it, appears on stamps of French-language countries.

Royaume De L'Arabie Soudite   (Fr. insc.) Kingdom of Saudi Arabia; appears on stamps of Saudi Arabia.

Royaume Du Cambodge   (Fr. insc.) Kingdom of Cambodia; appears on most stamps of Cambodia.

Royaume du Laos   (Fr. insc.) Kingdom of Laos; appears on stamps of Laos.

Rpf   (part of sur.) appears on Luxembourg stamps of 1926-39 for use under German occupation, 1940.

R.P.O.   Railway Post Office; also known as Travelling Post Office (T.P.O.) in many parts of the world. Post offices on railway trains process mail and cancel stamps with special impressions that include the name of the line, the time, and the date. The R.P.O. postmarks may also include the region or merely letters to indicate the name of the railroad. Some collectors have formed comprehensive studies of R.P.O. markings and have segregated their stamps by regions.

R.P.S.C.   Royal Philatelic Society of Canada.

R.P.S.L.   Royal Philatelic Society, London (England). The "L" for "London" is used to distinguish this organization from the photographic and other societies, especially philatelic organizations, authorized to use the designation "Royal".

R S A (insc.) Republic of South Africa. Appears on some stamps of the Republic of South Africa. Also used occasionally as a watermark.

RSM Republic of San Marino.

RUANDA (handstamped ovpt.) appears on stamps of Congo (German East Africa) while under Belgian occupation, 1916. In the same year other stamps were hand-stamped "URUNDI".

Ruanda-Urundi a former Belgian Trust Territory of about 21,234 square miles on the southeast coast of central Africa; became the Republic of Rwanda and the Kingdom of Burundi in 1962. Capital: Usum Bara. Stamps of Congo, overprinted or surcharged, were issued 1924-61.

Ruanda-Urundi (ovpt. and insc.) appears overprinted on stamps of Congo for use in Ruanda-Urundi (Belgian East Africa), 1924-9, 1941-2; also inscribed on issues of Ruanda-Urundi until 1961.

rubber blanket on an offset press, the sheet of rubber covering the transfer cylinder, which carries the image from the zinc plate to the paper.

rubber cement an adhesive containing rubber. While it may be useful for certain jobs, collectors should never use it for mounting postage stamps. This substance may attack the paper or the printing inks of postage stamps, causing them to change colour.

rubber rings a device used to make artificial watermarks in cheaper papers. Such watermarks are coarser and not so distinct as those obtained with dandy rolls.

ruble, rouble a silver coin of Russia, Armenia, and other countries. 100 kopecks equal 1 ruble. First struck in Russia in the seventeenth century, it became the standard coin under King Peter the Great in 1704. During the reign of Queen Catherine I in 1725, klippe or square rubles were struck.

Rueckporto (Ger.) return postage.

Rueckschein (Ger.) receipt.

rueckseitig (Ger.) on the back or reverse.

Ruhleben a First World War British prisoners' camp. Enough stamps, covers, cards, and related items exist for a well-formed collection to be made on this one wartime subject, sad but historical.

ruled paper paper printed with lines. The 1919 redrawn issue of stamps from Latvia were printed on paper with ruled horizontal blue lines. The 1886-1887 stamps of Mexico were printed on paper ruled both vertically and horizontally. These ruled

*Ruled paper
in stamp of
Mexico, 1887*

papers were used during paper shortages.

ruleteado (Sp.) rouletted.

Rumänien (sur.) appears on stamps of Germany for use in Romania under German occupation, 1918.

rund (Ger.) round.

Rundschreiben (Ger.) circular.

Rundstempel (Ger.) circular cancellation, round or ring cancellation.

rupee a silver coin of India, Ceylon, Burma, parts of Africa, and other eastern countries. In Ceylon 100 cents equal 1 rupee; in India 100 naye paisa equal 1 rupee; in Pakistan 100 pice equal 1 rupee. The name may be from the Sanskrit word for wrought silver. "Mahbubia" was the name given a silver rupee struck in Hyderabad in 1904.

rupia a silver coin of Portuguese India. 16 tangas equal 1 rupia. The rupia was comparable to the rupee of British India.

rupiah a silver coin of Indonesia. 100 sen equal 1 rupiah. The rupiah was the gulden of Dutch New Guinea.

Russell Eighth Avenue Post Office in New York City, New York, issued U.S. local stamps in 1854-8.

Russia formerly a kingdom, now a republic officially called the Union of Soviet Socialist Republics (U.S.S.R.), in east Europe and northwest Asia; area variously quoted as about 8,354,198 square miles, 8,599,776 square miles, and 8,662,400 square miles. Capital: Moscow. First stamps were issued in 1857.

Russian locals stamps issued in communities in Russia to serve the nearby areas where the government posts had not been established. They linked with other similar stamps to prepay the postal charges on mail sent on a chain-like system from one locality to another and then to the final destination. They are also known as Zemstvos.

Russian offices in China Russia maintained post offices in China and issued stamps there beginning in 1899.

Russian offices in Turkey   Russia maintained post offices in Turkey and issued stamps there beginning in 1863.

Russian Orthodox Cross design   appears in a circle handstamped on stamps of Latvia in 1919, and overprinted on Latvia stamps later in 1919. These issues were introduced during the occupation of Kurland by the West Russian army. The cross shown in a circle consists of one vertical bar with a small horizontal bar across it and with a wider bar just below and parallel to the top bar. Halfway below the wider bar and the bottom of the vertical bar, another bar at a 45-degree angle crosses the vertical bar. The top portion resembles a Cross of Lorraine.

Russie   (Fr.) Russia.

russisch   (Ger.) Russian.

Russisch-Polen   (ovpt.) appears on 1906-11 stamps of Germany for use in Poland under German occupation, 1915.

Russland   (Ger.) Russia.

Rustenburg   a town in the southwest central region of Transvaal about 70 miles west of Pretoria; issued stamps during the Second British Occupation in 1900 by handstamp-ing "V.R." in violet on former stamps of the South African Republic (Transvaal). "V.R." stands for "Victoria Regina", the Latin words for Queen Victoria. These stamps are listed with those of Transvaal.

rust stains on stamps   Collectors are advised to consult a chemist about the removal of such stains.

Ruthenia   a former province of Czechoslovakia; became part of Hungary in 1939. In 1939 issued one stamp in 3-koruna value, listed with stamps of Carpatho-Ukraine.

Rutherfordton, N.C.   This town in North Carolina issued postmasters' provisional stamps in 1861 as part of the Confederate States of America.

Rwanda (Rwandaise Republic)   a republic in central Africa of about 10,166 square miles. Capital: Kigali. First stamps were issued in 1962.

Ryukyu Islands (Nansei Islands)   a semi-autonomous island chain in the west Pacific Ocean under U.S. administration; about 848 square miles. Capital: Naha, Okinawa. Part of Japan until 1945, the islands have issued stamps since 1948.

S

S   in auction catalogues, means "specimen".

S   (ovpt.) may appear with crescent and star in an oval, on stamps of Straits Settlements for use in Selangor, a state in the Federation of Malaya, 1878-82.

S.A.   (Ger.) Sturm Abteilung, Storm Troops. Appears on essays made for proposed postage stamps depicting Hitler's Brown Shirts, the strong-arm men of the Nazi period before the Second World War. (Courtesy of H. P. H. Davies)

SAA   (airline) South African Airways. Point of origin: Transvaal.

S.A.A.E.I.   (airline) Societa Anonima Aero Espresso Italiana, Italy.

Saar   a German state of about 990 square miles. Capital: Saarbrucken. Saar was administered by the League of Nations from 1920 to 1935. It used overprinted stamps of Germany in 1920 and then Saar stamps inscribed "SAARGEBIET"; in 1935 was returned to Germany and used German stamps. It was occupied by France 1947, as a French Protectorate, then was returned to Germany in 1957. It used Saar stamps until 1959, and then stamps of the German Federal Republic.

Saare   (Fr. ovpt.) appears in 1920 on stamps of Germany and Bavaria for use in Saar, a German state on the French border. The League of Nations administered Saar, 1920-35.

SAARGEBIET   (ovpt.) appears on stamps of Germany for use in the Saar under administration by the League of Nations, 1920.

SAARLAND   (Ger. insc.) appears on stamps of Saar under German administration, 1957-9; these were replaced by stamps of the German Federal Republic.

Sabah   the former British colony of North Borneo on the northeast part of Borneo, in the Malay Archipelago. Capital: Jesselton. In 1963 Sabah joined with Malaya, Sarawak, and Singapore to form the Federation of Malaysia. In 1964 the first stamps of Sabah were overprinted stamps on 1961 pictorials of North Borneo. Subsequent postage stamps consisted of Malaysia issues, some with the added inscription "SABAH"

and arms.

SABAH   (ovpt.) appears on stamps of North Borneo issued on July 1, 1964, for use in Sabah. Sabah was the former British Crown Colony of North Borneo until the name was changed and the colony joined with Malaya, Sarawak, and Singapore to form the Federation of Malaysia in 1963. Sabah issued stamps with two inscriptions in 1965: "SABAH" and "MALAYSIA". Sabah now uses stamps of the Federation without a separate name on them.

S.A.B.E.N.A.   (airline) Société Anonyme Belge pour l'Exploitation de la Navigation Aérienne. Point of origin: Belgium.

Sachsen   (Ger.) Saxony.

SAE   stamped addressed envelope, for prepaid reply.

saegeartig   (Ger.) serrated.

S.A. Emprêsa de Viacao Aéreo Rio Grandense "Varig"   (airline) Point of origin: Brazil.

safety paper   strong paper chemically treated, tinted, or printed in such a manner as to expose attempts at alterations. Winchester paper is an example.

Sage key-type   French stamps designed by J. A. Sage. Also known as the Peace and Commerce key-type, depicting two human figures with a value tablet between them. Issued 1876-1900.

sägezahnartiger Durchstich   (Ger.) zig-zag roulette.

saggio   (It.) specimen of a postage stamp.

SAHARA   (ovpt.) appears on Spanish stamps of 1924 for use in Spanish Sahara (Spanish Western Sahara) in the same year.

Sahara espagnol   (Fr.) Spanish Sahara.

SAHARA ESPANOL   (ovpt.) appears on Spanish stamps of 1936-40 for use in Spanish Sahara, 1941-6.

Sahara Español   (Sp. insc.) Spanish Sahara; appears on stamps of Spanish Sahara.

Sahara Español Occidental   (Sp. insc.) Spanish Western Sahara; appears on stamps of Spanish Sahara, 1924-31.

S.A.I.D.E.   (sur.) appears with "23-8-1948" and Arabic words on two values of a former issue of Egypt to mark the first flights of Services Aériens Internationaux d'Egypte from Cairo to Athens and Rome on Aug. 23, 1948.

(See also ST.)

Saint-Christophe (Fr.) St. Christopher.
Sainte-Hélène (Fr.) St. Helena.
Sainte-Lucie (Fr.) St. Lucia.
Saint-Marin (Fr.) San Marino.
Saint-Thomas et Prince Iles (Fr.) St. Thomas and Prince Islands.
Salamanca a town in the state of Guanajuato, Mexico, situated in the southwestern corner of the state on the railroad to Guadalajara. In 1914, during the Mexican Civil War, Pancho Villa and Venustiano Carranza led the revolt in the North and referred to themselves as the "Gobierno Constitucionalista" (Constitutional Government). They overprinted Mexican stamps in captured towns with hand-stamped impressions. The issue for Salamanco bears an abbreviation "GBNO. CONST.", an overprint, and was issued in September 1914. See stamps of Mexico in stamp catalogues for the details.
Salem, N.C. This town in North Carolina issued postmasters' provisional envelopes in 1861, as part of the Confederate States of America.
Salem, Va. This town in Virginia issued postmasters' provisional stamps in 1861 as part of the Confederate States of America.
salient (her.) leaping, with both forepaws in the air.
Salisbury, N.C. This town in North Carolina issued postmasters' provisional envelopes in 1861 as part of the Confederate States of America.
Sällsynt (Swed.) scarce.
Salomon Iles (Fr.) Solomon Islands.
SALONICCO (sur.) appears on stamps of Italy, 1909-11, for use in Italian offices in Salonika.
Salonika or **Thessalonica** a seaport city of Greece. A variety of postage stamps trace the modern history of Salonika: surcharged stamps of Italy 1901-11, for use by Italian offices in Turkey; Russian stamps overprinted "Salonique", 1909-10, used in the Turkish Empire; and Turkish military, official, and newspaper stamps for use in Salonika, 1898 and subsequent years.
Salonique (ovpt.) appears on stamps of Russia, 1909-10, for use by Russian offices in Turkey.
salot, solot, or **lott** a copper coin of Siam (Thailand). 64 solots equal 1 tical. 2 solots equal 1 att.
saltire (her.) a diagonal cross.

salung or **mayon** a silver coin of Siam (Thailand). 4 salungs equal 1 tical.
S.A.M. (airline) Societa Aera Mediterranea. Point of órigin: Italy.
Samoa an archipelago east of Fiji in the southern Pacific Ocean, partially under New Zealand and partially under U.S. control; area about 1,209 square miles. Capital: Apia. As an independent kingdom Samoa issued stamps 1877-99; under German dominion stamps of Germany were overprinted, 1900-15; under British dominion and New Zealand mandate from 1914, stamps of German Samoa were surcharged, and then those of New Zealand were overprinted; Western Samoa was independent in 1962 and issued stamps. A set of stamps inscribed "Samoa" was issued in 1921.
SAMOA (ovpt.) appears on stamps of New Zealand for use in Samoa in 1914.
Samoa I Sisifo the revised name of Western Samoa introduced March 21, 1958, on the inauguration of the new parliament.
Samos an island department of Greece in the Aegean Sea off the west coast of Turkey; about 181 square miles. Stamps were issued in 1912-13 by a provisional government of Greece.
SAMPLE appears as an overprint or in perforated letters on postage stamps that are used as samples by security printers' salesmen.
sämsk-färgat (Swed.) buff.
San. Sanabria Air Post Catalogue.
S.A.N.A. (airline) Sociedad Argentina de Navigacia Aérea. Point of origin: Argentina.
S.A.N.A. (airline) Societa Anonima Navigazione Aerea. Point of origin: Genoa, Italy.
Sanabria a U.S. airmail catalogue, named after Nicholas Sanabria, who for many years operated a stamp business in New York City.
San Antonio, Texas This town issued postmasters' provisional envelopes in 1861, as part of the Confederate States of America.
sanar a silver coin of Afghanistan. 2 shahi equal 1 sanar. The coinage is similar to that of modern Persia (Iran), and includes the dinar, paisa, abbasi, quran, rupee, and tuman.
S.A.N.C. (airline) Sociedad Aéreo Navegación Comercial. Point of origin: Chile.
Sandjak d'Alexandrette (ovpt.) appears on stamps of Syria, 1938, for use in Alexandretta, a former French mandate in north Syria. The 1938 issue was surcharged with new values.
San Domingo or **Santo Domingo** the former

name of the Dominican Republic; also the first settlement on the island of Hispaniola.

Sandwich Islands former name of the Hawaiian Islands.

Sanitary Fair Stamps U.S. charity locals used to pay the carrying charges on mail from Sanitary Fairs (authorized by the U.S. Sanitary Commission) in different cities to the post offices in the local communities. The postage on each letter paid the remaining part of the delivery charges anywhere in the world. In 1864 the fair in Brooklyn, New York, raised $400,000 to aid the U.S. Civil War wounded.

San Marino a republic on the Italian Peninsula of about 38 square miles. Capital: San Marino. Stamps have been issued since 1877.

San Martin, José de (1778-1850) a South American soldier and statesman, who helped to liberate Argentina, Chile, and Peru from the Spaniards. He is honoured on many postage stamps.

sans filigrane (Fr.) unwatermarked.

sans gomme (Fr.) without gum.

sans serif printed characters without serifs or ticks on the end of strokes, such as the Gothic type.

sans trace de charnière (Fr.) never hinged.

Santander formerly a state, now a department of the Republic of Colombia in South America. Issued stamps in 1884 and some provisionals for Cucuta, the capital of the state, in 1900.

santim a coin of Haytay and Latvia. In Haytay, 100 santims equal 1 kurush; in Latvia, 100 santims equal 1 lat.

Saorstát Eireann 1922 (ovpt.) appears on stamps of Great Britain, for use in the Irish Free State.

SAR Syrian Arab Republic.

Sarawak a state of about 50,000 square miles in the Federation of Malaysia, in northwest Borneo on the China Sea; formerly a British Crown Colony. Capital: Kuching. Stamps known as the "White Rajahs" were issued in 1869.

SARKARI (ovpt.) appears on stamps of Soruth, a feudatory state of India for use as official stamps, 1929, 1933-49.

Sardaigne (Fr.) Sardinia.

Sardinia a Mediterranean island, formerly a kingdom, now part of Italy. Stamps were issued from 1851, superseded in 1862 by those of Italy.

Sarre (Fr.) Saar.

S.A.S. (airline) Scandinavian Airlines System. Point of origin: Stockholm, Sweden.

S.A.S. (airline) Servizi Aerei Speciali. Point of origin: Italy.

SASE self-addressed stamped envelope.

Saseno a small Albanian island of about 2 square miles in the Adriatic Sea. Italy occupied Saseno from October 1914 until 1947. Italian stamps overprinted "SASENO" were used in 1923, superseded by those of Italy until 1947, when the island was returned to Albania.

S.A.T.A. (airline) Sociedade Acoriana de Transportes Aereos, Lda. Point of origin: Lisbon, Portugal.

satang a bronze coin of Siam (Thailand). 100 satangs equal 1 tical. It was issued by king's order of November, 1908.

sats (Swed.) set.

Satz (Ger.) set; refers to type that was set correctly for proofs, but is not ready for printing.

Satzpreis (Ger.) price per set.

Saudi Arabia a kingdom of about 597,000 square miles, occupying most of the Arabian Peninsula. Capital: Riyadh. Between 1925 and 1932 overprinted stamps of Turkey and Hejaz were issued by Nejd and Hejaz; following the union of Nejd and Hejaz under the name "Saudi Arabia" in 1932, stamps were issues of Saudi Arabia.

SAURASHTRA (partial ovpt.) appears on stamps for use as revenue stamps of Soruth, a feudatory state in western India, in 1949.

Savannah, Ga. This town in Georgia issued postmasters' provisional envelopes in 1861, as part of the Confederate States of America.

saw-edge separation see SAW-TOOTH ROULETTE.

saw-tooth roulette a roulette resembling the teeth of a saw; in pairs of stamps or larger units it is clear that the tooth of one point

becomes the hollow in the adjacent stamp. Single postage stamps with this roulette often resemble perforated stamps.

Saxe (Fr.) Saxony.

Saxony a former kingdom, now part of central Germany; about 5,788 square miles. Capital: Dresden. Stamps were issued from

1850, superseded in 1868 by those of North German Confederation.

sc in auction catalogues, means "scrape(s)".

S.C. the small crown watermarks of Great Britain.

SCADTA or **S.C.A.T.A.** (airline) Sociedad Colombo Alemana de Transportes Aéreos. Point of origin: Colombia. This airline is now A.V.I.A.N.C.A.

Scandinavia (1) the ancient name of the land where Norsemen lived; (2) the modern collective name for Sweden, Norway, Denmark, and Iceland, but not including Greenland.

Scarpanto (It.) Karpathos.

Schattierung (Ger.) shade.

Schermack (nick.) U.S. stamps privately perforated by the Schermack Company of Detroit, Michigan, for use in their vending machines. Scott's U.S. Specialized catalogue lists three different types of vertical perforations.

schiefer (Ger.) slate.

schieferblau (Ger.) slate blue.

Schiff (Ger.) ship.

Schiffspostmarke (Ger.) ships post stamp.

Schiffspoststempel (Ger.) ship cancel.

schilling a coin of Germany. 16 schillings equal 1 mark. Originally money of account, the pound of silver was divided into 20 schillings of 12 denarii each.

schlangenartig durchstochen (Ger.) serpentine-rouletted.

Schlangenlinie (Ger.) serpentine.

schlangenliniger Durchstich (Ger.) serpentine roulette.

schlecht zentriert (Ger.) off centre.

Schlesien (Ger.) Silesia.

Schleswig a former duchy of the Danish crown; divided into North Schleswig (which joined Denmark in 1920) and South Schleswig (which remained part of Germany). A plebiscite issue of stamps appeared in 1930.

schmal (Ger.) narrow.

schmalrandig (Ger.) with narrow margins.

schmutzig (Ger.) soiled.

schraeg (Ger.) sloping.

Schraegeschrift (Ger.) italics.

Schreibschrift (Ger.) script.

Schriftstueck (Ger.) document.

schwach gestempelt (Ger.) lightly cancelled.

schwarz (Ger.) black.

schwarzblau (Ger.) blackish blue.

schwarzblaugruen (Ger.) blackish blue-green.

schwarzbraun (Ger.) blackish brown.

schwarzgrau (Ger.) black-grey.

schwarzgruen (Ger.) black-green.

Schweden (Ger.) Sweden.

Schweiz (Ger.) Switzerland.

Schweizer Reneke a community in the Second South African Republic. In 1900, during the Second British Occupation of the South African Republic, military authorities issued stamps overprinted on former regular-issues, reading "BESIEGED" in crude letters reading up or down. The same overprint was made in 1900 on stamps of the Cape of Good Hope. These are listed in catalogues with the stamps of Transvaal.

scientific aspects of philately Collectors have mixed feelings about the scientific aspects of stamp collecting. The positive thinkers claim that philatelists study their stamps to discover facts for themselves. The serious philatelists visit the manufacturers, paper mills and ink makers. The negative thinkers believe that stamp collectors as a group are not sufficiently trained to analyze stamps in a truly scientific manner.

SCINDE DISTRICT DAWK (insc.) Scinde District Post; appears embossed on stamps of the Scinde district of India in 1852.

Scotland stamps These are one of the regional issues by Great Britain in 1958. Other regionals include: Northern Ireland, Guernsey, Isle of Man, Jersey, and the combined region of Wales and Monmouthshire. These stamps resemble other British issues but have their own heraldic emblems.

Scott's catalogues postage stamp catalogues published by Scott Publications Incorporated of New York City. Most stamp dealers in Canada and the United States use the Scott catalogues to arrange and price their stock. The Scott catalogues give the locations of the stamp-issuing places and valuable data about coinage. Stamp designs are illustrated, and descriptions with many footnotes give valuable guidance to collectors.

Scott, John W. founder of Scott's catalogues and the famous stamp business under his

Scratched plate: caused hairlines in stamp design

name; called the father of American philately.

Scout's Fund (ovpt.) appears with the design of an animal's head on stamps of Siam for use as semi-postal stamps in 1920.

scratched plate a printing plate damaged by scratches, which show on some postage stamps as microscopic lines. (Illustration: p . 217)

screen (1) a ruled glass used in the production of halftones to break up the image into dots; also refers to the number of dots per linear inch; (2) a filtering device used in pulp and paper mills to remove knots and large dirt particles from the fibrous suspension; (3) a wire mesh device used in sprinkling and marbling edges of books.

script type type-face imitating handwriting.

scudo a silver coin of Italy and the Roman States. 100 bajocchi equal 1 scudo. The name derives from the Portuguese "escudo", meaning "shield". There was also a gold scudo.

Scutari See ÜSKÜDAR.

S.d.N. Bureau international du Travail (Fr. ovpt.) appears on stamps of Switzerland for use as official stamps by the International Labor Bureau, 1923-30, 1939, 1942-3.

SEACOM the code name of the South-East Asia Commonwealth Telephone Cable System, built jointly by Malaysia, Singapore, Australia, New Zealand, Canada, and Great Britain. It connects with the Trans-Pacific cable (see COMPAC). Malaysia marked the completion of the Hong Kong–Malaysia link of SEACOM on March 30, 1967, with two commemorative stamps showing the routes of the cables.

se in auction catalogues, means "straight edge".

sea floor postmark a special cancellation applied to mail in 1939-40 in a post office on the sea floor at Nassau, Bahamas. The 4-pence Bahamas stamps of 1938 featured the sea gardens. Similar issues in 1965 depicted a scene of a sea garden at Nassau on the 1-shilling stamps, and the 1914 Williamson film undersea project plus the 1939 sea floor post office on the 5-shilling stamps of 1965.

SEA GARDENS – NASSAU (insc.) appears on the 4-pence stamps of Bahamas in 1938, depicting the sea gardens of Nassau in the Bahamas.

seal a device impressed in wax for authentication.

sealing wax stamp refers to the ½-anna stamp of the Scinde district in India of 1852. It is the only postage stamp made of sealing wax.

sec (Fr.) dry.

sechs (Ger.) six.

secondary colours green, orange, and violet. Secondary colours are obtained by mixing two of the primary colours together.

secret dates See HIDDEN DATES.

secret marks dots, dashes, and extra lines added to postage stamps purposely to identify the products of one printer from those with issues of similar designs by another printer. Canada added proposed issue dates in microscopic figures on some issues. The secret marks on certain U.S. stamps created such interest that some catalogues enlarge the marks and give details about them. Naples and Great Britain also employed secret marks. Refer to stamp catalogues for details.

security overprint an overprint on stamps to prevent fraudulent use. Examples: a U.S. regular issue was overprinted "Kans. and Nebr." on May 1, 1929, to help prevent losses from post office robberies. Great Britain overprinted some 1873-80 stamps in large carmine numerals, "3d" on the 3-pence and "6d" on the 6-pence, to help prevent the public from removing cancels to use the stamps a second time. These British stamps are referred to as overprinted and not surcharged because the denominations remained the same.

Sedang (insc.) appears on bogus labels for a non-existant place.

SEDTA (airline) Sociedad Ecuatoriana de Transportes Aéreos, a German-controlled airline developed in Ecuador after the First World War. By 1941, the Pan American Grace Airways and the SEDTA lines provided international air connections for Quito, Guayaquil, and other Ecuadorian cities. After the United States became involved in the Second World War, SEDTA suspended operations.

Seebecks (nick.) stamps produced by N. F. Seebeck, an executive of the Hamilton Bank Note Co. of New York, for Honduras, Nicaragua, Salvador, and Ecuador. He agreed to supply these countries with

*Seebeck
stamp*

annual issues of postage stamps free of charge, in exchange for the privilege of printing more of the former stamps for his personal benefit.

seegruen (Ger.) sea-green.

SEGNATASSE or **SEGNA TASSE** (insc. and ovpt.) appears inscribed on postage-due stamps of Italy, San Marino, Vatican City, and Italian colonies; also overprinted on stamps of the Vatican City.

SEGURO POSTAL (Sp. insc.) appears on insured-letter stamps of Mexico.

Seguro Social del Campesino (part of ovpt., sur. and insc.) appears on postal tax stamps of Ecuador, 1935-6, 1938 for the benefit of the Social and Rural Workers' Insurance Fund.

sehr fein (Ger.) very fine.

Seidenfaden (Ger.) silk thread.

seize (Fr.) sixteen.

SEJM w WILNIE (insc.) appears on stamps of Central Lithuania.

Selangor a sultanate of about 3,160 square miles on the west coast of the Malay Peninsula. Capital: Kuala Lumpur.

SELANGOR (ovpt. and insc.) appears overprinted on Straits Settlements stamps for use in Selangor, a state in the Federation of Malaya, 1881-9; surcharged on Straits Settlements stamps for use in Selangor in 1891; inscribed on stamps of Selangor, 1892-1962.

selección (Sp.) selection.

selezione (It.) selection.

sello (Sp.) stamp.

sello conmemorativo (Sp.) commemorative stamp.

sello de certificado (Sp.) registration stamp.

sello de beneficiencia (Sp.) charity or semi-postal stamp.

sello de correo (Sp.) postage stamp.

sello de correo aéreo (Sp.) airmail stamp.

sello de correo de campaña (Sp.) field post stamp.

sello de paquete de ferrocarril (Sp.) railway parcel stamp.

sello de servico (Sp.) official stamp.

sello de tasa (Sp.) postage-due stamp.

sello de urgencia (Sp.) special-delivery stamp.

sello fiscal (Sp.) revenue tax stamp.

sello fiscal-postal (Sp.) postal revenue stamp.

sello para cartas retardadas (Sp.) too-late stamp.

sello para paquete postale (Sp.) parcel post stamp.

sello para periódicos (Sp.) newspaper stamp.

sello provisional (Sp.) provisional stamp.

Sello provisorio para REGISTRO (insc.)

appears on stamps also inscribed "CUNDINAMARCA", for use in 1883-6 as registration stamps for Cundinamarca, a state in Colombia, before it became a department in the newly constituted Republic of Colombia.

Selma, Ala. This city in Alabama issued postmasters' provisional envelopes in 1861 as part of the Confederate States of America.

sêlo aéreo (Port.) airmail stamp.

sêlo de correio (Port.) postage stamp.

sêlo de imposto de guerra (Port.) war tax stamp.

sêlo de registro (Port.) registration stamp.

sêlo militar (Port.) military postage stamp.

sêlo oficial (Port.) official stamp.

sêlo para encomenda de caminho de ferro (Port.) railway parcel stamp.

sêlo para expresso (Port.) special-delivery or express stamp.

sêlo provisório (Port.) provisional stamp.

selten (Ger.) scarce.

Seltenheit (Ger.) rarity.

selvedge or **selvage** the paper around panes or sheets of stamps, also called marginal paper.

semi-official airmail stamps labels made to prepay mail delivery charges of private companies; government-approved, but not regulated by post office departments. The best-known items originated in the northern parts of Canada and in Colombia following the First World War.

semi-postal stamps those issued usually with two separate denominations, one to prepay postal charges and the other to raise money for some predetermined project.

semis (nick.) semi-postal stamps, often called charity stamps.

sen a copper coin, although sometimes of iron, of Japan, the Malay Peninsula, and other countries. 100 sen equal 1 yen. 100 mon equal 1 sen. In Malaya 100 sen (cents) equal 1 dollar. The name of this early coin is from a Japanese word meaning "fountain".

senar a silver coin of Persia (Iran). 10 senars equal 1 kran.

Senegal a republic of about 74,112 square miles on the west coast of Africa south of the Senegal River; formerly a French colony. Capital: Dakar (St. Louis was the capital of Senegal as a French colony). Senegal used surcharged stamps of the French colonies from 1887 until 1892, and inscribed issues to 1941, when it became part of French West Africa. Senegal became a republic in 1958, and issued stamps;

it joined the Mali Federation in 1959-60, and has issued stamps of the Republic of Senegal since 1960.

Senegambia and Niger a temporary French administrative unit for Senegal and Niger possessions in Africa, later joined with part of French Sudan to become Upper Senegal and Niger. Stamps of French Colonies were issued for Senegambia and Niger in 1903, bearing the inscription "SÉNÉGAMBIE ET NIGER".

Senegambien und Niger (Ger.) Senegambia and Niger.

senkrecht (Ger.) vertical.

senkrechtes Paar (Ger.) vertical pair.

sensitized paper chemically treated paper, normally used for photographs. It was used in 1900 in Mafeking, Cape of Good Hope, for local postage stamps. These stamps portray Sgt. Major Goodyear (1-penny) and Gen. Robert S. S. Baden-Powell (3-penny). They would be the first stamps in a topical collection of Boy Scout stamps.

SEPAD Southeastern Pennsylvania and Delaware. The associated stamp clubs of these areas hold stamp exhibitions at eastern locations.

separation See PERFORATION; ROULETTE.

sept (Fr.) seven.

Serbia or **Servia** a former Balkan kingdom, now a republic in the Federal People's Republic of Jugoslavia; about 36,937 square miles. Capital: Belgrade. Stamps were issued for Serbia from 1866 until the formation of Jugoslavia after the First World War.

Serbie (Fr.) Serbia.

Serbien (Ger.) Serbia.

Serbien (ovpt.) appears on stamps of Bosnia for use in Serbia in 1916 under Austrian occupation; also appears on stamps of Jugoslavia for use in Serbia under German occupation, 1941.

série (Fr. and It.) set, series.

serie (Sp.) set, series.

series an issue of postage stamps.

serif the cross lines at top and bottom of a letter in type.

serpentine roulette a roulette comprised of wavy lines that resemble the movements of a serpent. For fifteen years, beginning in 1860, Finland issued postage stamps serpentine-rouletted in three distinct types, varying in the depth of the teeth. When these stamps are separated, they appear to have large perforations.

serrated roulette See ARC ROULETTE.

Service (ovpt.) appears in script letters, some also with a Turkish overprint, on

Serpentine roulette

regular issues of Turkey for use as official stamps, 1903-15.

SERVICE (ovpt. or insc.) appears on stamps for use by various governments, usually of English-language countries but also of native Indian states.

service postal (Fr.) mail service.

service postal intérieur (Fr.) domestic mail.

servicio (Sp.) service.

servicio aéreo (Sp.) airmail service.

SERVICIO/AEREO INTERIOR/10 Centavos/DE QUETZAL/1930 (Sp. sur.) appears on Guatemala airmail stamps for domestic use, 1930.

servicio oficial (Sp.) official service.

SERVICIO POSTAL MEXICANO (insc.) appears on official stamps of Mexico, 1884-93.

servizio (It.) official.

SERVIZIO / COMMISIONI (2-line insc.) appears on a set of three stamps of Italy issued July 1, 1913, for messenger service to prepay delivery charges on mail sent by government offices, and valid until March 15, 1925. The same stamps, surcharged "UNA LIRA", were issued by Italy on April 30, 1925, for the same service, and were valid until June 30, 1938.

Seschellen (Ger.) Seychelles Islands.

sesquicentennial a 150th anniversary of an event. The word often is inscribed on stamps, see, for example, the U.S. 1926 and 1927 stamps.

Sessional Papers Canadian government reports that include the postmaster-general's reports for the Province of Canada and later for the Dominion of Canada. These give the quantities of postage stamps by each denomination ordered in the year.

set a postal issue of two or more stamps, often with a common theme or subject. Stamps in sets are not always issued on the same day.

set-off a transfer of ink from one printed sheet to another.

se-tenant stamps postage stamps of different designs, colours, or values printed side by side, sometimes with advertisements or post office notices. Se-tenant stamps have been printed in sheets, panes, coils, booklet panes, and souvenir sheets.

Sevilla/ "VIVA ESPANA"/ Julio-1936 (3-line ovpt.) appears on stamps of Spain for use in the city of Seville, 1936.

sewing-machine perforations a type of roulette made by a sewing machine that is not threaded.

Seychelles a British Crown Colony of about 156 square miles formed of islands off the east coast of Africa in the Indian Ocean. Capital: Victoria. Issued stamps in 1890.

S. F. (ovpt.) Soldater Frimaerke. Appears on military stamps of Denmark, 1914-18. Privates and corporals serving on compulsory army duty were permitted one letter and postcard postage-free each week. In 1917 they received the overprinted stamps. In March 1919, the privilege ended with demobilization.

S. G. (ovpt.) Sudan Government; appears on official stamps of Sudan.

S.G. Stanley Gibbons postage stamp catalogues.

SGLS singles, as distinguished from pairs, strips, blocks, sheets, or panes of stamps.

SH. in an auction catalogue, means "souvenir sheet".

S H (insc.) appears on stamps of Schleswig-Holstein.

shades Any colour value made darker than the true colour is a shade of that colour. Tones lighter than the normal, true colours are tints. (Courtesy of John Sloan Gordon, A.R.C.A., artist)

shahi a copper coin of Persia (Iran) and Afghanistan. 4 shahi equal 1 abasi (abbasi). 1 shahi equals 2 puls or 50 dinars. The first coins of this name were of silver and were also used in the Deccan and other parts of India.

Shanghai a commercial city and treaty port in east China on the Hwang Pu River, thirteen miles from its mouth in the Yangtze delta. Stamps were first issued in 1865, and were discontinued in 1898.

SHANGHAI (sur.) appears on U.S. stamps for use by U.S. offices in China, 1919-22.

Shan States The Federated Shan States comprised the Northern and Southern Shan States, in east Burma. The original states flourished in the twelfth to sixteenth centuries, and became part of the old Burmese kingdom; overcome by the British in 1887; federated in 1922. Japan overran the entire region in 1942 and issued stamps 1942-3.

See Burma listings in stamp catalogues.

SHARJAH & DEPENDENCIES (insc.) appears on stamps of Sharjah, a Persian Gulf sheikdom under British protection. Chief town: Sharjah. Issued stamps in 1963.

S.H.C.A. (airline) Société Hellenique de Communications Aériennes, Hellenic Air Communications Co. Ltd. Point of origin: Greece.

SHCO (insc.) appears in a shield with a colourless cross on postal-tax stamps of 1925 for Mozambique (Portuguese East Africa) in the southeastern region of Africa.

sheep's eyes (nick.) the third issue of stamps of Brazil issued in 1850, with designs much the same as those of the 1843 and 1844

stamps, but smaller. Collectors called them "sheep's eyes"; the middle size were "goat's eyes" and the large stamps were nicknamed "bull's eyes".

sheet a complete unit of postage stamps as they were printed. Some of the sheets are made with hundreds of stamps arranged in smaller units called panes, booklet panes, miniature sheets, or souvenir sheets.

sheet fed refers to a printing press on which the paper is fed in single sheets, not from a roll.

Sheet F.O.G. in auction catalogues, indicates a complete sheet of stamps, of fine quality with original gum.

sheet numbers numbers struck on margins of stamps in consecutive order; should not be confused with plate numbers, on marginal paper of sheets or panes.

sheet watermark a large watermark covering most of the area of a sheet of stamps. As a result only a small portion, or else no part of the watermark appears in a single stamp. Examples: the Stamp Office watermark in 1854 of India and the Alex. Pirie & Sons script diagonal watermark 1868 on Canada 15-cent stamps (most stamps in the Pirie sheets do not have any part of the watermark).

Sheriﬁan Posts (also Cherifien or Cherifian Posts) The Sultan of Morocco gradually introduced a postal service among the chief towns of Morocco in 1892-3. Runners carried mail with prepayment noted by handstamps of the various towns. Following the formation of the Administration of Posts, Telegraphs, and Telephones (P.T. & T.) with French help in 1911 authorities issued local stamps in 1912. Morocco marked the fiftieth anniversary of the Sherifian Posts in 1962 by issuing three stamps with postal history subjects. The set also commemorated the First National Philatelic Exhibition Stamp Day on Dec. 15, 1962, and also the seventieth anniversary of the original postal service in 1892. See *Encyclopaedia of British Empire Postage Stamps*, Vol. II, by Robson Lowe, for details.

shift See SHIFTED TRANSFER.

shifted transfer duplicated lines in a steel-engraved plate made during an attempt to enter the stamp design a second time into the plate during the transfer process in plate making. The shifted transfer is made when the transfer press operator (or siderographer) puts the transfer roll under too much pressure during the second entry. This forces the impression of the first entry forward and creates a duplication when the plate is being made. It may cause increased thickness in the frames or even a doubling of lines printed on the stamps. Re-entries go through a similar process on used plates to restore them.

Shihr and Mukalla (partial insc.) appears on stamps of the Qu'aiti state in the Aden Protectorate, 1942.

shilling (1) a silver coin of the United Kingdom and British possessions. 12 pence equal 1 shilling. Struck about 1504 by King Henry VII, it was the first English coin to have a realistic portrait of the monarch. (2) a silver coin of British East Africa, Zanzibar, Eritrea, and other countries. 100 cents equal 1 shilling.

ship cancellation a special marking used to cancel stamps on mail posted at sea. Can-

cels read "posted at sea" with the ship name, "ship letter", or other similar marks, but not "paquebot", which is applied to mail at port post offices.

ship letter a letter bearing a postmark indicating in some way that the mail was transported at least part of the journey by ship.

ship (her.) Lyphads, galleys, and other ancient ships are fairly common as charges and as crests.

ship postage the charges made for transporting mail by ships of any kind.

ships on stamps a popular topical subject. Books and scores of articles have been written on this subject. Refer to the American Topical Association, Milwaukee, Wisconsin. (Dealers can supply the current address.)

short set low values in a series of stamps.

Showa stamps of Japan stamps of Japan issued since 1928. Showa designates the reign of Emperor Hirohito, and means "The period of bright tranquillity". (Credit: Harold Mayeda)

Shquiperise (insc.) appears on stamps of Albania.

Shqyptare (insc.) appears on stamps of Albania.

S.H.S. (ovpt.) appears on stamps of Bosnia and Herzegovina for use in 1918-19; also appears on stamps of Hungary for use in Croatia-Slavonia, 1918.

Siam See THAILAND.

Siberia part of northern Asia between the Ural Mountains and the Pacific Ocean, comprising the greater part of the U.S.S.R. Surcharged Russian stamps were issued in 1919 by an anti-Bolshevist government; the stamps of Far Eastern Republic and overprinted Russian stamps were issued in 1921-22 under a monarchist government in Priamur province.

Sibérie Fr.) Siberia.

Sicilia (insc.) appears on stamps of Two Sicilies.

Sicily See TWO SICILIES.

sideline collections any postage stamp or affiliated items formed into a collection of secondary interest to a collector. The quality and extent of a sideline collection depends on the degree of interest the owner has in the sideline.

siderograph an engraving produced by siderography.

siderographist or **siderographer** a man who operates a transfer press in a steel-engraving printing plant; he transfers the designs from steel dies to steel or copper plates. This process is entirely mechanical and does not involve hand engraving or retouching in the metal plates, which are separate hand operations.

siderography the process of transferring designs from steel dies to steel or copper printing plates. The transfer-press operator, known as a siderographer, uses the special machine called a transfer press to produce maximum-security printing plates for printing postage stamps, bonds, paper money or stock certificates. This kind of steel engraving is the most difficult type of printing to forge.

sideways watermarks those located sideways in relation to the stamp designs.

sidewise coils coil postage stamps, or roll stamps, with perforations down each side of every stamp (vertical perforations). The sidewise roll or coil stamps are imperforate top and bottom.

sieben (Ger.) seven.

Siege of Paris mail letters sent out from Paris during the Franco-Prussian war, 1870-1, by three transportation methods: balloon post, Moulin balls, and pigeon post. Philatelists do not agree on the exact number of balloon flights out of Paris from Sept. 23, 1870 to Jan. 28, 1871, but about 2,500,000 pieces of recorded mail left Paris during the siege.

Siegel (Ger.) seal.

Siegelabstempelung (Ger.) seal cancel.

Sierra Leone an independent state of about 27,925 square miles in the British Commonwealth since 1961; located between Guinea and Liberia on the west coast of Africa. Formerly a British colony and Protectorate. Capital: Freetown. Issued stamps in 1859.

Sievier's essays elaborate engine-turned steel-engraved designs in proposed stamps of Great Britain. R. W. Sievier also submitted embossed designs to the 1840 Treasury competition. These essays are sought by advanced philatelists specializing in Great Britain.

SIFILLUM NOV CAMB AUST (Lat. insc.) appears in a circular frame around the Seal of New South Wales, on the 1850-1 stamps of New South Wales, known as the Sydney Views because the seal depicts an early scene of Sydney, capital of the colony.

SIGILL CONSIL SANITATIS a disinfected mark, seal of the council of health, impressed on disinfected mail of central Europe. (Courtesy of Herbert Dube)

SIGILLUM SANITATIS a disinfected mark with or without a design; a seal of health impressed on disinfected mail in central Europe. (Courtesy of Herbert Dube)

signe (Fr.) sign.

signe de garantie (Fr.) mark of guarantee.

signed Sefi in auction catalogues, indicates that a stamp dealer named Sefi has guaranteed the philatelic item to be genuine.

signed Senf in auction catalogues, indicates that an item has been guaranteed by a stamp dealer named Senf.

signes secrets (Fr.) secret marks.

Silber (Ger.) silver.

silbergroschen a coin of Bremen and Prussia and other parts of Germany. 12 pfennig or 22 grote equal 1 silbergroschen.

Silesia See EASTERN SILESIA; UPPER SILESIA.

Silésie (Fr.) Silesia.

silk paper Stamp collectors consider there to be two types: (1) silk-thread paper, and (2) paper with short pieces of silk in the paper substance. The 1875-8 U.S. revenue stamps are some examples of the second type. When the threads are too small to see individually, the substance is called granite paper. See SILK-THREAD PAPER.

silk-thread paper a safety paper with threads of silk so arranged that one or more runs through the adhesive stamp or postal stationery stamp. This is used to help stop forgery. It is called Dickinson paper after the inventor.

silurian paper See GRANITE PAPER.

silver jubilees (nick.) British and Commonwealth postage stamps issued in 1935 to commemorate the twenty-fifth anniversary of the reign of King George V and his wife, Queen Mary.

silver overprints British military occupation stamps of Palestine were overprinted in silver and black in 1920.

Silver Weddings (nick.) the British Colonial 1948 series of postage stamps marking the twenty-fifth wedding anniversary of King George VI and his wife, Queen Elizabeth.

Simi or **Syme** an Italian island of about 25 square miles in the Dodecanese group, northwest of Rhodes. Italian stamps, overprinted, were used in Simi, 1912-32.

simplified catalogue a postage stamp catalogue omitting details or varieties.

simulated perforations designs, borders, or frames printed to resemble perforations. Example: the 1894-1902 Somali Coast stamps.

Sinaloa a state in western Mexico; issued provisional government stamps in 1923 during the revolution of 1923-4. These stamps are listed with those of Mexico in catalogues.

sin dentar (Sp.) imperforate.

Singapore a British Commonwealth island state of about 217 square miles off the Malay Peninsula south of Johore. Capital: Singapore. Issued stamps in 1948.

single one stamp, as opposed to a pair, block, pane, or sheet of stamps.

single, double, and treble letters By an English act of Queen Anne, 1710, three major classifications of letters were described. Postage on letters depended on the distance they passed from one place to another, the number of sheets in a letter, and the weight: (1) Single letters had one piece of paper weighing less than one ounce; any enclosure in a single letter caused it to become a double letter. (2) Double letters had two pieces of paper weighing less than one ounce. (3) Treble letters had three pieces of paper weighing less than one ounce.

single-line perforation the type made one line at a time by a perforating machine, as opposed to the comb type that strikes more than one row at a single stroke of the perforating pins.

single-line watermarks those in one line, as opposed to others in designs or text on two or more lines to complete the watermark. The Alexander Pirie & Sons watermark, Canada 1876, is an example.

singolo (It.) single.

sinister (her.) the left hand of the wearer of a shield; the spectator's right.

sinistro (It.) left.

Sinkiang formerly an outer dependency in western China, granted autonomy in 1946. Issued stamps 1915-45. See catalogues for details.

Sinking Fund Issues See CAISSE D'AMORTISSEMENT.

Sinn Fein labels propaganda stickers made in about 1907 by Irish rebels. Some are said to have been used for postage.

S.I.P. Society of Israel Philatelists.

Sir Codrington (insc.) appears under a portrait in a circular frame on the 5-drachma stamp of Greece, 1927. Later issues bore the corrected inscription, "Sir Edward Codrington". Sir Edward (1770-1851) was a British naval officer, and later vice-admiral (1821), who served as commander of the combined British, French, and Russian fleet that destroyed the Turkish and Egyptian fleet in 1827 at Navarino, a seaport in Greece.

Sirmoor (insc.) appears on stamps used in Sirmoor in the Punjab district of India.

S.I.S.A. (airline) Societa Italiana Serviz Aerei. Point of origin: Italy.

Sizilien (Ger.) Sicily.

skatiku a coin of Lithuania. 100 skatiku equal 1 auksinas.

skilling a silver coin of Denmark, Iceland, Sweden, and Norway. In Norway 120 skilling equal 1 specie daler. In Denmark 96 skilling equal 1 rigsbank daler. In Sweden 48 skilling banco equal 1 rixdaler banco (until 1858). In Iceland 96 skilling equal 1 rigsdaler. There was also a copper skilling of varying value.

skinned refers to a damaged stamp, with part of the paper front or back missing causing a thin area. As a rule, these are useless stamps.

Slav alphabet the alphabet universally called Cyrillic; named after the Slav apostles, Saint Cyril and Saint Methodius. The Russians, Serbians, and Bulgarians use Cyrillic words with certain differences among some letters. The Croats, Czechs, Slovaks, Slovenes, and Poles employ Cyrillic letters with a number of forms of the Latin alphabet. In the Cyrillic postage stamp words inscribed, surcharged, or overprinted, the letters are not sufficiently like the Latin alphabet to permit English-speaking people to read them. See the appendix.

sl cr in auction catalogues, means "slight crease".

Sld (insc.) soldi; coin name appearing on stamps of Austrian Offices for use in the Turkish Empire, 1867; also appears on stamps of Lombardy Venetia.

SL. DEF. slightly defective.

sleepers (U.S. nick.) a scarce stamp, often worth considerably more than catalogues indicate; sometimes called "pup" in England.

Slesvig (insc.) appears on stamps of Schleswig.

slogan cancellation the part of a duplex cancellation giving a government message. For example, post office departments employ instructions in duplex cancellations: "Protect your parcels / address distinctly / wrap carefully / insure." These should not be confused with advertising cancellations sponsored by the public.

Slovakia a province of about 18,921 square miles in east central Czechoslovakia between Poland and Hungary. Capital: Bratislava. Czechoslovakia surcharged stamps were first issued in 1939.

Slovenia a federated republic, part of the Federal People's Republic of Jugoslavia. Capital: Ljubljana. Stamps were issued for 1919-20 for Slovenia.

Slovensko (Czech. insc.) appears on stamps of Slovakia, 1939-44, a former province of Czechoslovakia.

Slovenský štát (ovpt.) appears on stamps of Czechoslovakia for use in Slovakia, 1939.

Slowakei (Ger.) Slovakia.

S.L.S. (airline) Slovenska Letecka Spoloeneost, Slovakia. Ceased operations in 1942. Following the Second World War this line merged with Ceskoslovenske Aerolinie of Prague, Czechoslovakia.

slurring blurring caused by slipping of a sheet or by a loose form during printing.

small caps capital letters smaller than regular capitals, often found in book founts and used for such things as running titles, sideheadings, and sub-heads.

small cents issues (nick.) the second issue of stamps of the Dominion of Canada, 1870 and in the following years to 1897. Also called the small Queens. The stamps were all smaller than the first issue, 1868, called the large cents or large Queens.

small thins in auction catalogues, indicates that small thin spots have been made in the stamps, often caused by hinges that do not peel.

smaragd (Ger.) emerald.

S. Marino (insc.) appears on stamps of San Marino.

Smirne (sur.) appears with values in para or piastre on stamps of Italy, for use by the Italian offices in Smyrna, part of the Turkish Empire, 1909-11.

Smith & Stephens City Delivery in St. Louis, Missouri, issued U.S. local stamps, but the date of issue is not definite.

S.M.O.M. Sovereign Military Order (of the Knights) of Malta. Italy refused recognition of any labels (postage stamps) the group planned. (Courtesy of *American Philatelist,* December 1966)

Smyrna or **Izmir** a coastal vilayet in western Turkey of about 4,826 square miles. Surcharged stamps of Italy were issued from Italian Offices in Turkey, 1909-22; also from Russian offices stamps were overprinted "SMYRNE" in 1909-10.

Smyrne (ovpt.) appears on stamps of Russia for use by the Russian offices in Smyrna, part of the Turkish Empire, in 1909-10.

soaking stamps the procedure of removing stamps from paper by putting them in water. Care should be taken to avoid soaking postage stamps printed in water-colour or fugitive inks.

sobre (Sp.) over, on; envelope cover.

sobrecarga (Port. and Sp.) overprint, surcharge.

sobrecarga de distrito (Sp.) district overprint.

sobrecarga local (Port.) local surcharge.

SOBREPORTO (Sp. insc.) appears on stamps of Colombia, 1866, used to pay the extra charges on mail to foreign countries

that had no postal agreements with Colombia.

SOBRE CUOTA PARA BULTOS POSTALES (Sp. insc.) appears on parcel post stamps of Mexico, 1950-4, indicating an extra fee on postal parcels. (Courtesy of Guillermo Tenunuri, Mexican tourism department)

sobretasa (Sp.) surtax.

SOBRETASA (Sp. ovpt.) appears on regular-issue stamps of Colombia in 1947 and 1950 for use as postal tax stamps. Although "sobretasa" is not used in Spain, "sobre" is a Spanish word meaning "on top of" or "over". Therefore, "sobretasa" indicates a charge on top of, or over, the normal postage rates being charged. (Courtesy of the Spanish Consulate, Toronto, Ontario)

SOBRETASA AEREA (insc.) appears on 1929 Colombia airmail stamps for use on foreign letters to pay the delivery charges from coastal places to the interior of Colombia. The stamps were often cancelled in the countries where mail originated.

soccer See FOOTBALL.

SOCIEDADE DE GEOGRAPHIA DE LISBOA (insc.) appears on the 1903-34 franchise stamps of Portugal. The stamps were provided to frank mail of the Geographical Society of Lisbon.

SOCIEDADE HUMANITARIA CRUZ DO ORIENTE (insc.) appears on Mozambique postal tax stamps, 1926-7. Mozambique is also known as Portuguese East Africa.

Société des Nations (Fr.) League of Nations.

Société des Nations (ovpt.) appears on various issues of Switzerland 1922-38, for use by the League of Nations.

Society for the Suppression of Speculative Stamps a group founded in May 1895 in England. Members tried to persuade governments to stop issuing speculative postal issues. They sent notices about speculative stamps to stamp papers, stamp collectors, and governments. They urged collectors to refrain from buying them and dealers to

Socked on the nose cancel

avoid such material. A similar group was formed in the United States, but neither society had much success.

socked on the nose slang for a cancel entirely within the area of a stamp. (Illustration: p. 225)

soi-disant provisionals Sir Edward Bacon described certain unlisted and unknown early Canadian provisional stamps by this term. "Soi-disant" is a French word meaning "self-styled" or "would-be". Refer to "The Postage Stamps of the British North American Colonies", compiled and published by the Philatelic Society, London, 1889.

soixante (Fr.) sixty.

soixante-dix (Fr.) seventy.

Sokol a Czechoslovakian gymnastic organization begun in 1872. It served as a model for other similar groups in Slavic countries. In 1938 Czechoslovakia commemorated the tenth Sokol summer games with three stamps portraying Jindrich Fügner, co-founder of the Sokol movement.

SOKOLSKI SLET LJUBLJANA (insc.) appears on two Jugoslavia semi-postal stamps of 1933 issued to mark the sixtieth anniversary meeting of the National Sokols (sports associations) at Ljubljana, in northwest Jugoslavia.

sol a silver coin of Peru, adopted in 1855. 100 centavos equal 10 dineros equal 1 sol. There are now multiples of this coin.

SOLDI (insc.) appears on oval stamps of Lombardy-Venetia (Austrian Italy) in 1861, embossed with a man's head or a heraldic coat of arms and without a country name.

soldiers' stamps Many countries authorized soldiers' and other service men's special stamps. Some were merely handstruck marks; others were special airgraphs and envelopes clearly marked for personal letters from men of the army, air force, and navy.

soldo a small copper or billon (alloy) coin of Italy, Lombardy-Venetia, and other countries. 20 soldi equal 1 lira. 100 soldi equal 1 florin. At one time the soldo was of gold, then of silver, now copper. The names "sol", "sou", and "soldo" derive from the Roman "solidus", the standard gold coin of early Europe.

SOLIDARITE 1947 (sur.) appears with new value on regular-issue 1926-46 stamps of Tunisia for use as semi-postal stamps.

Solomon Islands See BRITISH SOLOMON ISLANDS.

Somalia a republic in eastern Africa on the Gulf of Aden and the Indian Ocean; became an independent republic on July 1, 1960, formed by the union of Italian Somaliland and the former British Somaliland Protectorate. Proclamation of Independence stamps were issued on July 1, 1960. The area of Italian Somaliland was quoted as about 262,000 square miles, and the area of the (British) Somaliland Protectorate was said to be 68,000 square miles. The capital of the new state is Mogadishu (Mogadisico).

Somalia (ovpt.) appears on stamps of Italy for use in Somalia, a former Italian colony in eastern Africa on the Indian Ocean and Gulf of Aden, 1926-31.

Somalia Italiana (sur., ovpt., and insc.) appears as a surcharge with new values on stamps of Italy for use in Somalia (Italian Somaliland) in 1922-6; overprinted on Italian stamps for use in Somalia in 1926-30; inscribed on stamps of Somalia in 1934.

Somali Coast a French overseas territory of about 9,000 square miles on the Gulf of Aden; now known as the French Territory of the Afars and Issas. Capital: Djibouti (Jibuti). Stamps of Obock, overprinted or surcharged, were used 1894-1902. Then as a French overseas territory, Somali Coast issued stamps inscribed "COTE FRANCAIS DES SOMALIS".

Somalie Britannique (Fr.) British Somaliland.

Somaliland Protectorate a former British Protectorate in eastern Africa bordering on the Gulf of Aden at the north. Capital: Hargeisa. The first stamps of the Protectorate were contemporary stamps of India (1882-1900) overprinted "BRITISH/SOMALILAND" for use in 1903 and denominations in Indian currency of 16 annas to 1 rupee. The currency was finally changed on April 2, 1951, to the East African shilling of 100 cents at par with British sterling. Somaliland Protectorate became part of Independent Somalia in 1960.

Somerset House headquarters of the British Inland Revenue located on the Strand in London. Some British postage stamps were printed there, including the 1847-54 embossed issue.

Sonderausgabe (Ger.) special issue.

Sondermarke (Ger.) special stamp, such as a commemorative or semi-postal stamp.

Sonderpostmarke (Ger.) special postage stamp.

Sonderstempel (Ger.) special cancel.

SO/1920 (ovpt.) Silésie Orientale; appears on stamps of Czechoslovakia and Poland of 1918-20 for use in Eastern Silesia during the plebiscite that finally divided the former Austrian crown land between Poland and Czechoslovakia.

SONORA (insc.) appears on some Civil War issues of Mexico, 1913.

soprastampa (It.) surcharge, overprint.

SORUTH a feudatory state in west India of about 3,337 square miles. Capital: Junagarh. Issued stamps with no English inscriptions in 1864; then from 1877-1914 stamps were inscribed "SORUTH".

sottile (It.) thin.

SOUDAN (ovpt.) appears with Arabic text on 1884-93 stamps of Egypt for use in the Sudan, 1897. Also appears on Egyptian postage-due stamps of 1889 for use as postage-due stamps in the Sudan, 1897.

Soudan égyptien (Fr.) Sudan.

Soudan français (Fr.) French Soudan.

Soudan Français (insc.) appears on stamps of the French Sudan.

SOURASHTRA (insc.) appears on stamps of Soruth, 1923-29.

sous enveloppe (Fr.) in an envelope.

sous numero (Fr.) a sub number in stamp catalogues.

South Africa since 1961, a republic of about 472,494 square miles in southern Africa. Capitals: Pretoria as the Administrative centre and Cape Town for the Legislature. Issued stamps inscribed in English and Afrikaans, 1910-25; then inscriptions occurred in English and Afrikaans on every other stamp in the panes or sheets since 1925.

South Arabia, Federation of a British dependency in South Arabia, including Aden. Capital: Al Ittihad. First stamps issued in 1963.

South Australia a former British Crown Colony, now a state in the Commonwealth of Australia; about 380,070 square miles. Capital: Adelaide. South Australia issued stamps in 1855.

South Bulgaria formerly Eastern Rumelia; the name was changed after the province revolted against the Turks in 1885. See EASTERN RUMELIA.

Southern Cameroons part of the Federal Republic of Cameroun since 1961; a British Trust Territory 1960-1; previously part of the German protectorate of Cameroons. Issued 1953 stamps of Nigeria overprinted "CAMEROONS, U.K.T.T." in 1960-1.

Southern Nigeria part of the colony and protectorate of Nigeria, on the Gulf of Guinea in West Africa; formerly a British Crown Colony and Protectorate. Area about 90,896 square miles. Capital: Lagos. Stamps were issued in 1901. Stamps of Ni-

geria were used from 1914.

Southern Rhodesia A British territory of about 150,344 square miles south of the Zambesi River in southwest Africa. Southern Rhodesia was annexed to the Crown by an Order in Council, and in 1923 obtained a new constitution that provided for a governor to represent the king in Southern Rhodesia, and for a single House of Parliament of thirty members. This was a unique position in the British Commonwealth. Stamps inscribed "Southern Rhodesia" were issued in 1924, and in 1954 Southern Rhodesia became part of the Central African Federation, consisting also of Northern Rhodesia and the Nyasaland Protectorate. Stamp issues were inscribed "Rhodesia & Nyasaland" until Dec. 31, 1963, when the Federation was dissolved. Stamps inscribed "Southern Rhodesia" were used again when the state became an internally self-governing colony. See RHODESIA; NORTHERN RHODESIA; RHODESIA AND NYASALAND.

SOUTHERN/RHODESIA (2-line ovpt.) appears on British postage-due stamps of 1938-51 for use as postage-due stamps of Southern Rhodesia, 1951.

South Georgia a British territorial island of about 1450 square miles, located 1,100 miles east of Tierra del Fuego in the south Atlantic. Chief town: Grytviken Harbor. Issued stamps in 1944 overprinted on Falkland Islands stamps: "SOUTH GEORGIA/ DEPENDENCY OF". Issued stamps inscribed "South Georgia" in 1963.

South Lithuania a region in Lithuania including the district of Grodno, under German occupation during the First World War.

South Moluccas a part of Indonesia; privately issued stamps that were of no postal use.

South Orkneys or **South Orkney Islands** a group of islands in the southern Atlantic Ocean. First stamps, issued Feb. 21, 1944, were Falkland Island overprints; they were replaced in 1963 by stamps of British Antarctic Territory.

SOUTH ORKNEYS/DEPENDENCY OF (ovpt.) appears in red on stamps of Falkland Islands for use in the South Orkneys, 1944.

SOUTH PACIFIC / COMMISSION / FEB. 1947-1972 (3-line ovpt.) appears on Cook Islands $1 stamps issued Feb. 17, 1972. The South Pacific Commission is a regional body established by an agreement signed at Canberra, Australia, on Feb. 6, 1947, to

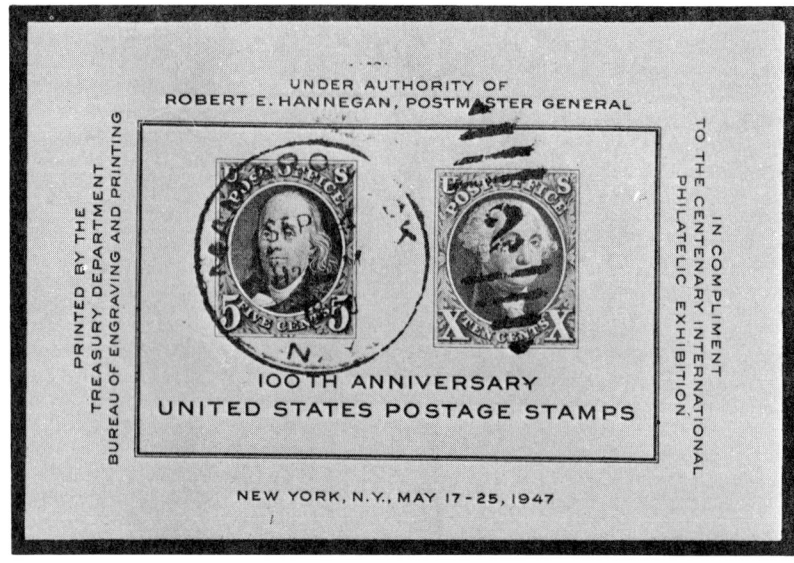

Souvenir sheet

advise participating governments on health, economic, and social matters of people in the Pacific Island Territories. Headquarters are in Noumea, New Caledonia.

South Russia the southern part of Russia on the Caspian and Black Seas. Russian stamps, surcharged, were used 1918-20 by the provisional government.

South Shetlands a group of islands north of Palmer Peninsula, formerly the Falkland Island Dependencies. Issued overprinted Falkland Island stamps in 1944.

SOUTH SHETLANDS/DEPENDENCY OF (ovpt.) appears in red on stamps of Falkland Islands in 1944 for use in the South Shetlands. These are listed with stamps of Falkland Islands in catalogues.

South Viet Nam a republic of about 66,000 square miles in South-East Asia; the southern portion of the former kingdom of Viet Nam. Capital: Saigon. First stamps were issued in 1955.

South-West Africa a territory of about 318,-099 square miles under administration of the Republic of South Africa on mandate of the League of Nations; a German colony before the First World War, first stamps were issued in 1923.

South West Africa (ovpt.) appears on stamps of South Africa, 1923-6, alternating with "Zuid-West Afrika", or "Suidwes-Afrika".

Southern Philatelic Association original name of the Society of Philatelic Ameri-

cans (SPA).

souvenir sheet a sheet containing one or more stamps; a commemorative inscription, and also items with no postal validity; for example, the souvenir sheets of labels issued by the organizers of many stamp exhibitions.

SOUV. SH. souvenir sheet.

sovrapprezzo (It.) surtax.

sower types (nick.) French postage stamps of 1903 and subsequent years featuring a woman sowing seeds in a field.

Sowjetische Besatzungs Zone (ovpt.) appears on stamps of Germany in 1948 for use in Germany under Russian occupation.

Sowjetische Zone (Ger.) Russian Zone.

sp in auction catalogues means "short perforation(s)".

SP in auction catalogues means "superb", the best possible condition for the stamp in question.

S.P.A. Society of Philatelic Americans.

S.P. Service Publique, public service; appears on 1881-93 stamps of Luxembourg for official use.

space filler a low-priced stamp to fill a space in a printed album. Mainly before 1900, many forgeries were made as space fillers.

Spain a state of about 193,144 square miles in southwest Europe, occupying the greater part of the Iberian Peninsula; formerly a kingdom. Capital: Madrid. First stamps were issued in 1850.

spandrel the three-sided area of a stamp design between the outer border or frame and the oval, curved, or circular frame enclosing the main part of the design, which may be a portrait, scene, or heraldic emblem.

Spanien (Ger.) Spain.

Spanisch-Guinea (Ger.) Spanish Guinea.

Spanisch-Marokko (Ger.) Spanish Morocco.

Spanish Guinea a Spanish colony on the Gulf of Aden; area variously quoted as about 10,040 square miles and 10,852 square miles. Stamps were first issued in 1902.

Spanish Morocco a republic of about 17,398 square miles on the northwest coast of Africa; formerly a Spanish protectorate. Capital: Tetuan. From 1903 Spanish Morocco used stamps of Spain overprinted, surcharged, or inscribed "MARRUECOS, PROTECTORADO ESPANOL"; then stamps of the republic were issued since 1956.

Spanish Sahara a Spanish colony in northwest Africa of about 105,409 square miles. Chief towns: Villa Cisneros, Rio de Oro and Smara, Saquiet el Hamra. First issued stamps in 1924.

Spanish West Africa a Spanish administration of about 117,000 square miles on the coast of northwest Africa. Capital: Sidi Ifni. Stamps were issued 1948-51.

Spargummi (Ger.) economy gum.

Sparta, Ga. This town in Georgia issued postmasters' provisional envelopes in 1861 as part of the Confederate States of America.

Spartanburg, S.C. This town in South Carolina issued postmasters' provisional stamps in 1861 as part of the Confederate States of America.

Spaulding's Penny Post in Buffalo, New York, issued U.S. local stamps in 1848.

spécial (Fr.) special.

special delivery stamps issues purposely made to prepay the special delivery services on mail.

special handling stamps stamps issued to prepay the fast delivery service on parcels, equivalent to first class mail. They do not pay postal charges. An example is the U.S. issue, 1925-9, with values from 10 to 25 cents.

special issue issues that draw attention to general facts and events, but do not commemorate specific dates, events, or anniversaries. They are issued one time and usually in limited quantities.

specialist a philatelist who concentrates his collecting activities to one phase of the hobby. Specialists often write articles about their collections for stamp publications.

specializing the collecting of some individual class or type of postage stamps or postal history items, excluding all other branches of the hobby.

specie daler a coin of Norway. 120 skilling equal 1 specie daler.

specimen an individual postage stamp or

Specimen stamp (Cyprus)

cover that has been marked "specimen".

SPECIMEN a word punched in postage stamps that were sent to the Universal Postal Union as examples of a country's stamps.

SPECIMEN (ovpt.) appears on stamps sent to the Universal Postal Union as examples of a country's stamps; also appears on postage stamps of the United States, 1851 and various other years; refer to Scott's U.S. Specialized catalogue for details.

spécimen (Fr.) specimen.

speculation Some people prefer to invest in stamps rather than buy stocks, bonds or real estate. Beginners are warned not to speculate in stamps until they have gained experience.

speculative issues postage stamps produced and sold in quantities above the normal postal requirements of the country that issued them. The production of large quantities of stamps and different issues at great frequency suggests that the postal authority responsible intends that stamp collectors will subscribe to such issues. Elaborate distribution arrangements are usually made to ensure penetration in all markets and the publicity afforded to speculative issues is usually first-rate.

Spence & Brown Express Post in Philadelphia, Pennsylvania, issued U.S. local stamps in 1848.

Sperati, Giovanni de (or Jean de Sperati) a

famous stamp forger. While a young man, he had learned engraving, lithography, printing techniques, and useful aspects of chemistry. He began to reproduce some San Marino stamps for his brother, a stamp dealer, and soon was deceiving stamp experts. On April 7, 1942, French customs officials prosecuted Sperati for forgery, but the case dragged on for ten years. Sperati was finally sentenced to two years in jail but was not required to serve the sentence because of his poor health and old age. In 1953, shortly before his death, he turned over all his stocks, forging materials, and formulae to the British Philatelic Association. Consult *The Work of Jean de Sperati.*

Sperati (nick.) a forgery or faked philatelic item made by Jean de Sperati.

spesso (It.) thick, usually in reference to papers.

Spezialkatalog (Ger.) specialized catalogue.

Spezial-Sammler (Ger.) collector of specialties.

sphinx a design in an oval frame appearing on 1867 stamps of Egypt, with no country name.

Spifs (Brit. nick.) stamps with perforated initials, designs, or numerals, or these combined; called "perfins" in Canada and the United States.

SPITFIRE (sur.) appears with new values on 1940 semi-postal stamps of Cameroun. Surtax funds were for the purchase of Spitfire planes for the Free French Army.

Spittal stamp an adhesive stamp from Spittal, near Salzberg, Austria. Some people claim that it preceded the 1-penny blacks of 1840. British experts and authorities say that the stamp was not a genuine postage stamp.

Spitze (Ger.) point, tip.

split a stamp cut into any portion other than halves, to pay a postal charge during a shortage of the correct denominations.

SPM (sur.) St. Pierre and Miquelon; appears on stamps of the French colonies for use in St. Pierre and Miquelon, 1885, 1891.

spoon a duplex type of cancellation where the two parts adjoin, and the left is shaped like the bowl of a spoon.

spoorwegen (Flemish insc.) appears with the French inscription "Chemins de Fer" on parcel post and railway stamps of Belgium since 1879. Some recent issues are inscribed "Colis Postaux – Postcolli".

sports on stamps Virtually every country since 1925, some earlier, has issued stamps with sporting designs. Books have been published on the subject as a popular top-ical collection.

spot a specific round, untagged area left by a cut-out for one of four small screws used to fasten the metal saddle on which Type I mats are mounted; most frequently found on the tagged 5-cent Washington 1966 coil. (Courtesy of Alfred G. Boerger)

spray watermark a watermark resembling a spray of flowers. An example is the Spray of Rose, of Great Britain 1867 and later issues. This is not to be confused with lotus or other flower designs or the sunbursts of Argentina.

springbok a South African gazelle noted for its ability to leap. A design of its head is used as a watermark in stamps of South Africa 1913 and later, and also as stamp designs since 1926.

Springfalz (Ger.) peelable hinge.

spurious false, illegitimate, counterfeit. The word is not used by philatelists because it is not sufficiently accurate.

squared circle a type of postmark having bars within a square area with a circular centre. The post office name, the date, and the time appear in most squared circle postmarks. These postmarks are so popular that numerous articles and at least two books have been written about them.

Squier & Co.'s City Letter Dispatch (later Jordan & Co.) in St. Louis, Missouri, issued U.S. local stamps in 1859-60.

Squipni (insc.) appears on stamps of Albania.

Squiptare (insc.) appears on stamps of Albania.

Sri Lanka, Republic of On May 22, 1972, Ceylon became a republic within the British Commonwealth, and changed its name to Sri Lanka. Ceylon ended its 157-year tie with the British crown in a glittering ceremony at Colombo. See stamp catalogues for details about the postage stamps.

Srodkowa Litwa (part of insc. and ovpt.) appears on 1920 stamps of Central Lithuania.

SSM (insc.) Socialistickeho Svazu Mladeze; appears on the Nov. 9, 1970, Czechoslovakia issue to commemorate the first congress of the Socialist Youth Union in Czechoslovakia.

S.S.T. supersonic transport, a type of fast aircraft.

st in auction catalogues, means "stain(s)".

(See also SAINT.)

St. Andrew's Cross two diagonal lines used in designs and fillers in stamp spaces left otherwise vacant, for example in stamps of

Austria and Germany. Also used as cancellations by Great Britain, India, and other countries during the Second World War.

St. Christopher an island of about 68 square miles southwest of Puerto Rico in the West Indies; a Presidency of the former Leeward Island Colony. Capital: Basseterre. Issued stamps in 1870, superseded by stamps of the Leeward Islands in 1890.

St. CHRISTOPHER - NEVIS - ANGUILLA (insc.) appears on stamps of St. Christopher-Nevis-Anguilla issued in 1952 to replace those inscribed "ST. KITTS-NEVIS".

St. Edward's crown watermark variety watermark errors in some British colonial stamps of 1950-2, resulting from wrong design bits placed on the dandy roll of the papermaking machine by workmen when they repaired the dandy roll. Gibbons Part One catalogue gives details.

St. Helena a British Crown Colony of about 47 square miles, 1,200 miles west of Angola, Africa, in the Atlantic Ocean. Capital: Jamestown. First stamps issued in 1856.

St. Kitts-Nevis a British Colony of about 155 square miles southeast of Puerto Rico in the West Indies; one of the presidencies of the former Leeward Islands Colony. Capital: Basseterre, St. Kitts. Issued stamps in 1903. Leeward Islands stamps were used concurrently with those of St. Kitts-Nevis until 1956.

St. Louis Bears (nick.) provisional stamps in 5-, 10-, and 20-cent values for St. Louis, Missouri, 1845-7. These were postmasters' provisionals used before the United States government issued adhesive postage stamps.

St. Louis City Delivery Company in St. Louis, Missouri, issued U.S. local stamps in 1883.

St. Louis, Missouri issued postmasters' provisional stamps in 1845-7.

St. Lucia a British colony of about 238 square miles in the West Indies; one of the Windward Islands group. Capital: Castries. Issued stamps in 1860.

Ste. Marie de Madagascar an island of about 64 square miles off the east coast of Madagascar; a French possession. Stamps were issued in 1894, superseded by those of Madagascar in 1896.

St. Pierre and Miquelon a French territory of about 93 square miles consisting of two small islands in the Atlantic Ocean south of Newfoundland. Stamps of French colonies were used, surcharged or overprinted, 1885-92. In 1892 French colonial stamps were used, inscribed "St. Pierre Et Mique-

lon". From 1909 stamps of St. Pierre and Miquelon were used.

St. Thomas and Prince Islands a Portuguese overseas territory of about 597 square miles consisting of islands off the west coast of Africa in the Gulf of Guinea. Capital: St. Thomas. Stamps have been issued since 1869 (Gibbons says 1870).

S. THOME E PRINCIPE or **S. TOME E PRINCIPE** (insc.) appears on stamps of the St. Thomas and Prince Islands, Portuguese Overseas territory of two islands in the Gulf of Guinea off the west coast of Africa.

St. Vincent a British colony of about 150 square miles in the West Indies; one of the Windward Islands. Capital: Kingstown. Issued stamps in 1861.

St. Vinzent (Ger.) St. Vincent.

staalgravure (Dutch) engraving on steel.

Stadt (Ger.) town, city.

STADT BERLIN POST (insc.) appears on stamps for use in the German provinces and the sector of Berlin under Russian occupation, 1948.

Stadtpost (Ger.) local (town) mail.

STADT-POST-BASEL (insc.) appears on stamps issued for Basel, a canton of Switzerland, 1845.

Stahlstich (Ger.) steel engraving.

stamp (1) to impress letters or designs by means of dies; (2) an instrument or hand-tool for making impressions; (3) a hand-tool for cutting blanks from paper; (4) a postage or excise stamp.

stampa (It.) printing.

stamp agency a philatelic section of a post office department where mint postage stamps and philatelic items my be purchased at face value.

Stampalia or **Astypalaia** an Italian island of about 44 square miles in the Dodecanese group in the Aegean Sea, west-southwest of Kos. Stamps of Italy were issued with overprints and surcharges under Italian occupation, 1912-32.

STAMPALIA (ovpt. and sur.) appears on stamps of Italy 1912-32 for use in Stampalia, one of the Aegean Islands that Italy occupied during the Tripoli War; ceded to Italy in 1924 by Turkey.

stamp artists and designers the men and women who create postage stamp designs. Many collectors need the information about designers and artists for write-ups in their collections. This data appears above the lists in Gibbons stamp catalogues.

stamp catalogues Hundreds of catalogues are published, some specialized. They include illustrations, current prices, and pertinent information about stamps. Scott's and Minkus catalogues lead in the United States, and Gibbons catalogues are most popular in Great Britain and the British Commonwealth.

stamp collecting the act of gathering postage stamps, mint as they came from post offices, used, or on their original letters. Many collectors save all three kinds and include the handstruck postage stamps used prior to the introduction of adhesive stamps in May 1840. Stamp collecting is the most popular hobby in the world; more people collect stamps than anything else. Stamp collecting offers the double advantages of pleasure and sound investments through the careful selection of top-quality postage stamps.

stamp dealers men and women who sell stamps to collectors. They form the hub of stamp collecting, since no great stamp collection, or prize winner in a large exhibition, was ever formed without the help of a stamp dealer.

STAMP DUTY (ovpt. and insc.) appears on postage stamps of Victoria, a former British colony now part of Australia, from 1885. These stamps are usually revenues.

stamp errors See ERRORS.

stamp exchange clubs organizations that solicit membership for the purpose of exchanging, buying, and selling stamps among themselves. They are usually commercial stamp clubs with members living in all parts of the world. Advanced philatelists do not join exchange clubs.

stamp hinge See MOUNT.

stamp mount See MOUNT.

stamp papers and magazines These contain useful information and articles of lasting interest to philatelists. Every collector should subscribe to some publication devoted to stamps and stamp collecting. Most national societies publish magazines of great value. Dealers can recommend papers.

stamp prepared but not issued Countries have prepared issues of postage and then not used them for various reasons, usually without announcements of the proposed stamps. For example, Canada prepared a series of peace stamps in about 1913, but did not issue them when war was declared in 1914.

stamp-removing box a small, airtight box made to remove stamps from pieces of paper, envelopes, or covers without damage to the stamps or the paper. It is most useful in removing stamps printed with aniline, fugitive, or water-colour inks, and stamps cancelled with fugitive inks. Such a box may be purchased for about five dollars or made free by the following directions. The necessary items are a box big enough to hold an envelope, a rack of plastic, and a small sponge or folded cloth. The box must have a tight-fitting lid to assure success. Scrap items around any home can be used – for example, any plastic container that held margarine, cheese, ice cream, or other foods. The rack must stand above the rubber sponge or cloth to prevent the stamps or envelopes (covers) from touching it. The rack can be made from a plastic fruit or vegetable basket bottom cut to fit above the sponge or moist cloth, which is put on the bottom of the box. The stamps usually can be lifted from paper in half a day. Experiments prove successful, but collectors are warned to handle the stamps with great care because they are moist and fragile after twelve to twenty-four hours in the closed box.

stamp size One particular stamp may vary in size depending on how it was printed; rotary-printed stamps have a greater dimension (height and width) than flatbed-printed stamps of the same design and denomination.

stamp sources Beginners should tell their relatives and friends to save stamps for them. Businesses often get foreign mail, and will save the stamps by request. If a tyro collector finds a large accumulation, he should consult an advanced collector for help. By joining a local club or a national society, new collectors can get help and information.

stamp tongs See TWEEZERS.

stamped envelope (1) an envelope with the stamp printed or embossed on it; (2) an envelope with an adhesive stamp already attached.

stämpel (Swed.) cancellation.

stämpelmärken (Swed.) tax paid by stamps, stamp marks.

stampless covers letters posted without adhesive postage stamps of any country, mainly prior to 1840. Modern letters sent by error without postage are not classified as stampless covers.

stamps on stamps postage stamp designs that feature other postage stamps.

standard (her.) a long flag tapering to a bifurcated end.

starched paper paper made with a starch content to help prevent the re-use of postage stamps. The cancellations could not be

*Stars: in margin of
stamp of United States*

removed without destroying the stamps. Charles F. Steel, manufacturing superintendent of the Continental Bank Note Company, filed his patent for this paper on March 15, 1875.

stark gestempelt (Ger.) heavily cancelled.

stars appear in margins of some U.S. stamps printed from flat plates. The stars distinguished plates with changes on the spacing of stamps mainly to improve the perforating process in manufacturing. Stars were also used on some rotary plates made to produce coils. See Scott's U.S. Specialized stamp catalogue for details.

statant (her.) standing, with all paws on the ground.

Staten Island Express Post in Staten Island, New York, issued U.S. local stamps in 1849.

Statesville, N.C. This town in North Carolina issued postmasters' provisional envelopes in 1861 as part of the Confederate

States of America.

STATI PARM or **STATI PARMENSI** (insc.) appears on stamps of Parma, 1852-60.

stationery authorized postcards, envelopes, airgraphs, wrappers, and other items printed with stamps on them and sold at post offices.

S.T.C. an abbreviation for "said to catalogue", meaning that a stamp lot has a value determined from a postage stamp catalogue such as Gibbons, Minkus, or Scott's. When "s.t.c." appears in auction catalogues, the auctioneer is quoting figures other than his own.

steam postage in India, a charge made on letters sent to post offices outside Bombay to connect with government packets sailing from Bombay. The charge is made on a mileage basis: for example, 14 annas on each letter from Calcutta to Bombay. Ship postage was extra. (Courtesy of Robson

Stamps on stamps

Lowe, London, England)

steel helmets or **tin hats** (nick.) Belgian stamps of 1919 portraying King Albert wearing a trench helmet.

steel-plate engraving (usually called "steel engraving") one form of intaglio printing; gravure is the other. Steel engraving is the art of hand-engraving designs on steel dies and then transferring them by means of a transfer press to steel plates to print stamps, paper money, and stock certificates. Not to be confused with line engraving, which is from copper plates only.

steel-plate engraving ink soft intaglio ink, with oil and water-resistant pigments, used for steel-plate engraving.

Steindruck (Ger.) lithography.

Stellaland an area of about 5,000 square miles in British Bechuanaland; formerly a Boer republic. Capital: Vryburg. Issued stamps in 1884.

stempel (Dutch) postmark.

STEMPEL or **STAMPEL** (insc.) appears on newspaper stamps of Austria, 1851-63, bearing the inscription "ZEITUNGS" but without a country name.

stempelmarke (Ger.) fiscal stamp, revenue stamp, or tax stamp.

stempelmarke als postmarke verwendet (Ger.) fiscal-postal.

stentryck (Swed.) lithography.

Stephan, Dr. Heinrich von a German postal reformer who made gradual reforms in the postal system of the North German Confederation after the 1863 Paris Conference. See UNIVERSAL POSTAL UNION.

stereotype a printing plate cast from a papier-mâché matrix or flong on which the type matter and designs have been impressed.

sterling British currency.

Stern (Ger.) star.

stet a proofreader's term, meaning "Do not change part marked; let it stand".

Steuer (Ger.) tax, revenue.

Steuermarke (Ger.) tax stamp.

Steuerentwertung (Ger.) fiscal cancellation.

Stich (Ger.) engraving.

Stichtiefdruck (Ger.) recess printed.

Stickney Press a rotary press used to print some postage stamps; invented by Benjamin R. Stickney (1871-1946), who was a mechanical engineer with the Bureau of Engraving and Printing in Washington, D.C.

stitch watermarks These are found in particular in the Canadian 3-penny beaver and the early U.S. and British embossed stamps of 1847-54. They are not watermarks in

the true sense of the word, and are the result of repairs sewn or stitched in the wire mesh that carries the wet substance toward the dry end of the machine. The repairs make impressions in the paper that resemble watermarks. Watermarks are made in the paper substance by projecting bits soldered to the dandy roll on a Fourdrinier paper-making machine.

stockbook a book with pockets of linen, card, paper, or plastic to hold stamps.

stockcards specially made sheets of light cardboard with narrow strips pasted on them to hold postage stamps. They are often made to fit binders, forming stockbooks.

Stock Exchange Forgery mysterious British forgeries of the 1870-3 1-shilling green stamps, made and used at the telegraph office in the London Stock Exchange. The persons who made the forgeries and used them were never caught, although the stamps had an estimated value of between £45,000 and £60,000. The forgeries are identified by a circular cancellation reading "Stock Exchange". The stamps were stuck on telegrams that were filed until 1898, when Charles Nissen, a London stamp dealer, found them on telegrams among waste paper he bought. The stamps have never been found used on covers.

Stockholm the capital of Sweden. Local stamps issued in 1856.

stock restant (Fr.) remainder.

storlek (Swed.) size.

stotinka or **stitinki** a copper coin of Bulgaria and Thrace. 100 stotinki equal 1 lev. This coin is also known as the kantem or canteim, and is equivalent to the centime.

Strafportomarke (Ger.) postage-due stamp.

straight edges These occur on stamps from the outside rows in a pane or sheet which has been guillotined or printed close to the paper margin. The normal perforation is not apparent on one or more sides of the outside stamps; hence the edges appear straight.

Stock Exchange Forgery:
genuine stamp and forge stamp

Straits Settlements a former British Crown Colony of about 1,356 square miles in southeast Asia on the Malay Peninsula. Capital: Singapore. Issued stamps in 1867.

stratosphere stamps (nick.) stamps of Belgium, Poland, and Russia issued mainly between 1932-8, when experiments were being conducted in the stratosphere.

streak the untagged area that parallels web direction in Type I tagging of U.S. stamps. (Courtesy of Alfred G. Boerger)

streetcar cancellations special markings indicating that the mail was carried on streetcars in some U.S. cities. With the increasing use of buses and motorized pick-up vehicles, the use of streetcars for mail collection and distribution decreased.

streifen (Ger.) strip.

strike the impression of a cancellation device.

Stringer & Morton's City Despatch in Baltimore, Maryland, issued U.S. local stamps in 1850.

strip three or more stamps in horizontal or vertical rows.

stripa (Swed.) strip.

stripping stamps the removing of stamps from paper.

striscia (It.) strip.

STT/VUJA (ovpt.) appears on stamps of Jugoslavia, 1945-50, for use in Trieste by the Jugoslav military government.

stuffer paper or card inserted in an envelope to hold it rigid in the cancellation process and through transportation to the point of delivery.

SU (ovpt.) appears in 1878-83 on Straits Settlements stamps for use in Sungei Ujong.

sovrastampa (It.) overprint or surcharge (some European countries do not distinguish between the two words).

subject the main part of a postage stamp design, such as a portrait, emblem, landscape, or building.

subject collecting collecting of stamps according to the subjects illustrated, as opposed to collecting stamps of a country in sets. Pictures on the stamps provide a guide for a collection. This is also called topical collecting, but it is not necessarily thematic collecting, which centres on themes like first day covers, postmarks, airmails, and provisional stamps.

subscrito (Port.) envelope.

sucre a silver coin of Ecuador. 100 centavos equal 1 sucre. It was named after de Sucre, a South American patriot who fought under Bolivar and whose portrait appears on most of the coins.

SUDAN POSTAGE TAX (insc.) appears on Sudan postage-due stamps.

Sudan a republic of about 967,500 square miles south of Egypt in northeast Africa. Capital: Khartoum. Issued stamps in 1897.

Suedafrika (Ger.) South Africa.

Suedaustralien (Ger.) South Australia.

Suède (Fr.) Sweden.

Suednigerien (Ger.) South Nigeria.

Suedrhodesien (Ger.) Southern Rhodesia.

suelto (Sp.) unfixed, not in a fixed position; single, separate.

Suez Canal Co. issued stamps inscribed "Canal Maritime de Suez" in July 1868, and discontinued in October. Many forgeries exist. These are listed with stamps of Egypt in Gibbons catalogues.

SUID-AFRIKA (Afrikaans insc.) appears on stamps of South Africa; alternate stamps had an English inscription.

Suidwes-Afrika (insc.) appears alternately with "South West Africa" on stamps of South West Africa from 1931.

Suisse (Fr.) Switzerland.

sujet (Fr.) subject.

S. UJONG (insc.) appears on 1891-94 stamps of Singei Ujong, formerly a non-federated state on the Malay Peninsula.

SUL BOLLETTINO (It. insc.) means "on the list"; appears on the left half of Italian parcel post stamps. The stamps were perforated in the centre; a post office clerk would keep the left half of the stamp and give the right half (with the inscription "SULLA RICEVUTA") to the sender of the parcel as a receipt. (Courtesy of Anthony Ruta and Mrs. Giraude)

SULLA RICEVUTA (It. insc.) means "on the receipt"; appears on the right half of Italian parcel post stamps. See SUL BOLLETTINO.

Sullivan's Dispatch Post in Cincinnati, Ohio, issued U.S. local stamps in 1853.

SULTANAT D'ANJOUAN (insc.) appears on French colonial stamps of the Navigation and Commerce type for Anjouan, one of the Comoro Islands in the Mozambique Channel between Madagascar and Mozambique.

Sumter, S.C. This town in South Carolina issued postmasters' provisional envelopes in 1861 as part of the Confederate States of America.

Sunday labels See BANDALETTE OR BANDEROLE.

Sunday Postal Tax stamps postal tax stamps of Bulgaria, issued 1925-41, compulsory on all mail for delivery on Sundays and holidays, but not paying postal charges. Proceeds were used to maintain a sanitorium for postal, telegraph and telephone employees in Bulgaria.

Sungei Ujong a former state in the west Malay Peninsula; became part of Negri Sembilan in 1895. Issued stamps in 1878.

SUNGEI UJONG (ovpt. and sur.) appears overprinted on stamps of the Straits Settlements in 1881 for use in Sungei Ujong. Also surcharged on Straits Settlements stamps for Sungei Ujong in 1891.

sunken die proof the proof of a stamp made on paper or light cardboard showing a depressed area the size of the die. A similar recessed area appears in etchings or aquatints.

suns designs resembling the sun, on watermarks of the 1892-5 and the 1896-7 stamps of Argentina; the issues are distinguished by the size of the watermarks.

Suomi (insc.) appears on stamps of Finland.

sulphite paper paper made wholly or in part from sulphite pulp.

sulphite process a process invented in 1866 by Tilghman in which wood is reduced to paper pulp by treatment with sulphurous acid and its calcium and magnesium salts, under controlled conditions of pressure and temperature.

sulphite pulp pulp made from resinous wood, such as spruce, by cooking under pressure with a solution of calcium bisulphite. It is used in writing and printing papers and in numerous specialty papers in which the cost of rags would be prohibitive.

Sup. in auction catalogues, means "superb".

superimpose to print over some other printing. Overprinted and surcharged stamps are examples of superimposed printing.

supplementary mail in the United States, the service of handling first-class mail to foreign places after the post-office closing time. Rates were doubled for this service. This is similar to late-fee services in other countries.

supporters (her.) realistic figures placed on either side of a shield as if to hold it securely.

surcharge (Fr.) overprint or surcharge. According to the late Louis Lamouroux, French stamp collectors do not distinguish between overprinting, which is additional printing on the face or back of stamps after the main printing had been done, and surcharging, which is overprinting with changes in price and often with other alterations.

SURCHARGE POSTAGE (partial insc.) appears on postage-due stamps of Trinidad,

Trinidad and Tobago, and the British West Indies colony of Grenada in 1892.

surcharge words or numerals and symbols printed on postage stamps to create new denominations, or for some purpose other than the original one.

surface-colored paper or **surface-tinted paper** paper with one side treated or printed.

surface-printing an inaccurate term for the letterpress printing process. This term has been used so long, mainly in Great Britain, that there is little hope of correcting it.

sur fragment (Fr.) on piece.

SURGOS (insc.) appears on special delivery stamps of Hungary, 1916-19.

Surinam (Dutch Guiana) a Netherlands territory of about 55,143 square miles in northern South America on the Atlantic coast. Capital: Paramaribo. As a colony until 1954, and then as a territory, Surinam has issued stamps since 1873.

sur pièce (Fr.) tied on, used on piece.

surtax an extra charge added to the total value of a stamp for charity or other use.

sur trois lignes (Fr.) on three lines.

Susse perforations privately made perforations in French stamps in 1861. The Susse Brothers, Parisian stationers, patented a machine in 1861 to perforate fifty stamps at one time. They hoped to get a contract from the French Post Office to perforate stamps, but when the negotiations failed they sold their machine to A. Maury, a postage stamp dealer in Paris. *The Stamp Collector's Magazine* of June 4, 1870, reported that the Susse perforating machine was used to turn large numbers of French

stamps into Susse varieties. The mint stamps are common, but used stamps on covers with the correct dates are exceedingly rare.

Svalbard (Norwegian insc.) Spitsbergen; appears on an issue of Norway in 1925 to mark the annexation of Spitsbergen.

svart (Swed.) black colour.

Sverige (Swedish insc.) appears on stamps of Sweden.

S.W.A. (ovpt.) appears with or without periods on stamps of South Africa for use in

South-West Africa, 1927-52.

Swarts' City Dispatch Post in New York City, New York, issued U.S. local stamps in 1849-53.

Swaziland an independent kingdom of about 6,700 square miles in southeast Africa; administered by Transvaal 1894-1906, then a British High Commission territory until 1968. Capital: Mbabane. Used Transvaal stamps from 1895 until 1933; then issued stamps of Swaziland.

SWAZIELAND (ovpt.) appears on stamps of the South African Republic (Transvaal) for use in Swazieland, 1889-95.

Sweden a kingdom of about 173,349 square miles in northwest Europe. Capital: Stockholm. First stamps were issued in 1855.

Swiss Industrial Fair (MUBA) an industrial and commercial show in Basel held annually, and important to the Swiss economy. Switzerland issued a publicity stamp on Feb. 21, 1966, to mark the fiftieth Industrial Fair. (Courtesy of Swiss PTT notice)

Switzerland (Helvetia) a republic in central Europe of about 15,940 square miles. Capital: Bern. First stamps were issued in 1843.

Switzerland postage-due stamps From 1878 to 1924, these had no inscriptions to indicate their purpose. After 1924, the stamps were inscribed "HELVETIA" but still had no words to suggest postage due; Swiss postage-due stamps were discontinued in 1954.

Sydney views (nick.) the first issues of New South Wales, 1850-1, featuring the Seal of the colony, a heraldic device depicting an early scene of Sydney, the capital.

syllabic characters characters used in the katakana or merely kana type of Japanese writing, one of three types with kanji and hiragana. The kana syllabic characters are employed to represent foreign words used in the Japanese language. In 1874, twenty-three of the katakana characters were employed in Japanese postage stamp designs. They appear in microscopic size in each stamp, and are illustrated in stamp catalogues as a guide. Some specialists believe they were a kind of secret mark to number the printing plates. All twenty-three are listed separately and priced according to rarity. See Japanese dictionaries and stamp catalogues for details.

syncopated perforations various types of perforations introduced in the Netherlands. See INTERRUPTED PERFORATIONS.

Syria a republic in Asia at the east end of the Mediterranean Sea; area variously quoted as about 76,030 square miles and 72,234 square miles. Stamps issued under French mandate, 1919-25, were those of France, surcharged or overprinted; Egyptian postal issues were inscribed "Syrie" in 1925-58; stamps of the United Arab Republic were used, 1958-61; from 1961 stamps of Syrian Arab Republic were used.

Syrie or **Syrienne** (insc.) appears on stamps of Syria, 1925-58.

Syrien (Ger.) Syria.

Szechwan or **Szechuan** a province in south-central China, the largest and most populous province in China proper. In 1933 stamps of China were overprinted for use exclusively in Szechwan. In 1940-1 stamps were issued for both East and West Szechwan. These are listed with stamps of China in stamp catalogues.

Szegedin Issue an issue for use in the autonomous city of Szegedin in southern Hungary in 1919. The stamps were issued by an anti-Bolshevist government in protest against the Russian control of Budapest.

T

T appears in a circular postmark above a denomination, sometimes hand-written, on handstruck postage-due stamps.

T The letter T stamped on envelopes indicates tax or postage-due, in accordance with the regulations of the Universal Postal Union.

T (insc.) appears, with one T in each corner and a numeral in the centre, on postage-due stamps of the Dominican Republic.

T (ovpt.) appears in a circle on stamps of Peru for use in Huacho in 1884, after the war with Chile.

T (ovpt.) appears in a triangle on regular stamps of Monaco in 1917 for use as postage-due stamps.

tab (1) marginal paper, especially the inscription margin on the bottom or side rows of stamps; (2) the binding edge of booklet panes. Tabs should not be removed from either kind of stamps.

Tabelle (Ger.) tabulation, listing.

tablet (1) (nick.) the French colonial keytypes called the Peace and Navigation issue; (2) the area of a stamp that includes the face value within a frame of any kind.

T.A.C.A. (airline) Transportes Aéreos Centro Americanos, Ltd. Point of origin: Guatemala.

tadpole variety a British 1953, Queen Elizabeth design 2-penny stamp with a flaw in the lower right thistle. It appeared on one stamp in a sheet.

T.A.E. (airline) Tráfico Aéreo Español. Point of origin: Spain.

tael a silver coin of China. 1 tael equals 10 mace or 100 candareen.

Tag (Ger.) day.

Tag der Briefmarke (Ger.) date of issue of a postage stamp.

tagged stamp a stamp with phosphor lines on the face side, for use in automatic machinery.

tagging the overprinting technique used to deposit phosphor materials. There are two types: (1) the experimental form of tagging, which was accomplished with four separated rubber mats and is referred to sometimes as Dayton printing; (2) an overprinting technique in which a continuous roller was used in lieu of the mats. These references are to stamps of the United States. (Courtesy of Alfred G. Boerger)

tagliato in due (It.) bisect.

T. A. Hampton City Despatch in Philadelphia, Pennsylvania, issued U.S. local stamps in 1847.

Tahiti an island of about 402 square miles in the Society Island group in the South Pacific, part of French Oceania. Capital: Papeete. Tahiti used stamps of the French Colonies surcharged or overprinted, 1882-1903, replaced by those of Oceania.

taille douce (Fr.) copper-plate engraving (correctly called line engraving); also, engraved copper plates used in intaglio printing.

tails (nick.) the last stamps in roll or coil postage. These often have paper attached to the bottom or right side of the last stamp.

Taisho stamps stamps of Japan issued 1913-27, with certain stamps appearing in the following Showa period. Taisho designates the reign of Emperor Yoshihito, 1879-1926. This is a specialized subject, similar to the Showa stamps. (Courtesy of Harold Mayeda)

Taiwan See FORMOSA.

Taksë (ovpt.) appears on postage-due stamps of Albania.

talari a silver coin of Ethiopia (Abyssinia). 16 mehalek equal 1 talari.

Talbotton, Ga. This town in Georgia issued postmasters' provisional envelopes in 1861 as part of the Confederate States of America.

taler or thaler a silver coin of Germany, once used all over Europe under different names. 30 silbergroschen or groschen equal 1 taler. First struck about 1518, it was replaced as a unit of German coinage by the mark in 1873. Many names are given to this type of large silver coin, including "dollar", "daler", "tallero", "peso", "ecu", "crown", "scudo", and "piastre".

tamanho (Port.) size.

tamaño (Sp.) size.

tamaño grande (Sp.) large size.

tandingen (Dutch) perforations.

tandning (Swed.) perforation.

tanga a copper coin of Portuguese India. 12 reis equal 1 tanga, and 16 tangas equal 1 rupia. Originally a silver coin equal to 60 reis, in 1787 it was struck from copper, and the value was lowered.

Tanganyika a republic of about 362,888 square miles in the British Commonwealth, on the Indian Ocean in southeast Africa; united in April 1964 with Zanzibar to become the United Republic of Tanganyika and Zanzibar, or Tanzania. Capital: Dar es Salaam. Issued stamps in 1961.

TANGER (ovpt.) appears on French stamps for use in French Morocco, 1918-24. Also appears on Spanish stamps of 1929 for use in the international city of Tangiers in Spanish Morocco.

TANGIER (ovpt.) appears on stamps of Great Britain for use in British offices in the International Zone of Tangiers from 1927-48.

Tanzania formerly Tanganyika and Zanzibar; a united republic within the British Commonwealth of about 363,732 square miles in southeast Africa on the Indian Ocean. Capital: Dar es Salaam.

TANZANIA, UGANDA, KENYA (insc.) appears on a stamp issued by Kenya, Uganda, and Tanzania on April 15, 1965, to promote safaris in the East African states.

Tapling Collection a famous British collection formed by the late Thomas K. Tapling, a renowned philatelist who bequeathed his stamp collection to the British Museum in London.

Tapling Medal an honorary medal made possible by the Royal Philatelic Society, London, and named after Thomas K. Tapling. The Medal was presented for the best paper read before the Society. Tapling formed one of the ten most notable collections of postage stamps and philatelic items in Europe. He served as vice-president of the Philatelic Society of London from 1881 until his death in 1913, and donated his collections to the British Museum. See also CRAWFORD MEDAL.

tard (Fr.) late.

target cancellation a type of postmark resembling the rings in a target. The "rings" are much heavier and fewer in number than the circles in a concentric ring cancellation.

T.A.R.S.A. (airline) Transportes Aéreos Rangueles, S.A. Point of origin, Argentina.

TASA (insc.) appears on postage-due stamps of Uruguay.

TASA POR COBRAR (insc.) appears on postage-due stamps of Cuba.

Tasmania originally Van Dieman's Land; a former British island colony of about 26,215 square miles southeast of Australia; one of the six colonies that united in 1901 to form the Commonwealth of Australia. Capital: Hobart. Issued stamps in 1853.

Tasmanie (Fr.) Tasmania.

Tasmanien (Ger.) Tasmania.

tassa gazzette (It. insc.) appears on newspaper tax stamps of Modena, Italy.

Tatsache (Ger.) fact.

tauschen (Ger.) to exchange.

Tauschpartner (Ger.) exchange or trade partner.

taux (Fr.) rate.

tavola (It.) plate.

TAX appears as a rubber-stamped impression on envelopes; also used to obliterate regular postage stamps of Papua to indicate that there is postage due.

TAX or **TAXE** appears enclosed in a frame of any shape or without a frame, on hand-struck postage-due stamps. The impressions usually have a space to show the amount of postage short-paid, and the amount is often written or stamped on mail by postal employees at the office of delivery. On some foreign mail, the figures in French currency may indicate the amount of postage short-paid but not the double amount that is actually due.

TAXA DE FACTAGIU (insc. and sur.) appears inscribed on 1895-1911 parcel-post stamps of Romania; also surcharged on the 1928 parcel-post stamps.

TAXA DE GUERRA (Port. ovpt.) war tax; appears on war-tax stamps of Portuguese territories; stamps of Macao have values in avos, those of Portuguese Africa in dollars, those of Portuguese India in rupias (Rp), and those of Portuguese Guinea in reis.

TAXA DE PLATA (sur. or insc.) appears on postage-due stamps of Romania.

TAXA DEVIDA (Port. insc.) appears on postage-due stamps of Brazil.

TAXA RECEBIDA (Port. insc.) appears above the design of an airplane on 1946 airmail stamps of Mozambique (Portuguese East Africa).

taxe (Fr.) fee.

TAXE A PERCEVOIR (Fr. insc.) appears on postage-due stamps of France and some French colonies. Also appears on postage-due stamps of Yemen (which Scott's says were used only for regular postage).

TAXE A PERCEVOIR T (ovpt.) appears on 1894 stamps of Ethiopia for use as postage-due stamps in 1905-7.

TAXE DE RETARD (Fr.) late fee.

Taxe Perçue (insc.) appears on 1947 Mozambique airmail stamps.

Taylor, Samuel Allen a famous forger, known for his creation of the so-called space fillers or bogus stamps for collectors; he reached his peak in about 1864. He also published the first philatelic paper in the United States, *The Stamp Collector's Record.*

Taylor-Made word used to describe doubtful philatelic items said to have been made by S. Allan Taylor, a Boston stamp dealer.

T.C. (ovpt.) appears on stamps of Cochin for use in the United State of Travancore-Cochin in 1950.

T.C. POSTALARI (insc.) appears on stamps of Turkey, 1931.

T.C.A. (airline) Trans-Canada Air Lines, now Air Canada. Point of origin: Canada.

T.C.E.K. (partial insc.) appears on Turkish postal tax stamps, 1946.

Tchad (ovpt.) appears on Middle Congo stamps of 1907-17 with the inscription "Chad".

TCHAD/A.E.F. (ovpt.) appears on postage-due stamps of France for use in Chad.

Tchécoslovaquie (Fr.) Czechoslovakia.

TCHONGKING (sur.) appears in 1903-4 on stamps of Indo-China for the use by the French offices in Tchongking, China.

TDLR Thomas De La Rue, British security printers.

T.D.S. town date stamp, a postmark with a town name and date.

tear W. a tear on the left (west) side.

TE BETAAL (insc.) appears on postage-due stamps of South-West Africa and of the Union of South Africa.

TE BETALEN (insc. and sur.) appears inscribed with no country name on postage-due stamps of the Netherlands and in dif-

ferent colours for Surinam, Dutch Indies, and Curaçao; also inscribed on postage-due stamps of South-West Africa and the Union of South Africa. Appears surcharged on stamps of the Netherlands and the Dutch Indies.

TE BETALEN/A PAYER bilingual inscrip-

tions on postage-due stamps of Belgium, the Congo, and Ruanda-Urundi.

teckning (Swed.) design.

Teese & Co. Penny Post in Philadelphia, Pennsylvania, issued U.S. local stamps in 1852.

teeth the projecting portions in a perforated stamp; the holes are the perforations; the projections in a serpentine roulette.

Teheran capital of Persia (Iran). Stamps were issued in 1902-9 overprinted "P L Teheran".

Teil (Ger.) part, section.

Teilgummi (Ger.) part gum.

Teilung (Ger.) separation, division.

teilweise (Ger.) partly, partial.

teinté (Fr.) coloured.

Telegrafenmarke (Ger.) telegraph stamp.

Telegrafenstempel (Ger.) telegraph cancel.

Telégrafos (Sp. insc.) appears on the 1883-8 telegraph stamps of the Philippines while under Spanish control.

telegraph cancels revenue cancels made by punched holes in stamps used on telegraph forms. Stamps having telegraph cancels are not kept in postage stamp collections.

Telegraph Despatch P.O. in Philadelphia, Pennsylvania, issued U.S. local stamps in 1848.

telegraph stamps stamps used to pay telegraph charges. In Great Britain, postage and revenue stamps serve this purpose. The well-known Stock Exchange forgeries were all found on telegraph forms.

Tellico Plains, Tenn. This town in Tennessee issued postmasters' provisional stamps in 1861 as part of the Confederate States of America.

Telos or **Piscopi** an Italian island of about 25 square miles in the Dodecanese group in the Aegean Sea. Italian stamps overprinted "Piscopi" were used 1912-32.

Temesvar or **Timişoara** a city in southwest Romania; formerly a city in Hungary. Hungarian stamps, overprinted, called the Temesvar issue, were used in 1919 under Romanian occupation. The city then became part of Romania.

tempo a bronze coin of Japan and Korea. 100 mon equal 1 tempo. It is an oblong coin, and its value has fluctuated.

Ten voordeele/van het/Roode Kruis (part of bilingual sur.) appears on 1945 semi-postal stamps of Ruanda-Urundi, formerly Belgian East Africa. The surtax was for the Red Cross.

T.E.O. (ovpt.) Occupied Territories of the Enemy; appears with denominations in milliemes on stamps of France for use in

Testing labels

Syria under French mandate; also appears with the overprint "Cilicie" on stamps of Turkey for use in Cilicia, 1919.

Termin (Ger.) date.

terne (Fr.) dull.

terraqueous globes a unique design on stamps of Italy, Dec. 29, 1956, to mark the first anniversary of the Italian entry to the United Nations. Each stamp shows two globes, one red and the other green, which become three-dimensional when seen through special glasses or under coloured acetate; the two globes appear to become one. Refer to *I Francobolli Dello Stato Italiano*, by the Italian Post Office.

Terre Adélie/Dumont D'Urville/1840 (3-line ovpt.) appears on 1948 Madagascar airmail stamps intentionally issued by the French postal authorities to establish their claim to Adélie Land in the Antarctic, a territory that Jules Dumont D'Urville discovered in 1840. Listed with stamps of Madagascar in catalogues.

Terre d'Edouard VII (Fr.) King Edward VII Land.

Terre de Victoria (Fr.) Victoria Land.

Terre-Neuve (Fr.) Newfoundland.

territoire de (Fr.) territory of; appears with a French place-name to distinguish the place of origin of the postage stamps.

TERRITOIRE/DE L'INNINI (Fr. ovpt.) appears on stamps of French Guiana, for use in Inini, 1932-40.

Territoire du Niger (Fr.) Niger Territory.

TERRITOIRE/DU NIGER (2-line ovpt.) appears on stamps of Upper Senegal and Niger of 1914, which have the inscription "AFRIQUE OCCIDENTAL FRANÇAIS. These were issued in 1921-6 for use in Niger, a former French colony in Africa north of Nigeria.

territorial covers mainly early U.S. mail from one of the territories before it became a state. For example, Arizona was organized as a separate territory in 1863 but did not enter the Union as a state until 1912. Thus letters of Arizona between 1863 and 1912 are territorial covers with territorial postmarks.

TERRITORIO DE IFNI (Sp. ovpt.) appears on stamps of Spain for use in Ifni, 1941-51.

TERRITORIOS ESPANOLES DEL GOLFO DE GUINEA (Sp. insc.) appears on stamps of Spanish Guinea.

TERRS. ESPANOLES DEL GOLFO DE GUINEA (Sp. insc.) appears on stamps of Spanish Guinea.

testing labels small pieces of paper, some printed like postage stamps, that are used for testing in vending machines.

Tete a district of about 46,600 square miles in west Mozambique, in southeast Africa, between Nyasaland and Southern Rhodesia; a Portuguese colony. Capital: Tete. The Vasco de Gama issue of various Portuguese colonies was used, surcharged "REPUBLICA TETE", in 1913; in 1914 stamps inscribed "TETE" on Ceres key-types of Portuguese colonies were used. Stamps of Mozambique were used after 1914.

tête bêche (Fr.) stamps or blocks of stamps printed upside down in relation to one another. Many booklet panes of stamps have been printed that way, and separated later to make stamp booklets. If possible these items should not be separated. (Illustration: p. 242)

tête d'ivoire (Fr.) ivory head.

tetragon In geometry, a plane figure with four sides and four angles, a quadrilateral. The 1967 Christmas stamps of Malta were in the shape of a tetragon.

TETUAN (ovpt.) appears on Spanish stamps for use by Spanish offices in Tetuán, Morocco, 1903-9.

teuer (Ger.) expensive.

Textanordnung (Ger.) arrangement of text.

text-book a manual of instruction; a standard work on a particular subject, used by students.

Thrace an ancient region on the eastern Balkan Peninsula, and now an area of about 90,000 square miles lying within Turkey, Greece, and Bulgaria. Turkish and Bulgarian surcharged stamps and Greek occupation issues were used 1913-20.

th. (sur.) for the German word "Tausend",

Tête bêche sheet arrangement

meaning "thousand". Appears on German official stamps, 1920-3.

th in auction catalogues, means "thin".

Thailand or **Siam** a kingdom in southeast Asia of about 198,247 square miles. Capital: Bangkok. Stamps were first issued in 1883. Most stamps except the first issue bear the name of the country in English as well as in Siamese. The first issue portrays King Chulalongkorn in three different

styles of frame designs. Later stamps bear portraits of royal persons, symbols, and scenes.

Thailand or **Thai** (insc.) appears on stamps of Thailand (Siam).

thematic collecting the collecting of stamps by themes, such as first day covers, airmails, postmarks, or prestamp covers. Not to be confused with topical collecting.

thematics British term for topicals, but considered incomplete in America. See THEMATIC COLLECTING; TOPICAL COLLECTING.

thermography or **thermographic process** a method of using special ink in postage stamp production to create raised effects that resemble steel engraving in stamps. The printer applies powder to wet ink, and heats the paper to make the powder set. Turkey issued stamps in May 1966 that used this thermographic process.

Thessalie (Fr.) Thessaly.

Thessalien (Ger.) Thessaly.

Thessalonica See SALONIKA.

Thessaly a region in eastern Greece, once under the domination of Turkey. In 1898 Turkey issued five stamps in a distinctive

octagonal shape for use by the Turkish occupation forces in Thessaly.

Thibet (Fr.) Tibet.

Thies provisional stamps of Bermuda. In 1860, J. H. Thies, the postmaster of St. Georges, Bermuda, made his own provisional stamps, from a postmarking device different from the Hamilton postmark used by W. P. Perot. Refer to stamps of Bermuda in catalogues for the designs.

thinned paper   stamp paper that has been damaged in some way other than in production.

Third Avenue Post Office   in New York City, New York, issued U.S. local stamps in 1855.

Thirkell position finder   a transparent sheet of plastic with markings of letters and figures, devised by Stanley Gibbons to describe the location of varieties, flaws, or anything noteworthy on stamps. See Stanley Gibbons catalogues.

Thomasville, Ga.   This town in Georgia issued postmasters' provisional envelopes in 1861 as part of the Confederate States of America.

Thrace Interalliée or **Thrace Occidentale** (ovpt.) appears on Bulgarian stamps for use in Thrace in 1919-20.

three-colour printing   the reproduction of a multi-coloured design or drawing by means of three separate printing plates, one for each of the primary colours, yellow, red, and blue.

three-penny Black Beaver   a mysterious Canadian proof of the 1851 issue, proofed in black on white ungummed wove paper. The late George Lowe, a Toronto, Ontario, stamp dealer, owned three Black Beaver proofs in about 1922. Each proof had been made in the upper left corner of the sheets that were about four by seven inches in vertical format. The 6-penny was in the middle of the sheets and a neat rectangular, upright hole appeared in the bottom right corner. The proofs from dies had been set in a diagonal line from top left to bottom right. While the 3-penny black proofs are known to exist, their original source has not been established positively.

Thuringen   (insc.) appears on stamps of Thuringia, a former German state, around the Thuringian Forest. Following the Second World War, Russia issued stamps for many towns and administrations, including the 1945-6 issues for Thuringia.

Thurn and Taxis   a princely family who operated the first organized mail service of Europe, from 1490 to 1867. In 1450, Frederick III, Emperor of the Holy Roman Empire, knighted Roger I, a member of the Thurn and Taxis family, and commanded him to establish communications in the Tyrol. Details of each member of the family who continued the mail service and who

are portrayed on the 1952 stamps of Belgium follow:

Francis of Taxis, first head postmaster of the Low Countries (1490-1517); gained control of the communication services in Central Europe; portrayed on the 80-centime stamp.

Jean-Baptiste of Thurn and Taxis, second head postmaster of the Low Countries (1517-36); portrayed on the 1-franc 75-centime stamp.

Francis the Younger, third head postmaster of the Low Countries, son of Jean Baptiste of Thurn and Taxis; died a few months after he became postmaster; not portrayed on the Belgian 1952 stamps.

Leonard I, Baron of Thurn and Taxis, fourth head postmaster, 1536-78 and again 1585-1612; expanded the territory for the family postal bureaus to Germany and surrounding countries to Burgundy. Rebels temporarily dispossessed the Taxis family and proclaimed Jean Hinckart, Lord of Ohain, as head postmaster, 1578-85. Leonard I regained the position in 1585. He is portrayed on the 2-franc stamp.

Count Lamoral I of Taxis, son of Leonard I, and fifth grand master of the post of the Low Countries (1616-24). Emperor Matthias granted the family of Thurn and Taxis the privilege of being grand masters of the Empire postal service, and Emperor Ferdinand II extended the grant to include the feminine branch of the Thurn and Taxis family. Lamoral I is portrayed on the 2-franc 50-centime stamp.

Leonard II, Francis Count of Thurn and Taxis, son of Lamoral I, sixth head postmaster of the Low Countries (1624-8); married Alexandrine of Rye, who when he died became Grand Mistress of the Thurn and Taxis posts for the Low Countries. Leonard II is portrayed on the 3-franc stamp.

Alexandrine of Rye, later the Countess of Thurn and Taxis, Mistress of the Post of the Low Countries (1628-45); portrayed on a 1960 commemorative stamp of Belgium.

Lamoral II, Claude-Francis Count of Thurn and Taxis, seventh head postmaster of the Low Countries (1650-76); son of Leonard II and Alexandrine of Rye. At first he renewed the licenses of all postmasters working under him, and then innovated a number of princely alliances that enhanced the nobility of the House of Thurn and Taxis. He is portrayed on the 4-franc stamp.

Eugene Alexander, Prince of Thurn and

Taxis, eighth head postmaster of the Low Countries (1676-1701); son of Lamoral II. In 1681 King Charles II of Spain renewed Eugene Alexander's licenses to continue as head postmaster of the Low Countries, upon receipt of 15,000 florins from Eugene Alexander. Eugene Alexander is portrayed on the 5-franc stamp.

Anselme-Francis, Prince of Thurn and Taxis, son of Eugene Alexander, ninth head postmaster of the Low Countries (1709-39). During French occupation of the Low Countries (1701-9), the Thurn and Taxis family lost their postal authority; the political problem continued up to the time of the French Revolution. Anselme-Francis is portrayed on the 5-franc 75-centime stamp.

Alexander Ferdinand, Prince of Thurn and Taxis, son of Anselme-Francis, tenth head postmaster of the Low Countries, 1739-46 and again 1748-73. Again during French occupation of the Low Countries (1746-8), French officials directed the postal service. Alexander Ferdinand is portrayed on the 8-franc stamp.

Charles Anseline, Prince of Thurn and Taxis, son of Alexander Ferdinand; eleventh head postmaster of the Low Countries, 1773 to November 1792 and again March to July 1793. Under his direction, stewards handled the administration of the provincial post offices. By order of the French Republic on Nov. 30, 1795, the Thurn and Taxis family lost their titles and privileges, and were forced to withdraw their postmaster services from the Low Countries; but Charles-Alexander, son of Charles Anseline, served one additional year as head postmaster. Charles Anseline is portrayed on the 10-franc stamp.

Charles-Alexander, Prince of Thurn and Taxis, son of Charles Anseline, twelfth and last of the Thurn and Taxis postmasters of the Low Countries; served as temporary administrator of the posts, March 1, 1814, to June 9, 1815. Following the French Revolution, the Treaty of Vienna placed the Low Countries under the sovereignty of William I. The Dutch postal system applied to Belgium, and the Thurn and Taxis administration of postal services came to an end in the Low Countries, but the family operated postal services in other parts of Europe. In 1852 the family issued adhesive postage stamps for the Northern and Southern Districts of German states. On July 1, 1867, Prussian stamps superseded these.

(Data courtesy of the Post Office Department of Belgium; translated by Wilfred Chauvin of Toronto, Ontario)

Tibet a country of Central Asia, and an outer dependency of China; area variously quoted as about 469,294 square miles, 463,200 square miles, and 471,660 square miles. Stamps were issued for use in Tibet only from 1912. The crude first issue for Tibet in 1912 is inscribed in Tibetan and English, "TIBET" on the left and "POSTAGE" on the right, but these words are not always easy to read. The central device represents the White Lion of Tibet. Chinese stamps surcharged in 1911 in pies and annas are stamps for the Chinese post offices in Tibet.

tical a silver coin of Siam (Thailand), sometimes countermarked for Burma. 100 satangs equal 1 tical. "Bat" is the Siamese name for this odd-shaped coin, known as bullet money. The coin is also known as tecul, tekal, tycal, or tickal.

tidningsfrimarke (Swed.) newspaper stamp.

tied on refers to a postage stamp (on an envelope, cover, or a piece of these items, or even on a piece of wrapping paper) with the postmark covering a portion of the paper and the stamp. This verifies that the postage stamp was used on the paper to which it adheres.

Tied Pen Canc. or **T.P.C.** a cancellation of lines, cross, or other pen and ink marks, other than writing, that defaces the stamp and extends to the paper bearing the stamp. Such a description indicates that the cancellation is shown in its entirety. This does not refer to cancellations in writing, which are manuscript cancellations.

Tiefdruck (Ger.) recess-printing or steel engraving.

tiefschwarz (Ger.) deep black.

tiefstehend (Ger.) placed low.

Tientsin (ovpt. and sur.) appears on stamps of Italy for use by Italian offices in Tientsin, China, 1917-21.

Tierra del Fuego a group of islands at the southern tip of South America, divided between Chile and Argentina. The name is Spanish for "Land of Erupting Fire". Julius Popper, a Romanian adventurer, issued one value of local stamps intended for use on mail to the mainland.

tiger key-types (nick.) also known as "the tigers"; the various issues of Negri Sembilan, Pahang, Perak, Selangor, Sungei, Ujong (inscribed "S. Ujong"), and later issues of the Federated Malay States, bearing designs of tigers.

tillägg (Swed.) addition, hence an extra

charge or surtax.

Tilleard Medal an honourary medal made possible by the Royal Philatelic Society, London, and named after J. A. Tilleard, an Honourary Secretary of the Royal Philatelic Society and of the former organization the Philatelic Society, London. Tilleard became Philatelist to King George V. See CRAWFORD MEDAL.

timbre (Fr.) stamp, stamp-office, stamp duty, postmark.

timbre adhésif (Fr.) adhesive stamp.

timbre avion (Fr.) airmail stamp.

timbre bord de feuille (Fr.) marginal copy, wing copy.

timbre classique (Fr.) classic stamp.

timbre commémoratif (Fr.) commemorative stamp.

TIMBRE COMPLEMENTARIO (Sp. insc.) appears on postage-due stamps of Mexico.

timbre coupé (Fr.) bisected.

timbre de bienfaisance (Fr.) charity stamp.

timbre de carnet (Fr.) booklet stamp.

timbre de la poste aeriénne (Fr.) airmail stamp.

timbre d'entrée (Fr.) admission stamp.

timbre de poste locale (Fr.) local postage stamp, one used in a limited region as opposed to a stamp used in the entire country or universally.

timbre de service (Fr.) official stamp.

timbre détaché (Fr.) single stamp, stamp off of a letter.

timbre en roulettes (Fr.) coil stamp.

timbre-exprès (Fr.) special delivery stamp.

timbre-fiscal (Fr.) revenue stamp.

timbre fiscal-postal (Fr.) fiscal-postal stamp.

timbre fiscaux (Fr.) fiscal stamp.

Timbre Imperial Journaux (insc.) appears on 1868 French newspaper stamps.

timbre lavé or **timbre nettoyé** (Fr.) cleaned stamp.

timbre-poste (Fr.) postage stamp, adhesive stamp.

timbre-poste émis par le gouvernement (Fr.) government postage stamp.

timbre pour colis postaux (Fr.) parcel-post stamp.

timbre pour exprès (Fr.) special delivery stamp.

timbre pour journaux (Fr.) newspaper stamp.

timbre pour lettre chargée (Fr.) registration stamp.

timbre pour lettre en retard (Fr.) too-late stamp.

timbre pour lettre par exprès (Fr.) express letter stamp.

timbre pour lettre recommandée (Fr.) registration stamp.

timbre pour poste locale (Fr.) city mail stamp.

timbre provisoire (Fr.) provisional stamp.

Timbres poste de l'Organisation des Nations Unies en Valeurs Suisses (Fr.) United Nations postage stamps in Swiss denominations. The first such stamps were issued Oct. 4, 1969.

TIMBRE TAXE (Fr. insc.) appears with numeral, but without country name, on postage-due stamps of the French Colonies, France, and Vietnam (1952).

timbre-taxe pour journaux (Fr.) newspaper tax stamp.

timbre-télégraphe (Fr.) telegraph stamp.

timbrologie (Fr.) philately.

Timor an island of about 13,094 square miles in the Malay Archipelago, northwest of Australia; the western half belongs to Indonesia and the eastern half is a Portuguese overseas territory. Eastern capital: Dili. Stamps of Macao, overprinted or surcharged, were used in 1885; then inscribed stamps for Timor were issued in 1887 and 1894, plus a Vasco de Gama issue in 1898, and subsequent provisionals and other types of Portugal and Portuguese colonial issues. (Gibbons gives 1886 as the date of the first overprinted issue.)

Tin Can Mail a mail delivery service introduced by W. G. Quensell for Niuafoou, Tonga, in which canoe men retrieved drums of mail for Tonga thrown into the sea from ships passing the island. Quensell impressed various cachets in English, French, German, and other languages on the back and front of letters he serviced, reading "Tin Can Mail" and foreign-language equivalents. He sent out more than half a million covers in the period 1919-40. When a volcano destroyed Niuafoou in 1946, the people were forced to leave and the service ended.

tinctures (her.) the metals, colours, and furs of heraldry.

tingido (Port.) tinted.

tin hats See STEEL HELMETS.

tint block an engraved, grained, or flat zinc or copper plate used to print a solid light shade as a background.

tint a gradation of colour obtained by mixing white with a colour.

tinted paper (1) stamp paper that retains the colour of printing ink after the stamp has been soaked in water. During the First World War some dyes in the printing inks used for U.S. stamps were soluble in water and thus formed solutions that tinted the stamp paper. (2) paper that is lightly coloured, such as azure paper.

Tintenstrich (Ger.) ink line.

TIPEX Third International Philatelic Exhibition, held Oct. 16-23, 1926, in Grand Central Palace, New York City. The United States issued a souvenir sheet of twenty-five stamps from the White Plains, New York, issue of Oct. 18, 1926, to commemorate the stamp show.

tipo (It.) type, mainly describing a type of watermark, but also refers to a type of design or postage stamp.

tipo desenho (Port.) type, design.

tipografia (Port.) typography, letterpress printing.

tipografía (Sp.) typography, letterpress printing.

tipo Romano (Port.) block letters.

tira (Sp.) strip, band.

tirada (Sp.) issue, edition, press-work, cast.

tirage (Fr.) printing, quantity. The word is used in press releases to indicate the number of stamps in an issue.

tiragem (Port.) issue, edition.

TIRANE (partial ovpt.) appears on 1931 airmail stamps of Albania to mark the first airmail flight from Tirana, Albania, to Rome, Italy, on July 6, 1931.

tiratura (It.) printing.

Tirol (Ger.) Tyrol.

title letters founts of type consisting entirely of capital letters and figures, used for title lines.

title page the page at the beginning of a stamp collection or book, containing the title or subject of the work.

tjänste (Swed. insc.) appears on official stamps of Sweden.

Tjeneste-Frimarke (insc.) appears on official stamps of Denmark.

Tjenestefrimerke (insc.) appears on 1925

official stamps of Norway.

tjock (Swed.) thick.

T.L. top left.

T Margin Blk. 4 PL V.F. O.G. in auction catalogues, indicates the top margin block of four stamps with a plate number in the

marginal paper, of very fine quality with the original gum.

Tobago a former British colonial island of about 116 square miles in the West Indies north of Trinidad; part of the colony of Trinidad and Tobago since 1913. Capital: Scarborough (also known as Port Louis). Tobago issued stamps in 1879.

Toenung (Ger.) shade.

Toga (insc.) appears on stamps of Tonga.

Togo a republic of about 39,934 square miles in west Africa between the Gold Coast and Dahomey; formerly a German protectorate. Capital: Lome. Stamps of Germany, overprinted, were in use 1897-1900; then German yacht key-types were inscribed for use in 1900-19. Under British occupation in 1914-16, stamps of German Togo and Gold Coast were surcharged or overprinted. Under French occupation in 1916-21, stamps of German Togo were used, surcharged, and under French mandate in 1922-56, types of various French colonies were overprinted. Since 1957 stamps of the republic of Togo have been used.

Tokelau Islands or **Union Islands** a group of islands of about 4 square miles in the central Pacific Ocean about 275 miles north of Samoa. Chief islands: Fakaofo, Atafu, and Nukonono. Formerly a part of the Gilbert and Ellice Islands colony; in 1926 transferred to New Zealand administration, but did not issue stamps until June 22, 1948.

Tolima formerly a state in Colombia, now a department. Issued stamps 1870-1904 and postmasters' provisionals in 1894.

toman a gold coin of Persia (Iran) and Bushire. 10 krans equal 1 toman. There are coins equivalent to 2, 5, and 10 tomans as well as halves and quarters.

tombstone postmark a type of postal marking with a circular top above a rectangular base, resembling an old-style tombstone. Some Liverpool tombstone ship letter handstamps were receiving marks, 1852-70.

toned paper paper with an off-white tint to the entire substance, often referred to as yellowish, bluish, or other descriptive colours.

Tonga or **the Friendly Islands** a group of islands of about 250 square miles south of Samoa in the South Pacific; a kingdom under British protection. Capital: Nukualofa. Issued stamps in 1886.

tongs See TWEEZERS.

Tonguin See TONKIN.

Tonkin a former French protectorate, now a department of Annam in French Indo-china. Annam and Tonkin issued stamps in 1888.

tono (Sp.) shade.

tönung (Ger.) shade.

TOO LATE a postmark sometimes used as a cancellation on the pence issues of stamps for the Province of Canada prior to Confederation. The impression "TOO LATE" indicated that the letter arrived after the departure of the mail that it had been intended to catch.

too-late stamps stamps issued to indicate a fee paid on mail after the post office was already closed. Victoria, Australia, issued postage stamps with this inscription, but some other places have used postal markings to indicate the same service with the words "late fee"; among these are Australia, Hong Kong, and Uruguay (1936).

To Pay (insc.) appears on postage-due stamps of Great Britain.

topical collecting the saving of postage stamps according to their illustrations: birds, animals, trains, flowers, and scores of others promoted by the American Topical Association (ATA).

top-side the side of a sheet of paper facing away from the wire during the manufacturing process.

torn stamps one of many kinds of damaged stamps that are not good for stamp collections, except for those torn for cancellation purposes. The early issues of Afghanistan are exceptions.

tornese a base silver and copper coin of the Two Sicilies and other Italian states. 200 tornesi equal 100 grana equal 1 ducat. The name is a modification of "gros tournois". Medieval French money was struck at Tours and Paris, and "tournois" is the general name for any coin struck at Tours.

Toscane (Fr.) Tuscany.

Toscano (insc.) appears on stamps of Tuscany.

Toskana (Ger.) Tuscany.

toughra, tughra, or **tugra** the monogram of the former sultans of Turkey. It is said to have originated in about 1360-5, when Murad I was sultan. He could not write, and dipped his three middle fingers into ink, then placed them on documents as his signature. This symbol appears on early stamps of Turkey.

Tour et Taxis (Fr.) Thurn and Taxis.

Touva (insc.) appears on stamps of Tannu Tuva.

Tovva (sur.) appears with new values on stamps of Tannu Tuva.

TOVVA/K8K/ POSTAGE (sur.) appears

on 1927 stamps of Tannu Tuva. Others, issued in 1927-33, were inscribed "TOUVA". Tuva Autonomous Region is the official name of the autonomous region of Soviet Russia in Asia between the Savan and Tannu Ola mountains. It was incorporated into the Soviet Union in 1945.

T.P.N.G. Territory of Papua and New Guinea.

T.P.O. travelling post office.

T.R. top right.

tr in auction catalogues, indicates a tear.

TR "Transito Reggio", an Italian postal marking applied to mail in transit through Reggio, a province in Italy.

T.R.D.S. temporary rubber date stamps. In many places throughout the world, temporary cancels and postal markings have been used for limited times. These are especially well known in the Bahamas, where they play such an important part in the postal history.

traço de pena (Port.) pen stroke.

traders stamps for exchange, usually duplicates.

Traffik an Austrian government-owned tobacco store that sells postage and revenue stamps.

trait (Fr.) stroke, line.

trait de plume (Fr.) pen stroke.

TRAITE DE VERSAILLES (ovpt.) appears in an oval frame on German stamps of 1906-20, for use in Allenstein, which became part of Germany.

trait d'union (Fr.) hyphen.

Transcaucasion Federated Republics (or officially, Transcaucasion Soviet Federated Socialist Republic) the former republics of Armenia, Azerbaidzhan (Azerbaijan), and Georgia, now part of the U.S.S.R.; about 71,255 square miles. Capital: Tiflis. Russian and Armenian stamps, overprinted and surcharged, were used in 1923, superseded by stamps of Russia.

transfer (1) the impression in recess in steel printing plates made by the transfer press roll; (2) the impression in relief on a transfer roll.

transferring the pulling of transfers from original designs and transferring them to the surface of a litho plate or stone.

transfer roll the steel roll (or wheel) on the transfer press. The operator rocks the transfer roll first over the hardened die to get the impression made on the roll. After the transfer roll is finished and hardened, the operator then rocks in the required number of stamp impressions in a steel plate. Transfer rolls are not used in any other printing plate manufacturing process.

Transilvania See TRANSYLVANIA.

transit marks postal markings struck usually on the back of envelopes, but sometimes on the front, at post offices where mail was transferred from one route to another. A transit mark is always struck somewhere between the point of origin and the place of the address. Envelopes or letters may have more than one transit marking.

Trans-Jordan See JORDAN.

Transjordanie (Fr.) Trans-Jordan.

Transjordanien (Ger.) Trans-Jordan.

Trans-Juba See JUBALAND.

Transkaukasien (Ger.) Transcaucasia (Transcaucasian Federated Republics).

transparente (Port. and Sp.) transparent.

transportation postmarks originally, postal markings struck in railroad post offices. Since the advent of airmail, transportation markings included mail with airmail or airport postmarks. Some collectors believe that ship postmarks should be included with transporation markings.

Transvaal a country of about 110,450 square miles in south Africa known as South African Republic until British occupation in 1877; became part of the Union of South Africa in 1910.

Transylvania or **Transilvania** a region of about 24,020 square miles in northwest and central Romania. Two Transylvanian issues of stamps in 1919 were overprinted Hungarian stamps.

trasparente (It.) transparent.

Trauermarke (Ger.) mourning stamp.

Travancore (insc.) appears on stamps of Travancore, an Indian feudatory state of

about 7,662 square miles. Capital: Trivandrum. Stamps issued in 1888.

TRAVELLING BOX a postmark used in Mauritius at least until 1957 on letters collected from the letter boxes in mail cars on railway trains. The marks ceased when railways stopped operating. (Courtesy of the postmaster of Mauritius)

T.R.D. temporary rubber datestamp.

Treasury (insc.) appears on official stamps of the United States, 1873, for use by the Treasury Department.

Treasury Board competition a contest held by the British Treasury Board in September 1939 to have people submit proposals for stamp designs. Of the more than 2,500 entries, none was used as it was presented. Perkins, Bacon & Co. Ltd. designed and printed the first adhesive postage stamps for Great Britain, the famous 1-penny black and 2-pence blue. The unsuccessful entries are called Treasury essays.

treasury roulette an experimental rouletting process used by Henry Archer in the various stages toward his development of perforated postage stamps.

Treaty Port cancels Many Hong Kong stamps of Queen Victoria issues were used in Shanghai, Amoy, and other Chinese cities known as the "Treaty Ports". Others were used in various cities of Japan. Treaty Port cancels are also found on King Edward VII and King George V stamps of Hong Kong.

Treaty Port issues (nick.) local postage stamps of certain Chinese cities where Great Britain and China had agreed by treaty to allow businessmen to operate trading establishments after the close of the First Opium War in 1842. China had no public postal system at that time, so the local posts were conducted by businessmen who issued their own stamps for commercial use.

treble letter See SINGLE, DOUBLE, AND TREBLE LETTERS.

treffen (Ger.) to meet.

treize (Fr.) thirteen.

Trengganu a country of about 5,050 square miles on the east coast of Malay Peninsula in southeast Asia. Capital: Kuala Trengganu. Issued stamps in 1910.

trennen (Ger.) to separate.

Trennung (Ger.) separation.

Trennungsart (Ger.) kind of separation.

Trennungslinie (Ger.) dividing line.

trente (Fr.) thirty.

trés beau (Fr.) very fine.

tres líneas (Sp.) three lines.

tresse (Fr.) a plait or braid-like design, sometimes used as decoration on the flaps of mid nineteenth-century envelopes.

trial or **trial printing** an essay or proof, an experimental procedure in postage stamp production.

trial colours Often before a postage stamp design is accepted, the stamps are prepared in proof form in the various colours. Such

Triptych

items are called trial colours, and may be prepared on either the actual paper for the issued stamps or on a type of proof paper.

triangles   (nick.) postage stamps printed in triangular format; originally the Cape of Good Hope issues, and finally any triangular-shaped stamps.

trident   a fork with three barbed prongs.

Trieste   (Free Territory of Trieste) a commercial seaport, with its surrounding area of about 285 square miles, at the head of the Adriatic Sea between Italy and Jugoslavia, established as a free territory by the United Nations in 1947, then divided between Italy and Jugoslavia in 1953. Stamps of Italy overprinted "A.M.G. F.T.T." were used in 1947-53 for Zone A. The Zone B

stamps were issued with various inscriptions, like "VUJA-STT", 1948-53.

Trinidad   an island in the Atlantic Ocean off the coast of Venezuela, ceded to Great Britain by the Treaty of Amiens in 1802; became part of the British colony of Trinidad and Tobago on Jan. 1, 1899, following an Order in Council in the previous year. Issued stamps 1851-1910. See TRINIDAD AND TOBAGO.

Trinidad and Tobago   since 1962, an independent state of about 1,980 square miles in the West Indies off the coast of Venezuela; formerly a British colony. Capital:

Port of Spain. The first stamps of Trinidad, in 1847, were locals known as the Lady McLeod stamps, and were issued by David Bryce, who owned the ship that carried mail to Port of Spain and San Fernando. Trinidad issued the first authorized stamps from 1851 to 1910, and became part of the British colony of Trinidad and Tobago in 1889. Tobago issued stamps in 1879-96. Combined colonial stamps were issued in 1913.

Trinité, Ile de la   (Fr.) Trinidad.

triple letter   See SINGLE, DOUBLE, AND TREBLE LETTERS.

triple transfer   In the steel-engraving process, occasionally the transfer press operator makes a third transfer of the design from the transfer roll to the postage stamp printing plate. When three sets of lines appear on the finished postage stamps, they indicate this third attempt at transferring the design.

Tripoli/di Barberia   (2-line ovpt.) appears on stamps of Italy for use by Italian offices in Tripoli, 1909.

Tripolis   (Ger.) Tripolitania.

Tripolitaine   (Fr.) Tripolitania.

Tripolitania   a province of about 350,000 square miles in north Africa; a former Italian colony now part of Libia. Capital: Tripoli. Various issues of Italian stamps were used, overprinted, in 1923-31; in 1926-34, inscribed stamps were issued. Stamps inscribed "Fiera Campionaria Tripoli" are listed with stamps of Libia in Scott's and with stamps of Tripolitania in Gibbons.

triptych   three postage stamps in one unit.

Tristan da Cunha   a group of islands of about 52 square miles between South America and the Cape of Good Hope; a dependency of St. Helena. Issued overprinted stamps of St. Helena in 1952, then inscribed issues in 1954. Previously, Tristan

had local stamps expressed in values of potatoes. A volcano erupted in 1961, forcing the people to leave the island, but many returned in 1963; they issued St. Helena stamps overprinted "TRISTAN DA CUNHA RE-SETTLEMENT, 1963".

Trockensiegel (Ger.) embossed seal.

trois (Fr.) three.

tropisch (Ger.) tropical.

trop tard (Fr.) too late.

trou (Fr.) hole.

Trucial States seven Arab sheikdoms on the Persian Gulf and Gulf of Oman, including Abu Dhabi, Ajman, Dubai, Fujairah, Ras al Khaimah, Sharjah and Dependencies, and Umm al Qaiwain. The Trucial States stamps went on sale in January 1961, but were declared invalid for postal use from Sept. 30, 1963. (Courtesy of G.P.O. London)

truncated postmark or **truncated cancel** a postmark with a portion of the shape cut off. Some postmarks formed of dots making a square had the bottom portion cut off to resemble a triangle; for example, the 1862 cancel of the ROPIT (Russian Company for Steam Navigation and Trade), agency in Jaffa with numerals 784 in the centre. Others had 785 for use in Alexandria, 782 for Alexandretta, 787 for Salonica, and 780 for Smyrna. Details are found in Parts One to Six of *Stamps of the Russian Empire Used Abroad*, by the British Society of Russian Philately, Publishers, in Bristol, England.

truquage (Fr.) faking.

Tschechoslowakei (Ger.) Czechoslovakia.

T.S. de C (Sp. ovpt.) Tribunal Superior de Cuentas, Superior Tribunal of Accounts. Appears on regular issue and airmail Honduras stamps of 1931.

tth in auction catalogues, means "tiny thinning".

t.t. one piece in auction catalogues, means "two tied to one piece".

TUC (insc.) Trades Union Congress; appears with a design on 1968 British stamps.

Tuerkei (Ger.) Turkey.

tuerkis (Ger.) turquoise.

tugrik a coin of Mongolia. 100 mung equal 1 tugrik.

Tullahoma, Tenn. This town in Tennessee issued postmasters' provisional envelopes in 1861 as part of the Confederate States of America.

Tumaco issue 1901 type-set stamps of Colombia made by subordinate postmasters who did not have authority to make them. They are listed with stamps of Colombia.

Tunisia a republic of about 48,300 square miles on the Mediterranean Sea in north Africa. Capital: Tunis. Stamps have been issued since 1888.

Tunisie (Fr.) Tunisia.

Tunis-Paeckchenmarke(n) (Ger.) Tunis package stamp(s).

tunn (Swed.) thin.

Tupfen (Ger.) spot, speckle.

Turkey a republic of about 295,116 square miles in southeast Europe and southwest Asia. Capital: Ankara. Stamps have been issued since 1863. Many issues have only Turkish inscriptions, but some bear the words "Emp. Ottoman" (Ottoman Empire) or "Postes Ottoman". The sultan's paraph, or signature, is the easiest means of distinguishing most Turkish stamps prior to 1923. In some issues the crescent and star

help to indicate Turkish stamps, while issues since 1926 bear the inscription "Turkiye". Octagonal military stamps with Turkish inscriptions were issued for the Turkish army in Thessaly.

Turkey postage-due stamps Turkey used regular issue stamps from 1863 to 1913. The 1914 and subsequent issues to 1926 included the French words "Chiffre Taxe". In 1926 postage-due stamps of Turkey were inscribed "Postalar Takse Pulu".

Turk, Iles de (Fr.) Turks Islands.

TURKIYE CUMHURIYETI POSTALARI (insc.) appears on stamps of Turkey.

TURKIYE POSTALARI (insc.) appears on stamps of Turkey.

TURK POSTALARI (insc.) appears on

stamps of Turkey.

Turks and Caicos Islands British Colony of about 166 square miles on south extremity of Bahamas in West Indies, former Jamaican Dependency. Capital: Grand Turk. Issued stamps in 1900.

Turks Islands a former dependency of Jamaica, of about 616 square miles at the southern extremity of the Bahamas in the West Indies; part of Turks and Caicos Islands, a British colony since 1848. Capital: Grand Turk. Issued postage stamps 1867-94. Combined issues for Turks and Caicos were introduced in 1900.

Turn und Sportfest (Ger.) gymnastics and sport festival.

Turquie (Fr.) Turkey.

Tuscaloosa, Ala. This town in Alabama issued postmasters' provisional envelopes in 1861 as part of the Confederate States of America.

Tuscany a former Lombard duchy, now a compartimento of central Italy; area about 8,890 square miles. Capital: Florence. Tuscany issued stamps 1851-9, then annexed to Sardinia in 1860.

tusche a type of India ink used for painting on stone or plate in the litho process.

Tuscumbia, Ala. This town in Alabama issued postmasters' provisional envelopes in 1861 as part of the Confederate States of America.

T.W.A. (airline) Trans World Airlines, Inc. Point of origin: United States.

tweezers or **tongs** a two-pronged device for grasping small objects, absolutely necessary in stamp collecting to handle stamps. Available at most stamp dealers' shops and offices.

twelve-penny black (nick.) the 1851 stamps of the Province of Canada (issued prior to Confederation). Despite the listings in stamp catalogues, these stamps were never printed on wove paper. This fact has been verified in about 1922 by George Lowe, who owned a stamp shop in Toronto, Ontario. It was also verified in later years by James N. Sissons, an internationally known auction specialist in stamps of British North America, and by Winthrop Boggs, author of *The Postage Stamps and Postal History of Canada*. The wove-paper claim may have originated with three proofs that Mr. Lowe owned of the three stamps of Canada issued in 1851. The 3-, 6- and 12-penny stamps were in black proofs on a single sheet of wove paper about four by seven inches in vertical format. The two proofs of 3-penny and 6-penny were made

with the impressions from the top left, the 6-penny in the middle and the space left open at the bottom right where a 12-penny proof had obviously been made but carefully cut out. The proof had not been gummed on the three sheets in Mr. Lowe's possession. (Few advanced collectors knew about these proofs, but Robert Lowe, son of George Lowe, verified the ownership and the facts stated above.) This proof sheet may have been the source of the 3-penny black, ungummed proof that has been a mystery for one hundred years. The late Dr. William Stericker, chemist and philatelic paper specialist, said that paper could miss the laid impressions at the sides of the sheets in the manufacturing processes. This could probably cause some 12-penny paper to resemble wove paper. See THREE-PENNY BLACK BEAVER.

twenty bet. 18/88 in auction catalogues, describes a lot containing stamps between two numbers from a postage stamp catalogue. Every stamp listed in the popular catalogues has a number. In this example the auctioneer is explaining that twenty stamps between the numbers 18 and 88 compose the lot.

20,000 Cruce/Linea Ecuatorial/PANAGRA/ 26-Julio-1951 (4-line ovpt.) appears on 1944 government palace-type airmails of Ecuador 3- and 5-sucre values, issued to mark the 20,000th crossing of the equator by aircraft of PANAGRA (Pan American Grace Airways).

two-colour press a two-cylinder press with two beds, which prints two colours on one side at the same feeding.

Two Pence (insc.) appears below a design of a throned queen on stamps of Victoria, Australia, 1852-4, with no country name.

Two Sicilies the island of Sicily and the lower half of the Apennine Peninsula, formerly a kingdom and now part of Italy. Capital: Naples. Naples issued stamps 1858-60, Sicily in 1859, and the Neapolitan provinces in 1861. Two Sicilies was annexed to Sardinia in 1860, and stamps were superseded by those of Italy in 1862.

tympan (Fr.) spandrel.

Type (Ger.) die.

type de surcharge (Fr.) type of overprint.

type-high a printing term meaning that other units in the form of materials, such as borders or designs, are as high as the type.

Typenerklaerung (Ger.) explanation of type.

Typensatz (Ger.) type setting or printing.

types small rectangular pieces of metal, having a letter or character set in relief at one end, used to reproduce the letter on paper by the printing process.

type-set in philately describes postage stamps or postal stationery produced by printers' type. Examples: early adhesive stamps of Hawaii, Fiji, and British Guiana, and scores of government-authorized postcards.

typewriter a desk machine for writing with type by pressing letters on a keyboard with the fingers; the impression is transferred to the paper by means of an inked ribbon.

typewritten stamps The Rev. E. Millar, a missionary in Uganda Protectorate, typed postage stamps in 1895; these are listed in stamp catalogues. During the British occupation of Long Island in the Aegean Sea in 1916, the British produced three types of stamps by typewriter; these are listed by Gibbons.

typographed inaccurate term for "letter-press-printed". Like the term "surface-printed", "typographed" has been used so long that any hope to correct it is futile.

typographie (Fr.) typography.

typography an inaccurate term for "letter-press printing".

U

U or **u**   used.

Ubangi-Shari or **Ubangi**   a former French colony in west Africa, now comprising Central African Republic. Stamps of Middle Congo were used at first, overprinted "OUBANGUI-CHARI-TCHAD", and later with the additional overprint or surcharge "AFRIQUE EQUATORIAL FRANÇAISE", 1915-27; these were superseded by stamps of French Equatorial Africa. Since 1959, stamps of the Central African Republic have been used.

U-Boot-Post   (Ger.) submarine mail. U-boat was a name given in 1916 to German submarines. German submarines carried mail to the United States during the First World War, but before the United States entered the conflict. See UNTERSEEBOOT-POST.

U.D.I.   Unilateral Declaration of Independence. Refers to the status of independent Rhodesia, as distinct from a negotiated status like that achieved by India and British colonies and possessions.

Ueberdruck   (Ger.) overprint.

Ueberdruckserie   (Ger.) overprint series.

uebereinander   (Ger.) one above the other; above one another.

Ueberschrift   (Ger.) title, inscription.

Uebersee   (Ger.) oversea, overseas.

Uebersetzung   (Ger.) translation.

Uebertrag   (Ger.) transfer.

UEPT   European Union of Posts and Telecommunications, established on Oct. 19, 1942 by Vienna Conference. Member countries were: Albania, Bulgaria, Croatia, Denmark, France, Germany, Hungary, Italy, the Netherlands, Norway, Romania, San Marino, and Czechoslovakia.

U G   appears typewritten with a numeral on thin laid paper for use in Uganda, 1895.

Uganda   an independent state of about 93,-981 square miles in east Africa; formerly a British protectorate comprised of Buganda and three provinces in the east, west, and north. Capital: Entebbe. The first stamps were typewritten by the Reverend Ernest Millar in 1895, the 1896 issue was typeset, and the 1898-1902 issue was inscribed. In 1902 overprinted stamps of British East Africa were used. Stamps of 1903-62 were inscribed "KENYA, UGANDA, TANGANYIKA". Stamps issued after October 9, 1962, were inscribed "Uganda".

U.H./10/Ctvs.   (sur.) appears on late-fee stamps of Ecuador, 1945.

UHURU   (insc.) freedom; appears on 1963 postage stamps of Zanzibar.

U.I.T.   (Fr.) L'Union Internationale des Télécommunications, for the International Telecommunications Union. The U.I.T. has been honoured on stamps by the United Nations in 1956 and by Vietnam in 1952.

U.J.A. issue   United Jewish Appeal stamps, a single commemorative issue of Israel on Dec. 26, 1962, to mark the twenty-fifth anniversary of the United Jewish Appeal in Canada and the United States and its work of supporting immigration and settlement in Israel.

Ukraine   a constituent republic of about 171,770 square miles in the U.S.S.R. on the north shore of the Black Sea. Capital: Kiev. Stamps in 1918-23 were those of Russia overprinted or those of Russian Offices in the Turkish Empire overprinted or surcharged; stamps of Soviet Russia were used since 1923.

UKRAINE   (ovpt.) appears in small type on stamps of Germany for use in the Ukraine, 1941-3.

Ukraine occidentale   (Fr.) West Ukraine.

U.K.T.T.   (partial ovpt.) United Kingdom Trust Territory; appears on Nigerian stamps of 1953 for use in Southern Cameroons, 1960-1.

ULTRAMAR   (Sp. insc. and ovpt.) overseas; appears inscribed with a year date on stamps of Cuba; also appears overprinted on Cuban stamps with manuscript devices for use in Puerto Rico, 1873-6; appears inscribed with values in avos or reis on stamps of Macao (Macau), 1910.

ultramarin   (Ger.) ultramarine.

ultra-violet rays   light rays shorter than violet rays in the spectrum, but invisible to the eye, used to detect the false documents or foreign matter in paper. Ultra-violet rays are also used to test fastness-to-light of inks and papers and to detect tagged stamps.

umbenannt   (Ger.) redesignated, renamed.

umgekehrt (Ger.) reversed.

Umlauf (Ger.) circulation.

UMM AL QIWAIN (insc.) appears on stamps of Umm al Qiwain, a shiekdom under British protection; formerly a trucial state in Arabia. Most of these stamps are unnecessary issues, and many are black-listed.

Umrandung (Ger.) frame, border.

Umrandungslinie (Ger.) frame line.

Umrechnungssatz (Ger.) rate of conversion, rate of exchange.

un (Fr.) one.

Un or **un** unused.

unbedeutend (Ger.) insignificant.

unbefugt (Ger.) unauthorized.

unbekannt (Ger.) unknown.

U.N.C.F. United Nations Children's Fund, formerly the United Nations International Children's Emergency Fund.

Undeliverable Mail Office the Canadian department formerly known as the Dead Letter Office.

underprinting designs, tints, words, or patterns that are printed on stamp paper before the stamp designs are printed, as a security measure. Burélage or moire patterns are examples of underprinting. Underprinting should not be confused with printing on the back of stamps.

Undersea Post Office a sea-floor post office located in the Sea Gardens off Nassau, the Bahamas, in a sphere of the undersea photosphere designed by John Williamson. It is illustrated on the 1965 5-shilling stamps of the Bahamas. The post office operated on Aug. 16, 1939, for the benefit of tourists, who had mail cancelled in an oval marking reading "SEA FLOOR/ Aug 16 1939/ Bahamas". The post office opened again on May 6, 1940, to mark the century of the first postage stamp, the penny black of Britain, and used a similar postmark. John Williamson experimented in undersea photography; an example of his work appears on the 4-penny stamps of 1938 in the Bahamas pictorial issues.

undulated heavy wavy lines.

UN ECAFE United Nations Economics Commission for Asia and the Far East.

UNEF United Nations Emergency Force. "UNEF 1957" appears four times in the marginal paper of each pane of fifty United Nations stamps issued April 8, 1957, to honour the UNEF.

UNEF (ovpt.) United Nations Emergency Force; appears on stamps of India in 1965 for use by the Indian United Nations Force in Gaza.

unemployment fund issues the postal tax stamps of Peru intended to raise money for unemployed people, 1931-6. Postal tax stamps must be used according to orders, but they do not pay postage charges.

unerforscht (Ger.) unexplored.

UNESCO United Nations Educational, Scientific, and Cultural Organization. The abbreviation has been used in inscriptions of various stamps, including the issues of Italy in 1950 and of the United States in 1955.

uneven margins In perforated stamps, these may be attributed to faulty alignment of the perforating machines in relation to the sheet of stamps. Perfect alignment pro-

duces stamps that have even margins on all sides. Imperforate stamps had to be cut from sheets or panes, but the same general conditions apply excepting imperforate stamps from the corners of sheets or sides had wide margins. Despite the uneven margins the value of such specimens is increased, either mint or used. Imperforate stamps with wide margins on any side are much scarcer than the stamps in the sheet or pane.

U.N. Force/(India)/Congo (3-line ovpt.) appears on stamps of India in January 1962 for use by Indian forces of the United Nations in the Congo.

U.N. Force W. Irian (ovpt.) appears in 1963 on stamps of Pakistan for use by the Pakistan United Nations Force in West Irian (West New Guinea), the western half of the island of New Guinea.

Ungarn (Ger.) Hungary.

ungebraucht (Ger.) unused.

ungefalzt (Ger.) unhinged.

ungenau (Ger.) inexact.

ungenuegend (Ger.) insufficient.

ungestempelt (Ger.) uncancelled.

ungezaehnt (Ger.) unperforated.

ungueltig (Ger.) not valid.

ungummed refers to stamps with no adhesive. They were frequently issued by tropical countries. China still issued stamps without gum in 1971.

ungummiert (Ger.) ungummed.

uni (Fr.) smooth.

UNIAO DOS ATIRADORES CIVIS (Port. insc.) appears on franchise stamps of Portugal for use by the civilian rifle clubs, 1899-1910.

UNICEF United Nations International Children's Emergency Fund. Appears on United Nations stamps of 1951, and on stamps of Austria, 1949.

unicorn a legendary beast with a horse's body and a single straight horn in the centre of its forehead.

UNIDO United Nations Industrial Development Organization. The U.N. Post Office issued 6- and 13-cent stamps on April 18, 1968, to honour UNIDO.

unified series stamps of Great Britain stamps used for both postage and inland revenue, with inscriptions to show their validity for either purpose, used mainly since 1881.

Union City, Tenn. This town in Tennessee issued postmasters' provisional envelopes in 1861 as part of the Confederate States of America.

Union de l'Afrique du sud (Fr.) Union of South Africa.

UNION/FRANCAISE (2-line insc.) appears on stamps of Laos, 1951 and other years.

Union Jack re-entry This occurs in the British 1-penny red stamp of 1847. A re-entry that was made in the stamp with letters L and K on plate 75, Die I, has the appearance of the British flag (the Union Jack). This is illustrated in the British section of Gibbons catalogues.

Union of South Africa (or South Africa) a former British Dominion established May 31, 1910, and comprised of the Cape of Good Hope, Natal, Transvaal, and the Orange Free State. The Union of South Africa became a republic in 1961. See SOUTH AFRICA.

UNION/PANAMERICANA (partial ovpt.) appears on regular-issue stamps of Guatemala for use as an airmail issue in 1940.

Union Post in New York City, New York, issued U.S. local stamps in 1846.

Union Postale (Fr.) postal union.

Union Square Post Office in New York City, New York, issued U.S. local stamps in 1852.

Uniontown, Ala. This town in Alabama issued postmasters' provisional stamps in 1861 as part of the Confederate States of America.

Unionville, S.C. This town in South Carolina issued postmasters' provisional stamps

in 1861 as part of the Confederate States of America.

unique stamp a stamp that is the only one of its kind known to exist. About 25 different world rarities are unique. The most famous is the British Guiana 1-cent magenta of 1856.

unissued stamps postal issues prepared but not placed on sale for a variety of reasons; for example: the Canadian stamp approved but not issued when King George VI died in February 1952; the 1-penny black stamps of Great Britain for official use, inscribed "V R" in the upper corner tablets, and never issued; and the 1-cent value for the Confederate States of America in 1862, which arrived after the postal rate had increased.

UNITAR United Nations Institute for Training and Research. Stamps were issued to honour this organization on Feb. 10, 1969, by the United Nations.

United Arab Republic a republic of about 386,198 square miles in northeast Africa and southwest Asia, formed by the union of Egypt and Syria in 1958. Capital: Cairo. Stamps were first issued in 1958.

United Nations Headquarters in New York City, issued adhesive postage stamps for the first time on Oct. 24, 1951. Five official languages appear on the stamps: English, French, Spanish, Russian, and Chinese.

United Nations Geneva Offices issued stamps in Swiss denominations for postal use at the Palais des Nations, Geneva, Switzerland. On Dec. 11, 1968, an agreement was signed in Geneva between Mr. Vittorio Winspeare-Guicciardi, Director-General of the United Nations Office at Geneva, and Mr. Vincente Tuason, President of the General Directorate of the Swiss Postal, Telephone and Telegraph Department (PTT), authorizing the issuance of United Nations postage stamps for all mail emanating from the Palais des Nations, the United Nations Office at Geneva. These stamps, which were introduced on Oct. 4, 1969, were similar to those valid for postage from the United Nations Post Office in New York, but their face values were in Swiss currency. (Courtesy of U.N. philatelic bulletin, 1969)

United Nations velvetones See VELVETONES.

United States 5-cent error in colour The United States issued 5-cent carmine colour stamps and rose colour stamps by error in the colours of the 2-cent stamps. Errors perforated 10 were issued on March 7, 1917 (Scott's no. 467). Collectors save either singles or the error in the centre of a block of nine (3 by 3) or two errors in a block of twelve in the middle of the blocks. The same mistakes took place in the imperforate 5-cent carmine stamps issued in March, 1917 (Scott's no. 485). A third time the mistakes were made, in the March 23, 1917, issue of 5-cent rose colour stamps in sheets of the normal 5-cent value perforated 11 (Scott's no. 505). Collectors seek all three varieties of the errors. See Scott's U.S. Specialized catalogue for details.

United States of America a federal republic in North America comprised of fifty states and the District of Columbia. Capital: Washington. Outlying possessions include Puerto Rico, Guam, American Samoa, Virgin Islands, and Panama Canal Zone. Declared independence from Great Britain on July 4, 1776. First adhesive stamps issued were 1842 carrier stamps for U.S. City Despatch Post authorized for use in New York City. Postmasters' provisional stamps came into use in 1845, mainly until the government issued postage stamps for the country on July 1, 1847.

United States of Indonesia See INDONESIA.

Universal Postal Union or **U.P.U.** an international organization formed to handle all subjects relating to the delivery and handling of mail and the related problems. The U.S. Post Office Department took the first steps to unite countries in co-operative postal work when Montgomery Blair, Postmaster General in President Lincoln's Cabinet, suggested that countries having diplomatic relations with the United States meet for discussion. The delegates met on May 11, 1863, in Paris, and agreed on a list of objectives for future action. The War between the States caused a delay in these activities for nearly ten years.

In September 1874, representatives of twenty-two countries met at Bern, Switzerland, in the hope of establishing a General Postal Union to bring an end to the high cost of international correspondence, the confusion of postal rates, and the uncertainty of mail delivery in other countries. The Postal Congress signed an International Postal Convention on October 9, 1874, and after it was ratified by the countries participating, the General Postal Union came into force on July 1, 1875. Three years later the organization changed its name to Universal Postal Union.

UNIVERSAL POSTAL UNION (insc.) appears on four stamps of Great Britain, with a portrait of King George VI but no country name, issued Oct. 10, 1949, to mark the seventy-fifth anniversary of the Universal Postal Union.

Universal Postal Union colours During the Washington convention of the U.P.U. in 1898, delegates decided to adopt certain colours to indicate postal rates. For example, in the United States and Canada 1-cent stamps were printed in green, 2-cent stamps in red or carmine, and 5-cent stamps in blue. Comparable rates in other countries had the same colours. At the Brussels convention in 1952 these regulations were abandoned.

unkenntlich (Ger.) unrecognizable.

Unkosten (Ger.) expenses.

UNKRA United Nations Korean Reconstruction Agency. Two 1955 sets of stamps mark Korea's industrial reconstruction.

unlisted stamps or **unlisted variety** Not all postage stamp varieties are listed in popular postage stamp catalogues. This does not indicate that the omitted stamp is a rarity or of great value.

unmittelbar (Ger.) immediate(ly).

unnecessary issue an issue that is not needed for postal use. Some collectors believe that most commemorative and special-issue stamps (wildlife stamps of Canada, for example) are not necessary. Most souvenir and some miniature sheets fall into the same class. Scott Publishing Co., New York, produce a small book *"For the Record"* filled with lists of unnecessary issues. It can save collectors money and give lasting advice.

UNO United Nations Organization. A number of countries have honoured various anniversaries of the United Nations and have inscribed "UNO" or "ONU" (the abbreviation for the French, Spanish, and Italian words for United Nations Organization) on their stamps.

unofficial city refers to the city in the cancellation of a first day cover that was cancelled on the correct date but not at the city designated by the post office department.

UNOGIL United Nations Observer Group in Lebanon. The abbreviation is inscribed on airletter sheets (aerogram) mailed from Beirut, Lebanon, in 1958.

unpaid letter stamp another name for postage-due stamp. The term is not always correct; for example, if a letter is short-paid, but has a stamp on it, it is partly paid, and the additional charge is postage due.

unperforated correct term for describing

postage stamps without perforations, although "imperforated" is frequently used.

unprinted lines on stamps These are the result of paper creases. Paper that is creased in the manufacturing process remains in place during the printing. When the stamps are soaked, or sometimes gently pulled apart, the unprinted lines may be seen.

unregelmaessig (Ger.) irregular.

UNRRA United Nations Relief and Rehabilitation Administration (discontinued). In 1944 and 1945 Haiti issued semi-postal stamps to raise funds for UNRRA. San Marino in 1946 and Honduras in 1953 issued stamps honouring UNRRA.

unsaubere Zaehnung (Ger.) rough perforation.

unsevered stamps stamps that are not separated; "unsevered" describes stamps on covers, a strip of stamps, or any other group of stamps not separated. The term is used most often in auction catalogues.

unsichtbar (Ger.) invisible.

UNSU United Nations Study Unit, of the American Topical Association, chartered by ATA on Sept. 10, 1963. This is not a United Nations agency.

UNSWS United Nations Social Welfare Seminar. The UNSWS for the Arab States was held Dec. 8-20, 1952, in Damascus, to implement programs in public health, maternal and child welfare, and similar matters. Syria issued four stamps of pictorial design overprinted in English and Arabic to mark the event.

un-tagged error in reference to United States stamps; the description of sheets of City Mail Delivery commemorative stamps that slipped through the Bureau of Engraving and Printing without being tagged. (Courtesy of Alfred G. Boerger)

UNTEA United Nations Temporary Executive Authority, created to mediate disputes and implement agreements between differing countries. The U.N. issued stamps inscribed "UNTEA" on Oct. 1, 1963. Netherlands New Guinea stamps were overprinted "UNTEA" when the U.N. took temporary control of the former colony, which was later named West Irian.

unten (Ger.) below, at bottom.

Unterabteilung (Ger.) subdivision.

Unterbrechung (Ger.) interruption, break.

unterbrochen (Ger.) broken, interrupted.

unterbrochene Zaehnung (Ger.) interrupted perforation.

Unterdruck (Ger.) burelage.

Unterrandaufdruck (Ger.) printing on lower margin.

Unterschied (Ger.) difference.

Unterschrift (Ger.) signature.

Unterseeboot-post (Ger.) submarine mail. Refers to the 1916 issues of the German Insurance Bank for use by commercial submarines of the German Ocean Shipping Line, for trade between Germany and the United States before the United States entered the First World War. The stamps were inscribed "German Insurance Bank, Berlin", and prepaid mail charges and paid for insurance. A second issue had a slightly revised design. Mail in the United States was delivered by post in plain envelopes or by messengers. (Courtesy of Dr. Frank Theubert)

ununterbrochen (Ger.) uninterrupted, continuous(ly).

unused describes a stamp that may be doubtful; usually without gum, and may have been used but not cancelled. Advanced philatelists frequently avoid the so-called unused stamps, and prefer mint or postally used stamps.

unverkaeuflich (Ger.) unmarketable, unsaleable.

unvollstaendig (Ger.) incomplete.

unwatermarked refers to a stamp without a watermark, although it may have come from a sheet with a sheet watermark.

unwesentlich (Ger.) unessential.

unwichtig (Ger.) unimportant.

UPAE (insc.) appears on Colombia commemorative stamps of Oct. 18, 1962, and on airmail stamps of the same day, issued to mark the fiftieth anniversary of the founding of the Postal Union of the Americas and Spain.

Upper Senegal and Niger former French colony in north west Africa, French Sudan since 1921, about 617,000 square miles. Capital: Bamako. Stamps of French colonial types inscribed "Senegal and Niger" were in use 1906-17; superseded in 1921 by stamps of French Sudan.

Upper Silesia a former province of Prussia, divided between Germany and Poland after a plebiscite in 1920. Plebiscite issues of stamps were used 1920-2.

Upper Volta (Fr. Haute Volta) republic north of Ghana in north west Africa, former French territory, about 113,000 square miles. Capital: Ouagadougou. Became a separate colony in 1919. Stamps issued 1920-33 were those of Upper Senegal and Niger overprinted and surcharged. From 1933-58 the country was divided with regions going to French Sudan, Ivory Coast and Niger Territory; it became a republic in 1958 and stamps were issued in 1959.

upplaga (Swed.) issue or edition.

UPU Universal Postal Union.

URGENCIA (Sp. insc. and ovpt.) appears on special-delivery stamps of Spain.

URGENTE (Sp. insc. and ovpt.) urgent; appears on special-delivery stamps of Spain.

Urkunde (Ger.) document.

Urkundenstempel (Ger.) documentary stamp.

urstempel (Ger.) die.

Uruguay a republic of about 72,153 square miles between Argentina and Brazil in South America. Capital: Montevideo. Issued stamps in 1856.

URUNDI (ovpt.) appears handstamped on stamps of Congo in 1916 during the Belgian occupation of German East Africa in the First World War. Other stamps were handstamped "RUANDA".

urval (Swed.) selection.

usado (Sp.) used.

usage provisoire (Fr.) provisional use.

usato (It.) used.

U.S. Automatic (nick.) the U.S. stamps privately perforated by the U.S. Automatic Vending Co. of New York City for use in their vending machines. Scott's U.S. Specialized stamp catalogue lists one endwise type with horizontal separations and one horizontal type with similar vertical slit and notch separations. A third type has vertical perforations and notches.

U.S.C.A.B. United States Civil Aeronautics Board.

usé (Fr.) worn.

used refers to a postage stamp or an item of postal stationery that has been postally used.

used abroad refers to postage stamps of one country authorized for use from another. Examples: the British stamps used from consular offices around the world. Refer to Gibbons stamp catalogues for detail.

used on cover refers to stamps used on original envelopes, wrappers, postcards, or labels clearly showing that the stamps were used.

Usküdar or **Scutari** a town in Turkey. Stamps of Italy surcharged "Scutari di Albania" were used, 1909-16.

U.S.P.O. United States Post Office.

U.S.P.O.D. United States Post Office Department. The abbreviation was used as a watermark in postal cards, 1873-5.

U.S.P.O. DESPATCH (insc.) appears on U.S. official 1851 issues of Carriers' stamps. The stamps paid delivery charges or a pick-up fee on letters going to the same city; they also paid the cost of delivery from one post office to another.

U.S.P.S. United States Postal Service; appears in U.S. watermarks, with usually one letter in each stamp of 1895-1910 and as single-line letters 1910-16 with one in each stamp.

U.S.T.C. (ovpt.) United States of Travancore-Cochin; appears on 1948 stamps of Cochin, for use in Travancore-Cochin, 1949.

Usual Tropical Stains in auction catalogues, refers to the brownish (or other colour) stains in postage stamps from tropical countries. For example, many mint sheets of stamps from Papua bear light brown stains varying in size.

utilisé à l'étranger (Fr.) used abroad.

UV short- or long-wave ultra-violet light.

V

V   appears as the design of the postal tax stamps of Cuba, 1942-4.

V   (insc.) appears in each corner of the 50-haleru personal delivery stamp of Czechoslovakia in 1937. The stamp is triangular and blue, and postage was prepaid by the sender. See D.

vagabond post   the service of private carriers who took mail with them as a favour or for a fee lower than the post office charged. These carriers, mainly travellers, carried so much mail in colonial America that they caused a reduction in postal revenues.

Valdosta, Ga.   This town in Georgia issued postmasters' provisional envelopes in 1861 as part of the Confederate States of America.

vale   (Sp. ovpt.) appears on various stamps of South American countries to indicate a surcharge.

Vale correo de 1911   (Sp. sur.) appears with new value on the back of Nicaragua revenue stamps used for postage in 1911.

valeur   (Fr.) value, denomination.

valeur supplémentaire   (Fr.) supplementary value.

Valevolle/per le stampe   (It. sur.) appears on Italy parcel post stamps of 1884-6 for regular issue stamps of 1890 to prepay printed matter.

Vallees D'Andorre   (insc.) appears on stamps of Andorra under French administration.

Valmy   (sur.) appears with new values on stamps of Cameroun for use as semi-postal stamps, 1943.

Valona or Vlona   a seaport town in southwest Albania on the Bay of Vlona; under Turkish rule until 1912, when Albanian independence was declared; under Italian occupation, 1914-20.

VALONA   (sur.) appears on Italian stamps for use in Valona, 1909-16.

Valore globale   (ovpt.) appears with new values on 1919 semi-postal stamps of Fiume for use as regular postage stamps, 1919-20.

valor suplementar   (Port.) supplementary value.

valor suplementario   (Sp.) supplementary value.

VALPARAISO MULTADA   (insc.) appears on 1894 postage-due stamps of Chile.

valuation of stamps   See APPRAISALS.

value   the denomination printed or surcharged on a postage stamp or an item of postal stationery.

value tablet   generally refers to a key-type stamp or a stamp with the value in a tablet type of design. Not all stamps have the value separate from the vignette.

Vancouver Island   part of the province of British Columbia on the west coast of Canada. Issued stamps from 1865 until British Columbia confederated with Canada in 1871.

Van Diemen's Land   See TASMANIA.

VAN DIEMEN'S LAND   (insc.) appears on stamps of Van Diemen's Land (now Tasmania), 1851-8.

vanlig   (Swed.) common.

vänster   (Swed.) left.

variedad   (Sp.) variety.

variedad de color   (Sp.) colour variety.

variedad de impresión   (Sp.) printing variety.

variedade   (Port.) variety.

variedade de cor   (Port.) colour variety.

variedade de impressão   (Port.) printing variety.

varietà   (It.) variety.

variété   (Fr.) variety.

variété de couleur   (Fr.) colour variety.

variété de planche   (Fr.) plate variety.

variété d'impression   (Fr.) printing variety.

variety   a stamp with some characteristic different from the normal state of the stamp.

V.A.R.I.G.   (airline) Viacão Aérea Rio Grandense, now S.A. Empresa de Viacão Aérea Rio Grandense. Point of origin: Brazil.

varnish bars   overprinted bars of varnish applied to the face of a stamp to help prevent the removal of a cancel.

Vasco de Gama types   1898 issue of Portugal and certain Portuguese colonies to mark the 400th anniversary of Vasco de Gama's discovery of the sea route to India.

V.A.S.P.   (airline) Viacão Aérea São Paulo. Point of origin: Brazil.

Vathy   (ovpt. and sur.) appears on French stamps for use by French offices in Vathy

Turkey, 1894-1900.

Vaticana (insc.) appears on Vatican City airmail stamps.

Vatican City an independent papal state of about 108.7 acres within the commune of Rome, Italy. Stamps have been issued since 1929.

Vaticane (insc.) appears on stamps of Vatican City.

vattenmärke (Swed.) watermark.

veck (Swed.) grease.

velletjes speciale (Dutch) souvenir sheets, miniature sheets.

velvetones a kind of picture postcard illustrating a postage stamp in its nearly complete design, mailed with a stamp of the same denomination and design cancelled on the face side, and another stamp on the back to prepay the postal charges. E. P. Haworth, a collector who lived in the United States, revived the use of velvetones in the United States and was instrumental in having all the U.N. stamps of the first issue and a score or more of the U.S. commemorative stamps made into velvetones and used on the first days of the issues. The Universal Postal Union stopped the use of velvetones, claiming that it was contrary to some U.P.U. regulations.

vending machine perforations special perforations in postage stamps made for sale in vending or affixing machines. Stamp catalogues list the vending machine perforations.

vending machine stamps See COIL STAMPS.

Venezia Giulia or **Venezia Tridentina** (ovpt.) appears on Italian or Austrian stamps for use in Austria, under Italian occupation, 1918.

venezolano See BOLÍVAR.

Venezuela a republic of about 352,143 square miles on the north coast of South America. Capital: Caracas. Issued stamps in 1859.

vente (Fr.) appears in press releases to indicate the day, also sometimes the location, of a postage stamp issue.

veraendert (Ger.) changed.

Verantwortung (Ger.) responsibility.

verbinden (Ger.) to connect.

Verbindung (Ger.) connection.

verblichen (Ger.) faded.

verbrannt (Ger.) burnt.

verbraucht (Ger.) used up.

verbunden (Ger.) connected.

verde (Sp. and It.) green.

verderben (Ger.) to spoil.

verdickt (Ger.) thickened.

verduennt (Ger.) thinned.

Verein (Ger.) club, association, union.

Vereinigtes Europa (Ger.) United Europe.

Vereinigte Staaten von Amerika (Ger.) United States of America.

vereinzelt (Ger.) isolated cases, sporadic.

verfaelscht (Ger.) falsified.

Verfaelschung (Ger.) falsification.

Verfahren (Ger.) method, process.

Verfassung (Ger.) constitution; condition.

vergato (It.) laid.

vergleichen (Ger.) to compare.

vergriffen (Ger.) sold out.

vergroessern (Ger.) to enlarge, magnify.

Vergroesserungsglas (Ger.) magnifying glass.

Verhaeltnis (Ger.) proportion.

verhaeltnismaessig (Ger.) relative(ly).

Verkauf (Ger.) sale.

Verkaufspreis (Ger.) sales price, selling price.

verkehrt (Ger.) reversed, inverted.

verkehrter Ueberdruck (Ger.) inverted overprint.

vernichtet (Ger.) destroyed.

Verschlussmarke (Ger.) label.

Verspätungsmarke (Ger.) too-late stamp.

Versteigerung (Ger.) auction.

Versteigerungsbedingungen (Ger.) condition of sale, regulation, rules of auction.

Versuch (Ger.) trial, experiment, test.

Versuchsdruck (Ger.) trial printing.

Versuchszaehnung (Ger.) trial perforation.

vert (Fr.) green.

Vert Crease L refers to a stamp with a vertical crease on the left side.

verteilen (Ger.) to distribute.

verteilt (Ger.) distributed.

vergé (Fr.) laid (paper).

verge (Port.) laid (paper).

vertical block a group of five or more stamps arranged vertically.

vertical half a bisected postage stamp cut in half from top to bottom, with each portion used as a single stamp.

Vertrag (Ger.) treaty, contract, agreement.

vervalsingen (Dutch) to forge or counterfeit.

Vervelle tête bêche stamps the 1-franc orange-vermilion stamps of France, 1849. Ernest Vervelle, a French stamp dealer, bought the unissued sheet of stamps from the estate of the printer of the stamps, Anatole Hulot.

Verwaltung (Ger.) administration.

Verwaltungsbezirk (Ger.) administrative district.

verwaschen (Ger.) blurred.

verwenden (Ger.) to use.

verwischt (Ger.) blurred.

Verzierung (Ger.) ornament.

VF in auction catalogues, means "very fine",

above average for the stamp in question.

V.G. very good.

V.G. Appear refers to a stamp that has faults, but has a very good appearance.

Vichy stamps (nick.) stamps of France and some French colonies issued during the Second World War, many of which portrayed Marshal Pétain.

VICTORIA (insc.) appears on postal tax stamps of Cuba, 1942-4.

Victoria former British Colony of about 87,884 square miles in south east part of Australia. One of 6 colonies uniting in 1901 to form Commonwealth of Australia. Capital: Melbourne. Issued stamps in 1850.

Victoria Land a section of Antarctica on the shore of Ross Sea and Ross Shelf Ice mainly included in the Ross Dependency. In 1911, during the expedition led by Robert Falcon Scott, New Zealand authorized the overprinting of the words "Victoria Land" on stamps of 1906. These are listed by Gibbons with stamps of New Zealand.

Victoria, Texas issued postmasters' provisional stamps in 1861 as part of the Confederate States of America.

Victorian key-types British colonial stamps designed by De La Rue from two different dies, portraying Queen Victoria. See illustrations in stamp catalogues.

Victories (nick.) peace commemorative stamps, mainly from the British Commonwealth, to mark the end of the Second World War. Belgium, France, the Netherlands, and the U.S. Post Office were among other authorities that issued peace or victory stamps after the war.

vielfach (Ger.) multiple.

vielfarbig (Ger.) multi-colour.

vier (Ger.) four.

Viereck (Ger.) square.

viereckig (Ger.) quadrangular.

viereckig geschnitten (Ger.) quadrangular cut.

Viererblock (Ger.) block of four.

Viererstreifen (Ger.) strip of four.

Viertel (Ger.) quarter.

vierzig (Ger.) forty.

Vietnam a former kingdom of about 123,-940 square miles in eastern Indochina, now divided into the two republics of North Vietnam and South Vietnam. Capital of the kingdom: Saigon. Stamps have been issued since 1951.

VIEZCA (ovpt.) appears on 5-centavos stamps of Mexico in 1914, for use as a revolutionary provisional in Viezca.

vif (Fr.) bright, intensive, vivid.

vignette (1) a typographic ornament or il-

lustration; the name derives from early Roman manuscripts, which were decorated with designs of vine leaves; (2) in postage

Vignette within frame on stamp of Lombardy-Venetia

stamps, the central part of the design, often within a frame.

vignette plate In printing stamps with two or more plates, the vignette plate or plates print the main part of the design, which is usually a portrait or landscape. These plates also called key plates.

vilayet one of the chief administrative divisions of Turkey.

Villa overprint (nick.) a monogram of Francisco Villa (or Pancho), on stamps of Mexico in 1914. See catalogues.

Vineta stamps vertical bisects of the 5-pfennig stamps of Germany, 1899-1900. When the stamps were in short supply on the German cruiser *Vineta* on April 13, 1901, they were bisected and each half surcharged "3 PF" by handstamp in bold-face type.

vingt (Fr.) twenty.

violett (Ger.) violet.

violettblau (Ger.) violet-blue.

violettbraun (Ger.) violet-brown.

violettgrau (Ger.) violet-grey.

violettpurpur (Ger.) violet-purple.

violettschiefer (Ger.) violet-slate.

violetteschwarz (Ger.) violet-black.

Virgin Islands (British) a British colony of about 59 square miles southeast of Puerto Rico in the West Indies. Capital: Road Town, Tortola. Issued stamps in 1866.

Virgin Islands (U.S.) formerly the Danish West Indies, now a U.S. territory comprised of approximately fifty islets totalling about 133 square miles. Capital: Charlotte Amalie. As Danish West Indies, stamps were issued 1855-1917; since 1917 stamps of the United States were used.

virgule (Fr.) comma.

visible au dos (Fr.) visible on the back.

Vi Vil Vinne (insc.) We will win; appears on the 20-ore stamps of Norway, 1943, issued by the exiled government of Norway in London, England, and used on mail posted at sea on Norwegian ships and in some camps in Great Britain.

viz. abbreviation of the Latin adverb, "videlicet", meaning "namely" or "it is clear"; usually used to indicate that examples follow.

vliegtuig (Dutch) plane, airplane, aeroplane.

Vlona See VALONA.

Voelkerbund (Ger.) League of Nations.

VOJENSKA POSTA (partial insc.) appears on 1919 stamps of the Czechoslovak Legion Post in Siberia, for use during the transit of the Czech force across Siberia after the Bolshevik Revolution.

Vojna Uprava / Jugoslavenske / Armije / appears with obliterating bars and new values on stamps of Jugoslavia for postage-due use in Venezia Giulia and Istria in 1947, authorized by the Jugoslav Occupation forces during the period of Jugoslav Military Government.

vol (Fr.) flight.

volk (Ger.) people, nation.

VOLKSDIENST (Ger. insc.) appears on semi-postal stamps of The Netherlands 1944, issued with a surtax for social service use.

Volksrust a town in South Transvaal on the Natal border in the Drakensberg mountains. In March 1902, Transvaal revenue stamps of an earlier period were overprinted "V.I.R.", (Victoria Regina Imperatrix, Latin for Queen Victoria, Empress). The stamps were authorized for use as postage, and are listed with stamps of Transvaal.

Volkstaat Bayern (Ger.) the people's state of Bavaria.

Volkstrachten (Ger.) native costumes.

Volkswohlfahrt (Ger.) public welfare.

vollkommen (Ger.) perfect(ly).

vollrandig (Ger.) full margin.

vollstaendig (Ger.) complete.

VOM EMPFANGER EINZUZIEHEN (Ger. insc.) collect from the receiver; appears with a coat of arms but no country name on postage-due stamps of Danzig, 1921-2.

Vom Empfänger Zahlbar (Ger. insc.) appears on postage-due stamps of Bavaria, 1862-76, and on Danzig issues, 1929-39.

Voor Het Kind (Dutch insc.) For the Child;

appears on Netherlands semi-postal or charity stamps with surtax to raise money for child welfare.

Voortrekker (Afrikaans) one of the original immigrants into the Transvaal. The word derives from the Dutch words "voor" (before) and "trekken" (trek). Voortrekkers are depicted on certain stamps of South Africa.

Vorausabstempelung (Ger.) pen-cancel.

voraus or **im voraus** (Ger.) in advance.

vorderseitig (Ger.) on the face or front side.

vorhanden (Ger.) existing.

vorhergehend (Ger.) previous.

Vorkriegsausgabe (Ger.) pre-war issue.

Vorlaeufer (Ger.) forerunner.

vorlaeufig (Ger.) temporary or provisional; refers to provisional postage stamps.

Vorlagestueck (Ger.) submission copy, specimen.

Vorschrift (Ger.) regulations.

Vorsicht (Ger.) caution.

VOX HIBERNIAE (Lat. insc.) voice of Ireland; appears on 1948-65 airmail stamps of Ireland.

VRI Victoria Regina Imperatrix, meaning Victoria, Queen and Empress. Refers to Victoria, Queen of England, 1837-1901.

V.R./ SPECIAL/ POST (vertical ovpt.) appears on 1895-6 stamps of Transvaal for use in Cape of Good Hope.

V.R./Transvaal (ovpt.) appears on stamps of the South African Republic, 1877-9, during the first British occupation of the republic.

Vryburg a town in Cape Province on a tributary of the Vaal River, occupied by the Boers during the Boer War. In 1899 the Boers surcharged some Cape of Good Hope stamps with the letters "Z.A.R." (South African Republic) and new values. These are listed with Cape of Good Hope stamps.

vuelo inaugural (Sp.) inaugural or first flight. The words occur in cachets of Mexico and other countries.

VUJA/STT (ovpt.) appears on stamps of Jugoslavia, 1945-50, for use in Trieste by the Jugoslav military government.

V VIA AEREA (part of insc.) appears on airmail stamps of Paraguay, 1929-31.

W

W. in auction catalogues, indicates a whole-sale lot.

waagerecht (Ger.) horizontal.

waagerechtes Paar (Ger.) horizontal pair.

Wadwhan a feudatory native state of India of 242 square miles. Capital: Wadwhan. Issued stamps in 1888.

Waffeln (Ger.) meshes.

Wales and Monmouthshire combined region stamps one of the regional issues by Great Britain in 1958. Other regionals include: Northern Ireland, Guernsey, Isle of Man, and Scotland. The stamps resemble other British issues but have their own heraldic emblems.

Wallis and Futuna Islands a French colony of about 100 square miles in the southwest Pacific Ocean. Chief towns: Mata Utu, Wallis Island, and Sigavé, Futuna Island. Stamps of New Caledonia, overprinted and surcharged since 1920 and inscribed since 1944, have been issued.

wallpaper covers During the American Civil War, paper became so scarce in parts of the South that some people made envelopes from wallpaper. These are scarce items.

Walterborough, S.C. This town in South Carolina issued postmasters' provisional envelopes in 1861 as part of the Confederate States of America.

Walton & Co.'s City Express in Brooklyn, New York, issued U.S. local stamps in 1846.

Walzendruck (Ger.) rotary printing.

wandering killers cancellations used in more than one post office, but all of the same numeral design. W. T. F. Castle refers to these cancellations in his book *Cyprus.* Larnaca, Cyprus, had six number 942 cancellers. It is probable that some of these cancellers were moved around the country when they were no longer needed at Larnaca. See WANDERSTEMPELS.

wanderstempels (Ger.) wandering postmarks. In 1895 and following years, the postal system of German Southwest Africa expanded so fast that new post offices opened before individual cancellation devices could be delivered from Germany. Postal men cancelled the stamps, then wrote or struck the post office name on the stamps. Sometimes they used pen and ink writing as cancels.

want list a list of a collector's needs sent to a dealer or pen-pal.

Wappen (Ger.) coat of arms.

WAR (ovpt.) appears 1916-7 stamps of British Honduras, for use as war tax stamps.

WAR/CHARITY/3.6.18. (3-line ovpt.) appears on January 1919 semi-postal stamps of Bahamas. The stamps were to be issued in June 1918, but were delayed until the following January.

War Dept. (insc.) appears on U.S. official stamps of 1873 for use by the War Department.

war effort stamps (nick.) stamps issued during wartime to show participation. Many countries issued stamps of patriotic designs, for example: the U.S. National Defence issue and the Overrun Countries issue; the Canadian wartime stamps of 1942-3; the four Australian stamps portraying three servicemen and a nurse; the two South African series, one in large format and the other about half-size but in the same basic designs.

Warrenton, Ga. This town in Georgia issued postmasters' provisional envelopes in 1861 as part of the Confederate States of America.

Warsaw issue stamps of the Warsaw local post that were not issued and that were surcharged in 1918 for use in the Polish territory occupied by Germany.

war tax stamps postage stamps that include a tax but were used as postage. Examples: Canadian stamps inscribed "WAR TAX" or "1T¢", 1915-16; many British colonies stamps overprinted "War", "War Tax", or "War Stamp", some with surcharges during the First World War; Spanish stamps inscribed "IMP^TO DE GUERRA 1874".

Wasserfarbe (Ger.) water-colour.

Wasserzeichen (Ger.) watermark.

Wasserzeichenabart (Ger.) watermark variety.

Wasserzeichen liegend (Ger.) watermak sideways.

Wasserzeichensucher (Ger.) watermark detector.

Waterlow paper   postage stamp paper made to the specifications of the security printers Waterlow and Sons, London. The 1898 pictorial issue of New Zealand was printed on thick, soft paper referred to as Waterlow paper.

watermark   an impression in the paper substance made by the devices on a dandy roll during the manufacturing process. Designs consist of figures, letters, leaves, fruit, animals, heraldic emblems, or a combination of these items. The first adhesive postage stamps in the world, the British 1- and 2-pence stamps of May 6, 1840, were watermarked with a small crown in each stamp. The watermarks are a security measure against forgery.

watermark bits   metallic devices attached to dandy rolls on paper-making machines. The bits impress the watermark designs in paper.

watermark dandy   dandy roll with a raised pattern that leaves an impression on the top surface of the wet web of paper.

watermark detector   usually a small black tray measuring two by three inches. A stamp placed on the tray reveals any existing watermarks when a few drops of benzine, white gasoline, or carbon tetrachloride is put on it. An electric watermark detector is a little plastic box with a hinged lid. Each box of the Philatector brand has five coloured filters in a disc in the lid. When a stamp is inserted in a slot and a light is turned on, the watermark can be seen under the proper colour in the disc. Watermark detectors also help distinguish types of papers, repairs, flaws, and fakes. They can be bought from stamp dealers.

watermarked paper   paper containing designs, numerals, letters, or any trademarks of the papermakers impressed in the paper substance when it is made.

watermark error   a mistake in a watermark in postage stamp paper, caused by the use of the wrong bits, or by the use of the wrong paper. This is not to be confused with various positions of watermarks, such as the doubled Cape of Good Hope inverts.

watermark rings   In cheaper grades of paper, the watermark is produced by means of rubber rings with raised designs. The watermark rings do not give as clear a watermark as the watermark dandy used on more expensive papers. See IMPRESSED WATERMARK; RUBBER RINGS.

watermark sideways or **watermark sidewise**   For the sake of economy or because of a problem in the security printers' plants, some postage stamps made for rolls are printed in such a way that the watermarks appear sideways, vertically instead of horizontally. Watermarks sideways may also occur if watermarked paper is placed into the printing machine on the side of the sheets, and not on the end as it should be to produce horizontal watermarks.

watermark stitch   See STITCH WATERMARKS.

watermerk   (Dutch) watermark.

way letter   Before Canadian Confederation in 1867, a regulation in New Brunswick and Nova Scotia required mail carriers on coach roads to accept letters for mailing when these were offered to the drivers at a distance of one or two miles, and not less, from the nearest post office. Couriers were instructed to place such letters in a locked leather pouch especially provided for the purpose, and to post them at the first post office, where the postmaster was instructed

to stamp them with the words "way letter". Later the postmark was used as an obliterator to cancel Canadian stamps.

Wayzatas   (nick.) the 1932 labels proposed

Wayzata: label for use between Wayzata, Minnesota, and Europe via Newfoundland

for use between Wayzata, Minnesota, and Europe, but never issued. Aerial World Tours of Minneapolis, Minnesota, planned to promote the first trans-Atlantic flight by an amphibian plane to carry mail and passengers, with the cost of the flight to be paid by airmail stamps, but the venture was halted.

WCAL (insc.) appears with a map of the world on stamps of Nationalist China (Formosa) issued on Sept. 25, 1967, to mark the First World Anti-Communist League Conference, held in Taipei.

Weatherford, Texas issued postmasters' provisional envelopes in 1861 as part of the Confederate States of America.

web-fed press a rotary press, such as postage stamp printing presses or newspaper presses, that use web rolls as compared to presses that print on sheets of paper.

web paper paper in continuous ribbon or rolls, not cut in sheets before it is printed and converted. Many U.S., Canadian, and British modern issues of postage stamps are printed from web paper.

Wedgwood £1 booklet a booklet of British postage stamps in low values, ½-, 2½-, and 3-penny, issued on May 24, 1972. Stamps feature the bas-relief portrait in Jasper ware (a kind of highly decorative ceramic vases, bowls, and other artistic works bearing unique figures in white on a Wedgwood-blue background) of Queen Elizabeth II, modelled by Arnold Machin. The stamps are known as the Machin types or designs, or merely the Machins of Great Britain.

Weimar Issue a German semi-postal issue of 1919. The stamps were surcharged "Furkriegs/besachadigte" (German, meaning "for war victims") and new values.

weiss (Ger.) white.

Weissrussland (Ger.) White Russia.

weit (Ger.) wide, far.

weldadigheidszegel (Dutch) charity stamp.

well centred refers to postage stamps with designs placed on the paper so that there are margins of equal width on all sides.

Wellenlinie (Ger.) wavy line.

Wells, Fargo & Co. an express company formed in 1852 by Henry Wells and William George Fargo for mail service between New York and California. In the spring of 1861, Wells, Fargo & Co. became agents for Russell, Majors and Waddell, the operators of the famous Pony Express that carried mail between St. Joseph, Missouri, and Sacramento, California, a distance of more than 1,960 miles. Wells, Fargo & Co. co-operated with the U.S.

Post Office to deliver mail to the new mining communities in the West. The company printed their name on U.S. postal stationery that had been made with 3, 6, 8, 10 and 18-cent stamps. The company paid full price for the envelopes they used for the prepayment of Pony Express mail charges on both letters and newspapers. This service continued until October, 1861, when the cross-country telegraph was completed and the Pony Express service between Missouri and California ended. Wells, Fargo & Co. continued to carry mail from New York to California, mainly to San Francisco, under a U.S. Post Office contract, until July 1, 1864. The company also carried mail on the West Coast as far north as British Columbia, the British Colony on the Pacific Ocean. During the years of mail delivery services, Wells, Fargo issued their own adhesive postage stamps as well as the stamped envelopes. The postage stamps and newspaper stamps were sold from 1861 to 1876. When the U.S. Post Office contract ended the company issues became obsolete. Fargo, North Dakota was named for William George Fargo.

Weltpostbuero (Ger.) Office of Universal Postal Union.

Weltpostverein (Ger.) Universal Postal Union.

Wenden a district in the province of Livonia annexed to Russia from Sweden in 1721, and divided between Latvia and Estonia after the First World War. According to some catalogues the first stamps were issued in 1862, but Gibbons states that the 1862 stamps in a circular design were merely essays, and that the first authorized postage stamps appeared in 1863 in a rectangular format.

WENDENsche KREIS BRIEF POST (Ger. insc.) appears on 1862 stamp of Wenden, classified by Gibbons as an essay. See WENDEN.

Werbeausgabe (Ger.) propaganda issue.

Wertangabe (Ger.) declaration of value, indication of value.

Wertaufdruck (Ger.) overprinted value.

Wertziffer (Ger.) numeral of value.

WESAK (insc.) appears on 1969 stamps of Ceylon. On the full moon day of the month of Wesak (May) Buddhists commemorate three great events – the Birth, Enlightenment, and Passing Away of the Buddha.

West-Berlin (Ger.) Berlin Western Sector.

Western Australia a former British colony of about 975,920 square miles in West Australia; one of six colonies uniting in 1901 to form the Commonwealth of Australia. Capital: Perth. Issued stamps in 1854.

Western Samoa an independent state of about 1,130 square miles in an archipelago east of Fiji in the South Pacific. Capital: Apia. See SAMOA.

Western Ukraine a former republic in east-central Europe taken over by Poland. Austrian stamps were used, surcharged, in 1918-19 under a short-lived provisional government.

Westervelt's Post in Chester, New York, issued U.S. local stamps and envelopes in 1863-5.

West Indies Federation a short-lived union formed in April 1958 by all British West Indies except the Virgin Islands and the Bahamas.

West Indies Federation (The) (insc.) appears on 1958 stamps of Antigua, Dominica, and St. Christopher-Nevis-Anguilla.

West Irian See WEST NEW GUINEA.

West New Guinea or **West Irian** a territory under Indonesian administration, comprising the greater part of the Vogelkop Peninsula and the west coastal region of New Guinea Island southeast of McCluer Gulf as far as Kaukenau. Formerly Dutch New Guinea, it was a region under U.N. Temporary Executive Authority from Oct. 1, 1962, until May 1, 1963. First stamps in 1962 were of Dutch New Guinea, overprinted "UNTEA". The 1963 issue was overprinted and surcharged "IRIAN BARAT" with new values on various issues of Indonesia. The subsequent stamps were inscribed "REPUBLIK INDONESIA".

Westtown, Pa. This town in Pennsylvania issued U.S. local stamps in 1853-70.

wet printing describes postage stamps printed on moistened paper. When the paper dries the stamps shrink to some degree, but not to a uniform size.

WFC World Forestry Congress. Meetings of the WFC have been commemorated by several postal issues: the third congress by Finland in 1949; the fourth congress by Persia (Iran) and India in 1954. The United Nations employed meter stamps, Dec. 11-22, 1954, that announced the sixth World Forestry Congress.

WFUNA (insc.) World Federation (of) United Nations Associations; appears on United Nations stamps of Jan. 31, 1966.

Wheatley Bond paper a brand name of bond paper used for some of the Argentine official postage stamps of 1918. The watermark "Wheatley Bond" was impressed in the paper.

white backs Some postage stamps have been printed on surface-coloured paper. The backs of these stamps were not printed in colours, and therefore they remained the natural colour of the paper. Collectors call these stamps white backs.

White Russia a former region of eastern Europe of indefinite boundaries, inhabited by the White Russians. Stamps said to be from White Russia were probably bogus labels, according to Scott's catalogue.

Whiting, Charles a British designer who submitted more than 100 designs of elaborate mechanically engraved patterns for the first British postage stamps of 1840. None were accepted but he received a £100 award for the Treasury competition.

Whittelsey's Express in Chicago, Illinois, issued U.S. local stamps in 1857-8.

WH Lot wholesale lot, consisting of more than one stamp of a type.

WHO World Health Organization. The WHO was founded in 1948 and assumed the activities of the U.N. Relief and Rehabilitation Organization. The WHO provides advisory and technical services to "forward the attainment by all people of the highest possible level of health". Assistance is given, on an advisory level, to help countries fight disease; while practical work is carried out in such fields as biological standardization, unification of pharmacopoeias, "early morning" service on epidemics, medical research, and publication of works of a scientific and technical nature. A special field of WHO activities is maternity and child care. (Courtesy of Crown Agents Stamp Bureau)

whole world collection or **worldwide collection** a collection of stamps from all parts of the world, in contrast to a specialized collection of one country, region, or a single type of stamp.

W.H.W. (sur.) appears with new values on regular-issue stamps of Danzig for use as semi-postal stamps for winter help.

Wiggins, Teape paper a general name for various postage stamp papers made by the companies that formed Wiggins, Teape and Company (1919), Limited. The company, located in London, has numerous subsidiaries in the British Commonwealth and in Argentina.

Williams' City Post in Cincinnati, Ohio, issued U.S. local stamps in 1854. These are listed in Scott's United States Specialized catalogue as carrier stamps.

Wilson, Sir John M. H., Bart, K.C.V.O. a Fellow of the Royal Philatelic Society,

Wing margins (left and right)

Winchester paper, with an engraved airmail stamp of Venezuela, 1932

London, and served as its president 1934-40, and as chairman of the Expert Committee since 1926; an Honorary Member for life. On his 1938 appointment as Curator of the Royal Collection, Sir John sold his British Colonial collection and some foreign sections as well. He is the author of *The Royal Philatelic Collection*, said to be the finest philatelic book ever published.

Winchester paper a brand name of security paper made with a decorative surface of semicircles printed in greyish blue, row on row. The name "Winchester Security Paper" appears in a thromboid. The surface prevents the postage stamps from being cleaned and used a second time. Venezuela airmail stamps of 1932 were printed on Winchester paper.

winged wheel watermarks three types of watermarks with the design of a wing projecting from a wheel, used in Italian stamps from May 1945 to January 1955. These watermarks are known in eight different positions. Refer to *I Francobolli Dello Stato Italiano*, the Italian government book.

wing margins British postage stamps with one wide margin on either left or right side.

Wings For Norway (insc.) appears in 1946 on a single stamp issue of Norway as a reminder of the training centre in Canada where Norwegian pilots received training during the Second World War. An additional inscription reads: "Little Norway/Toronto, Muskoka". Muskoka is a summer resort area just north of Toronto, Ontario. The stamps are listed with Norway regular-issue stamps in catalogues.

Winnsborough, S.C. This town in South Carolina issued postmasters' provisional

envelopes in 1861 as part of the Confederate States of America.

Winterhilfe (Ger.) winter relief.

Winterhilfswerk (Ger. insc.) appears on German semi-postal stamps with a surtax to help needy people in winter; for example, the German 1938 semi-postal series.

WINTERHULP (insc.) appears on Netherlands semi-postal stamps, 1944, with a surtax to aid the National Social Service and winter help.

WIPA (insc.) Wien Internationale Postwertzeichen-Ausstellung. Appears on a souvenir sheet of four stamps for the 1933 Vienna Philatelic Exhibition issue. The letters are also inscribed on each stamp in the souvenir sheet, and "Ausstellung Wien 1933" is inscribed on the selvedge (marginal paper) of the same souvenir sheets.

wire-marks impressions left on the bottom side of the paper web by the mesh of the wire cloth on the paper machine.

wire on a paper machine, the endless woven wire cloth suspending the pulp and water during the manufacturing process. Part of the water drains off from the suspension.

with-and-without watermark pairs postage stamp pairs in which one is with a watermark and the adjacent stamp is without a watermark. Occurs in the three airmail stamps of Newfoundland, 1931.

with center imprint in auction catalogues, describes an item (souvenir sheet, miniature sheet, pane, or sheet) with an imprint surrounded in the centre or imprinted at the centre of the top or bottom marginal paper.

without gum refers to a postage stamp from which the gum has been removed.

Witu a protected sultanate in the east coast

province of Kenya Protectorate in East Africa; proclaimed a German protectorate in 1885, but became British by agreement in 1890. The Sultan's post at Witu, under German protection, issued official stamps in 1889.

Wm. E. Loomis Letter Express   in San Francisco, California, issued U.S. local stamps in 1868.

WMK   watermark.

WMO   World Meteorological Organization; has specially inscribed stamps for postal use from the offices in Geneva, Switzerland. These stamps are catalogued with issues of Switzerland. Many countries have issued special or commemorative stamps to honour WMO.

WN   weun, a coin of Korea.

Wohltaetigkeitsausgabe   (Ger.) charity issue.

Wohltaetigkeitszuschlag   (Ger.) surtax for charity.

wohltatigkeitsmarke   (Ger.) charity stamp.

Wolke   (Ger.) cloud.

Wolmaransstad   a city in Transvaal that issued an overprinted stamp of Transvaal Republic in 1900, cancelled "V.R.I." and used during the Second British Occupation.

won   a coin of Korea, and the basis of the gold system of the country. 100 chun equal 1 won. The won corresponds to the yen of Japan and the yuan of China.

Wood & Co. City Despatch   in Baltimore, Maryland, issued U.S. local stamps in 1856-7.

woodblocks   (nick.) the Cape of Good Hope triangular stamps of 1861, printed by letterpress (incorrectly referred to as typographed or surface printed) from plates mounted on wood. These stamps were not printed from wood-engraved plates as the name suggests.

woodcut   (1) a printing plate of wood, having an illustration in relief with the background carved out; (2) a print obtained from a wood block of this kind. Some postage stamps, such as those of the Indian feudatory states, were printed from wooden plates.

wood engraving   (1) the art of cutting designs in relief upon a polished block of wood; (2) a print made from a block of this kind. See WOODCUT.

worn plate   a printing plate that has been used until portions of it are worn and produce low-quality impressions. In the 1800s, such postage stamp printing plates were repaired by retouching, or by re-entering the designs in the steel-engraved plates.

Wotton-under-edge   a British Maltese Cross cancel device that had all three frame lines cut (probably filed) without destroying the outline. Gibbons Great Britain Specialized catalogue illustrates thirty-two different Maltese crosses. The Mullingar cross also has cuts in the outer frame line.

wove paper   general term for paper which is not laid. The term "wove" refers to the imprint left on the surface of the paper by the woven wire on which the paper is made.

wr   in auction catalogues, means "wrinkles".

wrapper   a piece of paper usually long enough to wrap around a newspaper for mailing. This is a type of postal stationery, and is sold in post offices ready for use with stamps printed on it.

wreck covers   Mail saved from the wreckage of a train, aircraft, or ship often bears a post office stamp explaining why the mail was wet or damaged. Some collectors do not include air accident covers in this category. An excellent reference is *A History of Wreck Covers Originating at Sea, on Land, and in the Air*, by Adrian E. Hopkins.

write-up   the information that stamp collectors display with their postage stamp and cover collections.

Wunschliste   (Ger.) want list.

Württemberg   a former kingdom in southern Germany now part of Germany; about 7,530 square miles. Capital: Stuttgart. Stamps were issued from 1851 until superseded in 1902 by those of the German Empire. Official stamps were used until 1923.

WURTTEMBERG   (insc.) appears on stamps of Germany for use in Württemberg under French occupation, 1947-9.

W. Wyman   in Boston, Massachusetts, issued U.S. local stamps in 1844.

X

X appears on labels se-tenant, adjacent to postage stamps. The letter is printed in areas in sheets to prevent forgers from getting genuine paper. The X marks, called St. Andrew's crosses, should not be separated.

X an obliteration on Indian stamps of 1937-48, covering most of the area of the rupee value.

Xmas stamp (nick.) the map stamp of Canada inscribed "XMAS 1898", issued to mark the beginning of penny post (2-cents in Canada) to the places printed in red on the stamp. Also known as the Canadian map stamp.

X-ray examination of postage stamps Men have been able to detect fakes and forgeries by X-ray tests. For example, Dr. Herbert Pollock, of Chicago, Illinois, has been radiographing postage stamps for more than twenty years; W. H. S. Cheavin of London began the X-ray examination of stamps eleven years ago; and Charles F. Bridgman, of Rochester, New York, has proved the value of X-ray examination of stamps. (Courtesy of Charles F. Bridgman, in an interview on Oct. 17, 1956)

xylography the art of printing from wood blocks, which has been superseded by letterpress printing.

Y

y (Sp.) and; appears in some Spanish-language stamp inscriptions.

Y 1 appears in a cancel on Hong Kong stamps for use in Yokohama.

Y¼ (sur.) appears on the first stamps of Cuba and Puerto Rico, 1855-7.

Y and T Cat. in auction catalogues, refers to a lot catalogued by Yvert and Tellier, a French postage stamp catalogue.

Y.A.R. (insc.) appears on stamps of the Yemen Arab Republic.

YCA (ovpt.) appears on stamps of Peru in 1884 for use in the city as a result of the Chilean-Peruvian War of 1879-82.

Yacht key-types German colonial stamps featuring the Kaiser's yacht *Hohenzollern*. The stamps are usually in two formats: small for low values, and a large horizontal design for values in marks or other higher-value coinage.

yellowing the progressive discolouration of paper, caused by the action of air, gases, and light on paper impurities contained in the paper.

Yemen a kingdom of about 75,000 square miles in the southwest Arabian Peninsula.

Capital: San'a. Stamps have been issued since 1926.

yen a silver coin of Japan. The gold yen equals 100 silver sen and is the standard monetary unit of Japan. It is also a coin of Manchukuo.

Yin Yan (or Yang and Yin) a design resembling two quotation marks joined together, one upside down to the other, to form a circle. The design appears on stamps of Korea and in the country's flag. It symbolizes two opposing principles of existence that condition each other but also exclude one another, such as man and woman, or night and day.

ysabel canoe a type of native canoe shown on British Solomon Islands stamps, 1956.

yuan a silver coin of China and Manchukuo. 100 cents equal 1 yuan (Chinese dollar). The present issue of Chinese dollars, introduced in 1914, are known as "yuans" or "yuan dollars". "Yuan" is the Chinese word for "round coin".

Yugoslavia See JUGOSLAVIA.

Yunnan-Fou (ovpt.) appears on 1892-1906 stamps of Indo-China with Chinese characters, for use in Yunnan-Fou, a city in southern China, one of the French offices in China. Yunnan Fou, formerly Yunnan Sen, was later known as Kunming.

Yunnansen (ovpt.) appears on stamps of Indo-China with Chinese characters, for use by French offices in Yunnan-Sen, China.

Yvert et Tellier – Champion Catalogue the foremost French publication for stamp collectors.

Z

Zaehnung (Ger.) perforation.
Zaehnungsfehler (Ger.) perforation error.
Zaehnungsschluessel (Ger.) perforation gauge.
Z. Afr. Republiek (Afrikaans) Zuid Afrikaansche Republiek; South African Republic (Transvaal).
Zaire, Republique du the former Republic of Congo. "Zaire" (pronounced *zah-EER*) is the traditional name of the former Congo River. The first three postage stamps issued with the new name of the country went on sale Dec. 11, 1971; they marked the twenty-fifth anniversary of UNICEF. (Courtesy of the *Globe and Mail*, Toronto, Ontario)
Zambezia or **Zambesia** part of the Portuguese East Africa colony in Mozambique. Stamps were issued 1894-1917, superseded by those of Mozambique.
Zambia (insc.) appears on stamps of Zambia, formerly Northern Rhodesia and now an independent republic in southern Africa of 290,323 square miles. Capital: Lusaka. Issued stamps 1964.
Zanguebar See ZANZIBAR.
Zante one of the Greek Ionian Islands in Ionian Sea; about 156 square miles. Stamps were issued in 1941-43 under Italian occupation, and in 1943 under German occupation; they were superseded by stamps of Greece.
Zanzibar (Zanguebar, Zenj, or Zing) a former British protectorate, and later a republic comprising the islands of Zanzibar and Pemba with a total area of 1,020 square miles. First stamps were issues of India overprinted "Zanzibar" and placed on sale Nov. 10, 1895. Zanzibar united with Tanganyika on April 27, 1964, in one independent state known as the United Republic of Tanganyika and Zanzibar. The name was later changed to Tanzania, a combination of the two original names. See TANZANIA; TANGANYIKA.
Zanzibar (sur. and insc.) appears surcharged on stamps of France, for use by French offices in Zanzibar; after 1902, inscribed on stamps for use by French offices in Zanzibar.

Z.A.R. (sur.) Zuid Afrikaansche Republiek; appears with new values on stamps of Cape of Good Hope, issued in Vryburg in 1899 during the Boer War.
zegel (Dutch) stamp.
Zegelregt (insc.) appears on revenue (fiscal) stamps of the South African Republic. In 1895 they were overprinted "POSTZEGEL" for use as postage stamps in Transvaal.
zehn (Ger.) ten.
Zeichnung (Ger.) design.
Zeitungs (insc.) appears on Austrian newspaper or newspaper tax stamps.
Zeitungsdruck (Ger.) rotary press printing.
Zeitungsmarke (Ger.) newspaper stamp.
Zeitungsstempelmarke (Ger.) newspaper tax stamp.
Zelaya a province of Nicaragua.
Zemstvos Russian local postage stamps authorized in 1870. The local posts extended mail service throughout Russia, but at first were not operated by the government central post office. About 150 districts authorized their own local stamps to assist the Russian Imperial Postal Service.
Zenj See ZANZIBAR.
ZENTRALER / KURIERDIENST (2-line insc.) appears over a background with the letters "DDR" (the German Democratic

Republic, or East Germany) on official stamps of East Germany, 1956.
zentriert (Ger.) centred.
Zeppelin issues postage stamps of the world issued for mail carried on zeppelins, many of them on the *Graf Zeppelin*. Some popular issues of the United States and Germany illustrated the *Graf Zeppelin*. Other issues were overprinted or surcharged with a zeppelin design, such as the issue of Argentina, 1930.
Z grill name given to a grill in U.S. stamps.

William Stevenson, a specialist, could not decide what class a certain grill belonged in, so he used the letter Z to identify it. The name does not describe the shape.

zickzackartiger Durchstich (Ger.) sawtooth roulette.

Zieber's One Cent Dispatch in Pittsburgh, Pennsylvania, issued U.S. local stamps in 1851. Zieber's cancels were blots of colour on the locals. A chemical in the blots changed the colour of the paper, but did not damage the stamps. Known examples of the rarity are still in good condition.

ziegelrot (Ger.) brick-red.

Zierleiste (Ger.) ornamental bar.

Ziffer (Ger.) numeral.

Zifferzeichnung (Ger.) numeral design.

Zigarettenpapier (Ger.) cigarette paper.

zigzag paper paper watermarked or embossed with a design of short lines at sharp angles.

zigzag roulette a roulette with points in a regular pattern.

Zimska Pomac, Winterhilfe (sur.) appears with a design of a heraldic eagle and new values on stamps of Germany for use under German occupation of Laibach in the western half of Slovenia, 1944. These are listed with stamps of Jugoslavia in catalogues.

zinc a metal used in the manufacture of plates for the lithographic and letterpress printing processes. It is also one of the constituent metals of the alloys brass and German silver.

zincographer an engraver who uses zinc to make printing plates. This is not a common term.

zincography (1) the art of engraving or etching any kind of designs, pictures, or numerals on zinc plates. Zinc is most frequently used for plates made for newspaper reproductions; (2) the printing from zinc plates (sometimes called zincographs). The term is not used in popular works about printing, but it has been translated thus from foreign languages.

Zinj See ZANZIBAR.

zitronengelb (Ger.) lemon.

zloty a silver coin of Poland. 100 groszy equal 1 zloty. It is a name given the silver gulden of Poland.

ZOMERZEGEL 1950 (insc.) appears on Netherlands 1950 semi-postal stamps, with a surtax for social and cultural works. Subsequent issues also had the same inscription.

ZONA DE OCCUPATIE / 1919 / ROMANA (ovpt.) appears on stamps of Hungary, for use under Romanian occupation.

ZONA DE/PROTECTORADO/ESPANOL /EN MARRUECOS (4-line ovpt.) appears on Spanish stamps for use in Spanish Morocco, 1916-8. It appears without "ZONA DE" on stamps of Spain for Spanish Morocco in 1915.

ZONA / OCCUPATA / FIUMANO / KUPA (ovpt. and sur.) appears on stamps of Jugoslavia, for use under Italian occupation of the Fiume-Kupa zone.

Zuid Afrikaansche Republiek (Afrikaans) South African Republic.

Zuid-west Afrika (ovpt.) appears on stamps of South Africa for use in South-west Africa, 1923-30.

Zulassungsmarke (Ger.) admission stamp.

ZULASSUNGSMARKE DEUTSCHE FELDPOST (Ger. insc.) appears on military parcel post stamps of Germany, 1942-4.

Zululand a former British colony of about 10,427 square miles issued postage stamps from 1888 until 1896. Stamps of Natal were used after July 1898. Now the north-eastern part of Natal, in South Africa. Capital: Eshowe.

Zum Zumstein stamp catalogue.

Zumstein & Co. of Switzerland, publishers of the catalogues *Zumstein Europa*.

Zurich (insc.) appears in 1843 on stamps of Zurich, a Canton of Switzerland.

Zusammendruck (Ger.) se-tenant.

Zusammenfassung (Ger.) comprehension, summary.

Zuschlag (Ger.) surtax.

Zuschlagsmarke (Ger.) surtax stamp.

Zuschlagspreis (Ger.) price realized at auction.

Zustellungsmarke (Ger.) delivery stamp.

zu verkaufen (Ger.) for sale.

zwanzig (Ger.) twenty.

zwei (Ger.) two.

zweifach (Ger.) double.

zweifarbig (Ger.) bicoloured.

zweizeilig (Ger.) in two lines.

Zwischensteg (Ger.) gutter.

Zwischensteg-Zusammendruck (Ger.) gutter se-tenant.

zwoelf (Ger.) twelve.

Zypern (Ger.) Cyprus.

NON-LATIN EUROPEAN ALPHABETS

This section explains many of the words that appear in the Cyrillic and Greek alphabets on stamps of Bulgaria, Greece, Jugoslavia, and Russia. The words included are those the authors have most often been asked about. The non-Latin type was set by the printers of foreign-language newspapers in Toronto, whose help is gratefully acknowledged.

BULGARIA

Н. Р. БЪЛГАРИЯ
(insc.) appears on many stamps of Bulgaria. The first two letters are an abbreviation of the words meaning People's Republic.

НАРОДНА РЕПУБЛИКА
(insc.) appears on the first issue of the Bulgarian People's Republic stamps, September 1946.

ВЪЗДУШНА ПОЩА БЪЛГАРИЯ
(insc.) appears on airmail issues of Bulgaria, 1931 and subsequent years.

О. Ф.
(ovpt.) parcel post; appears with the design of an airplane on regular-issue stamps of Bulgaria issued Jan. 26, 1945. A second part of the 1945 issue was surcharged, and appears with a different aircraft design on 1944-type parcel post stamps of Bulgaria. The 100-lev stamp in this series was overprinted.

РЕПУБЛИКА БЪЛГАРИЯ
(insc.) appears on the first airmail stamps of the People's Republic of Bulgaria, in August 1947.

БЪРЗА ПОЩА
(insc.) appears on special delivery stamps of Bulgaria, 1939.

ТАКСА ДОПЛАЩАННЕ
(insc.) appears on postage-due stamps of Bulgaria, 1884 and subsequent years.

БЪЛГАРСКА
(insc.) appears on postage-due stamps of Bulgaria, 1932.

ЗА ДОПЛАЩАНЕ
(insc.) appears on postage-due stamps of Bulgaria, 1932-3.

ОБЩИНСКА ПОЩА
(insc.) appears on official stamps of Bulgaria, 1942.

ПОЩЕНСКИ КОЛЕТНИ ПРАТКИ
(insc.) stamps for parcels; appears on parcel post stamps of Bulgaria.

КОЛЕТНИ ПРАТКИ
(insc.) appears in vertical panels, one word on the left side and the other on the right, on parcel post stamps of Bulgaria.

ЮЖНА БЪЛГАРИЯ
(ovpt.) South Bulgaria; appears with the design of an heraldic lion in an octagonal frame on stamps of Eastern Rumelia, for use in South Bulgaria in 1885.

GREECE

ΑΡΚΑΔΙ
(insc.) appears on Greek stamps of 1930 featuring the Arcadi Monastery.

ΕΘΝΙΚΑ ΠΕΡΙΘΑΛΨΙΣ
(insc.) first aid; appears on the first postal-tax stamps of Greece, 1914.

ΕΚΘΕCΙC
(insc.) appears on postal-tax stamps of Greece in 1934. Since this issue, the Greek character C is not used in the revised alphabet. (Courtesy of James Zafeiropouos, translator)

ΕΛΛΑΣ

(insc.) appears on stamps of Greece, meaning Ellas, the name of modern Greece. The name of ancient Greece was Hellas.

ΕΛΛ. ΕΡ. ΣΤΑΥΡΟΣ

(insc.) appears on postal-tax stamps of Greece in 1924, with the design of a red cross. Proceeds were for the Red Cross Society.

ΕΝΑΡΙΘΜΟΝ ΓΡΑΜΜΑΤΟΣΗΜΟΝ

(insc.) appears on postage-due stamps of Greece, 1875-1943.

ΛΕΠΤΟΝ

(insc.) appears on postage-due stamps of Greece, 1875-1943.

ΛΕΠΤΑ

(insc.) appears on 1918 and 1924 postal-tax stamps of Greece.

ΔΡΧ

(part of insc. or sur.) an abbreviation of the Greek word for drachma, a coin; appears on many postage stamps of Greece.

ΚΟΙΝΩΝΙΚΗ ΠΡΟΝΟΙΑ

(insc.) appears on postal-tax stamps of Greece, 1939.

ΧΑΡΤΟΣΗΜΟΝ

(insc.) appears on postal-tax stamps of Greece in 1917 with a surcharge "K.II.", meaning Social Providence, and new values representing an extra tax. The stamps were formerly revenues or fiscal issues.

ΦΥΜΑΤΙΚΩΝ Τ.Τ.Τ.

(part of sur.) appears with a Cross of Lorraine on stamps of Greece for use as postal-tax stamps in 1944. Funds from the sales went toward the postal clerks' tuberculosis fund. Abbreviations in overprints and surcharges were used 1942-4.

ΠΡΟΝΟΙΑ ΠΡΟΣΩΠΙΚΟΥ Τ.Τ.Τ.

(3-line sur.) appears on stamps of Greece with new values for use as postal-tax stamps of Greece, 1946-51. Proceeds were for the postal employee's welfare fund.

ΕΛΛΗΝΙΚΗ ΔΙΟΙΚΗΟΙϹ

(ovpt.) appears on stamps of Greece for use in Albania (North Epirus) in 1940-1, during the Greek occupation of the region.

Ε * Δ

(ovpt.) appears on stamps of Greece for use in 1914 in Chios, an island in the Aegean Sea, claimed to be the birthplace of Homer. The Greek occupation forces used these overprinted stamps during the Balkan Wars.

ΣΑΜΟΥ

(insc.) appears on stamps of Samos, issues of the Provincial Government in 1912. Samos was an autonomous principality from 1832 until it joined with Greece in November 1912.

ΕΛΕΥΘΕΡΑ ΠΟΛΙΤΕΙΑ

(2-line insc.) free city; appears on stamps issued in 1912 for Icaria, an island in the Aegean Sea. The stamps were used when Greece occupied certain Aegean Islands during the Balkan Wars of 1912-13.

ΙΟΝΙΚΟΝ ΚΡΑΤΟΣ

(insc.) appears on postage stamps issued in 1859 for the Ionian Islands, a former British Protectorate. In 1864 the inhabitants requested Britain to cede the group of seven islands to Greece. Stamps of Greece are now used in the islands.

ΚΡΗΤΗ

(insc.) Crete; appears on stamps authorized by the government of Crete in 1900 and used until its union in 1913 with Greece.

ΗΠΕΙΡΟΣ

(insc.) appears on the provisional government postage stamps of Epirus, 1914.

ΕΛΛ. ΑΥΤΟΝ. ΗΠΕΙΡΟΣ

(insc.) appears with the design of a skull and crossbones and a double-headed eagle on the first issue of stamps for Epirus. These four stamps of 1914 were hand-stamped impressions in two colours each.

ΕΛΛΗΝΙΚΗ ΧΕΙΜΑΡΡΑ

(ovpt.) appears with the date 1914 on stamps of Greece issued in August 1914 for use in Epirus. Epirus was formerly a part of Turkey, but is now divided between Albania and Greece.

Β. ΗΠΕΙΡΟΣ

(vertical ovpt.) appears on regular-issue stamps of Greece for use in 1916 in Epirus.

ΚΟΡΥΤΣΑ

(insc.) appears on stamps of Epirus in 1914, in a series called the "Koritsa Issue".

ΔΙΟΙΚΗΣΙΣ ΔΥΤΙΚΗΣ ΘΡΑΚΗΣ

(3-line ovpt.) Administration of Western Thrace; appears on stamps of Greece for use in Western Thrace, part of a former Turkish province in southeastern Europe. The stamps were issued in 1920 during the Greek occupation of the region, and are listed with stamps of Thrace.

ΣΛΛ. ΔΙΟΙΚ. ΓΚΙΟΥΜΟΥ - ΛΤΖΙΝΑΣ

(part of 4-line sur.) appears with the design of a shield bearing a cross on stamps of Turkey. New values are printed at the bottom line of the surcharge.

ΕΛΛΗΝΙΚΗ ΔΙΟΙΚΗΣΙΣ

(part of control mark) Greek Administration. The control mark was used in 1913 in Alexandroupolis, a seaport city in Western Thrace, which is now a part of Greece. A similar surcharge was made on Bulgarian stamps in 1913 for use by the Greek occupation forces in Cavalla, a city in northeast Greece. The control marks served as postage stamps, and were printed in sheets of eight in three values to a sheet.

Ἑλληνική - Κατοχή - Μυτιλήνης

(3-line vertical ovpt.) appears on stamps of Turkey for use in 1912 in Mytilene (or Lesbos), a former Turkish island on the Aegean Sea annexed by Greece in 1913.

ΛΗΜΝΟΣ

(ovpt.) appears on various stamps of Greece in 1912 for use in Lemnos, an island in the Aegean Sea.

Σ.Δ.Δ.

(ovpt.) appears as an additional overprint on some stamps of Greece for use in 1947 in the Dodecanese, a group of twelve Greek islands in the southeastern part of the Aegean Sea near the coast of Turkey.

JUGOSLAVIA

ДРЖАВА С. Х. С. БОСНА И ХЕРЦЕГОВИНА

(ovpt. or sur.) Bosnia and Herzegovina; appears on stamps of Bosnia and Herzegovina in 1918 before the final union of the Serbs, Croats, and Slovenes, who formed the Kingdom of Jugoslavia.

КРАЉЕВСТВО С. Х. С.

(ovpt.) appears on stamps of Bosnia and Herzegovina in 1919 for use in the state before its final union to become Jugoslavia. The final letters are the abbreviation for the words meaning the Kingdom of Serbs, Croats, and Slovenes.

НЕДЕЉА ЦРВЕНОГ КРСТА

(insc.) Red Cross Week; appears on postal tax stamps of Jugoslavia in 1949 and subsequent years.

Ф. Н. Р. ЈУГОСЛАВИЈА

(insc.) Federated People's Republic; appears on official stamps of Jugoslavia in 1946.

КРАЉЕВIIНА СРБА: ХРВАТА: СЛОВЕНАЦА

(sur.) Kingdom of Serbia, Croatia and Slavonia; appears with changes in value on stamps of Bosnia and Herzegovina. These were 1919 postage-due stamps for the state before its final union to become Jugoslavia.

ЈУГОСЛАВИЈА

(insc.) appears on stamps of Jugoslavia.

ЗА ЦРВЕНИ КРСТ

(insc.) For the Red Cross; appears on the first issue of 1933 postal-tax stamps of Jugoslavia, with additional inscriptions in two other languages.

ДЕМОКРАТСКА - ФЕДЕРАТИ

(partial insc.) Democratic Federation. Appears on the first issue of semi-postal stamps of the Federal Republic of Jugoslavia in 1945. The surtax was for the Red Cross.

СРБИЈА

(insc. or part of insc.) appears on stamps of Serbia, 1866-1920.

К. С. ПОШТА

(insc.) Kingdom of Serbia postage; appears on stamps of Serbia in 1866-9.

К. СРБСКА ПОШТА

(insc.) Royal Serbian Mail; appears on 1866 stamps of Serbia.

ПОРТО МАРКА

(insc.) appears on postage-due stamps of Serbia, 1895-1920. Appears with an additional inscription on postage-due stamps of Jugoslavia, 1921-62.

ПОШТА

(insc.) postage; appears on stamps of Serbia, 1869 and subsequent years.

УСТАВ

(part of a bilingual ovpt.) appears on stamps of Montenegro, 1905, for the constitution issue.

ПОШТЕ ЦРНЕ ГОРЕ

(insc.) Post Office of Montenegro; appears on 1910 stamps of Montenegro.

НОВЧ

(insc.) appears on stamps of Montenegro, 1874-98. The word refers to the coin "novcic", expressing the denominations of the stamps in that period.

ЦРНА ГОРА

(ovpt. and insc.) appears as part of a bilingual overprint in 1941 on stamps of Yugoslavia for the Italian occupation of Montenegro. A similar overprint appears on stamps of Italy for use in 1941. The words are also inscribed on pictorial stamps for Montenegro during the same occupation.

ЦРНЕ ГОРЕ ТАКСЕНЕ БЕЉЕ-

(insc.) appears on postage-due stamps of Montenegro.

ПОШТЕ БИЉЕГА ЦР. ГОРЕ

(insc.) appears on stamps of Montenegro, 1874-98.

RUSSIA

СССР

(insc.) shortened form of Union of Soviet Socialist Republics; appears on most stamps of Russia since 1923.

МАРКА

(insc.) stamp; appears on many stamps printed in the Cyrillic alphabet.

ПОЧТА

(insc.) post; appears on many stamps printed in the Cyrillic alphabet.

ПОЧТОВАЯ МАРКА

(insc.) postage stamp; appears on many stamps printed in the Cyrillic alphabet.

АВИАПОЧТА

(insc.) appears on the first airmail stamps of Russia in 1922.

АВИАПОЧТОВАЯ

(insc.) appears on airmail stamps of Russia in 1927.

В ПОЛЬЗУ БЕСПРИЗОРНЫМ ДЕТЯМ

(insc.) in aid of homeless children; appears on semi-postal stamps of Russia.

РСФСР

(ovpt. and insc.) Russian Socialist Federal Soviet Republic; appears on many stamps printed in the Cyrillic alphabet.

ПОЧТА РУССКОЙ АРМІИ

Russian Army Post.

КРЫМСКОГО КРАЕВОГО ПРАВИТЕЛЬСТВА

(insc.) Crimean Regional Government; appears on stamps of 1919 for use in South Russia.

ВЕНДЕНСКАЯ УЕЗДНАЯ ПОЧТА

(insc.) appears on stamps for use in Wenden, the former seat of the Livonian knights in the Russian Empire province of Livonia. Issued stamps from 1862 to 1880, which are listed with stamps of Russia in catalogues.

ДОПЛАТА ЗОЛОТОМ

(sur. and insc.) addition to pay, or more to pay due in gold; appears on postage-due stamps of Russia. In 1924-5 Russian currency varied in value from one part of the country to another, but payment in gold was valid anywhere in the country.

О.К.С.А. РОССІЯ

(insc.) abbreviated form of the words meaning Special Corps, Army of the North; appears on stamps used by the Army of the North in 1919, listed with stamps of Russia.

ГОЛОДАЮЩИМ Р.С.Ф.С.Р.

(sur.) appears with new values on regular-issue 1918 stamps of Russia for use in 1922. This was an issue of the Russian Soviet Federated Socialist Republic as semi-postal stamps to raise funds for the Volga famine relief.

ПОМОЩЬ ГОЛОДАЮЩИМ ПОВОЛЖЬЯ

(insc.) in aid of the starving (people) in the Volga region; appears on postage stamps of the Russian Federated Socialist Republic in 1921.

РУССКАЯ ПОЧТА

(sur.) appears on stamps of Russia in 1921 with new values for the postal service of General P. Wrangel's army and of civilians from South Russia.

СПЕШНАЯ ПОЧТА

(insc.) fast post; appears on special delivery stamps of Russia.

КИТАЙ

(ovpt.) appears on stamps of Russia for use at the Russian Offices in China.

ОДНА МАРКА

(insc.) one markka (a Finnish coin); appears on 1867 stamps of Finland.

ПЕН

(insc.) abbreviated form of the word meaning pennia, a coin; appears on stamps of Finland issued under the Russian Empire, 1866-1916.

КОП.

(insc.) a short form of the word meaning

kopeck, a coin; appears on stamps of Finland issued under the Russian Empire.

УКРАІНСЬКА

(insc.) appears on postage stamps of the Ukraine Republic in 1918.

ДОПОМОГА ГОЛОДУЮЧИМ

(insc.) in aid of the starving; appears on semi-postal stamps of the Ukraine Republic in 1923.

КАРПАТСЬКА УКРАІНА

(insc.) appears on stamps of Carpathian Ukraine in 1918. Similar spellings appear on stamps of the Ukraine.

АЗЕРБАЙДЖАНСКАЯ

(insc.) appears on stamps of Azerbaijan.

БАКУ

Baku, the capital of Azerbaijan, a Soviet Socialist Republic on the west coast of the Caspian Sea. Issued stamps overprinted in 1922.

АМУРСКАЯ ОБЛАСТНАЯ

(insc.) appears on stamps of Amur province, Siberia, in 1920. Stamps were issued under the Communist regime, and are listed with stamps of Siberia.

БАТУМ: БАТУМ ОБ.

(sur.) appears on stamps of Russia, 1919-20, for use in Batum, a seaport on the Black Sea. Stamps were issued under the British occupation forces.

БАТУМСКАЯ ПОЧТА

(insc.) appears on the first stamps of Batum in 1919.

Н.А.П.В.П.

(sur.) appears handstamped with new values on stamps of Russia for use in 1921 in Siberia.